THE BLUE GUIDES

Albania
Austria
Belgium and Luxembourg
China
Cyprus
Czechoslovakia
Denmark
Egypt

FRANCE
France
Paris and Versailles
Burgundy
Normandy
Corsica

GERMANY
Berlin and Eastern Germany
Western Germany

GREECE
Greece
Athens and environs
Crete

HOLLAND
Holland
Amsterdam

Hungary
Ireland

ITALY
Northern Italy
Southern Italy
Florence
Rome and environs
Venice
Tuscany
Umbria
Sicily

Jerusalem
Malta and Gozo
Morocco
Moscow and Leningrad
Portugal

SPAIN
Spain
Barcelona

Switzerland

TURKEY
Turkey
Istanbul

UK
England
Scotland
Wales
London
Museums and Galleries of London
Oxford and Cambridge
Country Houses of England
Gardens of England
Literary Britain and Ireland
Victorian Architecture in Britain
Churches and Chapels of Northern England
Churches and Chapels of Southern England
Channel Islands

USA
New York
Boston and Cambridge

Detail from the polyptych of San Gregorio by Antonello da Messina (1473), Museo Regionale di Messina

BLUE GUIDE

Sicily

Alta Macadam

Atlas, maps and plans by John Flower

A&C Black
London

WW Norton
New York

Fourth edition 1993

Published by A & C Black (Publishers) Limited
35 Bedford Row, London WC1R 4JH

A CIP catalogue record of this book
is available from the British Library.

ISBN 0–7136–3784–6

Published in the United States of America by
WW Norton and Company, Inc
500 Fifth Avenue, New York, NY 10110

Published simultaneously in Canada by
Penguin Books Canada Limited
2801 John Street, Markham, Ontario L3R 1B4

ISBN 0–393–31054 X USA

Alta Macadam has been a writer of Blue Guides since 1970. She lives in Florence with her family (the painter Francesco Colacicchi, and their son Giovanni). Combined with work on writing the guides she has also been associated in Florence with the Bargello Museum and the Alinari photo archive. She is now involved in work for Harvard University at the Villa I Tatti in Florence. As author of the Blue Guides to Northern Italy, Rome, Venice, Sicily, Florence, Tuscany, and Umbria she travels extensively in Italy every year in order to revise new editions of the books.

For permission to reproduce the photographs in this book the publishers would like to thank **Mario Laurenza** (pages 73, 78, 85, 99, 185, 201, 212, 236, 263, 293), **Joe Cornish** (pages 87, 122, 134, 169, 194, 241) and the Museo Regionale di Messina (page 2).

The publishers invite readers to write in with comments, suggestions and corrections for the next edition of the Blue Guide. Writers of the most useful letters will be awarded a free Blue Guide of their choice.

Printed in Great Britain by The Bath Press, Avon

PREFACE

This new edition of Blue Guide Sicily has been rearranged to provide simpler and shorter itineraries of the island. Numerous small towns have been added to the text. Great care has been taken to provide practical details about hotels, restaurants and local transport, and sections have been added on visiting Sicily with children, and annual festivals. The landscape has been described in greater detail. A number of nature reserves have recently been instituted on the island: the protected areas of Vendicari and Zingaro stand out as beautiful stretches of coastline saved from 'development' by the efforts of the local population.

Since the last edition, the splendid Museo Archeologico Paolo Orsi has been reopened in Syracuse. It is one of the most interesting archaeological collections in Europe and is housed in a fine modern functional building. The palace of the Zisa in Palermo has been beautifully restored and its three floors opened to the public. It represents the most important Arab Norman secular building on the island. Museums reopened since the last edition of the book include the Museo Mandralisca in Cefalù, the Museo Alessi in Enna, and the museum on the island of Motya. New museums include the Museo delle Saline outside Trapani, the museum of prehistory in Trapani, a local ethnographical museum in Piana degli Albanesi, and the Museo Agro Forestale below Erice. In Marsala the Museo Archeologico di Baglio Anselmi has been enlarged, and in the province of Ragusa the Castello di Donnafugata opened to the public. Only two major museums on the island remain closed for long-term restoration: the Galleria Regionale in Palazzo Bellomo in Syracuse, and the Castello Ursino in Catania.

The detailed plans to restore and renovate the centre of Palermo drawn up in 1988–90 by three distinguished architectural planners and conservationists, and approved by the town council just before Leoluca Orlando was forced out of office as mayor of Palermo, have apparently been shelved. Thus a great chance to give this beautiful but decaying city the attention it deserves seems to have been lost. The depopulation of the centre of the city, where a vast number of houses have been in danger of collapse for years, continues at a frightening rate. Meanwhile Ragusa Ibla has provided a splendid example of how an old town centre can be preserved and revitalised. Numerous towns in Sicily, as in the rest of Italy, have been surrounded in the last few years by ugly modern suburbs: Gela, Bagheria, and Sciacca have become extremely disappointing places to visit as a result. The two major archaeological sites on the south coast, Selinunte and Agrigento are not protected as they should be: long term plans to create 'archaeological parks' here have still not been finalised. In the meantime an ugly dyke and tunnels have been built beside the temples at Selinunte, and in Agrigento the modern town is encroaching on the 'Valle dei Templi'.

Although the island could still do with more small hotels, especially in the interior, adequate accommodation is now to be found in all the main centres. The food of Sicily is extremely good and generally better than that on the Italian mainland. Many delicious local specialities are still produced. Prices in Sicily are generally lower than in the rest of Italy.

During my travels in Sicily for this new edition I received much generous help. I am particularly grateful to: the Assessorato Regionale del Turismo of Sicily; Daniela Cillino of the Azienda Autonoma Turismo of Palermo; the 'APT' of Palermo (especially Patrizia Cardinali and Lia Verdina), the 'APT' of Trapani, the Azienda Autonoma Soggiorno e Turismo of Agrigento, the

'APT' of Enna (in particular Dottoressa Agata Camilleri), the 'APT' of Ragusa (special thanks to Signora Burgio), the 'APT' of Syracuse (and Dottoressa Giusi Di Lorenzo), and the 'APT' of Messina. I would also like to thank Dottoressa Maria Amato of Noto, Signor Gallazzo of Modica, Professor Roberto Calia of Alcamo, and Giliana d'Agostino of Polizzi Generosa. I am most grateful to Eve Borsook for her invaluable help.

In the last few years Sicily has been much in the news because of the **Mafia**. It is necessary to underline that visitors to the island are in no way exposed to this problem. The Sicilians are extraordinarily hospitable and helpful, and the presence, since 1992, of Italian soldiers on the island has had no effect on every day life. Sicily is as safe a place to visit as any other part of Italy.

For years the island has been subjected to the 'protection' system of the Mafia who control almost every business transaction on the island, both private and state. Giovanni Falcone estimated that there were more than 5000 'men of honour' in Sicily, chosen after a rigorous selection process. He saw these men as true professionals of crime, who obeyed strict rules. A sentence passed in 1987, at the end of the largest trial ever held against the Mafia (the evidence for which had been collected by Giovanni Falcone), condemned hundreds of people of crimes connected with the Mafia. But this achievement in the battle against the Mafia was soon overshadowed when the anti-Mafia 'pool' of judges created by Antonino Caponnetto in 1983, and led by Giovanni Falcone, disintegrated because of internal dissensions and a belief on the part of Falcone that his attempt to fight the Mafia was being obstructed.

In 1992 this courageous Sicilian, who had raised the hopes of so many honest Italians, was assassinated together with his wife and bodyguards outside Palermo. Just a few months later his friend and fellow magistrate Paolo Borsellino was also murdered by the Mafia in Palermo. These tragic events were seen by many as a desperate blow in the battle against the Mafia, and the response from Rome which was to send in the army, which is still present in the island, produced much aggravation (and its only tangible result seems to have been to damage unjustifiably the island's tourist industry). In 1993 the arrest of Toto Riina, the acknowledged boss of 'Cosa Nostra', after more than twenty years 'in hiding' in Palermo, closely followed by the capture of Nitto Santapaola outside Catania, the head of the Mafia in that city since 1982, was greeted, not without some scepticism, as a step in the right direction.

However, since 1992, the whole question of the power of the Mafia has been placed on a different level. In 1992 the murder by the Mafia of Salvo Lima, Christian Democrat member of the European parliament and the most powerful politician on the island, was interpreted by many as a sign that he was no longer able to guarantee judicial immunity for Mafia bosses. In 1993 Giulio Andreotti, the most famous political figure in the country in the past four decades, was accused of collaboration with the Mafia. It now looks likely that a connection between the Mafia and the national political scene will be proved. A document just published by a parliamentary commission, entitled 'Mafia and politics' points the way to this conclusion. If this is the case the Mafia will lose two of its greatest strengths, its legitimacy and invisibility. The feeling in the whole country, particularly in Sicily itself, suggests the battle against the Mafia may one day at last be won.

CONTENTS

Maps and Plans

Maps

Town Plans

Ground Plans

EXPLANATIONS

Type. The main routes are described in large type. Smaller type is used for branch-routes and excursions, for historical and preliminary paragraphs, and (generally speaking) for descriptions of greater detail or minor importance.

Asterisks (*) indicate points of special interest or excellence.

Distances are given cumulatively from the starting-point of the route or sub-route in kilometres. Mountain heights have been given in the text and on the atlas in metres.

Hotels. A selection of hotels has been given in the text, with their official star rating in order to give an indication of price. In making the choice for inclusion, small hotels have been favoured, and those in the centre of towns, or in particularly beautiful positions in the countryside. For further information, see under Accommodation in the Practical Information section.

Restaurants. A small selection of restaurants has been given in the text. They have been divided into three categories which reflect price ranges in 1993: 'LUXURY-CLASS' RESTAURANTS where the prices are likely to be over Lire 60,000 a head (and sometimes well over Lire 100,000 a head). These include the most famous restaurants in Sicily and they usually offer international cuisine. '1ST-CLASS' RESTAURANTS where the prices range from Lire 35,000 and above. These are generally comfortable, with good service, but are not cheap. The third category, called 'SIMPLE TRATTORIE AND PIZZERIE' indicate places where you can eat for around Lire 25,000 a head, or even less. Although simple, the food in this category is usually the best value. For further information, see under Eating In Sicily in the Practical Information section.

Main roads are designated in the text by their official number. Motorways ('autostrade') always carry 'A' before their number.

Populations have been given from the latest official figures. They refer to the size of the Commune or administrative area, which is often much larger than the central urban area.

Plans. Double-page town plans are gridded with numbered squares referred to in the text thus: (Pl.1–16). On the ground plans and archaeological plans figures or letters have been given to correspond with the description which appears in the text.

Abbreviations. In addition to generally accepted and self-explanatory abbreviations, the following occur in the guide: APT Azienda di Promozione Turistica (official local tourist office); ENIT Ente Nazionale Italiano per il Turismo; fest. *festa*, or festival (i.e. holiday); FS Ferrovie dello Stato (Italian State Railways); TCI Touring Club Italiano.

A NOTE ON BLUE GUIDES

The Blue Guide series began in 1918 when Muirhead Guide-Books Limited published Blue Guide London and its Environs. Finlay and James Muirhead already had extensive experience of guide-book publishing: before the First World War they had been the editors of the English editions of the German Baedekers, and by 1915 they had acquired the copyright of most of the famous 'Red' Handbooks from John Murray.

An agreement made with the French publishing house Hachette et Cie in 1917 led to the translation of Muirhead's London guide, which became the first 'Guide Bleu', Hachette had previously published the blue-covered 'Guides Joanne'. Subsequently, Hachette's Guide Bleu Paris et ses Environs was adapted and published in London by Muirhead. In 1931 Ernest Benn Limited took over the Blue Guides, appointing Russell Muirhead, Finlay Muirhead's son, editor in 1934. The Muirheads' connection with the Blue Guides ended in 1963, when Stuart Rossiter, who had been working on the Guides since 1954, became house editor, revising and compiling several of the books himself. The Blue Guides are now published by A & C Black, who acquired Ernest Benn in 1984, so continuing the tradition of guide-book publishing which began in 1826 with 'Black's Economical Tourist of Scotland'. The series continues to grow: there are now more than 50 titles in print, with revised editions appearing regularly, and new titles in preparation.

HISTORICAL SUMMARY

The geographical position of Sicily in the centre of the Mediterranean has made her not only the prized possession of foreign powers, but also a battleground between warring nations. But her long history of foreign domination has often been coloured by a brilliant mixture of traditions and cultures which has produced some of the most remarkable art in the Mediterranean world.

The earliest prehistoric finds on the island are the Palaeolithic cave paintings on Levanzo and Monte Pellegrino. The first Neolithic culture so far recognised in Sicily is that known as 'Stentinello', named after one of its typical fortified villages near Syracuse. The Aeolian Islands became important because of the existence of obsidian, which was much sought after by the Mediterranean peoples. In the Bronze Age the islands were on the trade route between the Aegean Islands and the Western Mediterranean. The earliest inhabitants of Sicily of whom we have any written record are the *Siculi* in the E and the *Sicani* in the W. The *Elymni* are known to have occupied Segesta, Erice, and Entella; but evidence of their civilisation has only so far been found at Segesta. All these people, in the 15–10C BC, were in close commercial touch with the Aegeo-Mycenaean peoples of Greece. Recent archaeological evidence has suggested that the Phoenicians visited the west coast of Sicily to establish trading outposts (at Motya, San Pantaleo, and later Palermo) even before the Greek settlers began to arrive in the 8C BC. The Greeks established strongholds on the east coast at Naxos (c 735 BC) and Syracuse (734), going on into the next century with Lentini, Catania, Megara Hyblaea, Zancle, and Gela. Most of these settlements were separate from the Sicel villages, although in some cases (such as Morgantina, from the mid-6C BC), the two communities merged.

The 6C BC saw the beginning of the heroic age of tyrants with the notorious, if shadowy, figure of Phalaris, who ruled in Akragas probably from 570–555. The brothers Cleander and Hippocrates were succeeded in Gela by Gelon, who captured Syracuse in 485. He and his father-in-law, Theron, tyrant of Akragas, soon controlled nearly all of Greek Sicily, and Gelon became the most powerful figure in the Greek world after his decisive victory over the Carthaginians at the Battle of Himera in 480. This supremacy aroused the jealousy of Athens, but a massive Athenian attack (415) on Syracuse met with fatal disaster.

In the late 5C BC Dionysius the Elder dominated the affairs of the island for 38 years as the most powerful tyrant in Sicilian history. The Corinthian Timoleon brought greater prosperity to the island, while Agathocles extended control not only over Carthaginian Sicily, but also into North Africa. He became the first 'King' of Sicily. His successor, Hieron II, brought Sicily under Roman influence, and in 264 the First Punic War broke out between Rome and Carthage, with Sicily as one of the main battlegrounds. Continuous destructive fighting continued until the Carthaginian surrender in 241. In the Second Punic War Sicily again found herself in an important strategic position between Italy and North Africa. In 212 Syracuse finally fell to the Roman Marcellus, and by 210 Rome controlled the whole of the island including the former Carthaginian territories in the west.

Under Roman domination the Greek cities lost some of their autonomy. Extensive rural estates were established in the interior, and luxurious villas were built (typified by the villas found at Piazza Armerina, Patti, and Eloro). In the coastal towns public buildings were erected. The huge slave population on the island (increased by prisoners-of-war taken by the Romans in their battles in the east), led by Eunus in Enna and Cleon in Agrigento, revolted c 139. A second Revolt (c 104) led to cruel repressions by the Romans. In the early Imperial period Sicily lost importance as a Roman province.

During the 5C Sicily was the successive prey of the Vandals and the Ostrogoths, but in AD 535 it was conquered for Byzantium by Belisarius. The weak hold of the Eastern Emperors (although in the 7C Syracuse became the capital of the Byzantine Empire for 5 years) relaxed under the pressure of the Saracen invasion (827); fierce fighting for possession of the island continued for 50 years. Palermo fell to the Arabs in 831; Syracuse in 878. Muslim rule, accompanied by vast numbers of North African and Spanish settlers, was marked by a spirit of tolerance. Palermo in the 9C was one of the great centres of scholarship and art in the world, surpassed in size in the Christian world only by Constantinople. The fertility of the island was exploited to the full, and cotton, oranges, lemons, sugar cane, etc. were first cultivated at this time

In 1060 the Norman Count Roger de Hautville (1031–1101), with a handful of knights, seized Messina. By 1091 Roger was in control of the entire island. Norman rule was characterised by its efficiency, and willingness to adapt to the Arabic, Greek, and Roman traditions which already existed on the island. In 1130 Roger's son (1093–1154) was crowned King of Sicily as Roger II. At that time he was probably the wealthiest ruler in Europe, and his court in Palermo the most brilliant. Meanwhile Messina flourished as a supply base for the Crusaders.

In 1194 the crown was claimed by the Emperor Henry VI of Swabia, son of Barbarossa, in the name of his wife, Constance (daughter of Roger II) and the last of the Hautevilles was put to death. He was succeeded as Emperor and King of Sicily by his son Frederick II, 'stupor mundi', whose reign was marked by a prolonged struggle with the Papacy. His splendid court in Palermo, drawing on Islamic and Jewish, as well as Christian cultures, was famous throughout Europe for its splendour and learning. The Swabian line ended with the beheading of Conradin in 1268 and the Pope invested Charles of Anjou with the crown of Sicily and Naples. The hated Angevin rule was, however, soon terminated by the famous rebellion known as the Sicilian Vespers, which broke out at Palermo at the hour of vespers on Easter Tuesday, 1282. A French officer who had insulted a Sicilian bride on her way to church by insisting upon searching her for concealed weapons was immediately killed, and every Frenchman in Palermo was massacred. Every Sicilian town, except Sperlinga, followed suit by massacring or expelling its French garrison, and the Sicilians summoned Peter of Aragon to be their king. From that day for over four centuries Sicily was ruled by Aragonese princes and Spanish and Bourbon kings, a period in which the rebellious spirit of the islanders lay dormant. By the 16C Charles V had moved the centre of power W of the Mediterranean and Sicily lost much of her strategic importance.

After Napoleon failed to invade the island, the British took control of Sicily in the first years of the 19C and established a constitution for a brief time. Revolution broke out in 1848 against the Bourbons of Naples. Garibaldi fired the imagination of the Sicilian people and led an attack against Naples in 1860, thus paving the way for Italian Unification. But hard Piedmontese rule by Cavour soon proved unpopular. The Northern Italian cities took up a dominant position over the S, and the economic position of Sicily was to remain for a century a long way behind that in the rest of Italy. Violence increased in the ungovernable interior of the island. By 1900 Sicily was one of the main areas of emigration in the world. In 1931 40 per cent of Sicilians still remained illiterate.

The geographical position of Sicily meant that the Allies chose the island for their first important attack on Hitler in Europe. The capture of Sicily by the Allies in 1943 (Operation 'Husky') was accomplished in 38 days. During the Italian administration in 1944 Civil War broke out on the island. Regional administration was approved by Rome in 1946, and the first Assembly was elected in 1947.

This century has seen the power of the Mafia on the island steadily increase. In the 1980s a number of men in key positions, including magistrates, politicians, and members of the police force, who stood up to the Mafia were killed by them: General Carlo Alberto Dalla Chiesa, sent to Palermo as prefect in 1982 to deal with the problem of the Mafia was assassinated by them after only a few months in office. Rocco Chinicci, one of a group of investigating magistrates in Palermo was murdered in 1983. The journalist Gisueppe Fava, who became known for his outspoken opposition to the Mafia through his newspapaer 'I Siciliani', was killed by them in 1984. In 1987 a huge trial was held in Palermo, and hundreds of people were sentenced to life imprisonment for crimes connected with the Mafia. In 1992 two courageous judges, Giovanni Falcone and Piero Borsellino were assassinated by the Mafia.

Geography. Sicily, the largest and most important of the Mediterranean islands (25,708 sq km), owed its ancient name *Trinacria* to its triangular shape. The modern name *Sicilia* is derived from that of its ancient inhabitants, the Siculi. Physically it is a continuation of the chain of the Apennines on the one hand, and of the Atlas mountains on the other. But it appears that far from Sicily being joined at a comparatively recent epoch to Calabria, the Strait of Messina is actually narrower now than in former ages. The island is mountainous across the N and E, with plateaux in the centre, lowering towards the S, and fertile coastal plains. Etna, the largest volcano in Europe, dominates the E and much of the centre of Sicily. The island is notorious for its earthquakes. Fumarole, macalube, or diminutive mud-volcanoes, and thermal springs exist in a number of places. Within Sicilian waters are included many lesser islands: the *Aeolian* or *Lipari* Islands to the NE; *Ustica* to the NW; the *Egadi* to the W; and *Pantelleria* and the distant *Pelagian Isles* to the SW. Of the meagre rivers the largest are the *Simeto*, *Salso*, *Belice*, and *Platani*; most of the smaller streams are dry in summer. The island suffers from a shortage of water. Sicily numbers 5,008,000 inhabitants. Palermo, the capital, is the principal town; Syracuse, Agrigento, Messina, Catania, Caltanissetta, Trapani, Enna, and Ragusa are provincial capitals. The bulk of the population is devoted to agriculture. In the central uplands grain is the chief product, while in the coastal regions vines, olives, and fruit trees are grown; the most characteristic product is the 'agrumi', i.e. oranges, lemons, tangerines, etc. In general the sub-tropical lushness of the coastal areas is backed by arid hinterland. In the centre the immense expanses of steppe are sparsely populated. Sicilian waters are rich in fish, especially in the Strait of Messina where upwards of 140 species are known, including unusual deep-sea varieties. Wild flowers are particularly beautiful all over the island in spring.

THE ART AND ARCHITECTURE OF SICILY

Helen Hills

Sicily's strategic position, lying between Europe and Africa and linking the eastern and western Mediterranean and the Latin world with the Greek, resulted not only in its tumultuous history of successive invasions and conquests, but also in a unique cultural mixture which, in turn, stimulated the creation of rich and original works of art. The powers which ruled Sicily and those which traded with it, each left their distinctive cultural imprints; and individual artists, both foreigners working in Sicily, and Sicilians who had trained abroad, enriched these patterns. Yet the art history of Sicily is not simply a succession of disconnected impositions from foreign cultures; a strong local or Sicilian pride and conservatism nourished the development of insular and regional traditions which, during the most inventive periods, were fused with ideas coming from outside to create distinctive forms and styles quite peculiar to Sicily.

Sadly, the richness of Sicily's cultural heritage has not inspired the scholarly interest or political commitment it deserves. Many buildings which have survived the ravages of earthquakes, volcanic eruption and the bombardment of World War II now stand in desolate ruin, without hope of restoration, closed to the public and wasted. Paintings and sculpture have not fared much better: sales abroad, scandalous thefts, and over-restoration or poor conservation have dispersed or destroyed many irreplaceable and outstanding works. This pattern will continue so long as the necessary political will is lacking.

Prehistoric Art

Some of the finest manifestations of Palaeolithic art yet known have been discovered in Sicily. In a small cave at Cala dei Genovesi on the island of **Levanzo** are two distinct series of figures, one set incised, and the other painted, of c 8700 BC. The incised figures, of red deer, oxen, equids and other animals, are particularly vivacious. Another series of incised drawings (c 8000 BC), in one of the Addaura caves of **Monte Pellegrino**, is of particular interest because it features not only figures of animals such as are usually depicted in Quaternary art, but human figures as well, sometimes isolated and sometimes arranged in groups and drawn with the same naturalistic liveliness as the animals.

The earliest Neolithic culture known in Sicily, the **Stentinello**, may have covered much of the island by 3000 BC. Its pottery, decorated by impressions or incisions often made with the edges of shells, is finer and more compactly decorated than similar pottery of the same period elsewhere in the Mediterranean. In some of the sites of this civilisation (Stentinello, Lipari and especially Megara Hyblaea) more spirited pottery has been found, painted with red bands or flames on a light background, recalling the early painted ware of the Greek mainland. Painted wares were followed by others with incised spirals or complicated rolled handles. Each of these styles reflects an impact from outside, either casual landings or settlements, whose local nature accounts for the regional variations. The main sources were Anatolia, the Aegean, Cyprus and Syria, but contacts with north

Africa and Egypt can be inferred now and then. This rather disjointed development lasted throughout the so-called Copper Age (3rd millennium). Examples of the pottery, idols and jewellery can be seen in the Archaeological Museums in Palermo and Syracuse.

Cultural influences from Anatolia and the Aegean created the rock-cut chamber tombs which became ubiquitous in Sicily with little variation until the 5C BC. Most of the tombs are very simple, small oval, mitten-shaped rooms; but a few are more complicated architecturally with recessed doorways, pilasters and pillars in front of a prepared façade. Some fine tombs at **Sant'Angelo Muxaro**, in use from the 8C to the mid-5C BC, attain very grandiose dimensions and are comparable with Mycenean examples. At **Castelluccio**, near Noto, spiral motifs in relief of the 3rd or 2nd millennium BC sometimes decorate the stone slabs closing the tomb doorways, and these are the only examples of prehistoric stonecarving so far known in Sicily. As the population centres expanded in the Late Bronze and Iron Ages, so their necropoleis became larger and more conspicuous, giving rise to the thousands of tombs which honeycomb the hills at Pantalica, most of which date from the 13C to the 11C BC. Mycenean influences manifested themselves at **Pantalica** in the architecture of the so-called 'Anaktoron', or prince's palace, and in the form and decoration of pottery. However, in spite of its dolmens, strongholds, the variety of chamber tombs and Mycenean influence, Sicily does not display cultural or architectural sophistication until the arrival of the Greeks in the 8C BC.

Hellenic Sicily

ARCHITECTURE. Early Greek settlements were focussed on the south-east of Sicily, especially at Syracuse, founded 733 BC (Naxos, on the east coast, was founded c 735 BC). At first, Greek pottery was imported, but soon a flourishing pottery industry in decorated 'red figured' ware sprang up and architecture and graves were created in the Greek manner within Sicily. Greek Sicily was, and felt itself to be, fully Greek, not just a rude distant outpost. From the 6C BC Greek cities like Megara Hyblaea and Selinus (Selinunte) were planned in a rational way and had the characteristic Greek central square or agora, temples and cemeteries. But their most magnificent and influential monuments were the Doric temples which still stand, noble and unforgettable, in the dry Sicilian hills. The oldest of these, the temple of Apollo, or of Apollo and Artemis, built c 575 BC, at **Syracuse**, characterised by an enormous heaviness, is obviously a pioneer building. It was followed in the course of the next one and a half centuries at Himera, Akragas and elsewhere, but most grandly of all at **Selinunte** where at least nine temples were built in the long period of peace c 580–480 BC.

Sicilian Greeks were able to keep in step with old Greece through the continuous traffic between Sicily and the old Greek world; documentary evidence suggests the arrival of skilled craftsmen and architects summoned by Sicilian patrons. Indeed the influence of Greece is discernible in the reworking of designs during building. Nevertheless, distinctive Sicilian peculiarities developed in the temples: sculpted reliefs on friezes and pediments are much rarer than in Greece and the rule that a pteron (an external colonnade) should be more closely spaced along the sides than at the ends was gradually abandoned, as at **Selinunte Temple C**, whereas the differentiation was adhered to in Greece. Aesthetic considerations often prompted these changes; for instance the unorthodox elements of the unfinished temple at Segesta were designed to give the building a squat appearance in keeping with its situation in a wide valley.

The most remarkable Sicilian Greek building is the temple of Olympian Zeus at **Agrigento**, the largest of all the Doric temples and never finished. Its structure, plan and elevation, with its enormous engaged half columns and colossal Atlas figures, were all revolutionary. The conflict between Timoleon (sent in 346 BC with a small army after the Greek cities applied for assistance; and aimed at establishing a democratic government but with himself as *de facto* ruler) and Agathocles (391–289 BC, the 'tyrant of Syracuse' between 317 and 311; born at Thermae in Sicily), left its most dramatic architectural results at Gela, where, under Timoleon, a new city was built, culminating in the fortifications on Capo Soprano, which were completed during the reign of Agathocles. The beautiful masonry in almost perfect condition was recovered from the sand in 1953–54. But the most impressive image of Greek defenceworks is provided by the Castello Eurialo at Syracuse, the strategic position of which offered exemplary solutions to the defensive problems of the 4C BC.

Most of the Greek theatres in Sicily were modified or completely rebuilt when Sicily belonged to Rome. For example, at **Segesta**, the best preserved of all the Hellenic Sicilian theatres (of the 3C BC), the unusually high scena frons with architectural decoration was probably added early in the 1C and at Tyndaris the theatre was drastically altered by the Romans. Nevertheless it is clear that these buildings were conceived as part of a wonderful natural stage, taking careful advantage of dramatic views and slopes of the land around.

SCULPTURE. The rarity of sculpted reliefs on temples in Sicily in comparison with ancient Greece is most arresting and has not yet been convincingly explained. Of all the Greek cities in Sicily, Selinunte is the only one to have decorated its temples with sculptured metopes. These, therefore, are very important in the story of archaic sculpture. The oldest, belonging to Temple C, of the early 6C BC, are in flat relief, but others are almost in the round, and those of temple E, dated between 460 and 450 BC abound with life and movement.

The Roman Period

ARCHITECTURE. After Hieron II's switch away from Carthage to a partnership with Rome in 263 BC, the culture and civilisation of Sicily absorbed much from Rome. Most of the monuments of this era were public. The theatre of **Catania**, the aqueduct of **Termini Imerese**, the theatre and the naumachia of **Taormina** are representative. Only the central powers were willing to fund such expensive projects and consequently a number of similar buildings went up simultaneously in the most important towns of Sicily, as in the rest of Italy and the provinces. For instance, amphitheatres (which were sometimes converted theatres), in use until the late empire with gladiatorial games and jousting, frequently date from the Augustan age. However, the most spectacular sign of Roman wealth and luxury is the villa in the wooded valley at Casale near **Piazza Armerina**, near Enna. Probably built in the early 4C as the country retreat of Diocletian's colleague Maximian, it had nearly fifty rooms, courts, galleries, baths and corridors arranged in five complex groups and approached by an imposing entrance. Little remains of the sculpture, murals or marble architectural elements, but the mosaic pavements surpass in extent and inventiveness any others of their kind. Ranging from geometrical patterns to scenes of bathing, dancing, fishing, from theatrical performances to scenes of animal life and complicated narrative compositions drawn from Greek mythology, the mosaics create a wonderful display of trompe l'oeil effects, colours and designs. Despite their Roman imperial style, they are almost certainly the work of craftsmen imported from north Africa. Indeed, Roman Sicily did not develop a distinctive culture of its own: the marble portrait busts of local dignitaries, Roman emperors and Greek philosophers are exactly like those of Italy or Gaul.

The early catacombs in Syracuse also date from this period and the grandest of them exceed those of Rome in size and embellishment. The oldest, that of S. Lucia, was in continuous use for at least a century during the period of illegality before Constantine. There was little attempt at decoration during this period, but after the Edict of Toleration, the Syracusan Christians enlarged their underground cemeteries, and introduced new architectural and decorative elements. Higher social class was expressed by more carefully cut chambers with arched entrances and the creation of 'rotundas' in which sculpted sarcophagi were placed in groups.

The Byzantine Period

Of the years of Byzantine rule very little architecture, painting, or sculpture remains and the fragmentary pieces in the Palazzo Bellomo, Syracuse and elsewhere are a sorry contrast to the long duration of the dominion. A sketchy picture of architectural developments can be constructed, however, from the few surviving churches. Up until the 6C most churches were basilican in plan, ending in one or more semicircular apses, as at S. Pietro, Syracuse. Then the eastern provinces began to favour the centralised church in variations on the Greek cross. A few of these were erected in Sicily too, but the basilica seems to have remained the most common form. Hardly any fresco painting of this period has survived, although the remains in **S. Pietro, Noto**; **S. Maria della Rotonda, Catania**, and elsewhere show that painted decoration was the rule. The most important surviving frescoes, although severely damaged, are the six half-length figures of the saints covering the walls and ceiling of an oratory built in the catacombs of **S. Lucia, Syracuse**. Their style and spirit are Byzantine and their date is probably 8C. Paradoxically, Byzantine art is better represented in the Norman period.

The Norman Period

ARCHITECTURE. King Roger II de Hauteville (1093–1154; king, 1130–54) and his two successors were guided above all by a political desire not to antagonise unnecessarily any of their subjects, be they Latins, Orthodox or Muslims. As art tended to be controlled by the royal court, this tolerance manifests itself as a fascinating heterogeneous mixture of styles in the architecture, mosaics and woodwork, in the sculpture, coins and vestments of this period. Their architecture absorbed alien elements with particular grace, producing monuments of composite style, harmony and dignity. Secular, especially court, architecture, naturally inclined to Muslim models whose levels of refinement were unknown in the north. In Palermo the palaces of Favara, La Zisa and La Cuba, built or adapted to house royal and aristocratic families in splendour, show remarkable cultural heterogeneity: Muslim, Romanesque and Byzantine forms rub shoulders; Norman interlaced round arches, Muslim domes, honeycomb roofs and stilted pointed arches occur in compositions carrying Byzantine mosaics and classically proportioned columns. La Zisa is a particularly beautiful example.

The ecclesiastical architecture of the Norman period is its most celebrated achievement today. Indeed the interiors of Cefalù and Monreale cathedrals and of the Palatine chapel in Palermo are without equal in Europe. The first of these great Norman churches was Cefalù, begun in 1131 in a newly-founded bishopric and intended to reinforce monarchical, as opposed to papal, power. It is largely a northern, Romanesque church: tall, adorned with chevron patterning, and with a projecting transept and deep choir, flanked by chapels. But traditional Sicilian forms such as stilted pointed arches and columns set into angles were used.

A more complicated stylistic syncretism occurred at the Palatine Chapel in the **Royal Palace in Palermo**, built 1132–40. The ground plan is a combination of the Byzantine, centralised, inscribed cross plan and the south Italian longitudinal plan. The cupola, with its high drum and stepped squinches which oversail the wall, is of Egyptian Islamic derivation; and the wooden honeycomb ceiling of the nave, probably erected under William I (1154–66), belongs to the north African, Islamic world. Its paintings include Cufic inscriptions, Hellenistic scenes, and images traceable to Persian and Indian legends. It has been given many attributions, but it was probably executed by local Sicilians. The effect of the interior of this chapel is extraordinarily harmonious and tranquil; its richness is never strident because of the careful balancing of the colours and spatial rhythms.

La Martorana, Palermo, completed in 1143, is the only important church of this period which was not built for the Hautevilles, although its founder Admiral George of Antioch (died 1151) was an important figure at Roger II's court. His Greek Orthodox religion probably explains why the plan is of the Byzantine inscribed cross type. This seems to have been especially popular for Basilian monasteries: it occurs at **Trinità di Delia** near Castelvetrano and at **S. Antonio in Palermo**.

The climax of Sicilian Romanesque architecture is **Monreale Cathedral**, built by William II as his mausoleum and as a counterpoise to the power of the Archbishop of Palermo. Like the Palatine Chapel, it is a combination of a south Italian basilica and a Byzantine cross-in-square church, but its great size compelled the architect to do without vaults. As before, no attempt was made to fuse the Latin, Byzantine and Islamic ideas, but they are all handled on an unprecedentedly large and exhilarating scale.

It is the mosaic decoration of these buildings which contributes most to their splendour and constitutes Sicily's main claim to fame in the visual arts of the 12C. The Pantocrators in the choirs of Cefalù and Monreale with their ascetic reserve and haggard beauty attain a particularly deep spiritual intensity. The presence of Byzantine decoration in these Latin churches is explicable by the fact that they were royal foundations and the Norman kings were seeking to rival the Byzantine emperors. They were executed by important Byzantine craftsmen. Two styles are discernible: the elegant, humane, classical style of Cefalù and the Palatine Chapel; and the dynamic, late Comnenian style of Monreale (decorated 1185–90). Both styles profoundly influenced 12C Western painting, such as the Winchester Bible (c 1150–80). They are not, however, completely Byzantine. Their iconography reflects the outlook of their patrons (hence the early appearance of St Thomas Becket at Monreale). Whereas in a Byzantine church mosaic decoration consisted of an image of the world, the places sanctified by Christ's life and the feasts of the Church, in Sicily such decoration was didactic. At Monreale, for example, the Christian story from the Fall to the Last Judgement unfolds from the entrance eastwards (typically the Last Judgement is represented at the west end). This is the largest and most important Greek mosaic decoration of the 12C which exists anywhere.

Very few secular mosaics have survived, and of those that have hardly any have been dated. Most of the palaces built in the Conca d'Oro by Roger and his followers probably contained mosaic decorations. The Sala Terrena at La Zisa, probably set at the beginning of William II's reign, displays beautiful interlaced roundels, pairs of peacocks and other characteristic motifs, but the Norman Stanza in the Royal Palace at Palermo far exceeds this in sumptuousness. Despite clumsy restorations, the mosaics still glimmer brilliantly in greens and golds in this evocative room.

The fall of the Hauteville dynasty, however, put an end to these developments. A Court art, fostered by kings who were strangers in their country and executed by foreign artists, the mosaic work flourished and died with the Hautevilles and did not lead to the subsequent developments in mosaic art in Sicily.

SCULPTURE. The largest and most impressive group of sculpture of this period is the cloister of the Benedictine monastery at Monreale, created between 1172 and 1189. Here over 200 paired colonnettes, with twin capitals treated in single compositions, display an astonishing variety of styles and subjects. Sources of the styles and iconography include Arabic, Byzantine (the mosaics of Monreale Cathedral and Byzantine caskets were drawn upon), north French, Tuscan, Lombard and Campanian; but a general stylistic harmony exists because of the dominance of the classicising style of Campania. The royal porphyry tombs, free-standing under monumental sedicula, in the cathedrals of Palermo and Monreale are equally outstanding, but very different, examples of the sculpture of this period. The unique forms of their sarcophagi were derived from antique models. Some monuments reflect the style of contemporary Byzantine sculpture, such as the relief slabs from the Cathedral of Messina, now in the Museo Regionale, Messina.

MANUSCRIPTS. A particularly fine group of illustrated manuscripts was produced at Messina under the patronage of Richard Palmer, the English archbishop of Messina (1182–95). This exceptional work provides a tantalising glimpse of the patronage of one of the highly educated foreign prelates.

Thirteenth and Fourteenth Centuries

ARCHITECTURE. Unlike his predecessors, Frederick II did not endow monasteries or bishoprics; instead he devoted his building energies to creating a line of fortifications running from Germany to south Italy and Sicily. In Sicily this line tended to favour the east coast and internally towards Enna. Castles dominated the cities of this area and fortresses were erected at strategic points inland. The most characteristic of the Swabian castles are **Castello Maniace (Syracuse), Augusta** (begun 1232) and **Castello Ursino** (begun 1234) in Catania; the contemporaneity of their construction—or reconstruction—indicates the existence of an efficient technical organisation and illustrates Frederick's personal control over the castle building programme. The castles consist of quadrangular curtain walls with corner towers, a plan and spatial form derived from Byzantine and Muslim architecture. Castello Maniace, for instance, is square with round towers at the corners. Others, like the castle at Augusta, have towers in the middle as well as at the corners. Their original internal arrangement is best seen at Castello Maniace. Here the ground floor was originally unpartitioned but was divided by square bays with rib vaults resting on robust round columns, except for the central bay, which formed a small atrium. The atrium acquired a dominant role through its swollen size and luminosity in the castles of Catania and Prato in Tuscany. The Swabian castles are remarkable above all because they encase elegant apartments built in the Gothic style, as at Castello Maniace and Castello Ursino. This reflects the fact that in addition to their military function the castles were designed to house Frederick on his journeys through Sicily. Although these 13C castles, in their remote sites, are still awe-inspiring sights, little detailed research on them has been carried out or published. Thus we know very little about **Castello di Paternò**, an austere tower of volcanic rock commanding the wide Simeto valley, or the **Castello di Garsiliato** (recorded 1240) which rises in forbidding solitude in the immense valley of Gela; indeed, many buildings generally attributed to the Swabian period could date from other periods.

Frederick II did not give much impulse to the development of religious architecture. His direct involvement was restricted to the Murgo basilica near Lentini; but the religious orders initiated some important buildings like the Badiazza near Messina, a Cistercian church, or the Franciscan foundation at Messina. The **Murgo**, founded c 1225, demonstrates the continuity of Norman architectural forms in the use of Byzantine and Islamic motifs, but its plan is typical of Cistercian buildings and it has elements in common with contemporary castles: the side aisles of the basilica strongly recall the arcades of Castello Maniace. Similar elements occur in the Badiazza, whose rib vaults are among the most beautiful of 13C buildings and whose capitals include Byzantine, Burgundian and Cistercian types. Burgundian Gothic rib vaults, responds and portal capitals also appear in another important church, **S. Maria degli Alemanni** (c 1220) **in Messina**. They are combined with Romanesque elements which persist in the portal and interior capitals. Among the most remarkable churches is **S. Francesco, Messina** (founded 1254) whose architectual sophistication is illustrative of the axiom that the finest achievements of Italian Gothic architecture are often obtained by the simplest forms. Its eight nave chapels create interesting effects: too shallow to disturb the spatial unity of the nave, their undecorated pointed arches give the appearance of internal buttressing (a feature which originated among the mendicants in Catalonia and south France). Its apse is unexpectedly animated by the introduction of Gothic decoration elements not found elsewhere in the church.

With the fall of the Swabian monarchy and the break up of its central authority, 14C Sicily became tormented by factional struggles. As a result, the dominating 14C structural feature is the tower. The great feudal lords continued the well-tried building traditions established in the Swabian castles: the castle of **Naro**, for instance, reproduces the constructive system of Frederick II's castles in its use of round and quadrangular towers. Swabian forms also persisted in the castle at Mussomeli built by Manfredo Chiaramonte towards the mid 14C, and in that at Venetico, erected by the Spadafora in the first half of the 15C.

Castle building in the country was echoed in the towns by the erection of 'strong' houses, such as those of the Chiaramonte (begun 1307) and Sclafani (1329–30) at Palermo, or the tower houses of the 15C and early 16C still visible at Enna, Randazzo, Taormina and Alcamo. Of these the **Palazzo Steri** (Chiaramonte) **in Palermo** is the most interesting. Its lava inlay decoration and large windows belie the impression of a fortified castle given by the exterior. Inside, the painted ceiling, full of verve, dated 1377–80 and signed by three Sicilians, is the only surviving example of what may have been a widespread vernacular decoration.

PAINTING. Our knowledge of 14C painting is very cloudy because of the loss of many paintings and the inadequacy of research to date. Most important paintings executed in Sicily during the 14C were by foreigners and show Sienese influence. For instance, the elegant early 14C St Peter Enthroned in the Chiaramonte Collection, outstanding for the decorative brilliance of its design, recalls the work of Lippo Memmi and has been attributed to him. The important panel of 1346, signed by **Bartolommeo da Carmogli** (fl. 1346–after 1358) in the Galleria Regionale, Palermo, which shows the Virgin feeding Christ at the breast, is the earliest dated example of what became one of the key symbols of Italian painting for the rest of the 14C. Its predella is also interesting. It shows kneeling members of a flagellant confraternity, four of whom wear the hooded robes with circles cut into the backs to bare the body to the scourge, reflecting the fashion of violent self-mortification.

SCULPTURE. In sculpture as in painting the Sienese influence was marked in 14C Sicily. The wall tomb of Archbishop Guidotto de' Tabiati, dated 1333, in the Cathedral at Messina, signed by **Goro di Gregorio** (fl. 1324–43), a Sienese, shows the weaknesses and strengths characteristic of this period: in places the composition is swallowed up by the narrative and crowded figures make a hectic impression; but in the Annunciation the composition is more controlled and the clear lines and careful balance of the masses are most eloquent. Throughout the Gothic period, Sicilian sculpture betrays a certain clumsiness. Figure sculpture in particular, is often coarse and shows little appreciation of the living form. Ornament and relief display the continuing influence of Byzantine work. Not until the Gagini family came down from Geneva, some time in the late 1450s, was there established in Sicily a group of able sculptors.

Fifteenth and Sixteenth Centuries

ARCHITECTURE. Soon after 1400, Catalan art, often combined with Gothic forms from other sources, began to make its mark in Sicily. In architecture Catalan influences appeared throughout Sicily, but especially at Trapani, Syracuse, Ragusa, Modica and Palermo. The most significant building of the period occurred at **Palermo Cathedral**, and, as the capital was in closer contact with Barcelona than other towns, orthodox Catalan style was used for the sacristy (begun 1430) and the south loggia (1440s), and for the Flamboyant window added to the archipiscopal palace by Archbishop Simone da Bologna (1458–62); but on the whole Catalan influence in church architecture was limited to superficial details: doors and windows of typical shapes and with distinctive forms of vegetal ornament, in particular, of bands of leaves serving as capitals for a group of colonnettes, as in S. Pietro and S. Martino in Syracuse. **S. Giorgio Vecchio, in Ragusa**, is a perfect example of a Catalan Gothic façade transplanted to Sicily (cf. S. Martí Provençals, Barcelona), but usually doors and windows were plainer than comparable examples in Catalonia and Valencia. Elements associated with florid Gothic became increasingly evident during the 15C. Flowing tracery in place of a tympanum appears at S. Maria del Gesù in Palermo, in a chapel doorway, built by a family of Catalan origins probably in the second half of the 15C. But unlike cities where Gothic had taken stronger root, these elements never produced a thoroughly Flamboyant style.

In secular architecture the **Palazzo Aiutamicristo** (c 1495) and **Palazzo Abbatellis** (1488–95, by M. Carnelivari), both in **Palermo**, best represent the peculiar blend of south Italian and Spanish forms; their courtyards are closely akin to the courtyard of Palacio Velado, Avila; and the massive portal of the Palazzo Abbatellis, like a rope-bound raft, combines Castilian and Catalan designs. Secular architecture of this period reflects the metamorphosis of the ruling class. The castle-tower of the 14C, closed and defensive, hostile to the urban scene, and reflecting the military power of its owner, was replaced by the 15C palace, open and outward-looking, expressive of the civil and economic power of the aristocracy. Bankers were the patrons of the Palermitan palazzi Aiutamicristo and the Afflitto, both begun in the 1490s. On the whole, 15C palace architecture tended towards the solid block marked by a strong, but not over-stressed, horizontality. This was the result of the three distinct vertical divisions: the ground floor was for the services, stalls and kitchens; the grand *piano nobile* for the owner and reception rooms; and the attic housed the servants or cadet members of the family. Other characteristics of 15C Sicilian palaces include the vaulted entrance passage, patio, sunken garden, and a regular grid of rooms.

Sicilian architecture of the 15C was not sustained by humanism and remained somewhat inaccessible to Renaissance ideas; but great changes were wrought by two artists working in a mature Renaissance style who arrived in Palermo in the middle years of the century. **Francesco Laurana** (c 1420–79) had worked for Alfonso I in Naples, and was in Palermo from 1467–71 (and he may have returned later: the tomb relief of Abate Speciale now in the Galleria Regionale, Palermo, is dated 1495). His most significant work, the arch to the **Cappella Maestrantonio** in the church of S. Francesco d'Assisi, Palermo, executed in 1468, was the earliest important Renaissance work in Sicily. However, his advanced style was too aloof to take root and it was the sculptor-architect **Domenico Gagini** (fl. 1448–92)—founder of a dynasty of craftsmen which dominated Sicily for the next century—who effectively introduced the new style. Gagini, who had been trained in Genoa and worked in Naples on the triumphal arch of the Castelnuovo, arrived in Palermo in 1458/9 and stayed there until his death in 1492. Among his first documented works is the door to the church of S. Agostino (c 1470) in Palermo. It is a competent, if crudely executed, version of the style current in central and northern Italy, and soon doors of this type appeared all over Sicily, persisting long after the type had become old-fashioned in Lombardy and Tuscany. Domenico's gifted son, **Antonello** (1478–1536), carried on his tradition into the 16C. The gulf between him and local architects is well illustrated in the church of **S. Maria di Porto Salvo (Palermo)**, which he began in c 1527 in a Tuscan Quattrocento style, its chapels being articulated with orthodox pilasters and round-headed arches with more or less correct mouldings. But when Antonello died in 1536, it was impossible to find an architect able to complete it in the Renaissance style and it was finished in the Gothic tradition by Antonio Scaglione, a local architect.

S. Maria di Porto Salvo is one of a most interesting group of churches, almost all near the port of Palermo, dating from the last years of the 15C and the early 16C which demonstrate that the juxtaposition of Gothic and

Renaissance forms, which is so disconcerting to us, was not regarded as inappropriate by contemporaries. At **S. Maria della Catena** in Palermo, which was probably begun soon after 1502, columns crowned by 15C Florentine-style capitals stand on late Gothic pedestals, to which they are joined by French High Gothic bases, and carry Gothic rib vaulting; and a similar combination of Gothic and Renaissance elements appears in S. Maria Nuova.

The persistence in Sicily of certain architectural forms is particularly striking in this period. The unusual rustication and diamond-cut blocks of 16C buildings such as the Giudecca, Trapani, and Palazzo Steripinto, Sciacca, may derive from the prestigious rustication of the Hohenstaufen castles. However, the most obvious of these persistent architectural elements is the squinch. Inherited from Arab architecture and frequently found in Norman buildings in Sicily, the squinch was still being used in the 16C: the **Cappella Naselli** (built between 1517 and 1555) in S. Francesco, Comiso, and the remarkable **Cappella dei Marinai** in the Santuario dell'Annunziata, Trapani, are two instances out of many. In these later buildings the squinch is used with compelling conviction, not as an overworn cliché to be inserted where inspiration failed, and this raises questions about the significance it must have had for the architects.

Another Norman practice which survived into the 16C was the use of two or three superimposed columns for the pier of the crossing of a church. The most remarkable example of this occurs at S. Giorgio dei Genovesi, Palermo, built in an otherwise full Renaissance style between 1576 and 1591. These Sicilian forms have no bearing on the ideas developed in the rest of Italy.

SCULPTURE. A surprising amount of late 15C and early 16C sculpture survives in churches and museums scattered throughout Sicily. Quite unlike the pattern of development in north Italy, where ducal workshops provided focuses of development, in Sicily a single style tended to spread over the whole coastal area of the island. As in architecture, the main impetus came from **Laurana** and **Domenico Gagini**, both marble sculptors working in a style deriving from late Quattrocento Florence. Indeed, the similarity of their styles has created problems in attributing some works like the reliefs on the holy-water stoups in Palermo Cathedral and portrait busts (now in the Galleria Regionale, Palermo). **Domenico Gagini**'s style reflects that of late 15C Florence and particularly his interest in the work of Ghiberti and Buggiano, Brunelleschi's protégé. His Madonnas are exceptional for their suggestion of delicate movement: in his later works he departs from his early rigid frontal presentation of the image, creating a greater dynamic tension as in the figure on the tomb of Pietro Speciale in S. Francesco d'Assisi, Palermo, but on the whole his work and especially his portraits lack the sensitivity of Laurana's. Laurana executed an influential series of standing polychrome Madonnas, beginning with the one in Palermo Cathedral modelled on a Trecento Virgin by Nino Pisano in Trapani; others can be seen in the church of the Crocifisso in Noto and in the museum at Messina. They demonstrate Laurana's ability to fuse late Gothic and Renaissance ideas.

Antonello Gagini developed his father's work. He came to be considered the most significant Renaissance sculptor of Sicily, and his vast amount of work reflects his popularity. The period between 1510 and 1536 was particularly busy: not only did he have his usual studio work of statues, tombs and altars, but also the vast tribuna of Palermo Cathedral, remarkable for its combination of old and new styles and ideas, and for the introduction to Palermo of stucco as a material for sculpture. Indeed, Antonello and his workshop sculpted in marble, terracotta, 'mistura' (plaster and papier mâché mixed) and stucco, which meant that their work was available at a range of prices. Antonello's search for an ideal beauty, evident in the roundels in the Gancia, Palermo, of c 1500, was related to the contemporary classicising trend in Lombardy, and tended to produce rather sickly sweet Madonnas, such as the Madonna della Scala of 1503 in Palermo Cathedral.

Just as the ambivalence between Gothic and Renaissance forms persisted in architecture into the 16C, so it did in sculpture. A relief in the church of the Magione, Palermo, produced in the workshop of the Gagini in the late 15C or early 16C illustrates this well. Florentine Quattrocento-style figures stand between late Gothic twisted colonnettes and snuggle into shell niches below Gothic gables.

PAINTING. During the early 15C, Sicilian painting was markedly Spanish in character and showed little awareness of developments in the north. The most important paintings were by foreigners and most were in a Catalan style of which the early 15C polyptych in the church of S. Martino, Syracuse, by the so-called **Maestro di S. Martino**, is representative. The only major work in an independent 'Sicilian' style is the **Triumph of Death** in Palazzo Sclafani, Palermo.

However, **Antonello da Messina** (c 1430–79) dramatically altered the character of Sicilian painting in the late 15C. As no strong Sicilian stylistic tradition existed, he turned to movements abroad: three separate foreign experiences deeply affected his work. These were a training (probably in Naples) in the Flemish style and in the technique of oil painting; the influence of Giovanni Bellini during a stay in Venice; and the influence of the work of Piero della Francesca. The first half of Antonello's career is well documented, but almost entirely devoid of extant works. He seems to have been working from 1457–65 in and around Messina. Paintings of this period are dominated by Flemish forms, but show signs of his experimentation with the representation of spatial depth that had been developing in central Italy. During his most active period, 1473–77, Flemish influences, such as the work of Robert Campion, Petrus Christus or Memling, remained keen: the interior setting, decorated drapery and the fascination with precise rendering of reflected light in both the polyptych for the church of S. Gregorio of 1473 (now in the Museo Regionale, Messina) and in the Annunciation of 1475 (now in the Museo Regionale, Syracuse) are good examples of this; but Italian influences make themselves felt in the column dividing the Annunciation which recalls Piero della Francesca's Annunciations, and in the shape of the polyptych itself. In Venice, and especially from Bellini, Antonello learned how to handle architectural space. His **Virgin Annunciate** (Galleria Regionale, Palermo) displays this new mastery in the placing and perspectival treatment of the lectern and the Virgin's hand, which give a dramatic depth and solidity to the picture.

The influence of Antonello da Messina was widespread, especially amongst his descendants and relations who included **Jacobello di Antonello** (c 1455–90), **Antonello De Saliba** (1466/7–after 1535), **Salvo de Antonio** (fl. c 1493–1525) and **Marco Costanza** (15C). Their works, however, show none of Antonello's sense of inquiry and delight in experiment.

16C SCULPTURE. Because of its geographical position, Messina was in closer contact with the mainland than other towns in Sicily, and during the 16C artists from Florence and Rome frequently travelled there, attracted by its political and social importance. Of these, a pupil of Michelangelo, the Florentine **Giovanni Angelo Montorsoli** (1507?–63), who came to Messina in 1547, was the most important. He established in Sicily the Tuscan manner of the mid-century in both sculpture and architecture, reinstating the use of human and monstrous figures in sculpture, which had been lost largely because of Arab influence. Montorsoli's **Orion fountain** (begun 1547), with its Michelangelesque forms, was particularly influential both in Sicily and mainland Italy, and his **Neptune fountain** (begun 1557) was hardly less so. He left behind a long line of followers at Messina, principal among whom was **Martino Montanini** whose work, exemplified by the S. Caterina statue in the church of SS. Annunziata (1558/9) at Forza d'Agro, is a frostier version of Montorsoli's.

In Palermo the influence of Tuscan Mannerism was much weaker and, except for piecemeal scatterings, is restricted to one monument. In 1570 it was decided to embellish the square in front of the Palazzo Municipale with a fountain, and in 1574 the Fontana Pretoria, by the Florentine sculptor **Francesco Camilliani** (died 1586), originally intended for a Florentine villa, was duly inserted, with the necessary additions by Francesco's son, **Camillo** (fl. 1574–1603) and **Michelangelo Naccherino** (1550–1622). With this, Palermo tasted, albeit belatedly, the new language of Mannerist sculpture; but, unlike in Messina, no new school of sculptors formed, and the fountain remained an isolated case, even though its unusual figures were sometimes copied or adapted in later works of art.

16C ARCHITECTURE AND TOWN PLANNING. These fountains were part of flamboyant attempts to modernise the urban environment, by opening new streets, creating vistas marked by prestigious buildings or gates, improving the water supply, and so on, with which ambitious viceroys, courting popularity, sought to link their names. Religious orders also played an important role, demonstrating their power by building churches and convents. This process of renewal of the urban fabric, which was to be most significant at Palermo, began at Messina, where **Andrea Calamech** (1514–78) and Camillo Camilliani were entrusted with much of the work. A great deal of their work has been destroyed, but what survives reveals a new sturdy monumentality. Temporary architecture, designed for special religious or political occasions, was probably very influential. In Palermo, for instance, when the road to Monreale was opened between 1580 and 1584, the new gates of Porta Felice and Porta Nuova were erected, and the latter perpetuated ideas of the temporary triumphal arch put up for Charles V's celebrated visit of 1535.

Two of the finest streets of Palermo took their names from viceroys, the Via Toledo in the 1560s and the Via Maqueda in the 1590s, and ten years later another viceroy built a fine Baroque octagon at their intersection, the Quattro Canti, in imitation of Rome's Quattro Fontane. Begun by the Florentine architect, **Giulio Lasso**, most of the work was completed by **Smiriglio**. Monarchical, heavenly, and local references were combined in a ponderously impressive work, which hid, as it still does today, the slums of the poor behind its proud screens.

The return to Sicily of the Messinese **Giacomo Del Duca** (fl. 1540–1600), who had worked in Rome under Michelangelo in his later years, also contributed to the new phase of late 16C architecture in Messina. His understanding of Michelangelo's late style is visible in the remarkable church of **S. Giovanni di Malta**, Messina, on which he began work with Camilliani from about 1590: the use of giant pilasters and deep triangular *guttae* had repercussions in Sicilian architecture until the 18C. His establishment of a mature late 16C Roman style in a country with very different architectural traditions is unparalleled anywhere else in Italy. The vigour and monumentality of the tradition was perpetuated by **Natale Masuccio** (fl. 1560–70), a Jesuit architect, who had trained in Rome at the turn of the century and absorbed there a mixed Tuscan-Roman style from Bartolommeo Ammanati and Giuseppe Valeriani. Their influence can be seen in his Jesuit Novitiate in Trapani (begun before 1614) and the ruins of his Monte di Pietà in Messina.

Baroque Architecture

This is one of the most exciting periods of the architectural history of Sicily. The exuberant vivacity and inventiveness, the variety and exhilarating beauty of Sicilian Baroque architecture (including vernacular architecture) are unparalleled. In the more sophisticated buildings architects familiar with current styles in Rome worked to create, not slavish copies of Roman Baroque, but vigorous interpretations of that style from within Sicilian traditions. This is best seen in the work of **Rosario Gagliardi** (?1700–70). At their best Sicilian buildings occupy positions of dignity and authority in the field of European Baroque architecture.

The earthquake of 1693 which devastated most of the towns of south and east Sicily deeply affected the development of Baroque architecture on the island and our picture of it. Little remains of pre-1693 architecture in the earthquake zone, but that which does, such as **S. Sebastiano**, Acireale, suggests that it was highly decorated with scrolls, rustication and grotesque masks. This strange anthropomorphised architecture was rarely taken up again after 1693. The abruptness of this break and the inevitable self-consciousness of the new style makes the architecture of the east unlike that of the west where, particularly at Palermo, local traditions persisted as the most powerful force.

The new towns in the earthquake zone often enjoyed the benefits of new sites and plans. At Avolà **Angelo Italia** created a regular grid with large open piazzas, designed for safety in the event of another quake; but here and at Grammichele these new ideas were encased in a dramatic hexagon, derived from traditional military treatises. This approach, which cannot be appreciated within the town, contrasts strongly with the ideas used at Noto where the grid arrangement of the streets was exploited to create beautiful vistas punctuated by fine buildings to be enjoyed from within the city.

The buildings around the Cathedral square in Catania illustrate well the singleness of intention of the organisers of the rebuilding and the first style evolved after the earthquake. Its main characteristics were vigorous superficial decoration and multiform rustication. **G.B. Vaccarini** (1702–68), who arrived in Catania c 1730, introduced a completely different style which was to dominate Catanese architecture for several decades. From Rome, where he had trained in the early 1720s, he brought a number of new church plans and architectural features, especially windows, which show a thorough study of the great Roman Baroque architects and of Borromini in particular. In his best buildings, such as the **Palazzo Valle** (c 1740–50) or **S. Agata**, Vaccarini stretched out from these Roman ideas and created a unified movement and play of curves unthinkable in contemporary Rome. His introduction of certain Roman church plans to Sicily was seminal, but he always developed the Roman plans to achieve new effects. S. Agata, based on S. Agnese in Piazza Navona, is less centralised than its model (and its interior is lighter as a result of using stucco rather than marble). In contrast, the most active mid-18C local architect, **Francesco Battaglia** (fl. 1732–78), created in the *salone* of **Palazzo Biscari**, Catania, the most liberated Rococo decoration to be found in Sicily or south Italy. Vaccarini's later classicising style was continued by Stefano Ittar in S. Placido and the Collegiata; but the move towards the neo-classical use of orders and decoration is most marked in Antonio Battaglia's new staircase at the monastery of the Benedettini, 1749.

The most original architect in the south-east was **Rosario Gagliardi**, engineer to the town and district of Noto. Several churches have been grouped around his documented works, whose distinctive traits can perhaps best be appreciated at **S. Giorgio, Ragusa Ibla**, of 1744. Both here and at **S. Giorgio, Modica**, the hillside site is brilliantly exploited, and underlined by the façade design, in which the tower seems to burst from the central bay, itself a solution to the Sicilian belfry façade problem. The columns, canted boldly against the curved centres, and the pediments, flicked above the doorways, exploit a freedom never tasted by the Roman followers of Bernini and Borromini (if hinted at in some Roman façades, such as Martino Longhi's SS. Vincenzo ed Anastasio) and add dynamism to the design. The interiors of Gagliardi's churches, unlike those of the Roman architects and his fellow countryman and contemporary Filippo Juvarra, do not display great commitment to spatial experimentation, but they are full of fascinating details, some of which reveal an interest in Gothic forms. In Syracuse the masterpiece of Baroque architecture is **Andrea Palma**'s (1664–1730) cathedral façade (begun in 1728) which uses broken masses within a columnar façade to create a jagged and dramatic effect.

In Palermo ecclesiastical Baroque architecture shows greater continuity with insular architectural traditions. The basilican plan remained popular and the local (Norman) tradition of columnar arcades persisted, of which **S. Giuseppe dei Teatini**, begun 1612 by **Giacomo Besio**, is the most awe-inspiring example. Greater attention was given to plans consisting of a simple hall with shallow side chapels and apses, such as **Giacomo Amato**'s (1643–1732) **S. Teresa alla Kalsa**; this plan type was readily taken up by the many confraternities which blossomed in post-Tridentine Sicily. As in Catania, centralised plans were created more frequently but spatial experimentation was less important than in Rome.

A few Palermitan churches show that their architects were familiar with Roman Baroque architecture. **Paolo Amato**'s (1634–1714) SS. Salvatore (begun 1682), an elongated oval plan, is a much more spacious and flatter version of Rainaldi's S. Maria di Montesanto; and Giacomo Amato, who was in Rome from 1670 to 1687, derived the magnificent façades of S. Teresa (begun c 1686) and La Pietà (begun 1689) from Rainaldi's S. Maria in Campitelli and S. Andrea della Valle. These bold and majestic façades also incorporate traditional Sicilian elements, such as the circular window at the centre of the design, which would never have been used on a church on the mainland. This interest in Sicily's own traditions is shown equally in Angelo Italia's exceptional (if not wholly satisfactory) little church, S. Francesco Saverio (1684–1710), whose pierced hexagonal chapels were derived from Guarini's churches in Messina (tragically destroyed in 1908).

One of the most fascinating and peculiar aspects of Palermitan (and, to a lesser extent, Messinese) Baroque architecture is the use of cut and polished inlaid stones, known as *marmi mischi*, to cover the walls in a fabulous display of motifs, sometimes religious and symbolic, sometimes purely decorative. The practice seems to have begun with the use of flat panels of coloured marble on tombs; white reliefs were subsequently introduced and the rigid geometric forms were discarded: an early example is a tomb of 1637 in S. Domenico. Particularly fine examples of the fully developed form include the Cappella dell'Immacolata (c 1650) in S. Francesco d'Assisi, and the churches of the Casa Professa and S. Caterina, which incorporate low and high reliefs and statuary in complex iconographic programmes. Small biblical scenes were frequently depicted in marble on chapel walls and altarpieces in the 18C. The technical virtuosity in the Flight out of Egypt in S. Maria Miracoli is characteristic.

The exquisite stuccowork by **Giacomo Serpotta** (1656–1732) and his descendants displays similar concerns. Although indebted to earlier traditions of stucco work, the celebrated oratories of Serpotta surpass them by far in artistic sensibility and technique. In the Oratorio di S. Zita (1685–88), the walls appear to be draped in cloth, against which are set the Mysteries of the Rosary and the Victory at Lepanto, all delicately modelled in stucco. The paintings and frescoes around which Serpotta conceived his stuccowork still exist in the Oratorio del SS. Rosario di S. Domenico (c 1710–17), showing how harmonious and elegant these interiors must have been. Giacomo Serpotta's son, **Procopio**, allowed architecture a greater importance in his compositions, as in his masterpiece, the Oratorio of S. Caterina (1719–26). Although he strove to achieve his father's elegance and perfect finish of modelling, his figures are elongated and languid, and lack his father's verve and energy.

Palace architecture has suffered from disgraceful neglect in Palermo, but enough survives for us to appreciate the diversity of plans, the character of the façades and the most important features, such as doors, windows and staircases, on all of which creative energy was concentrated. Giacomo Amato's **Palazzo Cutò** (begun 1705) and **Palazzo Cattolica** (c 1720) combine innovative planning with the creation of impressive spaces and vistas. Similar theatrical effects are created by the most spectacular of Palermitan staircases at **Palazzo Bonagia** by **Andrea Giganti** (18C), probably executed in the 1760s. The interiors of 17C and 18C palaces have almost all been destroyed, but surviving examples show an imaginative gaiety rarely found outside Sicily. **Palazzo Gangi**, c 1770–90, for instance, boasts a spectacular suite of rooms culminating in the diaphonous Sala degli Specchi, whose unique ceiling is composed of a deeply coved upper shell, painted with allegorical frescoes, and a pierced lower ceiling suspended below. This creates an effect of shifting worlds, like a magic lantern.

Built by an extravagant and feckless aristocracy as retreats from the feverish capital during hot weather, the villas of Bagheria and Piana dei Colli are among the most inventive of Sicilian 18C buildings. Their simple façades, in keeping with their rustic setting, contrast with the grand and complex exterior staircases, which reflect the sophisticated life-style of the owners. Almost all these staircases are double; some are curved, as at the Villa Spina; others are jaggedly contorted, as at the Villa Palagonia. The latter was built by **Tomaso Napoli** (17C) who emerges as an outstanding architect here and at the Villa Valguernera (begun c 1709). He combined unusual forms, concave and convex curves, with ingenious and inventive planning involving the creation of many different shaped rooms, to achieve an overall effect of grace and flowing line.

It is important to remember that our picture of Baroque architecture in Sicily is very fragmentary, for two main reasons. First, in the 17C and 18C, temporary architecture and decoration erected to celebrate church festivals and political events were at least as important as permanent architecture. Although they are recorded in drawings and engravings, our impressions of these *apparati* are necessarily imperfect without being able to experience them in the round and bedecked with lights and colour. Second, much Baroque architecture has been destroyed. The ravages caused by the earthquake of 1693 prompted much fertile rebuilding; but much of the damage caused by subsequent earthquakes and by the bombing of World War II has never been attended to. Consequently, many 17C and 18C palaces and churches stand as empty shells, their once splendid features crumbling into meaningless rubble. This is the result of political irresponsibility, and it is horrifying to see.

Seventeenth Century Painting

17C painting is illuminated by the contributions of two outstanding foreign artists, Caravaggio and Van Dyck. **Caravaggio** (1571–1609/10), fleeing arrest in Malta, landed in Messina in 1608/9 and executed in Sicily at least five paintings, mainly for private patrons. His first work in Sicily, the **Burial of St Lucy**, (now in the Galleria Regionale, Syracuse), probably begun in early 1609, concentrates on the human aspects only of the divine drama, making an eloquent contrast between the helpless passivity, even distraction, of the mourners, and the empty but self-confident gestures of the officials. The **Adoration of the Shepherds** (1609, Museo Regionale, Messina), commissioned by the Messinese Senate as the high altarpiece of the church of S. Maria degli Angeli, is one of Caravaggio's most deeply felt and impressively simple works. Here the dignity he recognised in the poor and simple is intensely conveyed; even the resonant space accentuates the silent devotion of the shepherds.

Van Dyck's (1599–1641) visit to Palermo in 1624, although cut short by his fear of the plague raging in west Sicily, produced a remarkable group of pictures of S. Rosalia (now in New York, Houston and Ponce) and his grandest Italian altarpiece, the **Madonna of the Rosary** 1624–28 (finished in Genoa) still in the Oratorio del Rosario in S. Domenico. Although Sicily has retained only one of Van Dyck's Sicilian paintings, his influence is frequently apparent in local 17C painting, and in the work of **Pietro Novelli** (1603–47) above all.

Eighteenth and Nineteenth Century Architecture

During the 18C neo-classical architecture gradually took root all over Sicily, but particularly in Palermo, as a result of its close links with Naples, Rome and France. **Venanzio Marvuglia** (1729–1814), a Palermitan who had become deeply imbued with neo-classicism during his stay in Rome (1747–59), was the most significant architect of this style. With his Benedictine monastery, **S. Martino delle Scale**, near Palermo (1762–76), the curvaceous middle bays and flowing lines of Palermitan Baroque palaces are shrugged off and replaced by straight lines and planes. Of great significance is Marvuglia's use of a flat impost, rather than the traditional arcade, above the columns of the nave in the Oratory of S. Filippo Neri, in Palermo, built 1769. This was in accordance with Laugier's influential idea that the ancient Greek is the only true standard in architecture. However, Marvuglia's obvious feeling for the effect of simple masses and carefully thought-out proportions and his use of characteristic Sicilian balconies in the palaces of Riso-Belmonte and Constantino in Palermo push him far from the inflexible rigidity of some neo-classicists. Sicily's antiquity was very fashionable in 18C Europe and it was a Frenchman, **Léon Dufourny**, who first used again in Sicily the Greek Doric style when he built his pavilion in the Palermo Botanic Gardens, in 1787. This style was taken up all over Sicily for 19C public buildings, such as the theatre at Castelvetrano and the Ministry of Finance offices in Palermo.

Art Nouveau

Palermo is an important centre of Art Nouveau architecture, surpassed in Italy only by Turin and Milan. Its importance reflects the concentration of upper middle-class families gravitating around the Florio financial empire whose patronage provided the mainstay of Ernesto Basile's commissions. For it was **Ernesto Basile** (1857–1932), whose father **G.B. Basile** (1825–91) had created the heavy Corinthian Teatro Massimo, Palermo, who dominated the Art Nouveau style in Sicily. He was an able architect, keenly aware of Sicily's architectural traditions, without feeling bound to copy them slavishly. He borrowed heavily from Sicilian 15C motifs for the exteriors of his buildings, e.g. **Palazzo Bruno**, Ispica, and the **Villino Florio** in Palermo. Here Carnilivari, of whose work he had made careful measured drawings, was particularly important. By contrast, Sicilian Norman motifs are the predominant source for his interiors. Basile's characteristic fusion of structural and ornamental elements is best seen today in the **Villa Igiea** (1899), Palermo, whose dining room is the epitome of Basile's fantastic medievalism. Although most of his work was for private patrons, Basile also designed the theatre in Canicattì and the Palazzo Municipale in Licata (1930s). The interest of Basile's workshops in the revival of the applied arts contributed to the spread of Art Nouveau throughout Sicily, and to Catania in particular, where a number of good examples survive in the Viale Regina Margherita. Sadly, however, many fine Art Nouveau style villas have been demolished in the last twenty years.

Twentieth Century

20C architecture in Sicily is a dispiriting subject. Political irresponsibility has allowed ugly speculative schemes to stampede unhindered into the countryside, and to smother the coastlines with blocks of flats, tourist villages and holiday villas. Awareness of Sicilian traditions and of the distinctiveness of Sicilian culture, which were for centuries such important and invigorating forces in the island's architecture, has been cast aside, and the language these new buildings speak is the same inarticulate grunting that occurs everywhere in Europe where speculative gain has triumphed over artistic and social concerns.

GLOSSARY

For Greek architectural terms and vase types, see pp 35, 36, and 37.

ABACUS. Flat stone in the upper part of a capital.

ACROTERION. An ornamental feature on the corner or highest point of a pediment.

AEDICULE. Small opening framed by two columns and a pediment, originally used in classical architecture.

AGORA. Public square or market-place.

AMBO (pl. ambones). Pulpit in a Christian basilica; two pulpits on opposite sides of a church, from which the gospel and epistle were read.

AMPHIPROSTYLE. Temple with colonnades at both ends.

AMPHORA. Antique vase, usually of large dimensions, for oil and other liquids.

ANTEFIX. Ornament placed at the lower corner of the tiled roof of a temple to conceal the space between the tiles and the cornice.

ANTIS. *In antis* describes the portico of a temple when the side-walls are prolonged to end in a pilaster flush with the columns of the portico.

ARCHITRAVE. Lowest part of the entablature, horizontal frame above a door.

ARCHIVOLT. Moulded architrave carried round an arch.

ATLANTES (or *Telamones*). Male figures used as supporting columns.

ATRIUM. Forecourt, usually of a Byzantine church or a classical Roman house.

BADIA, *Abbazia*. Abbey.

BAGLIO. From the medieval word 'Ballium' meaning a large fortified building. It is now usually used to describe the warehouse of a wine distillery.

BALDACCHINO. Canopy supported by columns, usually over an altar.

BASILICA. Originally a Roman building used for public administration; in Christian architecture, an aisled church with a clerestory and apse, and no transepts.

BORGO. A suburb; street leading away from the centre of a town.

BOTTEGA. The studio of an artist; the pupils who worked under his direction.

BOULEUTERION. Council chamber.

BOZZETTO. Sketch, often used to describe a small model for a piece of sculpture.

BUCCHERO. Etruscan black terracotta ware.

CALDARIUM, or Calidarium. Room for hot or vapour baths in a Roman bath.

CAMPANILE. Bell-tower, often detached from the building to which it belongs.

CAMPOSANTO. Cemetery.

CAPITAL. The top of a column.

CARDO. The main street of a Roman town, at right angles to the Decumanus.

CARYATID. Female figure used as a supporting column.

CAVEA. The part of a theatre or amphitheatre occupied by the row of seats.

CELLA. Sanctuary of a temple, usually in the centre of the building.
CHIAROSCURO. Distribution of light and shade, apart from colour, in a painting.
CHIESA MATRICE (or Chiesa Madre). Parish church.
CHTHONIC. Dwelling in or under the ground.
CIBORIUM. Casket or tabernacle containing the Host.
CIPOLLINO. Onion-marble; a greyish marble with streaks of white or green.
CIPPUS. Sepulchral monument in the form of an altar.
CISTA. Casket, usually of bronze and cylindrical in shape, to hold jewels, toilet articles, etc., and decorated with mythological subjects.
CONSOLE. Ornamental bracket.
CRENELLATIONS. Battlements.
CUNEUS. Wedge-shaped block of seats in an antique theatre.
CYCLOPEAN. The term applied to walls of unmortared masonry, older than the Etruscan civilisation, and attributed by the ancients to the giant Cyclopes.
DECUMANUS. The main street of a Roman town running parallel to its longer axis.
DIORITE. A type of greenish coloured rock.
DIPTERAL. Temple surrounded by a double peristyle.
DIPTYCH. Painting or ivory tablet in two sections.
DUOMO. Cathedral.
ENTABLATURE. The part above the capital (consisting of architrave, frieze, and cornice) of a classical building.
EPHEBOS. Greek youth under training (military, or university).
EXEDRA. Semicircular recess.
EX-VOTO. Tablet or small painting expressing gratitude to a saint.
FIUMARE. Wide flat-bottomed torrent-bed filled with gravel, usually waterless.
FORUM. Open space in a town serving as a market or meeting-place.
FRESCO (in Italian, *affresco*). Painting executed on wet plaster. On the wall beneath is sketched the *sinopia*, and the *cartone* is transferred onto the fresh plaster (*intonaco*) before the fresco is begun, either by pricking the outline with small holes over which a powder is dusted, or by means of a stylus which leaves an incised line on the wet plaster. In recent years many frescoes have been detached from the walls on which they were executed.
FRIGIDARIUM. Room for cold baths in a Roman bath.
FUMAROLE. Volcanic spurt of vapour (usually sulphurous) emerging from the ground.
GIGANTOMACHIA. Contest of Giants.
GRAFFITI. Design on a wall made with iron tool on a prepared surface, the design showing in white. Also used loosely to describe scratched designs or words on walls.
GREEK CROSS. Cross with arms of equal length.
HELLENISTIC. The period from Alexander the Great to Augustus (c 325–31 BC).
HERM (pl. *hermae*). Quadrangular pillar decreasing in girth towards the ground, surmounted by a bust.
HEXASTYLE. Temple with a portico of six columns at the end.

HYPOGEUM. Subterranean excavation for the interment of the dead (usually Etruscan).
INTARSIA. Inlay of wood, marble, or metal.
KORE. Maiden.
KOUROS. Boy; Archaic male figure.
KRATER. Antique mixing-bowl, conical in shape with rounded base.
KYLIX. Wide shallow vase with two handles and short stem.
LOGGIA. Covered gallery or balcony, usually preceding a larger building.
LUNETTE. Semicircular space in a vault or ceiling, often decorated with a painting or a relief.
MARMI MISCHI. Inlay decoration of various polychrome marbles and pietre dure, used in church interiors in the 17C and 18C.
MEDALLION. Large medal, or a circular ornament.
MEGALITH. A huge stone (often used as a monument).
MEGARON. An oblong hall (usually in a Mycenean Palace).
METOPE. Panel between two triglyphs on the frieze of a temple.
MONOLITH. Single stone (usually a column).
NARTHEX. Vestibule of a Christian basilica.
NAUMACHIA. Mock naval combat for which the arena of an amphitheatre was flooded.
NYMPHAEUM. A sort of summer-house in the gardens of baths, palaces, etc., originally a temple of the Nymphs, and decorated with statues of those goddesses.
OCTASTYLE. A portico with eight columns.
ODEION. A concert hall, usually in the shape of a Greek theatre, but roofed.
OGEE (arch). Arch shaped in a double curve, convex above and concave below.
OINOCHOE. Wine-jug usually of elongated shape for dipping wine out of a krater.
OPISTHODOMOS. The enclosed rear part of a temple.
OPUS SECTILE. Mosaic or paving of thin slabs of coloured marble cut in geometrical shapes.
OSSUARY. Deposit of or recepticle for the bones of the dead.
PALAZZO. Any dignified and important building.
PANTOKRATOR. The Almighty.
PAX. Sacred object used by a priest for the blessing of peace, and offered for the kiss of the faithful, usually circular, engraved, enamelled or painted in a rich gold or silver frame.
PEDIMENT. Gable above the portico of a classical building.
PENDENTIVE. Concave spandrel beneath a dome.
PERIBOLOS. A precinct, but often archaeologically the circuit round it.
PERIPTERAL. Temple surrounded by a colonnade.
PERISTYLE. Court or garden surrounded by a columned portico.
PIETÀ. Group of the Virgin mourning the dead Christ.
PISCINA. Roman tank; a basin for an officiating priest to wash his hands before Mass.
PITHOS. Large pottery vessel.
PODIUM. A continuous base or plinth supporting columns, and the lowest row of seats in the cavea of a theatre or amphitheatre.
POLYPTYCH. Painting or tablet in more than three sections.

PREDELLA. Small paintng attached below a large altarpiece.

PRESEPIO. Literally, crib or manger. A group of statuary of which the central subject is the Infant Jesus in the manger.

PRONAOS. Porch in front of the cella of a temple.

PROPYLON. Propylaea. Entrance gate to a temenos; in plural form when there is more than one door.

PROSTYLE. Edifice with columns on the front only.

PULVIN. Cushion stone between the capital and the impost block.

PUTTO. Figure of a child sculpted or painted, usually nude.

QUADRIGA. Four-horsed chariot.

RHYTON. Drinking-horn usually ending in an animal's head.

SITULA. Water-bucket.

SQUINCH. Arched space at the angle of a tower.

STAMNOS. Big-bellied vase with two small handles at the sides, closed by a lid.

STELE. Upright stone bearing a monumental inscription.

STEREOBATE. Basement of a temple or other building.

STILTED ARCH. Round arch that rises vertically before it springs.

STOA. Porch or portico not attached to a larger building.

STOUP. Vessel for Holy Water, usually near the west door of a church.

STUCCO. Plasterwork.

STYLOBATE. Basement of a columned temple or other building.

TABLINUM. Room in a Roman house with one side opening onto the central courtyard.

TELAMONES, see *Atlantes*.

TEMENOS. A sacred enclosure.

TEPIDARIUM. Room for warm baths in a Roman bath.

TESSERA. A small cube of marble, glass, etc., used in mosaic work.

TETRASTYLE. Having four columns at the end.

THERMAE. Originally simply baths, later elaborate buildings fitted with libraries, assembly rooms, gymnasia, circuses, etc.

THOLOS. A circular building.

TONDO. Round painting or bas-relief.

TRANSENNA. Open grille or screen, usually of marble, in an early Christian church.

TRICLINIUM. Dining-room and reception room of a Roman house.

TRIGLYPH. Blocks with vertical grooves on either side of a metope on the frieze of a temple.

TRINACRIA. The ancient name for Sicily derived from its triangular shape.

TRIPTYCH. Painting or tablet in three sections.

TYMPANUM. Area above a doorway or the space enclosed by a pediment.

VILLA. Country-house with its garden.

XYSTUS. An exercise court; in a Roman villa the open court preceding the triclinium.

The terms Quattrocento, Cinquecento (abbreviated in Italy '400, '500), etc., refer not to the 14C and 15C, but to the 'fourteen-hundreds' and 'fifteen-hundreds', i.e. the 15C and 16C, etc.

Plan of Greek Temples

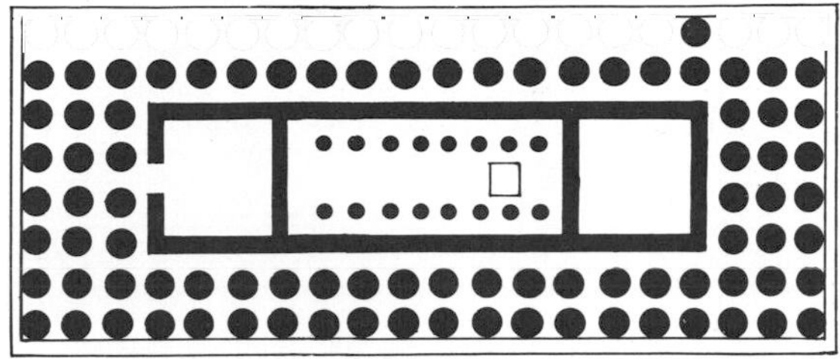

Dipteral
(Octastyle)

Parts of Greek Temple

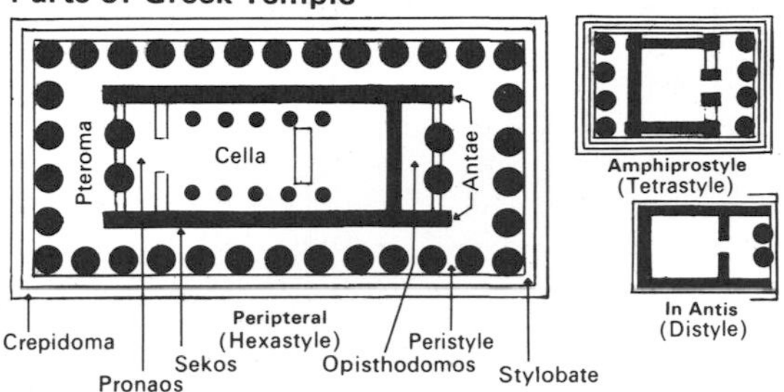

Walls

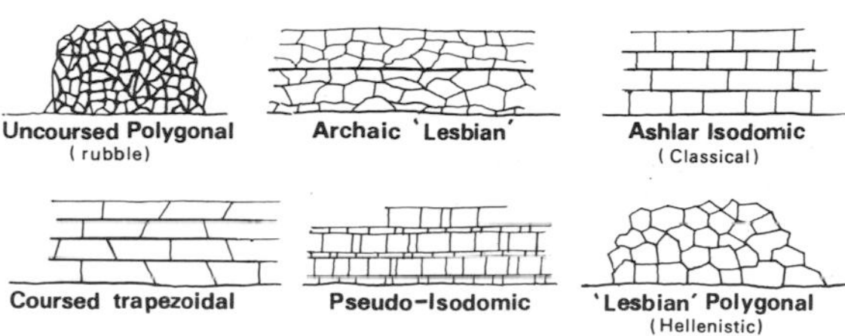

Greek Theatre

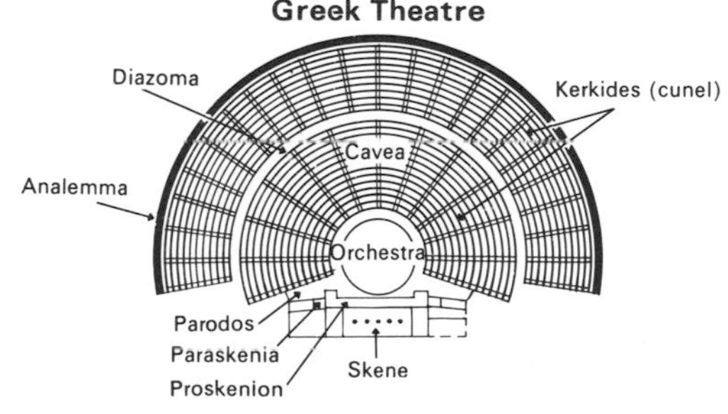

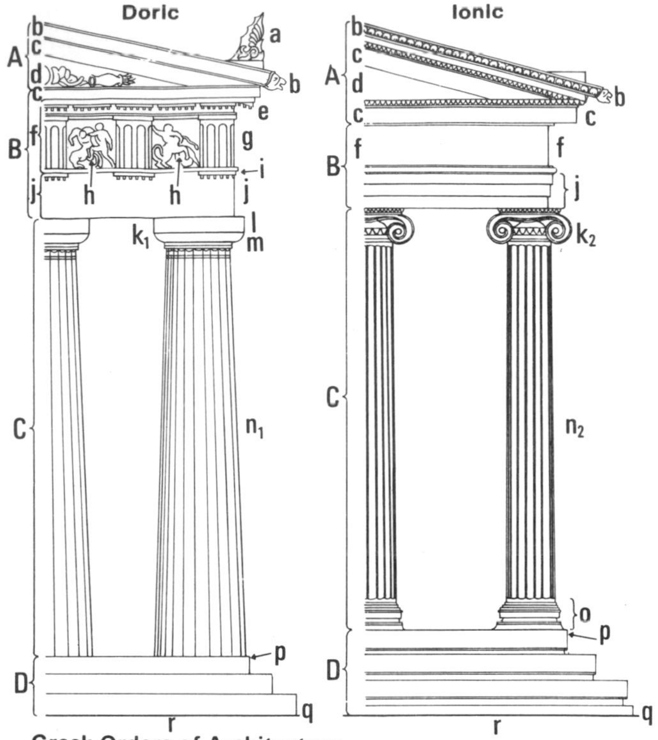

Doric Ionic

Greek Orders of Architecture

A. Pediment
B. Entablature
C. Column
D. Crepidoma
a. Acroterion
b. Sima
c. Geison or Cornice
d. Tympanum
e. Mutule & Guttae
f. Frieze
g. Triglyphs
h. Metope's
i Regulae & Guttae
j. Architrave or Epistyle
k_1 Capital (Doric)
k_2 Capital (Ionic) with Volutes
l. Abacus
m. Echinus
n_1 Shaft with flutes separated by sharp arrises.
n_2 Shaft with flutes separated by blunt fillets
o. Bases
p. Stylobate
q. Euthynteria
r. Stereobate

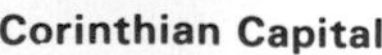

Corinthian Capital

Pergamene Capital

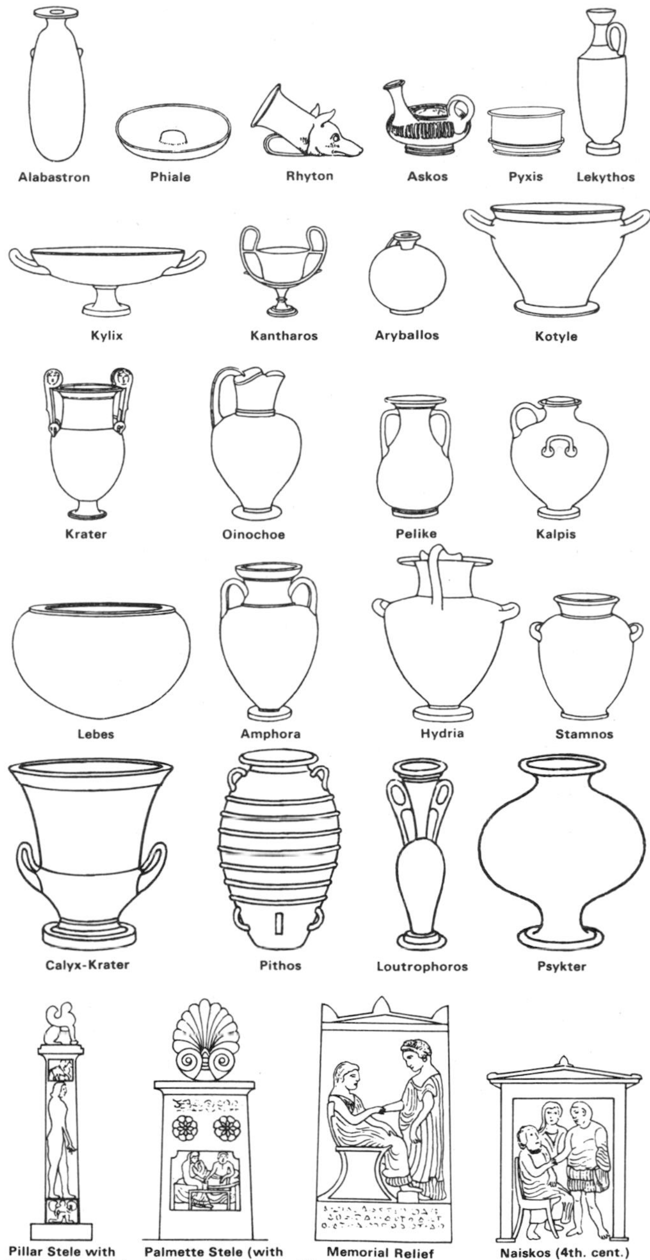
Alabastron
Phiale
Rhyton
Askos
Pyxis
Lekythos
Kylix
Kantharos
Aryballos
Kotyle
Krater
Oinochoe
Pelike
Kalpis
Lebes
Amphora
Hydria
Stamnos
Calyx-Krater
Pithos
Loutrophoros
Psykter
Pillar Stele with Sphinx (6th cent.)
Palmette Stele (with Anthemion) (5-4th. cent.)
Memorial Relief (5-4th. cent.)
Naiskos (4th. cent.)

BIBLIOGRAPHY

Topographical and General. Early travels that are still interesting, though the land they depict has greatly changed, are: *Houel* (*J.*): 'Voyage Pittoresque des Isles de Sicile, de Lipari, et de Malte' (Paris, 1782–87; 4 vols). *Goethe*: 'Italian Journey' (1786–88; Penguin translation by W.H. Auden and E. Mayer 1962, 1970). *Watkins* (*Thomas*): 'Travels in 1787–89 through Switzerland, Italy, Sicily, etc.' (1794; 2 vols). *Brydone* (*Patrick*): 'A Tour through Sicily and Malta' (1773; 2 vols). *Swinburne* (*Henry*): 'Travels in the Two Sicilies, 1777–80' (1790). *Hamilton* (*Sir William*): 'Observations of Mount Vesuvius, Mount Etna, and other volcanos' (1772). *Hare* (*Augustus*): 'Cities of Southern Italy and Sicily' (1883), *Sladen* (*Douglas*): 'In Sicily' (1901; 12 vols).

More modern works useful by way of general introduction are: *Guercio* (*Francis M.*): 'Sicily, the Garden of the Mediterranean' (2nd edn., 1954). *Quennell* (*Peter*): 'Spring in Sicily' (1952). *Berenson* (*Bernard*): 'The Passionate Sightseer' (1960). *Cronin* (*Vincent*): 'The Golden Honeycomb' (1954; 2nd edn. 1980). *Helbig* (*Konrad*): 'Sizilien' (Wiesbaden, 1966). *Fava* (*Giuseppe*): 'I Siciliani' (1980). *Simeti* (*Mary Taylor*): 'On Persephone's Island' (1986).

Less general and in some cases with highly individual viewpoints are: *Dolci* (*Danilo*): 'Banditi a Partinico' (1955); 'Inchiesta a Palermo' (1966; translated in 1959 and republished as 'Poverty in Sicily' in 1966), both remarkable accounts of Sicily in the 1950s. 'Sicilian Lives', a translation from Danilo Dolci was published in 1981. *Maxwell* (*Gavin*): 'God Protect me from My Friends' (1956), about the bandit Giuliano; 'The Ten Pains of Death' (1959) describes conditions among peasants of West Sicily. *Kubly* (*Herbert*): 'Easter in Sicily' (1957). *Diole* (P.): 'Seas of Sicily' (1955).

History. The most recent history of Sicily in three volumes (with comprehensive bibliographies) is: *Finley* (*M. I.*): 'Ancient Sicily' (1968), *Mack Smith* (*Denis*): 'Medieval Sicily', 'Modern Sicily' (1969). These have been revised and abridged by *Finley, Mack Smith* and *Christopher Duggan*: 'History of Sicily' (1986). *Dunbabin* (*T.J.*): 'The Western Greeks: the History of Sicily and South Italy from the Foundation of the Greek Colonies to 480 BC' (1948). *Boardman* (*J.*): 'The Greeks Overseas' (1964). *Thucydides:* 'The Peloponnesian War' (Penguin edn., trans. Rex Warner; 1954). *Mommsen* (*T.*): 'Provinces of the Roman Empire' (1886, 2 vols). *Gibbon* (*Edward*): 'Decline and Fall of the Roman Empire'. *Amari* (*M.*): 'Storia dei Musulmani in Sicilia' (2nd edn., Catania 1933). *Freeman* (*E.A.*): 'History of Sicily' (1891–94, 4 vols). *Norwich* (*John Julius*): 'The Normans in the South' (1967); 'The Kingdom in the Sun' (1970). *Douglas* (*D.C.*): 'The Norman Achievement' (1969). *Masson* (*Georgina*): 'Frederick II of Hohenstaufen' (1957). *Runciman* (*Stephen*): 'The Sicilian Vespers' (1958). *Croce* (*Benedetto*): 'Storia del Regno di Napoli' (Bari, 1925). *Italia* (*Alessandro*): 'La Sicilia Feudale' (Genoa, 1940). *Acton* (*Harold*): 'The Bourbons of Naples, 1734–1825' and its sequel 'The Last Bourbons of Naples, 1825–1861' (1957 and 1961). *Trevelyan* (*G.M.*): 'Garibaldi and the Thousand'; 'Garibaldi and the Making of Italy' (1909, 1911, many edns). *Trevelyan* (*Raleigh*): 'Princes under the Volcano' (1972). *Ahmad* (*Aziz*): 'A History of Islamic Sicily' (1976). *Romeo* (*R.*): 'Il Risorgimento in Sicilia' (Bari, 1970). *Di Stefano* (*F.*): 'Storia della Sicilia dal XI al XIX secolo' (Bari, 1977). *Peri* (*I.*): 'Uomini, Citta, e Campagne in Sicilia dall'XI al XIII sec.' (Bari, 1978). 'Storia della Sicilia'

(Napoli, 1979–80); part of this work was published as 'La Sicilia Antica' (1982) by Emilio Gabba and Georges Vallet (editors). 'Sikanie. Storia e Civilta della Sicilia Greca' (Milan, 1985).

Works on the **Mafia** include: *Stajano* (*Corrado*), ed.: 'Mafia: l'atto d'accusa dei guidici di Palermo' (Rome, 1986); *Leonardo Sciascia*, 'A Futura memoria' (1989); *Leoluca Orlando* 'Palermo' (1990); *Pino Arlacchi* 'Mafia Imprenditrice' and 'Gli uomini del disonore'; *Giovanni Falcone*, 'Cose di Cosa Nostra' (1991; translated into English in 1992: 'Men of Honour; the truth about the Mafia', London, Fourth Estate); and *Antonino Caponnetto*, 'I Miei giorni a Palermo' (1992).

Archaeology. *Guido* (*Margaret*): 'Sicily: an archaeological Guide' (1967, 1977). *Brea* (*L. Bernabo*: 'Sicily before the Greeks' (1957). The following provide specialised information: Angell (Samuel) and Evans (T.): 'Sculptured Metopes of Selinus' (1826). Randall-MacIver (D.): 'Greek Cities in Italy and Sicily' (1931). Whitaker (J.I.S.): 'Motya; a Phoenician Colony in Sicily' (1921). Sturzo (Luigi): 'Lost Morgantina' (New York, 1960). Vallet (Georges): 'Megara Hyblaea' (1983).

Art and Architecture. Bellafiore (Gius.): 'La Civilta artistica della Sicilia' (Florence, 1963). Pace (Biagio): 'Arte e Civilta della Sicilia Antica' (Rome, 1945). Dinsmoor (W.B.): 'The Architecture of Ancient Greece' (3rd rev. edn., 1950). Agnello (Giuseppe): 'L'Architettura Sveva in Sicilia' (Rome, 1935). Beltrandi (A.B.): 'Castelli di Sicilia' (1956). Giuffre (M.), 'Castelli e luoghi forti di Sicilia' (Palermo, 1980). Demus (Otto): 'The Mosaics of Norman Sicily' (1949). Waern (Cecilia): 'Medieval Sicily' (1910). Meli (Filippo): 'L'Arte in Sicilia' (Milan, 1929). Bottari (Stefano): 'Antonello' (Eng. edn., 1957); 'La Pittura del Quattrocento in Sicilia' (Florence, 1954). Mandel (G.): 'Antonello da Messina' (1967). Di Marzo (G.): 'I Gagini e la Scultura in Sicilia' (Palermo, 1883). Kruft (H. W.). 'Domenico Gagini' (Florence, 1972). Caradente (G.): 'Giacomo Serpotta' (Turin, 1967). Garstang (Donald): 'Giacomo Serpotta and the Stuccatori of Palermo, 1560–1790' (London, 1984). Blunt (Anthony): 'Sicilian Baroque' (1968). Gangi (G.): 'Il Barocco nella Sicilia Orientale' (1964); 'Il Barocco nella Sicilia Occidentale' (1968). Sitwell (S.): 'Southern Baroque Revisited' (1967). Boscarino (Salvatore): 'Sicilia Barocca. Architettura e Città, 1610–1760' (Rome, 1981). Agnello (Gius.): 'I Vermexio' (Florence, 1960). Borsook (Eve): 'Messages in Mosaic' (Oxford, 1990).

The following are accounts of individual cities: Bellafiore (Gius.): 'Palermo' (1971). Fagiolo (M.) and Madonna (M.L.): 'Il Teatro del Sole; la rifondazione di Palermo nel Cinquecento e l'idea della citta barocca' (Rome, 1981). Spatrisano (G.): 'Architettura del Cinquecento in Palermo' (Palermo, 1961). Hills (H.M.): 'Marmi Mischi a palermo' (Palermo, 1994). Guido (Margaret): 'Syracuse' (Syracuse, 1970). Agnello (Giuseppe) and Agnello (S.L.): 'Siracusa nel Medioevo e rinascimento' (Rome, 1964); 'Siracusa Barocca' (Caltanissetta, 1961). Trigilia (Lucia): 'Siracusa. Architettura e citta nel periodo vicereale (1500–1700)' (Roma-Siracusa, 1981). Accascina (Maria): 'Profilo dell' architettura a Messina dal 1600 al 1800 (Rome, 1964). Tobringer (Stephen): 'The genesis of Noto, an eighteenth-century Sicilian city' (London, 1982).

Literature. *Verga* (*Giovanni*): 'Cavalleria Rusticana'; 'Mastro-Don Gesualdo' (both translated into English by D.H. Lawrence, 1932, 1925); 'I Malavoglia ('The House by the Medlar Tree', 1950). Some of the short stories ('Novelle', 'Vita dei Campi', 'Novelle Rusticane', 'Per le Vie', etc.) have also been translated by Lawrence, and republished by Penguin as 'Little Novels of Sicily' in 1973. *Lampedusa* (*Giuseppe di*): 'Il Gattopardo' ('The Leopard' trans. 1960); 'I Racconti' ('Two stories and a memory', trans. 1962). *Federico De Roberto*: 'I vicere'. Much of the work of Luigi Pirandello is influenced by his native Agrigento. *Vittorini (Elio)*: 'Conversazione in Sicilia', 'Uomini e no', 'Il Garofano Rosso'. *Dacia Maraini*, a contemporary writer, has described her childhood in Sicily in 'Bagheria' (1993). One of the greatest Italian writers of this century was the Sicilian *Leonardo Sciascia* (1921–89), famous for his novels as well as his writings on the Mafia. His works include: 'Il Giorno della Civetta', 'Il Consiglio d'Egitto', 'A Ciascuno il Suo', the short stories published in 1973, 'Il Mare Colore del Vino', 'La Sicilia come metafora, 1979', etc. In English, recent translations include: 'Candido, or a dream dreamed in Sicily' (Manchester, 1979) and 'Sicilian Uncles: Four Novellas' (Manchester, 1986).

PRACTICAL INFORMATION

Getting to Sicily

Palermo and Catania are linked by air services with London. By sea, road, and rail Sicily is best reached from the Italian mainland. The shortest sea approach is by the ferry (car and rail) from Villa San Giovanni (35 minutes) and Reggio di Calabria (50 minutes) to Messina. A frequent hydrofoil service (passengers only) connects Reggio di Calabria with Messina (in 20 minutes). An overnight car ferry runs from Naples and from Genoa to Palermo.

Among the numerous **tour operators** who sell tickets and book accommodation, and also organise inclusive tours and charter trips to Italy are: Magic of Italy, Italian Chapters, Hayes and Jarvis, Citalia, Martin Randall Travel, Prospect Music and Art Tours Ltd, Specialtours, Swan Hellenic, Italian Escapades, and Italiatour.

Air Services between London and Sicily are operated by Alitalia (Tel. 071/602 7111). Flights to Palermo and to Catania usually run via Milan or Rome (direct flights in summer). Charter flights (often much cheaper) are also available to numerous cities in Italy. Details of these are available through travel agencies and listings sections in many of the national newspapers. All scheduled services have a monthly excursion fare, and a limited number of special reduced fares (usually only available if booked well in advance). The airline companies offer a 25 per cent reduction of the return fare to full-time students (12–26 years old) and young people between the ages of 12 and 21. Car hire schemes in conjunction with flights can also be arranged. For further details enquire at your local travel agent or the Italian State Tourist Board.

Flights from the Italian mainland are operated by Alitalia. A frequent air service connects Reggio di Calabria and Catania. There are also daily services from Rome and Milan to Palermo and Catania. Flights also operate from Naples, Pisa, Florence, and Cagliari to Palermo and Catania, and from Turin to Catania.

Railway Services. The most direct routes from Calais and Boulogne via Paris and Dijon (with sleeping compartments) are via Modane to Turin, Genoa, Pisa, and Rome or via Lausanne and Domodossola to Milan, Bologna, Florence, and Rome. From Turin, Genoa, and Milan main line trains (via Rome and Naples) run to Villa San Giovanni and Reggio di Calabria, and through carriages for destinations in Sicily (Palermo, Catania, and Syracuse) continue via the ferry to Messina. Overnight trains (with sleeping accommodation) daily from Milan and Turin via Rome to Palermo. Information on the Italian State Railways (and tickets and seat reservations) may be obtained in London from Citalia, Marco Polo House, 3–5 Lansdowne Road, Croydon, Surrey CR9 1LL (Tel. 081/686 0677) and Wasteels Travel, Platform 2, Victoria Station, London SW1V 1JY (Tel. 071/834 7066).

Bus Service. A bus service operates in two days between London (Victoria Coach Station) and Rome (Piazza della Repubblica) via Dover, Paris, Mont Blanc, Aosta, Turin, Genoa, Milan, Venice, Bologna, and Florence, daily from June to September, and once or twice a week for the rest of the year.

Reduction for students. Information in London from the National Express office at Victoria Coach Station, from local National Express agents, and in Italy from 'SITA' offices. From Rome daily coach services run by 'SAIS' to Messina (going on to Catania and Syracuse) and to Palermo (in c 12–13hrs).

By Car. British drivers taking their own cars by any of the routes across France, Belgium, Luxembourg, Switzerland, Germany, and Austria need only the vehicle registration book, a valid national driving licence (accompanied by a translation, issued free by the RAC, AA, and ENIT offices), insurance cover, and a nationality plate attached to the car. If you are not the owner of the vehicle, you must have the owner's permission for its use abroad. A Swiss 'motorway pass' is needed for Switzerland, and can be obtained from the RAC, the AA, or at the Swiss border.

The continental rule of the road is to drive on the right and overtake on the left. The provisions of the respective highway codes in the countries of transit, though similar, have important variations, especially with regard to priority, speed limits, and pedestrian crossings. Membership of the AA (Tel. 0256/20123) or the RAC (membership enquiries and insurance, Tel. 0345/331133; travel information service, Tel. 0345/333222) entitles you to many of the facilities of affiliated societies in Europe. They are represented at most of the sea and air ports.

Motorway routes to Italy from Europe. The main routes from France, Switzerland, and Austria are summarised below. From northern and central Italy the 'Autostrada del Sole' (A1) motorway continues to southern Italy.

A. The direct motorway route from France, bypassing Geneva, enters Italy through the **Mont Blanc Tunnel**. The road from Courmayeur to Aosta has not yet been improved. At Aosta the A5 motorway begins; it follows the Val d'Aosta. Just beyond Ivrea is the junction with the A4/5 motorway; the A5 continues S to Turin, while the A4/5 diverges E. At Santhia the A4 motorway from Turin is joined for Milan via Novara, or the A26/4 can be followed S via Alessandria, reaching the coast at Voltri, just outside Genoa. The 'Autostrada del Sole' (A1) leads S to Florence from Milan, or from Genoa the A12 motorway continues to Viareggio, where the A11 can be taken E to Florence to join the A1. The latter route avoids the Apennine pass between Bologna and Florence which carries very heavy traffic and can be subject to delays.

B. The most direct approach to Turin from France is through the **Monte Cenis Tunnel** from Modane in France to Bardonecchia. A road continues to Oulx where a motorway is under construction via Susa to Turin parallel to the old road. From Turin a motorway (A6) descends direct to the coast at Savona, or the motorway (A21, A26) via Asti and Alessandria leads to Genoa; either one joins directly the coastal motorway for Viareggio (where the A11 diverges for Florence). Alternatively, the A4 motorway leads from Turin E to Milan for the A1.

C. The **Coastal route from the South of France** follows the A10 motorway through the foothills with frequent long tunnels to enter Italy just before Ventimiglia. The motorway continues past Alassio, Albenga, and Savona (where the motorway from Turin comes in), to Voltri (where the A26 motorway from Alessandria comes in) and Genoa (with the junction of the A7 motorway from Milan). The coastal motorway continues to Viareggio where A11 branches left for Florence and the A1.

D. The approch to Italy from Switzerland (Lausanne) is usually through the **Great St Bernard Tunnel** (or by the pass in summer) which only becomes motorway at Aosta (see A, above).

E. Another motorway route from Switzerland is via the **St Gotthard Tunnel** (opened in 1980) and Lugano. The motorway (A9) enters Italy at Como and contnues to Milan where the A1 begins.

F. From Germany and Austria (Innsbruck) the direct approach to Italy is by the motorway over the **Brenner Pass**. The motorway (A22) continues down the Isarco valley to Bolzano and the Adige valley via Trento to Verona. Here motorways diverge W for Brescia and Milan, or E for Vicenza and Venice, or continue S via Mantua to join the A1 motorway just W of Modena.

From Milan and Florence the 'Autostrada del Sole' (A1) continues S to Rome, which is now bypassed well to the E, avoiding the congested ring-road around the capital (the 'Grande Raccordo Annulare'). At Caserta, just N of Naples, the A30 motorway diverges left to bypass Naples. At Salerno the A3 motorway (toll free) continues south via Cosenza to Reggio di Calabria, and the ferry for Messina. By this motorway Messina can comfortably be reached in a day from Naples.

CAR SLEEPER TRAIN SERVICES operate from Paris and Boulogne, Hamburg, Vienna, and Munich to Milan, Bologna, Rome, etc. Car transport by train in Italy is available from Turin, Milan, Bologna, Genoa, and Rome to Villa San Giovanni.

Sea Crossings. Car ferries on the Straits of Messina operate from Villa San Giovanni (c every 20 minutes) and Reggio di Calabria (for the same fare, but slightly less frequently) to Messina. The ferries are run by the State Railways (FS) and private companies (Caronte and Tourist Ferry). A frequent service is maintained, but there can be delays in the height of the summer. Frequent hydrofoil service operated by 'SNAV' between Reggio di Calabria and Messina. For further details, see Rte 28.

From Naples overnight car ferries (Tirrenia, Via del Mare, Palermo) operate daily to Palermo and several times a week to Catania and Syracuse. Car ferries (Tirrenia) also link Cagliari, Tunis, and Genoa to Palermo. Services by Grandi Traghetti (179 Via Stabile, Palermo) from Livorno and Genoa to Palermo. There is also a service run by Tirrenia from Malta to Syracuse. For services to the Aeolian Islands, see Rte 30. Advance reservation is advised, particularly for a cabin or if with a car.

THE CROSSING OF THE STRAITS OF MESSINA, the Fretum Siculum of the Romans. From Villa San Giovanni the ferry heads SW. Looking towards Messina the coast is overshadowed by the Monti Peloritani, whose highest peak, Monte Antennamare (1124m) is a little S of the white splash made by the town. Northwards the suburbs merge into small towns which extend to Cape Peloro or Punta del Faro, at the mouth of the strait, the site of the legendary whirlpool 'Charybdis', greatly feared by sailors in ancient times. The name of Cape Peloro recalls Pelorus, the pilot of Hannibal who was unjustly condemned to be thrown into the sea for misleading the fleet. The pylons that carry the power line from Calabria across the strait bear a single span of 3653m of unsupported cable and allow headroom for ships of 70m. To the S the coast may be seen as far as Cape Taormina, behind which rises the massif of Etna. Looking back towards the mainland, the beautiful Calabrian coast is sometimes in hot weather strangely magnified and distorted by the mirage called 'Fata Morgana'. Prominent on both shores are the giant pillars supporting the motorways. In the port of Messina the ferry passes the offices and houses of the naval base, and rounds Forte San Salvatore to enter the Stazione Marittima.

There is a long-term project to connect Messina and Reggio di Calabria by land: the latest plan, proposed in 1986, involves a SINGLE-SPAN SUSPENSION BRIDGE for road and railway 3300m long, carried on two pylons 400m high.

Passports or **Visitors Cards** are necessary for all British travellers entering Italy. American travellers must carry passports. British passports valid for ten years are issued at the Passport Office, Clive House, Petty France, London SW1, or may be obtained for an additional fee through any tourist agent. A 'British Visitor's Passport' (valid one year) can be purchased at post offices in Britain. You are strongly advised to carry some means of identification with you at all times while in Italy, since you can be held at a police station if you are stopped and found to be without a document of identity.

Money. In Italy the monetary unit is the Italian lira (pl. lire). Notes are issued for 1000, 2000, 5000, 10,000, 50,000, and 100,000 lire. Coins of 10, 20, 50, 100, 200 and 500 lire. The current exchange value is approximately 2200 lire to the £ sterling (1500 lire to the US dollar). Travellers' cheques and Eurocheques are the safest way of carrying money when travelling, and most credit cards are now generally accepted in shops and restaurants (but rarely at petrol stations). The commission on cashing travellers' cheques can be quite high. For banking hours, see under 'General Information', below. Money can also be changed at exchange offices ('cambio'), in travel agencies, some post offices, and main stations. Exchange offices are usually open seven days a week at airports and main railway stations. At hotels, restaurants, and shops money can sometimes be exchanged (but usually at a lower rate).

Police Registration is formally required within three days of entering Italy. If you are staying at a hotel the management takes care of this. The permit lasts three months, but can be extended on application.

Tourist Information

Italian Tourist Boards. General information can be obtained abroad from the Italian State Tourist Office ('ENIT'; Ente Nazionale Italiano per il Turismo), who distribute free an excellent 'Traveller's Handbook' (usually revised every year), and provide detailed information about Italy. In London their office is at 1 Princes Street, WIR 8AY (Tel. 071/408 1254); in New York at 630 Fifth Avenue, Suite 1565 (Tel. 2454822); in Chicago at 500 North Michigan Avenue, Suite 1046 (Tel. 6440990).

In Sicily the Regional State Tourist office is in Palermo: Assessorato Regionale del Turismo, 11 Via Notarbartolo (Tel. 091/6961111). The nine provinces of Sicily each have their own tourist boards, called the 'APT' (Aziende Autonome Provinciali per l'incremento Turistico). These provide invaluable help to travellers on arrival; they supply a free list of accommodation (revised annually), including hotels, youth hostels, and camping sites; up-to-date information on museum opening times and annual events; and information about local transport. They also usually distribute, free of charge, illustrated pamphlets about the province, sometimes with good town plans, etc. The headquarters are normally open Monday–Saturday 8–14, but in towns of particular interest there is sometimes a separate 'APT' information office which is often also open in the afternoon. Subsidiary information offices are sometimes open in railway stations, airports, or ports (usually in summer only). In addition, some local tourist boards ('Aziende Autonome di Turismo') still operate in the main tourist centres. All these offices are indicated, with their addresses in the main text below.

The nine head offices of the 'APT' of Sicily are as follows:

'APT' Palermo, 35 Piazza Castelnuovo (Tel. 091/583887).

'APT' Trapani, 15 Via Sorba (Tel. 0923/27273).

'APT' Agrigento, 255 Viale della Vittoria (Tel. 0922/401352).

'APT' Caltanissetta, 109 Corso Vittorio Emanuele (Tel. 0934/584499).

'APT' Catania, 5 Largo Paisiello (Via Pacini), Tel. 095/312124.

'APT' Enna, 413 Via Roma (Tel. 0935/500544).

'APT' Ragusa, 33 Via Capitano Bocchieri, Ragusa Ibla (Tel. 0932/621421).

'APT' Siracusa, 45 Via San Sebastiano (Tel. 0931/67710).

'APT' Messina, Via Calabria, isolato 301bis (corner of Via Capra), Tel. 090/675356.

Driving in Sicily

Temporary membership of the Automobile Club d'Italia ('ACI') can be taken out on the frontier or in Italy. The headquarters of 'ACI' is at 8 Via Marsala, Rome, and the head office in Palermo at 6 Viale delle Alpi (branch offices in all the main towns). They provide a breakdown service ('Soccorso ACI', Tel. 116).

Rules of the road. Italian law requires that you carry a valid driving licence when travelling. It is obligatory to keep a red triangle in the car in case of accident or breakdown. This serves as a warning to other traffic when placed on the road at a distance of 50 metres from the stationary car. It can be hired from 'ACI' for a minimal charge, and returned at the frontier. It is now compulsory to wear seat-belts in the front seat of cars in Italy. Driving in Italy is generally faster (and often more aggressive) than driving in Britain or America. Road signs are now more or less standardised to the international codes, but certain habits differ radically from those in Britian or America. If a driver flashes his headlights, it means he is proceeding and not giving you precedence. In towns, Italian drivers are very lax about changing lanes without much warning. Unless otherwise indicated, cars entering a road from the right are given precedence (also at roundabouts). Italian drivers tend to ignore pedestrian crossings. In towns, beware of motorbikes, mopeds and Vespas, the drivers of which seem to consider that they always have the right of way. In most towns in Sicily the traffic tends to be chaotic, the roads congested, and parking difficult. Visitors are strongly recommended to explore towns on foot.

Motorways ('Autostrade'). Italy probably has the finest motorways in Europe, although in the last ten years or so too many have been constructed to the detriment of the countryside. Tolls are charged according to the rating of the vehicle and the distance covered, although no tolls are charged on the motorway from Salerno to Reggio di Calabria, from Palermo to Catania, and from Palermo to Mazara del Vallo. There are service areas on most motorways open 24 hours. Some of the main motorways have 'SOS' points every two kilometres. Unlike in France, motorways are indicated by green signs (and normal roads by blue signs). At the entrance to motorways, the two directions are indicated by the name of the most important town (and not by the nearest town) which can be momentarily confusing.

In Sicily the motorways are a convenient and fast way of travelling for those restricted for time (and often provide spectacular views of the countryside). They traverse the difficult terrain by means of viaducts and tunnels, usually with little respect for the beauty of the landscape. Most travellers will prefer to take other roads (some of which are now much freer of traffic). Motorways link Messina to Catania, Catania to Palermo, Palermo to Trapani, and Palermo to Mazara del Vallo. The convenience of being able to reach Palermo from Catania in under three hours has transformed communications between the W and E half of the island. The motorway from Messina to Palermo has been awaiting completion for years (although work on the gap in the middle between Rocca Caprileone and Cefalù has recently been resumed). The project to build a motorway from Catania to Syracuse and (via the coast) to Gela seems to have beem shelved.

'Superstrade' are dual carriageway fast roads which do not charge tolls. They do not usually have service stations, 'SOS' points, or emergency lanes. They are also usually indicated by green signs.

Petrol Stations are open 24 hours on motorways, but otherwise their opening times are: 7–12, 15–20; winter 7.30–12.30, 14.30–19. There are now quite a number of self-service petrol stations open 24hrs operated by bank notes (Lire 10,000), usually near the larger towns. Unleaded petrol has become easy to find all over Sicily in the last few years. Petrol in Italy costs more than in England, and a lot more than in America.

Car Parking. Although most towns on the Italian mainland have at last taken the wise step of closing their historic centres to traffic, many town centres in Sicily (including Palermo) are still open to cars. This makes driving and parking extremely difficult. On approaching a town, the white signs for 'centro' (with a bull's eye) should be followed towards the historic centre. Car-parks are also sometimes indicated by blue 'P' signs; the best places to park near the centre have been mentioned in the main text below. Some car-parks are free and some charge an hourly tariff. In the larger towns it is usually a good idea to look for a garage which provides parking space (these usually have a blue 'P' sign and a blue-and-white striped entrance); tariffs are charged by the hour, by the day, or overnight. It is forbidden to park in front of a gate or doorway marked with a 'passo carrabile' (blue and red) sign. Always lock your car when parked, and never leave anything of value inside it.

Car Hire is available in the main Sicilian towns. Arrangements for the hire of cars in Italy can be made through Alitalia or British Airways (at specially advantageous rates in conjunction with their flights) or through any of the principal car-hire firms (the most well-known include Maggiore, Avis, and Hertz).

Roads in Sicily. The standard of roads on the island has improved in recent years. However, some of the main roads have rough stretches, while the condition of secondary roads can be unexpectedly good. The roads through the mountainous centre of the island are often very windy and slow.

Maps

Although detailed town plans have been included in this book, it has not been possible, because of the format, to provide an atlas of Sicily adequate for those travelling by car. The maps at the end of the book are only intended to be used when planning an itinerary. The Italian Touring Club publishes several sets of excellent maps: these are constantly updated and are indispensable to anyone travelling by car in Italy. They include the 'Grande Carta Stradale d'Italia', on a scale of 1:200,000. This is divided into 15 sheets covering the regions of Italy; Sicily is covered on the sheet (No. D19) entitled 'Sicilia'. These are also published in a handier form as an atlas (with a comprehensive index) called the 'Atlante Stradale d'Italia' in three volumes (the one entitled 'Sud' covers Sicily). These maps can be purchased from the Italian Touring Club offices and at many booksellers: in London they are obtainable from Stanfords, 12–14 Long Acre, WC2E 9LP (Tel. 071-836 1321) and the National Map Centre, 22–24 Caxton Street, SW1H 0QU (Tel. 071-222 2619).

The 'Istituto Geografico Militare' of Italy has for long been famous for its map production (much of it done by aerial photography). Their headquarters are in Florence (10 Viale Cesare Battisti). Their maps are now available at numerous bookshops in the main towns of Italy. They publish a map of Italy on a scale of 1:100,000 in 277 sheets, and a field survey partly 1:50,000, partly 1:25,000, which are invaluable for the detailed exploration of the country, especially its more mountainous regions; the coverage is, however, still far from complete at the larger scales, and some of the maps are out-of-date.

Public Transport

Railways. The Italian State Railways ('FS'; 'Ferrovie dello Stato') run five categories of trains. (1) 'EC' ('Eurocity'), international express trains (with a special supplement, approximately 30 per cent of the normal single fare) running between the main Italian and European cities (seat reservation is sometimes obligatory. (2) 'IC' (Intercity), express trains running between the main Italian towns, with a special supplement (on some of these seat reservation is obligatory, and some carry first-class only). (3) 'Espressi', long-distance trains (both classes) not as fast as the 'Intercity' trains. (4) 'Diretti', although not stopping at every station, a good deal slower than 'Espressi'. (5) 'Regionali', local trains stopping at all stations.

Trains in Italy are usually crowded especially on holidays and in summer; seats can be booked in advance from the main cities at the station booking office or at some travel agencies. The timetable for the train services changes on about 26 September and 31 May every year. Excellent timetables are published twice a year by the Italian State Railways ('Il Treno'; one volume for the whole of Italy) and by Pozzorario in several volumes ('Centro e Sud' covers Sicily). These can be purchased at news-stands and railway stations.

Fares and reductions. In Italy fares are still much lower than in England. Tickets must by bought at the station (or at agencies for the Italian State Railways) before starting a journey, otherwise a fairly large supplement has to be paid to the ticket-collector on the train. Time should be allowed for this as there are often long queues at the station ticket offices. Some trains carry first-class only; some charge a special supplement; and on some seats must be booked in advance. It is therefore always necessary to specify which train you are intending to take as well as the destination when buying tickets. If you purchase a return ticket, you must stamp it at automatic machines on the platform before boarding the train on the return trip (or write the date of the return by hand on the back of the ticket).

In the main stations the better known credit cards are now generally accepted (but there is a special ticket window which must be used when buying a ticket with a credit card). There are limitations on travelling short distances on some first-class 'Intercity' trains.

Children under the age of four travel free, and between the ages of four and twelve travel half price, and there are certain reductions for families. For travellers over the age of 60 (with Senior Citizen Railcards), the 'Rail Europ Senior' card offers a 30 per cent reduction on Italian rail fares. The 'Inter-rail' card (valid one month), which can be purchased in Britain by young people up to the age of 26 is valid in Italy. In Italy the 'Carta d'argento' and the 'Carta Verde' (both valid one year) allow a 20 per cent reduction on rail fares for those over 60, and between the ages of 12 and 26. The 'Biglietto Turistico di libera circolazione' ('Travel at Will Ticket') available to those resident outside Italy, gives freedom of the Italian railways for 8, 15, 21, or 30 days (and another scheme of this type is offered by the 'Italy Flexy Railcard'). These tickets can be purchased in Britain or at main stations in Italy (including Messina and Palermo). A 'Chilometrico' ticket is valid for two months for 3000 kilometres (and can be used by up to five people at the same time). There is a 15 per cent discount on Day Return tickets (maximum distance 50km), and on 3-Day Return tickets (maximum distance 250km). A 'Carta Blu' is available for the disabled, and certain trains have special facilities for them (indicated in the railway timetable; information from the main railway stations in Italy).

Left luggage offices are usually open 24 hours at the main stations; at smaller stations they often close at night. **Porters** are entitled to a fixed amount (shown on noticeboards at all stations) for each piece of luggage.

Restaurant Cars (sometimes self-service) are attached to most international and internal long-distance trains. A lunch tray brought to the compartment (including three courses and wine, and costing slightly less) is a convenient way of having a meal. Also, on most express trains, snacks, hot coffee and drinks are sold throughout the journey from a trolley wheeled down the train. At every large station good snacks are on sale from trolleys on the platform, and you can buy them from the train window. These include carrier-bags with sandwiches, drink, and fruit ('cestini da viaggio') or individual sandwiches ('panini').

Sleeping Cars, with couchettes or first- and second-class cabins, are also carried on certain trains, as well as 'Sleeperette' compartments with reclining seats (first-class only).

Train services in Sicily. Sicilian trains are now generally fast and comfortable, although in some places the service is infrequent. The two main lines, Messina to Palermo, and Messina to Catania and Syracuse have a frequent service, but almost all the fast trains are through trains from the Italian mainland (Naples, Rome, Milan, etc.), and more often than not subject to considerable delays. Work began in 1981 to electrify the main lines and install double tracks. Some of the minor secondary lines on the island have recently been closed and substituted by bus connections. With careful planning and with the help of the regional timetables (see above), it is still possible to reach many places by rail, and details of the lines have been given in the text below, although local bus services are now sometimes quicker and more frequent than train services.

Local Buses, run by numerous different companies, abound between the main towns in Sicily. It is however, at present, difficult to obtain local timetables in advance, details of which have been given where possible in the text. Since the improvement of bus services it is now easier to reach some destinations by bus rather than by rail; they are sometimes quicker and almost always more punctual than trains. The fastest way by public transport from Palermo to Catania is by the direct bus service along the motorway (service c every hour in 2 hours 40 minutes). Other comfortable express coaches run direct by motorway from Palermo to Trapani, and from Messina to Catania. Fares are normally comparable to rail fares and luggage is carried free of charge. The main bus companies operating on the island include 'AST', Piazza Marina, Palermo (Tel. 091/6254192), and 'SAIS', Via Balsamo, Palermo (Tel. 091/6166028).

Town Buses. It is almost always necessary to purchase tickets before boarding (at tobacconists, bars, newspaper kiosks, information offices, etc.) and stamp them on board at automatic machines.

Taxis. Taxis (yellow or white in colour) are provided with taximeters; make sure these are operational before hiring a taxi. They are hired from ranks or by telephone; there are no cruising taxis. A small tip of about 1000 lire is expected. A supplement for night service, and for luggage is charged. There is a heavy surplus charge when the destination is outside the town limits (ask roughly how much the fare is likely to be).

Accommodation

Hotels in Italy are now classified by 'stars' as in the rest of Europe. Since 1985 the official category of 'Pensione' has been abolished. There are five official categories of hotels, from the luxury 5-star hotels to the cheapest and simplest 1-star hotels.

A selection of hotels open in 1993 in Sicily have been listed in the text. They have been given with their official star rating in order to provide an indication of price. In making the selection for inclusion, smaller hotels have been favoured, and those in the centre of towns, or in particularly beautiful positions in the countryside.

Each provincial tourist board ('APT', see above) issues a free annual list of hotels giving category, price and facilities. Local tourist offices help you to find accommmodation on the spot; it is however advisable to book in advance, especially at Easter and in summer. To confirm the booking a deposit should be sent. Hotels equipped to offer hospitality to the disabled are indicated in the 'APT' hotel lists.

Up-to-date information about hotels and restaurants can be found in numerous specialised guides to hotels and restaurants in Italy. These include the red guide to Italy published by 'Michelin' ('Italia', revised annually). In Italian, the Touring Club Italiano publish useful information about hotels in 'Alberghi in Italia' (published about every year) and in the 'Guida Rapida d'Italia' (five volumes, one of which covers Campania, Puglia, Basilicata, Calabria, and Sicily). The guides published in Italian by 'L'Espresso' to hotels and restaurants in Italy are now issued (in a reduced single volume) in English every year. Other specialised guides include the 'Charming Small Hotel Guide: Italy' (Duncan Petersen).

There is still a lack of good small hotels in Sicily. The nine provincial capitals all have adequate hotels (although Enna, Caltanissetta, Ragusa, and Trapani have only a very small selection). The hotels in Erice, Taormina, and Agrigento are particularly good. The grading is not standard; a 3-star hotel in say, Taormina, may be better (and more expensive) than a 3-star hotel in a less fashionable town. Many large new hotels and tourist 'villages' have been built on the coasts of the island, which mainly cater for 'package' holiday makers.

Charges vary according to class, season, services available, and locality. These are listed in the annual list of hotels published by the local 'APT' office, and may not be exceeded. The total charge is exhibited on the back of the door of the hotel room. Breakfast (usually disappointing and costly) is by law an optional extra charge, although a lot of hotels try to include it in the price of the room. When booking a room, always specify if you want breakfast or not. It is usually well worthwhile going round the corner to the nearest bar for breakfast. Hotels are now obliged by law (for tax purposes) to issue an official receipt to customers; you should not leave the premises without this document.

Agriturism, which provides accommodation in farmhouses in the countryside, has recently been developed throughout Italy, although it is not yet as widely available in Sicily as in some other parts of the country. Terms very greatly from bed-and-breakfast, to self-contained flats, and is highly recommended for travellers with their own transport, and for families, as an excellent (and usually cheap) way of visiting the country. Some farms require a stay of a minimum number of days. Cultural or recreational activities are sometimes also provided, such as horse-back riding. Information from the head office of 'Agriturist' in Rome (101 Corso Vittorio Emanuele), who publish an annual guide to hospitality available in Italy, or the regional office of 'Agriturist' for Sicily in Palermo (14 Via Alessio di Giovanni, Tel. 091/346046). Information is also given by the local 'APT' offices.

Camping is now well organised throughout Italy. An international camping carnet is useful. In Sicily, camping sites are usually included in the local 'APT' hotel lists, giving details of all services provided, size of the site, etc.

In some sites caravans and campers are allowed. The sites are divided into official categories by stars, from the most expensive 4-star sites, to the simplest and cheapest 1-star sites. Their classification and rates charged must be displayed at the campsite office. Some sites have been indicated in the text, with their star ratings. Full details of the sites in Italy are published annually by the Touring Club Italiano and Federcampeggio in 'Campeggi e Villaggi turistici in Italia'. The Federazione Italiana del Campeggio have an information office and booking service at No. 11 Via Vittorio Emanuele, Calenzano, 50041 Florence (Tel. 055/882391).

Youth Hostels. The Italian Youth Hostels Association (Associazione Italiana Alberghi per la Gioventù, 44 Via Cavour, 00184 Rome, Tel. 06/4871152) has 52 hostels situated all over Italy. They publish a free guide to them. A membership card of the 'AIG' or the International Youth Hostel Federation is required for access to Italian Youth hostels. Details from the Youth Hostels Association, Trevelyan House, 8 St Stephen's Hill, St Albans, Herts, AL1 2DY, and the Americian Youth Hostel Inc, National Offices, PO Box 37613 Washington DC 20013-7613. In Sicily Youth Hostels are open at present only in Castroreale (May–October), Lipari (March–October), and Erice.

Eating in Sicily

Restaurants in Italy are called 'Ristoranti' or 'Trattorie'; there is now usually no difference between the two, although a 'trattoria' used to be less smart (and usually cheaper) than a 'ristorante'. Italian food is usually good and not too expensive. The least pretentious restaurant almost invariably provides the best value. Almost every locality has a simple (often family run) restaurant which caters for the local residents; the decor is usually very simple and the food excellent value. This type of restaurant does not always offer a menu and the choice is usually limited to three or four first courses, and three or four second courses, with only fruit as a sweet. The more sophisticated restaurants are more attractive and comfortable and often larger and you can sometimes eat at tables outside. They display a menu outside, and are also usually considerably more expensive.

In the text below a small selection of restaurants open in Sicily in 1993 has been given, which is by no means exhaustive. The restaurants have been divided into three categories to reflect price ranges in 1993: 'LUXURY-CLASS RESTAURANTS' where the prices are likely to be over Lire 60,000 a head (and sometimes well over Lire 100,000 a head). These are among the most famous restaurants in Sicily and they usually offer international cuisine. '1ST-CLASS RESTAURANTS' where the prices range from Lire 35,000 and above. These are generally comfortable, with good service, but are not cheap. The third category, called 'SIMPLE TRATTORIE AND PIZZERIE' indicates places where you can eat for around Lire 25,000 a head, or even less. Although simple, the food in this category is usually the best value.

Specialised guides, revised annually, to the restaurants of Italy (in the 'Luxury-class' and '1st-class' categories as described above) include the red guide published by Michelin ('Italia'), 'La guida d'Italia' published by l'Espresso (and now in a reduced English version) and 'I Ristoranti di Veronelli'.

Prices on the menu do not include a cover charge ('coperto', shown separately on the menu) which is added to the bill. The service charge is now almost always automatically added at the end of the bill. Tipping is therefore not strictly necessary, but a few thousand lire are appreciated. Restaurants are now obliged by law (for tax purposes) to issue an official receipt to customers; you should not leave the premises without this document ('ricevuta fiscale'). Fish is always the most expensive item on the menu in any restaurant.

Pizze (a popular and cheap food throughout Italy) and other excellent snacks are served in a 'Pizzeria', 'Rosticceria' and 'Tavola Calda'. Some of these have no seating accommodation and sell food to take away or eat on the spot. Typrical Sicilian snacks are 'arancini di riso', rice balls fried in breadcrumbs, filled with butter and cheese, or meat. For **picnics**, sandwiches ('panini') are made up on request (with ham, salami, cheese, anchovies, tuna fish, etc.) at 'Pizzicherie' and 'Alimentari' (grocery shops), and 'Fornai' (bakeries). Bakeries often also sell delicious individual pizzas, 'focacce' or 'schiacciate', bread or puff pastry topped or filled with cheese, spinach, tomato, salted anchovies, ham, etc; they also usually sell good sweet buns, rolls, and cakes. Some of the pleasantest places to picnic in towns have been indicated in the text below.

Bars (cafés), which are open all day, serve numerous varieties of excellent refreshments which are usually eaten standing up. The cashier should be paid first, and the receipt given to the barman in order to get served. If you sit at a table the charge is considerably higher (at least double) and you will be given waiter service (and should not pay first). However, some simple bars have a few tables which can be used with no extra charge (it is always best to ask before sitting down). Black coffee ('caffè espresso') can be ordered diluted ('alto', 'lungo', or 'americano'), or with a dash of milk ('macchiato'), with a liquor ('corretto'), or with hot milk ('cappuccino' or 'caffè-latte'). In summer cold coffee ('caffè freddo') and cold coffee and milk ('caffè-latte freddo') are served.

Sicily is particularly famous for its cakes and ice-creams. A PASTICCERIA (usually also a café) always sells the best cakes since they are made on the premises. Local specialities are still produced, and the best 'pasticcerie' have been indicated in the text below. Ice-creams should always be bought in a GELATERIA where they are made on the spot; bars usually sell packaged ice-cream only.

Sicilian Food is generally excellent and better than that to be found on the Italian mainland. Pasta dishes include 'pasta con le sarde', with fresh sardines, wild fennel, pine nuts and raisins; 'spaghetti alla Norma' or 'maccheroni alla Norma', with fresh tomato, basil, fried aubergine, and grated salted ricotta cheese; 'spaghetti al peperoncino', with red pepper and garlic (very spicy), 'pasta all'arrabbiata', with a dry anchovy sauce. The pasta dishes with fish sauces are usually served with dry roasted breadcrumbs, instead of grated parmesan cheese. Pasta is also often served with courgettes or broccoli. 'Pasta con la mollica' is spaghetti with capers, anchovies, green olives, garlic, and roasted breadcrumbs. 'Bottarga', dried tuna fish eggs, are also sometimes used as a condiment for pasta. A characteristic hors d'oeuvre dish is 'caponata', which contains aubergine, tomatoes, olives, capers, celery, onion, etc, served cold in a vinegar and sugar dressing. The olives of Sicily are famous. Broad beans ('fave', 'fagioli'), chick peas ('ceci'), and lentils ('lenticchie') are also often served (sometimes with pasta). 'Fave a maccu' is a rich dish made with mashed broad beans. On the west coast (Trapani and Erice) 'cuscus con pesce' is a traditional Arab dish (couscous) made from coarse semolina steamed in an earthenware pan with spices and onion, to which is added a 'zuppa di pesce' (fish stew), in a tomato sauce.

The fish in the seaside towns and villages (and on the islands) is usually extremely good, but, as elsewhere in Italy, it is generally a good deal more expensive than meat. Many varieties are served 'alla griglia' (grilled) or 'arrosto' (roasted). 'Zuppa di pesce' in Sicily usually consists of a variety of fish baked in a herb and tomato sauce. Shell fish is abundant, and is often served fried, in a 'fritto misto di mare'. 'Calamari ripieni alla griglia' are grilled whole squid filled with capers, salted anchovies, olives, garlic, pine nuts, raisins, pecorino cheese and breadcrumbs. Tuna fish ('tonno'; caught off the north coast and near the island of Favignana) and swordfish ('pescespada'; abundant near Messina in May, June and July), are delicious cooked 'alla griglia', 'in bianco' (in oil, water, and spices), or 'alla Siciliana' (with capers, red pepper, and herbs). 'Involtini di pesce spada' are grilled roulades of sword fish covered with breadcrumbs and oil. Sardines are cooked in a variety of ways, including 'sarde a beccafico', with bread-crumbs, grated cheese, pine nuts, salted anchovies, parsley, oil, sultanas, and lemon. Meat dishes include 'falsomagro', a meat loaf.

Good fruit (especially oranges, mandarines, tangerines, melons, and grapes) are always available in season. Prickly pears are ripe from September–November. The ice-creams and water ices ('granite') are famous, and can be made from roses and jasmine as well as the more traditional flavours. The confectionery of Sicily is justly renowned, and ricotta cheese, almond paste, and pistachio nuts are widely used. Particularly good and decorative are the marzipan fruits ('frutta di martorana'), biscuits made with egg whites, almonds and lemon rind ('dolci di mandorla'), and 'cannoli' (rolls of thin deep fried pastry, made with red wine and Marsala, filled with ricotta, candied fruits, bitter chocolate, and chopped pistachio). The 'cassata alla siciliana' is a delicious light cake filled with ricotta and candied fruits. 'Giuggiolena' is made with sesame seeds, honey, toasted almonds and orange rind. The confectionery of Modica (including chocolate) is particularly good.

Sicilian Wines. The local wines are usually excellent, and it is often advisable to accept the 'house wine' ('vino di casa'), white and red usually available. This varies a great deal but is normally a 'vin ordinaire' of average standard and reasonable price. The most famous Sicilian wines, widely known outside the island, are 'Corvo di Salaparuta' (red and white), and 'Regaleali' (red, white, and rosé). The commonest white wine is 'Bianco d'Alcamo'. Good red wines include 'Cerasuolo' produced around Vittoria, Ragusa, and Comiso, and 'Faro' still made by a few wine growers near Messina. A white wine called 'Capo Bianco' is also produced near Messina. The wine called 'Etna', produced on volcanic soil, can be white, red or rosé. 'Ciclopi' is also found around Etna. 'Mamertino Bianco' is produced near Castroreale. Near Catania the red 'Terreforti' is sold, and near Syracuse, 'Anapo' (white), Eloro, and Pachino (red). In the W of the island, wines produced near Agrigento include 'Menfi', 'Akragas' and 'Belice', and near Trapani the white 'Capo Boeo' is produced. In the Palermo area 'Casteldaccia' and 'Partinico' (white) can be found. Famous desert wines produced in Sicily are Marsala, Malvasia (from the Aeolian Islands), and Moscato (white Muscatel; from Pantelleria).

The **menu** which follows includes some of the dishes most often to be found in Italian restaurants (the Sicilian specialities are described on p 52).

Antipasti, Hors d'oeuvre
Prosciutto crudo o cotto, Raw or cooked ham
Prosciutto e melone, Ham (usually raw) and melon
Salame con funghi e carciofini sott'olio, Salami with mushrooms and artichokes in oil
Salsicce, Dry sausage
Caponata, a sweet-and-sour dish made with aubergine, tomatoes, olives, capers, onion, celery, etc., served cold with a vinegar and sugar dressing.
Frittata, Omelette
Sformato, Vegtables cooked in a bechamel sauce and baked in the oven
Verdura cruda, Raw vegetables
Antipasto misto, Mixed cold hors d'oeuvre
Antipasto di mare, Seafood hors d'oeuvre

Minestre e Pasta, Soups and Pasta
Brodo, Clear soup
Minestre, zuppa, Thick soup
Stracciatella, Broth with beaten egg
Minestrone, Vegetable soup
Spaghetti al sugo or *al ragù*, Spaghetti with a meat sauce
Spaghetti al pomodoro, Spaghetti with a tomato sauce
Penne all'arrabbiata, Short pasta with a rich spicy sauce
Tagliatelle, Flat spaghetti-like pasta, almost always home-made with egg
Lasagne, Layers of pasta with meat filling, and tomato and cheese sauce
Pasta al forno, timballo, pasta baked with meat, hard-boiled eggs, peas, etc.
Agnolotti, Ravioli filled with meat
Fettuccine, Ribbon noodles
Spaghetti alla carbonara, Spaghetti with bacon, beaten egg and black pepper
Spaghetti alle vongole, Spaghetti with clams
Spaghetti alla matriciana, Spaghetti with salt pork and tomato sauce
Cannelloni, Rolled pasta 'pancakes', with meat filling and cheese and tomato sauce
Tortellini, Small coils of pasta, filled with a rich stuffing, served either in broth or with a sauce
Cappelletti, Form of ravioli, often served in broth
Gnocchi, a type of pasta made from potato and flour
Ravioli or gnocchi verdi, Filled with spinach and ricotta cheese
Risotto, Rice dish

Pesce, Fish
Zuppa di pesce, Mixed fish, usually in a sauce (or soup)
Fritto di pesce, Fried fish
Fritto misto di mare, Mixed fried fish, often cuttlefish and prawns
Pesce arrosto, Pesce alla griglia, Roast, grilled fish
Aragosta, Lobster (an expensive delicacy)
Triglie, Red mullet

Sarago, a type of bream
Sarde, Sardines
Pescespada, Swordfish
Tonno, Tuna fish
Cernia, Sea perch
Calamari, Squid
Polipi, Octopus
Baccalà, Salt cod
Anguilla, Eel
Sogliola, Sole
Cozze, Mussels
Gamberi, Prawns
Dentice, Dentex
Orata, Bream
Sgombro, Mackerel
Trota, Trout
Seppie, Cuttlefish
Involtini di pesce spada, Grilled roulades of swordfish covered with breadcrumbs and oil
Sarde a beccafico, sardines cooked with breadcrumbs, grated cheese, pine nuts, salted anchovies, parsley, oil, sultanas, and lemon

Carne, Meat course
Vitello, Veal
Manzo, Beef
Agnello, Lamb
Maiale (*arrosto*), Pork (roast)
Pollo (*bollito*), Chicken (boiled)
Petto di Pollo, Chicken breasts
Pollo alla Cacciatore, Chicken with herbs, and (usually) tomato and pimento sauce
Bistecca, Steak (usually grilled over charcoal)
Stufato, Stewed meat served in slices in a sauce
Polpette, Meat balls (often served in a sauce)
Involtini, Thin rolled slices of meat in a sauce
Fegato, Liver
Tacchino, Turkey
Cervello, Brain
Animelle, Sweetbreads
Abbacchio, Roast sucking lamb
Costolette alla Milanese, Veal cutlets, fried in breadcrumbs
Saltimbocca, Rolled veal with ham
Bocconcini, as above, with cheese
Falsomagro, Meat loaf
Ossobuco, Stewed shin of veal
Spezzatino, Veal stew, usually with pimento, tomato, onion, peas, and wine
Bollito, Stew of various boiled meats
Fagiano, Pheasant
Coniglio, Rabbit

Lepre, Hare
Cinghiale, Wild boar

Contorni, Vegetables
Insalata verde, Green salad
Insalata mista, Mixed salad
Pomodori, Tomatoes
Funghi, Mushrooms
Spinaci, Spinach
Broccoletti, Tender broccoli
Piselli, Peas
Fagiolini, Beans (French)
Carciofi, Artichokes
Asparagi, Asparagus
Zucchine, Courgettes
Melanzane, Aubergine
Melanzane alla parmigiana, Aubergine in cheese sauce
Peperoni, Pimentoes
Finocchi, Fennel
Patatine fritte, Fried potatoes

Dolci, Sweets
Torta, Tart
Monte Bianco, Mont blanc (with chestnut flavouring)
Saint-Honoré, Rich meringue cake
Gelato, Ice cream
Zuppa Inglese, Trifle
Cassata, Cake filled with ricotta cheese and candied fruit

Frutta, Fruit
Macedonia di frutta, Fruit salad
Arance, Oranges
Uva, Grapes
Pesche, Peaches
Albicocche, Apricots
Mele, Apples
Pere, Pears
Fragole con panna, Strawberries and cream
Fragole al limone, with lemon
Ciliege, Cherries
Fichi, Figs
Fichi d'India, Prickly pears
Melone, Melon

Opening Times of Museums, Sites, and Churches

The opening times of **museums and monuments** have been given in the text but they vary and often change without warning; when possible it is always advisable to consult the local tourist office ('APT') on arrival about the up-to-date times. Many museums and archaeological sites in Sicily are now open seven days a week. State-owned museums and monuments, for long only open 9–14, fest. 9–13 and closed on Monday, are now sometimes also open in the afternoon on certain days, and do not all close on Mondays. However, there is no standard timetable and you should take great care to allow enough time for variations in the hours shown in the text when planning a visit to a museum or monument. Some museums, etc. are closed on the main public holidays: 1 January, Easter, 1 May, 15 August, and Christmas Day (although there is now a policy to keep at least a few of them open on these days in the larger cities; information has to be obtained about this on the spot). Admission charges vary, but are usually around Lire 2000 (generally lower than in the rest of Italy). British citizens under the age of 18 and over the age of 60 are entitled to free admission to State-owned museums and monuments in Italy (because of reciprocal arrangements in Britain). The 'Settimana per i Beni Culturali e Ambientali' is usually held early in December, when for a week there is free entrance to all State-owned museums, and others are specially opened.

Churches, although they usually open very early in the morning (at 7 or 8), are almost always closed for a considerable period during the middle of the day (11.30 or 12 to 16 or 17). Small churches and oratories are often open in the early morning, or for services only, but it is sometimes possible to find the key by asking locally. The sacristan will show closed chapels, crypts, etc., and sometimes expects a tip. Many pictures and frescoes are difficult to see without lights which are sometimes provided (operated by lire coins); a torch and binoculars are always useful. Some churches now ask that sightseers do not enter during a service, but normally you may do so, provided you are silent and do not approach the altar in use. An entrance fee is becoming customary for admission to treasuries, cloisters, bell-towers, etc. Sometimes you are not allowed to enter important churches wearing shorts or with bare shoulders.

Nature reserves in Sicily

Some of the most beautiful parts of the island are at last becoming protected areas. The two splendid coastal reserves of the Zingaro on the north coast, and Vendicari on the east coast, stand out not only as areas of extraordinary beauty and interest for their scenery, vegetation, and bird life, but also as examples of the success of the efforts of the local population to preserve them from 'development'. They are both only accessible on foot. The wooded areas of the island include the Nebrodi and Peloritani mountain ranges on the north coast, and tbe Bosco della Ficuzza, S of Palermo, one of the largest forests left on the island. A national park is projected to protect the Nebrodi. Beautiful walks (and rides) can be taken in the Madonie mountains, S of Cefalù, which became a Regional nature reserve in 1989. Etna, now a national park, remains one of the most fascinating areas of the island, despite the fact its lower slopes have been covered with new buildings.

Smaller areas, but with their own particular interest, which have recently been protected, where lovely countryside can be explored, include the Valle dell'Anapo and the Cava d'Ispica. The remote plateau of Pantalica is also very beautiful. A similar area, the Cava Grande at Cassibile, became a reserve in 1984. The salt marshes between Trapani and Marsala, interesting for their bird life, are partially protected, but the most beautiful accessible countryside here is on the island of San Pantaleo (Mozia). Capo Bianco and Torre Salsa, near Eraclea Minoa on the south coast is another lovely stretch of coastline, purchased by the 'WWF' in 1991, with interesting vegetation and birdlife. On the hillside below Erice the Museo Agro Forestale di San Matteo was opened in 1986, where a farm of some 500 hectares may be visited. The islands off the Sicilian coast are all of great natural beauty, particularly the Aeolian islands, Marettimo in the Egadi group, and Pantelleria. A marine reserve protects the splendid coastline of Ustica.

For information about protected areas and nature conservation in Sicily, contact the Direzione Azienda Foreste Demaniali, 97 Via Libertà, Palermo (Tel. 091/6256245). The headquarters of the Club Alpino Italiano ('CAI') is at 30 Via Agrigento, Palermo, and of the 'WWF' at 2H Via Calvi, Palermo.

Annual Festivals in Sicily

There are a number of traditional festivals in Sicilian towns which are of the greatest interest. At these times, the towns become extremely lively and, apart from the central procession or competition, numerous celebrations take place on the side, and local markets are usually held at the same time. They are particularly exciting events for children. Information from local 'APT' offices.

Spring. Carnival celebrations at Acireale, Termini Imerese, and Sciacca. Easter week is particularly important at Caltanissetta (Maundy Thursday), Trapani (Good Friday), Erice (Good Friday), Noto ('Santa Spina'; Good Friday), Castelvetrano (Easter Sunday), Prizzi (Easter Sunday; 'dance of the devils'), Modica, Caltagirone, Adrano, Enna, Piana degli Albanesi, San Fratello ('Festa dei Giudei'), and Castroreale. After Easter the 'Palio di San Vincenzo' is run at Acate, and in April Modica holds the 'Festa di San Giorgio'. On the first and second Sunday in May Syracuse celebrates 'Santa Lucia', and on the third Sunday in May the 'Infiorata' is held in Noto. On the last Sunday in May Ragusa Ibla commemorates 'San Giorgio', and Casteltermini holds the 'Tataratà' festival. Also in May 'San Gandolfo' is celebrated at Polizzi Generosa, and the 'Settimana delle Egadi' takes place at the end of May.

Summer. On the 3 June Messina has celebrations in honour of the 'Madonna della Lettera', and on 2 July Enna honours the 'Madonna della Visitazione'. At the end of June 'San Pietro' is celebrated in Modica and 'San Paolo' in Palazzolo Acreide. The famous 'Festa di Santa Rosalia' takes place in Palermo from 10–15 July. The 'Scala' is illuminated at Caltagirone on 24–25 July. On 6 August there are festivities in honour of 'San Salvatore' at Cefalù, and on 13–14 August the 'Palio dei Normanni' is held in Piazza Armerina. Messina has processions of the 'Giganti' and the 'Vara' on 13–15 August. Mistretta celebrates 'San Sebastiano' on 18 August, and Ragusa celebrates 'San Giovanni' on 29 August. On the last Sunday in August and the first Sunday in September the festa of 'San Corrado' takes place in Noto.

Autumn and **Winter**. In September a hazelnut fair is held in Polizzi Generosa and the 'Madonna della Luce' is celebrated at Mistretta. In Syracuse in December the 'Immacolata' festival takes place (8th) and the festa in honour of 'Santa Lucia' (13th). A festa is held on 26 December in Polizzi Generosa, and on 6 January the Epiphany is celebrated in Piana degli Albanesi. On 20 January festivities in honour of 'San Sebastiano' take place in Syracuse and Mistretta. In the first week in February the 'Sagra del mandorlo in fiore' is held in Agrigento. From the 3–5 February 'Sant'Agata' is celebrated in Catania. On 19 February there are more festivities in honour of 'San Corrado' in Noto.

Music and Theatre festivals. Music festivals are held in summer at Agrigento, Erice, Noto, Taormina, and Trapani. Summer theatre festivals include those at Segesta, Syracuse, Gibellina, and Pirandello's house near Agrigento. In Taormina in July an international film festival takes place. In November a music festival is held in the Duomo of Monreale, and in December a festival of folk music in Erice.

Local handicrafts in Sicily

It has become much harder to find locally made handicrafts on the island in the last ten years or so. Baskets are still made in a style distinctive to the island and sold at local weekly markets (and in some hardware shops; 'mesticherie'). Ceramics can also sometimes be found for sale, and are sold on the streets in Giarre and Santo Stefano di Camastra. Caltagirone still has numerous small potteries. Colourful rugs are woven in Erice. The traditional artisans' skill is now perhaps best seen in the sweets still produced in local 'pasticcerie' (some of the best of which are mentioned below in the main text).

Visiting Sicily with children

A holiday can often be marred for parents as well as children if too much serious sight-seeing is attempted in too short a time. Sicily has a variety of sights which may be of special interest to children and may help to alleviate a day of undiluted museums and churches. A golden rule when allowing a 'break' for an ice-cream is to search for a 'Gelateria' (rather than a bar) where the locally produced ice-creams are generally excellent.

A few suggestions are given below of places that might have particular appeal to children, listed in the order of the routes by which the book is divided. These include some important monuments which are likely to give a clear impression of a particular period of art or architecture, a few museums, and places of naturalistic interest. Local festivals, often with colourful processions, etc. (listed above) should not be missed if your visit coincides with one of them. Detailed descriptions of all the places mentioned below are given in the main text (and can easily be found by reference to the index at the back of the book).

Rte 1. Palermo: the street markets, and puppet theatre performances. The Cappella Palatina, and Palazzo dei Normanni (if it reopens), San Giovanni degli Eremiti, the park (and zoo) of Palazzo d'Orleans, the Puppet Museum, the park of Villa Giulia and the Botanical gardens, Palazzo Mirto, the Galleria Regionale, La Zisa, the gardens of Villa Malfitano, and the Museo Etnografio Siciliano Pitré.

Rte 2. Monte Pellegrino, the Duomo of Monreale (including the roof), the excavations of Solunto, the ethnographical museum in Piana degli Albanesi, the island of Ustica.

Rte 3. The castle of Caccamo, the ruins of Himera, the town of Cefalù (including the Rocca and the Museo Mandralisca), the Madonie mountains.

Rte 4. Segesta (the temple and theatre), the Museo Civico of Terrasini, the Tonnara di Scopello, the Riserva Naturale dello Zingaro, Custonaci.

Rte 5. The museums of Trapani: the Museo Trapanese di preistoria, the Museo Regionale Pepoli, and the Museo delle Saline.

Rte 6. The town of Erice (including the gardens of Villa Balio, and the Castello di Venere), and the Museo Agro-Forestale di San Matteo.

Rte 7. The Egadi islands and Pantelleria.

Rte 8. The island of Mozia, and, in Marsala, the Museo Archeologico di Baglio Anselmi, and the Stabilimento Florio.

Rte 9. The ruins of Selinunte and the Cave di Cusa.

Rte 10. The site of Eraclea Minoa.

Rte 11. The Bosco della Ficuzza.

Rte 12. Agrigento: the temples, the Museo Regionale, and the rock sanctuary of Demeter.

Rte 15. Enna: the 'passeggiata', as well as the numismatic collection in the Museo Alessi, the Castello di Lombardia, and the Rocca Cerere.

Rte 16. The town of Leonforte, including the 'Granfonte', and the castle of Sperlinga.

Rte 17. The mosaics in the Villa Romana at Casale near Piazza Armerina. The ruins of Morgantina.

Rte 18. Caltagirone: the 'Scala', the public gardens, and the Museo Regionale della Ceramica.

Rte 19. The town of Ragusa Ibla.

Rte 20. The Museo Ibleo delle Arti e delle Tradizioni Popolari at Modica,

Cava d'Ispica, the Castello di Donnafugata, and the ruins (and museum) of Camarina.

Rte 21. Syracuse: the town of Ortygia, the Duomo, the Fonte Aretusa, the Museo Archeologico Regionale Paolo Orsi, the catacombs of San Giovanni, the Latomia del Paradiso and Ear of Dionysius, the Greek Theatre, and the Amphitheatre.

Rte 22. The castle of Euraylus, the river Ciane, the town of Noto, Noto Antica, the ruins of Eloro, the nature reserve of Vendicari. In Palazzolo Acreide, the Casa-Museo ethnographical museum, the excavations of Akrai, and the 'Santoni'. The park of the Valle dell'Anapo, and the necropolis of Pantalica.

Rte 23. The excavations of Leontinoi.

Rte 24. Catania: Castello Ursino (when it reopens).

Rte 25. Excursion to the summit of Etna, the castle of Adrano, and the Castello Maniace at Bronte.

Rte 26. The castle of Aci Castello, a puppet performance in Acireale, Giarre (to see the ceramics sold on the streets), and the Alcantara gorge.

Rte 27. Taormina: the town, the Theatre, the public gardens, the Madonna della Rocca and the Castello, and the excavations of Naxos.

Rte 28. Messina: the Museo Regionale, the Punta del Faro, and the Monti Peloritani (the road to Maria Santissima di Dinnamare).

Rte 29. The castle of Milazzo (when it reopens), Capo Milazzo, the excavations of Tindari, the mosaics of the Roman villa at Patti.

Rte 30. The Aeolian islands.

Beaches in Sicily

The sea around Sicily has suffered from pollution in recent years, as it has around the rest of Italy, and much of the coastline has been disfigured by new building. The industrial zones of Augusta and Gela should be avoided by visitors at all costs. Some of the prettiest unspoilt beaches can be found near Noto, at Cala Bernardo and Lido di Noto. The south coast is generally the least spoilt part of the island, with good beaches especially around Porto Palo (S of Menfi, near Selinunte) and at Torre di Monterosso, S of Siculiana. Farther E are the small resorts with some good beaches of Marina di Ragusa, Donnalucata, Cava d'Aliga, and Marina di Modica. The rocky coast around Acireale and Taormina is popular for sea bathing. On the north coast there are fine (but crowded) beaches at the resorts of Cefalù and Mondello. There are rocky beaches on Capo di Milazzo. N of Castellammare del Golfo there is a remarkable stretch of unspoilt rocky coastline (only accessible by paths) at Cala Bianca, Cala Rossa and Baia Guidaloca, and sea bathing is allowed in the beautiful nature reserve of Zingaro on the promontory of Capo San Vito. San Vito lo Capo has become a seaside resort, with good beaches. The best sea bathing of all is to be found on the islands, especially the Aeolian islands, Marittima, Ustica, and Pantelleria.

Planning a visit to Sicily

The 30 routes in this Guide follow a roughly circular route of the island (which can be made by car or by public transport) from Palermo, to Trapani and Erice, Selinunte, Agrigento, Enna, Ragusa, Syracuse, Catania, Taormina, Messina, and back long the N coast to Palermo. The places mentioned below should not be missed. As many days as possible should be devoted to the city of Palermo and its environs (notably Monreale). Selinunte may then be reached via Segesta and the west coast (Trapani, Erice, the island of Motya, and Marsala), or, for those with less time, direct from Palermo (in this case Segesta can be visited on a detour or in a day from Palermo). Agrigento, reached from here along the south coast via Eraclea Minoa, deserves a visit of at least two days. The numerous medieval hill-towns and spectacular countryside in the interior of the island can be explored from Enna (reached via Caltanissetta from Agrigento). Piazza Armerina with the famous mosaics in its Roman villa and the ruins of Morgantina are near Caltagirone, another inland town. The coast road from Agrigento runs via Gela. In the SE corner of the island are the fine Baroque towns of Ragusa, Modica, and Comiso. The exploration of Syracuse and its environs (Castle of Euraylus, Noto, Palazzolo Acreide, and the necropolis of Pantalica) requires at least 3 days. Catania, which can be visited in a day, is a good centre for the ascent of Etna and a circular tour of the foothills. The road back to Messina passes Naxos and Taormina, where at least one night should be spent. On the road between Messina and Palermo, Tindari and Cefalù should not be missed.

General Information

Season. Sicily is famous for its cloudless skies and mild winters, and even in the rainiest months, November and December, there are usually many days of Indian summer. July and August are apt to be very hot, and the sirocco, which can blow for four or five days at a time, raises the temperature to 40 degrees Cent. It is often very windy near the Straits of Messina, and even in summer the sea here can be chilly. In March it is possible in the region of Etna to combine sea-bathing with winter sports. The best months for travelling in Sicily are March, April, May, June, September, October, and November.

Public Holidays. The Italian National Holidays when offices, shops, and schools are closed are as follows: 1 January, Easter Monday, 25 April (Liberation Day), 1 May (Labour Day), 15 August (Assumption), 1 November (All Saints' Day), 8 December (Immaculate Conception), Christmas Day and 26 December (St Stephen). Each town keeps its Patron Saint's day as a holiday.

Italy for the disabled. Italy is at last catching up slowly with the rest of

Europe in the provision of facilities for the disabled. All new public buildings are now obliged by law to provide access for the disabled, and specially designed facilities. In the annual list of hotels published by the local 'APT' offices, hotels which are able to give hospitality to the disabled are indicated. Airports and railway stations provide assistance, and certain trains are equipped to transport wheelchairs. Access is allowed to the centre of towns normally closed to traffic for cars with disabled people, where parking places are reserved for them. For all other information, contact local 'APT' offices.

Telephones and **Postal Information**. Stamps are sold at tobacconists (displaying a blue 'T' sign) and post offices (open 8.10–13.25, Monday–Saturday). Central offices in main towns are open 8.10–19.25. It is always advisable to post letters at post offices or railway stations; collection from letterboxes can be erratic. There are numerous public telephones all over Italy in kiosks, bars and restaurants. These are now usually operated by coins, telephone cards, or metal disks (200 lire) known as 'gettone'. These and telephone cards can be bought from tobacconists, bars, some newspaper stands, and post offices.

Working Hours. Government offices usually work Monday– Saturday from 8–13.30 or 14. Shops (clothes, hardware, hairdressers, etc.) are generally open from 9–13, 16–19.30, including Saturday, and for most of the year are closed on Monday morning. Food shops usually open from 8–13, 17–19.30 or 20, and for most of the year are closed on Wednesday afternoon. From mid-June to mid-September all shops are closed instead on Saturday afternoon. **Banks** are usually open from 8.20–13.30, and for one hour in the afternoon (usually c 14.30–15.30), every day except Saturday and Sunday. They close early (about 11) on days preceding national holidays.

Public Toilets. There is a notable shortage of public toilets in Italy. All bars (cafés) should have toilets available to the public (generally speaking the larger the bar, the better the facilities). Nearly all museums now have toilets. There are also toilets at railway stations and bus stations.

Health Service. British citizens, as members of the EC, have the right to claim health services in Italy if they have the E111 form (issued by the Department of Health and Social Security). There are also a number of private holiday health insurance policies. First Aid services ('Pronto Soccorso') are available at all hospitals, railway stations, and airports. **Chemist Shops** ('farmacie') are usually open Monday–Friday 9–13, 16–19.30 or 20. On Saturdays and Sundays (and holidays) a few are open (listed on the door of every chemist). In all towns there is also at least one chemist shop open at night (also shown on the door of every chemist). For emergencies, dial 113.

Crime. Pick-pocketing is a widespread problem in towns all over Italy; it is always advisable not to carry valuables in handbags, and be particualrly careful on public transport. Crime should be reported at once to the police, or the local 'carabinieri' office (found in every town and small village). A detailed statement has to be given in order to get an official document confirming loss or damage (essential for insurance claims). Interpreters are provided. For all emergencies, dial 113.

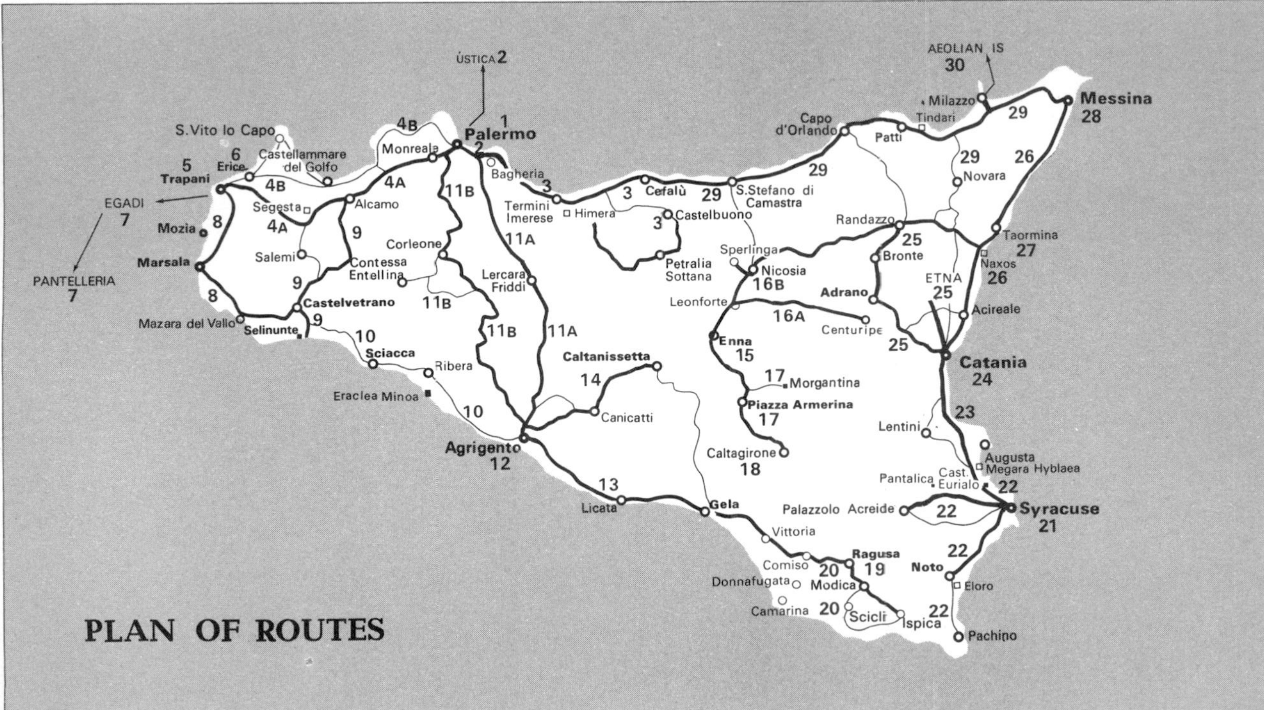

PLAN OF ROUTES

1

Palermo

PALERMO (730,800 inhab.), the capital of Sicily and her most interesting city, is situated on a bay on the N coast at the foot of Monte Pellegrino, a beautiful headland. One of the largest and most important cities in the world from the 9C to the 12C, Palermo still possesses some of the great Arab-Norman buildings erected at that time: the Cappella Palatina, La Martorana, San Giovanni degli Eremiti, the Zisa, and, a few kilometres outside the city, the cathedral of Monreale. Numerous delightful Baroque churches and oratories survive from later centuries. The Archaeological Museum and the Regional Gallery contain outstanding collections.

The bustling streets and animated markets give the town an Oriental aspect. The 'Conca d'Oro', a small plain enclosed by limestone hills, which surrounds the city, was once filled with dark groves of orange, lemon, and carob trees, but it has been smothered in the last few decades with ugly tower blocks. In the historic centre, suffering from depopulation, a large proportion of the houses are in danger of collapse, and there are numerous decaying slum areas around bomb sites which have been neglected since the last War. In 1988–90 detailed plans to restore and renovate the centre of the city were drawn up by three distinguished architects and conservationists, together with the town planning office. These were approved by the town council in 1990, the first sign that the city may evenutally receive the careful attention it deserves. Palermo enjoys a superb climate. **Plan on p 8 of the atlas section**.

Information Offices. 'APT' Palermo, 35 Piazza Castelnuovo (Pl. 6; Tel. 091/583887). Subsidiary offices at the railway station, the airport, and (in summer) at the port. 'Azienda Autonoma di Turismo', Villa Igiea, 43 Salita Belmonte (Tel. 091/540122). 'Assessorato Regionale del Turismo' (Sicilian Regional Tourist Board), 11 Via Notarbartolo.

Airport. *Punta Raisi*, 32km W (motorway). Internal and international services. Coach services in connection with flights run by Prestia & Comandé to Via Emerico Amari (Pl. 7), and the central railway station.

Railway stations. *Centrale* (Pl. 16) for all State Railway services; *Notarbartolo* (N of Pl. 1), subsidiary station on the Trapani line.

City Buses run by 'AMAT' tend to be overcrowded and very slow because of the traffic conjestion in the centre of the city. Tickets (1000 lire; or 3000 lire valid for 24hrs) must be purchased at tobacconists, kiosks, etc. and stamped at automatic machines on board. Many of the lines serve the railway station and follow the Corso, Via Maqueda, or Via Roma for part of their course. For buses to muonuments in the outskirts of the town, see Rtes 1E, 1F, and 1G.

Country Buses. There is a wide network of services from Palermo run by various bus companies, including those listed below. Daily services from VIA BALSAMO (beside the railway station; Pl. 16): 'SAIS' c every hour to Catania (via the motorway in 2hrs 40mins), and, less frquently to Enna (in c 2hrs); also to Taormina, Cefalù and Messina. 'Segesta' to Trapani (via Alcamo); 'Cuffaro' to Agrigento, and 'Randazzo' to Piazza Armerina. From PIAZZA MARINA (Pl. 12): 'Trepanum' to Segesta; 'Stassi' to Erice, and 'AST' to Ragusa and Syracuse. For services to the environs of Palermo, see Rte 2.

Maritime Services. Port, Molo Vittorio Veneto (Pl. 8). Overnight ferry service run by 'Tirrenia' (Via del Mare, beside the Port) to Naples, Cagliari, Tunis; and Genoa. Services run by 'Grandi Traghetti' (179 Via M. Stabile) from Molo Santa Lucia to Livorno and Genoa. Hydrofoil and ferry services run by Siremar (120 Via Crispi) to Ustica.

Car Parking is extremely difficult in the centre of Palermo (where no major roads have yet been closed to private cars). Most 3- and 4-star hotels have parking facilities or garages (at extra cost). There are some garages and 'ACI' car-parks in and near Piazza Castelnuovo (Pl. 6) and Piazza Verdi (Pl. 11).

An **underground railway** is under construction which will link the SE suburb of Brancaccia to the main railway station, and that of Notarbartolo, with the Parco della Favorita, Sferracavallo, and Punta Raisi airport.

Hotels. 5-star: 'Villa Igiea' (beyond Pl. 3) in a remarkable Art Nouveau building on the sea at Acquasanta, 3km N of the city (see Rte 2A) in a large park with tennis courts and swimming pool. 4-star: 'Grande Albergo & delle Palme' (a; Pl. 7), 398 Via Roma, in another historic building (formerly Palazzo Ingham), 'Politeama Palace' (h; Pl. 6), 15 Piazza Ruggero Settimo, 'President' (i; Pl. 3), 228 Via Crispi, 'Jolly' (b; Pl. 16), Foro Italico. 3-star: 'Sole Grande Albergo' (e; Pl. 11), 291 Corso Vittorio Emanuele, 'Mediterraneo' (f; Pl. 7), 43 Via Rosolino Pilo; 'Touring' (g; Pl. 7), 126 Via Mariano Stabile, 'Europa' (j; Pl. 2), 3 Via Agrigento. 2-star: 'Sausele', 12 Via Vincenzo Errante, 300m SW of the Stazione Centrale, 'Villa Archirafi' (k; Pl. 16), 10 Via Archirafi, 'Liguria' (l; Pl. 7), 128 Via M. Stabile. 1-star: 'Letizia' (n; Pl. 12), 30 Via Bottai, 'Petit' (o; Pl. 7), 84 Via Principe di Belmonte, 'Orientale', 26 Via Maqueda (d; Pl. 15); and many others.

At MONDELLO (see Rte 2A): 4-star: 'Mondello Palace', with golf course and swimming pool. 3-star: 'Splendid Hotel La Torre', in a fine position by the sea (swimming pool), 'Conchiglia d'Oro'. 2-star: 'Esplanade'.

Camping Sites on the coast N of the city at Sferracavallo: 2-star: 'Trinacria', and 1-star: 'Dell'Ulivo'.

Restaurants. Luxury-class: 'Charleston', 71 Piazzale Ungheria; 'Chamade', 22 Via Torrearsa; 'Da Renato', Via Messina Marine; 'Regine', 4 Via Trapani (for fish); 'La Scuderia', 9 Viale del Fante. 1st-class: 'A Cuccagna', 21 Via Principe di Granatelli; 'Da Zio Aldo', Piazza Ignazio Florio; 'Friend's Bar', 138 Via Brunelleschi; 'Trattoria del Buongustaio', 79 Via Venezia. Simple trattorie and pizzerie: 'Stella', 104 Via Alloro; 'Primavera', Piazza Bologna; ''Ngrasciata', 12 Via Tiro a Segno; 'Bellini', Piazza Bellini; 'Peppino', 49 Piazza Castelnuovo; 'Al 59', 59 Piazza Verdi; 'Antica Focacceria di San Francesco' (sandwiches), 58 Via Paternostro. Vegetarian restaurant: 'Cotto e Crudo', 45 Piazza Marina.

Restaurants at MONDELLO are well known for fish: Luxury-class: 'Chamade Mare' and 'Le Terrazze'; 1st-class: 'Calogero', 'Franco', 'Il Gambero Rosso'. Pizzeria: 'Da Totuccio'. Vegetarian restaurant: 'Giardino dei Melograni'. At SFERRACAVALLO (1st-class): 'Al Delfino'.

Cafés or bars ('pasticceria' which make their own delicious savoury snacks, cakes, sweets, etc.) include: 'La Martorana', 196 Via Vittorio Emanuele; 'Roney', Via Libertà; 'Mazzara', Via Generale Magliocco; 'Extra Bar', Piazza Politeama; 'Preferita', Via Villareale. There are a number of cafés with tables outside off Via Ruggero Settimo, in Via Principe di Belmonte (Pl. 7; closed to traffic).

Picnic Places. Well kept public parks near the centre of the town include the Villa Giulia (Pl. 16), the Giardino Inglese (Pl. 2), and the Parco d'Orleans (Pl. 14).

Police Station: (Questura), 11 Piazza della Vittoria (tel. 210111); for emergencies, tel. 113.

English Church: (Holy Cross; Pl. 7), 118 Via Stabile; services in winter only.

Theatres. 'Politeama Garibaldi', Piazza Ruggero Settimo; 'Biondo', 260 Via Roma (prose and concerts); the 'Massimo' has been closed for many years. CONCERTS are held in the churches of San Salvatore and San Giuseppe, and in the 'Sala Scarlatti' of the Conservatorio, 45 Via Squarcialupo. PUPPET THEATRES: performances at the Museo Internazionale delle Marionette (see Rte 1D), 1 Via Butera (tel. 328060), and periodically at various small theatres in the city (it is advisable to telephone in advance for information): 'Cuticchio', 95 Via Bara (Pl. 11; Tel. 323400); 'Opera dei Pupi', Vicolo Ragusi (Tel. 329194), and 'Teatro Bradamante', 25 Via Lombardia (Tel. 6259223).

Markets. The street markets of Palermo are justly famous, and should not be missed even by the most hurried visitor. The biggest are: VUCCIRIA (Pl. 11), for produce (especially fish); BALLARÒ (Pl. 15), for produce (and some 'antiques'); CAPO (Via Sant' Agostino; Pl. 10, 11), for clothes and produce; PAPIRETO (Piazza Peranni; Pl. 10), for 'antiques' and 'junk' (although this is now in decline). There is a food market open all afternoon and evening in Corso Scina (Pl. 3).

Annual Festivals. *Festino di Santa Rosalia* (10–15 July), with celebrations including theatre performances, concerts, fireworks and a street procession with the statue of St Rosalia on a huge cart drawn by horses; pilgrimage (with a torchlight procession) to the shrine on Monte Pellegrino, 3–4 September. A Music Festival is held for a week in November in the cathedral of Monreale.

History. *Panormus*, a Phoenician colony of the 8–6C BC, was never a Greek city, despite its Greek name signifying 'all harbour'. It was, instead, an important Carthaginian centre, hotly disputed during the First Punic War, and not finally acquired by Rome until 254 BC. It became a municipium, and after 20 BC, a flourishing colony. After the invasions of the Vandals and Ostrogoths it was reconquered for the Byzantine emperors in 535 and remained in their possession until 831, when the Saracens captured it after a prolonged resistance. Under Muslim rule it was made capital of an emirate and rivalled Cordoba and Cairo in oriental splendour. Taken by Roger de Hauteville in 1072, it again reached a high state of prosperity under his son King Roger (1130–54), and became the centre of trade between Europe and Asia. Under the brilliant court of Frederick II of Hohenstaufen (1198–1250), 'stupor mundi', the city became famous throughout Europe for its learning and magnificence.

The famous rebellion of the 'Sicilian Vespers' put an end to the misrule of Charles of Anjou in 1282. A long period of Spanish domination, which became increasingly tyrannical, led to the gradual decline of the city, despite an insurrection of 1646. By the treaty of Utrecht (1713) Sicily was allotted to Victor Amadeus of Savoy, who was, however, forced to exchange it for Sardinia (1718) in favour of the Neapolitan Bourbons. Under their rule the island suffered more than ever, though Ferdinand IV established his court at Palermo in 1799 during the French occupation of Naples. The city was granted a temporary constitution in 1811 while under British protection. In the 18C it was the largest town in Italy after Naples. The city rebelled against misgovernment in 1820 (when Sir Richard Church was relieved of his governorship), 1848, and in April 1860. On 27 May 1860 Garibaldi and the Thousand made a triumphal entry into the city.

Parts of the centre of Palermo were badly damaged from the air in 1943, and bomb sites still remain. Much illegal new building has taken place in the Conca d'Oro since the War which has spoiled the once beautiful environs. Perhaps the most neglected city in Italy, a vast number of houses in the historical centre have been in danger of collapse for years, and the population of this area has dwindled to some 35,000 (from 125,000 in 1951), which represents a mere five per cent of the total population of the municipal area. An enlightened city government in 1988–90 produced a period of optimism and there was real hope that the beautiful old centre of the city would at last receive the careful attention it deserves, and that it would be revitalized after restoration.

Famous natives of Palermo include Alessandro Scarlatti (1660–1725), the composer, Stanislao Cannizzaro (1826–1910), the chemist, and Vittorio Emanuele Orlando (1860–1952), prime minister of Italy in 1917–19 and brilliant jurist. Though educated in Palermo, Sergius I (pope, 687–701) is now thought to have been born at Antioch. M.W. Balfe produced his first opera 'I Rivali di se stessi' in Palermo in 1830, and William Harris (c 1796–1823), the English architect, died here of malaria contracted while excavating Selinunte. Ippolito Nievo (1831–61), the patriot-novelist, was drowned when his ship the 'Ercole' disappeared without trace between Palermo and Naples. Constantine of Greece died here in 1923 (commemorative plaque at Villa Igiea).

Art. The Norman domination, with its architecture showing a strongly oriental tinge, has left many magnificent buildings, including the Palazzo della Zisa and Palazzo dei Normanni, the Cappella Palatina, La Martorana, and, in the environs, Monreale cathedral. All these buildings also have especially remarkable mosaic decoration. Architecture and painting in the early 15C was influenced by Catalan masters, as can be seen from the South Porch of the cathedral and Palazzo Abatellis. Matteo Carnelivari was the most important architect working in Palermo at this time. Francesco Laurana, the Renaissance sculptor came to work in Palermo in the middle of the 15C. Another extremely influential sculptor here in the second half of the 15C was Domenico Gagini; his style was continued into the following century by his son Antonello. The dramatic 15C fresco of the Triumph of Death (now in the Galleria Regionale) is the most important Sicilian work of this period.

Numerous splendid Baroque churches were erected in Palermo, many of them by the local architect Giacomo Amato (1643–1732). From the mid 17C to the end of the 18C the interiors of many churches were lavishly decorated with coloured marbles and mosaic inlay. The delightful stuccoes of Giacomo Serpotta (1656–1732) are best seen in the oratories of Santa Cita, San Domenico, and San Lorenzo. Pietro Novelli of Monreale was the greatest Sicilian painter of the 17C. Venanzio Marvuglia (1729–1814) produced some fine neo-classical buildings in Palermo, and the city is particularly rich in Art Nouveau architecture. Ernesto Basile (1857–1932) here built some monumental edifices in eclectic styles.

Topography. The ancient town, bounded by two inlets of the sea, occupied an elliptical area centering on the present cathedral. Its main street (now the W half of the Corso Vittorio Emanuele) was known as the Cassaro Vecchio, a name derived from Castrum or the Arabic Kasr (castle). The Saracen citadel, called Khalisa, grew up to the S of the harbour. By the mid 16C the harbour had dried up to its existing proportions and the plan of Palermo from then on hinged on two main thoroughfares: the Cassaro, extended to the E in 1565 and prolonged to the sea in 1581, and the Via Maqueda (laid out c 1600), running roughly parallel with the coast. These bisect one another at the Quattro Canti. In the 19C and 20C the city expanded towards the N, with its focus at Piazza Verdi (Pl. 10).

A. The Centre of the City

The monumental crossroads known as the **Quattro Canti** (Pl. 11) was laid out in 1608–20 by Giulio Lasso at the central intersection of the four longest and staightest streets of the city. It was named Piazza Vigliena after the Duke of Vigliena, Spanish viceroy in 1611. The four decorative façades bear fountains with statues of the seasons, the four Spanish kings of Sicily, and of the patronesses of Palermo (Cristina, Ninfa, Oliva, and Agata). It is now a confined and busy road junction, but at either end of Corso Vittorio

Emanuele can be seen Porta Nuova and the sea beyond Porta Felice, while Via Maqueda has a vista of the hills surrounding the Conca d'Oro.

A few steps along Via Maqueda to the SE, PIAZZA PRETORIA (Pl. 11) is almost entirely occupied by a fountain designed by the Florentines Francesco Camilliani (1554–55) and Michelangelo Naccherino (1573). The great basin, designed for the garden of a Florentine villa, and installed here in 1573, is decorated with numerous statues (some of them damaged by vandals). PALAZZO DELLE AQUILE (formerly Palazzo Senatorio), named after the eagles which decorate its exterior, is the town hall. It was built in 1463, enlarged in the 16C, and over restored in 1874. On the top of the façade is a statue of St Rosalia by Carlo d'Aprile (1661).

One side of the piazza is closed by the flank and dome of the church of SANTA CATERINA (1566–96). The interior (usually closed), especially the choir, is an elaborate example of Sicilian Baroque, with its striking effects of sculptural decoration and marble veneering (executed in the early 18C). In the right transept is a St Catherine by Antonello Gagini (1534). The frescoes in the cupola are by Vito d'Anna (1751).

In the adjoining Piazza Bellini the majestic campanile of La Martorana stands next to the three little red domes of San Cataldo, raised above part of the E wall of the Roman city and surrounded by a few trees; it is fitting that these two beautiful churches founded by two of Norman Sicily's greatest statesmen, should survive together in the centre of the city.

***La Martorana** (Pl. 11; open 8.30–13, 15.30–dusk; fest. 8.30–13) or Santa Maria dell'Ammiraglio, is a Norman church founded c 1140 by George of Antioch, admiral of King Roger. It was presented in 1433 to a convent founded in 1194 by Eloisa Martorana. The Sicilian Parliament met here after the Sicilian Vespers. Since 1935 it has shared cathedral status with San Demetrio in Piana degli Albanesi, with offices according to the Greek rite.

EXTERIOR. The Norman structure survives on the N and S sides, although a Baroque façade was inserted in 1588 on the N side when the Norman narthex was demolished and the atrium covered. The present entrance (A) is beneath the splendid 12C *CAMPANILE which survived the alterations (only its red dome is missing).

INTERIOR. The central Greek-cross plan of the tiny original church can still be detected, despite the Baroque alterations at the W end and the prolongation of the chancel in 1683. The walls at the W end are heavily decorated with Baroque marble and frescoes which at first overpower the original mosaic decoration which remains on and around the central cupola. The ***mosaics**, probably by Greek craftsmen, date from the first half of 12C; in the dome (B), Christ and four angels, and, in Arabic lettering, a quotation from a Byzantine hymn; around the drum, Prophets and Evangelists; on the triumphal arch, the Annunciation; in S apse (C) St Anne, in N apse (D), St Joachim; in the side vaults, four evangelists, the Nativity, and the Dormition of the Virgin. The transennae in front of the apses and the mosaic pavement are also Norman. At the W end are two more original mosaic panels (restored; set in Baroque frames) from the destroyed portico: to the left (E), George of Antioch at the feet of the Virgin, and, to the right (F), Roger crowned by Christ. Also here are frescoes by Borremans (1717), and in the embrasure of the S portal (G) is a carved wooden door of the 12C. Above the main altar (H) is a good painting of the Ascension (1533) by Vincenzo da Pavia. SE of the church are cloistral arches of the 12C Casa di Martorana.

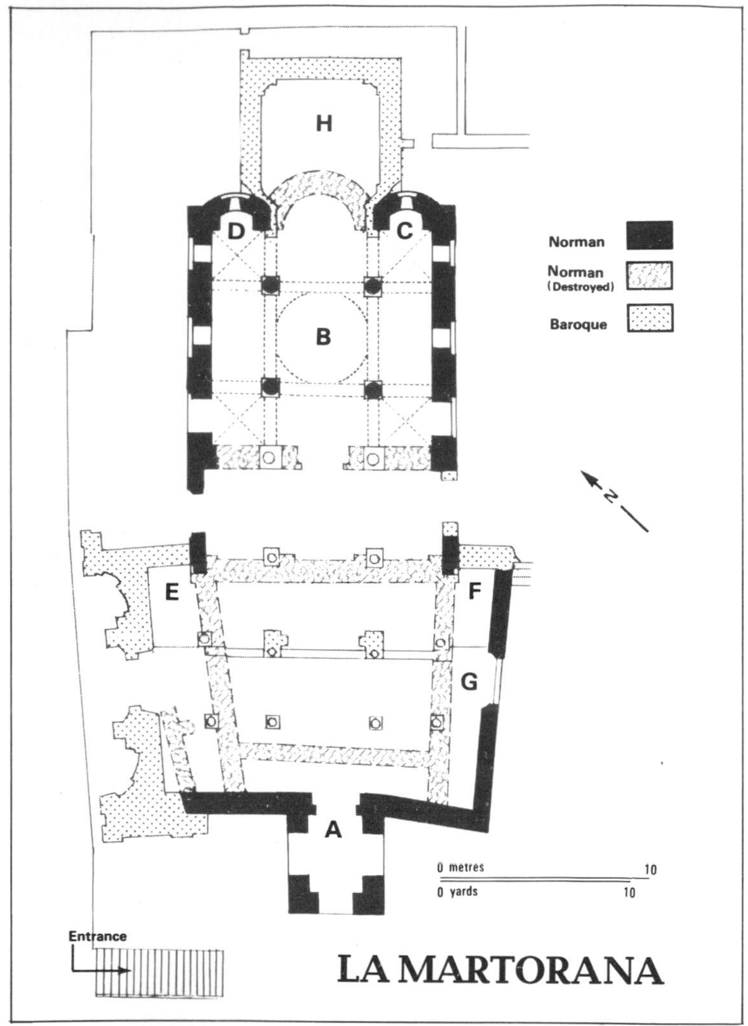

Opposite the campanile is the ***Cappella di San Cataldo** (ask for the key at La Martorana). It was founded by Maio of Bari, William I's chancellor; because of his early death in 1160 the interior was never decorated. After 1787 it served as a post office, and it was restored in 1885. The fine exterior has blind arcading round the windows and pretty crenellations at the top of the wall. In the centre rise three small red domes pierced by little windows. The simple plan of the interior has three aisles ending in apses and three domes high up above the central aisle. The beautiful old capitals are all different. The original mosaic floor and lattice windows survive.

On the opposite side of Via Maqueda the ex-Convent of the Teatini di San Giuseppe is now occupied by the University (the building was modified in the 19C). The small Geological Museum founded here in the early 19C is now at No. 131 Corso Tuköry (Pl. 15), and open to students.

A little farther along Via Maqueda Via Ponticello (right) leads to the **Gesù** (or church of the Casa Professa; Pl. 15; open 7–10.30, 17–18.30), the first church to be erected in Sicily by the Jesuits (1564–1633). The splendid *INTERIOR was beautifully decorated in the 17C and 18C with colourful marble intarsia and sculptures (especially good in the nave chapels, 1665–91). It was well restored after severe damage in the last war. The inside façade has very fine 18C sculptural decoration. In the S aisle, the second chapel has paintings of two saints by Pietro Novelli, and the fourth chapel has a statue of the Madonna by the school of Gagini. The presbytery also has remarkably good marble decoration.

Beside the church can be seen the fine Baroque atrium of the Casa Professa, now partly occupied by the BIBLIOTECA COMUNALE, founded in 1760. It has over 250,000 volumes, and more than 1000 incunabula and MSS. The area to the S, the QUARTIERE DELL'ALBERGHERIA is one of the poorest in the city, and was much devastated by bombing in 1943. The bright produce stalls in the street markets of Piazza Ballarò and Piazza del Carmine stand out against a background of drab houses, while above the scene towers the fantastic dome of the church of the **Carmine** with its telamones and colourful majolica tiles (1681). The interior (usually closed) contains altars in the transepts by Giuseppe and Giacomo Serpotta (1683–84), paintings (in the sanctuary) by Tommaso de Vigilia (late 15C), a statue of St Catherine by Antonello Gagini, and a Madonna by the Gagini School. Near here in Via delle Mosche was born in 1743 Giuseppe Balsamo, better known as Count Cagliostro, whose story fascinated Goethe when he was in Palermo in 1787. The church of SAN NICOLÒ (Pl. 15) preserves a tower once part of the 14C fortifications of the town.

Beside the church of the Gesù, Vicolo della Casa Professa leads back to Via Maqueda through Piazza dei Santi Quaranta Martiri. Here the sturdy tower (with a Catalan window) of the 15C Palazzo Marchesi forms the base of the campanile of the Gesù.

In Via Maqueda is Palazzo Comitini by Nicolò Palma (1771), and, on the opposite side of the road, the long façade (mid 18C) of Palazzo Santa Croce, which has a good courtyard. In the church of Sant' Antonino (Pl. 15) Fra Umile of Petralia, the sculptor, is buried. From here Via Lincoln leads to the Central Station and the sea.

B. The Cathedral and the Cappella Palatina

On the SW corner of the Quattro Canti stands the church of **San Giuseppe dei Teatini** (Pl. 11). The upper church, built by Giacomo Besio of Genoa (1612–45), was the scene of two popular assemblies called by Giuseppe D'Alessi during the revolt of 1647.

In the beautiful Baroque INTERIOR, in addition to the 14 monolithic columns in the nave, eight colossal columns of grey marble support the well-proportioned central dome. The frescoes of the nave roof are copies of the originals by Filippo Tancredi; those in the dome are by Borremans; the stuccoes are remarkable. The two large angels holding the stoups on either side of the entrance are by Marabitti. In the fourth S chapel, with pretty marble decoration, is a statue of the Madonna by the school of Gagini. In the S transept, beneath the altarpiece of St Andrea Avellino by Sebastiano Conca is a charming frieze of child-musicians, and the altar has a bas-relief of a Madonna amidst angels, both by Federico Siragusa (1800). In the choir vault are fine reliefs, with full length figures, by Procopio Serpotta. In the chapels flanking the choir are (right) a Crucifix by Fra Umile da Petralia and (left) reliefs by Filippo Pennino, and an 18C statue of St Joseph. In the N transept, above an altar of marble mosaic (probably late 17C), is a painting of St Gaetano by Pietro Novelli.

The Corso or Cassaro Vecchio, with its bookshops, passes Piazza Bologni, with an unsuccessful statue of Charles V by Scipione Li Volsi (1630), and several fine palazzi (in poor repair). Only the façade remains of Palazzo Riso-Belmonte on the Corso (facing Piazza Bologni). This abandoned shell was once the grandest of Marvuglia's works (1784). Farther along the Corso is the church of **San Salvatore**, built in 1682 by Paolo Amato. Also damaged in the war, its oval *interior has been well restored. It is frequently used for weddings, but is otherwise only open at 11.30 on fest. or for concerts.

On the opposite side of the Corso is the BIBLIOTECA CENTRALE DELLA REGIONE SICILIANA, recently reopened after restoration. It occupies the former Jesuit college, and is entered by the portal of the adjacent church of Santa Maria della Grotta. It owns over 500,000 volumes and many ancient MSS (particularly of the 15C and 16C).

Just beyond opens Piazza della Cattedrale, with the elaborate flank of the cathedral beyond a garden of palm trees enclosed by a balustrade bearing statues of saints. The ***Cathedral** (Pl. 10; Assunta; closed 12.30–15.30), a building of many styles not too skilfully blended, is still a striking edifice with its sharp lights and shades and the golden colour of its stone.

The present cathedral, on the site of an older basilica which did duty as a mosque in the 9C, was founded in 1185 by Walter, Archbishop of Palermo (known as 'Gualtiero Offamiglio'). Building continued for many centuries and in the 15C much of the exterior acquired a Catalan Gothic style. The incongruous dome was added by Ferdinando Fuga in 1781–1801. Baroque and neo-classical elements predominate in the interior.

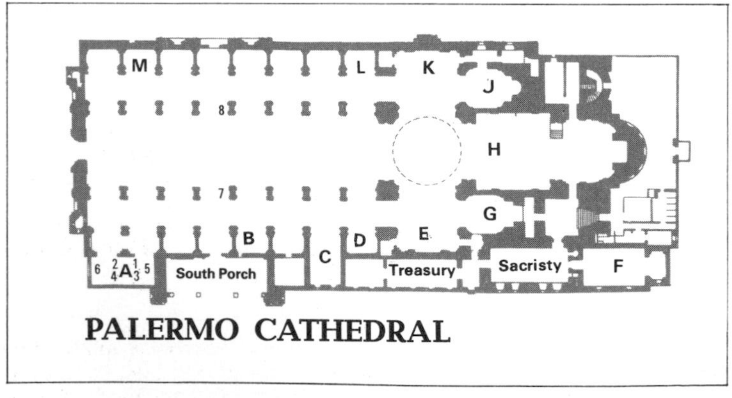

PALERMO CATHEDRAL

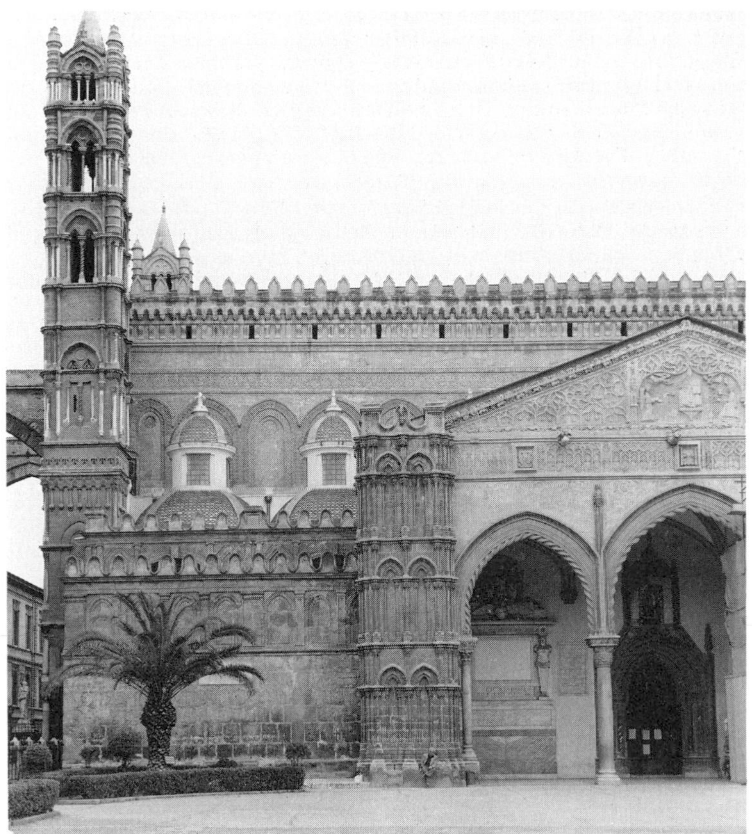

The south porch of the Duomo, Palermo

EXTERIOR. The façade, turned towards the SW on Via Matteo Bonello, is a fine example of local Gothic craftsmanship (13–14C). The doorway dates from 1352. Two powerful Gothic arches span the road to a Norman tower transformed into the campanile in the 19C. The E end, with three apses and two towers matching those at the W end, is practically original 12C work. The usual entrance is from the garden through the great *SOUTH PORCH, a splendid Catalan Gothic work of 1453. The column on the left, probably preserved from the earlier mosque, is inscribed with a passage from the Koran. The fine doorway by Antonio Gambara (1426) has wooden doors by Francesco Miranda (1432).

INTERIOR. The aisled nave has been spoilt by Fuga's alterations. In the SOUTH AISLE the first two chapels (A) enclose ***six royal tombs**, four canopied and two set in the wall. They were moved here from the choir in the 18C and have been enclosed (making it difficult to see them). On the left in front is the tomb (1) of Frederick II (died 1250) and Peter II (died

1342); the similar tomb on the right (2) contains the ashes of Henry VI (died 1197). At the back, beneath mosaic canopies (3,4), are the tombs of Roger II (died 1154), and his daughter Constance (died 1198), wife of Henry VI, with two porphyry sarcophagi brought from the cathedral of Cefalù. On the left (5), is the sarcophagus of Duke William (died 1338), son of Frederick II of Aragon; the Roman sarcophagus on the right (6) contains the body of Constance of Aragon (died 1222), wife of the emperor Frederick II.

In the NAVE are statues of saints from a high altar by the Gagini and (7) a canopied stoup by Giuseppe Spadafora and Antonino Ferraro (1553–55). In the fourth chapel (B), altarpiece by Pietro Novelli, and in the sixth chapel (C), reliquary urns of saints of Palermo, and, used as an altar frontal, the tomb slab of St Cosma (died 1160). The seventh chapel (D) has a fine altar of 'marmi mischi' (1713). In the SOUTH TRANSEPT (E), altarpiece by Giuseppe Velasquez and, above the altar, a bas-relief of the Dormition of the Virgin by Antonello Gagini (1535).

The TREASURY (open daily 9–12, 16–18, except fest.) contains the ***crown of Constance of Aragon**, made by local craftsmen in the 12C, found in her tomb (see above) in the 18C. Also displayed here are the contents of some of the other royal tombs, 18C and 19C copes, chalices and altar frontals. The SACRISTY has two fine portals by Vincenzo Gagini (1568). The inner sacristy (F: usually closed) has a Madonna by Antonello Gagini (1503). The interesting CRYPT (closed indefinitely) contains archbishops' tombs, including that of Giovanni Paternò (died 1511) by Antonello Gagini, and 'Gualtiero Offamiglio' (died 1190), as well as Roman sarcophagi.

In the chapel (G) to the right of the choir is a silver coffer containing the relics of St Rosalia by Francesco Rivelo, Giancola Viviano and Matteo Lo Castro (1631). The reliefs on the walls are by Valerio Villareale (1818). In the CHOIR (H) the statues of apostles and Christ (difficult to see) on the altar are fragments of Antonello Gagini's high altar; the stalls date from 1466. In the chapel on the left (J) is a domed ciborium in lapis lazuli (1663) and the funerary monument of Bishop Sanseverino by Filippo and Gaetano Pennino (1793). NORTH TRANSEPT (K). An early-14C wood Crucifix donated by Manfredi Chiaramonte has been removed for restoration: the marble statues of the mourners at the foot of the Cross are by Gaspare Serpotta and Gaspare Guercio. On the altar is a high relief with scenes of the Passion by Fazio and Vincenzo Gagini. NORTH AISLE. Seventh chapel (L), statue of the Madonna by Franesco Laurana and his pupils. In the nave (8) is a stoup attributed to Domenico Gagini (damaged) of finer workmanship than the one opposite. The second chapel (M) has an Assumption and three reliefs by the Gagini, once part of the high altar.

PALAZZO ARCIVESCOVILE, across the busy Via Bonello, has a portal of 1460 which survived the rebuilding in the 18C. The **Museo Diocesano** was founded here to house fragments from the cathedral and works of art from destroyed churches. It has been closed for many years. The contents include paintings by Zoppo di Ganci, Carlo Maratta, Antonio Veneziano, Gera da Pisa, Riccardo Quartararo, Antonello Riccio, Pietro Ruzzolone, Vincenzo da Pavia, Antonello Crecenzio, Pietro Novelli, Mario di Laureto, Giuseppe Velasquez, and Giorgio Vasari. The sculpture includes works by the Gagini, Pietro da Bonitate, and Gabriele di Battista.

Behind Palazzo Arcivescovile, in a lane, is the ORATORIO DEI SANTI PIETRO E PAOLO (usually closed) which contains stuccoes by Giacomo Serpotta and Domenico Castelli (1698) and a 17C ceiling-fresco by Filippo Tancredi. The entrance can be seen from Via Bonello. On the other side of Via Bonello is the LOGGIA DELL'INCORONAZIONE (Pl. 10), erected in the 16–17C using earlier columns and capitals. It takes its name from the tradition that the kings used to show themselves to the people here after their coronation. Behind is the Cappella dell'Incoronata, a Norman building partly destroyed in 1860. Via Bonello leads into Via Papireto and Piazza Peranni, with an antique and junk market.

On the other side of the Corso is PIAZZA DELLA VITTORIA, occupied by Villa Bonanno, a public garden planted with palm trees in 1905. Partially protected by a roof are some remains of three Roman houses, the only buildings of this period so far found in the city. At the centre of the old city and in front of the Royal Palace the piazza has been used throughout Palermo's history for public celebrations. The garden adjoins Piazza del Parlamento with a monument to Philip V of Bourbon, at the foot of the huge Palazzo dei Normanni. Spanning the Corso is the PORTA NUOVA, a triumphal gateway celebrating Charles V's Tunisian victory (1535), reconstructed after damage by lightning in 1667 (with a conical top).

***Palazzo dei Normanni** (or **Palazzo Reale**; Pl. 14) stands on the highest part of the old city. It was built by the Saracens, enlarged by the Normans, and later restored by the Spaniards who added the principal façade. It has always been the palace of the rulers of the island, and here the splendid courts of Roger II and Frederick II 'stupor mundi' held sway over Europe. Since 1947 it has been the seat of the Regional Assembly. The long façade (1616) hides the apse of the famous Cappella Palatina: at the right end is the massive Torre Pisana, part of the Norman palace.

The entrance (A) to the ****Cappella Palatina** (Pl. 14) is at the rear of Palazzo dei Normanni (reached by the steps down from the piazza to the left of the façade, and Corso Re Ruggero). It is open 9–12, 15–17; Sat 9–12; fest. 9–10, 12–13, although it is sometimes closed to visitors without warning when weddings are being held. A monumental staircase (C; 1735) leads up to a loggia overlooking the fine courtyard (B; 1600). A side of the loggia is occupied by the flank of the chapel, a jewel of Norman-Saracenic art built by Roger II c 1132–40.

The interior, famous for its wonderful mosaics, is one of the finest works of art of its kind in Italy. The light changes constantly: it should, if possible, be visted at different times of the day. Set into the wall of the loggia is a pillar (right) with an inscription (behind glass) in Greek, Latin, and Arabic relating to a water-clock built by Roger in 1142. Beside the portico of seven column with modern mosaics the chapel is approached through the original NARTHEX (D; now the baptistery, with a mosaic font). Two beautifully carved mosaic doorways with bronze doors lead into the gracious INTERIOR (illuminated on request; but difficult to see at present while the ceiling and side aisles are covered for restoration). A small aisled basilica in form, with a raised choir and a cupola above the central bay, it shows the perfection reached by this style of architecture. The ten antique columns of the nave are of granite and cipollino; the *ceiling is of splendid Saracenic workmanship. The ambo and paschal candlestick are good examples of the richest Norman marble decoration. The pavement and lower part of the walls are made of white marble inlaid with red, green and gold patterns, which combine in a delightful harmony of colour and design with the mosaics of glass and plaster on a gold ground above.

The ***mosaics** were commissioned by Roger II and completed by his son William I at an unknown date. They follow a carefully worked out design intended to celebrate the monarchy of Roger II, and the subjects seem to have been chosen with particular reference to the Holy Spirit and the theology of light. The earliest and finest mosaics are in the E part of the chapel and are thought to have been the work of Byzantine Greeks

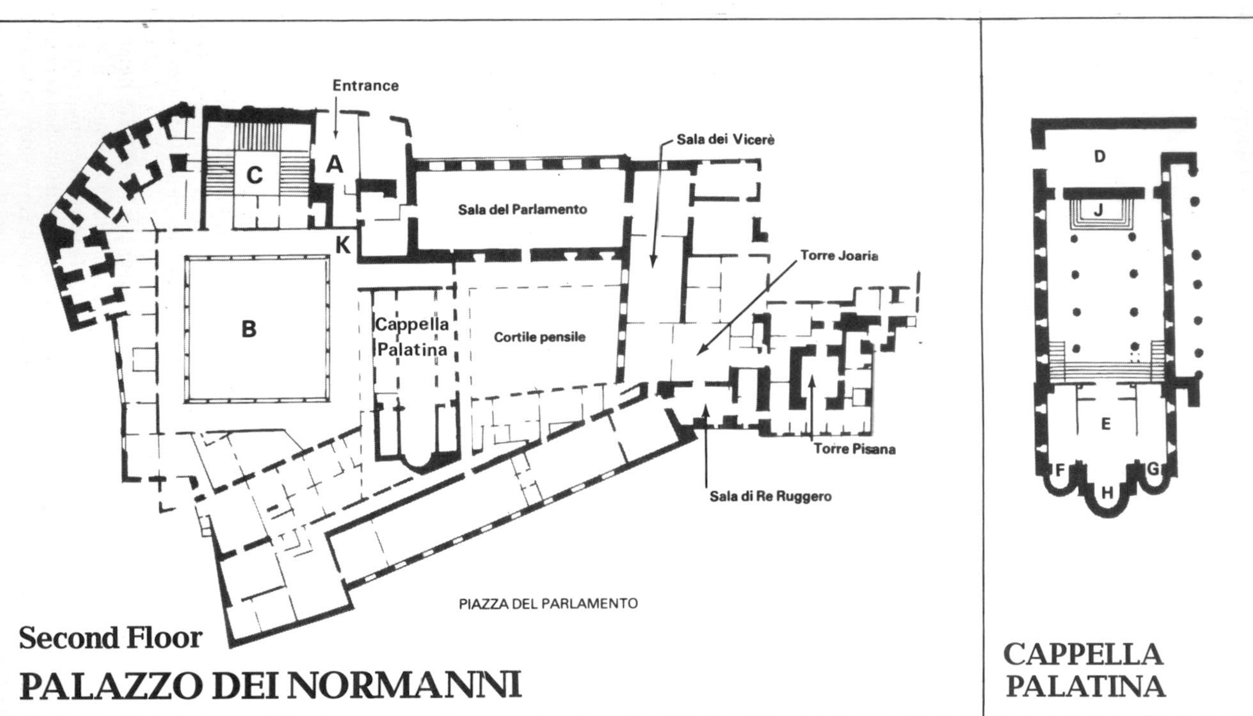
Entrance
A
C
K
B
Sala del Parlamento
Sala dei Viceré
Cappella Palatina
Cortile pensile
Torre Joaria
Torre Pisana
Sala di Re Ruggero
PIAZZA DEL PARLAMENTO
Second Floor
PALAZZO DEI NORMANNI
D
J
E
F
G
H
CAPPELLA PALATINA

(c 1140–50). Here the splendour of the mosaics is increased by the use of silver as well as gold tesserae. SANCTUARY (E). In the cupola, Christ surrounded by angels and archangels; on the drum, David, Solomon, Zachariah, and St John the Baptist; on the pendentives, Evangelists. On the triumphal arch, Annunciation. In the right apse (F) Nativity; on the upper part of the right wall, Joseph's Dream and the Flight into Egypt; on the nave arch, Presentation in the Temple; in the middle of the right wall, Baptism, Transfiguration, and the Raising of Lazarus; and on the lower part of the right wall, Entry into Jerusalem. On the lower part of the left wall, five bishops of the Greek church (among the best preserved mosaic figures in the building), and, on the arch, three female saints. In the left apse (G), Madonna and St John the Baptist. In the main apse (H), Christ Pantocrator, above a late-18C mosaic of the Virgin.

The mosaics in the NAVE were probably the last mosaics to be executed in the chapel (c 1150–71), and are Roman rather than Greek in style. They illustrate the book of Genesis in two tiers of scenes between the clerestory windows and in the spandrels of the arches. The cycle begins in the upper tier of the S wall nearest to the sanctuary, showing the first seven days of the Creation up to the Creation of Eve. The sequence continues in the upper tier of the N wall (beginning at the W end) with the Fall up to the Building of the Ark. The lower tier of the S wall (from the E end) illustrates the Flood up to the Hospitality of Lot, and continues in the lower tier of the N wall (W end) with the Destruction of Sodom and continues up to Jacob's Dream and his Wrestling with the Angel, which is the last scene in the sequence (nearest to the sanctuary).

In the AISLES are scenes from the lives of Saints Peter and Paul, also executed after the mosaics in the E part of the church, possibly by local artists. The sequence begins at the E end of the S aisle with Saul leaving Jerusalem for Damascus and the last scene in this aisle shows St Peter's escape from Prison. The cycle continues at the W end of the N aisle with Saints Peter and John healing the lame man at the temple gate, and the last scene in this aisle, nearest to the sanctuary, shows the Fall of Simon Magus. Above the recomposed Norman throne on a dias at the WEST END (J) is a 15C mosaic of Christ enthroned between Saints Peter and Paul. The SACRISTY and TREASURY are usually closed.

The former **Royal Apartments** have been closed indefinitely to the public. Situated on the top floor of the palace they were mostly decorated in the 19C. The most interesting room is the so-called *SALA DI RE RUGGERO with delightful mosaics of 1140, including hunting scenes. The Regional Assembly meets in the Sala del Parlamento decorated in 1700 by Giuseppe Velasquez. From the observatory at the top of the Torre Pisano Giuseppe Piazzi discovered the first asteroid (Ceres) on 1 January 1801. Other Norman parts of the palace include the vaulted armoury, the treasure-chamber, and the dungeons.

Across Corso Re Ruggero is PALAZZO D'ORLEANS (Pl. 14), the seat of the Regional President, with a pretty park (with a small zoo) open to the public. This was the residence of the exiled Louis Philippe (1809) at the time of his marriage with Marie Amélie, daughter of Ferdinand IV, and birthplace of his son Ferdinand Philippe (1810–42), ancestor of the Comte de Paris.

Via del Bastione skirts the great wall of Palazzo dei Normanni. In Piazza della Pinta (Pl. 14) is the little Oratorio della Compagnia della Madonna della Consolazione (San Mercurio, in poor repair). The stucco decoration in the interior has recently been attributed as an early work to Giacomo Serpotta.

San Giovanni degli Eremiti, Palermo

Via dei Benedettini, an extremely busy road, leads from here to the church of ***San Giovanni degli Eremiti** (Pl. 14; open Tues, Wed and Fri, 9–12.30, 15–17; Mon, Thurs and Sat, 9–13.30; fest. 9–13). This is perhaps the most romantic building of Norman Palermo, because of its small luxuriant garden, carefully tended, which somewhat protects it from the noisy road. It was built by Roger II in 1132–48, and is now deconsecrated. Paths lead up through the beautiful garden, with splendid palm trees, cactus and papyrus plants, and flowering jasmine, overshadowed by five charming red domes, the tallest one crowning the campanile of the little CHURCH. In the bare interior the nave is surmounted by two domes divided by an arch (pierced by a window). At the E end are three apses and three smaller domes, the one on the left part of the campanile.

To the right an inconspicous opening leads into an older structure, probably a MOSQUE, consisting of a rectangular hall with cross vaulting and once divided by a row of pillars. Adjoining this (seen from the right of the entrance to the church) is a portico of five arches, whose inner wall is now the right wall of the church, and an open courtyard. The little CLOISTER of the late 13C has twin columns bearing pointed arches which surround a delightful garden.

C. San Domenico and the Museo Archeologico Regionale

From the Quattro Canti, Corso Vittorio EmanuelePal;Corso Vittorio Emanuele leads E towards the sea. A short way along on the left is the fine Baroque church of SAN MATTEO (1662; open on weekdays at 17, and on fest. at 10.30). It contains statues by Giacomo Serpotta and frescoes by Vito d'Anna (1754). At the next intersection VIA ROMA diverges left; this is one of the main thoroughfares of the city running N from the station. On the right is SANT'ANTONIO (Pl. 11), reconstructed after the earthquake of 1823 in the Chiaramonte style of the original; the 14C campanile was shortened at the end of the 16C. The church occupies the most easterly eminence of the old city.

The maze of small streets below is the scene of a busy daily market known as the VUCCIRIA (the area around Piazza Caracciolo, Piazza Garraffello, etc.) where produce of all kinds is sold on the streets, including fish. It is one of the most colourful sights in the city. In Piazza Garraffello, with a damaged statue of the 'Genius of Palermo' is Palazzo Lo Mazzarino, still owned by the family. Many of its precious contents were stolen in 1989.

Beyond opens Piazza San Domenico, in the middle of which rises the Colonna dell'Immacolata by Giovanni d'Amico (1724–27), crowned by a Madonna by Giovanni Battista Ragusa. The large church of **San Domenico** (Pl. 11; open 7.30–11.30; Sat and Sun also 17–18.30), rebuilt in 1640, has a tall façade of 1726. Since the middle of the last century the church has served as a burial place for illustrious Sicilians.

INTERIOR. S aisle: on the left wall of the first chapel is the funerary monument of Francesco Maria Emanuele di Villabianca by Leonardo Pennino (1802). Second chapel, altarpiece of the Crucifixion by Paolo Fondulli (1573); third chapel, fine marble decoration on a design by Gaspare Serpotta and a *statue of St Joseph by Antonio Gagini. Beyond the fourth chapel with an altarpiece attributed to Rosario Novelli, the fifth chapel has the funerary monument of Enrico Amari by Domenico Costantini (1875). The sixth chapel has a painting of St Vincent Ferrer by Giuseppe Velasquez (1787). SOUTH TRANSEPT. Altarpiece of St Dominic by Filippo Paladino, and on the left wall, monument to Giovanni Ramondetta by Giacomo Serpotta and Gerardo Scudo (1691). Chapel to the right of the sanctuary, good bas-relief of St Catherine attributed to Antonello Gagini; neo-classical monument by Benedetto de Lisi (1864); a relief of the Trinity (1477) by Rinaldo Bartolomeo; a small Pietà in high relief by Antonello

Gagini, and a pretty little stoup. The two fine organs date from 1781; beneath the one on the right is a small Turrisi Colonna funerary monument, with a female figure by Antonio Canova.

The SANCTUARY has 18C choir stalls. The chapel to the left of the sanctuary has Gaginesque reliefs including a tondo of St Dominic, and the tomb of Ruggero Settimo (1778–1863) who convened the Sicilian parliament in this church in 1848. NORTH TRANSEPT. On either side of the altarpiece by Vincenzo da Pavia are funerary monuments by Ignazio Marabitti. NORTH AISLE. Tomb of Pietro Novelli, the painter (1608–47). Fourth chapel, altarpiece of St Raimondo by Filippo Paladino; third chapel: on the left is a statue of St Catherine by Antonello Gagini (1528), with reliefs on the base, and on the right, a statue of St Barbara by his school. The second chapel has a terracotta statue of St Catherine of Siena, and the first chapel an altarpiece by Andrea da Trapani. On the left is a Lancellotti funerary monument by Leonardo Pennino (1870), and on the right a tomb by Valerio Villareale. The fragmentary 14C CLOISTER which was part of the first church built on this site by the Dominicans is being restored.

Behind the church, in Via Bambinai, is the **Oratorio del Rosario di San Domenico** (ring for the custodian at the shop at No. 16 Via Bambinai; fee). It contains a famous altarpiece by Van Dyck, representing the *Virgin of the Rosary with St Dominic and the patronesses of Palermo. The artist painted it in Genoa in 1628 having left Palermo because of the plague. The wall-paintings of the Mysteries are by Novelli, Lo Verde, Stomer, Luca Giordano and Borremans. Giacomo Serpotta's graceful *stuccoes (1720) display amazing skill. In its fine piazza is the church of SANTA MARIA DI VALVERDE (closed). Its sumptuous Baroque interior (1694–1716) was designed by Paolo Amato. The main altarpiece is by Pietro Novelli.

The street continues as Via Squarcialupo. The next large church on the left is **Santa Cita** (or Santa Zita; Pl. 11; closed for restoration), rebuilt in 1586–1603. Much damaged in 1943, it is still surrounded by bomb sites. The INTERIOR contains fine but damaged *sculptures by Antonello Gagini (1517–27): in the apse behind the altar is a marble tabernacle surrounded by a triumphal arch, both superbly carved; in the second chapel on the left of the choir is the sarcophagus of Antonio Scirotta; and more sculptures by the same artist are in the second chapel on the right of the choir. The chapel of the Rosary has splendid polychrome marble decoration (1696–1722) and the sculpture in the niches is by Gioacchino Vitaliano.

Adjoining the left side of the church is the **Oratorio del Rosario di Santa Cita** (or Zita; if closed, ring at No. 3 Via Valverde). It is approached through a pretty (if poorly kept) garden and loggia. The *INTERIOR is one of the best of Serpotta's works (1685–1717). The stucco reliefs of New Testament history and (entrance wall) of the Battle of Lepanto are especially fine. The altarpiece of the Madonna of the Rosary (1702) is by Carlo Maratta.

Nearly opposite Santa Cita is the fine 14C doorway of the Conservatorio di Musica. Beyond is the isolated church of **San Giorgio dei Genovesi** (Pl. 7; deconsecrated and usually locked; sometimes used for exhibitions), a church built for the Genoese sea-captains by Giorgio di Faccio in 1576–91. It has a graceful façade. The aisled *interior is in the purest Renaissance style. Marble tomb-slabs (17C and 18C) cover the floor of the nave. It contains paintings attributed to Luca Giordano, Bernardo Castello of Genoa, and by Palma Giovane.

Beyond opens the untidy PIAZZA DELLE TREDICI VITTIME, where an obelisk commemorates 13 partriots shot by the Bourbons on 14 April 1860.

A huge steel stele, 30m high, was set up here in 1989 to commemorate victims in the struggle against the Mafia. A fence protects recent excavations of 10C Arab buildings, and part of the Norman fortifications of the city (restored in the 16C).

To the SE lies the Cala (see Rte 1D). The PORT of Palermo extends from the Cala northward. Remains of the Fortezza del Castellammare, used in the 12C as a prison, and from the 13C onwards as barracks, were partially restored in 1988–91. Along the quay (where the ferries dock) runs Via del Mare.

In front of Piazza San Domenico (see above), across Via Roma, the narrow Via Monteleone leads up behind the huge Post Office (1933) to the Oratorio di Santa Caterina d'Alessandria (closed) with notable stuccoes by Serpotta's son, Procopio (1719–26). Just beyond is the church of **Sant' Ignazio all'Olivella** (Pl. 11), begun in 1598. The fine INTERIOR (open 7.30–11, 17.30–19; fest. 7.30–12.30) has a barrel vault designed by Venanzio Marvuglia (1772) with frescoes by Antonio Manno (1790). S aisle: first chapel, Filippo Paladino, St Mary of Egypt; the second chapel has beautiful 17C decorations in 'marmi mischi'. In the S transept, altarpiece by Filippo Paladino. The high altarpiece of the Trinity is by Sebastiano Conca and in the sanctuary are two statues by Ignazio Marabitti. In the N transept is an interesting altarpiece, of unusual design, of the martyrdom of St Ignatius by Filippo Paladino (1613). N aisle: the fifth chapel was sumptuously decorated in 1622 and has an altarpiece of St Philip Neri by Sebastiano Conca (1740) and two statues by Giovanni Battista Ragusa. The third chapel is also elaborately decorated with polychrome marble and precious stones and an altar frontal in relief. The small fresco in the vault of the Pietà is by Pietro Novelli. In the first chapel the altarpiece of the archangel Gabriel is by Pietro Novelli.

The ORATORIO DI SANT'IGNAZIO OLIVELLA is unlocked on request by the sacristan and entered by a small door in the S transept. It has an interesting neo-classical interior of 1769 by Venanzio Marvuglia, with good capitals by Filippo Pennino. It is lit by pretty chandeliers. In the presbytery is an elaborate sculpture with angels and cherubs by Ignazio Marabitti. The façade of the oratory, on Piazza Olivella, is also by Pennino.

Adjoining the church is the former monastery of the Filippini, now the seat of the ***Museo Archeologico Regionale** (Pl. 7), one of the most interesting collections in Italy, illustrating the history of western Sicily from prehistoric times to the Roman era. It is arranged around two charming 17C cloisters. It is open 9–13.30; Tues and Fri, also 15–17; fest. 9–12.30. The rooms are numbered in the text and on the plans in their logical sequence. The collection was formed at the beginning of the 19C when it belonged to the University. During the century it acquired various collections, including that of Casuccini, the most important colelction of Etruscan material outside Tuscany. It also houses finds from excavations in the W part of the island, notably those of Selinunte.

In the centre of the CHIOSTRO MINORE is a triton from a 16C fountain. Off this cloister (right; **Room 2**; partially closed but visible from Room 3) is a collection of under-water discoveries, including a marble statue, a Roman copy of a 4C BC original, fished up off Cape Boeo. Rooms 3 and 4 contain **Egyptian and Punic sculpture**. **R 3**. Two Phoenician sarcophagi of the 5C BC found near Palermo. In the centre of **R 4**, male torso of 6C BC: on the wall, the 'Pietra di Palermo', a black diorite slab whose hieroglyphic inscription records the delivery of forty shiploads of cedar-wood to Pharaoh

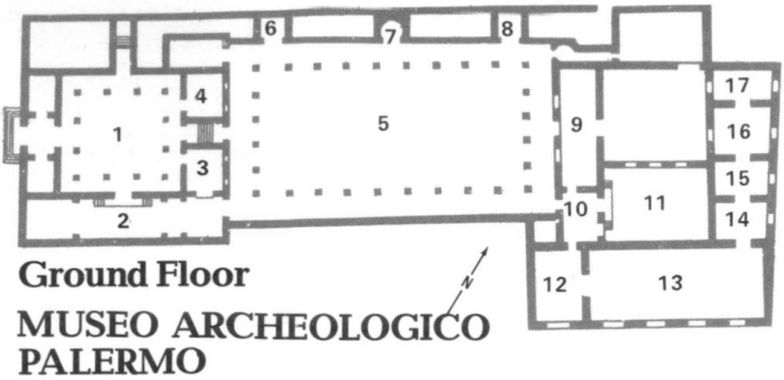

Snefru (c 2700 BC); Punic inscription to the sun god Baal-Hammon, on white stone from Lilybaeum; male figure (4C BC) of Egyptian type.

The pretty CHIOSTRO MAGGIORE (**5**) has palms and flower-beds and a papyrus pool in the centre. In the arcades are Roman fragments: in niches: Zeus enthroned (6), derived from a Greek type of 4C BC, and colossal statue of the emperor Claudius (8), both restored by Villareale; also an interesting funerary stele with three portrait busts (40–30 BC). On the right: sarcophagi, cippi, and stelae. At the far end, **Room 9** has Greek inscriptions, the majority from Selinunte. **Room 10** contains stelae from Selinunte, and a dedicatory inscription to Apollo from Temple G. Steps lead down to **R 11** in which have been gathered fragments of Temple C; part of the entablature has been assembled. **Room 12** contains a cornice of lion head ***water-spouts** from the Doric temple of 'Victory' at Himera (2nd quarter of 5C BC), discovered by Pirro Marconi in 1929–30.

Room 13 contains the famous **metopes of Selinunte**, the most important treasures of the museum. These sculpted panels once decorated the friezes of the temples at Selinunte, and they show the development in the skill of the local sculptors from the early 6C BC to the end of the 5C BC. On either side of the entrance are three delicate female heads and fragmentary reliefs from temple E. Beneath the windows are six small **Archaic *metopes**, sculptured in low relief, from an early-6C temple, perhaps destroyed by the people of Selinunte themselves to repair their citadel, in the time of Dionysius the Elder (397–392 BC). They represent scenes with Demeter and Kore (one with a quadriga), three dieties, a winged sphinx, the Rape of Europa, and Hercules and the Cretan bull. Facing the windows is a reconstruction, incorporating original fragments, of a frieze and cornice with three triglyphs and three fine **Archaic *metopes** from Temple C (early 6C), representing a quadriga; Perseus, protected by Athene, beheading the Gorgon; and Heracles punishing the pigmies Cercopes. Also on this wall are parts of two metopes from Temple F, with scenes from the gigantomachia (5C BC). Opposite the entrance, four splendid **Classical *metopes** from Temple E (early 5C) show Herakles fighting an amazon, the wedding of Zeus and Hera, the punishment of Actaeon, who is attacked by dogs in the presence of Artemis, and Athene overcoming a titan. In the centre of the room is the small bronze statue found in a tomb at Selinunte in 1882, known as the '***ephebus of Selinunte**'. It was stolen from Castelvetrano in 1962,

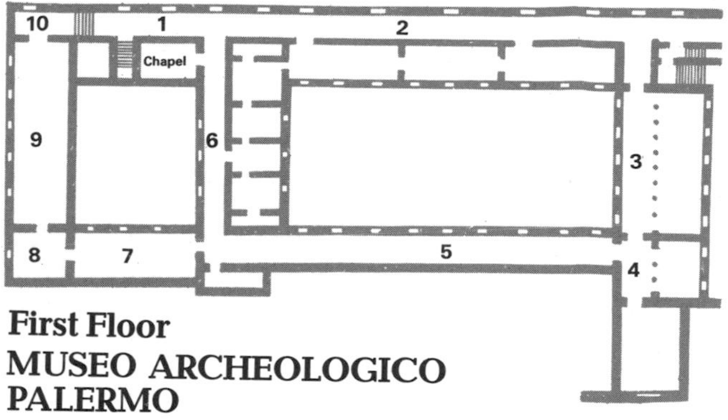

and recovered in 1968. During its recent restoration certain defects in the original casting were detected; a somewhat enigmatic work, it is thought to be a local product of c 480–460 BC.

Rooms 14–17 contain the Casuccini collection of **Etruscan antiquities** from Chiusi. Particularly interesting are the urns and tombs in high relief, a number of panels with delicately carved bas-reliefs (many with traces of painting), and a magnificent *oinochoe of bucchero ware (6C BC) portraying the story of Perseus and Medusa, perhaps the finest vase of its kind in existence.

The **First Floor** is reached from the small cloister. The long NORTH GALLERY (**Rooms 1 and 2**) displays **finds from Greek and Roman sites in western Sicily**, arranged topographically. Selinunte, Lilybaeum, Randazzo, the Lipari Islands, and Marsala are especially well represented. Between the cases, containing vases, terracottas, bronzes, etc., are sepulchral stelae from Marsala painted with portraits of the deceased, and sections of lead water-pipes, showing junction points and stop-cocks, from the Cornelian aqueduct at Termini Imerese. **Room 3** contains terracotta figures, mainly from Gela, Himera, and Palazzolo Acreide. In **Room 4** are more terracottas, and a 5C kylix fished from the sea off Termini Imerese. The long SOUTH GALLERY (**5**) contains some of the 12,000 terracotta votive figures found in the sanctuary of Demeter at Selinunte which demonstrate their chronology by the evolution of their design. The WEST GALLERY (**6**) contains some of the more important recent finds from sites in Palermo (fine vases).

A few steps lead up to **Room 7** with **large Roman bronzes**. The famous ***ram** is a superb sculpture dating from the 3C BC, probably modelled on an original by Lysippos, and formerly one of a pair. Up until 1448 it was in the Castello Maniace in Syracuse; in the 18C it was admired by Jean Houel and Goethe in the Palazzo Reale in Palermo. The second ram was destroyed in the 19C. The ***athlete fighting a stag** is a Roman copy of a 3C BC original. It decorated a fountain at Pompeii, and was donated to the museum by Francesco I. **Room 8** is devoted to Greek sculpture. In the centre, satyr filling a drinking cup, a Roman copy from Torre del Greco of a Praxitelean original; portrait of Aristotle, Roman copy of an original of c 330 BC; herm of a bearded Dionysus, another Roman copy; beautiful **5C *reliefs and stelae**, and a fragment of the frieze of the Parthenon. **Room 9**. Roman sculpture: Roman matron; priestess of Isis (from Taormina); reliefs of vestal virgins, and Mithras killing the bull, sarcophagus of 2nd half of 2C. On the floor, mosaic pavement (3C AD). Beyond a small vestibule (**10**), with Roman fragments, is the landing at the head of the stairs. Nearby is a small chapel (usually closed), part of the 17C convent.

The **Second Floor** surrounds the Chiostro Maggiore. It contains a superb collection of ***Greek vases** (see p 37 for vase types). At the top of the stairs to the right is the SHORT GALLERY with proto-Corinthian pottery of the 7C BC. In the central wall case: 6C plate with horses, and a fragment of an amphora with elaborately dressed figures; (2nd central case): 6C oinochoe from Selinunte, and various aryballi.

The LONG GALLERY has a splendid series of Attic black-figure vases (580–460 BC). Among the lekythoi with figures on a white ground is one (2nd central case) showing the sacrifice of Iphenegea, signed by Douris. In the 3rd central case, large krater with a quadriga and dionysic scenes, and two amphorae with Hercules. In the 5th central case red-figure stamnos with Hercules and the hydra (480–460 BC). In the room at the end (right) are displayed red-figure vases including a kylix decorated by Oltos, a hydra with the judgement of Paris, and a bell-shaped krater with dionysic scenes. Another room displays mosaic pavements (1C BC–4C AD), mostly from Piazza Vittoria in Palermo. The wall paintings here include five of the 1C BC from Soluntum, and a fragment (1C AD) from Pompeii. The room at the end of the next long corridor contains Italiot vases (4–3C BC), many with reliefs and traces of painting from Puglia, Campania, and Sicily. The last LONG GALLERY contains the collection of prehistoric and Early Bronze Age material which comes mainly from north-west Sicily. Here are displayed casts of the fine incised drawings (late Palaeolithic) of hooded figures and animals from Cave B at Addaura on Monte Pellegrino. Nearby are the bones of elephants, rhinoceros, and hippopotami found in Via Villafranca, Palermo.

The pretty Via Bara, in front of the museum, leads past one of Palermo's puppet theatres to PIAZZA VERDI (Pl. 10, 11), laid out at the end of the 19C and now one of the most central squares in the city. It is dominated by the **Teatro Massimo**, a huge Corinthian structure begun by Giovanni Battista Basile and finished by his son Ernesto (1875–97). In Europe its stage is exceeded in size only by that of the Paris Opera. It has not been in use since 1973; modifications are being carried out in order to adapt it to present-day theatrical needs and safety standards.

Via Maqueda returns downhill to the S towards the Quattro Canti. Beside a bomb site, the third turning right, Via Sant'Agostino, is given over to a street market (clothes, household goods, food, etc.; cars are banned). On the right, hidden behind the stalls, is the flank and bell-tower of the church of **Sant'Agostino** (Pl. 11). The unusual tall side portal (restored) is attributed to Domenico Gagini. The FACADE, on via Maestri dell'Acqua, has a late-13C portal decorated with lava mosaic and a beautiful 14C rose-window. In the side porch is a Roman sarcophagus. The hall INTERIOR (open 7–12, 16–18) was decorated with gilded stuccoes by Giacomo Serpotta and assistants from 1711, including numerous cherubs, statues, and lunettes over the side altars. SOUTH SIDE. Second altar, 17C Flight into Egypt; third altar, Olivio Sozzi (attributed), St Nicholas of Tolentino; fifth altar, two frescoes of the 16C and 14C (the latter removed). The pretty organ dates from the 18C. NORTH SIDE. Fourth altar, Zoppo di Ganci, St Thomas of Villanova and stories from his life. On the left of the second altar, monument to Francesco Medici, with his bust (surmounted by a cockerel) by Ignazio

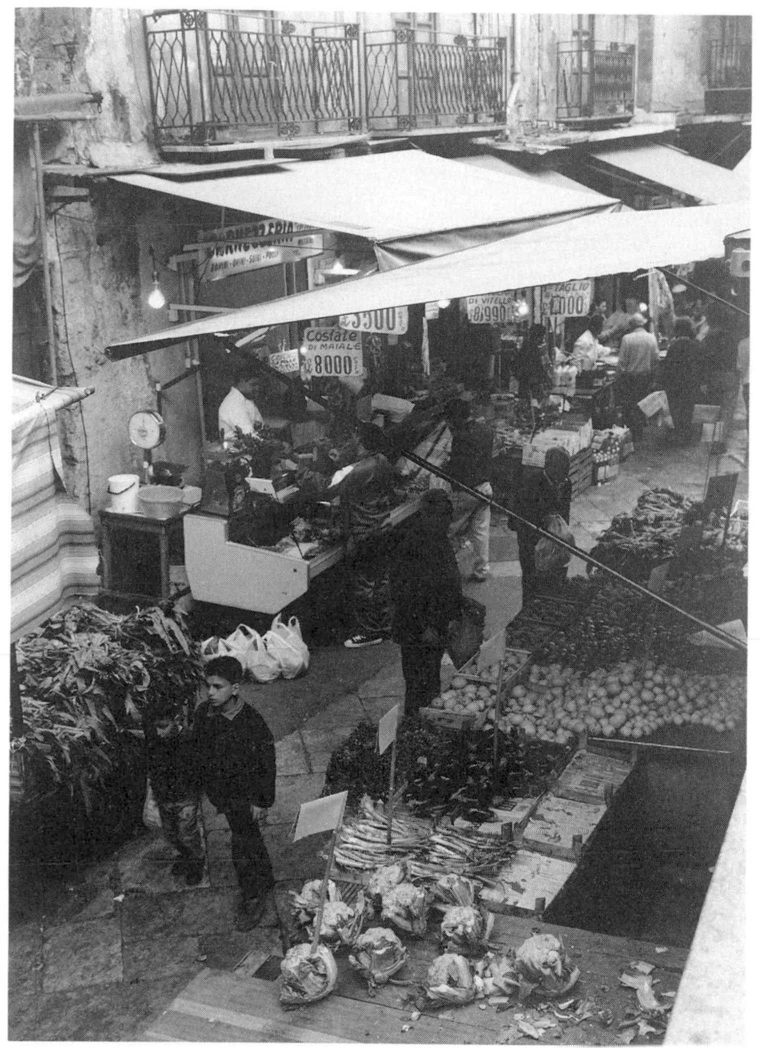

The Quartiere del Capo, Palermo

Marabitti. The pretty 16C cloister, with tall pulvins above its capitals, surrounds a charming garden. The fine Gothic entrance to the chapter house was exposed here in 1962 and restored.

The long Via Sant'Agostino winds on down to the Mercato del Capo where the colourful food market begins. The QUARTIERE DEL CAPO (Pl. 10), historically one of the poorest areas of the city, has a maze of narrow streets. In Via Porta Carini (right) are three churches: on the right, SANT'IPPOLITO

(1583) with a façade of 1728. It contains a 14C Byzantine fresco of the Madonna and 18C paintings including the high altarpiece of the martyrdom of St Ippolito by Gaspare Serenario. The church of SAN GREGORIO was built in 1686–88. Opposite is the church of the CONCEZIONE (1612) with a beautifully decorated 17C interior. The Capo market continues as far as Via Papireto (Pl. 10) which leads back (left) to the Cathedral.

D. San Francesco d'Assisi and the Galleria Regionale di Sicilia

Corso Vittorio Emanuele leads E from the Quattro Canti towards the sea. Beyond Via Roma, the narrow Via Paternostro diverges right for the 13C church of ***San Francesco d'Assisi** (Pl. 12; open 7–11, 16–18). The FACADE has a beautiful portal with three designs of zigzag ornamentation (1302) and a lovely rose-window.

INTERIOR (inconspicuous lights in most of the chapels). The church was damaged by earthquake in 1823 and again by bombs in 1943, after which it was well restored. The Franciscan nave of 1255–77 is flanked by beautiful chapels added in the 14–15C. Eight statues by Serpotta (1723) decorate the W door and nave. SOUTH AISLE. Above the door, fine sculpted arch of 1465; second chapel, altarpiece of St George and the dragon in high relief and carved roundels by Antonello Gagini (1526); third chapel, Madonna attributed to Antonio Gagini flanked by 15C statues of saints. The Gothic fourth chapel contains a beautiful 15C Madonna by a Catalan sculptor and the sarcophagus of Elisabetta Omodei (1498) attributed to Domenico Gagini. Beyond the side door and another Gothic chapel is the sixth chapel with three bas-reliefs by Ignazio Marabitti (including the altar frontal). The seventh chapel has interesting 14C decoration in lava. The chapel to the right of the sanctuary has splendid polychrome marble intarsia decoration (17–18C; carefully restored after war damage). The eight figures of Sicilian saints are by Giovanni Battista Ragusa (1717). The altarpiece of the Immacolata in mosaic is on a design by Vito d'Anna and below is an elaborate marble altar frontal. The SANCTUARY has fine choir stalls (being restored) carved and inlaid in 1520 by Giovanni and Paolo Gili. The chapel to the left of the sanctuary has good marble decoration and an 18C wood statue of St Francis.

NORTH AISLE. Eighth chapel: a bust of St John in polychrome terracotta attributed to Antonello Gagini has been removed for safety. The four statuettes of the Virtues are attributed to Pietro da Bonitate. By the door into the sacristy, tomb effigy of the young warrior Antonio Speciale attributed to Domenico Gagini (1477) with a touching inscription above it. The fifth chapel has a 14C portal with zig-zag ornamentation and remains of early frescoes on the intrados. The fourth chapel, the CAPPELLA MASTRANTONIO has an ***arch** superbly sculpted by Francesco Laurana and Pietro da Bonitate (1468; restored in 1992), the earliest important Renaissance work in Sicily. On the left wall of the chapel, Madonna and saints attributed to Vincenzo da Pavia. Second chapel: highly venerated silver statue of the Immacolata (1647; protected by a curtain), and on the left wall remains of a fresco of St Francis. In the first chapel (light on the right), with a fine 16C portal, Madonna and Child with St John, by Domenico Gagini (with a beautiful base), and a relief of the Madonna.

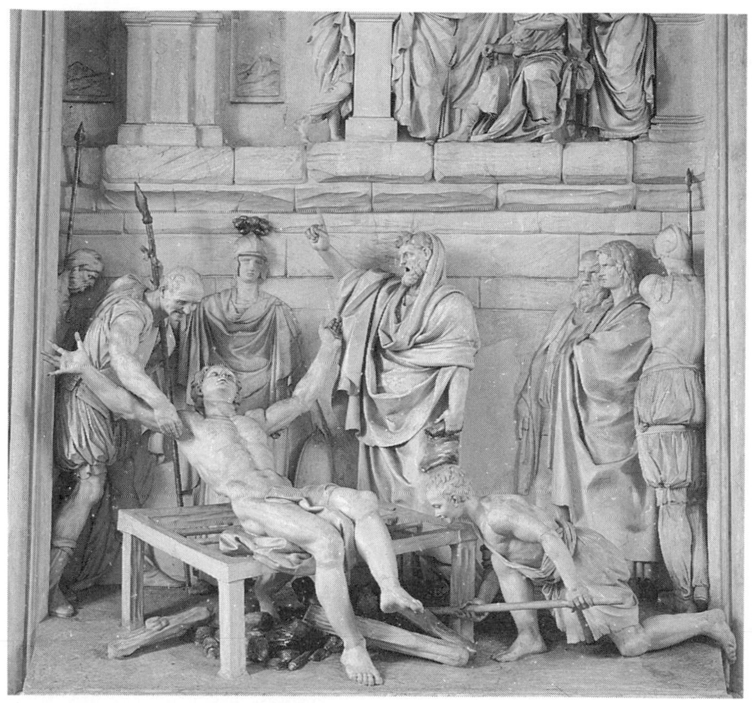

Detail of the Martyrdom of St Lawrence by Giacomo Serpotta in the Oratorio di San Lorenzo, Palermo

To the left of the church is the ***Oratorio di San Lorenzo** (entrance at No. 5 Via Immacolatella: the custodian lives off the courtyard and will open the oratory on request; tip). The interior, designed by Giacomo Amato is decorated with stuccoes illustrating the lives of St Lawrence and St Francis, perhaps the masterpiece of Giacomo Serpotta (1699–1707). Ten symbolic statues, eight vivacious little reliefs, and the Martyrdom of St Laurence above the door, the whole encircled by a throng of joyous putti, make up a well-balanced and animated composition. The modelling of the male figures above the windows is especially skilful. The 18C mahogany benches have carved supports, and beautiful mother-of-pearl inlay. The Nativity, by Caravaggio (1609; almost his last known work), stolen from the altar in 1969, has never been found.

In Via Paternostro, opposite San Francesco, is the huge Palazzo Cattolica (No. 48) with a double courtyard by Giacomo Amato (c 1720).

Via del Parlamento leads back to the Corso. Beyond the Fontana del Garraffo (designed by Paolo Amato in 1698; damaged), the Corso runs between the large Piazza Marina (described below) and the CALA, a shallow basin used as a mooring for the fishing fleet, all that remains of the ancient harbour which, until Norman times, extended far into the old town. On the left is SANTA MARIA DI PORTO SALVO (open for services), a Renaissance church mutilated in the replanning of 1564. It was begun in c 1527 by Antonello Gagini, and the interior was completed by Antonio Scaglione. Farther on in the Corso, also on the left, is the late-15C church of SANTA MARIA DELLA CATENA (Pl. 12; 1502–34), probably the work of Matteo Carnelivari, which takes its name from the chain that used to close the Cala. A flight of steps leads up to the three-arched porch, which, with its two corner-pilasters, exhibits an ingenious combination of the Gothic and Renaissance styles. Three doorways (in poor repair) by Vincenzo Gagini admit to the elegant interior (open at 9am on Sundays).

The lower end of the Corso, the 'Cassaro Morto' was virtually destroyed in 1943; here is the reconstructed PORTA FELICE (1582–1637). There is no arch between the two monumental pillars so that the tall 'vara' of St Rosalia could pass through on her festival. Just out of the piazza here, at No. 1 Via Butera, is the *MUSEO INTERNAZIONALE DELLE MARIONETTE (Pl. 12; open daily 9–13, 16–19; fest. closed), with a delightful collection of puppets illustrating the history of Sicilian puppet theatres. In Palermo, the puppets are between 80cm and 1m high, weigh about 8kg, and have articulated knees. Each theatre owns about 100 puppets and about 70 different backcloths. In Catania, the puppets are between 1.10m and 1.30m high, weigh about 25kg, and the knee is not articulated. Each theatre owns about 50 puppets and about 500 different backcloths. Puppet shows are held in the small theatre. There are also puppets from Naples and Calabria, and a collection of shadow puppets from Malasia, Cambodia and Java.

The FORO ITALICO (Pl.12), a wide thoroughfare always busy with traffic, runs along the sea front, with a splendid view of Monte Pellegrino. This was once a fashionable esplanade: part of the huge area to seaward, reclaimed by pouring in war debris has recently been planted with palm trees. The long 17C façade of the damaged Palazzo Butera stands above the terraced Mura delle Cattive immediately to the right.

The Foro Italico continues to Via Lincoln. Here is the entrance to the ***Villa Giulia** (Pl.16), or La Flora, a delightful garden laid out in 1777, with beautiful trees and flowers, much admired by Goethe in 1787. In the centre are four 'prospetti', or niches in the Pompeian style, and a sundial fountain; towards the sea is a statue of the 'Genius of Palermo', by Marabitti. The *ORTO BOTANICO, adjoining the Villa on the SW, is remarkable for its subtropical vegetation (adm. 9–12.30; Saturdays 9–11; closed Sundays and fest.; entered by the side gate). The entrance pavilion was built in the Greek Doric style in 1789 by Léon Dufourny; Marvuglia worked on the decoration and added the side wings. The botanical garden, one of the best in Europe, was opened to the public here in 1795. It has ficus trees, bamboo, date palms, lotus trees and tropical plants from all over the world.

PIAZZA MARINA (Pl. 12; cf. above), once a shallow inlet of the sea, was reclaimed in Saracen times. Here 16C Aragonese weddings and victories were celebrated by jousting; later, in the proximity of two prisons (the Vicaria and that of the Inquisition), public executions were held here. The centre is occupied by the GIARDINO GARIBALDI, with fine palms and fig-trees, and incredible huge old banyans. On the corner by the Corso is the church of SAN GIOVANNI DEI NAPOLETANI (1526–1617; open only for exhibitions). The harmonious interior has a magnificent contemporary organ by Raffaele La Valle, with its choir-loft ornamented by 15 panels, perhaps the work of Vincenzo da Pavia, and a St John the Baptist by Zoppo di Ganci. Also overlooking Piazza Marina are the Renaissance church of Santa Maria dei Miracoli (1547; the good interior has also been closed indefinitely) and Palazzo San Cataldo, a reconstruction incorporating some windows of a Renaissance palace (in the side street).

Salita Partanna leads out of the piazza to Via Merlo where (at No. 2) an 18C gateway leads into **Palazzo Mirto** (Pl. 12; open daily 9–13.30, Tues, Thurs and Fri, also 15–17). The main façade on Via Lungarini, with a double row of balconies, dates from 1793. The residence of the Lanza-Filangeri family since the early 17C, it was donated by them, together with its contents, to the Sicilian Region in 1982. The well-kept interior is interesting as a typical example of a princely residence in Palermo with 18C and 19C decorations, including a little 'Chinese' room. The contents include furniture (mostly 18C and 19C), Capodimonte porcelain, Murano glass, etc. On the ground floor, near the delightful stables (1812) are displayed the funerary stele of Giambattista and Elisabetta Mellerio (c 1820) by Antonio Canova, purchased by the Sicilian Region in 1978 to prevent their export.

On the E side of Piazza Marina is the huge PALAZZO CHIARAMONTE, known as Lo Steri (i.e. Hosterium), occupied by the law courts from 1799 until 1972. The building was restored in 1984 for the University Rector (sometimes open for concerts or exhibitions).

Begun in 1307 by the Chiaramonte family, it became the palace of the viceroys. From 1605–1782 it was the seat of the Inquisition; the graffiti which survive on the prison walls provide a fascinating historical record of the persecutions. The exterior, though deprived of its battlements, retains several of its original windows. Inside are two rooms with wooden ceilings painted by Simone da Corleone and Cecco di Naro (1377–80), in Saracenic style. The inner courtyard, surrounded by a loggia with pointed arches, has two fine three-light windows on the left. In the courtyard on the right of the palazzo is the charming façade of the chapel of Sant'Antonio Abate.

Via 4 Aprile leads out of the square to the narrow old Via Alloro with its dilapidated palaces, and the flank of **La Gancia** (Pl. 12), or Santa Maria degli Angeli, a 15C church, entered by the side door (usually open 10.30–12.30 on fest.; at other times ring at the convent in the little piazza on the right of the façade). The fine exterior dates from the 15C.

In the INTERIOR (lights in each chapel) the wooden ceiling and fine organ (over the W door; perhaps by Raffaele La Valle) date from the transformation begun in 1672. South side. Second chapel (right): Antonello Crescenzio, Madonna with Saints Catherine and Agatha (signed and dated 1528; removed for restoration), Pietro Novelli (attributed), Holy Family; fourth chapel: Antonello Gagini (attributed), seated Madonna (the head of the Christ Child is modern); fifth and sixth chapels, inlaid marble panels with scenes of the Flight into Egypt: outside is a pulpit made up of fragments of sculpture by the Gagini. The chapel on the right of the choir has fine marble decoration and stuccoes by Giacomo Serpotta. On the choir-piers are two tondoes of the Annunciation attributed to Antonello Gagini. In the chapel to the left of the choir are more stuccoes by Serpotta, and a Marriage of the Virgin by Vincenzo da Pavia. North side. On the wall (high up), St Francis by Zoppo di Ganci. Sixth chapel, two fine reliefs (one of the Descent into Limbo) by Antonello Gagini; third chapel, Pietro Novelli, San Pietro d'Alcantara; second chapel, Vincenzo da Pavia, Nativity.

The adjoining convent is famous in the annals of the revolution of 4 April 1860. Its bell gave the signal to the insurgents; Francesco Riso, their leader, was mortally wounded; 13 were captured and shot; while two hid for five days in the vaults of the church, before escaping by the 'Buca della Salvezza', a hole in the wall next to Palazzo Patella.

Next to the church in Via Alloro is **Palazzo Abatellis** (sometimes called

'Patella'; Pl. 12), designed in 1488–95 by Matteo Carnelivari for Francesco Abatellis, master-pilot of Sicily, in a style combining elements of the Renaissance with late Catalan Gothic. Much altered internally during its occupation by Dominican nuns from 1526 until 1943, when it was damaged by bombs, the palace was freely restored in 1954 as the home of the ***Galleria Regionale di Sicilia**, with a fine collection of Sicilian sculpture and paintings (open daily 9–13.30; Tues, Thurs, Fri also 15.30–19.30; fest. 9–12.30). The exhibits are well documented and have been beautifully selected and arranged, gaining much from their appropriate surroundings.

A *doorway of original design admits to the pleasant courtyard. The GROUND FLOOR is devoted principally to **sculpture**. A door on the left leads into **Room 1**. Here are displayed 16C wooden sculptures, a 12C Arab door frame carved in wood; and a painting of the Madonna with saints by the workshop of Tommaso de Vigilia. Beyond, **R 2**, the former CHAPEL, is dominated by a famous large ***fresco of the Triumph of Death**, detached from Palazzo Sclafani. Dating from c 1449 it is of uncertain attribution, thought by some scholars to be the work of Pisanello or his school. It was restored in 1992. Death is portrayed as an archer on a spectral horse, piercing the contented and successful (right) with his arrows, while the unhappy and aged (left), among whom are the painter and a pupil, pray in vain for release.

A corridor (**3**) containing Saracenic ceramics, including a magnificent majolica vase of Hispano-Moresque type (13–14C) from Mazara del Vallo, and a fragment of a wooden ceiling (Siculo-Arabic, 12C) from Palazzo dei Normanni, leads to three rooms devoted to LATE-15C AND EARLY-16C SCULPTURE. **R 4** contains works by **Francesco Laurana**, principally a *bust of Eleonora of Aragon, his masterpiece. The bust of a young boy here has recently been attributed to Domenico Gagini (c 1469), who also sculpted (with assistants) the Madonna del Latte. **R 5** is devoted to the Gagini; notable are a marble statuette of the Madonna and Child, the Tabernacle of the Ansalone, with the Madonna del Buon Riposo (1528), and the head of a young boy, all by Antonello Gagini, and the Madonna della Neve (1516) by his workshop. In **R 6** are architectural fragments, including carved capitals.

The FIRST FLOOR is reached by a staircase from R 6, or from the courtyard. It contains the **Pinacoteca**, with its wonderful series of SICILIAN PAINTINGS, including 13–14C works, still in the Byzantine manner, and later works showing the influence of various schools (Umbrian, Sienese, Catalan, and Flemish): **R 1**. (left) Raising of Lazarus, and Christ in Limbo, two small paintings, perhaps Venetian, of the 13C; painted 13C Crucifix; Madonna in mosaic in a Byzantine style (early 14C); Antonio Veneziano, Madonna and Child; Bartolommeo da Camogli, Madonna dell'Umiltà (1346). In **R 2** (left) are paintings of the late 14C and early 15C. Giovanni di Pietro, St Nicholas; Turino Vanni, Madonna and saints; 'Master of the Trapani Polyptych', Madonna del Fiore; Gera da Pisa, Saints George and Agatha.

A short corridor (**R 3**), with a triptych, Madonna between Saints Agatha and Barbara, dated 1423, by a painter of the Marchigian school, leads on to the NORTH WING. **R 4** contains SICILIAN PAINTINGS OF THE EARLY 15C, including several Coronations of the Virgin by the same unknown Master, and works by the 'Master of the Trapani Polyptych'. **R 5**. LATE 15C. Paintings and frescoes by Tommaso de Vigilia; Pietro Ruzzolone, Crucifix; Coronation of the Virgin, polyptych from Corleone, by an unknown hand. In a little room off the hall, 16C custodia from Palermo. Beyond, in **R 6**, is a precious collection of works by **Antonello da Messina**, including his masterpiece, *Virgin Annunciate, and Saints Gregory, Augustine, and Jerome; also, Madonna, attributed to Marco Basaiti. **R 7**, the upper half of the chapel, overlooks the Triumph of Death (see above), and is devoted mainly to Riccardo Quartararo, notably Saints Peter and Paul, and Coronation of the Virgin. Also here is a 15–16C wood group of the Pietà. A number of 16C works of uncertain attribution are displayed in **R 8**: these include 'Master of the Pentecost', Pietà, and Pentecost; Andrea da Salerno, Saints John the Baptist and John the Evangelist; and a copy (1538) by Crescenzio of Raphael's 'Spasimo' (formerly in the church of Santa Maria dello Spasimo, see below).

In the SOUTH WING, **R 9** is devoted to 15–16C FLEMISH PAINTINGS: Annunciation, in the style of the Master of Flémalle; Mabuse, *Malvagna Triptych of the Virgin and Child between Saints Catherine and Barbara (on the outside, Adam and Eve), a painting of extraordinary detail; works of the 16C Antwerp and Bruges schools. **R 10** (left). Jan van Scorel, St Mary Magdalen; Tuscan school (dated 1563), portrait of a young man. **R 11** is devoted mainly to works by Vincenzo da Pavia: Deposition, St Conrad the Hermit, and two scenes from the Life of the Virgin. ROOM 12. Giuseppe Cesari, Andromeda; Mattia Preti, Christ and the Centurion; Pietro Novelli, communion of St Mary of Egypt; Van Dyck (copy), Madonna, his early masterpiece; Leandro Bassano, portrait of a man; Palma Giovane, Deposition.

At the end of Via Alloro is the church of **La Pietà**, with a splendid Baroque FACADE by Giacomo Amato (1678–84). The INTERIOR is a particularly striking example of local Baroque architecture. The delightful vestibule has stuccoes by Procopio Serpotta and frescoes by Borremans. The W end is filled with a splendid nuns' choir, and four cantorie in gilded wood decorate the nave. The fresco in the vault is by Antonio Grano (1708). On the S side, the first altar has a painting of Dominican saints by Antonio and Francesco Manno, and the second altar a Madonna of the Rosary by Olivio Sozzi. The high altar has a tabernacle in lapis lazuli. On the N side, the third altar has a Pietà (in a good frame) by Vincenzo da Pavia and the second altar, St Dominic by Olivio Sozzi.

On the opposite side of Via Torremuzza is the church of SAN MATTIA (closed), also by Amato. Facing Piazza Kalsa is the façade (1686–1706) of the church of **Santa Teresa**, one of the best works of Giacomo Amato. In the INTERIOR, on the S side: first altar, Giovanni Odazzi, Holy Family (1720); second altar, Ignazio Marabitti, marble Crucifixion group (1780–81). The high altarpiece is by Gaspare Serenario (1746) and the two statues of female saints in the sanctuary are by Giacomo Serpotta. N side: the second altarpiece is by Guglielmo Borremans (1722) and the first altarpiece by Sebastiano Conca.

In Piazza della Kalsa (Arabic 'khalisa', 'pure') are the remains of the 19C Palazzo Forcella, built on the bastions facing the sea. The QUARTIERE DELLA KALSA (Pl. 16) is a very poor area of the city, badly damaged by bombs in the last War. Behind Santa Teresa, Via dello Spasimo leads through the Kalsa near the partially destroyed church of Santa Maria dello Spasimo (1506), for which Raphael painted his Jesus falling beneath the Cross ('Lo Spasimo di Sicilia') now in the Prado at Madrid, having been presented to Philip IV in 1661.

The road continues across a huge open bomb site; at the far end is the fine Norman apse of the church of ***La Magione** (Pl. 16) which stands in majestic isolation, painstakingly restored since the bombs in World War II devastated the neighbourhood. It was founded by Matteo d'Aiello before 1151 as the Chiesa della Trinità for the Cistercians, but transferred to the Teutonic Knights in 1193 by the Emperor Henry VI as their mansion, from which it takes its name. It is a precious example of Arab Norman architecture. The FACADE has three handsome and very unusual doorways. The beautiful tall INTERIOR (open 7.30–11.30, 16–18.30) has a fine apse decorated with six small columns. Above the 14C stone altar hangs a painted Crucifix. The contents include statues of Christ and the Madonna and Child by the Gagini school, a 15C marble triptych, and a tabernacle of 1528. The custodian shows the charming little Cistercian CLOISTER (c 1190) around a garden; one walk with twin columns and carved capitals has survived. A room off the cloister contains a detached 15C fresco of the Crucifixion with its sinopia. Outside is a delightful garden of palm trees and a monumental 17C gateway on Via Magione.

Via Magione leads to Via Garibaldi, a dilapidated street with some handsome palaces and numerous balconies. Here is the huge PALAZZO AIUTAMICRISTO, built by Matteo Carnelivari in 1490, with Catalan-Gothic elements (doorway at No. 41; the courtyard, in a sad state of disrepair, is entered from No. 23). Here Charles V was entertained on his return from Tunis in 1535. Via Garibaldi, and its continuation Corso dei Mille mark the route followed by Garibaldi on his entry into the city. At the end is Piazza della Rivoluzione, the scene of the outbreak of the rebellion of 1848, inspired by Giuseppe La Masa. Surrounded by papyrus plants is a bizarre fountain, known as 'il genio di Palermo', with the statue of a king entangled in a serpent. Here is the 16C Palazzo Scavuzzo and the church of San Carlo (1643–48) with an elliptical interior (closed). Beyond is Piazza Aragona at the top of Via Alloro (see above). At No. 54, some way along on the right, stood Palazzo Bonagia, almost totally destroyed in the last war. The remarkable Baroque staircase in the courtyard attributed to Andrea Giganti survives, propped up by scaffolding behind a closed gateway.

The other end of Piazza Aragona leads into Piazza della Croce dei Vespri, where the graves of many French victims of the 'Vespers' were marked in 1737 by a Cross (copy of 1873; recently broken). Two sides of the piazza are occupied by the fine 18C Palazzo Valguarnera-Ganci, with pretty balconies, still owned by the family. Visconti used the sumptuous Salone degli Specchi here for the setting of the scene of the great ball in his film 'Il Gattopardo', based on the novel by Giuseppe di Lampedusa. The Art Nouveau palace in the piazza has an amusing portal and balcony. Nearby is the church of **Sant'Anna**, with a fine Baroque FACADE begun in 1726 by Giovanni Biagio Amico, with sculptures by Giacomo Pennino and Lorenzo Marabitti, on designs by Giacomo Serpotta. The INTERIOR dates from 1606–36. On the W wall are two paintings by Giuseppe Albina. South aisle. Second chapel, 17C altarpiece of the Holy Family and two good paintings from the life of the Virgin. The third chapel has a 17C painting of St Rosalia with a view of Monte Pellegrino and the port. In the S transept are frescoes by Filippo Tancredi. In the sanctuary is a 16C organ case.

Via Roma leads back (right) to Corso Vittorio Emanuele and the Quattro Canti.

E. The Zisa and the Convento dei Cappuccini

Since these monuments are outside the central area of the city they are best reached by car or bus. For the Zisa, bus No. **24** (black) from Via Volturno; inconspicuous request stop in Via della Zisa. For the Cappuccini, bus No. **27**. For the Cuba, Cubula, and Villa Tasca, bus Nos **8, 9**.

***La Zisa** (Pl.9; Arab, 'el aziz', 'magnificent') is one of a group of palaces built by the Norman kings in their private park of Genoard (used as a hunting reserve) on the outskirts of Palermo. Begun by William I c 1164–65 and completed by his son, it is the most important secular monument of Arab-Norman architecture to survive, and is purely Islamic in inspiration. After years of neglect, it was beautifully restored in 1974–90. The structure had to be consolidated throughout, but the unity of its remarkable design of geometrical perfection (on three floors) has been preserved. It is now surrounded by a railing beside a humble piazza while beyond rise the tower blocks of the city. From Via della Zisa (and the bus-stop; see above) it is usually necessary to follow the railings around the front of the building as only the gate on the far side is kept open (9–13.30).

The palace is known to have been used by Frederick II, but it was already in disrepair in the late 13C. It was fortified by the Chiaramonte in the 14C. By the 16C it was in a ruined state and was drastically reconstructed by the Spanish Sandoval family who owned it from 1635 to 1806. It was expropriated by the Sicilian government in 1955 but then abandoned until part of the upper floors collapsed in 1971. A remarkable restoration programme was begun in 1974 and it was finally opened to the public in 1990.

The fine EXTERIOR has a symmetrical design, although the two-light windows on the upper floors were all destroyed in the 17C by the Sandoval, who set up their coat of arms on the façade and altered the portico. In William's day the sandstone was faced with plaster decorated in a red and white design. The small pond outside, formerly part of a garden in Arab style, collected the water from the fountain in the ground floor hall, which was fed by a nearby Roman aqueduct. A damaged inscription in Cufic letters at the top of the E façade has not yet been deciphered.

The beautiful INTERIOR of the palace, on three floors, can be visited. The exceptionally thick outer walls (1.90 metres on the ground floor), the original small windows, and a system of air vents (also found in ancient Egyptian buildings) kept the palace protected from the extremes of heat and cold. The rooms were all vaulted: the square rooms with cross vaults and the oblong rooms with barrel vaults. Amphorae were used in the structure of the vaults in order to allow for the foundations of the floors above. Some of the vaults have had to be reconstructed in reinforced concrete. The pavements (very few of the original ones remain) were in tiles laid in a herring-bone pattern, except for the ground floor hall which was in marble. The miniature stalactite vaults (known as 'mouqarnas') which decorate niches in some of the rooms and the intrados of many of the windows are borrowed from Arab architecture.

On the GROUND FLOOR are explanatory plans and a display illustrating the history of the building. A model in plexiglass shows where it had to be reconstructed (after its partial collapse in 1971) and where iron girders have been inserted to reinforce the building. The small rooms here were originally service rooms or rooms used by court dignatories. The splendid central *HALL, used for entertainments, has niches with stalactite vaults derived from Islamic architecture. Around the walls runs a mosaic freize which expands into three ornamental circles in the central recess. The Norman mosaics (which recall those in the Sala di Re Ruggero in the Palazzo Reale), show Byzantine, Islamic, and even Frankish influences. A fountain gushed from the opening surmounted by the imperial eagle in mosaic and flowed down a runnel towards the entrance to be collected in the fish pond outside. A majolica floor survives here, and the faded frescoes were added in the 17C. The little columns have beautiful capitals. On the inner side of the entrance arch is a damaged 12C inscription in large stucco letters.

Two symmetrical staircases used to lead up to the FIRST FLOOR (replaced by modern iron stairways). Here the living rooms are connected by a corridor along the W front. Numerous fine vaults survive here, and a series of air vents (see above). Egyptian Muslim objects, including metalwork and ceramics, are displayed in some of the rooms, as well as amphorae found in the vaulting. On the TOP FLOOR is a remarkable central hall with columns and water channels which was originally an open atrium surrounded by loggias, used in the summer. The small rooms on either side were probably a harem. From the windows there is a view of the hills surrounding the Conca d'Oro beyond modern tower blocks. There are plans to recreate the garden and park around the palace.

Outside to the N of the Zisa, in Via dei Normanni, the church of GESÙ, MARIA, E SANTO STEFANO incorporates a Norman chapel built at the same time as the palace. In Piazza Zisa is the 17C church of the ANNUNZIATA, with Sandoval funerary monuments.

From the Zisa, Via Whitaker and Via Serradifalco lead N to VILLA MALFITANO (Pl. 5; open 9–13 except fest.) built for Joseph (Pip) and Tina Whitaker by Ignazio Greco in 1887. It is surrounded by a magnificent park (nearly 7 hectares) of rare trees and plants collected by the owners, including yuccas, bamboos, white judases, and a giant 'ficus magnoloides'. This was the centre of English society in Palermo at the beginning of the century, and here the Whitakers were visited by Edward VII in 1907 and by George V and Queen Mary in 1925. Pip Whitaker, descendant of the famous Marsala wine merchants, was owner and excavator of Motya (see Rte 8) and the house was left by his daughter on her death in 1971 to the Joseph Whitaker Foundation, and it is used for exhibitions.

To the S, at No. 38 Viale Regina Margherita, is the Villino Florio, one of Ernesto Basile's best works (1890). It has been partially reconstructed after a fire in 1962. In Via Dante are a number of Art Nouveau houses.

To the S is the **Convento dei Cappuccini** (beyond Pl. 9, 13; open 9–12, 15–17), famous for its catacombs in which the bodies of wealthy citizens, bishops, friars, children, etc. were interred until 1881. A friar conducts visitors to the macabre underground passages with about 8000 bodies, some naturally mummified.

From Piazza Cappuccini Via Pindemonte leads (right) to Via La Loggia where are the scant ruins of the Norman PALAZZO DELL'USCIBENE (or Scibene, formerly Mimnermo), built at the time of William II as a summer residence for the archbishops of Palermo. A hall with niches decorated with stucco shells has all but disappeared.

Outside Porta Nuova (Pl. 14) begins Corso Calatafimi which leads to Monreale. On the left is a huge charitable institute built in 1735–38 by Casimiro Agretta; the church façade is by Marvuglia (1772–76). On the corner is a fountain of 1630, the only one to survive of the many which used to line the road. Opposite is the vast ALBERGO DEI POVERI (Pl. 13), an interesting building by Orazio Furetto (1746–72), recently restored and now used for important exhibitions. There follow a series of barracks including (on the left) the Caserma Tuköry (No. 100; c 1km from the gate) which encloses ***La Cuba** (Arab, 'kubbeh', dome), a Norman palace built by William II (1180) in imitation of La Zisa (closed for security reasons; and covered for restoration). On the outer wall is an Arabic inscription, and inside are the remains of a hall with a small cupola decorated with stuccoes.

Farther on in the Corso, opposite a 'Standa' department store and behind No. 575 a short road leads right to the remains of the 18C VILLA DI NAPOLI (now derelict). Here is the entrance to the delightful orchard which still surrounds the **Cubula**, although ugly new buildings have engulfed the square in the last decade or so. The gate is unlocked by the custodian who lives at the house beside the villa on the left; a path leads to the little pavilion with its characteristic red dome, built by William I. It is the only one to survive of the many which used to decorate his private park in this area (cf. above).

Farther on, across the busy Viale della Regione Sicilia, the Corso passes close to the **Villa Tasca** (see atlas p 16), with a *garden (admission by previous appointment), remarkable for its araucarias and palms.

F. The northern district of the city and La Favorita

Bus Nos **1**, **3**, **19**, **25**, and **40** for Viale della Libertà. Bus Nos **14** or **15** for La Favorita.

Via Maqueda is continued N by Via Ruggero Settimo, with numerous cinemas, shops, and cafés, to the double Piazza Ruggero Settimo and Piazza Castelnuovo. Here rises the huge **Politeama Garibaldi** (Pl. 7), a 'Pompeian' theatre (1874, by Giuseppe Damiani-Almeyda) crowned by a bronze quadriga by Mario Rutelli. In part of the building is housed the **Gallery of Modern Art**, founded in 1910, with 19C and 20C works, mostly by artists from Sicily and southern Italy (open 9–13; Tues and Fri also 16–20; closed Mon), including Domenico Morelli, Antonio Mancini, Giovanni Boldini, Corrado Cagli, Carlo Carrà, Felice Casorati, Gino Severini.

To the S, in Via Roma, is the Grande Albergo e delle Palme (formerly Palazzo Ingham). Here Richard Wagner stayed with his family and completed 'Parsifal' in 1882. The building was modified in 1907 by Ernesto Basile.

Viale della Libertà (Pl. 2; 6), a wide avenue (one-way S) laid out in 1860, with trees and some pretty Art Nouveau houses, leads N past the GIARDINO INGLESE (Pl. 2), a delightful well-kept public garden, designed at the end of the last century. Via Generale Dalla Chiesa, a street parallel to the Viale, records General Carlo Alberto Dalla Chiesa who was assassinated by the Mafia here in 1982 (plaque), along with his wife and chauffeur, after just five months in office as Prefect of Palermo. Nearby, towards the sea is the UCCIARDONE (Pl. 3), built in 1837–60, and now a maximum security jail. A special wing was added in the late 1980s to house a number of huge collective trials which resulted in the condemnation of hundreds of people for crimes connected with the Mafia. Two of the courageous judges who collected evidence for these trials, Giovanni Falcone and Paolo Borsellino, were assassinated by the Mafia in Palermo, together with their bodyguards, in 1992.

Across Via Notarbartolo Viale della Libertà passes (left; No. 52) the head office of the Banco di Sicilia with the MUSEO ARCHEOLOGICO DELLA FONDAZIONE MORMINO (open 9–13, 15–17; Sat 9–13; closed fest.), which contains good archaeological material, a numismatic collection and a philatelic collection (1860, from Naples and Sicily).

Viale della Libertà ends in the circular Piazza Vittorio Veneto. From here Via d'Artigliera (right) leads shortly to Piazza dei Leoni at the S entrance (c 4km from the Quattro Canti) to **La Favorita** (see atlas p 16). This large area of woods and gardens at the foot of Monte Pellegrino is a public park (nearly 3km long), traversed by a one-way road system; it now contains a hippodrome and other sports facilities. On Viale del Fante bounding the W side of the park are the Stadio Comunale (right) and the Istituto Agrario (left).

Just beyond Piazza Niscemi is the main entrance (c 7km from the Quattro Canti) to the formal PARCO DELLA FAVORITA, an estate bought by Ferdinand of Bourbon in 1799, and laid out by him in the taste of the early 19C. The *PALAZZINA CINESE (being restored), a charming building in a Chinese style by Venanzio Marvuglia was occupied by Ferdinand and Maria Carolina in 1799–1802 during their enforced exile from Naples. The collection of English prints was a gift from Nelson who in 1799 shared with the Hamiltons the neighbouring town house of the Palagonia family. Nearby is the ***Museo Etnografico Siciliano Pitrè** (open 9–13.30; closed Fridays), founded in 1909 by Giuseppe Pitrè, an outstanding collection illustrating Sicilian life from its customs, costumes, popular arts (painted carts, ex-votos, etc.), musical instruments, implements, and objects of common use.

In the PIANA DEI COLLI, the area between Monte Pellegrino and Monte Castellaccio (see atlas p 16), are a number of villas built in the 18C as summer residences by the Palermitan nobility. They are notable for their ingenious design (often with elaborate outside stairs). In this century many of them have been engulfed by new buildings or left to decay; the publication of a recent study of 60 of them may hopefully provoke interest in their preservation. In Piazza Niscemi (see above) is the Villa Niscemi, and across Via Duca degli Abruzzi is the small early 18C Villa Spina in its park. Nearby is Villa Lampedusa built in 1770 and now in a state of abandon. This was bought by the Principe di Lampedusa, Giulio Tomasi c 1845, and described in 'Il Gattopardo' by his great grandson Giuseppe Tomasi.

Farther W, off Via Nuova is Villa Pantelleria (c 1730), now the seat of the Centro Internazionale di Musica, Cultura, e Arte Popolare 'Django Reinhardt'. In the district of San Lorenzo is the Convitto Nazionale (now used by the Red Cross), the grandest of this group of villas, built in 1683. Near here is the new district of 'Z.E.N.', notorious for its social problems. Off Via San Lorenzo is Villa Amari built in 1720 by Count Michele Amari di Sant'Adriano (now abandoned) and Villa Boscogrande (1756). Across Via Tommaso Natale is the well preserved Villa De Cordova. In the district of Resuttana is Villa Terrasi with early 18C frescoes by Vito d'Anna.

At Acquasanta, on the coast, reached by Via Imperatore Federico from the S entrance of the Favorita, is the VILLA IGIEA (see atlas p 16; buses from the centre of Palermo, Nos 3, 27, 31, and 39), now a 5-star hotel, in a large park. A remarkable Art Nouveau building, it was built as a sanatorium by the Florio at the end of the 19C, and transformed into a hotel in 1900 by Ernesto Basile. Nearby is Villa Belmonte, a neo-classical building by Venanzio Marvuglia (1801). For Monte Pellegrino and Mondello, see Rte 2A.

G. The southern district of the city: Santo Spirito and San Giovanni dei Lebbrosi

These churches are best visited by bus; for Santo Spirito Bus No. **2** or **42**; for S. Giovanni dei Lebbrosi, Bus No. **11**, **26** or **31**.

From the station Corso Tuköry leads W to Porta Sant'Agata (follow the signs for 'Policlinico/Ospedale'). Here Via del Vespro (Pl. 15) diverges left; beyond the Policlinico and just across the railway are the flower stalls and stonemasons yards outside the cemetery of SANT'ORSOLA, in the midst of which is the church of **Santo Spirito** or **dei Vespri** (15–20 minute walk from the station; open 9–12). This fine Norman church (1173–78) was founded by Walter, Archbishop of Palermo. It has a pretty exterior with arches and bands of volcanic stone and lattice-work windows. The interior has a restored painted wood ceiling and a painted wood Crucifix of the 15C. It was in front of this church at the hour of vespers on Easter Tuesday (31 March 1282), that the famous revolution of the Sicilians broke out against their Angevin overlords.

From Porta Garibaldi near the Station Corso dei Mille (Pl. 16) leads S to the Oreto; this ancient thoroughfare was used by Garibaldi and his men on their entrance to the city. Just across the river is the *PONTE DELL' AMMIRAGLIO, a fine bridge built by George of Antioch in 1113, and extremely well preserved. Since the river has been diverted it is now surrounded by a well kept garden and busy roads. Here took place the first skirmish between the Garibaldini and the Bourbon troops, on 27 May 1860. A short way beyond is Piazza Scaffa. On the left of the Corso, hidden behind crumbling edifices (and now approached at No. 38 Via Salvatore Cappello), is **San Giovanni dei Lebbrosi**, one of the oldest Norman churches in Sicily. It is surrounded by a well-kept garden of palms; the custodian lives next to it, ring at the gate (16–17.15; Sundays 8–11.30). Traditionally thought to have been founded by Roger I in 1072, it was more probably erected at the time of Roger II when it became a leper hospital. The fine interior has been restored.

From Piazza Scaffa (see above) Via Brancaccio leads S through the unattractive suburb of Brancaccio. Via Conte Federico continues to the **Castello del Maredolce** (or **Flavia**) in ruins and almost totally engulfed by tower blocks. The palazzo, once surrounded on three sides by an artificial lake, was built by the emir Giafar in 997–1019, and was later used by the Norman kings and Frederick II. A chapel was built here by Roger II. To the S across the motorway is the ruined 18C church of San Ciro near which the Grotto dei Giganti yielded finds of fossil bones.

Much further S beyond ugly new suburbs and the ring road and motorway (at present very difficult to find by car; across the ring road to the right at the end of Via Loreto) is the church of **Santa Maria di Gesù**, preceded by a terraced graveyard. The church has been restored; if closed, ring at convent. The simple chapel of 1426 was enlarged laterally in 1481, and a presbytery was added, with two fine Gothic arches. Here are the arcade and colonnettes of the tomb of Antonio Alliata, by Antonello Gagini (1524), and a monument to a lady of the Alliata family, by the workshop of Domenico Gagini (1490–1500). In a chapel off the nave is a statue in wood of St Francis, by Pippinico; a Baroque niche contains a wooden statue of the Madonna (late 15C). The atrium, the funerary chapel of the Bonet family, has a wooden ceiling of the late 12C. The main doorway, with a frieze of the Apostles, dates from c 1495, by the workshop of Domenico Gagini. Outside the presbytery is the Gothic CAPPELLA LA GRUA; the frescoes, probably by a Spanish artist of the late 15C, have been removed for restoration, and will be returned to the main church.

MONTE GRIFONE (832m), the hill overlooking Palermo from the SE, may be reached either from Santa Maria di Gesù or from San Ciro (see above). On its N slope is the ravine of the Discesa dei Mille ('descent of the Thousand'), above which an obelisk (337m) marks the site of Garibaldi's encampment of 26 May 1860.

2

Environs of Palermo

A. Mondello and Monte Pellegrino

Bus **15** for Mondello; Bus **12** for Monte Pellegrino.

From the N end of the Parco della Favorita (see Rte 1F) a road traverses the suburb of (8km) Pallavicino to run beneath the W slope of Monte Pellegrino, reaching the shore among the numerous villas of (11km) **Mondello** (for hotels and restaurants, see the beginning of Rte 1). This is one of the most noted bathing resorts in Sicily, whose sandy beach extends for 2km from Monte Pellegrino to Monte Gallo. A garden city was laid out here by a Belgian society in 1892–1910, although the bay has been filled with new buildings since the second World War. At its N end is the old fishing village of Mondello with a medieval tower, while at the S end is Valdesi from which Lungomare Cristoforo Colombo returns towards the centre of Palermo following the rocky coast at the foot of Monte Pellegrino via Vergine Maria, Arenella and Acquasanta (see Rte 1F). Inland from Mondello is Partanna, now part of the same comune, where the unusual Villa Partanna survives from 1722–28. From Mondello a road crosses Monte Pellegrino, see below.

Monte Pellegrino (606m), described by Goethe as the most beautiful headland in the world, lies between the Mondello road and the sea; it rises sharply on all sides except the S. The rock, in places covered with trees and cacti, has a remarkable golden colour. Almost certainly the ancient *Heirkte*, the headland was occupied by Hamilcar Barca in the First Punic War and

Monte Pellegrino, Palermo

defended for three years (247–244) against the Romans. In the ADDAURA CAVES on the N slopes prehistoric rock carvings have been discovered since 1952 (for adm. apply to the Soprintendenza Archeologica, next to the Museo Archeologico in Palermo). The incised human and animal figures date from the Upper Palaeolithic period: they include an exceptionally interesting scene of uncertain significance with seventeen human figures.

The direct approach from Palermo is from (3km) Piazza Generale Cascino, near the fair and exhibition ground called the 'Fiera del Mediterraneo'. From here Via Pietro Bonanno, crossing and recrossing the shorter footpath, mounts towards the Santuario di Santa Rosalia. A flight of steps mounts and zigzags up the 'Scala Vecchia' (17C) between the Primo Pizzo (344m; left), with the prominent Castello Utveggio, built as a hotel in 1932 (its terrace provides the best *view of the city) and the Pizzo Grattarola (276m).

A small group of buildings marks the SANTUARIO DI SANTA ROSALIA (428m; 13km from the centre of Palermo), a cavern converted into a chapel in 1625, containing a statue of the saint, by Gregorio Tedeschi, and her coronation, by Nunzio la Mattina. The water trickling down the walls is held to be miraculous and the grotto is filled with an extraordinary variety of ex-votos. This was the hermitage of St Rosalia, daughter of Duke Sinibald and niece of William II. She died here in 1166, and is supposed to have appeared to a man on Monte Pellegrino in 1624 to show him the cave where her remains were, since she had never received a Christian burial. When found, her relics were carried in procession through Palermo and a terrible plague then raging in the town miraculously ceased. She was declared patron Saint and the annual procession in her honour, with a tall and elaborate carriage drawn by animals, became a famous spectacle.

A steep road on the farther side of the adjoining convent mounts to the summit, from which there is a wonderful view extending from the Aeolian Islands to Etna. Another road from the sanctuary leads to a colossal 19C statue by Benedetto De Lisi of St Rosalia on the cliff edge.

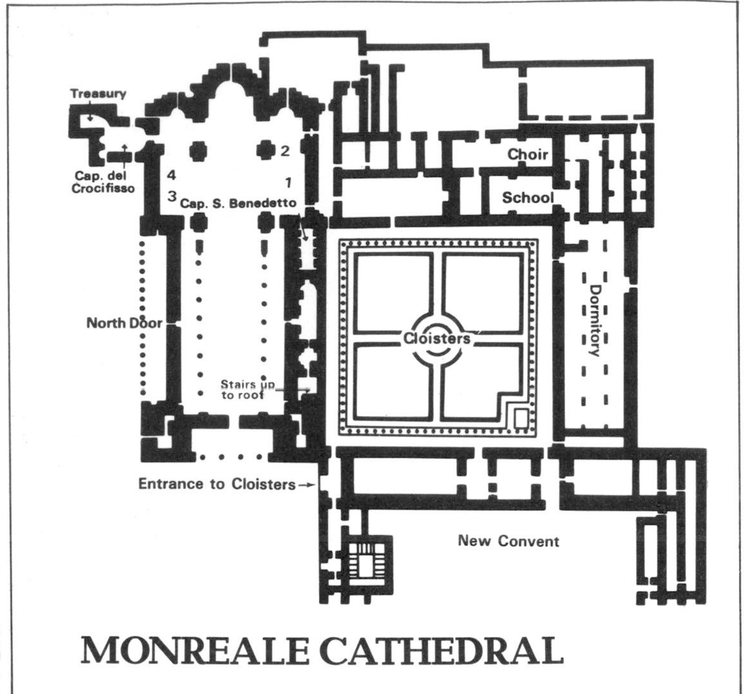

B. Monreale

Monreale, 8km SW of the city, is approached by Corso Calatafimi from Porta Nuova (see Rte 1E). Bus No. **8/9** from Via Mariano Stabile (Pl. 6; frequent service in 20–30 minutes).

MONREALE grew up around William II's great church. On a hill (310m) overlooking the Conca d'Oro, it is now a small town (23,700 inhab.) with fine views. 3-star hotel: 'Carrubbella Park'. The road from Palermo climbs up to Piazza Vittorio Emanuele with the N side of the ****Cathedral** (dedicated to the Assumption; open 8–12.15, 15.30–18.30), the last and most beautiful of the Norman churches in Sicily, built to contain one of the most remarkable mosaic cycles ever produced. Begun c 1174 by William II and already near to completion by 1183, it was one of the architectural wonders of the Middle Ages. The FACADE, facing the adjoining Piazza Guglielmo, flanked by two square towers (one incomplete) and approached by an 18C porch, has a fine portal with a bronze *door signed by Bonanno da Pisa (1186). The splendid apse, decorated with interlacing arches of limestone and lava, can be seen from Via del Arcivescovado (see below). The entrance is beneath the portico along the N side built in 1547–69 by Gian Domenico and Fazio Gagini, with elegant benches. Here the portal has a mosaic frieze and a bronze *door by Barisano da Trani (1179).

The INTERIOR (102m by 40m), remarkably simple in design but glittering with golden and coloured mosaics, gives an immediate impression of majesty and splendour. It is the conception of the Cappella Palatina carried out on a magnificent scale. Beyond the rectangular crossing, surmounted by a high lantern, with shallow transepts, is a deep presbytery with three apses, recalling the plan of Cluniac abbey churches. The stilted arches in the nave are carried on 18 slender columns with composite capitals, of Roman origin, all of granite except the first on the S side, which is of cipollino. The ceiling of the nave was restored after a fire in 1811; that of the choir bears the stamp of Saracenic art. The handsome marble slabs decorated with mosaic on the lower part of the walls were installed in the 19C.

The magnificient series of ***mosaics** have recently been beautifully restored (the numerous coin-operated lights are essential to see the exquisite details). It is not known whether Greek or local craftsmen trained by Greek mosaicists were involved in this remarkable project, and the exact date of its completion, thought to be around 1182, is uncertain. The large scenes chosen to illustrate the theme of Christ's Ascension and the Assumption of the Virgin fit an overall scheme designed to celebrate the Norman monarchy and to emphasise its affinity with Jerusalem. All the scenes bear detailed inscriptions in mosaic.

Above the arcade in the NAVE begins the Genesis cycle in a double tier, starting on the upper tier at the E end of the South side with the Creation and continuing round the W wall and along the N side to end (on the lower tier) with the dream of Jacob and Jacob wrestling with the Angel. In the CROSSING and TRANSEPTS the story of Christ is illustrated from the Nativity to the Passion. The piers in the transept are covered on all sides with tiers of saints.

In the AISLES scenes show the Ministry of Christ. On either side of the PRESBYTERY are scenes from the life of St Peter and Paul, whose figures are represented in the side apses. In the MAIN APSE is the mighty half-length figure of Christ Pantocrater, the most imposing of all such figures in Sicily. Below is the enthroned Madonna with angels and apostles, and lower still, on either side of the E window, figures of saints including Thomas Becket, executed within ten years of his martyrdom; Henry II of England was William II's father-in-law. Above the original royal throne (left; restored) William II receives the crown at the hands of Christ; above the episcopal throne (right; reconstructed) William offers the cathedral to the Virgin. The floor of marble mosaic dates in its present form from 1559.

CHAPELS. The transept S of the choir contains the porphyry sarcophagus of William I (*1*; died 1166) and that of William II (*2*; died 1190) in white marble (1575). Here is the CAPPELLA DI SAN BENEDETTO (1569), with a relief of the saint by Marabitti (1760). On the N of the choir are the tombs (*3*; reconstructions of 1846) of Margaret, Roger, and Henry, the wife and sons of William I, and an inscription (*4*) recording the resting-place (1270) of the body of St Louis when on its way back from Tunis; his heart remains buried here.

The TREASURY (adm. fee), which contains precious reliquaries, is entered through the splendid 17C Baroque CAPPELLA DEL CROCIFISSO, by whose entrance is a marble tabernacle by the school of the Gagini. At the SW corner of the nave is the entrance (fee) to the *ROOF. Stairs (180 steps) and walkways lead across the roof above the cloisters and round the apses of the cathedral. The view of the Conca d'Oro and the coast is now marred

Detail of the twelfth-century cloisters of the Duomo of Monreale (engraved in 1875)

by high modern buildings; the plain was described by Augustus Hare at the end of the last century as a 'vast garden of orange and olive trees'.

On the S side of the church are the lovely ***cloisters** (usually open 9–18; fest. 9–13); a masterpiece of 12C art, with pointed arches borne by twin columns of every imaginable design, with delicate and varied capitals. Many of the colonnettes are decorated with mosaics or reliefs; the seventh from the NW corner is signed on the capital. In the SW corner a single column in a little enclosure of its own forms a charming fountain. The N wall is pierced by a doorway and eight two-light windows with a decoration of limestone and lava like that of the apse. The South Walk is surmounted by a fine Norman wall (possibly predating the cloisters) of the ruined dormitory of the Monastery, built for Cluniac Benedictines.

A pleasant public garden is entered on the right of the façade of the new CONVENT (1747; now a school). The convent has a grand staircase with two large paintings (removed for restoration): St Benedict distributing bread, symbolising his Rule, to all the monastic and knightly orders, the masterpiece of Pietro Novelli (1635) who was born at Monreale in 1608, and the Discovery of a treasure revealed by the Virgin to William II in a dream, by Giuseppe Velasquez (1797). The BELVEDERE behind, with traces of the old monastic wall and exotic plants, has a lovely view of the Oreto valley.

In Piazza Vittorio Emanuele, surrounded by palm trees, is a fountain with a triton by Mario Rutelli. The restored 18C Municipio occupies part of the Norman palace (remnents of which can be seen from behind). In the council chamber is a Madonna with two saints (terracotta), attributed to Antonello Gagini (1528), and an Adoration of the Shepherds, by Mathias Stomer (17C). Behind the Municipio is Via Arcivescovado, from which can be seen the magnificent exterior of the E end of the Duomo. The Choir School here incorporates some arches and windows of the Norman palace which originally had an entrance to the Duomo. The medieval districts here (where the houses are decorated with numerous plants) and between Via Cassara and Via Roma are worth exploring.

The little town also possesses some fine Baroque churches. The CHIESA DEL MONTE in Via Umberto I contains stuccoes by Serpotta and his school and the Madonna of the Constellation, by Orazio Ferraro (1612). Higher up, on the left, is the COLLEGIATA, with large 18C paintings in the nave by Marco Benefial, a 17C Crucifix (on the external wall of the presbytery), and a stucco Crucifixion by Omodei (16C; on the high altar). Higher still is the Madonna delle Croci, with a fine view. In the other direction, in Via Roma, is the 18C COLLEGIO DI MARIA, and, at the end of Via Pietro Novelli, the church of SAN CASTRENSE, with a pretty 18C interior with stuccoes by the school of Serpotta and a high altarpiece by Antonio Novelli (1602).

From the N side of the town a lonely road (9.5km) leads to San Martino delle Scale. It ascends to Portella San Martino from where a path ascends through a pinewood to (c 20 minutes) the *CASTELLACCIO (766m), the SW summit of Monte Cuccio, a splendid viewpoint. The castle was a fortified monastery built by William II as a hospice for the convent of Monreale. It then passed to the Benedictines, and was badly damaged by Manfredi Chiaramonte in the 14C. Towards the end of the 18C it was abandoned and fell into ruin until in 1899 it was purchased by the Club Alpino Siciliano. The road continues downhill to San Martino delle Scale (see below).

C. San Martino delle Scale and Baida

Bus Nos **22 red** and **23** to Baida; bus from Piazza Verdi to San Martino delle Scale; coach excursions in summer and on holidays to San Martino.

From Piazza Indipendenza (Pl.14), Via Cappuccini and its continuation Via Giuseppe Pitrè lead W; beyond Altarello and a military airfield the road mounts to (5km) BOCCADIFALCO, a large suburb on a crag (175m) at the entrance to the Valle del Paradiso.

A road to the right by the clock-tower leads to (1.5km) **Baida**, an isolated hamlet backed by a crescent of hills that rise in Monte Cuccio to 1050m. The Convento di Baida (for adm. ring at No. 41 Via del Convento) was built in 1377–88 by Benedictine monks, expelled by Manfredi Chiaramonte from the Castellaccio (see above), on the site of a 10C Saracen village ('baidha', white). The foundation was already in decline in 1499 when Giovanni Paternò took it over as a summer residence for the archbishops of Palermo; in 1595 it passed to the Observantine order. The church, its original Gothic façade pierced by a portal of 1507, preserves a fine 14C apse, and a statue, by Antonello Gagini, of St John the Baptist; traces of the 14C cloister remain.

The road follows Valle del Paradiso, climbing between pine-clad slopes, to (11km) **San Martino delle Scale** (500m; 2-star hotels: 'Messina' and 'Ai Pini'), a hill-resort. The huge Benedictine ABBEY OF SAN MARTINO, possibly founded by St Gregory the Great, was rebuilt after 1347 by Archbishop Emanuele Spinola and the Benedictine Angelo Sisinio, and enlarged c 1762 by Venanzio Marvuglia. It now shelters a college. The church (closed 12.30–16.30), dating from 1561–95 (with part of the 14C masonry in the N wall) contains carved choir-stalls by Benvenuto Tortelli da Brescia (1591 97); St Benedict, and the Madonna with Saints Benedict and Scholastica, both by Pietro Novelli; six altarpieces by Lo Zoppo di Ganci; and St Martin, by Filippo Paladino. The fine organ in the apse was made in 1650 by Raffaele La Valle. The sacristy contains vestments of 16–18C, paintings attributed to Annibale Carracci and Guercino, and a reliquary by Pietro di Spagna. The carved doorway into the Convent dates from the 15C; nearby is a stoup of 1396. In the convent, at the foot of the splendid grand staircase (1786) by Marvuglia, is a group of St Martin and the beggar, by Marabitti. A statue of St Benedict, by Benedetto Pompillion, stands in the graceful monastic cloister (1612; altered and enlarged in the 18C). The Oreto fountain is by Marabitti (1784). The refectory ceiling is frescoed by Novelli (Daniel in the Lions' den).

The return may be varied by taking the road which ascends to Castellaccio; from there to Monreale and Palermo, see Rte 2B.

D. Bagheria and Solunto

BUS services run by 'AST' from Palermo (Piazza Lolli and the railway station) to Bagheria. A few trains a day on the Messina line stop at Bagheria (14km in c 10 minutes) and 'Santa Flavia-Solunto' (16km in c 15 minutes). The Palermo–Bagheria line was the first to be opened on the island in 1863.

Bagheria and Solunto are best approached from Palermo by the coastal road via Ficarazzi (and not by the motorway). Palermo is left by the Foro Italico (Pl. 12) which passes Villa Giulia. N113 traverses the old suburbs of the city where fish is sold on the side of the road. At (7km) Acqua dei Corsari, the Agrigento road and approach to the motorway exit of 'Vill-abate' diverge to the right. The old road continues through (10km) FICARAZZI with (right) a huge 15C castle transformed into a villa at the beginning of the 18C. Its monumental staircase descends to the level of the road.

Beyond the ancient Eleutherus the road enters (14.5km) **Bagheria**, a country town (35,400 inhab.), once famous for its 18C Baroque villas amidst orange groves and vineyards. It has been suffocated by uncontrolled new buildings in the last 30 years, and has become notorious (together with Altavilla and Misilmeri) as a centre of Mafia activities. The villas are suffering from neglect, and only two of them are now open to visitors. 1st-class restaurant 'Il Vespro' (French cuisine) and trattoria 'Don Ciccio'.

The Palermo road passes close to the conspicuous VILLA DEI PRINCIPI DI CATTOLICA, a fine building of c 1737, now in an ugly setting. It houses the Pinacoteca Civica di Bagheria, with a large collection of paintings by Renato Guttuso (1912–87), a native of Bagheria, and other contemporary artists. It is open 9–13, 17–19 excluding Mondays and fest. (ring for custodian at the side entrance). In the garden is the bright blue marble tomb of Guttuso by Giacomo Manzù.

Near the villa, beyond a railway crossing (right), begins the long Corso Butera which passes the fine PALAZZO INGUAGGIATO, attributed to Andrea Giganti (1770) before reaching the piazza in front of the 18C Duomo. At the far end of the Corso can be seen VILLA BUTERA, built in 1658 by Giuseppe Branciforte (façade of 1769). In the grounds, now engulfed by modern buildings, the 'Certosa' (ruined) was built to house a collection of wax figures of historical characters dressed in the Carthusian habit.

In front of the Duomo begins Corso Umberto which ends in the untidy Piazza Garibaldi beside (left) a garden gate (guarded by two monsters) of VILLA PALAGONIA (ring for the custodian; open 9–12.30, and for two hours in the afternoon before dusk). The garden, and vestibule and hall on the first floor may be visited. The fine building was erected in 1705 by Francesco Gravina, Prince of Palagonia (and his architect Tommaso Maria Napoli). His eccentric grandson Ferdinando Gravina Alliata lived in rooms decorated in a bizarre fashion, including the hall with its ceiling covered with mirrors set at strange angles (now very damaged) and its walls encased in marble with busts of ladies and gentlemen. The oval vestibule has frescoes of four labours of Hercules. The villa is famous for the grotesque statues of monsters, dwarfs, strange animals, etc. set up on the garden wall by Ferdinando (their effect now sadly diminished by the houses which have been built just outside the wall). At the time these carved figures were not to everyone's taste; when Goethe visited the villa in 1787 he was appalled by them.

Opposite is the entrance gate to the avenue which leads up to VILLA VALGUARNERA (not visible from here and closed to the public). Built by Tommaso Napoli c 1713–37, this is the most handsome of the Bagheria villas (most of its contents were stolen in 1988). The statues above the parapet are by Marabitti. Off Via IV Novembre is VILLA TRABIA (mid 18C), perhaps by Nicolò Palma, with a façade of 1890. It is surrounded by a neglected park. Near the railway station is the early-18C Villa Cutò.

Solunto can be approached directly from Bagheria (signposted from Piazza Garibaldi) or off the Palermo road (N113). At Santa Flavia (where the

Municipio occupies the Villa Filangeri, c 1750), Via Porticello diverges towards the sea. On the left (signpost) is the road up to the solitary ruins of **Solunto** (open daily 9–two hours before sunset), in a beautiful position on the slope of Monte Catalfano (374m).

The ancient town of *Solus* is thought to have replaced a Phoenician settlement in the vicinity of the same name (perhaps at Cozzo Cannita where traces of walls have been found), destroyed in 397 by Dionysius of Syracuse. It was built in the 4C BC on an interesting grid plan similar to the urban layout of some Hellenistic sites in Asia Minor. It fell to the Romans, who named it *Soluntum*, in 254 BC and had been abandoned by the beginning of the 3C AD. It was discovered in 1825 and still much of the site remains to be excavated.

The entrance is through a small MUSEUM with good plans of the site, and Hellenistic capitals, two female statues, architectural fragments, etc. A Roman road mounts the side of the hill past Via delle Terme (with remains of BATHS) and bends round to the right into the wide VIA DELL'AGORA. This, the main street, traverses the town to the cliff edge overlooking the sea; it is crossed at regular intervals by side streets with considerable remains of houses on the hillside above. Beyond Via Ciauri and Via Perez is the stepped Via Cavallaro on which are some of the columns and architrave of the so-called GYMNASIUM (restored in 1866), really a sumptuous house. This stretch of Via dell'Agora is beautifully paved in brick.

The next stepped road, Via Ippodamo di Mileto, links two small hills. Here on the slope of the hill above (right) is the so-called CASA DI LEDA on three levels. Above four small shops on Via dell'Agora, is an oblong cistern and courtyard off which are rooms with mosaic and tiled floors and traces of wall paintings. Farther up Via Ippodamo di Mileto are more interesting houses.

Farther on in Via dell'Agora, beyond a large SANCTUARY (on the corner of Via Salinas), the road widens out into the large AGORA with brick paving in front of nine rectangular exedrae along the back wall thought to have been used as shelters for the public. On the hillside above are traces of the THEATRE and a small BOULEUTERION probably used for council meetings. The hillside higher up may have been the site of the ACROPOLIS. Via dell'Agora next passes a huge public CISTERN, part of a complex system of storage tanks (many vestiges of which are still visible), made necessary by the lack of spring water in the area. On the edge of the cliff, in Via Bagnera is a small Roman villa with mosaics and wall paintings.

At the foot of the cliff lie several fishing villages amidst orange groves (although new building has taken place here in recent years). The view along the coast towards Cefalù, with the Aeolian Islands and Etna, is magnificent. In the foreground are the medieval castle of Solanto and the bay of Fondachello with the villas of Casteldaccia (famous for its wine) amid luxuriant vegetation on the slopes behind.

The return to Bagheria (9km) may be made by the picturesque coast road round Monte Catalfano. Beyond the delightful little fishing village of PORTICELLO (with an important fish market), it passes to landward of CAPO ZAFFERANO, an isolated crag of great geological interest, and for a while the road follows a ledge above the sea with sheer eroded rock above. On the cape grow dwarf palms, and (in spring) wild orchids. As the road rounds Capo Mongerbino to Aspra, the whole Gulf of Palermo comes into view.

E. Piana degli Albanesi

ROAD, 24km. BUSES ('Prestia & Comandè') several times a day from Via Balsamo and Piazza Stazione.

Palermo is left by Corso Pisani which starts from the SW corner of Piazza Indipendenza (Pl.13, 14). Beyond the ring-road, a fast road (partly on stilts) continues for Altofonte. At Villa Ciambra a byroad diverges left to avoid the incredibly steep and narrow main street of the grim little town of (11km) ALTOFONTE (350m). It takes its alternative name, Parco, from a former hunting-lodge of King Roger. The small Norman church was the oratory of his castle. Beyond the town the road traverses a ridge with pine woods (with views back of Palermo and the sea, and across the valley to Monreale). On the left of the road near some tall television masts is an obelisk commemorating Garibaldi (signposted; car-park), from which there is a fine view.

The road now follows the Vallone del Fico, beside the bare limestone hills at the foot of Monte Grifone. After a sharp right turn it descends through vineyards with views of oddly-shaped hills.

The road climbs again round the Pizzo dalla Moarda to (24km) **Piana degli Albanesi** (once *dei Greci*; 720m), the most interesting of the 15C Albanian colonies (6100 inhab.) in Sicily. The inhabitants still use their native tongue, are Catholics of the Byzantine-Greek rite, and wear traditional costume for weddings, etc. The most characteristic ceremonies take place at Easter and Epiphany. Here Garibaldi planned the tactics that led to the capture of Palermo. Piana is known for its excellent bread, cheeses, and 'cannoli'.

In the pleasant main steet, Via Giorgio Kastriota, is the cathedral church of SAN DEMETRIO (usually open 10–12.30). On the W wall is a 19C painting of St Nicholas by Andrea d'Antoni (a pupil of Giuseppe Patania). On the N wall of the church is a small Byzantine Madonna and Child. The statues are attributed to Nicolò Bagnasco, and the damaged apse frescoes are by Pietro Novelli. The iconostasis was decorated with paintings in 1975.

The main street leads uphill to the piazza beside the church of the MADONNA ODIGITRIA (usually closed), on a design by Pietro Novelli. Just out of the square is the church of SAN GIORGIO, the oldest church in the town built in 1495. On the S side is a mosaic by the local artist Tanina Cuccia (1984) and a painting of St Philip Neri by Giuseppe Patania. The iconostasis has 20C paintings. On the N side is a fresco of St Anthony Abbot by Antonio Novelli and a delightful equestrian statue of St George, fully armed. Other churches of interest include San Vito (18C, with statues) and Santissima Annunziata (with a fresco by Pietro Novelli).

At the lower end of the main street, a stable block (No. 207) has been converted into a library, cultural centre, and an interesting ETHNOGRAPHICAL MUSEUM, arranged by the local inhabitants in 1988 (open 9–13, Tues and Thurs also 15–19; Sat and fest. 9–13, 15–19). The delightful exhibits illustrate the peasant life of the community, and some of the traditional costumes (and 18C jewellery) worn by the women of Piana are preserved here.

A byroad leads S from Piana to the Portella della Ginestra (4km), where there is a memorial to the peasants killed here by Salvatore Giuliano in 1947. The main road continues SE of the town and passes near the LAGO DI PIANA DEGLI ALBANESI, a pretty reservoir formed in 1923 by an impressive dam between two high mountains (Kumeta and Maganoce, 1200m and

900m), across the Belice river. This road continues towards the beautiful Bosco della Ficuzza (23km), described in Rte 11B.

F. Ustica

Ustica is a pretty island of just over 8.5 square kilometres and 1100 inhabitants, which lies 58km NNW of Palermo. It is especially remarkable for its rocky shore and beautiful sea bed, much visited by skin-divers. The first marine reserve in Italy was established here in 1987.

Information Offices. 'Pro-Loco', Piazza Longo, Ustica (Tel. 091/8449190); Comune di Ustica, Tel. 091/8449190; 'APT di Palermo' (see Rte 1).

Maritime services. From Palermo daily boat in 2½hrs and daily hydrofoils in 1½hrs (more expensive). Information from 'Siremar', 120 Via Crispi, Palermo. Less frequent services from Naples and Civitavecchia.

Hotels. 3-star: 'Grotta Azzurra'; 2-star: 'Patrice', 'Stella Marina'. Also rooms to let.

The island is the summit of a huge submerged volcano: its highest hills rise to c 240m above sea level. The vegetation includes cultivated fields of wheat and low vineyards, as well as olives, almonds, and fruit trees, with hedges of prickly pear. It has interesting bird life. The name of Ustica from the Latin 'ustum' (burnt) is derived from the colour of its black volcanic rock. Excavations have proved that it was inhabited in prehistoric times and in the Roman era. It declined under the attacks of Barbary pirates who defeated all attempts to colonise it in the Middle Ages. In 1763 it was repopulated from the Aeolian Islands by the Bourbons who laid out the village round its port on geometric lines. For long used as a place of exile and as a prison, in the Fascist era the Rosselli brothers and Antonio Gramsci were held here as political prisoners. In September 1943 Italian and British officers met in secret on the island to discuss details of Italy's change of sides.

Above the little port is the Rocca della Falconiera (157m) built by the Bourbons on the site of a settlement of the 3C BC, also inhabited in Roman times. The Torre Santa Maria, once used as a prison, has been restored to house an Antiquarium. On the N tip of the island, at Faraglioni, are excavations of the biggest Prehistoric fortified village so far found on the island. On the west coast, from Punta di Megna to Punta Spalmatore is the RISERVA NATURALE MARINA, a protected area where fishing is prohibited and boats have to keep offshore. Swimming is allowed only at the N and S ends of the reserve (limited access). The Bourbon Torre della Spalmatore is used as the reserve headquarters. Just to the S, near the lighthouse at Punta Gavazzi, a buoy in the sea marks an underwater archaeological itinerary for skin-divers, with a number of finds from various wrecks left in situ. The island has numerous beautiful marine grottoes, notably the Grotta dell'Acqua and Grotta della Colonna near the port, where boats can be hired. A mini-bus service operates on the island, and donkeys may also be hired.

3

Palermo to Cefalù (and the Madonie mountains)

Road, N113, 67km.—14km Bagheria—37km **Termini Imerese**—49km Buonfornello (for **Himera**)—67km **Cefalù**.

The Palermo–Messina **Motorway** (A19, A20) runs parallel to this route with exits at Termini Imerese, Buonfornello (for Himera and Collesano), and Cefalù.

Railway. Train services c every hour from Palermo to Termini Imerese (in c 20 minutes) and to Cefalù (in 50 minutes) on the main Palermo–Messina line. BUS services run by 'SAIS' from Palermo (Via Balsamo) to Termini Imerese and (once a day) to Cefalù.

Information Office. 'APT' Palermo, Tel. 091/583887.

From Palermo to (14km) Bagheria and Solunto, see Rte 2D. Beyond (23km) Altavilla Milicia can be seen the prominent ruins of the Chiesazza, a church built by Robert Guiscard in 1077. At (33km) Trabia there is a well preserved castle on the shore.

37km **Termini Imerese** (27,000 inhab.; hotels) is situated on the slopes of a hill (113m), and divided into an upper and lower town. Much new building has taken place here in recent years.

Thermae Himerenses, of mythical origin, was captured by the Carthaginians after the sack of Himera (see below). The name is thought to have come from the two neighbouring Greek cities of Thermae and Himera; the inhabitants of the latter were settled in Thermae in the 5C BC. In 307 BC it was ruled by Agathocles (361–289), a native of the town and the most ferocious of the tyrants of Syracuse. Its most prosperous period followed the Roman conquest. Its thermal mineral waters were praised by Pindar.

The main approach passes (right) part of a Roman aqueduct. In the spacious piazza in the upper town the 17C CATHEDRAL (extensively restored in 1986) has four statues of 1504–06 in its modern front. Beneath the tower (right) is a fragment of a Roman cornice (in poor condition). It contains a sculpted Madonna del Ponte, by Ignazio Marabitti and a Crucifix, painted on both sides, by Pietro Ruzzolone (1484). In the chapel to the left of the choir are reliefs by Marabitti and Federico Siragusa. Beyond the 17C Palazzo Comunale is the MUSEO CIVICO (usually open 9–13.30 except Monday). It contains interesting archaeological material from Thermae and Himera, including lion-head waterspouts and ancient inscriptions. Other sections display 15C reliefs, paintings (including a small 14–15C altarpiece with St Christopher and other saints in Byzantine style), etc.

In Via Mazzini, to the W, are the CHIESA DEL MONTE (now an auditorium), burial place of local dignatories since the 16C (containing 16C and 17C Sicilian paintings; sometimes open in the afternoon), and SANTA MARIA DELLA MISERICORDIA (usually closed), with a *triptych (Madonna with Saints John and Michael), ascribed to Gaspare da Pesaro (1453). From the belvedere, behind the cathedral, there is a fine view of the coast. Viale Iannelli leads W to the church of SANTA CATERINA (often closed) whose frescoes of the life of the saint are probably by Nicolò and Giacomo Graffeo (15–16C; much damaged) of Termini. In the delightful public garden laid out in 1845, beyond, are fragments of a Roman curia (1C BC–1C AD), opposite which are the remains of an amphitheatre (1C AD). In the lower town are the Terme (the Grand Hotel here was begun in 1890 on a design by Giuseppe Damiani Almeyda), with some remains of the Roman baths.

A pretty road through olive groves leads up to **Caccamo** (8600 inhab.; 'Randazzo' bus services from Palermo and Termini Imerese), 10km S in a fine position in the mountains (521m), a little town of ancient origins, with steep narrow streets. The huge 12C *CASTLE, one of the major Norman strongholds on the island, several times restored, was the residence of the Duke of Caccamo until the beginning of this century. Extensive restoration work began in 1986; it is shown by the custodian (ring at the house on the main road opposite the war memorial, preferably at 12 and 16.30).

In the pretty small Piazza del Duomo (car parking) the DUOMO has a good 17C façade (ring if locked). Founded in 1090, it was altered in 1477 and 1614. St George features in a number of fine works of art which decorate the church (note the relief above the door by Gaspare Guercio, and the 15C triptych in the S aisle). The font and bas-relief of the Madonna with angels and saints are by Domenico Gagini and his workshop. Higher up in the town is the church of SANTISSIMA ANNUNZIATA, its Baroque façade flanked by two earlier towers. Inside is a carved 16C organ case. Beyond, SANTA MARIA DEGLI ANGELI (1497; ring at the convent) has a fine relief of the Madonna and Child over the door. Inside it preserves its original ceiling and a statue of the Madonna by Antonello Gagini. The church of SAN BENEDETTO ALLA BADIA (1615) has a majolica pavement and stuccoes by Giacomo and Precopio Serpotta.

The road descends from Termini and a huge industrial plant (partly abandoned) occupies the low coastal plain. Just before (49km) BUONFORNELLO (2-star camping site 'Himera'), on the bank of the Fiume Grande (or Imera Settentrionale) is the site of **Himera** (open daily 9am–two hours before sunset), with a conspicuous modern antiquarium on the hillside above the road. This was a colony of Zancle, founded in 648 BC and destroyed in 409 BC by Hannibal, nephew of Hamilcar. It was the home city of Stesichorus (born c 630 BC), the lyric poet, and the scene of a great defeat of the Carthaginians by Theron of Agrigento and Gelon of Syracuse (480 BC). On the right of the main road (just across the railway line) are the ruins of a DORIC TEMPLE, peripteral and hexastyle, probably built to celebrate the victory over the Carthaginians, and known as the 'Temple of Victory'. It measures 22m by 55m and had 14 columns at the sides and 6 in front. The cella had a pronaos and opisthodomus in antis. Only the lower part of the columns and part of the cella walls survive. It was discovered in 1823 and excavated by Pirro Marconi in 1929–30 when the splendid lion head water-spouts from the cornice were taken to the Archaeological Museum in Palermo.

Off the main road, just beyond, a byroad (left; signposted) leads up to the museum and the areas of the city excavated since 1963. The MUSEUM (open daily 9–16.30, 9–18 in summer) was opened in 1984 to house finds from the site while excavations continue. The material is well displayed and labelled in a building of strikingly modern design, and there are good plans etc. of the site. The first section displays finds from the temples in the sacred area on the hill top, including a votive deposit with fragments of metopes. The second section has material from the city and necropoli, including ceramics, architectural fragments, and votive statues. There is also a section devoted to finds from recent excavations in the surrounding territory, including Cefalù and Caltavuturo.

Just above the museum are excavations ('restored' in 1986) of part of the city. A path or rough road (keep right; the custodians of the Museum will act as guides) continues up to the plateau where a track (marked by two iron posts) leads past two little huts to the edge of the hill overlooking the plain towards the sea. Here is the AREA SACRA (surrounded by a fence) with a temenos enclosing the bases of an altar and four temples (7–5C BC). Another enclosure to the left contains traces of houses. The view extends along the coast as far as Solunto (Rte 2D). In the other direction the track leads away from the sea to more excavations of houses beside an olive grove. Three necropoli have been identified in the surrounding area. There are long-term plans to protect the extensive site in an archaeological park.

At Buonfornello the motorway (A19) from Palermo to Catania (207km) diverges S away from the coastal motorway (A20) for Messina. It runs through the centre of the island passing magnificent scenery via Enna (128km from Palermo), described in Rte 15. It also provides the fastest approach to the interesting little hill towns of Polizzi Generosa and Petralia Soprana and Sottana (reached from the 'Tre Monzelli' exit, 34km S of Buonfornello), in the Madonie mountains (see below).

67km **CEFALÙ** (14,500 inhab.), a picturesque little town with an old port, clustered beneath an isolated rock. It has a remarkable urban structure and one of the finest Norman churches in Sicily. In its well kept streets numerous buildings have recently been restored. Because of its excellent beaches Cefalù has become a resort in recent years and much new building has taken place on the outskirts.

Information Office. 'Azienda Autonoma', 77 Corso Ruggero (corner of Via Amendola), Tel. 0921/21050.

Railway Station, Via Gramsci, 500m SW of Corso Ruggero. Trains on the Palermo–Messina line c every hour from Palermo in 50 minutes.

Buses ('SAIS') from Palermo (once a day).

Car Parking in Piazza Colombo on the sea front (Corso Ruggero is closed to traffic).

Hotels. The nearest to the old centre are: 2-star: 'La Giara', 40 Via Veterani; 'Villa Belvedere', 13 Via dei Mulini; 'Delle Rose', Via Gibilmanna; 'Riva del Sole', 25 Viale Lungomare Colombo. 1-star: 'Locanda Cangelosi', Via Umberto I. Large modern 3-star hotels on the beaches to the W near Santa Lucia and E near Caldura, many with swimming pools and tennis courts, including 'Kalura' and 'Le Calette'.

Camping Sites on the coast W of the town at Contrada Ogliastrillo (3-star): 'Costa Ponente' and 'Sanfilippo'.

Numerous **Restaurants** all over the town. 1st-class: 'Osteria del Duomo', 5 Via Seminario; 'Kentia', 15 Via Nicola Botto; 'Osteria Magno', Via Amendola (also pizzeria). Trattorie and pizzerie: 'Da Nino' and 'Al Gabbiano-da Saro' on the Lungomare.

Cafés (with tables outside) in Piazza del Duomo.

Picnic places on the 'Rocca' hill above the town, on the bastion of Capo Marchiafava, or on the sea front near the port.

Hydrofoil services in summer to the Aeolian Islands (three times a week): information from the tourist office.

Annual Festival on 6 August (San Salvatore).

History. Founded at the end of the 5C or early 4C BC, its name *Cephaloedium* comes from the head-like shape of the rock which towers above. In 307 BC it was taken by Agathocles of Syracuse. In 857 it was conquered by the Arabs. In 1131 Roger II rebuilt the town on the sea, and constructed the magnificent cathedral which became head of a powerful bishopric.

Corso Ruggero (closed to traffic) leads through the little town. At the beginning on the right is the former hotel Barranco next to the sandstone façade of MARIA SANTISSIMA DELLA CATENA (1780; closed) preceded by a high portico with three statues. On the right of the facade are a few large blocks from the old walls (late 5C BC) on the site of the 'Porta Terra', the main entrance to the old town. The Corso continues past (right) Vicolo dei Saraceni (signposted for the 'Tempio di Diana') beyond which begins a path up to the Rocca (described below), and then runs slightly downhill. On the left is the restored OSTERIA MAGNO with a good 13C triple window high up on its façade and (in Via Amendola) windows decorated with black lava. On the left are a series of nine picturesque straight parallel streets which lead downhill to Corso Vittorio Emanuele with a view of the sea beyond. They were laid out by Roger II in 1130. The Corso continues past the tall plain façade of the 16C church of the Annunziata (closed). To the right opens the little piazza in front of the 15C church of the Purgatorio (formerly Santo Stefano Protomartire) with outside stairs and a decorative portal.

Beyond on the right opens the piazza with palm trees which slopes up to the ***Duomo**, a splendid edifice begun by Roger II in 1131, and intended as his burial place, but still unfinished at the time of his death in 1154. It was consecrated in 1166 by which time it was probably completed. It is in a particularly effective setting with the formidable cliff (or 'Rocca') rising immediately behind it. Excavations during restoration work have revealed Roman remains on this site. It is preceded by a raised terrace surrounded by a balustrade with statues (this gate is closed; entrance from the S door). The unusual FACADE is flanked by two massive towers with fine windows. Above the narthex built by Ambrogio da Como in 1471 can be seen a double row of blind arcades. The beautiful exterior of the S side and transept are visible from Via Passafiume. The building has been the object of controversial restorations in recent years.

The basilican INTERIOR (closed 12–15.30 or 16) has 16 ancient columns with Roman capitals supporting stilted Gothic arches. The open timber roof of the nave bears traces of painting (1263). The stained glass windows high up in the nave were installed in 1985–90. The crossing is approached through an arch borne by huge columns. The sanctuary is still being restored: the 15C painted Cross here is attributed to Tommaso de Vigilia.

The presytery is decorated with exquisite ***mosaics** carried out for Roger II in a careful decorative scheme, reflecting Greek models. They are the best preserved and perhaps the earliest of their kind in Sicily. The apse, vault, and possibly the lunettes of the side walls are thought to be the work of Greek craftsmen. In the apse is the splendid colossal figure of Christ Pantocrater holding an open book with the Greek and Latin biblical text from John 8:12 ('I am the Light of the world, he who follows me will not walk in darkness'). On the curved apse wall below are three tiers of figures: the Virgin in prayer between four archangels, and the Apostles in the two lower registers. In the vault are angels and seraphims. On the left wall of the presbytery are prophets, deacon martyrs, and Latin bishop saints, and on the right wall, prophets, warrior saints, and Greek patriarchs and theologians. These standing figures were probably carried out c 1164 by Greek or possibly local craftsmen.

The S aisle and lower walls of the sanctuary were 'restored' (i.e. stripped of their Baroque decoration) in the 1970s. In the chapel to the right of the sanctuary is a statue of the Madonna by Antonello Gagini. On the left pilaster of the sanctuary, high up in a niche, is a statue of the annunciatory angel (the Madonna and niche on the right pilaster have been removed). In the neo-classical chapel to the left of the sanctuary is an elaborate 18C silver altar. The redesigned marble and mosaic episcopal and royal thrones were dismantled in 1985, and the 12C font with lions has been removed.

From the N aisle is the entrance to the charming CLOISTER (closed indefinitely for restoration) which had three galleries of twin columns with charming capitals (including Noah's Ark and 'Trinacria' symbol) supporting Gothic arches. There is a fine view of the cathedral and the rock behind.

In Piazza del Duomo is Palazzo Maria, with medieval traces, and the 17C Oratorio del Santissimo Sacramento beside the neo-classical Palazzo Legambi. Opposite is Palazzo Vescovile (1793) next to the 17C Seminario Vescovile with a hanging garden. Opposite the Duomo is the huge ex-monastery of Santa Caterina restored and enlarged in the 18C and in 1857, and again undergoing a drastic restoration. Via Mandralisca leads down to the **Museo Mandralisca** (open daily 9–12.30, 15.30–18), the exterior of which is also being restored. The collection was founded by Enrico Pirajno, Baron Mandralisca (1809–64). On the ground floor is a mosaic from Cefalù (1C BC). Stairs lead up to ROOM 1 with a vase showing a vendor of tuna fish (4C BC) and a numismatic collection from the Greek period up to the last century (most of it recovered after a theft in 1989). ROOM 2 has Veneto-Cretan paintings and other 15–18C works. In Room 3 is the famous ***portrait of a man by Antonello da Messina** (c 1465–72), the jewel of the collection, and one of the most striking portraits in Sicily. The sarcophagus in the form of an Ionic temple dates from the 2C BC. ROOM 4 has archaeological material, including Italiot vases from Lipari (320–300 BC), and a well preserved kylix. Beyond ROOM 5 with a display of minerals, the last room (6) has Mandralisca's remarkable collection of c 20,000 shells.

The Corso continues down to end at Via Porpora which leads right to a restored square tower in a gap between the houses. Outside the tiny postern gate here can be seen a fine stretch of the megalithic walls (5C BC) built onto the rock. In the other direction Via Carlo Ortolani di Bordonaro leads past (right) Piazza Francesco Crispi with the church of the Madonna del Cammino. Here modern steps lead up to a 17C bastion (Capo Marchiafava) where a 14C fountain has been placed (good view). Via Ortolani continues down towards the sea and ends beside a terrace overlooking the little port, with picturesque old houses on the sea front.

From here Via Vittorio Emanuele leads back past the church of the Badiola (12–17C), recently restored next to its convent (the old portal survives on the corner of Via Porto Salvo). On the other side of the Corso the 16C Porta Pescara has a lovely Gothic arch through which can be seen the sea. Beyond, the Discesa Fiume with wide steps curving down past a few trees leads to a medieval LAVATOIO (restored in the 16C and in 1991), a public fountain. A spring famous since antiquity, it was converted into an Arab bath-house.

From Corso Ruggero and Vicolo dei Saraceni steps and a path lead up (in c 1 hour) to the ROCCA; the summit (278m) commands a fine view. Here the so-called 'Temple of Diana' has walls made out of huge polygonal blocks and a carved architrave over the entrance. It was probably a sacred edifice built in the 5–4C BC over an earlier cistern. Stretches of castellated walls can also be seen here as well as numerous cisterns and ovens. Virtually nothing remains of the castle where Charles of Salerno passed his imprisonment.

The **Madonie Mountains** are best visited from Cefalù. They lie between the Imera Settentrionale to the W and the Pollina river to the E. The Pizzo

Carbonara (1979m) is the second highest mountain on the island (after Etna). This area of some 40,000 hectares was at last protected as a nature reserve known as the PARCO NATURALE REGIONALE DELLE MADONIE in 1989. The vegetation in the upland plains and mountains includes beech trees, chestnuts, oaks, poplars, cork trees, and a rare species of fir, recently saved from extinction. Manna is still extracted from the bark of Manna ash trees around Pollina and Castelbuono. The area can also be approached from the Palermo–Catania motorway ('Tre Monzelli' exit, 34km S of Buonfornello, see above). Marked trails provide beautiful excursions for walkers, riders, and cyclists with mountain bikes. An unattractive ski resort has been built at Piano Battaglia. Information about the park from the 'APT' of Palermo (see Rte 1), 'CAI' (Club Alpino Italiano), 30 Via Agrigento, Palermo, or the 'Ente Parco' at Petralia Sottana.

The 17C SANTUARIO DI GIBILMANNA, 14km S of Cefalù in a beautiful position on the tree-clad slopes of the Pizzo Sant' Angelo (2-star hotel 'Bel Soggiorno'), is a centre of pilgrimage, especially on 8 September. The vegetation includes olives, cork trees, pinewoods, and chestnut trees. On the nearby Cozzo Timpa Rossa (1006m) stands the observatory (1952) of the Istituto Nazionale di Geofisica.

FROM CEFALÙ TO COLLESANO, PIANO BATTAGLIA, PETRALIA SOTTANA AND SOPRANA, AND POLIZZI GENEROSA, 90km. The road runs W along the coast to (14.5km) Campofelice di Roccella and then S (passing the restaurant 'Mari e Monti' in Contrada Pizzillo) across the mountains to (27km) **Collesano**. This little medieval town (4600 inhab.) has several interesting churches including the Duomo which contains a painted Crucifix of 1555, a fine carved tabernacle of 1489 by Donatello Gagini, and a Madonna with angels by Zoppo di Ganci. In Santa Maria la Vecchia is a statue of the Madonna by Antonello Gagini. From Collesano there is a direct road S to Polizzi Generosa (25km), see below. At (32.5km) MUNCIARRATI a road climbs S to the wooded plateaux of Piano Zucchi (1085m) and the ski grounds of (48km) PIANO BATTAGLIA (1646m; youth hostel and alpine refuges), lying below the Pizzo della Principessa (1975m), one of the highest of the range.

An ugly modern road on stilts continues to (73km) **Petralia Sottana** (3800 inhab.; 1-star hotel 'Madonie', 81 Corso Paolo Agliata) on a hillside (1000m) enclosed by the Madonie mountains. The attractive Corso Paolo Agliata passes Santa Maria della Fontana (16–17C) and the 18C church of San Francesco before reaching Piazza Umberto I (with a view of the Imera valley). The Chiesa Madre, with a pretty campanile, was rebuilt in the 17C. It contains a fine sculpted altarpiece of 1501, and a 17C statue of the Madonna and Child.

The road for Petralia Soprana continues uphill past the church and convent of the Santissima Trinità (being restored) with a marble ancona by Gian Domenico Gagini (1542) and traverses pine woods before emerging on a hillside with a view of **Petralia Soprana**, one of the most interesting and best preserved little towns in the interior of the island, in a beautiful position (1147m). *Petra* was important in the Roman era, and in 1062 it passed into the hands of Count Roger. One rock-salt mine survives here. The exteriors of the attractive old stone houses have not been covered with plaster as in numerous other Sicilian towns.

In the central Piazza del Popolo is a large war memorial by Antonio Ugo (1929) and the neo-Gothic town hall (1896). Via Generale Medici leads up past (left) the fine façade of San Giovanni Evangelista (1770; closed) to Piazza Fra Umile with a bust commemorating Fra Umile da Petralia (Pintorno: 1588–1639), the sculptor who was born here. On the right is the 18C Oratorio delle Anime del Purgatorio with a bellcote and very worn portal. Further up is Piazza dei Quattro Cannoli with a pretty 18C fountain and palace.

Beyond on the right a wide flight of steps leads down to the DUOMO, consecrated in 1497, with a delightful 18C portico (recently restored). At one end is a squat tower and at the other is the 15C campanile with a two-light window in which have been placed two quaint statues of St Peter and St Paul. The gilded and white stucco decoration in the interior was carried out in 1859. On the N side the first altar has a fine painted statue of the Madonna and Child, and the fourth altar a marble statue of the Madonna (della Catena). The fifth altar has a high relief of the Pietà with symbols of the Passion. In the chapel to the left of the sanctuary is an 18C gilded wood altarpiece. The realistic Crucifix in the sanctuary is the first work of Fra Umile da Petralia (c 1624). The polychrome statues of St Peter and St Paul are by the Neapolitan sculptor Gaetano Franzese (1764), and the large painting of their martyrdom is by Vincenzo Riolo. On the fifth altar on the S side is a beautiful *Deposition, attributed since its recent restoration to Pietro Novelli or the school of Ribera. Above the Duomo is the 18C domed circular church of SANTISSIMO SALVATORE (closed) built on the site of a Norman church. It contains 17–18C statues.

From the other side of Piazza del Popolo (see above) Via Loreto leads uphill past a pretty courtyard, several nice small palaces, and the 16C church of San Michele (recently restored) with a miniature bellcote and fountain on its W front. The street ends in the charming piazza (paved with pebbles) in front of the handsome façade of SANTA MARIA DI LORETO (being restored). The façade of 1750 is by two local sculptors named Serpotta and the two little spires on either side are decorated with coloured stones. It is preceded by a wrought iron gate of 1881. The beautiful interior has a carved high altarpiece attributed to Gian Domencio Gagini or Antonio Vanello (with a Madonna attributed to Giacomo Mancini). It also contains paintings by Vincenzo Riolo, 18–19C statues, and a delightful sacristy of 1783. On the right a lane (Via Belvedere) leads out under an arch to a terrace beside the apse of the church, with a splendid view which takes in Etna on a clear day.

On the edge of the hill, below Corso Umberto, is the church of SAN TEODORO (closed) founded by Count Roger and rebuilt in 1759. Here in 1991 was discovered an interesting sarcophagus decorated with animal carvings.

From Petralia Sottana N120 continues E across the mountains. At Bivio Geraci a byroad (N286) leads N to GERACI SICULO (1077m), with a ruined castle (1072), the seat of the Ventimiglia before they moved to Castelbuono, to which the road continues (described below). The church of Santa Maria della Porta contains a Madonna and Child by Domenico Gagini and his workshop (1475). The main road continues to GANGI, the birthplace of Giuseppe Salerno, known as 'Lo Zoppo di Ganci', whose Last Judgement adorns the church. Attached to the castle is a Renaissance chapel attributed to the Gagini family (early 16C). Here the 'Queen of Gangi', a famous leader of the Mafia, was arrested by the government of Mussolini. The road continues along the Sperlinga valley, closely shut in by hills. Sperlinga, in the province of Enna, is described in Rte 16.

17km W of Petralia Sottana (reached by N20 and a turning right) is **Polizzi Generosa** (917m), beautifully situated at the head of the Imera valley, with the Madonie mountains behind. It is a delightful little town which received its name 'Generosa' from Frederick II in 1234. It once boasted 76 churches within its walls, and many of them now belong to local confraternities (who have the keys).

Information from the 'Vigili Urbani' in Piazza Umberto. 'Agriturist' **accommodation**: 'Il Pavone', Contrada San Nicola; 'La Sorgente di Iside', Contrada Chiaretta; 'La Ginestra', Contrada Santa Venera. 1st-class **restaurant** 'Itria', 3 Via Itria; **pizzeria** 'Il Pioniere'. **Bus services** run by 'SAIS' four times a day from Palermo (in 1hr 15 mins) and twice a day from Cefalù. Annual **festivals** include San Gandolfo (in May), a hazelnut fair in September, and 26 December when a huge bonfire is lit in front of the ruined church of La Commenda.

From the small Piazza Umberto, where all the main roads converge, Via Cardinale Rampolla (with pretty stone and brick paving) leads up to the **Chiesa Madre** with a charming 16C porch and two very worn statues of St Peter and St Paul. A Gothic portal has been exposed beside the Renaissance doorway. In the S aisle is a painting of the Madonna of the Rosary by Zoppo di Ganci. At the end of the aisle, a chapel on the right (closed by a grille) contains some fine *sculptures, including the sarcophagus of Beato Gandolfo da Binasco (recomposed) by Domenico Gagini; reliefs by the Berrettaro family, and a fragment of the Last Supper by Domenico Gagini and his workshop. In the sanctuary are two precious large triptychs: the one on the right with the Madonna enthroned amidst angels is attributed to the 'Maitre au feuillage en broderie' (early 16C), and the one on the left (with the Visitation) dates from the 16C. In the Cappella Ventimiglia (left of the sanctuary) are interesting funerary monuments and in the left transept are 18C statues. The font (with a pagan base) at the W end dates from 1488. The decorative organ was made in the 18C. Beside the Duomo is SAN GANDOLFO LA POVERA (1622) with a high altarpiece of St Gandolfo by Zoppo di Ganci.

The road continues up to the church of SAN FRANCESCO, founded in 1303, now used as an auditorium. On the left opens Piazza Castello with the ruins of the so-called castle of the Regina Bianca. In the walled garden here two rare fir trees (of the Nebrodi type) survive. A little museum (open on Sunday) in the piazza illustrates the natural history of the Madonie mountains. Below San Francesco is the church of SAN NICOLÒ DE FRANCHIS (locked) founded in 1167 by Peter of Tolouse, with a bellcote. Nearby is SANTA MARGHERITA (or the Badia Vecchia), a 15C church (being restored). It has delicate white and gold stucco decoration and a pretty W end. The barrel vault and sanctuary have 19C pictorial decorations, including a copy of Leonardo's Last Supper.

Another road from Piazza Umberto leads up to remains of the circular 'Torre di Leo' named after a family who purchased it in 1240 next to the church of SAN PANCRAZIO DEI GRECI (locked), recently restored, which contains a painting by Zoppo di Ganci. From its terrace (when the gate is open) there is a wonderful view of the mountains.

The main street of the little town, Corso Garibaldi, also starts in Piazza Umberto. It leads past the centrally-planned church of SAN GIROLAMO (deconsecrated and kept locked) by Angelo Italia with an amusing doorway. Next to it is the ex-COLLEGIO DEI GESUITI, a large building now occupied by the town hall and prefecture. The fine interior courtyard with loggias on two levels and a single balcony on the top storey has recently been restored. In the morning visitors are allowed up to the top storey where an open balcony has a fine view over the rooves of the town (and the ruined church of the Commenda below). The Corso continues past a flight of steps (right) which lead up to the large PALAZZO CARPINELLO with a long low façade. The Corso ends at a terrace known as the BELVEDERE with a magnificent view: the motorway from Palermo to Catania is reduced to a winding stream in the distant valley below, while to the E rise the Madonie mountains. The ancient church of SANTA MARIA LO PIANO here, seat of the Teutonic Knights, contains 17C paintings. Via Malatacca leads down from the Corso towards SANT'ANTONIO ABATE (closed) with a red Arabic dome crowning its campanile (once a mineret). Inside is another painting by Zoppo di Ganci. The old Arab district here has interesting one-storey houses.

The main road (N120) continues W and crosses the Palermo–Catania motorway at the 'Tre Monzelli' exit and then ascends through cultivated uplands N to **Caltavuturo** (635m), a 16C town with stepped streets. It lies in a superb position beneath outcrops of red rock and the ruined fortress taken from the Saracens by Roger I. High above (left) on a precipitous crag (813m) is the fortress-village of SCLAFANI. The road crosses the Salito and then climbs over the Portella di Cascio (401m) with a wide panorama of the Madonie mountains. Up until the 1970s this formed part of the 72km circuit used for the 'Targa Florio' motor race, first run in 1906. N 120 now descends to join the coast road (N113), 10 km E of Termini Imerese (see above).

Another approach to the Madonie is via Castelbuono. From Cefalù N113 continues along the coast towards Messina. Behind the headland of Cefalù there is a view of the promontory of La Kalura, with extraordinary rock formations. The road skirts the sea, crossing and recrossing the railway. 9km, turning for Castelbuono. The road goes beneath the incredibly high motorway viaduct under construction to complete this stretch of the Palermo-Messina motorway. It continues up a wooded valley to (23km) **Castelbuono**, a little town (9900 inhab.) in the Madonie (423m), the former seat of the Ventimiglia princes of Geraci. (2-star hotel 'Villaggio dei Fauni' in località San Guglielmo; 'Francesco Crispi' refuge in località Piano Sempria).

The road leads up past a 16C fountain with a statue of Venus to Piazza Margherita, with a fountain. Here the MATRICE VECCHIA of 1350 is preceded by a loggia. It contains a marble ciborium attributed to Giorgio da Milano (late 15C), a huge polyptych attributed to Pietro Ruzzolone, and statues and frescoes of the 16C. A 15C Crucifix has recently been restored. Also in the piazza is a building owned by the Ventimiglia in the 14–16C and used as a prison from the 18C up to 1965. A MUSEUM (open daily 9–13, 15–19) was arranged here in 1989 and named after the naturalist Francesco Minà Palumbo (1814–99), a native of Castelbuono. It contains a display illustrating the extraction of manna (used for medicinal purposes) from the trunks of Manna ash trees in the Madonie (a local industry which survives here). There is also an archaeological section (Prehistoric finds) and examples of glass produced here from the late 16C to the end of the 18C. A road continues uphill past the town hall to the CASTLE (open daily 9–13, 15–19) built by the Ventimiglia in 1316. Off the courtyard (being restored) is a chapel with white stuccoed putti on a gold ground by the school of Serpotta (1683). Behind the castle the terrace has a view of the Madonie and the little hill town of Geraci Siculo.

From the Matrice Vecchia a road (signposted) leads up to a piazza with palm trees and a memorial surrounded by cannon used in the First World

War. Here is the MATRICE NUOVA begun at the beginning of the 17C (and rebuilt in 1830). It contains a painted Cross attributed to Pietro Ruzzolone, stucco altars, and a 16C triptych. There are good tombs in the Ventimiglia chapel in the church of SAN FRANCESCO (reached by the road which leads up to the right of the Matrice Nuova). Sant'Antonio has a fine portal.

The road continues S across the Madonie to Geraci Siculo (see above).

Another byroad off N113, 14km E of Cefalù, leads up to the hill town of POLLINA (730m) where the church has works by Antonello Gagini. A theatre was built on the hillside here in 1979.

The coast road (N113) between Cefalù and Messina is described in Rte 29.

4

Palermo to Trapani and Erice

A. Via Segesta

Road, N186 and 113, 96km.—8km **Monreale**—28.5km Partinico—45km **Alcamo**—60km **Segesta**—62.5km Calatafimi—96km **Trapani**.

Motorway, A29 and A29 dir., 107km. A29 follows the coast (see Rte 4B), and at 24km diverges left from the Punta Raisi motorway. At 66km, A29 dir. leaves the A29 motorway (which continues S for Mazara del Vallo), passes directly below the temple of **Segesta** (exit at 75km), and continues into (107km) **Trapani**.

Railway, 126km in c 2hrs. To 'Alcamo diramazione', 79km in 1hr 15mins–2hrs; to 'Segesta Tempio', 94km in 1hr 40mins (1 train a day; the station is 20 minutes' walk from the temple). Frequent direct **Buses** ('Segesta') to Trapani via the motorway in 2½hrs.

Information Offices. From Palermo to Partinico, 'APT' Palermo (Tel. 091/583887), and from Alcamo to Trapani, 'APT' Trapani (Tel. 0923/27273).

Palermo is left by Corso Calatafimi (Pl.13) and the road passes below (8km) **Monreale** (described in Rte 2B). Beyond the long steep high street of Pioppo it climbs to 531m, and takes a sharp turn right to enter the barren Nocella valley, where the scenery is at once much prettier and there are fewer houses. The road emerges above the plain of Partinico with a fine view of the sea coast. The realigned road passes above (26km) Borgetto, with its church towers capped with tiles. To the W the coastline ends in Capo San Vito.

28.5km **Partinico** (bypass; 29,500 inhab.), an agricultural town. Here Danilo Dolci, a man deeply involved in the plight of Sicily's poverty-striken, moved in 1955 to found his principal centre (known as Mirto, a remarkable local school). In Piazza Duomo is a fountain of 1716. The Biblioteca Comunale nearby has an archaeological collection (unlocked on request) with finds from Monte Iato and Rocca d'Entella, and a local ethnographical collection. From the Duomo Corso dei Mille leads to a neo-classical bandstand (1875) near the 17C church of San Leonardo (being restored) with works by the school of Novelli. Opposite is the church of the Carmine (1634).

In the hill town of MONTELEPRE (trattoria 'Monte d'Oro'), where much ugly new building has taken place, 8km NE, the bandit Salvatore Giuliano 'reigned' for seven years before he was caught and killed in 1950 at the age of 27. A road leads S from Partinico past the Lago di Poma formed by the Iato dam to (17km) SAN CIPIRELLO. The dam built at the instigation of Danilo Dolci, and run by a local cooperative greatly improved the agriculture in the area. Here, on Monte Iato, recent excavations (open to visitors in summer) have brought to light remains of the ancient city of **Jetae** (the Roman *Iaitas*), a town which flourished from the 4C BC until it was destroyed by Frederick II in the 13C. The best preserved remains date from the Hellenistic period and include a theatre, a temple, and a large villa on two floors with a peristyle and 25 rooms. The agora has also been partially uncovered. The site is being excavated by the University of Zürich. In the town the Museo Civico (usually open 9–13) contains finds from the site including statues.

At the complicated intersection outside Partinico the road bears left (signposted to Alcamo). It traverses a flat cultivated plain and soon enters the province of Trapani. Alcamo, approached on a new road which negotiates the low hills by viaduct and tunnel (unlit), is well seen ahead on a low ridge.

45km **Alcamo** is an agricultural town (43,200 inhab.; 1-star hotel 'Miramare'), with numerous fine 18C churches. Founded at the end of the 10C, it derives its name from the Arab 'Alqamah'. It was the birthplace of the 13C poet Cielo or Ciullo, one of the earliest masters of Italian literature. In Piazza Bagolino (car park) the terrace has a panorama of the plain stretching towards the sea. Beyond the 16C Porta San Francesco (or Porta Palermo; being restored) Corso VI Aprile leads into the town. On the left is the church of SAN FRANCESCO D'ASSISI, founded in 1348 and rebuilt in 1716. It contains a beautiful marble altarpiece attributed to Giacomo Gagini (1568), statues of St Mark and Mary Magdalene by Antonello Gagini, and a 17C painting of the Immacolata by Giuseppe Carrera. The Corso continues past the ex-church of San Tommaso (c 1450) with a carved Gothic portal. Opposite, next to a convent, is the church of SANTI COSMA E DAMIANO (closed), a domed centrally planned building of c 1721 by Giuseppe Mariani. It contains two stucco statues by Giacomo Serpotta and two altarpieces by Guglielmo Borremans.

The Corso crosses Via Rossotti with a view left of the castle and right of San Salvatore. The well-preserved CASTELLO DEI CONTI DI MODICA was built c 1350. On a square plan with four towers, it is being restored and a local ethnographical museum is to be opened here. SAN SALVATORE stands next to the monastery of the Badia Grande. It contains allegorical statues by Bartolomeo Sanseverino (1758), a follower of Serpotta. The vault fresco and high altarpiece are by Carlo Brunetti (1759–60). The statue of St Benedict is by Antonino Gagini (1545). Nearby is the church of the Annunziata, a Catalan-Gothic building in ruins (without a roof).

The Corso continues past the ex-church of the Madonna del Soccorso (15C; being restored) with a portal attributed to Bartolomeo Berrettaro to the CHIESA MADRE. Founded in 1332, it was rebuilt in 1669 by Angelo Italia and Giuseppe Diamante, with a fine dome. In the interior are columns of red marble quarried on Monte Bonifato. The frescoes in the vault, cupola and apse are by Guglielmo Borremans. South side: second chapel, Crucifix by Antonello Gagini (1523); fourth chapel, late 16C sarcophagus with portraits of two members of the De Ballis family; fifth chapel, marble relief by Antonello Gagini. In the chapel to the right of the choir, Last Supper by Giuseppe Carrera (1613). In the adjoining chapel (right) are two fine Gothic arches and a beautiful fresco fragment of the Pentecost (1430). In the chapel to the left of the choir, Lorenzo Curti, wood statue of the Madonna (1721). On the altar of the N transept, statue of St Peter by Giacomo Gagini (1556). The inner door of the sacristy (beyond the wood door in the N aisle) is decorated with carvings of fruit attributed to Bartolomeo Berrettaro. North side: third chapel, high relief of the Transition of the Virgin by Antonello Gagini; first chapel, painting of the Madonna by Giuseppe Renda (late 18C). Opposite the Chiesa Madre is the ex-church of San Nicolò di Bari with a fine portal of 1563.

The Corso continues to Piazza Ciullo, the centre of the town. On the corner is SANT'OLIVA, built by Giovanni Biagio Amico in 1724. It was restored in 1990 after a fire in 1987 destroyed the 18C frescoes and stuccoes in the vault of the nave. The lovely interior has altars beautifully decorated with marble. On the fourth S altar is a statue of *St Oliva by Antonello Gagini (1511). The high altarpiece is by Pietro Novelli and on the left wall is a marble tabernacle by Luigi di Battista (1552). On the N side are 18C statues and a marble group fo the Annunciation by Antonino and Giacomo Gagini (1545). The CHIESA DEL COLLEGIO (1684–1767) has a theatrical façade on Piazza Ciullo. It contains 18C stuccoes and altarpieces. Corso VI Aprile continues from Piazza Ciullo past 18C and neo-classical palaces to the church of SANTI PAOLO E BARTOLOMEO (1689) with a splendid interior decorated by Vincenzo and Gabriele Messina and Antonino lo Grano. The oval Madonna del Miele dates from the end of the 14C or beginning of the 15C.

In Via Amendola is the church of the ROSARIO (SAN DOMENICO) which contains a fresco attributed to Tommaso de Vigilia. Beyond the castle (see above) and the large Piazza della Repubblica is the church of SANTA MARIA DEL GESÙ (1762). Beneath the portico is a portal attributed to Bartolomeo Berrettaro (1507). It contains a 16C altarpiece of the Madonna and saints with the counts of Modica, and a statue of the Madonna and Child attributed to Bartolomeo Berrettaro or Giuliano Mancino. In Via Caruso is the BADIA NUOVA (or San Francesco di Paola) rebuilt in 1699 by Giovanni Biagio Amico. The pretty interior has stucco statues by Giacomo Serpotta and an altarpiece of St Benedict by Pietro Novelli.

On MONTE BONIFATO (825m), 2km S of the town, planted with conifers and pine trees, is a ruined Norman castle of the Ventimiglia with the chapel of the Madonna dell'Alto (*view). The medieval 'Fontanazza' here is a huge reservoir or thermal edifice.

The road descends from Alcamo through vineyards into the valley of the Fiume Freddo. The attractive landscape with vineyards has been spoiled by the intrusion of the motorways (raised on stilts) from Palermo to Trapani and to Mazara del Vallo. The pretty viaducts of the railway offer a striking contrast in scale. As the road begins to curve it passes some lovely old farmhouses and pine, eucalyptus and olive trees. There is a distant view of the temple of Segesta (its site now marred by two motorway tunnels directly below the eminence on which it stands) and the sustaining wall of the theatre on the skyline of Monte Barbaro.

60km, turning right for the temple and theatre of **SEGESTA** (3km), two of the most splendidly sited classical monuments in existence. From the old road, the view of the famous temple on a bare hill in deserted countryside backed by the rolling hills W of the Gaggera is unforgettable. It has been admired by travellers for centuries. The theatre is on a second, higher hill to the E.

The site has recently been enclosed (open daily 9–dusk). 'Segesta Tempio' station (for train services, see the beginning of this route) is 20 minutes' walk from the temple. A small café is usually open (except for two hours at mid-day). A classical drama festival is held in the theatre every two years.

Segesta, also origially known as *Egesta*, was the principal city of the Elymians, who are now thought to have come from the eastern Mediterranean, probably Anatolia. It was rapidly Hellenised, and was in continual warfare with Selinunte from 580 onwards. Its mint was one of the most important on the island. It sought the alliance of Athens in 426. After the destruction of Selinunte in 409 Segesta became a subject-ally of Carthage, and was saved by Himilco (397) from the attacks of Dionysius of Syracuse. In 307, however, Agathocles sacked the city, and changed its name to 'Dikoeopolis'. It resumed its old name under the protection of Carthage, but treacherously murdered the Carthaginian garrison during the First Punic War, after which it became the first city in Sicily to ally itself to Rome. It declined during the Arab period and was then abandoned.

The ancient city which covered the slopes of Monte Barbaro is still largely unexcavated, and the site of the necropolis has not yet been identified. Sporadic excavations have taken place since the end of the 18C, when the temple was first restored. The theatre was excavated in 1822. The important sanctuary at the foot of Monte Barbaro was discovered in 1950.

From the car-park a path (flanked by two posts on which the Fascist symbol survives) and steps lead up past agave plants to the **Temple** splendidly sited on a low hill (304m) on the edge of a deep ravine formed by the Pispisa river, across which is a hillside covered with pine woods. It is one of the grandest existing monuments of Doric architecture, and since it has no cella, scholars are still in doubt whether it represents an unfinished temple or was instead an open peristyle used by a cult. It is thought to have been constructed by a Greek architect c 424–416 BC. It is peripteral and hexastyle with 36 unfluted columns (c 9m high, 2m wide at base) on a stylobate 58m by 23m. The high entablature and the pediments are intact. The bosses used for manoeuvring the blocks of the stylobate into position remain. Refinements include the curvature of the entablature and the abaci. The building is inhabited by birds, but the sound of the motorway now disturbs this wonderfully romantic spot.

From the car-park a road (1km; closed to cars; shuttle bus every half hour) climbs up Monte Barbaro to the theatre. A prettier and more interesting approach (with spectacular views back down the hill of the temple) is by the path which roughly follows the road (a steep climb of 20–30 minutes). At the foot of the hill can be seen conspicuous excavations of part of the walls (and gate) of the ancient city. Above a sheepfold, yellow signs mark various excavations including an upper line of walls (2C BC) and a cave dwelling (reused in Roman times; protected by a wood roof). Beside the car park near the top of the hill are two enclosures, the higher one has remains of medieval houses built over public buildings from the Hellenistic era and the lower one has a monumental Hellenistic edifice, reconstructed in the Roman period. A path continues towards the theatre with a splendid view of the temple below. On the right is an enclosure with a ruined church (12–15C), and on the summit of the hill remains of a 12–13C castle.

The **Theatre** is in a wonderful position near the summit of Monte Barbaro (415m). It looks towards the gulf of Castellammare beyond Monte Inici (1064m), while inland to the E rise more high mountain ranges. It is one of the best preserved ancient theatres in existence, built in the mid 3C BC or

Temple of Segesta

possibly earlier. With a diameter of 63m and two rows of seats, it could hold 3200 spectators. The exterior of the cavea was supported by a high polygonal wall, which is particularly well preserved at the two sides. Beneath the cavea a grotto with late Bronze Age finds was discovered in 1927 by Pirro Marconi. The theatre has been damaged by the sight and sound of the motorway in the valley below.

In Contrada Mango at the foot of Monte Barbaro to the E near the Gaggera river is a large Archaic SANCTUARY (not fully excavated), of great importance. The temenos measures 83m x 47m. It is thought to date from the 7C BC. A huge deposit of pottery sherds dumped from the town on the hill above has also come to light here. The rough footpath (c 3km) is no longer practicable.

The road passes below (62.5km) CALATAFIMI (left; 8400 inhab.), damaged in the earthquake of 1968 (see below). The town was frequently visited by Samuel Butler in 1893–1900, author of 'Erewhon', who travelled much in Southern Italy. 2km SW (signposted 'Pianto Romano', off N113) an obelisk commemorates Garibaldi's victory here on 15 May 1860. A cypress avenue leads to the monument by Ernesto Basile (1892) on which are inscribed Garibaldi's words on reaching the hill after his disembarkation from Marsala ('Qui si fa l'Italia o si muore'). There are fine views from the hilltop. N113 turns NW in full view of the imposing Monte San Giuliano, with Erice on its summit.

65km, turning for Salemi, 12.5km S in the Valle del Belice, described in Rte 9. The road from Castellammare is joined on the outskirts of (96km) **Trapani** (described in Rte 5).

B. Via the coast

Road, N113 and 187, 102km.—16.5km Isola delle Femmine—67km **Castellammare del Golfo** (Scopello, 10km, Riserva Naturale dello Zingaro, 12km)—90.5km, turning for **San Vito lo Capo** (24km)—104km **Trapani**.

Motorway, and **Railway**, see Rte 5A.

Information Offices. From Palermo to Trappeto, 'APT' Palermo (Tel. 091/583887); from Castellammare del Golfo to Trapani, 'APT' Trapani (Tel. 0923/27273).

Palermo is left through its N suburbs and the Parco della Favorita (see atlas p 16). The road passes between Monte Pellegrino and Monte Castellaccio in the Piana dei Colli, described in Rte 1F. Just before the road reaches the sea at (13km) Sferracavallo the motorway to Punta Raisi Airport (which runs parallel to N113) diverges left. This route skirts the small bay overshadowed by the beautiful headland of CAPO GALLO, rising (527m) vertically from the sea (and now a protected area). It turns W along the coast to (16.5km) ISOLA DELLE FEMMINE, facing an island of the same name. It is now surrounded by an industrial zone which has polluted the sea, and hampered its development as a tourist resort (3- and 2-star hotels). 24km CARINI (20,500 inhab.; 3- and 2-star hotels), which gives its name to the gulf the road now skirts, lies 4km S. It has interesting stalactite caverns. Its fine 16C castle has been acquired by the state in an attempt to save it from ruin.

The road rounds the base of Monte Pecoraro (910m) before reaching TERRASINI, with a huge holiday centre. Here the Museo Civico is divided into three sections: a natural history museum (with an important ornithological collection) at No. 4 Via Calarossa; an archaeological section in the town hall, and a large collection of Sicilian carts in Via Roma. The lovely gulf of Castellammare comes into view which stretches away to Capo San Vito, with a striking background of mountains. Despite a lot of new building it still has olive groves and plantations of orange trees. 49km Trappeto, the village where Danilo Dolci (see Rte 4A) founded his 'Borgo di Dio' in 1952. Just before Alcamo Marina, where the road enters the province of Trapani, the picturesque medieval castle of Calatubo stands prominent on an isolated hill to the S (well seen from the motorway).

67km **Castellammare del Golfo**, a port (14,500 inhab.; 3-star hotel 'Al Madarig', 7 Piazza Petrolo; trattoria 'Da Totò', 7 Corso Mattarella) important for its tuna fisheries in the Middle Ages. It was notorious for its Mafia connections in the 1960s and 1970s. The old centre has a particularly interesting plan with numerous long straight parallel streets sloping down at an angle to the sea. The 18C Chiesa Madre has a 17C majolica statue of the Madonna. The 14C castle (signposted), at the end of the promontory, is approached over a narrow bridge with a view of the port on the left. A road (signposted 'Porto Turistico') descends to the harbour at the foot of the castle headland, with its colourful houses and boats, and a number of trattorie. On the other side of the cape, the seaboard has been planted with palm trees.

FROM CASTELLAMMARE DEL GOLFO TO SCOPELLO AND THE RISERVA NATURALE DELLO ZINGARO, 14km. The road (signposted 'Scopello') diverges right from the Trapani road just outside Castellammare. Paths lead down to Cala Bianca, Cala Rossa, and Baia Guidaloca, beautiful bays on the rocky coast, where the sea is particularly transparent. The narrow road then skirts the sea with a pebbly beach and a few pizzerie near a defensive tower (3-star and 2-star camping sites). The road then becomes wider and climbs uphill past some unattractive new houses, with a view ahead of hills. At a fork, the left-hand road ends at **Scopello** (10km), a tiny picturesque village (1-star hotels 'Torre Bennistra', 'Tranchina' and 'la Tavernetta', with cafés and restaurants). From the little piazza (with a large drinking trough) an archway leads into the old paved courtyard with a few trees of an 18C *'baglio' surrounded by one storey houses.

From below the village the right-hand fork of the road continues along the coast above the ***Tonnara di Scopello** an important tuna fishery from the 13C up to the middle of this century. It is well seen on the sea below the road, beside fantastically shaped rocks on which are ruined defensive towers. The buildings have been beautifully preserved (now private property, but visitors are welcome from 9–19). A footpath leads down to the sea front where hundreds of anchors are piled up beside the picturesque old buildings and a little cove. The life of the fishermen here was vividly described by Gavin Maxwell in 'The Ten Pains of Death' (1959).

The coast road continues for another 2km past some unattractive holiday houses and ends at the S entrance to the ***Riserva Naturale dello Zingaro**, a nature reserve (open daily: car-park; information office at Scopello, Tel. 0924/596100), the first of its kind in Sicily. Local protest in 1981 succeeded in blocking the construction of a road here which was begun in 1976 and was to have connected Castellammare to San Vito lo Capo, and open up the area to development. Now these 7km of unspoilt coastline can be explored on foot along marked paths (no cars are allowed). The well preserved landscape is particularly beautiful, and interesting for its bird life. A museum is open (9–16 in winter, and 8–21 in summer) illustrating the peasant life of the area. Swimming is allowed. The Grotta dell'Uzzo, also in the reserve, was inhabited in the Paleolithic era. There is another entrance to the park on its N border, approached by the road from San Vito lo Capo, see below.

The main road from Castellammare to Trapani (N187) continues across the base of the peninsula of San Vito Lo Capo, passing S of Monte Sparagio (1110m). It climbs past the turn for Balata di Baida, after which it traverses fields where yellow melons are grown, and low vineyards. There is a view ahead of the mountain of Erice. 90.5km Baglio. Turn for Custonaci and the promontory of Capo San Vito (24km).

4.5km CUSTONACI with a sanctuary and a number of marble quarries. On the outskirts, a rough road (signposted 'Grotte Mangiapane') leads past an old quarry to a tiny abandoned borgo built inside a huge cave at the foot of the beautiful Monte Cofano. On either side of the paved street are little houses with courtyards, bread ovens, etc, and high above the cave serves as a second roof. A road leads SW along the coast and around the foot of Monte San Giuliano to Trapani, see Rte 5. The road for San Vito Lo Capo continues through Purgatorio, beyond which it becomes much prettier passing barren hills (it is being realined). It descends through the wide picturesque main street of (15km) CASTELLUZZO, with one-storey houses and palm trees, and then straightens to pass plantations of almonds and olive trees on the plain which descends to the seashore. There is a splendid view back of the beautiful headland of Monte Cofano, with Erice in the distance. The road passes beside the interesting little 16C domed 'Cubola di San Crescenzia', derived from Arab models.

24km **San Vito lo Capo** at the tip of the cape has recently been developed as a seaside resort (4000 inhab.) with good beaches. 3-star hotel 'Capo San Vito', 29 Via Tommaso; 2-star 'Egitarso', 94 Via Lungomare, and others. Camping sites: 2-star 'Soleado', 1-star 'La Fata'; in località Salinella, 4-star 'El Bahira'. Laid out on a regular plan in the 18–19C most of the houses are decorated with colourful plants. The unusual church, a square fortress, was a 13C sanctuary which was fortified by order of Charles V in 1526 to defend it against pirate raids. The road continues around the beautiful promontory of Monte Monaco and passes a disused tuna fishery prominent on the left, and soon the Gulf of Castellammare comes into view. The deserted road (signposted 'Calampiso') continues high above the shore across bare hills through an African landscape, with dwarf palm trees, giant carobs, and broom and wild flowers in spring. Beyond the holiday village of Calampiso (hidden below the road) the right fork continues to an unsurfaced road which ends at the N entrance to (34km) the **Riserva Naturale dello Zingaro** (described above).

The main road (N187) for Trapani continues with a good view right of the summit of Monte Cofano beyond bare hills. The sea can be seen just before the road enters the straggling unattractive town of VALDERICE, where a spectacular road diverges right for **Erice** (see Rte 6). 104km **Trapani**, described in Rte 5.

5

Trapani

TRAPANI, the most important town on the W coast of the island (73,000 inhab.), lies below the headland of Mount Erice, with the Egadi islands usually visible offshore. Its old district occupies a scimitar-shaped promontory between the open sea on the N and the port and salt-marshes on the S, but from inland the town is approached through extensive modern suburbs laid out on a dreary chessboard pattern. Trapani has a number of unusual churches (not all of them open) by the local architect Giovanni Biagio Amico (1684–1754), and the Corso is given distinction by its interesting monumental buildings. The collection of decorative arts in the Museo Pepoli is one of the best on the island, and attests to the traditional skill of the native sculptors, silversmiths, and jewellers (particularly famous for their works in coral).

Trapani is the capital of a province in economic decline and has become one of the most important centres of Mafia activity in recent years. It has interesting environs including the beautiful little hilltown of Erice, the promontory of Capo San Vito stretching N beyond the splendid headland of Monte Cofano, and, to the S, the lovely island of Motya and the town of Marsala. The classical site of Segesta can be reached easily from Trapani. It is also the port for the Egadi islands and Pantelleria. The ancient industry of extracting salt from the marshes has recently been revived, and documented in a new museum.

Information Offices. 'APT' Trapani, 15 Via Sorba (Tel. 0923/27273). Information Office, Piazza Saturno (Tel. 0923/29000).

Railway Station, Piazza Umberto. Trains to Palermo, Marsala, and Castelvetrano.

Buses from the centre of the town to the Museo Pepoli (Nos 1, 10, and 11). The Corso may be reached by buses from the station or Villa Margherita which terminate in Piazza Generale Scio (near the Museo di Preistoria, at the end of the promontory). For Erice services from the bus station in Via Malta and from Via Fardella. Bus services run by 'Autoservizi Segesta' for Palermo from Piazza Marina. 'AST' services to places of interest in the province from Via Malta.

Car Parking on Lungomare Dante Alighieri or in Via Mazzini (near the railway station).

Airport at Birgi, 18km S. Services to Palermo, Pantelleria, Rome, etc. (and sometimes to Milan in summer). There are plans to introduce flights to Tunis. Bus from Corso Italia, in front of the Agenzia Salvo.

Maritime services. Ferries from Molo della Sanità to Tunis and Cagliari weekly. To Pantelleria daily ferry (in 4–5 hours) and hydrofoils ('Snav'). Boats ('Siremar') and hydrofoils from Via Ammiraglio Staiti daily to the Egadi Islands (boats in c 50 minutes; hydrofoil in 15–20 minutes).

Hotels. 3-star: 'Nuovo Russo', 4 Via Tintori, and 'Vittoria', 4 Via Francesco Crispi. 1-star: 'Moderno', 20 Via Genovese and 'Messina', 71 Corso Vittorio Emanuele. Two kilometres N of the centre on the coast, 3-star 'Astoria Park', Lungomare Dante Alighieri. Better accommodation of all categories is to be found at Erice, on the hill above the town (14km), see Rte 6.

Youth Hostel 'Ostello della Gioventù G. Amodeo' (run by the 'APT' of Trapani) at the foot of the hill of Erice on the Martogna road. Another youth hostel is open in summer only in Via delle Pinete, Erice.

Camping sites at San Vito lo Capo, see Rte 4; 1-star site at Lido Valderice.

Restaurants. Luxury-class: 'P & G', 1 Via Spalti. 1st-class: 'Da Peppe', 54 Via Spalti; 'del Porto', 45 Via Ammiraglio Staiti; 'Meeting', 321 Via Fardella; 'Il Salotto', 10 Via Burgio. Trattorie: 'I Trabinis', Porta Galli (Arab cuisine), 'La Carbonella', Via Fardella. The 'Trattoria del Sale' at the Museo del Sale (località Nubia) 5km S of the town (described below) serves good meals if ordered in advance (booking: Tel. 0923/867442).

Cafés or bars ('pasticceria') who make their own pastries and snacks include: 'Fiorino', Via Fardella and Via Cuba, and 'Colicchia', Via delle Arti. A good place to **picnic** is in the gardens of Villa Margherita.

Annual Festivals. Passion procession of the 'Misteri' on Good Friday; 'Musicale Trapanese' in the Villa Margherita in July; and classical theatre festival at Segesta every two years in summer (next in 1995).

History. *Drepana* or Drepanon, which occupied the promontory in ancient times, was the port of Eryx (see Rte 6), but was raised to the status of a city when Hamilcar Barca transferred here part of the population of Eryx in 260 BC. It was captured for the Romans by Catulus in 241. It acquired strategic importance as the maritime crossroads between Tunis, Anjou and Aragon in the 13C; here King Theobald of Navarre died of typhoid contracted near Tunis (1270), and here on the 'Scoglio del Malconsiglio', a rock at the extreme end of the cape, John of Procida is supposed to have plotted the Sicilian Vespers with his confederates. Edward I of England, who landed at Trapani on his return from the crusades in 1272, here received the news of his accession to the throne. The city was specially favoured by Peter of Aragon, who landed at Trapani as

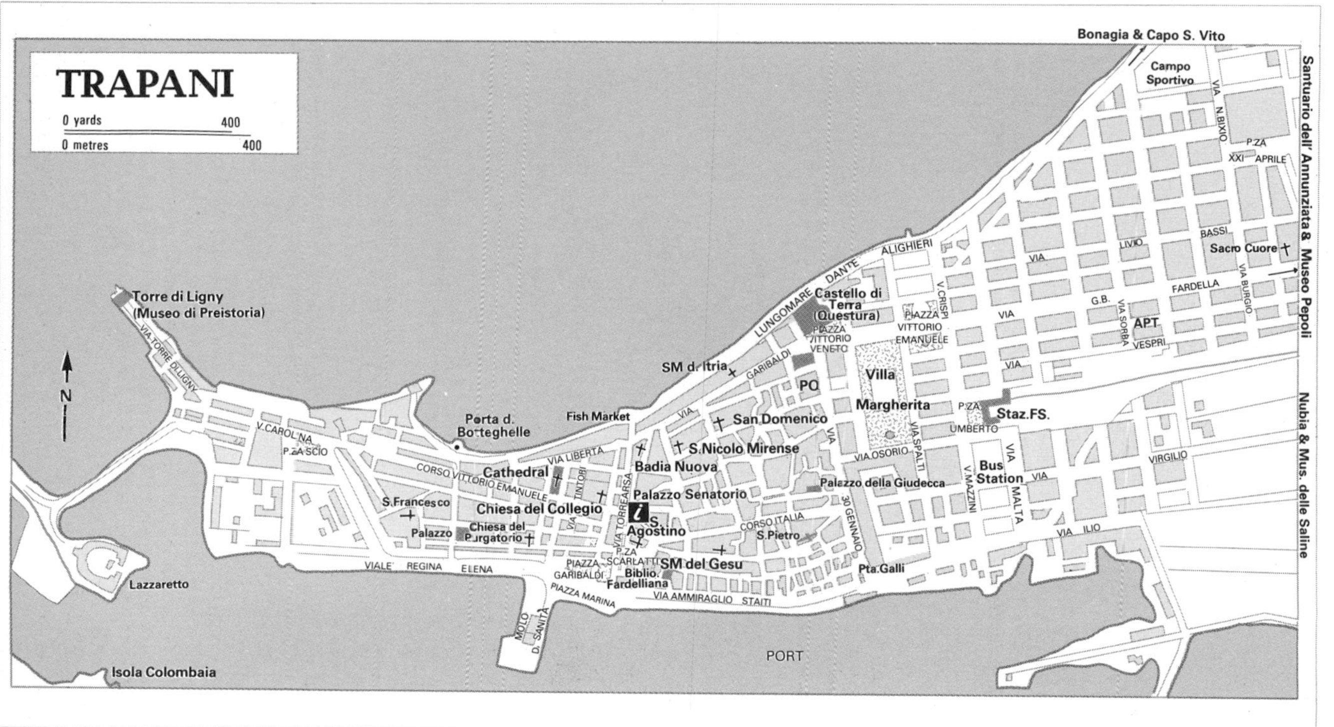
TRAPANI
0 yards 400
0 metres 400
N
Torre di Ligny (Museo di Preistoria)
VIA TORRE DI LIGNY
Lazzaretto
Isola Colombaia
V.CAROLINA
P.ZA SCIO
Porta d. Botteghelle
Fish Market
VIA LIBERTA
CORSO VITTORIO EMANUELE
Cathedral
S.Francesco
Chiesa del Collegio
Palazzo
Chiesa del Purgatorio
VIALE REGINA ELENA
TINTORI
VIA TORREARSA
Badia Nuova
Palazzo Senatorio
S. Agostino
P.ZA SCARLATTI
PIAZZA GARIBALDI
Biblio. Fardelliana
SM del Gesu
PIAZZA MARINA
MOLO D. SANITA
VIA AMMIRAGLIO STAITI
PORT
SM d. Itria
GARIBALDI
S.Nicolo Mirense
San Domenico
CORSO ITALIA
S.Pietro
30 GENNAIO
Pta.Galli
Palazzo della Giudecca
LUNGOMARE DANTE ALIGHIERI
Castello di Terra (Questura)
PIAZZA VITTORIO VENETO
PO
Villa Margherita
VIA OSORIO
VIA SPALTI
PIAZZA VITTORIO EMANUELE
V.CRISPI
P.ZA UMBERTO
Staz.FS.
V.MAZZINI
Bus Station
VIA MALTA
VIA ILIO
VIRGILIO
G.B.
VIA SORBA
APT
VESPRI
LIVIO
FARDELLA
VIA BURGIO
BASSI
Sacro Cuore
VIA N.BIXIO
P.ZA XXI APRILE
Campo Sportivo
Bonagia & Capo S. Vito
Santuario dell' Annunziata & Museo Pepoli
Nubia & Mus. delle Saline

the saviour of Sicily in 1282, and by Charles V. Nunzio Nasi (1850–1935), a native, represented Trapani in parliament for 40 years. In 1940 and again in 1943 the city suffered many air raids and naval bombardment, the district of San Pietro being razed to the ground. Floods caused by the lack of adequate drainage since the construction of new buildings at the foot of Mount Erice afflict the E end of the city; in 1976 16 people were drowned.

From the large Piazza Vittorio Emanuele (1869), planted with palm trees, and with a monument to the king by Giovanni Duprè (1882), Viale Regina Margherita skirts the N side of VILLA MARGHERITA, a lovely garden of tropical trees laid out in the late 19C, to PIAZZA VITTORIO VENETO, the modern centre of administration. Here the early 20C buildings include the fine post office (1924; being restored). Restoration is also in progress of the old CASTELLO DI TERRA, a castle which has been reconstructed during the centuries and which was converted into a barracks in the 19C. The outer walls have survived, but a modern building is being built inside them to house the Questura. The streets to the N give access to the sea front, with a good view of the old city on its promontory.

Via Garibaldi leads towards the old centre past the 18C Palazzo Fardella Fontana, with an elaborate window above its portal, and the 18C Palazzo Riccio di Morana decorated with stuccoes. The 17C church of SANTA MARIA DELL'ITRIA has a façade completed in 1745. Inside is a sculptural group of the Holy Family by Andrea Tipa. Beyond is the 19C red-brick Palazzo Staiti opposite the 18C Palazzo Milo. The Salita San Domenico (with steps and pretty cobbles) leads up to the church of **San Domenico** (often closed), with a blind 14C rose window. In the interior is a remarkable wood Crucifix (thought to date from the 14C) in an 18C chapel by Giovanni Biagio Amico in the N aisle. Near the entrance is a fresco fragment of the 15C. The sanctuary preserves the sarcophagus of Manfred, son of Frederick III of Aragon. A chapel behind has fresco fragments (14C and 15C), recently discovered. The Baroque frames, pulpit, and organ are interesting. The remarkable '*Misteri', twenty groups of figures in wood and paste carved in the 17–18C, by local artists, including Andrea Tipa, are kept here. They are taken through the town on Good Friday in a colourful procession. Nearby, to the S, is the church of SAN NICOLÒ MIRENSE, with a 16C marble tabernacle on the E wall and in the left transept a striking sculptural group of Christ between the two thieves, a realistic 18C work in wood and paste by a local sculptor. Via delle Arti and Via della Badia lead back to Via Garibaldi on which is the 17C façade of SANTA MARIA DEL SOCCORSO (or the BADIA NUOVA), with a fine interior (usually closed). A short way back along Via Garibaldi is the church of the CARMINELLO (or San Giuseppe), with an 18C portal with bizarre twisted columns. It was built in 1699 and the statue in the apse of St Joseph and the young Christ Child is a charming 18C sculpture by Antonio Nolfo (an earlier version of the statue, probably used for processions, is kept in the sacristy). A wood Crucifix is attributed to Giacomo Tartaglio.

From the Badia Via Torrearsa leads right, past the 16C church of the CARMINE with a fine exterior with tall pilasters and a high cornice (recently restored) to the sea front beyond a pretty market building of 1874. Fish is sold under the portico and produce in the piazza around a fountain with a statue of Venus. Via Torrearsa leads in the other direction to PALAZZO SENATORIO, used as municipal offices, built in 1672 with an eccentric theatrical façade with statues on the upper part.

From here the handsome wide **Corso Vittorio Emanuele** leads towards the end of the promontory. On the right is the CHIESA DEL COLLEGIO DEI GESUITI, built c 1614–40 by Natale Masuccio, with a Baroque façade by Francesco Bonamici (1657). The interior, with stuccoes by Bartolomeo Sanseverino, has been closed for restoration for many years. The sacristy has beautifully carved cupboards in walnut by Pietro Orlando (18C). Beyond the monumental ex-Collegio dei Gesuiti (now a school) is the **Cathedral of San Lorenzo** (1635) with a very unusual façade built by Giovanni Biagio Amico in 1743 preceded by a portico (being restored). On the S side (fourth altar) is a Crucifixion attributed to the local 17C artist Giacomo Lo Verde, and on the N side (second altar) is a painting of St George by Andrea Carreca, and (fourth altar) a fine painting of the Deposition (showing Flemish influence).

In front of the cathedral Via Giglio leads to the church of the PURGATORIO (closed) with a fine tiled dome and elaborate façade by Giovanni Biagio Amico. In Via San Francesco is a building (awaiting restoration) built in the 17C as a prison, with four caryatids on its façade, and, on the opposite side, the church of the IMMACOLATELLA, with a delightful apse by Giovanni Biagio Amico (1732).

The Corso continues past (left) the 18C Palazzo Berardo Ferro, with a courtyard, and then Palazzo Alessandro Ferro (1775), decorated with busts. Beyond on the right is the little Porta delle Botteghelle (13C), outside of which can be seen the defensive fortifications which protected the town from the sea. The Corso, now at the narrowest part of the promontory (the sea can be seen at either end of the side streets), becomes less interesting. Some 800m farther on (buses to Piazza Generale Scio), Via Torre di Ligny bears right and ends at the TORRE DI LIGNY, a fortress built in 1671 by the Spanish Viceroy, on the tip of the promontory. It has been well restored to house the **Museo Trapanese di Preistoria** (open 9–13, 16–20 except Mon), beautifully arranged on two floors. The province of Trapani is one of the areas richest in Prehistoric finds on the island. Among the exhibits are stone artefacts and pebble-tools from the Lower Paleolithic period; finds from caves (including tombs in the Grotta dell'Uzzo); material from Tunis (Upper Paleolithic); and Neolithic artefacts in ossidian and flint. An important section is dedicated to the incised drawings (Upper Paleolithic) and cave paintings (Neolithic) from the Cala dei Genovesi cave on the island of Levanzo (see Rte 7). Numerous fossils and animal remains (elephants, etc.) are displayed, found in caves on Monte Cofano and Capo San Vito. In the central case of the upper room is a bronze helmet of 5–4C BC. Admission is sometimes granted to the balcony on the roof of the fort from which there is a fine view.

From beside the Torre di Ligny there is a fine view across the bay to the ISOLA COLOMBAIA which was the base of the Roman siege operations in 241 BC. An Aragonese castle here, the CASTELLO DI MARE, was restored in later centuries, and in 1714 the octagonal lantern was added by Giovanni Biagio Amico. It was used as a prison up until the 1960s and is now being restored and may be opened as a museum (and connected to the mainland by a wooden bridge). The boulevards which skirt the harbour return to the town past (left) the so-called 'Palazzo', a 14C building several times enlarged.

Near the S end of Via Torrearsa (see above) is the restored Templars' church of SANT'AGOSTINO, with its 14C rose-window and portal (now used as a concert hall). The Saturn fountain here is on the site of a 14C fountain. Nearby is the BIBLIOTECA FARDELLIANA in the ex-church of San Giacomo, with a fine Mannerist façade. Opened to the public in 1830, it contains important manuscripts, and 90,000 vols (open 10–13, 16–19; Sat 9–13). In the rebuilt district of San Pietro is **Santa Maria del Gesù** (closed), a church with a transitional 16C façade and a Renaissance S doorway bearing an Annunciation in a Catalan-Gothic style. The fine simple interior, golden in colour, contains a *Madonna in enamelled terracotta by Andrea della Robbia under a marble baldacchino by Antonello Gagini. Farther E in the former Jewish district is the unusual PALAZZO DELLA GIUDECCA, its embossed tower and 16C windows recalling the Plateresque style of Spain.

At the landward end of the town (c 4km from the centre; bus Nos 1, 10 and 11) is the **Santuario dell'Annunziata** (sanctuary of the Madonna di Trapani), founded in 1315 and rebuilt in 1760. Little remains of the 14C structure except the W front with a rose-window which overlooks a well kept little garden with palm trees. The campanile dates from 1650. The entrance is through the N door on the main road. The interior (open 7–12, 16–19) was redesigned in the 18C by Giovanni Biagio Amico. Off the right side opens the CAPPELLA DEI PESCATORI, a beautiful little chapel built in 1481, perhaps an adaption of an earlier chapel. On the left of the presbytery is the CAPPELLA DEI MARINAI, another lovely chapel built in the 16C in a mixture of styles. From the sanctuary, with a pretty apse, two fine 16C doorways lead into the CAPPELLA DELLA MADONNA; here another arch, with sculptures by Antonino Gagini (1531–37) and a bronze gate of 1591 (by Giuliano Musarra), gives access to the inner sanctuary containing a highly venerated statue of the *Madonna and Child by Nino Pisano or his bottega, known as the 'Madonna di Trapani'. Below it is a tiny silver model of Trapani by Vincenzo Bonaiuto, who also made the silver statue in the Cappella di Sant'Alberto, on the right of this chapel. The sacristy has good 18C cupboards.

In the former Carmelite convent, entered on the right of the façade of the church, is the ***Museo Regionale Pepoli** (open 9–13.30, Tues and Thurs also 15–18.30; fest. 9–12.30). This includes a municipal collection formed in 1827, a group of paintings which belonged to General Giovanni Battista Fardella, and a large collection donated by Count Agostino Pepoli in 1906. The museum was opened here in 1914 (and rearranged in 1965). The exhibits are beautifully arranged and well labelled. The entrance is through the paved 16–17C cloisters, with palm trees. The rooms are un-numbered but described below in their logical sequence. GROUND FLOOR. Room I contains architectural fragments and Arab funerary inscriptions (10–12C). Room II. Sculpted portal by Bartolommeo Berrettaro; *stoup of 1486 from the Annunziata, resembling those in Palermo cathedral; works by the Gagini, notably a figure of St James the Great, by Antonello (1522). In the room on the left is a macabre guillotine.

The grand staircase (begun in 1639 and decorated in the 18C) leads up to the FIRST FLOOR where Rooms III–XI are devoted to paintings of the Neapolitan and local schools. Room III, 'Master of the Trapani Polyptych', Madonna and Child with saints (from the church of Sant'Antonio Abate), Roberto di Oderisio, Pietà (c 1380). In Room IV are three paintings by Il Pastura (Antonio del Massaro). Room VI contains St Francis receiving the Stigmata, attributed to Titian, and works by the local painters Andrea Carreca (1590–1677) and Giacomo Lo Verde. Room VII has 17C Neapolitan works. Outside, at the end of a corridor (used for temporary exhibitions) are four cases of 17C Sicilian jewellery. In Rooms XII–XXI is a ***collection of decorative arts**, most of them made by local craftsmen in the 17C–19C, including silversmiths, jewellers, and sculptors. Particularly remarkable are the charming ***crêche figures**, the best by Giovanni Matera (1653–1718), and Nativity scenes. Room XVII contains elaborate 17C objects in coral, a skill for which Trapani is particularly famous, notably a Crucifixion and candelabra by Fra Matteo Bavera; 16C silver works from Nuremburg, and jewellery made in Trapani. Room XXI, majolica, made locally, and from Faenza and Montelupo. The small prints and drawings collection includes works by Stefano della Bella and Jacopo Callot. The archaeological collection in Rooms XXIII–XXIV contains finds from Erice, Selinunte, and Motya, and coins of the 5C BC. The flag of 'Il Lombardo', the ship sailed by Garibaldi and the Thousand, is preserved in Room XXV.

The secondary road to Marsala (which runs to seaward of the railway and the main N115 road) leads out of the town from the port and crosses the salt-pans where a number of windmills (some with sails), which used to be used to refine the salt, survive to the right and left of the road. On the right a turning (signposted) leads to NUBIA, on the edge of the sea c 5km S of Trapani, where the **Museo delle Saline** was opened in 1988 (9–13, 13.30–17.30 except fest.). This illustrates the ancient industry of extracting salt which still takes place here and in a number of other salt-pans in the marshes between Trapani and Marsala. Piles of salt, protected by tiles, can usually be seen in the area. The museum is housed in a 17C building which was used as a store and dormitory for the workers. In the centre of the building is a windmill once used for refining the salt (this process is now carried out at a refinery). The exhibits illustrate the various stages in extracting the salt, an industry which from the 15C up to the beginning of the 20C was extremely important to the local economy. From February to March sea-water is pumped by a mill (seen from the window) from a canal into the beds, and then into salt pans which decrease in depth to allow the salinity of the water to increase. When the sun has evaporated the water from the last pan the harvest begins in July. The salt is then piled up and protected from humidity by tiles. Particularly good fish are caught in the pans in December, and there is interesting bird life in the marshes which became a protected area in 1991. A restaurant here is open if booking is made in advance (see above).

Lungomare Dante Alighieri leads N along the sea shore from the centre of the town, skirting the foot of Mount Erice. It passes SAN CUSOMANO where the windmill of a salt-pan is being restored, near a tuna fishery. Ships are protected from the low islands offshore here by a lighthouse. Beyond the unattractive Pizzolungo with marble quarries the road passes BONAGIA where the picturesque tuna fishery (signposted 'tonnara') is being restored. Beside the pretty little fishing port are hundreds of rusting anchors and a fine tall tower. The road continues through the plain, where numerous small holiday houses have been built, towards Custonaci and the beautiful headland of Monte Cofano, described, together with San Vito lo Capo in Rte 4.

Erice, which can be reached with ease from Trapani, is described in Rte 6, and the area to the S of Trapani, including Mozia and Marsala is described in Rte 8. For the Egadi islands and Pantelleria, see Rte 7.

6

Erice

***ERICE** is a silent little medieval town (600 inhab.) in a remarkable position perched on top of an isolated calcareous hill (751m), high above the sea. It is often shrouded in mist (and chilly in winter) which contributes to its feeling of isolation from the rest of the world. It was famous in ancient times for its important sanctuary of Venus; white doves sacred to the goddess still inhabit the town. The *view to the N of MONTE COFANO, one of the most beautiful promontories on the coast of Sicily, is unforgettable. The reddish colour of its sheer rock face changes according to the weather and time of day. To the SW there is another remarkable view of Trapani and the Egadi Islands, and, on a clear day, Cape Bon in Tunisia. The grey stone houses of Trapani (mostly dating from the 14C to 17C), hidden behind their high courtyard walls, and the beautifully paved streets unusually clean and deserted, give the town an austere aspect. The perfect triangular shape of the town makes it difficult to find ones bearings, despite the fact it is so small. It has particularly good hotels and restaurants, and many of its houses are occupied only in the summer months by residents of Trapani or Palermo who come here on holiday to escape the heat.

Information Office. 'Azienda Autonoma', 11 Viale Conte Pepoli.

Approaches. Three roads ascend the hill from Trapani. The most spectacular leaves the E end of the town at Raganzili (Via Martogna) beside the disused cableway station and ascends in 14km. It passes beneath the cableway and begins to climb through pine woods, with fine views of Trapani and the Egadi Islands. Higher up it rounds the wooded hill to reveal Monte Cofano and Capo San Vito in the distance. It then traverses an upland plain with a few vineyards and a picturesque group of abandoned farmhoues on a promontory. It passes the turn for the Museo Agro Forestale di San Matteo, described at the end of this route. It then joins the road from Valderice and traverses thick woods before entering Erice. Another road (constructed by the Bourbons in 1850) diverges left from N187 outside Trapani and climbs in 10.5km to the summit. The longest road (17km) diverges from N187 at Valderice.

Bus from Trapani in c 40 minutes (the cableway at the end of Via Fardella at Raganzili has been out of action for many years).

A FOOTPATH from Trapani starts at Casa Santa (Borgo Annunziata) and ascends through pine woods in c 2 hours.

Car Parking outside Porta Trapani.

Hotels. 4-star: 'Ermione', Via Pineta Comunale; 3-star: 'Moderno', 67 Via Vittorio Emanuele, 'Elimo', 75 Via Vittorio Emanuele; 2-star: 'Edelweiss', Vicolo San Domenico.

YOUTH HOSTELS: 'Ostello della Gioventù G. Amodeo' at the foot of the hill on the Martogna road; 'Ostello della Gioventù, C.S.I.', Via delle Pinete (open in summer only).

Restaurants. 1st-class: 'Moderno', 67 Via Vittorio Emanuele, 'Elimo', 75 Via Vittorio Emanuele; 'Al Ciclope', 45 Viale Nasi; 'Monte San Giuliano', 7 Via San Rocco; 'Cortile di Venere', 31 Via Sales. Trattorie: 'La Pentolaccia', 17 Via Guarnotti; 'La Vetta da Mario', Via Fontana; 'Nuovo Edelweiss', Piazza Umberto I; 'Al Cantuccio', Piazzale San Giovanni; 'Ulisse', Via Chiaramonte.

Cafés or bars ('pasticceria') with good snacks and excellent pastries include: 'Tulipano', and 'Maria Grammatico' both in Via Vittorio Emanuele; 'San Carlo', Via Palma; 'Del Convento' and 'Silvestro' both near San Domenico.

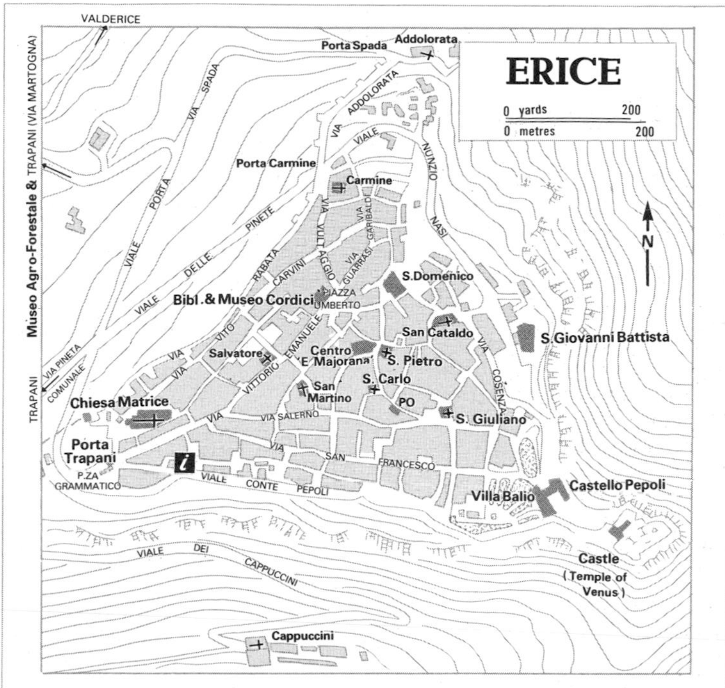

Picnic places in Villa Balio or in the pine woods below the walls (off Viale delle Pinete).

Annual Festivals. Procession of the 'Misteri' on Good Friday. Festivals of medieval and Renaissance music (in summer) and of folk music (in December).

History. *Eryx*, an Elymian city of mythical origin, was famous all over the Mediterranean for the magnificent temple of the goddess of fertility, known to the Romans as Venus Erycina. On this splendid site, naturally defended, and visible for miles around it was a noted landmark for navigators from Africa. An altar was first set up here by the Sicani and the sanctuary became famous during the Elimian and Phoenician period. In 415 BC the inhabitants of Segesta took the Athenians to see its rich treasury. Taken by Pyrrhus in 278 BC it was destroyed in 260 by Hamilcar. The Roman consul L. Junius Pullus captured the hill in 248 and was besieged by Hamilcar, who was himself blockaded by a Roman army, until the Punic cause was lost by the naval victory of Catulus. The cult of Venus Erycina reached its maximum splendour under the Romans and the sanctuary was restored for the last time by Tiberius and Claudius. The Saracens called the place *Gebel-Hamed*, which Count Roger, who had seen St Julian in a dream while besieging it, changed to *Monte San Giuliano*, a name it kept until 1934. The city thrived in the 18C when the population was around 12,000. It has long been noted for the beauty of its women. A local industry which survives here is the weaving of brightly coloured cotton rugs.

The entrance to the town is by PORTA TRAPANI, beyond which Via Vittorio Emanuele climbs steeply uphill. A street leads left to the **Chiesa Madre** (Assunta), which has a beautiful fortified Gothic exterior. The porch dates from 1426. The detached *CAMPANILE was built as an Aragonese look-out tower in c 1315 by Frederic III, several years before the foundation of the church. The INTERIOR (entered by the S door; at present only open at 11am

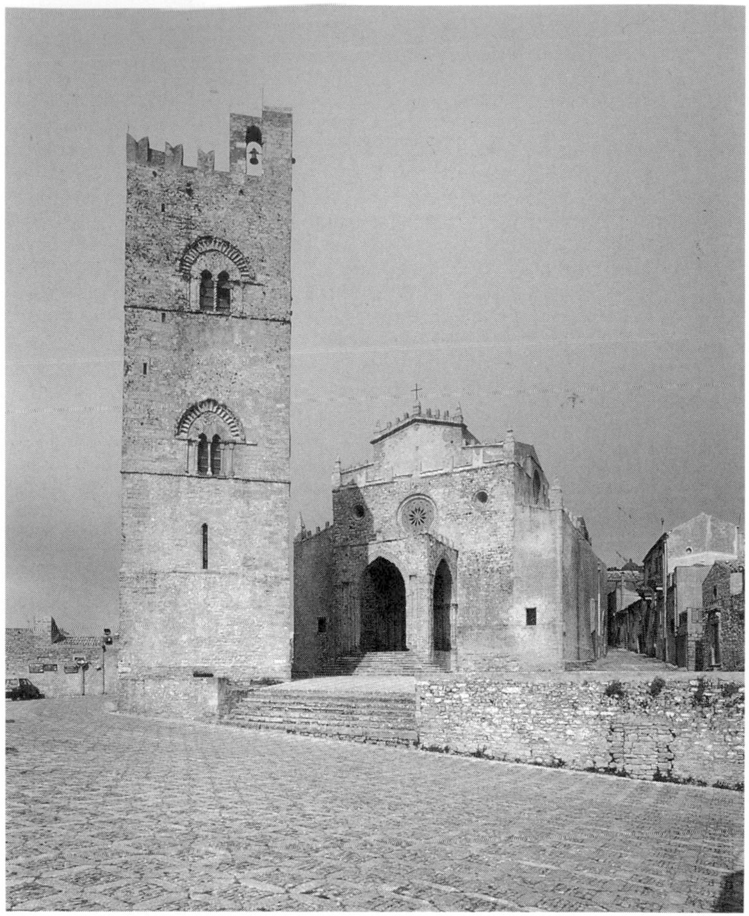

The Chiesa Madre, Erice

on Sunday) received its impressive neo-Gothic form, with an elaborate cream-coloured vault, in 1852. The apse is filled with a huge marble altarpiece by Giuliano Mancino (1513). The 15C painting of the Madonna of Custonaci over the altar to the left was replaced in 1892 by the present copy. Over a side altar (right) is a Madonna, once attributed to Francesco Laurana, but now thought to be by Domenico Gagini (1469; note the fine base).

Via Vittorio Emanuele continues steeply uphill past several old shop-fronts and characteristic courtyards. At a fork Via Vittorio Emanuele continues left past the huge old ruined Gothic church of San Salvatore beside a lovely old narrow lane which leads downhill (and has a distant view of the sea). To the right Via Bonaventura Provenzano ends at a house with a Baroque doorway and window near the closed church of SAN MARTINO (with another Baroque portal, and an interesting 15C statue of the Madonna). Just before reaching Piazza Umberto, a flight of steps leads down left to the monumental doorway with four columns of San Rocco (closed). The 'Circolo' here is an old-fashioned private club.

In the central **Piazza Umberto** are a few cafés, a pretty palace now used by a bank, and the long 19C building which houses the town hall and the **Biblioteca and Museo Comunale Cordici** (open 8.30–13.30; or on request), named after the local historian Antonino Cordici (1586–1666). The library was founded in 1867 with material from the suppressed convents of the city. It now has c 20,000 volumes. In the entrance hall is a beautiful relief of the Annunciation by Antonello Gagini, one of his finest works (1525), and a number of inscriptions. Upstairs in the well-arranged small MUSEUM are interesting local archaeological finds (including an Attic head of Venus, 5C BC); a 15C well-head; 16–18C church vestments; a painting by the local 17C artist, Andrea Carreca; and a wood crucifix by Pietro Orlando (also 17C).

Via Guarrasi leads ahead out of the piazza and immediately on the left a stepped lane (Via Argentieri) leads down across Via Carvini into Via Vultaggio which continues to wind down past a church with a classical façade. The delightful interior was restored in 1954 by an American benefactor. It has white stucco decoration in very low relief on the walls and the barrel vault, a worn tiled pavement, fine woodwork, and popular votive statues. On the right is the 14C Palazzo Militari with Gothic traces next to the Gothic church of the Carmine. Here is PORTA CARMINE, with a worn headless statue in a niche, on its outer face.

The ***walls** here, which stretch from Porta Spada to Porta Trapani protected the only side of the hill which has no natural defences: on all the other sides the sheer rock face made the town one of the most impregnable fortresses on the island. The walls are constructed on huge blocks of rough stone which probably date from the Elimian period, above which can be seen the square blocks added by the Carthaginians. The masonry in the upper parts, with stones of smaller dimension, date from the 6C BC. The defences were strengthened in the Roman era and in the Middle Ages, and six postern gates and 16 medieval towers survive. Inside the gate the stepped Via Addolorata leads down past a well preserved stretch of the walls, with a distant view ahead of Monte Cofano, to the church of the ADDOLORATA (or Sant'Orsola; closed), surrounded by a little garden. It has an interesting 15–16C plan. Here are kept the 18C sculptures of the 'Misteri' taken in procession through the streets of Erice on Good Friday. In this remote and picturesque corner of the town is the Norman PORTA SPADA.

From Porta Carmine (see above) Via Rabatà (which has lost its traditional paving) leads back to Porta Trapani skirting the walls (less well preserved here) with a number of postern gates. Tiny narrow alley-ways lead up left to Via Carvini and Piazza Umberto.

From Piazza Umberto (see above), in front of the museum, Via Antonio Cordici leads up out of the piazza past a few shops to Piazza San Domenico with a pretty Baroque palace. The ex-church of SAN DOMENICO, with a classical porch, has been restored as a lecture hall for the Centro Majorana (see below). From the right side of the church Via San Cataldo leads downhill (and right) past a neo-Gothic electricity tower to the bare façade of SAN CATALDO (open for services only) on the edge of the old town. It was founded before 1339, and rebuilt in 1740–86. It contains a stoup of 1474 by the workshop of Domenico Gagini, and a painting by Andrea Carreca.

Further downhill and to the right, beyond a less picturesque part of the town, is the church of SAN GIOVANNI BATTISTA (deconsecrated, and kept locked) on the cliff edge, with a pretty 15C dome, and an ancient side doorway. It contains a statue of St John the Evangelist by Antonello Gagini, and of St John the Baptist by Antonino Gagini. There is a good view from Via Cusenza.

From Piazza San Domenico (see above), Via Guarnotti leads up right to the church of SAN PIETRO (open for services) with an 18C portal. The beautiful white interior by Giovanni Biagio Amico (1745) has a worn tiled pavement. Beside it is an arch over the road and on the right (at No. 26) a convent has been restored as the headquarters of the CENTRO INTERNAZIONALE DI CULTURA SCIENTIFICA 'ETTORE MAJORANA. Founded in 1963, this has become a famous centre of learning where courses are held for scientists from all over the world.

Via Guarnotti continues past the bare façade of the closed church of San Carlo. On the right is the post office and downhill on the left is a pleasant piazza with a statue in front of the church of SAN GIULIANO (deconsecrated, used by a religious community), with an elegant 18C campanile. The road continues down past a very old shop front and crosses Via Porta Gervasi (with a view left of the church of San Giovanni Battista with its dome, see above). A ramp leads up right to ***Villa Balio**, delightful public gardens (with ilexes) laid out in 1870 by Count Agostino Pepoli on the summit of the hill, with wonderful views. It has a monumental entrance with a double staircase on Via San Francesco. Above is the CASTELLO PEPOLI (no admission), a Norman castle reconstructed in 1875–85 by Count Pepoli, with a 15C tower restored in 1973. The splendid view from the terrace on the left takes in Monte Cofano, the sea coast, and San Giovanni Battista on the side of the hill. Below can be seen the abandoned neo-Gothic 'Torretta' in trees, also built by Count Pepoli.

A ramp leads down from the gardens beside the castle to Viale Conte Pepoli, on the S edge of the hill which continues left to end beside the 17C steps up to the **Castello 'di Venere'** (open daily 8.30–13.30), on the edge of the rock. Above the entrance to the castle is the coat of arms of Charles V and a Gothic window. The disappointing interior is poorly kept. The ruined Norman walls surround the sacred area, once the site of the famous Temple of Venus (see above), many fragments of which are embedded in the masonry of the castle. A few very worn Roman fluted column drums can be seen here and the so-called 'Pozzo di Venere', once thought to be a piscina, was probably a silo. A mosaic pavement discovered in 1932 has disappeared. The view is breathtaking.

About 5km below the town the interesting MUSEO AGRO FORESTALE DI SAN MATTEO was opened in 1986 (open daily 8.30–17.30). It is reached from the Raganzili road (described at the beginning of this route). About 3km below Erice a signposted turn leads in c 500m to the gates of the estate owned by the forestry commission. A rough road (c 1km) continues to the museum in the lovely old Baglio di San Matteo, arranged in five rooms around the courtyard. The exhibits include wine and olive presses, farm carts, saddle and tack, agricultural implements, and household objects. There is also a natural history section. The beautifully kept farm of c 500 hectares may also be visited, where wildfowl, Tibetan goats, and work horses (a Sicilian breed known as 'San Fratello', until recently threatened with extinction) are raised. The site is spectacular with fine views towards Capo San Vito, and the vegetation includes dwarf palm trees, cypresses, fruit trees and woods (experimental replanting is carried out). A path leads past a little palaeochristian oratory below ground level. A smithy and carpentry shop operate on the estate. A huge reservoir to collect rain water is conspicuous on the hillside.

The promontory of Capo San Vito is described in Rte 4, and the town of Trapani, at the foot of the hill, in Rte 5.

7

The Egadi Islands and Pantelleria

The **Egadi Islands**, consisting of Favignana, Levanzo and Marettimo, lie 15–30km off the west coast of Sicily. They are reached by boat and hydrofoil from Trapani. The inhabitants were once famed as skilled fishermen; fish are now far less abundant. Oil wells were sunk in the sea here a few years ago despite local efforts to preserve the sea from pollution. The sea between Favignana and Marsala is of great interest to underwater archaeologists. The varied bird life includes migratory species from Africa in the spring. The islands, much visited by skin-divers, were declared a marine reserve in 1988.

Information Offices. 'APT' Trapani (Tel. 0923/27273); 'Pro Loco', Piazza Matrice, Favignana (Tel. 0923/921647).

Maritime Services from Trapani. Daily ferries from Molo Sanità to Favignana (in 50 mins) and to Levanzo in 1hr 20mins. Once a week in 2hrs 40mins to Marettimo. Hydrofoils (several times a day) from Via Ammiraglio Staiti in 25 minutes to Favignana and Levanzo, and once a day in 55 minutes to Marettimo. The ferries are cheaper than the hydrofoils.

Bicycles can be hired on Favignana.

Hotels. Favignana: 3-star: 'Approdo di Ulisse' (open June–November); 1-star: 'Egadi'; and others. Levanzo: 1-star: 'Paradiso'. Rooms to let available on all the islands.

Camping Sites. On Favignana: 3-star 'Egad'; 1-star: 'Quattro Rose'. Free camping is allowed on Levanzo and Marettimo.

Annual Festival called the 'Settimana delle Egadi' at the end of May.

History. These islands were the ancient 'Aegades' or 'Aegates', off which Lutatius Catulus routed the fleet of Hanno in 241 BC in one of the most famous Roman victories over Carthage. In the middle of the 16C the islands were given to the Genoese Camillo Pallavicini, from whom they were purchased in 1874 by the Florio.

Favignana, 17km from Trapani, is the biggest island of the group (19 sq km) and the seat of the comune (3500 inhab.). It is flat and has a rather bare landscape, mostly used as pastureland. It has good swimming. The little medieval town was refounded in 1637 by the Genoese family of Pallavicini, and now the town hall occupies the Palazzo Florio built in 1876 for Ignazio Florio by Giuseppe Damiani Almeyda. On the opposite side of the port is the huge tuna fishery bought by the Florio in 1874 from the Pallavicini. There is a project to restore the fine buildings as a marine research centre.

On Favignana the traditional method of tuna fishing known as 'la mattanza' has been practiced in spring according to a precise ritual since ancient times. The tuna fisheries here were the most important in the Mediterranean. The catch has drastically declined in recent years due in part to modern fishing techniques, polluted water, and disturbance of the water by motorboats and hydrofoils. The spectacle still usually takes place between 15 May and 15 June if the fish are sighted.

Levanzo (10 sq km), 15km from Trapani, has no springs and supports a population of just 200. It also has an austere barren landscape, and few beaches. It is famous for its prehistoric caves, notably the *'GROTTA DEL GENOVESE', which has the most interesting Prehistoric wall paintings in Italy, discovered by chance in 1950. The cave paintings date from the Neolithic period, and the incised drawings from the Upper Paleolithic period. A footpath leads across the island from the port to the cave (which can also be reached by boat; enquire for directions at the port).

Marettimo (12 sq km) is the most isolated of the Egadi islands, 38km from Trapani. It is wild and mountainous, rich in springs and beautiful grottoes, and is the best preserved of the three islands. With a little Arab-like village, it has a population of just 800. It has no hotels, but a few trattorie. Samuel Butler suggested that this was the island described as Ithaca in the Odyssey, and the islets of Le Formiche were the rocks hurled by Polyphemus at Ulysses (see Rte 26).

Far away to the SW, about 110km from the Sicilian mainland (and only 70km from Tunisia) lies **Pantelleria** (7500 inhab.), the largest island (83 sq km) off the Sicilian coast. It has beautiful wild scenery, and interesting volcanic phenomena including hot springs (the last eruption was in 1891). Its central conical peak rises to a height of 836m. The sea bathing is exceptionally good. It is a sanctuary for migratory birds. Capers, figs, and sweet raisin grapes called 'zibibbo' are cultivated here despite the lack of spring water, and it is especially famous for its wine 'moscato di Pantelleria' (the 'moscato passito' is a white desert wine). The cube-like whitewashed houses, called 'dammusi', with thick walls and domed roofs, are Arabic in origin.

Information Offices. 'Pro-loco', Via San Nicola (Tel. 0923/911838); 'APT' Trapani (Tel. 0923/27273).

Maritime Services. Ferries daily from Trapani (Molo della Sanità) in c 5hrs, and hydrofoils in c 2hrs 30mins.

Air services from Trapani (twice a day in 30mins) and from Palermo once a day in 1hr 20mins (and from Rome). Connecting bus from the airport to the town of Pantelleria.

Cars and mopeds may be hired at the port.

Hotels. 3-star: 'Port Hotel', 43 Via Borgo Italia; 2-star: 'Agadir', 1 Via Catania; 'Miryam', 1 Corso Umberto. In località Bue Marino, 2-star: 'Turistico Residenziale', and others, most of them larger. Rooms to let available locally.

History. Archaeological evidence has proved the island was inhabited in the Neolithic era. Later a Phoenician settlement, it was taken by the Romans in 217 BC, and called by them 'Cossyra'. After its conquest by Roger I in 1123 it remained a Sicilian possession. During World War II it was used as a base for harrying allied convoys; reduced by heavy bombardment during May 1943 it was taken from the sea on 11 June with 11,000 prisoners, allied casualties being reported as 'one soldier bitten by a mule'. It has been used as a place of exile for political prisoners. It now has Italian and US military installations. Irregular mafia activities here in recent years have threatened to spoil the island, which has become a fashionable place to have a summer villa.

The port of Pantelleria had to be rebuilt after the Second World War. In Località Mursia 58 prehistoric tombs known as 'sesi', were discovered by

Paolo Orsi in the 19C. These large domed tumuli were built in blocks of lava. Only 27 have survived, notably the 'Sese Grande'; the others have either fallen into ruin or been engulfed by new buildings.

The beautiful inland crater lake of 'BAGNO DELL'ACQUA' (or the 'Lago di Venere') is about 6km from the port. It is fed by a hot water spring and is 500m in diameter and 2m above sea level. The fine rocky coast is best seen from a boat (which can be hired at the port). Some of the best swimming on the island can be had at the 'Arco dell'Elefante'.

8

Trapani to Motya, Marsala and Mazara del Vallo

Road, N115, 53.5km.—19km, turning right for **Motya** (4km)—31.5km **Marsala**—53.5km **Mazara del Vallo**.

The main road (N115) between Trapani and Marsala bears heavy traffic and has numerous traffic lights; it is worth taking the secondary coastal road here. This leaves Trapani on the seaward side of the railway and passes the salt marshes and the turn for Nubia, with the interesting Museo delle Saline (c 5km S of Trapani), described at the end of Rte 5. It then passes close to the airport of Birgi and the island of Motya.

Buses ('AST') from Trapani (Via Malta) to Marsala and Mazara del Vallo. The landing-stage for Motya is c 1km away from Ragattisi where the bus between Trapani and Marsala stops.

Railway, 52 km in c 1 hour (the trains continue to Castelvetrano, see Rte 9). To Marsala in c 40 minutes. The trains stop at Ragattisi, the nearest station to the landing stage for Motya (c 1km).

Information Office. 'APT' Trapani, Tel. 0923/27273.

Between Trapani and Marsala are salt marshes (now a partially protected area), with interesting bird life. Some salt-pans are still worked here, and the landscape is characterised by piles of salt protected by tiles, and windmills once used for refining the salt. The coastal plain is reminiscent of North Africa, dotted with white cube-shaped houes, palms, and monkey puzzle trees. Beyond Marsala the plain is densely cultivated with olives, low vineyards and market gardens (tomatoes are grown in the green houses).

The road leaves Trapani and bypasses Paceco. In the plain of Falconaria, where Frederick II defeated the allied French and Neapolitans in 1299, it passes under the motorway from Palermo to the airport of Birgi. 19km Granatello. Turning (signposted 'Stazione di Ragattisi') for Motya on the island of San Pantaleo. In just over two kilometres this byroad crosses the railway at a level crossing; ahead a narrow road (signposted 'Motya'), in Contrada Spagnola, continues straight towards the sea past a windmill on the left, and then bears left to the edge of the lagoon in front of the island of San Pantaleo. A boatman is here every day (9–13.30; 15–17, or 15–19 in summer) who takes visitors across to the island in c 10 minutes (3000 lire return trip). There is a splendid view from the water's edge of the island of San Pantaleo with its pine trees, just to the left of which is the island of Favignana. Behind San Pantaleo can be seen Levanzo, and to the left in the distance is Marettima. On the far right the headland of Erice is prominent beyond salt pans and windmills and piles of salt.

San Pantaleo is one of three islands in the beautiful shallow lagoon, known as **Lo Stagnone**, protected from the sea by the Isola Longa. The lagoon (2000 hectares) has an average depth of just over 1m, and is abundant in fish (now threatened by the polluted water). Since at least the 15C salt has been extracted from the marshes, and after a period of decline, the industry is showing a slight revival. Pyramidal heaps of salt roofed with red tiles line the shore, and a few salt-crushing windmills survive.

The ***Island of San Pantaleo** (2.5km in circumference), with the remains of the Phoenician ***MOTYA** (*Mozia*) may be visited every day. It lies just 1km offshore, an oasis of luxuriant vegetation, a sanctuary for birds, with sweet-smelling plants, palm trees and pinewoods. The low vineyards on the island produce an excellent wine. The ruins are unenclosed and the views are delightful.

Admission daily 9am to sunset. The museum is closed from 13–15.

Sandwiches and drinks are available at a custodian's house, and it is a lovely place to picnic.

History. Motya was founded in the mid 8C BC by the Phoenicians as a commercial base. By the mid 6C BC the island was entirely surrounded by defensive walls, 2400m long and over 2m thick. In his determination to wipe out the Carthaginians from the W of the island, Dionysius I of Syracuse brought a huge army here in 398 BC. During the fierce battle which ensued the tyrant's fleet was trapped in the lagoon; he brilliantly resolved the situation by constructing a 'road' of logs nearly 4km long, along which his ships were dragged to the open sea where he finally defeated the enemy. By the following year the Carthaginians had moved their headquarters to Lilybaeum. The island was owned by Joseph (Pip) Whitaker (1850–1936), a distinguished ornithologist and member of the famous family of Marsala wine-merchants. He began the excavations here around 1913, and on the death of his daughter Delia in 1971 the island became the property of the Joseph Whitaker Foundation. Three families live on the island, and excavations continue every year.

The boat crosses the lagoon with a view left of the island of Favignana and right of Mount Erice beyond the salt-pans. It docks near a stretch of the fortifications of the Punic city. A path leads to a group of houses and the Whitaker villa, appropriately used as a MUSEUM, reopened in 1988. It was founded in 1925, and some of the showcases brought at that time from Edinburgh and Belfast are still used. The material, delightfully displayed, comes from excavations at Motya, Lilybaeum, and Birgi, carried out by Whitaker and (in the last few years) by the Italian State. It includes Phoenician ceramics, the earliest dating from the 8C BC, and Greek ware including proto-Corinthian and Corinthian vases, and Attic black- and red-figure vases. Other finds from the island include Phoenician glass, alabaster, and jewellery. Among the sculptural fragments is a metope from the North Gate showing two lions attacking a bull, distinctly Mycenaean in style (end of 7C or beginning of 6C BC), and a marble crater with bas-reliefs (Augustan period). The splendid marble *statue of a young man (perhaps a charioteer, or a magistrate) in a tight-fitting tunic was found on the NE side of the island in 1979. This remarkable work is thought to be by a Greek master and to date from c 440 BC.

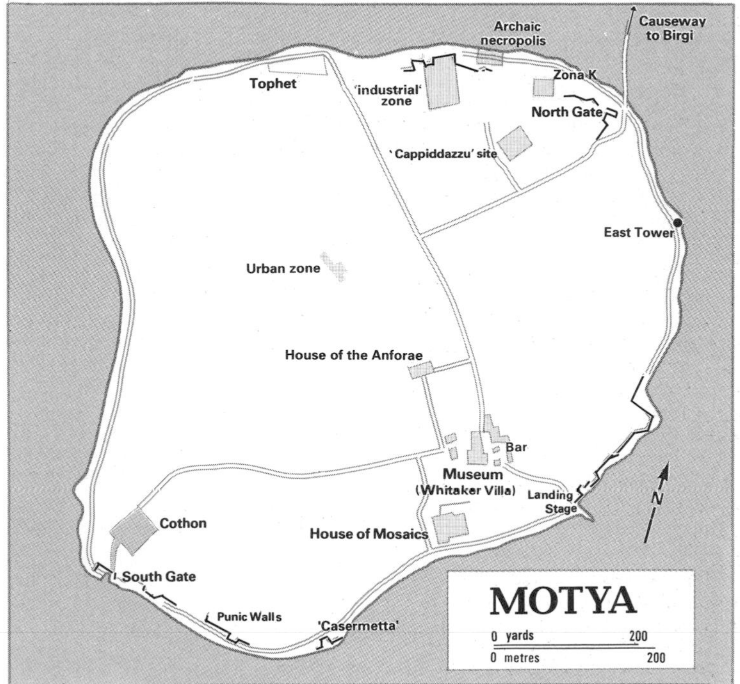

From beside the custodian's house a path (not signposted), flanked by bushes, leads to the waterfront beside the COTHON and SOUTH GATE. This small basin (50m by 40m) within the walls is thought to have been an artificial dock used for repairing ships. A paved canal with ashlar walls of the 6C BC, thought to be its seaward entrance, has also been excavated. A path leads along the edge of the shore past an enclosure near a clump of pine trees where excavations have unearthed a building probably used for military purposes (and known as the 'CASERMETTA'). There are fine views across the lagoon of the piles of salt on the mainland, and of the Egadi islands. The path ends at the HOUSE OF THE MOSAICS, surrounded by rich vegetation, with bases of columns and interesting pebble mosaics showing a panther attacking a bull, a griffin chasing a deer, etc. (4–3C BC).

The path continues along the water's edge past the landing stage and the impressive FORTIFICATIONS (late 6C BC), the best preserved stretch on the island. The EAST TOWER preserves its flight of steps. Beyond some recent excavations (protected by a roof) is the imposing NORTH GATE, with a treble line of defences. It defended a CAUSEWAY, now just submerged (but up to a few years ago practicable for a horse and cart) which was built in the late 6C BC to link the island to the mainland (and a necropolis at Birgi). It is 7km long and just wide enough for two carts to pass each other. There is a fine view of Erice from here, beyond the low islands of the lagoon. A path leads inland through the N gate to CAPPIDDAZZU, probably a sacred area. Above the level of the path is an edifice with mosaic remains. To the right is a field with low vines and two enclosed areas, the farthest of which, on the edge of the sea, is the ARCHAIC NECROPOLIS with tombs dating from the 8–6C BC. Nearby a fence surrounds an 'industrial area', known as 'ZONA K', with interesting kilns, similar in design to some found in Syria and Palestine. Here the most recent excavations have taken place (and the remarkable Greek statue, now in the museum, was found). The largest enclosure is the TOPHET, a Punic sacrificial burial ground dedicated to the goddess Tanit and to the god Baal Hammon, where child sacrifices were immolated (replaced after the 5C BC by animal sacrifices). The tombs are protected by low rooves. Excavations here produced cinerary urns, votive terracotta masks, and stelae (some with human figures). From the Tophet a path, marked by low olive trees, leads back through a vineyard in the centre of the island towards the museum. It pases (right) an enclosure with remains of the CASA DELLE ANFORE, so called because a huge deposit of amphorae was found here. Nearby are four conspicuous white pylons once used for generating electricity for the island.

Boats can sometimes be hired (enquire on the island) to visit the lovely Stagnone lagoon, with its three small islands, including the large Isola Longa (admission only with special permission), which has luxuriant vegetation and some abandoned salt-works.

31.5km **MARSALA** (80,800 inhab.), a pleasant town with a 16C aspect, and an attractive open seafront on Capo Boeo, the site of the Carthaginian city of Lilybaeum. It gives its name to a famous dessert wine still produced here in large quantities from the vineyards along the coast, and stored in huge 'bagli'. It is the most important wine-producing centre on the island.

Information Office. 'Pro-loco', 45 Via Garibaldi.

Railway Station, Via Fazio, on the line from Trapani to Castelvetrano.

Buses from Piazza del Popolo to Motya, Trapani, Palermo, Mazara del Vallo, Castelvetrano, and Agrigento.

Maritime Services from Molo Dogana for the Egadi Islands and Pantelleria.

Car Parking on Lungomare Boeo, or outside Porta Garibaldi.

Hotels. 3-star: 'Stella d'Italia', 7 Via Rapisardi; others (3-star and 2-star) on the outskirts.

Restaurants. Luxury-class: 'Delfino', 672 Lungomare Mediterraneo. 1st-class: 'Garibaldi', 35 Piazza Addolorata; 'Marinella di Gnaziu u Pazzu', 38 Lungomare Boeo; 'Capo Lilybeo', 40 Lungomare Boeo; 'Marsha-Hallaa', 1 Viale Veneto; 'Zio Ciccio', 112 Lungomare Mediterraneo; 'Stella d'Italia', 7 Via Rapisardi; 'Villa Favorita', 27 Via Favorita (on the S outskirts). Trattorie: 'Belvedere', Via Vaccari, and 'Kalos', Piazza della Vittoria.

Cafés or bars ('pasticceria'). 'Enzo e Nino (Tiffany)', Via 11 Maggio; 'De Gaetano', Via Rapisardi.

Picnic places near the sea front on Capo Boeo.

History. *Lilybaeum*, founded by the Carthaginians in 396 BC, near the headland of Capo Boeo, the western extremity of Sicily, and peopled from Motya (see above), was their strongest bulwark in Sicily, and succumbed to the Romans only after a siege of ten years (250–241). As the seat of the Roman governor of Sicily it reached its zenith. It kept its importance as an avenue of communication with Africa during the Saracen dominion under the name 'Marsa Alí' or 'Mars-al-Allah', the harbour of Ali or God, but declined after 1574 when Don Juan of Austria (illegitimate son of Charles V) almost completely blocked its port to protect it from Barbary pirates.

The wine trade was founded by John Woodhouse in 1773 when he made the first shipment of the local white wine to Liverpool, conserving it on its month-long journey by adding alcohol. Marsala became popular in England as an alternative to madeira

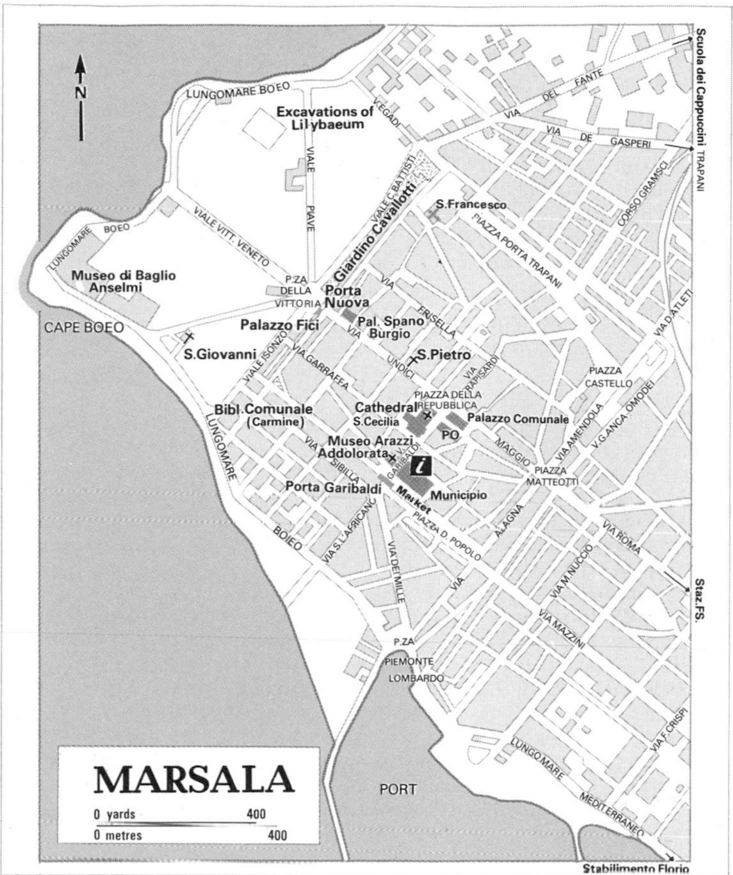

and port. In 1798, after the Battle of the Nile, Nelson placed a large order of Marsala for his fleet. In 1806 Benjamin Ingham and his nephew Whitaker also took up trading in Marsala with great success; by 1812 they were exporting the wine to America. Production on an even grander scale was undertaken by Vincenzo Florio (died 1868), one of Sicily's most able businessmen. In 1929 the establishments of Woodhouse, Ingham Whitaker, and Florio were taken over by Cinzano, and merged under the name of Florio. The house of Florio continues to flourish along with many other companies, including Pellegrino and Rallo (all of which welcome visitors).

Here Garibaldi and the Thousand made a landing on 11 May 1860, being unobtrusively assisted by two British warships which were there for the protection of the wine merchants. Marsala was heavily damaged in 1943 by allied air attacks.

The town is entered by the monumental PORTA GARIBALDI, formerly the 'Porta di Mare', reconstructed in 1685. On the left is the church of the ADDOLORATA, with a fine circular domed 18C interior, and a venerated popular statue of the Madonna wearing a black cloak. Municipal offices occupy a restored 16C military building, behind which is the market square.

Via Garibaldi continues to the central Piazza della Repubblica with the idiosyncratic PALAZZO COMUNALE (the town hall) which has original lamps on its upper storey. Opposite is the flank and dome of the 17C church of San Giuseppe (being restored).

The **Cathedral** (San Tommaso di Canterbury) has a Baroque front completed in 1957. The first church on this site was built in 1176–82 and dedicated to St Thomas Becket. A new building, begun in 1607 and completed in 1717 was ruined when the dome collapsed in 1893, and it was partly rebuilt in this century.

The pleasant INTERIOR, with pretty tiled floors in the side chapels, has interesting 17C paintings and sculptures. SOUTH SIDE: first chapel, unusual statue of the Assunta and two reliefs on the side walls, all by Antonino Gagini. Second chapel, 15C statue of the Madonna, and a tomb with the effigy of Antonio Grignano (died 1475) attributed to Domenico Gagini. In the third chapel is an elaborate statue of the 'Madonna dell'Itria', and the tomb of Giulio Alazzaro with an amusing effigy, both by Antonino Gagini. The fifth chapel has a 15C Crucifix and an expressive popular statue of the Virgin in mourning. In the SOUTH TRANSEPT is a good altarpiece of the Presentation in the Temple by Antonello or Mariano Riccio, and the tomb of Antonio Lombardo, who donated the tapestries to the cathedral (now in a museum, see below). In the chapel to the right of the sanctuary is an unusual statue of the Madonna (wielding a club), attributed to Giuliano Mancino, and a tomb with an effigy of Antonio Liotta (died 1512), also attributed to Mancino. On either side of the sanctuary are two statues, one of St Vincent Ferrer attributed to Giacomo Gagini and one of St Thomas the Apostle by Antonello Gagini. In the apse is a 17C painting of the Martyrdom of St Thomas in a good frame. In the chapel to the left of the sanctuary is a beautiful gilded marble altarpiece of the Passion (behind the altar) begun in 1518 by Bartolomeo Berrettaro and finished by Antonello Gagini (1532; four of the panels have been set into the walls). NORTH SIDE. In the sixth chapel is a charming polychrome wood statue of the 'Madonna del Carmelo', and in the second chapel is another wood statue of the Madonna (1593), and two frescoed ex-votos with scenes of Marsala. A 17C silver statue of St Thomas of Canterbury, formerly outside the choir, has been removed for safety.

Behind the Duomo, in Via Giuseppe Garraffa is the little **Museo degli Arazzi** (open 9–13, 16–18), opened in 1985 to display eight precious *TAPESTRIES given to the cathedral in 1589 by Antonio Lombardo, archbishop of Messina (1523–95) born in Marsala and buried in the cathedral. He became ambassador to Spain, and the tapestries depicting the Capture of Jerusalem (made in Brussels between 1530 and 1550) are known to have come from the Palazzo Reale of Philip II in Madrid. They have been beautifully restored, and have to be kept in darkened rooms.

Via XX Maggio leads out of Piazza della Repubblica (see above). The convent of San Pietro, with a massive pointed tower, is now used as a sports centre. A street on the left leads towards the former church of the Carmine, now the Biblioteca Comunale. The piazza here is used as an open-air theatre in summer. Nearby, in a pretty square with a Baroque fountain is the ex-church of SANTA CECILIA, with a Baroque façade, where concerts are held. In via XX Maggio, just before Porta Nuova, is the façade (left) of Palazzo Fici (in poor repair) with a tall palm tree in its delightful Baroque courtyard. Opposite is the 19C Palazzo Spanò Burgio (No. 15), with a collection of contemporary art opened in 1988.

Outside the gate is the entrance (right) to the GIARDINO CAVALLOTTI, lovely public gardens with huge ficus trees, magnolias, and ornamental araucarie. Between Piazza della Vittoria and the sea front extends **Cape Boeo**, an open area (closed to traffic, and protected from new buildings) with lawns and trees. Some picturesque old 'bagli' on the sea front are used as restaurants, and one of them houses the Archaeological Museum. Capo Boeo was the site of **Lilybaeum**, the excavations of which are reached by Viale Piave. A ROMAN VILLA (surrounded by a fence and covered for protection; officially open at the same time as the museum, see below, but often kept locked) dates from the 3C AD, and was built over in the Arab period. Around the impluvium are four mosaics of wild beasts attacking each other (thought to represent circus animals), probably the work of African craftsmen. There are remains of baths and other rooms with mosaics, including a head of Medusa, the symbol of Trinacria, the four seasons, etc. Nearby are more recent excavations including part of the walls, a necropolis, a Roman road, a Roman vomitorium, etc.

On the tip of the promontory is the BAGLIO ANSELMI, a former Marsala distillery and wine cellar, which has been restored as the ***Museo Archeologico di Baglio Anselmi** (open daily 9–14; Wed and Sat, also 15–18; fest. 9–13, 15–18). From the entrance hall can be seen the spacious courtyard of the balio, planted with palm trees; the museum is arranged in two huge vaulted warehouses. The display begins in the hall on the left (and on the left wall), with Prehistoric material from the Marsala area, in particular from Motya. Beyond, two showcases have Phoenician finds from the tophet of Motya. The finds from the Phoenician necropoli of Lilybaeum are displayed chronologically with explanatory diagrams and photographs, and include ceramics, funerary monuments, sculptures, terracottas, and 'Tanagra' figurines. On the end wall are fragments of funerary monuments, stele, and edicole with carved inscriptions or paintings (3–2C BC) from Motya and Lilybaeum. Also here are fragments from a large mausoleum in local stone covered with a fine layer of white and polychrome stucco (its hypothetical form has been reconstructed in a drawing). A small room displays epigraphs. On the right wall of the hall are finds from Roman Lilybaeum (3–4C AD), and in the centre of the room a model of the excavations on Cape Boeo. In show cases are fragments of wall paintings, a hoard of coins, lamps, and a fragment of a female statuette of the 3C AD. In the centre, two mosaics (5C AD and 3C AD) and an 'opus sectile' pavement from the 4C AD. The display ends with photographs of Palaeochristian finds, and a case of ceramics including Siculo-Norman ware. The last case illustrates the discovery of a Norman wreck offshore in 1983, with a few finds from the boat.

The other splendid hall on the right contains the *PUNIC SHIP, discovered by Miss Honor Frost in 1971 off the Isola Longa, in the Stagnone lagoon N of Marsala (see above), and subjected to a long and delicate process of restoration under her supervision. The well-preserved poop was recovered from the seabed and the rest of the hulk, 35m long, was carefully reconstructed in 1980. Manned by 68 oarsmen, it is thought to have been sunk on its maiden voyage during the First Punic War. It is unique as the only warship of this period so far discovered; it is not known how the iron nails resisted the corrosion of the sea. The ship has been partly reconstructed around the original wood which is conserved beneath a huge tent which makes viewing awkward. Drawings illustrate the original appearance of the ship. At the end of the room are two cases of objects found on board, including remains of ropes, a sailor's wooden button, a bone needle used for making nets, corks from the amphorae, a brush, and a few ceramic fragments. Around the walls are piled underwater finds, including numerous amphorae.

Nearby is the conspicuous little church of SAN GIOVANNI, covering the so-called Grotto of the Sibyl which was probably the shrine of a Roman water-cult (recently restored; usually open in summer).

The road, lined with palms, continues along the sea front (with ugly modern buildings on the left) past the former Baglio Woodhouse (the entrance is marked by two round towers in front of a jetty and next to a chapel built by the English). In the harbour only the base remains of the monument commemorating the Landing of the Thousand, by Ettore Ximenes, which was destroyed in the war. There are long-term (and controversial plans) to reconstruct it. The road passes a number of old 'bagli', and, beside two tall palm trees, is the huge STABILIMENTO FLORIO (see above; open to visitors Mon–Thurs 8.30–13, 14.30–18; Fri 8–14; closed Sat and Sun). The monumental buildings were designed in 1833–35 by Ernesto Basile around a huge inner courtyard planted with trees. Visitors are shown the historic cellars and invited to taste the wine (free of charge). In the small museum a letter is preserved from Nelson, Duke of Bronte to John Woodhouse in 1800 with an order for Marsala for his fleet. In the grounds are the tomb-stone of John Woodhouse, and the neo-classical villa built by Ingham.

N of the town, in the SCUOLA DEI CAPPUCCINI are remains of a huge Punico-Roman necropolis (open in summer). To the S, on N115, the former Baglio Amodeo, one of the oldest Marsala warehouses, is surrounded by a beautiful garden and is open as a restaurant (Villa Favorita). At contrada Ponte Berbaro (also off N 115) is a private wine museum (Cantina Montalto), with a restaurant (previous booking only).

Some 10km outside the town, in the contrada Biesina, the MUSEO DI VILLA GENNA contains an interesting local collection of artisans' tools, etc. (closed indefinitely).

he road continues S past a line of Marsala warehouses and then traverses a plain rich in vineyards, but where much ugly new building has taken place.

53.5km **Mazara del Vallo**, the most important fishing town in Italy (49,000 inhab.) at the mouth of the Mazaro. It has a pleasant waterfront and busy harbour. The town, built in golden-coloured tufa, has a distinctly Arab flavour; in recent years the ancient 'Casbah' of the city in the Pilazza district has been repopulated by Tunisians. Much uncontrolled new building has taken place on the outskirts in the last few decades. It was damaged by earthquake in 1980.

Information Office 'Pro Loco', 9 Piazza della Repubblica.

Railway Station, Piazza de Gasperi, on the line from Trapani to Castelvetrano.

Bus station, Piazza Matteotti.

Hotels. 3-star: 'Hopps'; 2-star: 'Mediterraneo'.

Numerous **trattorie**, mostly on the water front.

History. Mazara was an emporium of Selinunte and fell with it in 409 BC. It was held by the Carthaginians until 210 BC when it came under Roman dominion. Here in 827 the Saracens, called in by the governor Euphemius to abet his pretensions to the Imperial purple, gained their first foothold in Sicily. There followed the most important period in the town's history, when it became the main city in the Val di Mazara. It was finally captured by Count Roger in 1075; and here the first Norman parliament in Sicily met in 1097.

The **Cathedral** was founded in 1093 and rebuilt in 1690–94. Above the W door, which faces the sea, is a 16C sculpture of Count Roger on horseback. The interior contains a *Transfiguration in the apse by Antonello Gagini (finished by his son Antonino, 1537). The two statues of St Bartolomeo and St Ignazio are by Ignazio Marabitti. In the S aisle is a sculpted portal by Bartolomeo Berrettaro. In the vestibule of the chapter house are two Roman sarcophaghi. A small MUSEUM contains the tomb of Giovanni Montaperto (1495) by Domenico Gagini, church silver, vestments, etc. Off the N side is a chapel with a 13C painted Cross, and in the chapel of the Madonna del Soccorso is a Byzantine fresco in a niche of Christ pantocrator.

Between the cathedral and the sea front is a PUBLIC GARDEN with fine trees on the site of the Norman castle, a ruined wall of which faces the busy Piazza Mokarta at the end of the main Corso Umberto I. On the other side of the cathedral is the 18C PIAZZA DELLA REPUBBLICA, with a statue by Marabitti (1771) and the handsome PALAZZO DEL SEMINARIO (1710) with a double portico. Via San Giuseppe leads to the church of SANTA CATERINA decorated in 1797 by Giuseppe Testa, with a statue of the saint by Antonello Gagini (1524). On the other side of Piazza della Repubblica Via XX Settembre leads to Piazza Plebiscito with the 18C church of SANT'IGNAZIO and the COLLEGIO DEI GESUITI (1675–86). This now houses the municipal libraray and archives and the MUSEO COMUNALE which has Roman finds from the area and two interesting sculpted elephants which bore the columns outside the W porch of the Norman cathedral. A section dedicated to the history of the local fishing industry is also to be opened here.

The **harbour** lies at the mouth of the river Mazaro which is normally filled with the fishing fleet during the day (except on Saturdays). This is the most interesting part of the city (with the Tunisian district around Via Porta Palermo and Via Bagno). A short way upstream stands the little Norman-Byzantine church of SAN NICOLÒ REGALE with a crenallated top (recently restored; usually open on Sundays). The Lungomazaro continues along the river past the fish market to the bridge from which there is a splendid view of the boats. Farther upstream are caves, once inhabited. The 'marrobbio', a curious tidal movement of the sea, probably due to variations in the atmospheric pressure near the mouth of the river, now rarely occurs.

2km outside the town is the church of the MADONNA DELL'ALTO erected in 1103 by Giulitta, daughter of Count Roger.

A motorway (A29 for Palermo) runs on stilts parallel to N115 across the small plain from Mazara del Vallo to Castelvetrano, which is described, together with Selinunte in Rte 9.

9

Palermo to Castelvetrano and Selinunte

Road, N186, N113, and N119, 117.5km. To (45km) Alcamo, see Rte 4A. N119 diverges left.—90km Santa Ninfa (for Gibellina Nuova and Salemi)–104km **Castelvetrano**—117.5km **Selinunte**.

The **Motorway**, A29 for Castelvetrano (107km) runs roughly parallel to the road. At 66km it diverges left from the Trapani motorway (see Rte 4) and runs S down the valley of the Fiume Freddo.

Railway. To **Castelvetrano** 121km in 2–3 hours via Alcamo diramazione; a bus service has substituted the branch line from Castelvetrano to **Selinunte**, 14km in 25mins.

Information Office. 'APT' Trapani, Tel. 0923/27273.

From Palermo to (45km) **Alcamo**, see Rte 4A. N119 turns S and becomes sinuous, mounting to (77km) the old town of **Gibellina** (400m), below a ridge of sulphur-bearing hills, abandoned when it was totally destroyed in the earthquake of 1968 which badly damaged this area of the VALLE DEL BELICE. 531 people died and thousands were made homeless. Reconstruction has been scandalously slow and tens of thousands in the area lived in temporary shelters for many years (and many people have not yet been rehoused). Legal proceedings are in progress for embezzlement, etc. Where new towns have been built (see Gibellina) they tend to have a design which shows little consideration for the needs of the local population. Part of the ruins of Gibellina have been 'covered' by the sculptor Alberto Burri with cement as a work of 'Land Art'. The inhabitants have been moved some 20km W to the new town of Gibellina Nuova, described below. During a summer festival open-air theatrical performances are held here.

Above POGGIOREALE (also destroyed in the earthquake), 7km E of the old town, excavations in 1970 revealed part of a town and its necropolis (with 7C and 6C BC tombs). SALAPARUTA, 3km S of Gibellina, has been abandoned since the earthquake and a new town partially reconstructed. 90km SANTA NINFA, also badly damaged in the earthquake. Here a road diverges right for Gibellina Nuova (5km) and Salemi (12km).

The new town of **Gibellina Nuova** (5000 inhab.) has been built since 1968 on the plain near the motorway and railway station of Salemi in an unattractive site, unpleasantly hot in summer. It is approached by a colossal concrete 'star' over the motorway. The architecture of the new town is disappointing and numerous modern sculptures have been set up in its streets in highly questionable taste. The town has a sad atmosphere and seems to have nothing to do with the traditional farming culture of the area. The Museo Elimo has local Elymnian and Greek archaeological material, and there is a local Ethnographical Museum.

Salemi probably represents 'Halicyae', a town of the ancient Sicani or Elymians. Here Garibaldi, three days after landing at Marsala, assumed the function of dictator in Sicily in the name of Victor Emmanuel II. The town was badly damaged in the earthquake of 1968 when a third of the population (12,400 inhab.) were housed in huts on the edge of the town.

The centre was abandoned and the houses shaken by the earthquake declared unsafe (marked 'o' beside the doorways). The Cathedral and Cappuccino monastery were destroyed. The church of the Collegio (near the summit of the hill), with its twisted Baroque columns either side of the entrance, has been given Cathedral status. The imposing castle of the mid 13C has fine vaulted rooms. The Collegio dei Gesuiti has been restored to house the MUSEO CIVICO (for admission enquire at the Biblioteca Comunale). It contains sculptures attributed to Domenico and Antonello Gagini and Francesco Laurana, and a section on the Risorgimento.

On the outskirts of the town is the interesting palaeochristian basilica of San Miceli, with mosaic pavements. From Salemi the undulating 'Strada di Salemi' leads W to Marsala, see Rte 8.

The main road continues past a turning for **Partanna** (5km S), an agricultural centre (12,000 inhab.) badly damaged in 1968. Some of the inhabitants are still housed in temporary shelters. It preserves a Norman castle (rebuilt in the 17C), in the courtyard of which is a damaged coat of arms sculpted by Francesco Laurana who stayed here in 1468. The Chiesa Matrice has been partially reconstructed after it was almost totally destroyed in the earthquake. It contains stuccoes by Vincenzo Messina, an organ by Paolo Amato, and a statue of the Madonna by the bottega of Laurana.

The main road continues along a pretty ridge (parallel to the motorway) to (104km) **CASTELVETRANO** a town (32,000 inhab.) in the centre of a wine and oil producing area, which is also known for its cabinet-makers. To the S the view falls away across the cultivated plain towards the sea and the ruins of Selinunte. The simple architecture of many of the houses, with internal courtyards, is interesting, although it was also damaged in the earthquake of 1968. Here the body of the bandit Giuliano (see Rte 4A) was found in 1950.

Information Office, Piazza Garibaldi.

Railway Station, Piazza Amendola, on the Trapani line.

Hotels. 3-star: 'Selinus', 2-star: 'Zeus'. There are now 3-star and 2-star hotels, and 1-star camping sites on the coast at Selinunte, see below.

Annual Festival. 'Aurora' on Easter Sunday morning, with a traditional procession, etc.

The centre of the town is the cramped and oddly shaped PIAZZA GARIBALDI, planted with trees. The DUOMO (usually entered by the side door in Piazza Umberto I) is a 16C church with an unusual flowery portal. The central roof beam has preserved its painted decoration. Two triumphal arches are bedecked with white stuccoes of putti, festoons, and angels, by Antonino Ferraro and Gaspare Serpotta (who also executed the four saints in the nave). In the presbytery is gilded decoration by Antonino Ferraro and an Assumption by Orazio Ferraro (1619). The chapel to the right of the sanctuary has a wood Crucifix of the 16C, and the chapel to the left of the sanctuary, a marble Gaginesque statue, and, on the wall, a painting attributed to Pietro Novelli. Off the left aisle, the Cappella della Maddalena has fine decoration, especially in the dome, by Tommaso Ferraro. The detached campanile dates from the 16C. On the corner of Piazza Umberto I is an elaborate fountain (1615) with a statue of a nymph by Orazio Nigrone.

In Piazza Garibaldi is the church of the the PURGATORIO with a decorative 18C façade (now used as an auditorium), and the neo-classical TEATRO SELINUS (1870; by Giuseppe Patricolo). Via Garibaldi leads downhill past

Via Francesco la Croce on the corner of which is the Biblioteca Comunale. New premises have been prepared here for a MUSEUM, but it has never been opened. The small collection includes some finds from Selinunte (ceramics and coins) and a statue from the church of the Annunziata (the head attributed to Francesco Laurana). The famous bronze statuette known as the 'Ephebus of Selinunte' (5C BC) stolen from here in 1968, has been displayed since its recovery in the archaeological museum in Palermo.

From the top of Via Garibaldi, Via Fra Pantaleo leads downhill SE to Piazza Regina Margherita with a little public garden, and two churches. SAN DOMENICO, with a plain façade, contains a riot of Baroque terracotta *stuccoes by Antonino Ferraro (late 16C), and unusual funerary monuments. It was damaged in 1968 and the E end is still covered for restoration. On another side of the piazza is the church of SAN GIOVANNI BATTISTA with an elaborate façade and a green cupola. The interesting interior (also damaged in 1968) is closed during restoration work. It contains a good statue of its patron by Antonello Gagini, 1522, and three 17C paintings (temporarily removed), formerly attributed to Gherardo delle Notti. In Viale Roma is a private museum of Sicilian carts.

About 3km W of the town is the church of the ***Santissima Trinità di Delia**. It is reached by taking the road downhill from Piazza Umberto I and continuing straight ahead (signposted 'Trinità di Delia'), leaving the Trapani/Agrigento road on the left. After c 1km, at a fork, the road (unsignposted) continues left past a gravel works and straight on (signposted 'Lago di Trinità). It passes a small eucalyptus wood and then skirts the white wall of the farm which incorporates the church. The key is kept at the modern house on the right. The chapel, dating from the 11–12C, is a very fine building derived from Arab and Byzantine models. It was beautifully restored in 1880, and contains 19C family tombs. The crypt beneath is entered by an outside stairway. In the churchyard in a little wood is a romantic tombstone by Benedetto Civiletti, erected by the Saporito family. Beneath the hill is the large dammed Lago Trinità.

The road (N115 and N115d) and railway run S across the plain to the extensive ruins of the ancient city of (117.5km) ***SELINUNTE**, on the edge of the sea (superb views along the coast to the E). The town with its acropolis occupied a terrace above the sea, between the river Selinon and the marshy depression now called Gorgo di Cottone or Galici, and possessed a harbour at the mouth of each valley. An important group of temples lay to the E of this site, and a necropolis to the N. The sandy soil is overgrown with wild celery, mandrake, acanthus, and capers. This is perhaps the most impressive of the Greek cities of Sicily, since the ruins have never been built over in modern times. However, the site has recently been damaged by the construction of a huge dyke, with tunnels, beside Temple E, and the long-term plans to enclose the site in a park (270 hectares) in an attempt to discourage clandestine excavations and preserve the area from new buildings have so far come to very little. A new entrance and ticket office have been built near the E group of temples but are not in use. MARINELLA, once a simple fishing village, has been untidily and pretentiously developed as a resort.

Information Office of the 'APT' Trapani on the site near the E group of temples.

Hotels. 2-star: 'Alceste' and others (3-star, 2-star, and 1-star); numerous **restaurants** and cafés in Marinella.

Buses from Castelvetrano (the stop near the disused railway station is a 5-minute walk from the E group of temples).

Admission daily 8.30–dusk. Entrance fee for the Acropolis. The visit, best started early in the morning, takes at least 2–3 hours (it is a lovely place to picnic). A music and drama festival is celebrated in August near Temple E.

History. Selinunte was colonised from Megara Hyblaea, probably as early as 651 BC. It takes its name (*Selinous*) from the wild celery (Greek, selinon), which still grows here in abundance. Its most prosperous period was the 5C BC, when the great temples were built, and the city was laid out on a rectangular plan. After the battle of Himera Selinunte allied itself with Syracuse against Carthage, and in 409 BC the Carthaginians, summoned to the help of Segesta, the mortal enemy of Selinunte, sent an army of 100,000 under Hannibal, son of Gisco, which took Selinunte by assault before the allied troops of Agrigentum and Syracuse could arrive. The city was sacked and destroyed, and a later settlement led by Hermocrates, a Syracusan exile, was dispersed by Carthage in 250, and the population resettled at Lilybeaum. It is thought, however, that the utter destruction of every building, scarcely a single column being left upright, must have been due to earthquakes, rather than to the hand of man.

The site was rediscovered in the 16C; but systematic excavations were begun only in 1822–23 by the Englishmen William Harris and Samuel Angell, after a fruitless dig had been made in 1809–10 by Robert Fagan, British consul-general in Sicily. Harris and Angell found the famous metopes of Temple C: Harris died of maleria contracted while excavating here. In 1956–58 12 streets were excavated, and in 1973 excavations were begun to the N, on the site of the ancient city. The most recent excavations have been in the area of the Temple of Malophoros. A bronze statue (Phoenician, 12–11C BC) of Reshef found hereabouts is the first archaeological confirmation that the Phoenicians traded here before the foundation of Carthage. It is, at present, kept in the Museo Archeologico in Palermo.

The temples are distinguished by letters as their dedications are still under discussion. They were the only temples in Sicily to be decorated with sculptures; many of their beautiful metopes are displayed in the archaeological museum in Palermo (described in Rte 1C). All except Temples B and G are peripteral and hexastyle and all are orientated. The measurements given in the text refer to the temple stylobates. Many architectural fragments bear remains of intonaco (plaster), and throughout the site are underground cisterns, built to collect rainwater. Beside most of the temples are sacrificial altars.

The main road from Castelvetrano, before entering Marinella, passes (right) a huge ugly dyke beside an untidy car park which is at present the entrance to the E group of temples. A new car park and entrance to the whole site (including the acropolis) are to be opened near here. The **East Group of Temples** consists of the ruins of three large temples. Beside the modern dyke and tunnel is TEMPLE E, which measures 67.7m by 25.3m, and was probably dedicated to Hera or Aphrodite. It is a Doric building of 490–480 BC; four of its metopes discovered in 1831 and now in the Palermo archaeological museum attest the beauty of its sculpture. Toppled by an earthquake, its colonnades were reconstructed in 1958. A small ANTIQUARIUM near the car park shows the various stages in its restoration, and contains a few architectural fragments found on the site. A new museum may one day be opened in the farmhouse near Temple G (cf. below). TEMPLE F, the oldest on this hill (c 560–540 BC), totally ruined, had a double row of columns in front and 14 at the sides. It may have been dedicated to Athena or Dionysius. Part of one column rises above others which are now only a few metres high.

The farthest N, beyond the road, is TEMPLE G, probably dedicated to Apollo or Zeus; octastyle in form, it ranks second in size (110 by 50m) after the Olympieion at Agrigento among Sicilian temples. Its columnar arrangement (8 by 17) is matched only by the Parthenon. It was laid out before the

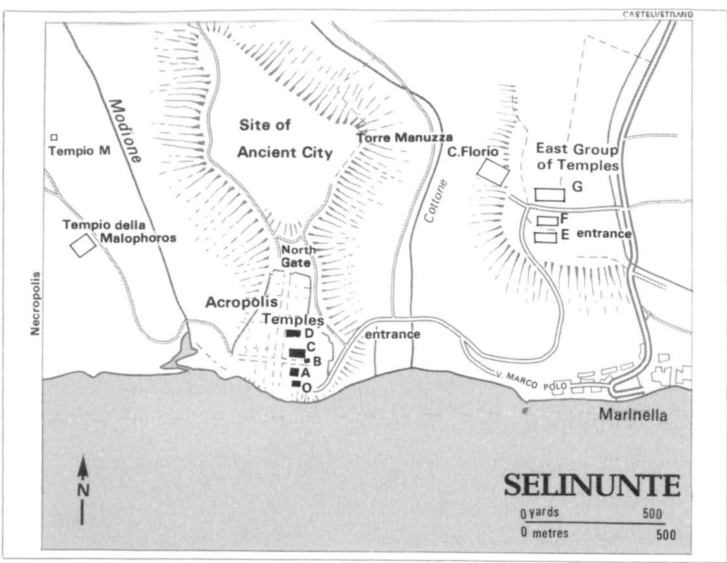

end of the 6C and left incomplete in 480. One column alone remains standing, and the ruins are now very overgrown. The columns, over 16m high with a base diameter of 3.4m, were built up of drums, each weighing c 100 tons, from the quarries at Cusa. As each drum was placed in position it was caused to revolve around a central pivot, until, by the attrition of sand inserted for the purpose, it rested absolutely truly on the drum beneath. The fact that many of the columns are unfluted implies that the temple was never completed. The cella, preceded by a pronaos of four columns, had three aisles, the central aisle being open to the sky. At one end are huge blocks from the quarries; the fallen capitals give some idea of the colossal scale of the building. The enormous stylobate is in itself a marvel of monumental construction. There is a fine view of the plain filled with olive trees and the restored farmhouse ('BALIO FLORIO') which is eventually to become a MUSEUM. The handsome spacious building has been restored but closed for many years.

The old road can be followed on foot from the temple hill down across the Gorgo di Cottone (site of one of the ancient harbours) to the acropolis; this can also at present be reached by car along the upper road from Marinella. It ends at a car-park (and ticket office) beside the massive double walls of the **Acropolis**. Five towers and four gates have been located along their length, and they date from around 307–306 BC. A path continues up to the custodian's house and a group of buildings used as excavation offices. Beside an abandoned house near a group of palm trees a path and steps lead up to the complicated ruins of the acropolis which is traversed by two principal streets at right angles, with lesser streets running parallel. In front of the custodian's house are the stylobate of TEMPLE O, whose superstructure has entirely disappeared, and the stylobate of TEMPLE A (40m by 16m; 36 columns), with some fluted drums. The cella was one step higher than the pronaos and the adytum one higher still. Between the cella and

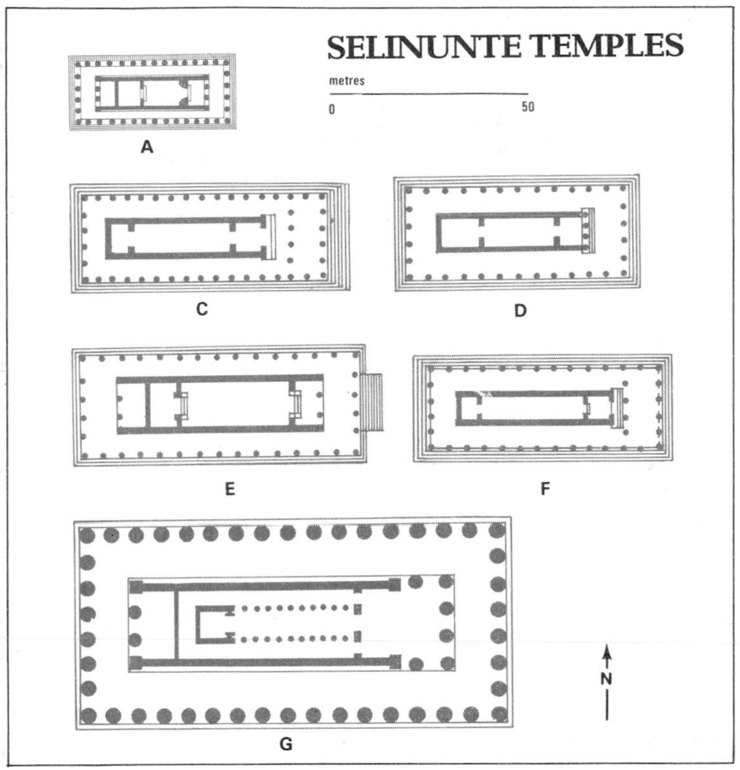

pronaos two spiral staircases led up to the roof. Fragmentary ruins of a propylaea exist to the E. Temples A and O, built in 490–480 BC, and identical in form and dimension, were the latest and probably the most perfect of the Selinuntine temples. In front of Temple O a sacred area has been excavated, thought to date from after the destruction of the city in 409 BC.

A path, which follows the E–W thoroughfare of the city, leads left in front of the pronaos of Temple A past a mosaic pavement which has the representation of the Punic goddess Tanit, to reach the wide main N thoroughfare of the city, which should now be followed N. On the right, on the highest point of the knoll are the remains of the great TEMPLE C (63.7m by 24m), dating from the early 6C, and probably dedicated to Apollo; the famous metopes in the Palermo archaeological museum were found here in 1823. The colossal columns (6 by 17), some of which were monolithic, are nearly 2m in diameter at the base, except for the corner-columns which are even thicker; they fell during an earthquake in Christian times, burying a Byzantine village that had grown up in the 5C (Crosses are carved on some of the architectural fragments). The N colonnade was re-erected in 1925–27. Part of the sacrificial altar remains. To the S of the temple is a MEGARON (17.6m by 5.5m), dating from 580–570 BC. In the E corner of the temenos a STOA has been excavated which was probably built at the same time as the

Reconstruction of Temple C at Selinunte

Acropolis walls (late 6C). To the right is the small TEMPLE B, a prostyle aediculum with pronaos and cella.

Beside a small pine tree is TEMPLE D which flanks the road. It dates from 570–554 BC; the stylobate, which carried 34 columns, measures 56m by 24m. Some of its blocks still have their bosses. Fronting a road near the temple is a row of modest constructions, thought to have been shops, each with two rooms, a courtyard, and stairs up to the living quarters on the first floor. Nearby are the foundations of the TEMPLE OF THE SMALL METOPES, so-called because it is thought the 6 small metopes now in the Palermo Museum belong to it; it had a simple cella and adytum and measured 15.2m by 5.4m.

The NORTH GATE, one of the main gates of the city, is well preserved. Outside it is a sophisticated defence system once thought to date from the time of Hermocrates, but probably constructed by Agathocles in 307–306 BC. The fortifications include three semicircular towers, and a second line of walls c 5m outside the earlier ones which were reinforced after their destruction by Hannibal in 409 BC using material from the acropolis including capitals. The imposing remains are explained here in a diagram.

The ANCIENT CITY, orientated N–S, is still being excavated: recent research has suggested it may originally have extended beyond the (later) perimeter wall to the N, and into the valleys of the Cotone and Modione rivers. Another area of the city farther N, on the sand-covered hill of Manuzza, may have had a slightly different orientation. Farther N was a necropolis (probably on the site of a prehistoric burial place).

A larger **Necropolis** ('Manica-lunga, Timpone Nero'), however, lay on the right bank of the Modione, which can be crossed in front of the farm called Gaggara. Here the interesting **Sanctuary of Demeter Malophoros** consists of a sacred area enclosed by walls. It is now approached by a propylaea (late 5C) and portico. In the centre is a huge sacrificial altar, and beyond, the temple (a megaron), thought to have been built c 560, with a Doric cornice. Nearby are the scant remains of two other sacred precincts, one of them dedicated to **Zeus Meilichios** with two altars, where numerous stelae carved with a male and female head were discovered. More than 5000 terracotta figurines have been found in the vicinity. Another temple is being excavated to the S. Near a spring, some 200m N, a sacred edifice has recently been excavated and called **Temple M**. This may in fact be an altar or a monumental fountain of the 6C BC. The necropolis proper extends for some kilometres to the W; several tombs and heaps of bones are still visible. It has recently been suggested that this necropolis did not belong to the city of Selinunte.

FROM SELINUNTE TO THE CAVE DI CUSA, 18km. Off the road between Selinunte and Castelvetrano a pretty byroad (signposted) leads through extensive olive groves and vineyards to (10km) CAMPOBELLO DI MAZARA, a wine-producing centre (11,800 inhab.), with a Crucifix by Fra Umile da Petralia.

From here a road (signposted) leads S towards Tre Fontane on the coast. At a crossroads by the ruins of the Baglio Ingham (a little beyond which, in a field on the left, lies a column drum abandoned on its way to Selinunte) a right turn continues past a sewage plant to end at (18km) the entrance (open daily 9am to sunset) to the ancient quarries used for the construction of the temples of Selinunte known as the ***Cave di Cusa**. The beautiful peaceful site is surrounded by olive and orange plantations, and vineyards, and ancient olive trees grow among the ruins. The quarries have not been worked since the destruction of Selinunte in 409 BC. The various processes of quarrying may be studied, from the first incisions in the rock to the empty spaces left by the removal of completed drums for columns. A block, still attached to the rock, seems to have been intended for a capital. Around each column carved out of the rock a space of c 50cm allowed room for the stonemason. Close together stand four drums which have been carved for the whole of their length and await only to be detached at their bases. The large cylindrical masses of stone (c 3m by 2m) were probably intended for Temple G. It is thought that wooden frames were constructed around the columns and they were transported to Selinunte on wheels of solid wood strengthened by iron bands and pulled by oxen or slaves.

10

Castelvetrano to Agrigento

Road, N118B and N115, 91.5km.—34km **Sciacca**—63km, turning for **Eraclea Minoa**—87km Porto Empedocle—91.5km **Agrigento**.

The pretty, narrow-gauge **railway line** along the coast has been closed: a **bus service** has taken its place. To Sciacca in 1½hrs; to Agrigento in 3½hrs (with a change at Ribera).

Information Office. 'APT' Agrigento (Tel. 0922/26926).

From Castelvetrano the new road (which ruins the landscape since it is raised on stilts) traverses the cultivated valley of the Belice, which meanders lazily through a wide and deep channel. There are occasional glimpses of the sea and the oddly shaped white promontory of Capo San Marco, beyond vineyards, citrus plantations, and fields of artichokes.

19km, turning for MENFI (13,000 inhab.), which lies 2km S of the road. The town was laid out on a regular plan in 1698, and the houses arranged around courtyards off the main streets, many of which were made uninhabitable by the earthquake in 1968. Several of its damaged chuches are propped up with scaffolding, and some of the inhabitants still live in temporary shelters along the road outside the town. A new town is being built on the higher ground above.

12km N lies SANTA MARGHERITA DI BELICE where the country house described by Lampedusa in 'Il Gattopardo' as 'Donnafugata' was destroyed, together with most of the town, in the 1968 earthquake. **Sambuca di Sicilia** (7000 inhab.) is 17km NE of Menfi. It old centre preserves its Islamic lay-out (near Piazza Navarro). The church of the Concezione has a 14C portal and the church of the Carmine contains 19C stuccoes and a statue of the Madonna attributed to Antonello Gagini. In Palazzo Panitteri is a museum of 19C wax models. The Chiesa del Collegio and Cappuccini have works by Fra Felice da Sambuca (1734–1805). To the N are the excavations of Adranone and Contessa Entellina, described in Rte 11B. A byroad (7km) lead S from Menfi to PORTO PALO, a fishing village beyond woods. There are good beaches on the unspoilt coast here. Camping sites: 3-star 'La Serenella' in contrada Torrenove, and 1-star 'La Palma' in contrada Fiori.

The main road (still raised on stilts) continues through beautiful countryside with a good view of the sea before reaching the ugly outskirts of (34km) **SCIACCA** (40,000 inhab.) a spa town known since Roman times, when it was the 'thermae' of Selinunte. It has been engulfed by new buildings, and many of its monuments are in poor repair. A local ceramic industry flourished here in the 16C and 17C, and a few artisans' workshops survive in the town.

Information Office. 'Azienda Autonoma', 84 Corso Vittorio Emanuele (Tel. 0925/22744). 'Azienda Autonoma delle Terme', 2 Via Agatocle (Tel. 0925/27577).

Buses. Frequent services to Agrigento (in 1hr 45 mins) and to Palermo (in 2hrs 30 minutes).

Hotels. 3-star: 'Grande Albergo delle Terme' and 'Garden', Via Valverde.

Camping Sites on the sea: 2-star: 'Baia Makauda', and 1-star 'Gioventù'.

Restaurants. 1st-class: 'Hostaria del Vicolo', Vicolo Sammaritano 10. Trattoria: 'Ardizzone Maria', 4 Via della Dogana.

Annual Festival. Carnival procession with allegorical floats, etc.

A road descends towards the centre of the town. Beside part of its old fortifications is the unusual PORTA SAN SALVATORE (1581), a fine work by local stonemasons. Beside it is the eccentric façade of the CARMINE with a half finished neo-classical lower part and an asymmetrical 13C rose-window. The dome, with green tiles, dates from 1807. The church contains a good painting of the Transition of the Virgin, the last work of Vincenzo da Pavia, completed by Giampaolo Fondulli in 1572.

A short way up Via Geradi (left) is the STERIPINTO a small fortified palace in the Gothic Catalan style (in very poor repair). It is interesting for its façade, with diamond-shaped stone facing, erected in 1501 by Antonio Noceto. Opposite the Carmine, on the other side of Via Incisa, is the N portal, sculpted in 1468 by Francesco Laurana and his workshop, of the church of SANTA MARGHERITA (closed many years ago). It contains polychrome stuccoes by Orazio Ferraro. Beyond is the Gothic portal of the ex-church of San Gerlando and the abandoned Ospedale di Santa Margherita. Opposite are the late-Gothic Palazzo Perollo-Arone and the 15C Torre di Pardo, both ruined by modern alterations.

Corso Vittorio Emanuele continues into the central PIAZZA ANGELO SCANDALIATO planted with trees and with a long terrace from which there is a view of the old houses rising in terraces above the fishing harbour. Here is the huge ex-COLLEGIO DEI GESUITI (now the town hall), begun in 1613, with a fine courtyard. The Corso continues to the dilapidated Piazza Duomo where the DUOMO (called the 'Basilica') has statues by Antonino and Gian Domenico Gagini on its façade. It was rebuilt in 1656 by Michele Blasco, and the vault fresco is by the local artist Tommaso Rossi (1829). It has some good sculptures including a statue of the Madonna of 1457, a marble ancona with reliefs by Antonino Gagini, and (on the high altar) the Madonna 'del Soccorso' by Giuliano Mancino and Bartolomeo Berrettaro.

The Corso continues to PIAZZA FRISCIA with pretty 19C public gardens with tropical plants, in a pleasanter part of the town. Via Agatocle leads right past a new THEATRE to the edge of the cliff. Here is the NUOVO STABILIMENTO TERMALE, a pink spa building in Art Nouveau style built in 1928–38. The sulphureous waters (32 degrees cent.) are used in thermal swimming pools (open June to October) and mud bath therapy. The Grand Hotel was built next door in 1952.

From Piazza Friscia Via Valverde leads up to the gardens in front of the church of SANTA MARIA DELLE GIUMMARE (or Valverde), its façade tucked in between two castellated Norman towers; the restored chapel in the left tower has an interesting interior. The elaborate 18C Rococo decoration in the main church is the work of Ferraiolo. The vault was frescoed by Mariano Rossi (1768). Also in the upper town is SAN NICOLÒ LA LATINA, a simple 12C church (in bad repair). Above is the ruined CASTLE of the Spanish Luna family. Their feud with the Perollo clan in 15–16C became notorious under the name of 'caso di Sciacca' (the 'Sciacca affair'); it was resolved only after the population of the town had been reduced to almost half its size. In Piazza Noceto, with the 16C Porta San Calogero, are three churches including SAN MICHELE (1614–20) which contains an 18C cantoria, a Gothic wood Crucifix, and a 16C marble bas-relief.

7km NE of Sciacca rises **Monte Kronio** (or **Monte San Calogero**; 388m) which has caves with interesting steam vapours, known since Roman times. A spa hotel is open here from April to November. The sanctuary of San Calogero (1530–1644) has a statue of the saint by Giacomo Gagini. Two kilometres outside the town, on the Agrigento road, is the 'CASTELLO INCANTATO' (well signposted), a park with olive and almond trees where thousands of heads were sculpted in wood and stone by a local sculptor Filippo Bentivegna (died 1967).

Caltabellotta, 20km NE of Sciacca, is a little town (5200 inhab.) in a beautiful position on a commanding height (849m). Here the peace ending the War of the Vespers was signed in 1302. The Norman church (usually locked) has statues by the Gagini. The castle sheltered Sibylla, queen of Tancred, and her son William III in 1194 shortly before they succumbed to their fate at the hands of Henry VI. The church of the Salvatore, below the rock face, has a late Gothic portal. On the outskirts is the hermitage of San Pellegrino (17–18C; now derelict). 7km below Caltabellotta is the little town of SANT'ANNA, founded in 1622.

Beyond Sciacca the road passes untidy suburbs, which finally give way to olives, vineyards, and citrus fruit plantations (protected from the wind by net screens). 50km, turning for RIBERA (5km), a town (18,000 inhab,) founded in 1627 by Luigi, Prince of Paternò, and named in honour of his Spanish wife, Maria de Ribera. It was the birthplace of Francesco Crispi (1818–1901), the statesman. The town is a centre of market gardening (oranges, strawberries, etc.).

N386 leads N from Ribera to VILLAFRANCA SICULA (18km), founded in 1499, but damaged in 1968, and BURGIO (20km), an agricultural town with a local ceramics industry founded in the 16C and a bell-foundry. A castle survives here and in the church is a Madonna by Vincenzo Gagini. The N386 winds N towards Corleone via Chiusa Sclafani (37km) to Bisacquino (42km; described in Rte 11B).

63km, turning for (4.5km) the excavations of ***Eraclea Minoa**, in a magnificent isolated position on the sea at the mouth of the ancient Halykos (now the Platani). The road follows the lovely meandering river valley and climbs the low hill past vineyards. Beyond (4km) the turning for the seaside village (3-star camping site: 'Eraclea Minoa Village') an unsurfaced road continues for the last 500m. Here can be seen part of the town DEFENCES which were improved in the 4C (when the length of the walls was increased to c 6km). Above the dirt road on the left are the foundation of a circular Greek tower and stretch of well preserved wall (ending in a square Roman tower). The continuation of the walls has been lost in landslides. A splendid view extends along the wooded shore and white limestone cliffs to CAPO BIANCO, beyond the river. The beautiful coastline here, which includes TORRE SALSA, with interesting vegetation and birdlife (where sea turtles survive) was saved from development in 1991 when part of it was purchased by the World Wildlife Fund. The MAIN ENTRANCE TO THE EXCAVATIONS of Eraclea Minoa is beside the ruins of Hellenistic houses.

The name suggests an origin as a Minoan colony; a legend that Minos pursued Daedalus from Crete and founded a city here was reiterated by Diodorus who records that Theron Akragas found the bones of Minos at Minoa. A colony of Selinunte was founded on this site in the 6C, and the name Heracleia was probabaly added later in the century by Spartan emigres. The Halykos formed the boundary between the Greek and Carthaginian territories in Sicily. The town thrived during the 4C when it was resettled by Timoleon, but it seems to have been uninhabited by the end of the 1C BC. The first excavations took place in 1907 (and they were resumed in 1950–61).
Admission daily 9 to dusk. No refreshments are available, but it is a beautiful place to picnic.

A small ANTIQUARIUM (open 9–15 or 16) houses finds from Eraclea Minoa, and has instructive plans of the area so far excavated. A path leads on through the beautifully kept site where the visible remains (excavations in progress) date mainly from the 4C. The THEATRE was built at the end of the 4C. The soft sandstone has been covered in perspex for protection. On the hillside in front was the site of the CITY. Under cover is the so-called GOVERNOR'S HOUSE: part of the wall decoration and mosaic pavement survives. Also here is a little altar for sacrifices (under glass). Outside excavations have revealed three levels of destruction; the level of the Archaic city is at present being uncovered. The second line of the walls (built when the E part of the town was abandoned) is visible nearby. A path (or steps) lead up to the top of the hill above the theatre and a paved path leads over the hillside to the line of WALLS to the NE, with square towers built in the 4C BC.

The main road skirts a reservoir and passes below (67km) MONTALLEGRO, rebuilt in the 18C below its abandoned predecessor on the hill (a grotto here has produced finds from the Early Bronze Age to the Copper Aage). A byroad leads N to CATTOLICA ERACLEA (10km), founded in 1610. 78km SICULIANA, on a low hill to the left of the road, with a prominent domed church (1750–1813). The castle dates from 1350. Much new building has taken place on the plain. Camping sites (1-star) at Siculiana Marina. A byroad leads down to the pretty coast (with good beaches) beside the TORRE DI MONTEROSSO.

82.5km REALMONTE, with almond plantations. A byroad along the coast here leads to Punta Grande, near which are the 'SCALA DEI TURCHI', remarkable white rocks of limestone and sandy clay which have been eroded by the sea into fantastic shapes. Nearby are the excavations of the VILLA ROMANA DI DURRUELI dating from the 1C AD.

87km **Porto Empedocle**, an ugly industrial town (17,700 inhab.; 4-star hotels) with cement works, and a fishing port (in decline), now engulfed by high-rise buildings. On the inner mole, built in 1749–63 partly of stone from the temples of Agrigento, is a massive tower. It is the port for the Pelagie islands.

The **Isole Pelagie** lie about 205km SW of the Sicilian mainland (and 113km from Tunisia). They consist of three flat and barren islands, Lampedusa, Linosa and Lampione, off which there is good fishing (especially noted for sardines and anchovies). They fell to the allies without resistance in June 1943; Lampedusa surrendered to an English airman who landed by accident having run out of petrol. A ferry leaves from Porto Empedocle every evening in summer, and six times a week in winter (departure at 23.00) and arrives at Linosa around 7am and at Lampedusa at 9am. There is also a direct air service from Palermo and Trapani to Lampedusa. In summer a hydrofoil runs between Lampedusa and Linosa.

Lampedusa is the largest of the three islands with an area of 20 sq km and 5100 inhabitants. It has 3-star hotels including 'Baia Turchese' and 'Le Pelagie' and numerous 2-star and 1-star hotels. Camping sites: 2-star 'La Roccia', and 1-star 'Lampedusa'. Although it has a beautiful coast with excellent swimming, its beaches are not as clean as they might be, and it has some unattractive new buildings and noisy traffic. The ISOLOTTO DEI CONIGLI, just offshore, has been declared a nature reserve (sea turtles can still sometimes be seen here). Lampedusa has important US and Italian military installations; the Libyans made an unsuccessful attack in 1986 when two missiles fell 2.5km short of the island. **Linosa**, 42km N of Lampedusa, has an area of 5.3 sq km and 452 inhabitants. Volcanic in origin, it is the most fertile of the islands, and has colourful houses. It has one hotel (3-star 'Algusa'). It has been used as a place of exile for Mafia detainees. **Lampione**, with an area of just 1.2 sq km, is uninhabited.

Just beyond Porto Empedocle a road (signposted; 500m) diverges right for Caos where the BIRTHPLACE OF LUIGI PIRANDELLO, is now a delightful small museum. Admission daily 9–12, 15–17 (or 19 in summer). It can be reached by bus from Agrigento (Piazza Marconi). Nearby, under a wind-blown pine, the ashes of the writer (1867–1936) are buried according to his wishes beneath a 'rough rock in the countryside of Girgenti'. At a festival here in July plays by Pirandello are perfomed in the open-air. At Villaseta, a new housing estate, the direct (signposted) road for the modern town of Agrigento now diverges left on a fly-over above the river valley; the old road which continues straight on offers a much prettier approach. It traverses the valley of the temples before ascending to the centre of (91.5km) **Agrigento**, see Rte 12.

11

Palermo to Agrigento

A. Via Lercara Friddi

Road, 129.5km. 7km Acqua dei Corsari. N121—30km, turning for Bagni di Cefalà—60km Bivio Manganaro. N189—64.5km Lercara Friddi—129.5km **Agrigento**. This is the most direct route.

Railway, 139km; in c 2hrs. The railway leaves the Messina line beyond Termini Imerese, ascends the Torto valley to Roccapalumba-Alia (where the Catania line diverges), and at Lercara joins the road which it then closely follows to Agrigento.

Information Offices. From Palermo to Castronuovo di Sicilia, 'APT' Palermo (Tel. 091/583887). From there to Agrigento, 'APT' Agrigento (Tel. 0922/26926).

There are no **hotels** on this route.

Palermo is left by the old coastal road towards Messina; in the suburb of (7km) Acqua dei Corsari, N121 diverges right past the entrance to the Catania and Messina motorway, and follows the valley of the ancient Eleutheros. The plain has been filled with new buildings but some persimmon plantations survive here. Prominent to the right above the road is the ruined castle of (16km) MISILMERI. It takes its name from the Arab 'Menzil el Emir' ('village of the Emir'). Here in 1068 Roger de Hauteville defeated the Saracens, thus paving the way for the Norman domination of Sicily. A byroad leads right to BELMONTE MEZZAGNO (7km), founded in 1752 with a theatrical church built in 1776.

At (23.5km) Bolognetta N118 diverges right for Corleone (see Rte 11B). 30km Ponte Buffa. The old road (3km) to the W crosses the Cefalà beside the *BAGNI DI CEFALÀ, a remarkable bath house dating from the 10–11C, considered the most interesting Arab edifice left on the island (open daily except fest. 9–13.30). The baths have a splendid barrel vault and a pretty arch with two capitals and columns at one end. The water used to bubble up here at 33 degrees cent., but since 1989 the spring has been dry, and the baths, in use up until a few years ago, have lost much of their character after their recent restoration. The cufic inscription on a frieze of tufa which runs around the top of the outside wall has virtually disappeared. From here the castle of CEFALÀ DIANA is very prominent on a rock outcrop to the S.

A byroad leads E from Ponte Buffa to BAUCINA (5km) founded in 1626. The church has a wood Crucifix by the school of Salvatore Bagnasco. The road goes on to CIMINNA (10km) which has a number of interesting churches including the Chiesa Madre with 17C stuccoes by Scipione and Francesco Li Volsi and St John the Baptist by Paolo Amato. Off the main road at 39km is a turn for the little hill town of MEZZOJUSO (3km; 534m), of Arab origins. Settled by Albanians in the 15C, several of its churches still have services according to the Greek rite. A monastery here has a restoration laboratory for antique books. The deserted landscape changes as the road crosses the fertile valley of the San Leonardo, and then climbs up round VICARI, whose ruined castle was built by Count Roger, offering views of extraordinary beauty. At (60km) Bivio Manganaro this route turns S leaving N121 to continue through the centre of the island towards Enna and Caltanissetta.

64.5km LERCARA FRIDDI (660m) was founded in 1605 and was important in the 19C and early 20C for its sulphur mines. A number of 18C churches survive here. The road now joins the railway and follows the Platani valley. Side roads to the right lead up into the hills for (76km) CASTRONUOVO DI SICILIA where the churches contain 18C stuccoes by Antonio Messina, and the Chiesa Madre has works by the Gagini, and (79km) CAMMARATA, a little medieval town.

89.5km Acquaviva Station. The ruined Chiaramonte castle of MUSSOMELI stands 13km E on an impregnable crag. Here in 1976, at the age of 83, died Genco Russo, considered one of the most famous Mafia bosses. The valley narrows between odd-looking sulphurous hills. To the W is CASTELTERMINI, which has an interesting festival on the last Sunday in May known as the 'Tataratà'. This was once a sulphur mining town; the last mines were closed down in 1988, and those at Cozzo Disi and Ciavolotta may become museums. SUTERA rises above the left of the road at the foot of the gypseous outcrop of Monte San Paolino (819m; surmounted by a chapel).

Beyond (114km) Comitini, a byroad (right; 2km) leads to ARAGONA (12,000 inhab.), founded in 1606, with an interesting street plan. From here a rough road leads to the VULCANELLI DI MACALUBE, tiny conical volcanoes, 0.5–1m high, filled with salty bubbling mud. 129.5km **Agrigento**, see Rte 12.

B. Via Corleone

Road, 173km. N121.—23.5km Bolognetta. N118—40.5km Bivio Lupotto (turning for the **Bosco della Ficuzza**)—57km **Corleone** (for Contessa Entellina, 42km)—80km Prizzi—95.5km Santo Stefano Quisquina—155km Raffadali—173km **Agrigento**.

This route runs through pretty, sometimes magnificent mountain scenery on a road bearing little traffic.

An alternative route from Palermo runs via Piana degli Albanesi (see Rte 2E) from where a beautiful minor road continues, to join the route described below at (41km) Bivio Lupotto.

Information Offices. From Palermo to Prizzi 'APT' of Palermo (Tel. 091/583887); from there to Agrigento 'APT' of Agrigento (Tel. 0922/26926).

From Palermo to (23.5km) Bolognetta, see Rte 11A. N118 bears right past (29km) MARINEO, at the foot of an oddly shaped rock. The castle (partly abandoned and partly inhabited) was reconstructed in 1559 by Matteo Carnelivari.

The road continues above the artificial lake of Scanzano through woods. At (40.5km) Bivio Lupotto it joins the alternative road from Palermo via Piana degli Albanesi (see above). A byroad (5km) leads past an obelisk marking the entrance to a former Bourbon hunting estate to end at the village of **Ficuzza**, dominated by the PALAZZINA REALE, a handsome building in sandstone with numerous chimneys and two clocks (now used by the Forestry Commission). It was built by Venanzio Marvuglia in 1803 as a hunting lodge for the Bourbons. Behind it extends the *BOSCO DELLA

FICUZZA, a splendid forest beneath the mountain wall of ROCCA BUSAMBRA (1613m). This is the most extensive and interesting wooded area of its kind left on the island, noted for its fine trees, plants, and wild life. Several rough roads and paths traverse the woods although much of it is fenced off for protection.

The main road continues from the obelisk, lined in places by pines and cypresses, through beautiful countryside beneath yellow and red rocks. A rough byroad on the left leads to the 'Gorgo del Drago', the source of the river Frattina, a lovely green oasis in the barren countryside.

57km **Corleone** (11,400 inhab.) nestled in the hillside, but now surrounded by ugly buildings. It is notorious for its Mafia gang whose boss Totò Riina ruled 'Cosa Nostra' for many years until he was arrested in 1993 after more than 20 years 'in hiding' in Palermo.

The town of Saracen origin has a Lombard colony established here by Frederick II in 1237. Traces of its importance as a medieval town can be seen in the old centre which preserves some fine palace doorways in its narrow streets. The Chiesa Madre (if closed, ring at the inconspicuous N door approached from the road on the left of the outside steps through a gate) contains some interesting wood statues (16–17C), wood stalls by Giovanni Battista Li Volsi, and paintings (on the transept altars) by Fra Felice da Sambuca, and (first N chapel) by Tommaso de Vigilia (Adoration of the Magi). The public gardens, laid out in 1820, are well kept.

FROM CORLEONE TO CONTESSA ENTELLINA, 43km. N188C, a road with good mountain views, leads S. 22km BISACQUINO, an Arab citadel and then a medieval fortress town. Narrow winding byroads lead W to (43km) **Contessa Entellina** (524m), a charming mountain-village, colonised by Albanians in 1450. Nearly half the population (2100 inhab.) had to be rehoused after the earthquake in 1968 (see the Valle del Belice, Rte 9). It takes its surname from *Entella* a town of the Elymi situated c 13km NW on a high isolated rock which stands out above the surrounding hills. On the extensive plateau excavations are in progress of the city: so far the fortifications have been identified, part of the medieval rocca, and a building of 4–3C BC. At the foot of the hill were the necropoli.

The Olivetan abbey of SANTA MARIA DEL BOSCO, about 14km S, reached from the road to Bisacquino, has a church (1676–1757) attributed to Vanvitelli, to be restored after serious damage in 1968. It contained a terracotta of the Della Robbia school, two large cloisters (one of the 16C), and a fresco of the Miracle of the Loaves (in the refectory). About 9km S, on the road to Sambuca di Sicilia (described in Rte 10), at MONTE ADRANONE (1000m) excavations were begun in 1968 of the ancient city of *Adranon*. This was an indigenous settlement occupied by a Greek city in the 6C BC, probably founded by Selinunte. It was destroyed at the end of the 5C by Carthage. The Carthaginian settlement was conquered by Rome in 263 BC and the site abandoned. Beside the small Antiquarium are part of an Iron Age necropolis including the so-called Tomba della Regina with an interesting entrance. Tombs of the 5C and 4C BC have also been found here. Other remains include walls and the S Gate, a sanctuary, and part of the Acropolis to the NE.

From Bisacquino a road continues S via Burgio and Villafranca Sicula to Ribera (see Rte 10), and another road leads E via Palazzo Adriano to rejoin this route near Prizzi (see below).

From Corleone the road turns SE. The scenery becomes wilder with curious outcrops of rock, appropriately named 'Imbriaca' ('drunken'). Near (80km) a lake, the medieval town of PRIZZI stands above the road to the left. An interesting traditional 'dance of the devils' takes place here on Easter Sunday. Excavations on the Montagna dei Cavalli in the vicinity have revealed 4–3C BC remains thought to belong to the ancient city of *Hippana*.

10km SW is the little town of PALAZZO ADRIANO, a late 15C Albanian colony with its main monuments in Piazza Umberto I. Shortly beyond, this route is joined by a road from Lercara Friddi (Rte 11A), and climbs to the Portella Mola overlooking the artificial lake of Piano del Leone. Beyond a summit-level of 902m it drops to (95.5km) SANTO STEFANO QUISQUINA (5800 inhab.). In the pleasant little town the Chiesa Madre has an altarpiece of the Resurrection of Lazarus by the Carracci school. The Santuario di Santa Rosalia on a hill to the E, has frescoes by the Manno.

104km BIVONA (5000 inhab.), with a number of fine churches. Just beyond (114km) Alessandria della Rocca, a byroad left runs to San Biagio Platani (15km).

This is an alternative route (42km; 3km shorter than the main road) which rejoins the main route at Raffadali. The road traverses rugged farming country where animals are still much in use, through San Biagio Platani to SANT'ANGELO MUXARO, possibly the site of the ancient *Kamikos*. Prehistoric tombs pepper the hillside. Those near the foot of the road which mounts to the village date from the 11–9C BC; the higher domed tombs were used in the 8–5C BC. A double chamber tomb (torch useful) lies a short way below the third hairpin bend of the road. The road continues through Sant'Elisabetta to Raffadali (see below).

N118 descends past (124km) CIANCIANA, founded in 1640, to cross the Platani and rises again to (142.5km) RAFFADALI (420m), a town of 14,200 inhabitants, where the church contains a Roman sarcophagus depicting the Rape of Proserpine. A prehistoric necropolis on the hill of BUSONE has yielded finds including a number of statuettes of a female divinity made from pebbles. 149km, turning right for JOPPOLO GIANCAXIO, a pretty village in a fine position with an 18C castle and church. 173km **Agrigento**.

12

Agrigento

AGRIGENTO (56,300 inhab.) once one of the most prosperous of the Greek cities on the island, preserves a remarkable series of Doric temples of the 5C BC, unequalled except in Greece itself. The medieval and modern city, on the site of the ancient acropolis, crowns a narrow ridge overlooking a valley which stretches towards the distant sea, and in the midst of which, on a second lower ridge stand the classical ruins. The beautiful 'Valle dei Templi' is now disturbed by a network of busy roads, and the ugly high buildings of the modern city have encroached on the valley. Long-term plans to preserve the archaeological zone as a national park have still not been finalised and illegal new building has even been allowed to take place in this area. Agrigento is the capital of one of the poorest provinces in Italy, and the town has a serious lack of water. Uncontrolled new building here caused a disasterous landslide in 1966. **Plan on p 5 of atlas section**.

Information Offices. 'Azienda Autonoma', 123 Via Atenea (Tel. 0922/20454), with its headquarters at 73 Via Empedocle. 'APT' Agrigento, 255 Viale della Vittoria.

Railway Stations. 'Agrigento Centrale' is the terminus for all trains. The different lines, however, all converge at 'Agrigento Bassa', 3km N, where connections are made. Services to Palermo, Caltanissetta, etc.

Buses. No. 10 from Piazza Marconi for the Valle dei Templi (resquest stops at the Museum, and, lower down, for the temples at the 'Posto di Ristoro'). Buses traverse the upper town along Via Atenea. Buses from Piazza Fratelli Rosselli to Porto Empedocle, to San Leone on the sea; and to Palermo, Catania, Sciacca, and Gela. From Piazza Marconi to the birthplace of Luigi Pirandello, see Rte 10.

Car Parking. There are car-parks near the archaeological museum, and at the 'Posto di Ristoro' near the temples. In the upper town parking is extremely difficult (underground car-parks are being built); best in Piazza Fratelli Rosselli or Viale della Vittoria.

Hotels. In a beautiful quiet position in the 'Valle dei Templi': 4-star 'Villa Athena' (Pl. a). Near the temples (on Via dei Templi): 4-star: 'Della Valle' (Pl. b), and 3-star: 'Colleverde' (Pl. c). In the upper city: 3-star 'Del Viale' (Pl. d), 12 Via del Piave, and 'Pirandello' (Pl. e), 5 Via Giovanni XXIII; 2-star 'Belvedere' (Pl. f), 20 Via San Vito, and 'Bella Napoli' (Pl. g), 6 Piazza Lena.

Camping sites (3-star) near the sea at San Leone (7km).

Restaurants. Luxury-class: 'Le Caprice', Via Panoramica; 'Taverna Mosé', Contrada San Biagio; 'Kalos', Piazza Aldo Moro. 1st-class: 'l'Ambasciata di Sicilia', 2 Via Giambertoni (off Via Atenea); 'La Francescana', Via Atenea; 'Leon d'Oro', 7km outside the city at San Leone. Trattorie: 'Da Lillo', Via Bac-Bac; 'La Forchetta', Piazza San Francesco; 'Trattoria Atenea', Via Atenea.

Cafés or bars ('pasticceria', with good pastries and snacks). 'Saieva', Viale della Vittoria; 'Amato', Via Atenea; 'La Promenade', Via Passeggiata Archeologica; 'La Preferita', Via Atenea; 'Patti', Piazza Aldo Moro. Delicious sweets, made by nuns, can be purchased at the convent next to the church of Santo Spirito, see below.

Good places to **Picnic** in the 'Valle dei Templi'.

Theatres. The 'Teatro Pirandello' in the upper town has been restored but has still not been reopened. A new open-air theatre the 'Teatro della Valle' has been built in the 'Valle dei Templi'.

Annual Festivals. The 'Sagra del mandorlo in fiore', an international festival of folklore, is held at the temples around the first week in February when the almond blossom is in flower. In August and September a music festival is held in the Teatro della Valle at the road junction beneath the Temple of Hera. For one week in July there is a festival of plays by Pirandello at his birthplace near Porto Empedocle (see Rte 10).

History. Agrigento, the *Akragas* of the Greeks and the 'Agrigentum' of the Romans, claims Daedalus as its legendary founder, but seems almost certainly to have originated as a colony from Gela (581 BC). From 570 to 555 the city suffered under the tyranny of Phalaris, though the bull-cult (of Moloch?) which he introduced was more likely Rhodian than Carthaginian, and the story (related by Pindar) that he sacrificed his enemies by hurling them alive into a red-hot brazen bull is probably apocryphal. Under the wise rule of Theron (489–472), in alliance with his son-in-law Gelon of Syracuse, the soldiers of Akragas defeated the Carthaginians at Himera (480), captured that city, and so extended their wealth and power that Pindar (who lived in the city) described Akragas as 'the fairest city of men'. Its population was then about 200,000. Its breed of horses was renowned, and the racing chariot found on many coins minted here may derive from their constant successes at the Olympic Games. Conflict with Syracuse led to defeat in the field, after which Theron's dynasty gave place to a republican government. In 406 the Carthaginians, under Hannibal, son of Gisco, and Himilco, took the city and burned it after a siege of eight months. Timoleon conquered the Carthaginians (340) and rebuilt the city, but it was taken by the Romans in 261 and again in 210, and remained in their possession till the fall of the Empire. It fell into Saracen power in 827, and was delivered in 1087 by Count Roger, who founded the bishopric.

The present town occupies the acropolis of the Greek city. The name of *Girgenti*, abandoned in 1927, was derived from Kerkent, a Saracen corruption of Agrigentum. The most famous native of Akragas was Empedocles (c 490–430), 'a poet, a physician, a patriot, and a philosopher'. His contemporary Acron, the physician, succeeded in stopping the Athenian plague of 430 BC, through the invention of fumigation. Luigi Pirandello (1867–1936), the dramatist, was a native of the district.

The medieval and modern city

The old part of the town occupies the summit of Monte Camico (326m); its modern suburbs extend along the ridge to the E below the Rupe Atenea, and the city is expanding down the hillsides to the N and S. Three connected squares effectively divide the centre of the town; the area to the W contains the old city. To the N is the huge PIAZZA VITTORIO EMANUELE (250m) where the roads from Palermo and Enna enter the city; here is the circular post office. To the S is PIAZZALE ALDO MORO, with a garden, and farther S still, and at a lower level, lies PIAZZA MARCONI with the CENTRAL STATION; opposite, at a confused intersection, the straight tree-lined Viale della Vittoria runs for over 1km along the edge of the ridge below modern buildings; while Via Crispi descends to the 'Valle dei Templi'.

VIA ATENEA, the long main street of the old town leads W from Piazzale Aldo Moro. Via Porcello (right) and the stepped Salita Santo Spirito lead steeply up to the abbey church of **Santo Spirito** (if locked, ring for the custodian at No. 2 in the piazza, or at the convent), founded c 1290 for Cistercian nuns. The nuns still make exquisite sweets ('frutti di martorana', marzipan friuts, 'kus-kus', with pistachio and cocoa, etc.) which may be purchased here. A Gothic portal survives and inside are good stuccoes (c 1693–95), by Serpotta and his school. The statue of the Madonna enthroned is by the workshop of Domenico Gagini. Part of the CONVENT was restored in 1990 to house part of the MUSEO CIVICO (open 9–13 except fest.), formerly in Piazza Luigi Pirandello (see below), with a miscellany of objects, poorly labelled. It is approached through an over restored cloister, and up a modern flight of stairs. The two rooms on the top floor (with views of the sea) contain a local ethnographical collection (agricultural implements, domestic ware, etc.). On the floor below is archaeological material and remains of frescoes. Steps lead down to the 'stanza della Badessa' in a tower with a Gothic vault and a painted 15C Crucifix. Another room has architectural fragments including a carved marble doorway and a Crucifix. The fine dormitory has good vaulting and an exhibition of international folk costumes, as well as a collection of butterflies and shells. On the ground floor a chapel with a Gothic vault has a crèche, with charming domestic scenes, made by a local craftsman in 1991. The chapter house is also shown. The paintings which belong to the Museo Civico are still in the old museum building and not on view. They include works by Pietro Novelli, Luca Giordano, and Fra Felice da Sambuca.

Farther on in Via Atenea is the unfinished façade of Santa Rosalia beside the PURGATORIO or San Lorenzo (containing elegant statues by Giacomo Serpotta). The lion to the left of the church sleeps above the locked entrance to a huge labyrinth of underground water channels and reservoirs, built by the Greek architect Phaiax in the 5C BC. Beyond the neo-Gothic exchange building the street widens at the undistinguished Piazza Nicola Gallo, once the centre of the old city, with a club in a neo-classical building. Beyond the church of San Giuseppe, at the top of the rise, Via Atenea descends to Piazza del Municipio (now renamed Piazza Luigi Pirandello). On the right is the Baroque façade of San Domenico; occupying the former convent (mid 17C) are the Municipio and the fine TEATRO PIRANDELLO (restored and due to be reopened shortly).

To the right of San Giuseppe (see above) Via Bac-Bac and then the stepped Via Saponara (signposted) mount steeply to (right) to **Santa Maria dei Greci** (usually open 8.30–9.30, 15.30–16.30; longer hours in summer), preceded by a courtyard with a palm tree and a cypress. The custodian lives at No. 8 Salita Sant'Alfonso, behind the church to the left. This small basilica was built with antique materials, on the site of a Doric temple, perhaps that of Athena begun by Theron in the 5C BC. The interior preserves a painted wood ceiling (now very worn) and fragments of charming 14C frescoes. Parts of the temple may be seen here, and in a passage (entered from the churchyard) below the N aisle are the stumps of six fluted columns on the stylobate.

The alleys on the N side join Via del Duomo. The **Duomo** (San Gerlando), though altered at the E end in the 17C is basically a 14C building with an unfinished CAMPANILE (to the SW) that shows in its Gothic windows a mixture of Arab-Norman and Catalan influences. The North Aisle was dislodged in the disastrous landslide of 1966, but has since been restored. The church is entered by the side door at the top of a double flight of steps. INTERIOR. A single round arch divides the nave into two parts; to the W the tall polygonal piers support an open painted roof of 1518, to the E a coffered ceiling of 1603. At the end of the S aisle is the chapel of the Norman St Gerland (who refounded the see after the Saracen defeat), with a silver reliquary by Michele Ricca (1639). Opposite, in the N aisle is the tomb of Gaspare de Marino, by Andrea Mancino and Giovanni Gagini (1492), and other Baroque funerary monuments, and fragments of 15C frescoes. A curious acoustical phenomenon ('il portavoce') permits a person standing beneath the cornice of the apse to hear every word spoken even in a low voice near the main doorway, though the reverse is not true.

The **Museo Diocesano** in a modern building (also damaged in the landslide) has been closed since 1966. The contents of the treasury are housed in the Museo Archeologico Regionale (see below), and the sarcophagus from the chapter house is displayed in the church of San Nicola. The SEMINARIO (17–18C) has an arcaded courtyard, off which (shown on request) is a Gothic hall with a double vault, remains of the Chiaramonte Steri (14C).

In Via del Duomo is the long façade of the BIBLIOTECA LUCCHESIANA, founded here in 1765 as a public library by the Bishop of Agrigento. It is shown by volunteers on weekday mornings while the fine building is being renovated; its treasures number 40,000 volumes (including Arab MSS. still housed in the original presses of 1765).

The 'Valle dei Templi' and the ancient city

The ancient city, encircled by a wall, occupied the angle between the rivers Hypsas and Akragas (now the Fiume di Sant'Anna and the Fiume di San Biagio) which meet near the coast to flow into the sea.

The museum and all the main ruins are linked by road. On foot at least a whole day should be allowed for the visit. Those with less time should not miss the Museum, the temples on the Strada Panoramica, and the Temple of Zeus.

The Temples of Concord, Hera and Herakles are unenclosed. The Temple of Zeus and the Hellenistic and Roman Quarter are open 8.30– dusk. The Museum is open 9–17, fest. 9–12.30.

The temples should, if possible, be seen at several different times of the day, especially in the early morning and at sunset; and at night when floodlit. In early spring, when the almond trees are in bloom, they are particularly beautiful.

A. The Temples of Herakles, Concord, and Hera

Viale Crispi (bus) descends from the modern city past the Hellenistic and Roman Quarter and the Museum (see below) to (c 3km) the car-park and café, known as the 'Posto di Ristoro', near the main temples. Here the *VIA SACRA (closed to cars) diverges left. It traverses the ridge on which the temples of Herakles, Concord, and Hera are built. The delightful countryside survives undisturbed here with beautiful groves of almonds and ancient olive trees. At the beginning on the right a footbridge leads above a deep sepulchral street to the **Temple of Herakles**, a heap of ruins showing traces of fire, with nine columns upright, eight of them re-erected in 1922–23 by the munificence of Captain Alexander Hardcastle. This is probably the oldest visible temple of Akragas (built c 500 BC). It was peripteral and hexastyle (67m by 25m) and had 38 columns (6 by 15), 9.9m high and 2m in diameter, and a cella (perhaps roofless) with pronaos and opisthodomus in antis. Anciently it was famed for its statue of Hercules, which Verres attempted to steal, and for a painting of the infant Hercules strangling the serpents, by Zeuxis. Beyond, on the Via Sacra is the VILLA AUREA (admission only with special permission) surrounded by a luxuriant and beautifully kept garden.

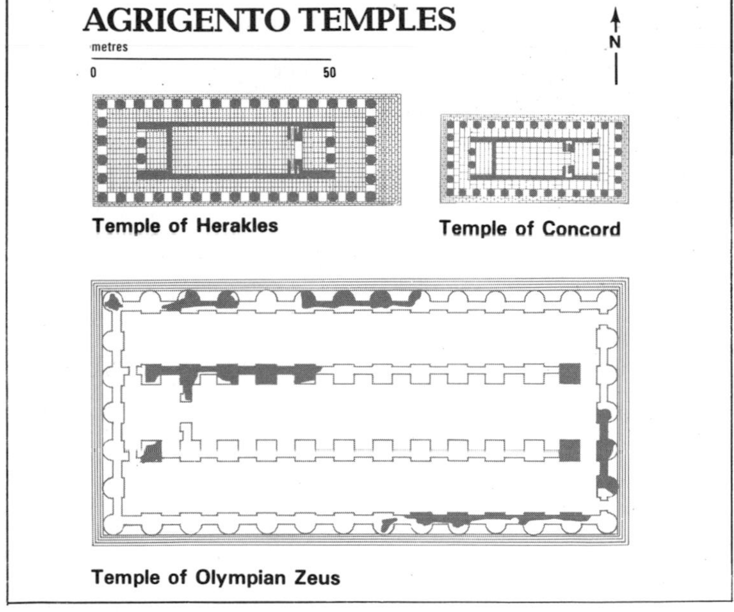

In the forecourt is a bust of Captain Alexander Hardcastle set up in 1984 as a memorial to him. This eccentric Englishman repaired the villa in 1921 and, with his brother Henry, a parson, lived here until Alexander's death in 1933. The Captain provided substantial funds to restore and excavate the ancient city, supporting the work of Pirro Marconi. He also took an interest in the modern city, and provided an aqueduct from there to the temple valley. In gratitude the Italian government made him a 'commendatore' of the 'Corona d'Italia' and the Home Office allowed him to wear the insignia. The Villa now contains an antiquarium (material from the Pezzino Necropolis, and excavations in Contrada Mosè), and in the garden are tombs and underground cisterns.

Farther up on the left is a PALAEOCHRISTIAN NECROPOLIS. Here are Christian tombs cut in the surface of the rock, as well as extensive CATACOMBS (if closed, usually unlocked on request by a custodian at the Temple of Zeus) with subterranean passages extending below the road. In the field here are two tholos tombs thought to date from the 5C BC.

The road continues up to the so-called ****Temple of Concord**, best preserved of all Greek temples except the Theseion at Athens, which it recalls in its majestic symmetry and rich colour. For preservation reasons, it is sadly no longer possible to enter the building. The name occurs in a Latin inscription found here, but has no real connection with the temple (although a tradition persists among the inhabitants of Agrigento that the temple should be visited by a husband and wife on their wedding day). The building, which probably dates from about 430 and was only slightly harmed by the Carthaginians, stands on a stylobate of four steps (39.3m by 16.9m) and is peripteral and hexastyle with 34 Doric columns (6 by 13), 6.8m high including the capitals, with a diameter of 1.4m at the base. The intercolumniations of the façades become narrower towards the sides (to accommodate the corner metopes); this is one of the earliest instances in Sicily of this refinement in temple design. The cella has a pronaos and an opisthodomus, both in antis. From the E end of the cella two spiral staircases mount to the architrave. The complete entablature survives at both ends.

The excellent state of preservation of the temple is explained by the fact that it was converted into a church by San Gregorio delle Rape (i.e. of the turnips), bishop of Agrigento, in the 6C AD. It was restored in the 18C, but the arches of the nave remain in the cella walls. The material of this and of the other temples is easily eroded oolitic limestone, formerly protected by white stucco made of marble dust, and brightly painted above the capitals, and now burnt by the sun to a rich tawny gold.

From the temple can be seen the pretty building of the Villa Athena hotel with a neo-classical loggia beside two palm trees. The lovely road, now more peaceful, continues parallel to the ancient city WALLS; in the inner face are many Byzantine tomb recesses. There is a view on the left of the cemetery to the right of which can be seen San Biagio (see Rte 12D) beside a clump of trees. In the far distance radio masts mark the Rupe Ateneo. Above the road, c 1km farther E, stands the much ruined but picturesque ***Temple of Hera**, called the 'Temple of Juno Lacinia', from a confusion with a temple dedicated to Hera on the Lacinian promontory at Croton. It resembles the Temple of Concord in form, but is slightly smaller and older (c 450 BC). A landslide in 1976 threatened its stability and the entrance is still fenced off. The stylobate, on a massive artificial platform, measures 38m by 16.8m. Of its 34 columns (6 by 13), 6.4m high with a base-diameter of 1.3m, nine have fallen. Traces of a fire (which probably occurred in 406) are still visible, and the work of the Roman restorers was ruined by an earthquake. To the E is the sacrificial altar; to the W an ancient cistern.

Temple of Concord, Agrigento

Looking W there is a good sight of the outer face of the wall, in some places carved out of the natural rock, clinging to the brow of the hill. Nearby are the scant remains of GATE THREE, and, outside the walls, an ancient roadway (with deep ruts) can still be seen. In the other direction, at the foot of the hill, are numerous roads and a new open-air theatre.

B. The Temple of Olympian Zeus and the Sanctuary of Chthonic Divinities

At the 'Posto di Ristoro' (cf. above) is the entrance (admission see above) to the Temple of Olympian Zeus and the excavations which extend to the westernmost edge of the temple ridge. The custodians of the ancient monuments of Agrigento have their office here: they are helpful and informed. Enquire here for admission to areas found closed or for the key to sites normally kept locked (cf. the text).

Beside the entrance is the vast, complicated heap of ruins of the ***Temple of Olympian Zeus**, or **Olympieion**, thought to have been begun by the Carthaginian prisoners taken at Himera, and left unfinished in 406: its destruction, due in part to the Edict of Olympia (6C AD), and in part to earthquakes, was completed by quarrying in the 18C, much of the stone going into the foundations of Porto Empedocle.

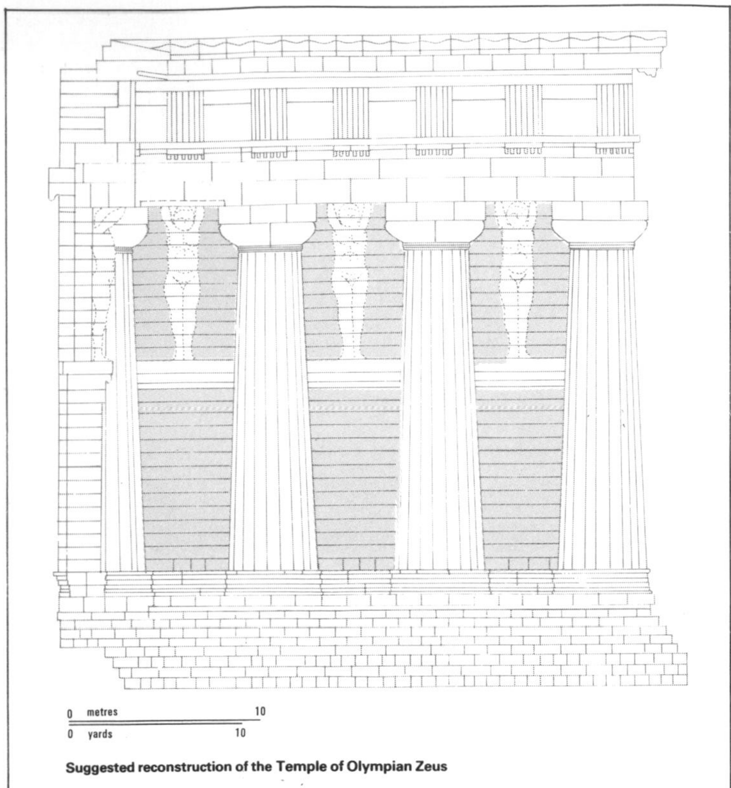

Suggested reconstruction of the Temple of Olympian Zeus

This huge Doric temple (110.1m by 52.7m, virtually a double square), is the largest Doric temple known, and is unique in form among Greek temples. It was built of comparatively small stones (each capital was composed of three blocks) and then covered in stucco. It is heptastyle and pseudoperipteral, i.e. the seven columns at each end and the 14 on each side were engaged in the walls, being rounded externally and presenting a square face towards the interior. In between the semi-columns, 16.7m high and 4m thick at the base, were 38 colossal telamones set on the outer wall; their exact arrangement is still under discussion (cf. below). In the E pediment was represented a Gigantomachia, and in the W pediment the capture of Troy. The cella was divided into three aisles, separated by square pillars (to support the vast roof).

Little remains in position except the stereobate, which alone, however, is sufficient to convey an impression of the immensity of the monument. Part of the N wall survives (note the outer face), and the foundations of the aisle pillars. To the E, beyond the wall which (curiously) 'blocked' what is thought to have been the entrance, are the foundations of the altar platform. All around the temple is a heap of ruins, amid which lies a copy of a GIGANTE (7.6m high), one of the telamones; the original 19C reconstruction is displayed in the Archaeological Museum. The U-shaped incision visible on many stones is believed to have facilitated their raising by ropes. Near the SE corner, below one of the colossal fallen capitals, is a small temple of archaic date with a cella divided by piers. The AGORA of the ancient city is thought to have been to the E (near the modern car-park).

To the W is a complicated area of excavations including remains of houses, and traces of an L-shaped portico which enclosed a sanctuary and a tholos on a spur beside GATE FIVE, its carriage-way obstructed by masonry, which apparently fell in Greek times. It was probably a double gate defended by a tower. On the other side of the gate are various shrines, that together formed the **Sanctuary of the Chthonic Divinities**, which were entirely enclosed by a precinct wall, a portion of which is visible on the W side. Here is the misnamed TEMPLE OF CASTOR AND POLLUX. The four columns bearing a portion of the architrave, which have been used as the picturesque symbol of Classical Sicily, are a reconstruction of 1836 now known to incorporate elements from more than one building on this site.

Superimposed ruins show the existence of shrines dedicated to the cult of the earth-goddesses as early as the 7C BC. Of this period are the structures on the N side, notably the pairs of altars, one circular and one square. To the S of these, remains exist of two unfinished temples of the 6C; the third is that formerly misascribed to Castor and Pollux, which was probably of the same plan as the Temple of Concord; and a fourth was built, just to the S, in Hellenistic or Roman times. To the last belong many of the fallen column-drums and the well-preserved altar E of the platform.

Beyond the custodians' hut is an ARCHAIC SANCTUARY, recently excavated on the edge of the hill. From here two columns of the Temple of Hephaistos (or Vulcan) can be seen on the hill across a delightful fertile little valley, with orange trees and old farm houses. The pretty footpath from here to the temple is now difficult to find; the temple is therefore best reached from the main road (see Rte 10D). The high rise buildings of the modern town of Agrigento are conspicuous from here. Beneath the ugly Morandi road viaduct the PEZZINO NECROPOLIS (admission from Via Dante) has recently been excavated.

C. The Museo Regionale Archeologico and the Hellenistic and Roman Quarter

On the main road, about 1km uphill from the 'Porto di Ristoro' (cf. the plan), is the ***Museo Regionale Archeologico** (admission see above; car-park off the road just above the museum), one of the finest museums in Sicily, spaciously arranged in a building of 1967. It is approached through a garden and the 15C cloisters of the convent attached to the church of San Nicola (see below). In the cloisters is a long bench carrying an inscription to Herakles and Hermes found in the 'Agora' zone of the city.

GROUND FLOOR. **Room I**. Early and Late Bronze Age material from sites near Agrigento, including a small Mycenaean amphora (probably found at Porto Empedocle), and painted vases. Also, prehistoric objects found in Agrigento beneath the classical area. **Room II** contains objects from Gela (6–7C BC), including Corinthian and Rhodian ware (note the head of a bull), as well as locally made vases; votive statuettes from Licata (late 4C BC).

Room III displays a superb collection of ***vases**, including a group of outstanding Attic vases, from the mid 6C BC to the early 3C BC. The following description follows the cases in sequence from the top of the steps left in a clockwise direction around the four halls (see p 37) for the nomenclature of vases). On the walls are photos of some of the most famous vases found in Agrigento and now in other museums. CASE I: Attic black-figured vases, including a fine amphora; CASE 2: red-figured kraters; CASE 3: Attic red-figured vases including a lekythos with Nike sacrificing (460–450 BC), and a krater with Dionysiac scenes (c 440 BC); CASE 4: krater showing Perseus and Andromeda in polychrome on a white ground, a rare example of c 430 BC, and a stamnos (440–430 BC) showing a sacrifice to Apollo; CASE 5: a small red-figured krater with a bull led to sacrifice, and several kraters and stamni with banqueting scenes (some by the 'Painter of Lugano', c 400 BC); CASE 6: Hellenistic vases. At the end of the hall, fine marble statue of a warrior (damaged); belonging to the Early Classical period, this may have adorned part of the pediment of the Temple of Herakles (c 480 BC). Two cases by the window and CASE 7 contain vases (4C BC) from Campania. CASES 8 and 9: vases from Apulia (4C BC); CASE 10: Attic red-figured vase of the first half of the 5C BC, including two kraters by the 'Harrow Painter', and a krater showing the burial of a warrior; CASE 11 and 12: black-figured Attic vases of the end of the 6C BC, including a lekythos with Herakles and the hydra; and a large amphora with four gods and a quadriga by the 'Painter of Dikaios'.

Room IV. Architectonic fragments including a remarkable variety of lion-head water spouts from various buildings (including the Temple of Herakles, and the Temple of Demeter). **Room V**. Statuettes and heads in terracotta, notably, female votive statues; (CASE 45) askos, the mule of Dionysos (late 6C BC, from Favissa), and the mask of a negro of the same date; two cases of moulds; (CASE 51) head of Athena with a helmet (c 490 BC); (CASE 55) head of a kouros (500 BC). On the end wall are delicate bas-relief friezes, including some showing the telamones. Beyond the steps which descend to Room VI, CASE 59 on the balcony displays the head of a kouros (?) of c 540 BC, and a female bust of the end of the 6C BC. Other cases here contain finds from the area near the Temple of Herakles, including architectonic fragments in terracotta. Steps descend to **Room VI** devoted to the Temple of Zeus. Here is displayed the ***Gigante** (7.6m high), one of the telamones from the temple, which was recomposed from fragments in the 19C; along the wall are three colossal telamone *heads. The blocks of stone were originally covered with plaster. Plans and models suggest possible reconstructions of the temple, and the controversial position of the telamones. The recent discovery of a leg attached to a block of stone of one of the statues has shown that their feet must have been further apart than is here indicated. **Room VII** contains fragments of wall-paintings (recomposed) and mosaics (including three in small tesserae of animals) from the Roman Quarter. **Room VIII** (inscriptions) and **Room IX** (coins) are opened only on special request.

Room X is reached from the balcony through Room V. Among the Greek and Roman sculpture here is a statuette of Apollo, or the river-god Akragas, known as the Ephebus of Agrigento (c 480 BC). Nearby is displayed material found in the Bouleuterion, including coins. A corridor, overlooking a little garden with two Roman statues, has panels illustrating the political history of Akragas. **Room XI**, has finds from various necropoli, notably that at Contrada Pezzino, the oldest one in Agrigento and the one that has produced the richest finds (early 6C–3C BC). The miniature vases were found in children's tombs. The fine alabaster *sarcophagus of a child, with charming childhood scenes (ended by illness and death), a Hellenistic work of the 2C BC, was found recently near Agrigento. At the end of the room is another Roman sarcophagus. From the window here can be seen new excavations in progress. **Room XII** has an introductory display of prehistoric material, and finds from Sciacca; in **Room XIII** are objects from the province of Agrigento, including finds from the Grotto dell'Acqua Fitusa, and from Sant'Angelo Muxaro. The fragments of ochre are thought to have been used to colour vases. Material from Eraclea Minoa is displayed in **Room XIV**, and Greek and Roman helmets; busts from Licata; bronze cooking utensils, etc. **Room XV** contains a splendid red-figured *krater from Gela (5C BC). In perfect condition, it displays the battle of the amazons. Photographs on the walls show other vases, now in the Gela museum. **Room XVII** has finds from Caltanissetta (notably a fine red-figured krater showing horsemen of 450–440 BC).

The museum is left past **Room XVIII** (opened only on special request) which houses the contents of the TREASURY OF THE CATHEDRAL: especially noteworthy are two reliquaries of Limoges-enamelled copper, a portable altar-stone with Byzantine enamels (13C), an ivory crozier, and a Madonna attributed to Guido Reni.

Outside the museum is the entrance to an area of excavations. The BOULEUTERION (or ekklesiasterion) was built in the 4–3C BC and transformed into an odeon in the Imperial era. It was used for the meetings of the 'boulé', a political ruling body. It could hold some 300 people; the participants are thought to have stood. The narrow divisional rows are carved into the rock. In one corner is the so-called ORATORY OF PHALARIS, a prostyle building in antis, probably a late-Hellenistic shrine, which was transformed into a Gothic chapel.

A footbridge crosses an area with remains of late-Hellenistic houses, and Imperial Roman buildings (mosaics). The early-13C church of **San Nicola** has a curious façade made up of a Gothic doorway in strong relief between antae with a Doric cornice (the material probably came from a Roman edifice nearby). It is kept locked and only opened for weddings. The architecture of the interior, reconstructed in 1322, and altered in 1426, is interesting. In the second chapel (right) the magnificent *SARCOPHAGUS was brought here from the chapter house of the Duomo. With great delicacy and purity of style it portrays four episodes in the story of Hippolytus and Phaedra; it derives from Classical Greek models but is Attic or even Roman workmanship of the 2–3C AD. In 1787 it was much admired by Goethe as the best preserved Classical relief he had seen. In the third chapel is a venerated wooden Crucifix. From the terrace there is a fine view of the valley of the temples.

On the opposite side of the main road is the entrance to the enclosure (behind a green fence) with the conspicuous remains of the **Hellenistic and Roman Quarter** (admission see above) of the city. Here an area of c 120 sq m has been excavated, exposing four cardines, running N and S, with their complex of buildings sloping downwards from E to W in a series of terraces. The quarter was first developed towards the end of the 2C BC and its civic life lasted probably to the 4C or 5C BC. The drainage system is elaborate and traces of stairs show that buildings were of more than one storey. Houses, of sandstone blocks, are built around a peristyle, or with an atrium; many of their rooms have good pavements (the best, which include the Casa della Gazella and the Casa del Maestro Astratista, are covered for protection).

Beside the entrance excavations are in progress and an ancient *ROAD (reached by steps beneath a modern foot bridge) can be followed through delightful countryside to join the Via Sacra near the Temple of Concord (cf. Rte 12A). This was the cardine which led from the city to the temple ridge.

D. San Biagio, the Rock Sanctuary of Demeter, and the Temples of Asklepios and Hephaistos

Since the distances are great these monuments are best visited by car.

From Viale Crispi opposite the Hotel Della Valle, a road to the left crosses a main road and continues to the cemetery. Here a gate on the left (signposted) is usually kept unlocked (9–17). Beyond it an unsurfaced road can be followed on foot for c 200m to the edge of the cliff. On the hillside above is **San Biagio** (locked). This Norman church was built on the cella of a small temple begun after the victory at Himera in 480, and dedicated to Demeter and Persephone. The pronaos and stylobate of the temple protrude beyond the apse of the church. To the N are two large round altars. The temple was approached by the ancient track with deep wheel ruts still clearly visible mounting the side of the hill. On the rock face a marble plaque records excavations here by Alexander Hardcastle (cf. Rte 12A).

On the edge of the cliff the line of the **walls** can clearly be seen from the Rupe Atenea (see below), above San Biagio, to the Temple of Hera; beyond the view extends along the temple ridge and to the sea beyond. Just outside the walls and below the cliff edge is the entrance gate to the **Rock Sanctuary of Demeter** (unlocked by a custodian). The long steep flight of steps was constructed in the rock face in this century; they lead down through a delightful garden to the sanctuary. Beside two natural caverns in the rock (in which were found numerous votive busts and statues dating from the 5–4C BC) is a tunnel which carries a terracotta aqueduct from a spring far inside the hill. In front is a complicated series of cisterns on different levels and remains of what may have been a monumental fountain. The sanctuary was formerly thought to antedate the foundation of the city by some two centuries, but some scholars now believe it was constructed in the 5C BC.

From the cemetery (cf. above) another unsurfaced road (signposted) leads along the wall of the cemetery to (200m) an interesting wedge-shaped BASTION that guarded the vulnerable spot where a valley interrupts the natural defence line. To the N is GATE ONE. Captain Alexander Hardcastle (cf. above) was buried in the cemetery beside a hole in the wall: he was responsible for excavating the ancient walls here.

The **Rupe Atenea** (351m) a rocky hill, the highest part of the town, now crowned with masts and aerials, was part of the acropolis of Akragas. It is reached by road (unsignposted) from above the hospital through an unattractive part of the town. It is now military property and has little interest since the ruins of a large ancient building found here are inaccessible. The wide view is marred by modern buildings on all sides.

Viale Crispi continues downhill from the Hotel Della Valle (cf. above), and the Strada Panoramica diverges left passing near the GELA GATE (GATE TWO) which guards a steep defile, and continues to the Temple of Hera (described in Rte 12A). Those on foot can continue along the Via Sacra to rejoin the main road at the 'Posto di Ristoro'.

Just below the 'Posto di Ristoro' the main road (the ancient road to the sea) descends through the rock on the site of the PORTA AUREA (GATE FOUR). This was the main gate of Akragas built over in Byzantine times. Just before the roundabout on the high ground to the left is a Roman funerary monument, miscalled the TOMB OF THERON, a two-storeyed edifice with a Doric entablature and Ionic corner-columns. It stands on the edge of a huge Roman cemetery (1C BC–5C AD) which extends eastwards below the line of the walls (here much ruined by landslides).

The Gela road runs E from the roundabout beneath the temple ridge and walls and the first unsurfaced road on the right (signposted) leads through a field of almonds to a farm beside the little ***Temple of Asklepios** on the bank of the Fiume San Biagio (near a medicinal spring). Excavations are in progress here and the site has recently been enclosed (sometimes unlocked on request at the custodians' office at the entrance to the Temple of Olympian Zeus, see Rte 10B). This is a small Doric temple in antis with a pronaos, cella, and false opisthodomus. In spite of its size, it shows the advanced techniques of construction (including convex lines) associated with the (contemporary) Parthenon. The stairway is preserved between the cella and pronaos. This is the temple mentioned by Polybius in his account of the Roman siege of 262, and it contained the statue of Apollo by Myron whose adventures are chronicled by Cicero.

From the roundabout (see above) the Porto Empedocle road leads in c 500m to the bottom of a little valley where, just before a bridge, an unsurfaced road (unsignposted) diverges right. This should be followed as far as the high railway viaduct. From here steps (signposted) lead up past plants of agave and aloe to the **Temple of Hephaistos** (or **Vulcan**) beyond a charming field of almonds near a branch railway line and right beside a primitive farmhouse. The temple, hexastyle and peripteral, was built c 430 BC and two columns remain upright. The cella was partly built over a small archaic temple of the early 6C. A marble stone beneath the stylobate on the S side records excavations here in 1930 by Alexander Hardcastle. From here the irregular line of WALLS is pierced by GATES SIX, SEVEN, EIGHT, and NINE.

The seaside resort of **San Leone**, at the mouth of the Akragas, lies 4km S of Porta Aurea (see above). **Porto Empedocle**, and Pirandello's birthplace are described in Rte 10.

13

Agrigento to Gela

Road, N115, 73.5km—40km Licata—73.5km **Gela**.

Buses follow the coast from Agrigento to Gela.

Information Offices. From Agrigento to Licata, 'APT' Agrigento (Tel. 0922/26926). For Gela and environs, 'APT' Caltanissetta (Tel. 0934/21089).

From the crossroads below the 'Valle dei Templi' N115 leads E from Agrigento. The road traverses lonely country planted with almond trees, olives, and vineyards, and passes below (28.5km) PALMA DI MONTECHIARO (25,000 inhab.) founded in 1637 by the Prince of Lampedusa, ancestor of Giuseppe Tomasi di Lampedusa (1896–1957), author of 'Il Gattopardo'. Published posthumously, the book describes his great-grandfather Giulio Tomasi (1815–85). The town, notorious for its poverty and its mafia, is surrounded by hundreds of half-constructed houses (now abandoned concrete shells) begun by emigrants. The conspicuous Chiesa Matrice is a fine building (1666–1703) by Angelo Italia approached by a theatrical flight of steps. The 17C Lampedusa palace is in urgent need of repair.

The road descends to the rocky coastline dotted with medieval defence works and the plain (now disfigured with new buildings) surrounding (40km) **Licata** (bypass; 3-star hotel 'Al Faro', and others), an unattractive town (41,200 inhab.), suffering from economic decline. It occupies the site of Phintias, the city founded by the tyrant of the same name from Gela (see below). In the PALAZZO DEL MUNICIPIO (1935), designed by Ernesto Basile, are preserved antique reliefs and a 15C triptych; also a Madonna by Domenico Gagini (1470).

The Corso leads past Palazzo Canarelli, decorated with grotesque heads. Beyond (left) is SAN FRANCESCO; its fine convent (now a school) was reconstructed in the 17C and the marble façade added in 1750 by Giovanni Biagio Amico. Behind, Piazza Sant'Angelo is surrounded by pretty 18C buildings. The 17C church of Sant'Angelo has a façade and cupola attributed to Angelo Italia. The Corso ends at the DUOMO where a chapel in the S transept, elaborately decorated in 1600–1705, preserves a wooden Crucifix which narrowly escaped destruction at the hands of the raiding Turks in 1553. In Corso Roma is the church of SAN DOMENICO, with two paintings by Filippo Paladino. The MUSEO CIVICO (open 8.30–14 except fest.) in Piazza Linares contains local archaeological material from the Prehistoric and Greek periods, including Hellenistic votive statuettes, ceramics, and red-figure vases from a necropolis of the 5C BC.

Off the mouth of the Salso (the ancient Himera) Attilius Regulus defeated the Carthaginian fleet in 256 BC, but in 249 a convoy of Roman transports for Africa was driven ashore by the Carthaginians in a tempest. Landings were effected here by the 7th Army in 1943.

A road leads inland from Licata to RAVANUSA (24km), founded in 1621, near which on Monte Saracino, excavations have revealed a prehistoric site, Hellenised at the end of the 7C BC. 5km W is CAMPOBELLO DI LICATA, founded in 1681.

The road skirts the shore past (51km) FALCONARA with its 15C castle in an oasis of palm trees around a large fountain (a custodian lives near by). Beyond are cotton fields and market gardens (protected from the wind by cane fences).

73.5km **GELA**, an important port and now the fifth largest town in Sicily (79,000 inhab.). Uncontrolled new building has rendered it perhaps the ugliest city on the island. The huge petro-chemical plant which dominates the E side of the town faced serious accusations of pollution in 1979; not only the sea but also the atmosphere in the town suffer from its vicinity. In 1983 5000 inhabitants occupied the town hall destroying documents in protest against the chaotic local administration. Business is controlled by a mafia racket which results in numerous murders here every year. The superb Greek fortifications of Gela testify to its ancient importance.

Information Office. 'Azienda Autonoma', Via Bresmes (Tel. 0933/913788).

Hotels. 3-star: 'Mediterraneo'; 2-star: 'Sole', and others.

History. The modern city, known until 1927 as *Terranova*, was founded by Frederick II in 1230, on the site of Gela, a colony of Rhodians and Cretans established in 689 BC. Gela soon rose to importance, and sent out a colony to Akragas in 582. It had an important influence on the Hellenisation of the local settlements in the interior of the island. The site of the city corresponded roughly to the area of the medieval town and the present historical centre. Under Hippocrates (498–491) the city reached its greatest prosperity, but Gelon, his cavalry-commander and successor, transferred the seat of government and half the population to Syracuse in 485. Aeschylus died at Gela in 456. In 405 the town was destroyed by the Carthaginians, but Timoleon refounded it in 339. The new city was larger than the earlier one and received a new circle of walls. Phintias, tyrant of Akragas, transferred its inhabitants in 282 to his new city at the mouth of the Himera (see Licata, above), and Gela disappeared from history. Hieron I of Syracuse and the ancient comic poet Apollodorus were among the distinguished natives of Gela.

At the E end of the town is the fine **Archaeological Museum** (open daily 9–13, 15–18; rearranged in 1985). It contains some of the painted vases by which Gela is best known, and which are exhibited in most of the museums of Europe. Notable also: a small altar of the 6C BC, showing Hercules slaying Alkyoneus; Attic red-figured lekythoi, one by the Nikon painter, and one on white ground showing Aeneas and Anchise (460–450 BC); the head of a horse of the early 5C BC; female statuettes, antefixes, etc. A magnificent hoard of c 1000 silver coins, none later than 490 BC, stolen in 1973, has been recovered. Near the museum (excavations in progress) part of Timoleon's city on a terraced grid plan with shops and houses (c 339–310 BC) has been uncovered, above the ruins of a small sacred enclosure. Farther E, in the garden on the site of the ACROPOLIS of the earliest city, stands a single (re-erected) column of a temple probably dedicated to Athena (5C), and the basement of a second earlier temple also dedicated to Athena.

The Corso traverses the long untidy town; at a fork the left-hand road continues for another 1.5km to the sand dunes of CAPO SOPRANO at the W end (over 3km from the museum) with the remarkable ***Greek Fortifications** (admission 9–dusk every day). Excellently preserved after centuries beneath the sand, they extend for several hundred metres, and reach a height of nearly 13m. The lower course is built of stone, while the top is finished with brick (preserved behind glass). The walls were begun by Timoleon in 339 BC and completed under Agathocles. Their height was regularly increased to keep ahead of the encroaching sand, a danger today removed by the planting of trees. The foundations of the brick angle towers are visible. Nearby were found the remains of a barracks and a well, and a circular medieval kiln. Close by, entered from Via Scavone or Via Europa, are the remains of GREEK BATHS (4C). The hip baths are provided with seats.

FROM GELA TO CALTANISSETTA, 67km. A fine road traverses the plain of Gela and then ascends through hills with a view ahead of (19km) BUTERA, perched on a flat rock. The princes of this picturesque old hill-town reached the height of their importance under the Spanish rule, when the Barresi family held the title. The Chiesa Madre has a Madonna painted by Filippo Paladino, and a 15C triptych of the Madonna with saints (the central panel is in the sacristy). The Castle (11C) has been closed indefinitely for restoration. The views are magnificent.

5km N of Butera begins a fast road for Caltanissetta, off which at 31km a road diverges right for MAZZARINO (10km), founded by the princes of Butera, whose palazzo survives. Its churches preserve Branciforte funerary monuments and paintings by Filippo Paladino. Another road leads W to RIESI (5km), where in 1978 Giuseppe di Cristina, considered one of the most powerful Mafia bosses, was killed. Nearby 10,000 people were present at his funeral. The main road continues to (67km) Caltanissetta, see Rte 14.

From Gela the Centrale Sicula (N117 bis) leads N through open country, and then woods of eucalyptus and cork trees, to (45.5km) Piazza Armerina (see Rte 17); another good road (N417) branches right via (34km) Caltagirone (see Rte 18) for (99km) Catania

(Rte 24). Both roads pass IL CASTELLUCCIO, a remarkable ruined castle on a small mound sticking sharply up in the fertile Gela valley (with extensive plantations of artichokes), by a war memorial to the battle of 1943 (see above).

14

Agrigento to Caltanissetta

Road, N640, 57km.—22km, turning for Racalmuto (5km)—33km, turning for Canicattì (5km) and Naro (16km)—57km **Caltanissetta**. This is a busy road with heavy traffic.

Railway, 71km in 1hr 30mins.

Information Offices. From Agrigento to Canicattì, 'APT' Agrigento (Tel. 0922/26926); from there to Caltanissetta, 'APT' Caltanissetta (Tel. 0934/584499).

The road descends from Agrigento from the N side of Piazza Vittorio Emanuele, and at the Quadrivio Spinasanta begins the main (signposted) road to Caltanissetta. There is a good retrospective view of the natural rock defences of the old city and of the walls of Agrigento. The road traverses pretty country as it undulates across low hills where the extensive vineyards are now covered with plastic, with wide views in every direction.

9km, turning for FAVARA, with a castle of the Chiaramonte family (1275; enlarged in 1488), damaged and 'restored'. At 22km a road diverges left for **Racalmuto** (5km). This little town, the Arabic 'Rahal-maut', was the birthplace of Leonardo Sciascia (1921–89), one of the greatest Italian writers of this century, who is buried here. He is famous for his novels as well as his perceptive writings on the problems which afflict the island, in particular the Mafia. He left his library to the town, where he lived for most of his life, and a foundation was inaugurated here in his memory in 1992. Another native was Pietro d'Asaro (1597–1647), called 'il Monocolo', whose paintings can be seen in the churches of Racalmuto.

33km, turning for **Canicattì** (5km S; 34,500 inhab.), a market town of some importance and a railway junction. Notorious for its remoteness, it has come to be synonymous with 'Timbuctoo' in the Italian language. It is surrounded by fertile hills clad with olives and almonds, and to the N are disused sulphur mines. The little town of NARO, (10km SW) stands on a hill top (520m), once defended by battlemented walls (1263). It has early 17C churches and a Chiaramonte castle (13–14C). 7km N of the main road is SERRADIFALCO which gave a ducal title to Domenico Pietrasanta (1773–1863), author of an important work on Siclian antiquities. 49km, turning for SAN CATALDO, 3km N, a little town (625m), set amid wooded hills.

57km **CALTANISSETTA**, a pleasant provincial capital (62,500 inhab.), with 17C and 18C works in its churches and an interesting local archaeological museum.

Information Offices. 'APT' Caltanissetta, 109 Corso Vittorio Emanuele (Tel. 0934/584499); information office, 20 Viale Conte Testasecca (Tel. 0934/21089).

Railway Stations. CENTRALE, Piazza Roma, with services via Canicattì to Agrigento, Gela, Ragusa, and Syracuse. The station of CALTANISSETTA XIRBI, 7km N, is on another line between Palermo, Enna, and Catania.

Buses. Frequent services (usually faster than the trains) from Piazza della Repubblica for Palermo and Catania ('SAIS'); for Piazza Armerina ('ASTRA') and for towns in the province.

Car Parking is difficult: one hour limit in Corso Umberto. Space sometimes available in Via Francesco Crispi and Via Kennedy.

Hotels. 4-star 'San Michele', Via Fasci Siciliani; and three 3-star hotels.

Restaurants. 1st class: 'Il Vicolo', beside the Duomo; 'l'Altro Mondo', Via Nicolò Palmieri; Trattorie: 'Delfino Bianco', Via Scovazzo; 'l'Oca Bianca', 37 Via Moncada.

Café ('pasticceria') 'Romano', Corso Umberto.

Picnic places in Villa Cordova.

Theatre. 'Teatro Baufremont', Salita Matteotti, for concerts and prose.

Annual Festival on Maundy Thursday, when the 'Misteri' are carried in procession. At present they are kept in the church of San Pio X in Via Napoleone Colajanni.

History. The name of the town was for long thought to be derived from that of the ancient Sikel city of *Nissa*, with the Arabic prefix 'Kal' at' (castle). Excavations in 1989 on Monte San Giuliano (or 'del Redentore') yielded 7C–6C BC finds. The site was then abandoned until the Roman period. After its conquest by Count Roger in 1086 it was given as an appanage to his son Jourdain, and passed subsequently into the hands of Corrado Lancia (1296) and the Moncada family (1406). The province was an extremely important centre of sulphur mining from the 18C up until the early 20C (the last mines were closed down in the 1970s), and potassium salt was also extracted in the area.

In the central Piazza Garibaldi is a fountain by Michele Tripisciano (1860–1913), a talented local sculptor, whose statues also decorate Corso Umberto I, the Municipio and the public gardens. Here is the pink façade of the **Duomo** (1570–1622), damaged in the last war. The *vault-painting, Guglielmo Borremans' masterpiece (1720), has been well restored. In the second S chapel is a wood statue of the Immacolata (1760). In the chapel to the right of the sanctuary, wood statue of the archangel Michael by Stefano Li Volsi, and two marble statues of the archangels by Vincenzo Vitaliano (1753). The high altarpiece is by Borremans, and the organ dates from after 1653. In the N transept is a painting by Filippo Paladino, and in the second N chapel is a Crucifix attributed to Fra' Umile da Petralia. The church of SAN SEBASTIANO, opposite, has an unusual façade (1891) and at the E end is a fine 17C wood statue of the titular saint.

Corso Umberto I leads up to the church of **Sant'Agata**, built on a Greek-cross plan in 1605. In the interior is fine marble intarsia decoration, especially on the two side altars. The N altar (with a delightful frontal with birds) is surmounted by a statue of St Ignazio by Ignazio Marabitti. The high altarpiece, a good work by Agostino Scilla, is flanked by statues by Salvatore Marino (1753), and above are putti by Marabitti. The first N chapel has frescoes by Borremans (including an Assumption in the vault, and a Nativity on a side wall).

A street on the left side of the Duomo leads down to SAN DOMENICO with a delightfully shaped Baroque façade fitting an awkward site. Inside are two good paintings: the Madonna of the Rosary by Filippo Paladino (1614) and St Vincent Ferrer by Guglielmo Borremans (1722). From here can be reached (in ten minutes) the 14C church of SANTA MARIA DEGLI ANGELI (closed). Sadly ruined, it preserves its W door. Beyond a warehouse, on a fantastic rock, stand the shattered ruins of the CASTELLO DI PIETRAROSSA, residence of Frederick III of Aragon.

To the S, near the station, in Via Napoleone Colajanni, is the **Museo Civico** (admission 9–13 except fest.), with a particularly interesting archaeological collection from sites in the province. There are long-term plans to move it to a new building. ROOM 1. Objects from tombs at Gibil Gabib, including fine kraters (many with animal illustrations), and black and red-figure vases; figurines found recently on Monte San Giuliano (on the N outskirts of Caltanissetta), the earliest portrayal of the human figure so far discovered in Sicily. Dating from the Early Bronze Age, they are thought to have been used in a prehistoric sanctuary. The Arabic finds date from 996 to 1020 AD. ROOM 2 displays material from Sabucina (cf. below), dating from 1270–1000 BC; red-figure kraters and a lekythos on a white ground (c 500 BC); child's doll and shell necklace; unique votive model of a Greek temple in terracotta (6C BC) from Sabucina. ROOMS 3 and 4 display finds from Capodarso, and Mimiani, including a bronze helmet of the 6C BC. On the floor below is a sculpture gallery (temporarily closed), with notable works by Michele Tripisciano (cf. above).

Near the public gardens the Seminario Vescovile houses a small MUSEO D'ARTE SACRA with 17C and 18C vestments and two paintings by Borremans. At No. 73 Viale della Regione is a MUSEUM OF MINERALOGY, with a collection of some 3000 minerals, and scale models of sulphur mines, some 500 of which existed in the provinces of Caltanissetta and Agrigento.

A minor road (N191) leads S from Caltanissetta to the site of the ancient city of **Gibil Gabib** (the name is dervied from the Arab 'Gebel Habib') discovered in the 19C. A necropolis here has yielded finds from three periods of occupation: 7C BC, 6C BC and the 4C BC.

FROM CALTANISSETTA TO ENNA, N122 and N117bis, 34km (motorway, 31km). The old road to Enna leaves Caltanissetta from Piazza Garibaldi, to the right of the town hall. After 3km it meets the Palermo road, 500m along which, at the end of a curve (and right on the road) is the **Abbazia di Santo Spirito**, a basilica founded by Roger and his wife Adelasia (probably between 1086 and 1093), and consecrated in 1153. It was attached to a fortified building, parts of which now form the sacristy. The church has a fine treble apse, recently restored. The charming small interior (ring at the door on the right marked 'Abbazia', 11–12, 17–18) contains a large font below an interesting painted Crucifix dating from the 15C. On the walls are three detached 15C frescoes which have been restored. The striking 17C fresco of Christ in benediction was repainted in 1974. On the arch of the apse is the dedication stone (1153), and nearby is a little Roman cinerary urn (1C AD), with rams' heads, birds and a festoon. A 17C sedan-chair, with its original fittings, which used to be used as a confessional has been removed to the priest's house (shown on request).

The Enna road (see above) continues beneath Monte Sabucina, and just beyond a modern shrine conspicuous on a little hill on the right of the road is (5km) a turning (signposted) for the site of **Sabucina** (2.5km).

The road climbs up past several disused mines, and there is a view up to the right above an overgrown mine of the line of walls of Sabucina, just below the summit of the hill. After 2km the asphalted road ends beside recent excavations of a necropolis and the new circular museum building (still closed). An unsurfaced road continues downhill for another 500m to a gate by a modern house at the entrance to the site (open daily 8–dusk), in a fine position with wide views. Monte Sabucina was first occupied in the Bronze Age. A thriving Iron Age village was then settled by the Greeks in the 6C BC. The city declined after the revolt of Ducezio in 450 BC. The long line of Greek fortifications with towers and gates were built directly onto the rock. Sacred edifices can also be seen here. The rich material from the necropoli is displayed in the Museo Civico at Caltanissetta (see above).

The main road traverses the forbidding Terra Pilata, a sterile upland of white clay affording a fine retrospective view of Caltanissetta. It descends to cross the Salso by (12km) Ponte Capodarso, a graceful bridge built in 1553 by Venetian engineers, and passes under the Gela 'superstrada'. A rough road leads left for 5km to the archaeological zone of CAPODARSO, an ancient city which had disappeared by the beginning of the 3C BC. Part of the walls and necropolis survive. Finds from the site are kept in the museum in Caltanissetta (see above).

The main road continues left past bare hills and wild olives. After the turning (19km; right) for Piazza Armerina, the Enna road follows a barren river valley beneath yellow and white hills, past some attractive isolated farmhouses. The landscape becomes greener, with more trees, on the approach to (34km) **Enna** (see below), the masts of which soon come into view on the left, surrounded by new buildings.

15

Enna

ENNA, known as the 'Belvedere della Sicilia' from its wonderful position on the gentle slope of a precipitous hill (931m), is the most interesting inland town (29,300 inhab.) on the island. The most impregnable stronghold in Sicily, it was for centuries the only town in the interior. The view of the medieval hill town of Calascibetta from Enna is exceptional. The evening 'passeggiata' (when Via Roma is closed to traffic) is a remarkable spectacle. Much ugly new building has taken place in recent years on the S edge of the hill and in the valleys beneath, even though the town is the capital of one of the poorest provinces in Italy.

Information Offices. 'APT' Enna, Via Roma (Tel. 0935/500544). 'Azienda Autonoma', 6 Piazza Colajanni.

Railway Station, in the valley, 5km from the town centre, on the Palermo–Catania line.

Buses. Bus Station, Viale Diaz. Services run by 'SAIS' to Catania (via the motorway in 1hr 20mins), Palermo, Taormina and Messina, Caltanissetta and Agrigento, Caltagirone, Piazza Armerina (in 45mins), Nicosia, Leonforte, Adrano, and Palermo.

Parking in Piazza Prefettura and Piazza Umberto I.

Hotel. 3-star: 'Grande Albergo Sicilia', 5 Piazza Colajanni.

Restaurants. 1st-class: 'Ariston', 365 Via Roma; 'Tiffany', 467 Via Roma, 'Centrale', 9 Piazza VI Dicembre. Trattoria and pizzeria: 'le Arcate', 4 Via de Gaspari.

Picnic places in the Castello di Lombardia.

Theatres. 'Teatro Garibaldi' for concerts and prose. Open air performances in summer in the Castello di Lombardia.

Annual Festivals. The religious ceremonies in Holy Week culminate with a procession on Good Friday. On 2 July, festivities in honour of the 'Madonna della Visitazione'.

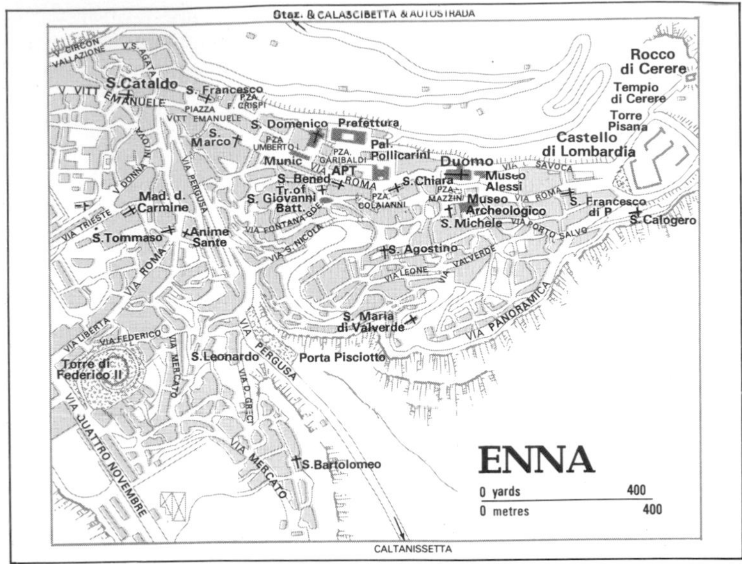

History. The city occupies the site of *Henna*, a Siculian stronghold subjected to Greek influences perhaps from Gela as early as the 7C BC. The lengendary scene of the rape of Proserpine (see below), and the centre of the cult of Ceres or Demeter, her mother, to whom Gelon erected a temple in 480 BC, it fell by treachery to Dionysius I of Syracuse in 397. In 135 BC the First Servile War broke out here under the slave Eunus, and the town was taken in 132 by the Roman army only after two years' siege. The Saracens, who took it in 859 by crawling in one by one through a sewer, named it 'Kasr Janna' (Castrum Ennae); and it was not captured by the Normans until 1087. From then on the town was known as *Castrogiovanni* until in 1927 it became the chief town of a new province. Some damage was caused by bombing in 1943.

The short Via Sant'Agata leads into Piazza Vittorio Emanuele the centre of the city, recently planted with trees and illuminated with pretty lamp-posts. On the N side is the bold flank of SAN FRANCESCO, with its fine 16C tower. On the left opens Piazza Crispi which has a splendid view across the valley to Calascibetta, and, on a clear day to Etna. The bronze statue on the fountain is a copy of Bernini's Rape of Proserpine. Via Roma, the principal street, continues uphill traversing a series of piazze. In Piazza Umberto I, with trees and decorative lamp-posts, is the neo-classical Municipio, which incorporates the Teatro Garibaldi. The Baroque façade of SAN BENEDETTO (or San Giuseppe) decorates Piazza Coppola, off which is the 15C tower of SAN GIOVANNI BATTISTA with Gothic arches, and crowned by an Arabic cupola, beside an incongruous modern building.

On the N side of Via Roma the tower of the PREFETTURA (1939) rises from Piazza Garibaldi. SANTA CHIARA, in Piazza Colajanni, is a war memorial and burial chapel. Two majolica pictures (1852) decorate the tiled pavement, one celebrating the advent of steam navigation, and the other the triumph of Christianity over Mohammedanism. The bronze statue of Napoloeone Colajanni (1847–1921), in the piazza outside, is by Ettore Ximenes.

The view to the SW takes in the Torre di Federico II (see below) surrounded by new tower blocks. Here PALAZZO POLLICARINI retains one or two Catalan-Gothic features. Via Roma continues up towards the Duomo past several narrow side streets on the left which lead to the edge of the hill.

The **Duomo**, founded in 1307 by Eleonora, wife of Frederick II of Aragon, and damaged by fire in 1446, was slowly restored in the 16C. The strange front with a 17C bell-tower, covers its Gothic predecessor. The transepts and the polygonal apses survive in their original form (they can be seen from the courtyard of the Museo Alessi, see below). The S door is also partly original.

The interesting INTERIOR (being restored) has dark grey basalt columns with splendid bases, carved with grotesques, and Corinthian capitals (1550–60; the work of various artists including Gian Domenico Gagini who carved the symbols of the Evangelists on the first two at the W end). The nave ceiling is the work of Scipione di Guido, who probably carved the stalls as well. On either side of the W door are 16C statues of the Annunciation. The two stoups in the nave date from the 16C, and at the E end of the nave are richly carved 16C organ lofts. The altarpieces on the S side are by Guglielmo Borremans (the painting of Saints Lucilla and Giacinto on the second altar is particularly good). In the presbytery are five *paintings of New Testament scenes by Filippo Paladino (1613). The late-15C painted Crucifix at the E end was restored in 1990. In the chapel to the right of the sanctuary is 18C marble decoration and a painting of the Visitation attributed to Filippo Paladino. There are more works by Borremans in the N transept and on the fourth N altar. The Renaissance font is preceded by an interesting screen.

The ***Museo Alessi** (open 9–13, 16–19 except Mon) was reopened in 1987 in a building behind the E end of the Duomo. It is named after Canon Giuseppe Alessi (1774–1837), a native of Enna, who left his remarkable collection to his brother intending that he should donate it to the church. The church instead had to buy it in 1860 and it was first opened to the public in 1862. It is beautifully arranged. In the BASEMENT are church vestments of the 17C and 18C. On the GROUND FLOOR. The 'Sala Alessi' has interesting small paintings collected by Alessi, together with his portrait. The other room has paintings from various provenances, including a Pietà with symbols of the Passion (late 15C), St John the Baptist and St John the Evangelist attributed to Antonello Crescenzio ('Il Panormita'); the Mystical Marriage of St Catherine by Antonio Spatafora (1584); a striking 16C Madonna and Child, and St Peter the fisherman by the school of Ribera. In the CORRIDOR are works by 19C local painters.

On the FIRST FLOOR is exhibited the ***Treasury** of the Duomo, with splendid 16C and 17C works, one of the richest on the island. In the large room the 16C pieces include a monstrance by Paolo Gili (1536), and four reliquaries by Scipione Di Blasi (1573). There are fine views from the windows of the valley and Calascibetta. In the room beyond is a cupboard made in 1750. The room at the other side of the stairs contains 18C and 19C silver and two large paintings by Zoppo di Ganci. In the little adjoining room is a precious gold *crown, encrusted with jewels and enamels, made for a statue of the Madonna in 1653 by Leonardo and Giuseppe Montalbano and Michele Castellani, and a beautiful 16C jewel in the form of a pelican.

The GALLERY has the remarkable ***Numismatic collection** made by Alessi, one of the most important in Sicily. The Greek, Roman, and Byzantine coins are arranged topographically and include many in bronze used in everyday transactions. A section of Roman coins is arranged chronologically. Alessi's charming archaeological collection (with some of his original labels) is also displayed here. It includes missiles (glandes) used in the Servile war, bronzes, pottery, etc. In the last room the Egyptian Ushebti figurines (664–525 BC), which also formed part of the Alessi collection and were presumably found in Sicily, are of the greatest interest.

Across Piazza Mazzini the pretty 15C PALAZZO VARISANO was restored in 1985 to house the **Archaeological Museum** (or **Museo Varisano**; open daily 9–13.30, 15.30–18.30; fest. 9–13.30). The collection is beautifully displayed and includes finds from: Calascibetta and Capodarso (7C BC local products), including the prehistoric rock tombs of Realmese; Enna (Greek, Roman, and medieval ceramics, including an Attic red-figure krater); Cozza Matrice (where the necropolis was in use from the Bronze Age up to the 5C BC) and prehistoric material from the lake of Pergusa. There is also a collection of coins; interesting Hellenistic objects from Rossomanno (and an unusual bronze belt or necklace of the 6C BC); and material from Assoro, Agira, Cerami and Pietraperzia.

Via Roma continues up to the **Castello di Lombardia** (or 'Cittadella'; open daily 8–18.30), built by the Swabians and adapted as his residence by Frederick III of Aragon. One of the best preserved medieval castles on the island, six of the 20 towers remain. Outside is a First World War memorial by Ernesto Basile (1927). On the left steps lead up to the entrance to the castle. The first courtyard is filled with a permanent open-air theatre used in summer. Beyond the second court, planted with trees, the third has remains of a church, and (beneath a roof) tombs carved in the rock. Here is the entrance to the *TORRE PISANA, which can be climbed by a modern flight of stairs. The view from the top takes in Etna, Centuripe on top of its hill, and the lake of Pozzillo. In the other direction the edge of the lake of Pergusa can be seen, and Calascibetta.

At the edge of the hill, beyond the castle, are the unenclosed remains of the **Rocca Cerere**, where traces of antique masonry may mark the site of the Temple of Demeter. High steps lead up to the summit with a view of Etna straight ahead. To the left can be seen the lake of Pozzillo and Centuripe, and Calascibetta.

The lower town is reached by following the other branch of Via Roma, which takes a sharp turn to the S below Piazza Vittorio Emanuele. On the right are the churches of SAN TOMMASO, with a 15C tower and a marble altarpiece by Giuliano Mancino (1515), and the CARMINE (behind San Tommaso), with another 15C campanile and a curious stair-tower. On the left, near the SW end of Via Roma, rises the octagonal TORRE DI FEDERICO II, surrounded by a public garden, a Swabian work recalling the towers of Castel del Monte (it can sometimes be climbed on request).

Enna is a good centre for visiting the famous mosaics in the Roman villa near Piazza Armerina, and the excavations of Morgantina (see Rte 17). The secondary roads in the province often traverse spectacular countryside, and small towns of interest include Leonforte, Sperlinga, and Nicosia, described below.

Calascibetta from Enna

16

The province of Enna

A. Leonforte and Centuripe

Road from Enna, 71km.—4km, turning for CALASCIBETTA (2km)—22km **Leonforte** (ASSORO, 6km E)—35km Agira—50km Regalbuto—63km, turning for **Centuripe** (8km S).

A road descends from Enna at Piazza Garibaldi. In the valley it joins N121 which passes under the motorway and at 4km a by road leads left to climb up to the hill town of **Calascibetta** (691m) on a flat-topped hill, which is particularly picturesque when seen from a distance (and provides one of the most delightful views from Enna). The narrow main street (keep left) leads up to the DUOMO which is to be reopened after restoration. Its 16C column bases are similar to those in the Duomo at Enna. There is a good view from the terrace.

A one-way street leads back down to Piazza Umberto where the signposted road to Enna leads downhill past the church of the CAPPUCCINI, on the edge of the hill. It contains a splendid large altarpiece of the Epiphany by Filippo Paladino, in a huge wooden frame.

The REALMESE necropolis (unenclosed), 2km NW of Calascibetta, is well signposted. Here some 300 rock tombs (850–730 BC) have been found.

The main road undulates through farming country with some orange groves. Near the railway station of Pirato is a lovely old abandoned country villa. There is a view ahead of the distant hills, and views back of Enna. The road begins to climb past some old pink farm houses (mostly abandoned) and olive trees. On the approach to Leonforte there is a good view across the valley of the little town with the conspicuous Palazzo Baronale preceded by its defensive wall, and, at the bottom of the hill in trees, the back wall of the 'Granfonte'.

22km **Leonforte** (603m) is a delightful little town founded in 1610 by Nicolò Placido Branciforti, where in 1833 John Henry Newman nearly died of fever. Via Porta Palermo leads to Corso Umberto, just before which, below the road to the left, is the DUOMO (17C–18C), with a striking façade in a mixture of styles. It contains numerous interesting wood statues.

A very short steep road can be followed on foot downhill past the church of Santo Stefano to the church of the Carmelo beside the delightful *GRANFONTE (built in 1651 by Nicolò Branciforte) an abundant fountain of 24 jets (it can also be reached by car from Via Porta Palermo). The water is collected in a stream which follows a picturesque lane downhill. Beside it is the gate of an overgrown botanical garden, with palms and orange trees. From here can be seen the defensive walls and turret in front of the Palazzo Baronale.

Just beyond the Duomo is Piazza Branciforte with the impressive façade of the 17C PALAZZO BARONALE, and, at the end, a stable block built in 1641 (the town used to be famous for horse-breeding). The well-proportioned Corso leads gently up through a pretty circular piazza. Beyond, a side street (left) leads to the church of the CAPPUCCINI. It contains a huge high altarpiece of the *Calling of St Matthew by Pietro Novelli (in a large dark wood frame). On either side are niches with Gaginesque statues. A finely carved arch (1647) precedes the Branciforte funerary chapel, with the sumptuous black marble sarcophagus (1634) of Caterina di Branciforte, supported on four lions.

A byroad leads E from Leonforte to **Assoro** (6km), another interesting little town. Occupied in the Greek and Roman period, it was taken by the Arabs in 939, and by the Normans in 1061. The road leads up past the campanile of the ex-church of Santa Caterina to Piazza Umberto I, with a view from its terrace. The side façade of Palazzo Valguarnera (see below) is connected by an arch to the porch of the CHIESA MADRE (San Leone), with a square bell tower. It is entered by a Catalan doorway and has an unusual interior with twisted columns and a carved and painted wood roof, and early 18C stucco decoration. In the raised and vaulted presbytery is a fine marble ancona (1515) with statues and reliefs, and two early 16C Valguarnera funerary monuments on the side walls. Over the nave hangs a painted Crucifix (late 15C). The high altar has three Gothic statues. To the left of the presbytery is a double chapel, the first with Gothic vaulting and bosses, and the second with Baroque decoration. Here is a carved processional Crucifix attributed to Gian Domenico Gagini, and two 17C sarcophaghi. In the nave are some particularly interesting 16C polychrome gilded wood statues.

The main façade of the Duomo faces Piazza Marconi, and here the front of PALAZZO VALGUARNERA has a balcony with grotesque heads. Also here is the Baroque portal of an oratory.

N121 continues from Leonforte and at 24km leaves a turning for Nicosia and Sperlinga (see Rte 16B) on the left. The road becomes prettier with wide views ahead of the mountains beyond the little town of (35km) **Agira** (bypass), on a conical hill (670m). The ancient *Agyrion* was a Sicel city colonised with Greeks by Timoleon (339 BC). Traces have been found here of Roman houses with mosaic pavements, a temple on what must have been the acropolis, and necropoli of the 4–3C BC. Diodorus Siculus, the historian, who lived in the Augustan era was born here: in his description of Timoleon's city he declares the theatre was the most beautiful in Sicily after that of Syracuse. It was the scene of the miracles of the apocryphal St Philip of Agirò, possibly a Christianised form of Herakles, the tutelary deity of the town. The town is now of little interest, and the churches are usually kept closed (the largest of which is Sant'Antonio da Padova, with a dome, built in 1549, in the lower town).

Beyond Agira a fine road diverges left to **Troina** (29.5km; 3-star hotel 'La Cittadella dell'Oasi', località San Michele), on a steep ridge, the highest town (1120m) in Sicily. Its early capture by the Normans (1062) is recalled by Norman work (1078–80) in the Chiesa Matrice, which has a good 16C campanile. Parts of the Greek walls remain, and the Belvedere has a splendid *view.

The road continues from Agira past (left; well signposted) a Canadian Military Cemetery (490 graves) in a clump of pine trees on a small hill, beautifully kept. The road descends, negotiating hair-pin bends, through lovely countryside with almonds, prickly pear, and agave. It skirts the pretty artificial lake of POZZILLO, its shores, with some woods, used as pasture-land. The road runs straight through the main piazza of (50km) REGALBUTO, where the church has a campanile crowned by a spire. It has some fine 18C buildings and a public garden. Beyond bare red and ochre hills on the left there is a splendid view ahead of Etna.

The road descends to the plain with its bright green citrus friut plantations, many of them protected by 'walls' of olive trees, and Centuripe can be seen on its hill to the right. On the left a subsidiary crater of Etna is now prominent. 63km, turning (signposted) for Centuripe. The byroad winds up past citrus groves and olives and then crosses barren hills with a few almond trees. There are views of Adrano and Biancavilla on the lower slopes of Etna. Outside Centuripe the terraced hillside shows how they were once cultivated.

71km **Centuripe**, a small town occupying a commanding position (719m) astride a ridge facing Etna, aptly named 'il balcone della Sicilia' by Garibaldi when he arrived here in 1862. The key-point in several Sicilian campaigns, it was destroyed for rebellion by Frederick II (1233) and reconstructed in 1548 after a further sack by Charles I of Anjou. Its capture by the Allies in 1943 decided the Germans to abandon Sicily. Once called *Centorbi*, it was the birthplace of the physician Celsus (fl. AD 14–37). The town centre, now surrounded by ugly new buildings, is the piazza near the 17C pink-and-white Duomo. On the edge of the cliff a pine avenue leads to the remains of a monument possibly of Roman (2C AD) origin (locally known as 'Il Corradino' in allusion to the Swabian Corrado Capace who is supposed to have built a castle here). There are fine views. A new museum, built to display the local Hellenistic and Roman finds, has never been opened.

In the valley (Vallone Difesa), E of the town, excavations beneath and near the church of the Crocifisso have revealed an important Augustan edifice, known as the 'Sede degli Augustali'. On Monte Calvario (Contrada Panneria) is a Hellenistic house, and to the NW in Vallone dei Bagni, is a large Roman thermal edifice with five huge niches.

Beyond the Centuripe turning (see above), N121 continues E and crosses the Simeto by the Ponte del Maccarone, about 1km below a huge aqueduct (31 arches) constructed in 1761–66. Adrano, 17km E of Centuripe, is described together with Etna in Rte 25.

The fastest route back to Enna from Centuripe is via the lonely road which continues S across barren yellow hills to join the A19 motorway at Catenanuova, 41km E of Enna.

B. Nicosia and Sperlinga

ROAD FROM ENNA, N121, N117, 48km. From Enna to (22km) Leonforte, see Rte 16A. N117 43km, junction for **Nicosia** (5km E) and **Sperlinga** (6km N).

From Enna to (22km) Leonforte, see Rte 16A. 2km outside the town, N117 diverges left for Nicosia and Sperlinga. The beautiful road, one of the prettiest in the centre of the island, leads down through farming country past ruined old houses, with views of the rolling hills, alongside remains of a disused railway viaduct. There are views back of the hill of Calascibetta in front of the high rock of Enna, and a distant view ahead to the E of Etna. The road reaches a summit level of 858m to reveal a splendid view across the Salso valley to high hills, with Sperlinga conspicuous on the left (the sheer rock on which its castle is built is prominent to the right of the village). The road continues above the Salso valley with Sperlinga still visible, through countryside where cattle and sheep are grazed (and a few mules are still used by the farmers as a means of transport), and then descends to cross the Salso (with the ruined railway viaduct upstream).

43km, junction for Sperlinga (left; described below) and (right; 5km) **Nicosia** (700m; 3-star hotel 'Pineta' in località San Paolo), a place of some importance in the Middle Ages. The local dialect betrays the Lombard and Piedmontese origins of its early colonists. The town is now surrounded by ugly buildings, and its monuments are in poor repair. It was damaged by a landslide in 1757, earthquake in 1968, and flood in 1972.

PIAZZA GARIBALDI is at the centre of the town, with the Palazzo di Città by Salvatore Attinelli (early 19C), and the elegant portico of the CATHEDRAL (San Nicola). The decorative 14C W door is in extremely poor repair; the entrance is by the S door. The imposing campanile, struck by lightning some years ago, has been partially rebuilt. In the interior the vault was decorated by the Manno brothers in the early 19C. On the W wall is the organ by Raffaele La Valle. On the S side, in the second bay is a *Martyrdom of St Placido by Giacinto Platania, and in the third and fifth bays, the Immacolata and Holy Family both by Filippo Randazzo. The pulpit is attributed to Gian Domenico Gagini. In the S transept is a Gaginesque statue of the Madonna della Vittoria. Over the crossing, in the octagonal vault, surrounded by 17C paintings by Antonio Filingelli, is a huge statue of St Nicholas by Giovanni Battista Li Volsi, a very unusual sight. In the chapel to the right of the high altar, venerated wooden Crucifix by Fra Umile di Petralia, carried in procession through the town on Good Friday. In the presbytery the carved stalls are by Stefano and Giovanni Battista Li Volsi (c 1622; with a relief showing the old town of Nicosia). In the chapel to the left of the high altar is delightful polychrome marble decoration, and in the N transept, a statue of St Nicholas by Filippo Quattrocchi, and the funerary monument of Alessandro Testa by Ignazio Marabitti. On the N side are statues by Giovanni Battista Li Volsi (fifth and second bays), and a font by Antonello Gagini. Above the nave vault (difficult of access) the original 15C painted wood ceiling is preserved.

Opposite the S door of the Duomo is the fine 18C Palazzo Vescovile. From behind the E end of the Duomo Via Francesco Salomone leads up past Palazzo La Motta Salinella (right) with an amusing façade, and the ruined convent of San Domenico. Ahead is an isolated carved portal in front of a modern building, and on the right (behind two palm trees) the 18C portal of San Giuseppe (in poor repair and closed) with two statues. Via Ansaldi continues up to the ex convent of San Vincenzo Ferreri (1555) with an interesting closed balcony at the top of its façade for the nuns. It contains frescoes by Guglielmo Borremans.

Farther uphill to the left is SANTA MARIA MAGGIORE built in 1767. The campanile crashed to the ground in 1968 and in 1978 the bells were rehung on a low iron bracket beside the façade. Beside the interesting W door can be seen several houses built into the rock face. The interior contains a huge marble ancona at the E end, finished by Antonello Gagini in 1512, a statue of the Madonna in the N transept, and two statues by Li Volsi. There is a view from the terrace of the modern buildings of the town, and the church of San Salvatore perched on a rock. Via Carlo V and Via del Castello climb up behind Santa Maria Maggiore to the ruins of the Norman CASTLE.

From Piazza Garibaldi (see above) Via Fratelli Testa leads down past the closed churches of SAN CALOGERO (with a good ceiling and works by Filippo Randazzo) and Sant'Antonio Abate. On a rock outcrop at the top of the hill can be seen the portico and campanile of SAN SALVATORE, rebuilt in the 17C. Via Testa ends at Via Li Volsi with (left) the church of the CARMINE which contains two statues of the Annunciation attributed to Antonello Gagini. At the top of Via Li Volsi, lined with trees, can be seen the Baroque façade of Palazzo Speciale propped up by concrete pillars.

In SAN MICHELE (just E of the town) is a 16C font and two wooden statues by Giovanni Battista Li Volsi.

From Nicosia N117 continues N through the Nebrodi mountains via Mistretta to the coast at Santo Stefano di Camastra, described in Rte 29.

From Nicosia to Randazzo, 82km. N120 leads E from Nicosia through a particularly beautiful landscape, with frequent glimpses of Etna in the distance. The fields are dotted with 'pagliari', conical huts of straw and mud. On the approach to (21km) Cerami there is a spectacular view (left) of the hill town of CAPIZZI, one of the highest villages in Sicily. After his victory at the Battle of Cerami in 1063, Roger I presented four Saracen camels to Pope Alexander II in Rome. A road leads left to the artificial lake of Ancipa with its huge dam. 33km Troina is described in Rte 16A.

From now on Etna towers ahead, while the road winds below the heights of the Nebrodi, through rugged country, passing below CESARO, with remains of its castle.

At 65km it crosses the Simeto. A short way beyond a road leads left to Castello Maniace (open to the public; described in Rte 25). 82km **Randazzo**, at the foot of Mount Etna (described in Rte 25). From here to Fiumefreddo di Sicilia on the E coast, see Rte 25.

From the road junction (see above), 5km W of Nicosia, the Sperlinga road leads NW in 6km. **Sperlinga**, the only Sicilian town which took no part in the 'Vespers', is a delightful little place laid out beneath its conspicuous castle rock. The road enters the town past the 17C church of Sant'Anna (closed for restoration) and on the right yellow signs indicate grottoes used as houses up until a few years ago. They are preserved as a little museum (approached by steps up the Salita del Municipio by a very tall palm tree; key with Signora Siracusa at No. 15).

The main road continues and then a road (signposted right) leads up past the large 17C Duomo to a car-park just below the entrance to the medieval *CASTLE (open 9–12; if closed apply at the Municipio), built on the sheer rock face. Two grottoes are used as a local ethnographical museum with tools, pots, baskets, agricultural implements, etc. Steps lead up across a small bridge (on the site of the drawbridge) through the double entrance. Restoration work is in progress, and a little church is being rebuilt. Stables, carved out of the rock in the Middle Ages, were later used as prisons. In one room are old photographs of Sperlinga, some taken during the occupation in 1943 by Robert Capa (1913–53). From a terrace a flight of high steps hewn into the rock leads up to the battlements from which there are splendid views.

N120 continues W from Sperlinga towards Gangi, Petralia Soprana and Sottana, and Polizzi Generosa, all described in Rte 3.

The rest of the province of Enna, including the Lago di Pergusa, Morgantina, and Piazza Armerina, is described in Rte 17.

17

Piazza Armerina and Morgantina

Road from Enna, 33km, N561, N117bis. 9km **Lago di Pergusa**—22km, junction with N117bis—30km Madonna della Noce crossroads (for Aidone,7km, and **Morgantina**, 11km)—33km **Piazza Armerina**.

Buses ('SAIS') from Enna via Pergusa to Piazza Armerina (in 45mins) and to Aidone in 1hr.

Information Office. 'APT' Enna, Tel. 0935/500544.

A fast road leads S from Enna to (9km) the **Lago di Pergusa** (3-star hotel 'Riviera' and 2-star 'Miralago'), the only natural lake on the island. Its sheet of brackish water (182 hectares), now polluted and drying up, has no visible outlet. The vegetation on the shores, and birdlife have been virtually destroyed since the 1950s. Although it has been developed as a resort, access to the lake is limited since it is encircled by an incongruous motor racing track. According to legend the lake occupies the chasm through which Pluto carried Proserpina off to Hades:

...Not that faire field
of *Enna*, where Proserpin gathring flours
Her self a fairer Floure by gloomie *Dis*
Was gatherd, which cost *Ceres* all that pain
To seek her through the World;
(Milton, 'Paradise Lost'.)

On a hill above the lake (signposted) excavations (not open to the public) were begun in 1978 of the necropolis, city and walls of COZZO MATRICE.

The road continues through open farming countryside and at 22km joins the main road (N117 bis). This traverses thick woods, the result of a scheme, initiated in 1926 to clothe the area with pine, eucalyptus, cypress, and poplar trees (replanting is now taking place). The 'Parco Ronza' here has picnic areas and a little wildlife enclosure. 30km Madonna della Noce crossroads where the road for Aidone and Morgantina diverges left (see below).

33km **PIAZZA ARMERINA**, a brisk small town, was little known to travellers before the discovery of the Roman villa at Casale, but, with 22,300 inhabitants, it now rivals Enna as the most important centre of the province. It has interesting Baroque monuments. In 1295 Frederick of Aragon here summoned the council that decided to contest his brother's attempt to cede Sicily to Charles II of Anjou.

Information Office. 'Azienda Autonoma', 15 Via Cavour.

Buses ('SAIS') from Piazza Generale Cascino to Enna (in 45mins).

Hotel. 3-star 'Villa Romana', 18 Via De Gasperi.

Restaurant. 1st-class: 'Bellia', on the N117 bis.

Annual Fesival on 13–14 August, the 'Palio dei Normanni'.

A number of streets converge at the central PIAZZA GARIBALDI, with its five palm trees. Here is the 18C Palazzo di Città next to the church of the Fundrò (or San Rocco), with a carved tufa doorway. Between them Via Cavour leads up past a former electricity station, restored as the seat of the Pretura. Farther uphill is the ex-convent of San Francesco (now a hospital) with an elaborate balcony high up on the corner.

The road continues past the 17C Palazzo del Vescovado (in very poor condition) to Piazza del Duomo, at the top of the hill, with a pretty view from its terrace. Here is a statue to Baron Marco Trigona (1905), who was responsible for financing the rebuilding of the **Duomo** in 1627. The façade was added in 1719 and the dome in 1768. The fine campanile (c 1490; covered for restoration), survives from an earlier church.

The entrance is by one of the side doors. In the INTERIOR the crossing and transepts decorated in white and blue are unusually light and spacious. On the high altar is a copy of a venerated Byzantine painting, the Madonna delle Vittorie preserved behind in a 17C silver tabernacle. It is said to have been given by Pope Nicolas II to Count Roger. Three of the 17C paintings in the sanctuary are by Zoppo di Ganci. In the little chapel on the left of the sanctuary (above the door of which is a painting of the Martyrdom of St Agata by Iacopo Ligozzi) is a *Cross, painted on wood, attributed to a Provençal artist (1485). The altarpiece in the N transept of the Assumption of the Virgin is by Filippo Paladino. The organ is by Donato del Piano (1760). The font is surrounded by a Gaginesque portal which survives from the earlier church. An equestrian statuette of Roger and a reliquary by Simone d'Aversa (1392–1405) are among the cathedral's treasures, which may one day be exhibited in a museum. Also in the piazza is the fine brick façade of the large 18C PALAZZO TRIGONA.

The picturesque Via Monte leads downhill through an interesting part of the town, while Via Floresta leads down past the back of Palazzo Trigona with its Renaissance loggia (partly blocked up and altered) and ends in Piazza Castello. Here are the overgrown 14C CASTLE and four pretty small 17C palaces. The road continues down past the college of the Gesuiti, the charming façade of SANT'ANNA (18C), and the 17C façade of SANT' IGNAZIO DI LOYOLA (preceded by an outside double staircase) to end in Piazza Garibaldi.

To the E of the centre, in Piazza Umberto I, is SAN GIOVANNI DEI RODI (now used by a youth club; enquire locally for the key). This plain 13C chapel of the Knights of St John is lit by lancet windows. Nearby are the eccentric façade of Santo Stefano, and the Teatro Garibaldi (1905; disused). Downhill are the fine public gardens in Villa Garibaldi near the 16C church of San Pietro. On the rise to the S the CHIESA DEL CARMINE preserves a campanile and cloister of the 14–15C.

To the N of the town, is the Norman church of SANT' ANDREA (open on Sundays; at other times enquire locally for the key). Dating from 1096 the austere interior contains 13–15C frescoes, including one of the Crucifixion of the titular saint.

1km W of the town, reached from the road to Casale (see below), a rough track (3km) climbs the Piano Marino (or Amerino) to the little church of SANTA MARIA DI PLATEA where the Byzantine Madonna delle Vittorie (see above) was found. Nearby are the ruins of a castle, traditionally thought to have been founded by Count Roger. The views are delightful.

At MONTAGNA DI MARZO, c 15km NW of Piazza Armerina, recent excavtions have revealed a sanctuary of Demeter and Kore, in use from the 6C–3C BC. Votive statuettes and coins have been found here.

The famous ****VILLA ROMANA** lies 5.5km SW of the town, in the contrada of CASALE, off N191. The road (signposted) leads under a high road viaduct and then along a pretty valley. It passes the church of Santa Maria del Gesù, with a double portico, beside the cemetery, before ending at a car-park and modern restaurant/café.

This luxurious country mansion must have belonged to one of the wealthiest men in the Roman Empire, who may possibly have been Diocletian's co-Emperor Maximian (Maximianus Herculeus). It lay in a wooded and sequestered site at the foot of Monte Mangone; the nearest Roman town was Philosphiana (Soffiana), 5km S. In richness and extent the villa can fairly be compared with Hadrian's Villa at Tivoli or Diocletian's Palace at Split (Spalato), but while enough stands of the walls to give an idea of the elevation, it is for the extent of the polychrome mosaics covering the floors that the building is unique.

The **Villa**, which consists of four distinct though connected groups of buildings on different levels, appears to date in its entirety from the early 4C, and to have succeeded a more modest 2C dwelling. The mosaics are of the Roman-African school (probably 4C AD). The buildings seem to have been kept in a habitable state up to the Arab invasion. From c 1000 they were occupied until their destruction by William the Bad (c 1160), when they were abandoned to a few cottagers, and soon obliterated by a landslide. The buried ruins remained unnoticed until 1761 and it was not until 1881 that any but spasmodic excavations were put in hand; in 1929 and again in 1935–39 the work was continued, and finally, from 1950, with official assistance, the main structure of the building was exposed, under

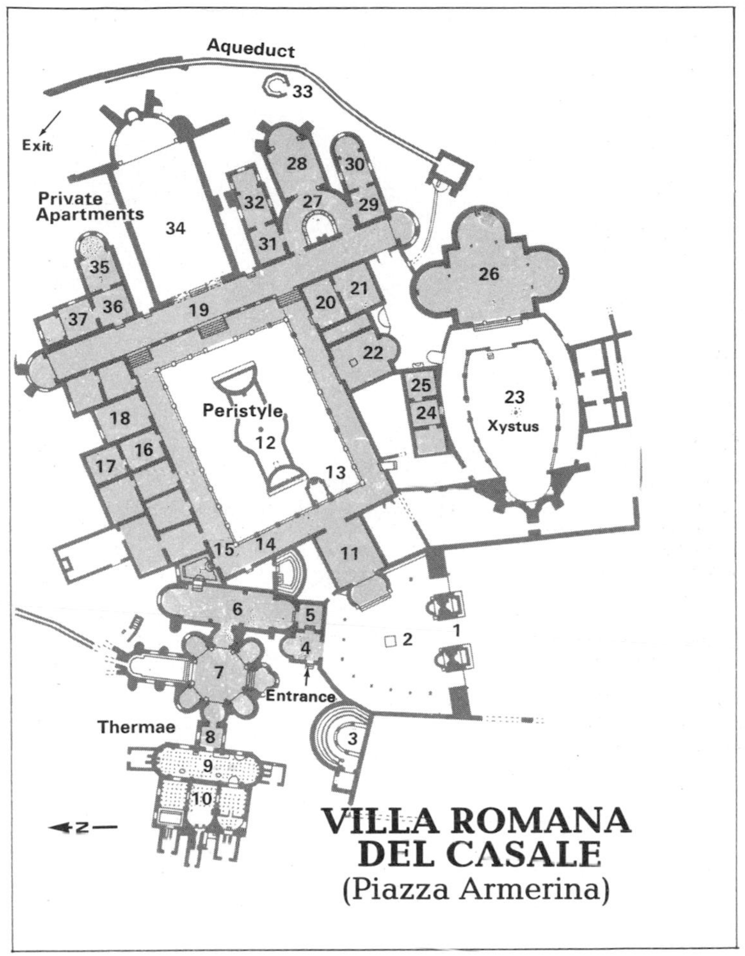

the direction of Vinicio Gentili; the slaves' quarters and the outbuildings still remain to be explored. The mosaics have had to be extensively restored after damage from a flood in 1991. In 1992 rooms 23–26, and room 34 were still closed for restoration.

Most of the site has been protected against the weather by a plastic shelter, its shape designed to give an idea of the original villa. This description follows the order in which it is possible to view the rooms from platforms and elevated walkways; the plan is numbered in the same order. The plan shows the lay-out of the villa without the protective structure; for clarity, however, the parts enclosed have been shaded. **Admission**: daily 9am–one hour before sunset. The site is beautifully kept.

From the ticket office a modern path leads down past the thermae (see below). While excavations are in progress the present entrance is through

Detail of a mosaic in the Villa Romana near Piazza Armerina

an aediculum (4). The ENTRANCE (1) to the villa, recalling in its massive form the Roman triumphal arch, had two fountains on each face, fed probably from a reservoir in the attic story. The ATRIUM (2) is a huge polygonal court surrounded by a portico of marble columns. To the left are the remains of the GREAT LATRINE (3; originally entered on the W side), the marble seats of which are lost. The aediculum (4), designed for a statue of Venus, gives access to the **thermae**. The vestibule (5) was the entrance to the long narthex (6), which can now only be viewed from the peristyle (see below). The FRIGIDARIUM (7), an octagon with radiating apses of which two served as vestibules, four as apodyteria, and two, larger than the rest, as plunge baths, was covered with a dome. The mosaics show robing scenes and, in the centre, marine myths. Those in the adjoining room (8), depicting the massage of bathers by slaves, suggest its use as an aleipterion, a function consistent with its position between the cold baths and the TEPIDARIUM (9) and CALIDARIA (10) which lie beyond. In both these the partial disappearance of the floor has exposed the hypocaust beneath.

From the atrium (cf. above) is the entrance to the villa proper, through the TABLINUM (11) to the **peristyle** (12), a quadriporticus of ten columns by eight, interrupted on the E side by an arch. It has been laid out as a garden, and in the centre is a large fountain. Immediately opposite the entrance is an aediculum (13), the shrine of the patron deity of the house, decorated with a mosaic showing an ivy motif. The peristyle walks are paved with mosaic, divided by geometrical borders into panels, in which animal heads are framed in laurel wreaths.

Off the W walk opened a small court giving access to the SMALL LATRINE (14), a sumptuous construction whose brick drain, marble hand-basin, and pictorial decoration attest the standards of imperial Roman comfort. From here it is possible to look down into the SALONE DEL CIRCO (6; the narthex of the thermae), so called from the scenes of the Roman circus depicted in its mosaic floor, the most extensive of their kind known. The obelisk has recently been identified as the obelisk of Constantius II in the Circus Maximus in Rome which received this form in AD 357. Adjacent is a vestibule (15; another entrance to the thermae). Its coloured mosaic, a mother with a boy and girl and two slave-girls carrying bathing necessities and clean clothing, is doubly interesting for the style of dress, and because it probably represents the imperial household in a family scene.

The majority of the rooms on the N side of the peristyle have geometrical mosaics, several of them damaged by Norman structural alterations. Representations of the Seasons figure in one (16); another (17) shows fishing scenes with amorini. The most interesting is that called the *Piccola Caccia (18), where a number of hunting scenes are depicted in great detail.

From the E walk steps ascend to the AMBULACRUM (19), a corridor (64m long) running the width of the building to isolate the private apartments and closed at either end by an exedra. An arcade overlooked the peristyle. The corridor is paved throughout with a wonderful series of ***hunting scenes** ('Venationes'), one of the finest Roman mosaics known. In the exedrae are personifications of two Provinces, flanked by wild beasts, representing perhaps two opposing points of the Mediterranean, since the landscape between them is divided in the centre by a sea full of fish on which sail large galleys, in which exotic animals are being transported. The hunting scenes are notable for the number of species of wild animals, for the fidelity with which they are depicted in action (note the position of the leopard on the antelope's back, and the tigress rescuing her cub), and for the dignified figure robed in Byzantine splendour, perhaps a portrait of Maximian himself.

At the SE corner of the peristyle is an ante-room (20), and, beyond, the SALA DELLE DIECI RAGAZZE (21), whose late mosaic (4C) shows ten girls performing gymnastic exercises, clad in 'bikinis'. In one corner is part of an earlier geometric pavement which was ruined by damp. Adjacent is a summer living-room (22) with a damaged mosaic representing the Orphic myth; again the animals are lovingly depicted.

Steps descend from the building, and, outside, a path skirts the apse of the triclinium (see below) to enter the **xystus** (23), a large elliptical court surrounded on three sides by a portico and closed at the W end by a wide exedra. Rooms 24 and 25 (to the N) are adorned with mosaics of vintage and fishing scenes. From the E end, with charming mosaic decoration, steps lead up to the TRICLINIUM (26), a room 12m square with deep apses on three sides. The theme of the central pavement is the *Labours of Hercules, the violent episodes being combined into a single turbulent composition. Ten of the labours can be distinguished, those missing being the Stymphalian Birds and the Girdle of Hippolyte. In the apses: the Glorification of Hercules; Conquered Giants; Lycurgus and Ambrosia. The tonal shading of the figures is remarkable.

A path leads round the outside of the triclinium and follows the line of the aqueduct to enter the **private apartments**. The S group is approached above the semicircular atrium (27; with a mosaic of cupids fishing), divided by a tetrastyle portico into a nymphaeum and an ambulatory. On either side a vestibule leads into a bed-chamber, while the centre opens into a living room (28), whose walls were decorated with marble; the mosaic shows Arion surrounded by Naiads and marine creatures and is the best known representation of this myth. The S vestibule (29), decorated with nursery scenes leads into a bed-chamber (30) in which the mosaic shows dramatic scenes; the musical instruments and the indication by Greek letters of musical modes are of unusual interest. Off the N vestibule (31), with its stylised tableau of Eros and Pan, is a bed-chamber (32) with scenes of inexperienced young hunters, those in the centre already amusingly routed by their quarry.

Outside the building is a small latrine (33). In the large BASILICA (34; closed in 1992), the throne room in which guests were received, the apse is decorated with marble intarsia. The N group of apartments consists of a chamber (35) with a decorative mosaic depicting a variety of fruit, and an antechamber (36) with a large mosaic of Ulysses and Polyphemus. The adjoining chamber (37) has a perfectly preserved floor in 'opus musivum' with a faintly erotic scene in its 12-sided centre panel. The exit follows a path around the outside of the buildings back to the entrance.

From Piazza Armerina N117 bis descends towards the distant sea at Gela (see Rte 13), with open views across plantations of prickly pear.

Aidone lies 10km NE of Piazza Armerina. From the Madonna della Noce crossroads on the Enna road (see above), a byroad leads E for Aidone (7km) and Morgantina. It descends gently as it traverses lovely woods of pine and eucalyptus trees.

The little town of **Aidone** (889m) is built of the local red stone. In the upper part of the town (poorly signposted), in a restored 17C Capuchin convent, is an ARCHAEOLOGICAL MUSEUM (open daily 9–13.30, 15.30–18.30), with a well-displayed collection of finds from Morgantina (see below). The entrance is through a charming little church with wood statues. On the ground floor ROOM I contains Bronze and Iron Age finds from the Cittadella, the area of Morgantina occupied before the Greek era. This includes material from huts inhabited by the 'Morgetica' colony. A spiral staircase leads up to ROOM II which continues the display from Cittadella, with Corinthian and Attic ceramics, antefixes with gorgons' heads (6C BC), a large red-figure krater by the Euthymides painter, an Attic Corinthian krater with birds, and lekythoi. ROOM III contains a fine collection of ceramics from the agora zone of Serra Orlando (including a plate with three fish), and from the houses excavated on the W and E hills (including statues). Also here are numerous votive statuettes and large *busts of Persephone (3C BC) from the three sanctuaries of Demeter and Kore so far found in the district. Another room on two levels has a delightful display of household objects, cooking utensils, agricultural implements, toys, masks, etc. found at Morgantina.

The extensive remains of the ancient city of ***Morgantina** (open every day, 9am–dusk) lie some 4km beyond Aidone in beautiful deserted countryside, dotted with farms, with pastureland for cattle and sheep. The new approach road diverges left from the main road before entering Aidone and continues E for 2km. A good paved road (1km) diverges left at a fork

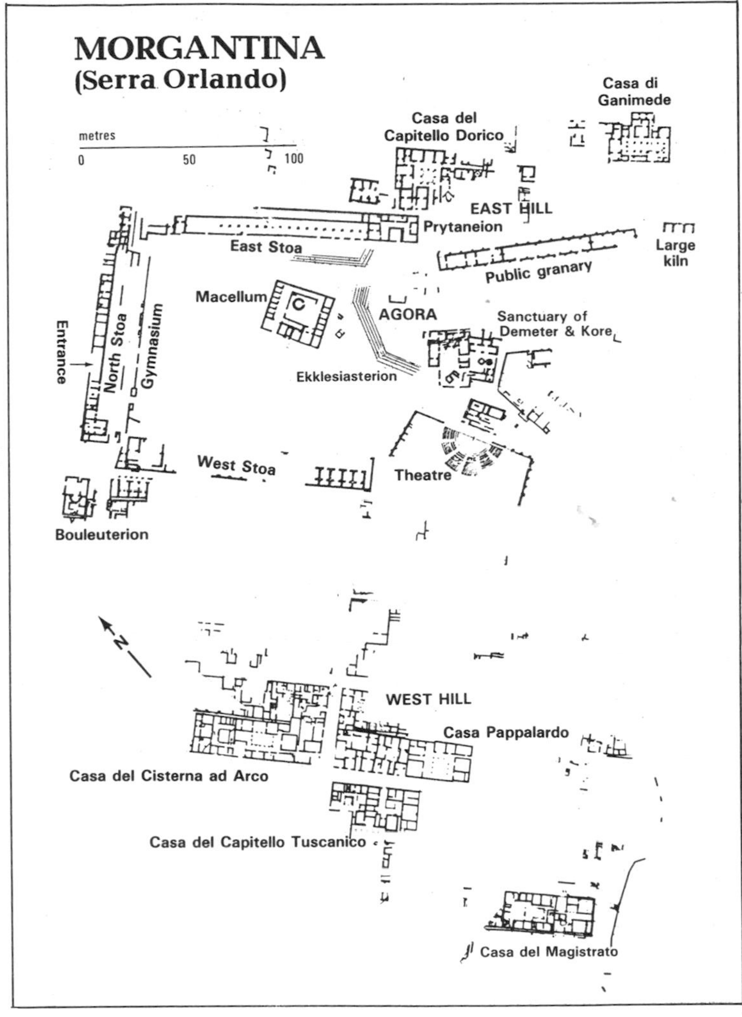

(signposted) with spectacular views. On the right, behind a green fence and under a plastic roof, is a sanctuary of Demeter and Kore (4C BC), still being excavated. Beyond is a car-park beside olive trees, but cars can normally continue down along the rough stone road for another kilometre to the entrance to the excavations, beyond which is a small car-park (and a café and trattoria on the left).

The huge site (c 20 hectares) occupies the long tufa ridge of SERRA ORLANDO to the W and the conical hill of CITTADELLA (578m) to the E; they are separated by a deep valley. The city was in the centre of a rich agricultural plain near the source of the river Gornalunga. A colony of the Sikels, called 'Morgeti' was founded c 850 BC on the Cittadella on the site of an Early Bronze Age settlement. Signs of Greek occupation here date from the 6C BC, but the Cittadella was abandoned after its sack by Ducetius in 459 BC. The new city was built on Serra Orlando, and it probably reached its zenith in the reign of Hieron II (269–215 BC). Having sided wrongly in the Second Punic War, it was given in 211 by the victorious Romans to their Spanish mercenary Moericus. By the time of Augustus it had lost importance. The site was identified in 1955 by Princeton University, and excavations continue.

The main excavations consist of the area of the agora laid out in the 3C BC and the houses on the two low hills to the E and W of the agora. The entrance, by a group of cypreses, to the **agora** is through the NORTH STOA, with remains of the GYMNASIUM. A numer of Hellenistic lava millstones have been placed here. This area of the UPPER AGORA was also enclosed on the W and E side by a stoa. At the extreme right-hand corner, at the foot of the hill, are remains of shops and a paved street (excavations in progress here and on the slope of the W hill) near the BOULEUTERION, where the Senate met. In the centre of the upper agora, surrounded by grass, is the large rectangular MACELLUM, added in 125 BC, a covered market with shops, around a tholos. The long EAST STOA (87m) consisted of a narrow portico. A monumental fountain (under cover) with two basins has been excavated at its N end, and at its extreme S end is the so-called PRYTANEION. In the centre of the piazza is a monumental three-sided *flight of steps, 55m wide, which descends to the lower polygonal AGORA. These are thought to have served as an EKKLESIASTERION for public assemblies. Beside the steps is a SANCTUARY OF DEMETER AND KORE with two round altars (under cover). Behind this, built into the hillside, is the THEATRE. To the right, beyond a long terracotta conduit, are shops in the hillside, part of the West Stoa (see above).

In front of a conspicuous ruined house in the centre of the site, a rough lane leads up along the fence (with fine views) in c 15 minutes to the **west hill**, with a residential district. It passes the large so-called 'CASA DEL MAGISTRATO' with 24 rooms, on the slope of the hill near the walls (well preserved here outside the fence). It follows the outer wall of the house and continues to the top of the hill where a number of houses have been excavated, separated by roads on a regular grid-plan. Here the 'CASA DEL CAPITELLO TUSCANICO' has some good floors; across the street, near a large olive tree, is the 'CASA PAPPALARDO', a luxurious house with more mosaics. To the N, partly covered by a bulding for protection, is the 'CASA DELLA CISTERNA AD ARCO', with a cistern beneath a low arch, and several mosaics. On the N side of the hill (near the approach road to the site) new excavations are in progress of another house (covered for protection).

On the other side of the Sanctuary of Demeter and Kore (see above), at the foot of the east hill is the large oblong PUBLIC GRANARY, with a small pottery kiln (under cover), and, at the other end (by the fence), a larger kiln for tiles and bricks with elaborate ovens (also under cover). A stepped street zig-zags up the **east hill** to the 'CASA DEL CAPITELLO DORICO', just below the summit. Beyond an old farmhouse on the extreme right, in a little group of almond trees, is the 'CASA DI GANIMEDE' built c 260 BC, and destroyed in 211 BC, with two columns and mosaic fragments in two little huts (seen through glass doors). The Ganymede mosaic is particularly interesting as one of the earliest known tesserae mosaics. There is a fine view of the agora and, on a clear day, of Etna to the east. A lane leads back past the farmhouse and down towards the exit.

To the E of the site can be seen the hill of the **Cittadella** (reached from here by a rough road in c 3km), which was separately fortified. On the summit is a long narrow temple of the 4C BC. Here a hut village of the 'Morgeti' (850–750 BC) was excavated, and rock hewn tombs of Siceliot type yielded considerable finds of pottery. Parts of the WALLS (7km in circumference) of Serra Orlando and the W gate can be seen near the approach road to the site.

18

Caltagirone

FROM ENNA TO CALTAGIRONE, N117bis, N124, 62km. To (33km) Piazza Armerina, see Rte 17. The fast road continues S past woods and plantations of poplars, with the duomo of Piazza Armerina prominent on the skyline. The views widen out and around San Cono are fields of prickly pear. At 45km N124 diverges left for Caltagirone. The narrow, winding road traverses the main street of SAN MICHELE DI GANZARIA (1st-class restaurant 'Pomara'), on a hillside overlooking a wide plain with rolling hills in the distance. Across the brow of the hill the landscape changes with fields of light soil, some rock outcops, and dry stone walls. Many farmhouses here have been abandoned. 62km Caltagirone.

CALTAGIRONE, one of the most flourishing inland towns of the island (38,500 inhab.) is situated in the province of Catania. The old town, with pleasant Baroque and Art Nouveau buildings, is built on three hills (608m), to which it owes its irregular plan and narrow streets and its medieval name 'Regina dei Monti'. It has been noted throughout its history for its ceramic ware, and numerous artisans workshops are still active here (and their wares are exhibited in a permanent exhibition at No. 7/9 Via Vittorio Emanuele). The use of majolica tiles and terracotta finials is a characteristic of the local architecture.

Information Office. 'Azienda Autonoma', 3 Via Volta Libertini (off Via Emanuele Taranto), Tel. 0933/53809.

Railway Station, Piazza della Repubblica, built in 1975 in the modern town. It is about 500m from the public gardens. On the Catania–Gela line, it has services to Catania in c 2hrs.

Buses from the railway station to Catania and Piazza Armerina ('AST'); to Palermo and Gela ('SAIS'), to Catania ('Etna Trasporti'); and to Ragusa and its province ('Ditta Petrelli').

Hotel. 2-star 'Casa Donato' (with restaurant), Via Porto Salvo, 2km below the old town.

Restaurants. Trattorie: 'San Giorgio', Viale Regina Elena; 'Pub 2/4', 24 Via Rosa; 'La Baita', 117 Viale Milazzo. Outside the town at Bosco San Pietro, Contrada Corvacchio, trattoria 'la Quercia'.

Picnic places in the public gardens.

The 'Politeama' **Theatre** is being restored.

Annual Festivals. The 'Scala' is illuminated with oil lamps on 24–25 July, when there is also a ceramics fair. Processions, etc. during Easter week and an exhibition of terracotta whistles.

History. Traces of one or more Bronze Age and Iron Age settlements have been found in the area. The Greek city, together with other centres in central and southern Sicily, came under the influence of Gela. The present name is of Arabic origin ('kal' at', castle and 'gerun', caves). The town was conquered by the Genoese in 1030, and destroyed by the earthquake of 1693. A bombardment of July 1943, caused more than 700 casualties. Antonuzzo Gagini (c 1576–1627) died at Caltagirone, where his son Gian Domenico was probably born. The politician Luigi Sturzo (1871–1959) is a much honoured native of the town.

In the central Piazza Umberto I the BANCO DI SICILIA occupies a building of 1783 by Natale Bonaiuto. Via del Duomo leads to the **Cathedral**, which was completely transformed in 1818. In the S aisle are altarpieces by the Vaccaro, a family of local painters (19C), and in the S transept an unusual carved Crucifix attributed to Giovanni de' Mattinari (1500). Beyond is the CORTE CAPITANIALE, a delightful one-storey building decorated in the 16–17C by Antonuzzo and Gian Domenico Gagini (in very poor repair). In Piazza del Municipio is the neo-classical façade of the ex-Teatro Comunale, which serves as an entrance to the GALLERIA LUIGI STURZO, an unusual monumental building inaugurated in 1959 and used for exhibitions. The MUNICIPIO has an impressive façade of 1895.

Here begins the splendid long flight of 142 steps known as the ***Scala**, with colourful majolica risers, predominantly yellow, green, and blue on a white ground. They were designed by Giuseppe Giacalone in 1606, and altered in the 19C. They provide a tiring climb up to SANTA MARIA DEL MONTE, once the mother church. The Baroque façade is by Francesco Battaglia and Natale Bonaiuto and the campanile is by Venanzio Marvuglia. Inside (usually locked) is a Madonna attributed to the workshop of Domenico Gagini. Higher up is the ex-church of SAN NICOLA which houses a private local ethnological museum (sometimes opened on request). There are interesting medieval streets in this area.

From near the foot of the steps Via Luigi Sturzo leads up past the church of Santa Maria degli Angeli with a 19C façade and a series of interesting palaces, some of them from the Art Nouveau period, to San Domenico (left; closed). Opposite is the splendid façade of SAN SALVATORE by Natale Bonaiuto (1794). It has a pretty octagonal interior (being restored) with a Gaginesque Madonna. A modern chapel contains the tomb of Luigi Sturzo (1871–1959; see above). Via Sturzo ends at SAN GIORGIO, rebuilt in 1699, preserving a beautiful little *Trinity, attributed to Roger van der Weyden (a fragile painting in poor condition). From the terrace (left) there is a fine view of the countryside.

The pleasant Corso Vittorio Emanuele passes several fine palazzi, and the Art Nouveau post office, on the way to **San Giacomo**, rebuilt in 1694–1708; at the side a pretty flight of steps ascends through the base of the campanile. In the interior, above the W door, the marble coat of arms of the city is by Gian Domenico Gagini. In the N aisle is a blue-and-brown portal (formerly belonging to the baptistery), and the blue-and-gold arch of the Cappella del Sacramento by Antonuzzo Gagini. In the N transept is the charming little Portale delle Reliquie, also by Antonuzzo, with bronze doors by Agostino Sarzana. In the chapel to the left of the sanctuary (behind glass doors) is a silver urn, the masterpiece of Nibilio Gagini (signed 1604). In the sanctuary are paintings by Filippo Paladino, and a processional statue of St Giacomo by Vincenzo Archifel (1518).

Just to the S of Piazza Umberto I (see above) is a massive building built as a prison in 1782 by Natale Bonaiuto. It is an interesting stone edifice with

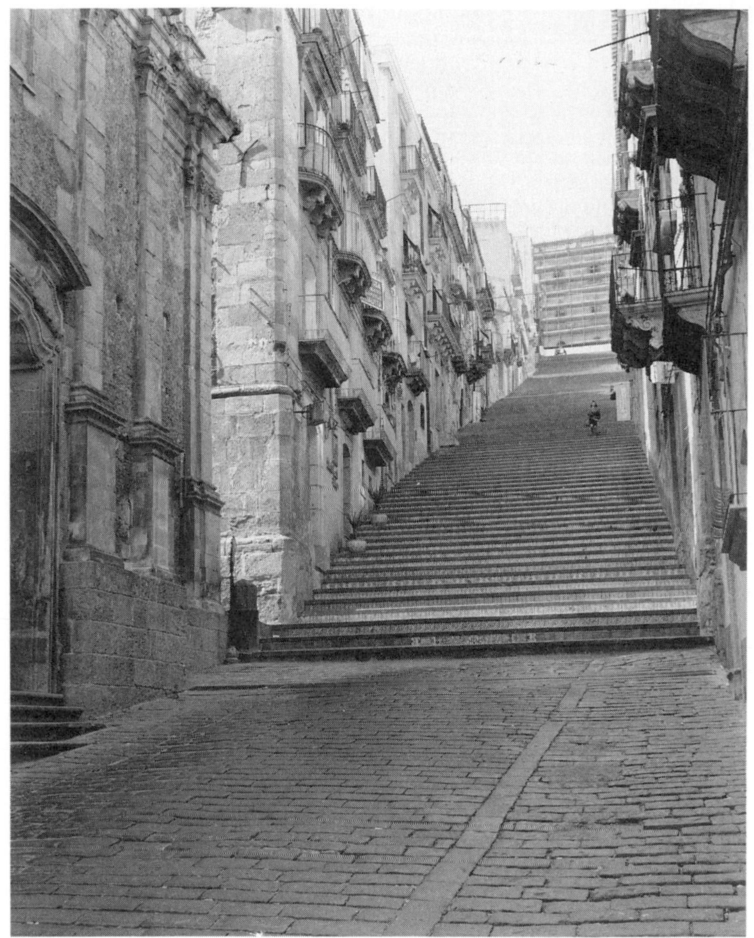

The 'Scala' in Caltagirone

an interior court and double columns, still undergoing restoration. It now houses the **Museo Civico** (open 9–13; Tues and Fri also 16–19; closed Mon), founded in 1914. On the stairs are architectural fragments and 19C terracotta vases by Bongiovanni Vaccaro. Beyond a room with modern local ceramics, the second room (temporarily closed) has a small archaeological collection. Another room contains the gilded throne of St Giacomo (16C, by Scipione di Guido) and a bishop's 19C sedan chair. The collection of 19C paintings by local artists include works by Giuseppe, Francesco and Mario Vaccaro. Beside the museum is the good façade, also by Bonaiuto, of SANT'AGATA (closed).

Beyond an 18C viaduct, on Via Roma, are the delightful **Public Gardens** laid out in 1846 by Giovanni Battista Basile. The exotic trees include palms, cedars of Lebanon, and huge pines. The vegetation has been threatened by the construction of a new road tunnel. There is a long balustrade on Via Roma decorated with pretty ceramics from the workshop of Enrico Vella, and throughout the gardens are copies of terracotta vases and figures by Giuseppe Vaccaro and Giacomo Bongiovanni. There is also a fountain by Camillo Camilliani and a decorative bandstand. The palace of Benedetto Ventimiglio, also on Via Roma, is preceded by a colourful ceramic terrace.

Beside the gardens is the **Museo Regionale della Ceramica** (open every day 9–18), entered through the scenographic TEATRINO (1792) by Natale Bonaiuto. From the top of the steps there is a view beyond a War Memorial by Antonio Ugo, with four palm trees, to the pretty hills (with the town on the left). The museum contains a fine collection of Sicilian ceramics from the prehistoric era to the 19C. The rooms are un-numbered and the exhibits poorly labelled, and the main room was closed in 1992. In the corridor to the right are 17C and 19C ceramics from Caltagirone. Beyond a room with 18C and 19C works, the archaeological material is displayed, including Hellenistic and Roman terracotta heads and figurines. Cases 19 and 20 contain fragments from Caltagirone (5–4C BC) and a bas-relief in stone with sphynxes (6C BC). Prehistoric pottery from San Mauro and Castelluccio is exhibited in cases 21 and 22. In case 26 is a krater depicting a potter at his wheel protected by Athene (5C BC). Case 27 contains the Russo Perez collection, including 5C BC red- and black-figure vases.

In the courtyard are exhibited bases used in various potteries from the 11C to the 13C. In the large room on the left are Arab Norman stuccoes from San Giuliano, 10–12C Arab Norman pottery, and medieval works (case 48 onwards). In the room by the entrance are 17C and 18C works from Caltagirone including tiles, and in a little room beyond is exhibited part of a 17C tiled floor, and elaborate 17–18C ecclesiastical works.

On a lower level is a large hall with 17–19C ceramics from Palermo, Trapani, Caltagirone and Sciacca, including blue enamelled vases and pharmacy jars. The fine collection of terracotta figures includes works by Giuseppe Bongiovanni (1809–89) and Giacomo Vaccaro (1847–1931).

Via Santa Maria di Gesù leads S from the public gardens to (10 minutes) the church of SANTA MARIA DI GESUÙ (1422), with a charming Madonna by Antonello Gagini.

Grammichele, 15km E of Caltagirone (approached by an old road or by a new 'superstrada'), was founded by Nicolò Branciforte, Principe di Butera, to house the people of Occhiolà, destroyed in 1693. Its remarkable concentric hexagonal plan is preserved around Piazza Umberto I with some pleasant small Baroque palaces. In the hexagonal piazza are a medley of houses between the six roads and the well sited Chiesa Madre begun in 1723 by Andrea Amato next to the Palazzo Comunale (1896, by Carlo Sada).

N124 continues from Grammichele to VIZZINI, 17km further E on a spur (619m), which occupies an ancient site, perhaps that of *Bidis* recorded by Cicero, and claims to be the scene of Verga's 'Mastro Don Gesualdo' and 'Cavalleria Rusticana'; the latter claim is contested by Francofonte, 15km NE.

Catania may be reached from Caltagirone by the fast N417 (65km) which follows the Caltagirone valley. A less direct road to Catania (N385; 80km) bypasses PALAGONIA (29.5km), just beyond which, on the road is the 7C shrine of Santa Febronia. This area is well known for its oranges.

13km S of Palagonia is **Militello in Val di Catania**, a pleasant town where the churches contain paintings by Vito d'Anna, Olivio Sozzi, Pietro Ruzzolone (attributed; St Peter enthroned) and others. Beside the Chiesa Madre is the Museo di San Nicola with 17C and 18C works, including vestments, church silver, sculpture and paintings. The half-ruined SANTA MARIA LA VETERE, outside the town to the E, has a porch supported on lions and a good doorway of 1506.

Ragusa, described in Rte 19, is about 60km S of Caltagione, reached by a fast road (N124 and N514). A new 'superstrada' leads E from Caltagirone passing S of Grammichele (see above), to join (15km) N514 which continues S down a wide valley with fine views. The vegetation includes olives, almonds and carob trees on the plain stretching down towards the sea. After (29km) the turn for Vittoria the landscape changes and the fields are now divided by low dry-stone walls characteristic of the province of Ragusa.

19

Ragusa

The upper town of **Ragusa** (68,800 inhab.) is an elegant provincial capital laid out after the earthquake of 1693. It occupies a ridge (502m) that runs from W to E between two deep gorges, and has expanded across the river gorge to the S, where high bridges now connect it to the modern town. Beyond a declivity at its E end, on an isolated spur below, is ***Ragusa Ibla**, a beautiful quiet old town, one of the best preserved in Sicily. It is connected to the upper town by a steep winding road (and steps), and has exceptionally fine Baroque palaces and churches.

Information Office. 'APT' Ragusa, 33 Via Capitano Bocchieri, Ragusa Ibla (Tel. 0932/621421).

Railway Station, Piazza del Popolo, in the newest part of the upper town; subsidiary station of 'Ragusa Ibla' at the bottom of the hill of Ibla on N194. On the line between Gela, Modica, Noto, and Syracuse, it has services to Syracuse in c 2hrs.

Buses. Bus No. 3 every half hour from the upper town (Corso Italia) to Ibla (Piazza della Repubblica and Piazza Pola). No. 1 from the main railway station to Ibla. Country buses from Piazza del Popolo run by 'AST' and 'Etna Trasporti' to Catania, Syracuse, Enna, and Agrigento (via Gela). Services in summer to Camarina and other places on the sea.

Car Parking. In the upper town: Via Natalelli, or Piazza Libertà; in Ibla, Piazza Duomo.

Hotels. In the upper town: 3-star: 'Rafael', 40 Corso Italia; and 'Montreal', 14 Via San Giuseppe.

Camping Sites on the sea at Marina di Ragusa and Santa Croce Camerina.

Restaurants. In Ibla: (1st-class) 'Il Barocco', 'Il Saracino', and 'Antica Macina'. Luxury-class fish restaurants at Marina di Ragusa.

Picnic places in the public gardens (Giardino Ibleo) in Ibla.

Annual Festivals. 'Festa di San Giorgio' on the last Sunday in May in Ibla; 'Festa di San Giovanni' in the upper town on 29 August.

History. Ragusa Ibla occupies the site of the Siculian Hybla Heraea. The county of Ragusa, created in 1091 by Roger for his son Godfrey, was united in 1296 by Manfredi Chiaramonte with that of Modica. After the earthquake of 1693 a new town arose to

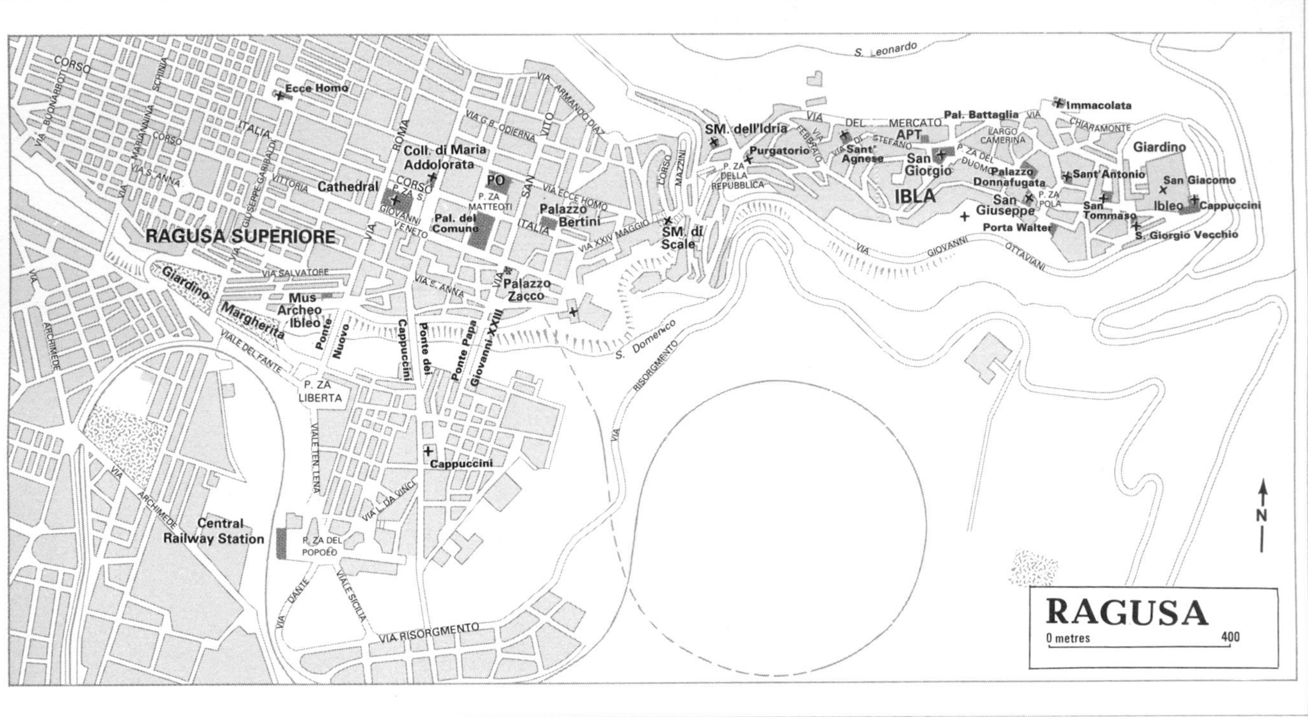

RAGUSA
0 metres
400
N
IBLA
RAGUSA SUPERIORE
Central Railway Station
Cathedral
Ecce Homo
Mus Archeo Ibleo
Giardino
Margherita
Ponte Nuovo
Ponte dei Cappuccini
Ponte Papa Giovanni XXIII
Cappuccini
Palazzo Zacco
Palazzo Bertini
PO
Pal. del Comune
Coll. di Maria Addolorata
SM. di Scale
SM. dell'Idria
Purgatorio
Sant' Agnese
San Giorgio
APT
Pal. Battaglia
Immacolata
Palazzo Donnafugata
San Giuseppe
Porta Walter
San Tommaso
Sant'Antonio
Giardino
San Giacomo
Ibleo
Cappuccini
S. Giorgio Vecchio
S. Leonardo
S. Domenico
VIA RISORGMENTO
VIA GIOVANNI OTTAVIANI
CORSO MAZZINI
P. ZA DELLA REPUBBLICA
VIA DEL MERCATO
VIA FEBBRAIO
VIA DI STEFANO
VIA CHIARAMONTE
LARGO CAMERINA
P. ZA DEL DUOMO
P. ZA POLA
VIA XXIV MAGGIO
VIA ECCE HOMO
VIA ARMANDO DIAZ
VIA SAN VITO
VIA G.B. ODIERNA
P. ZA MATTEOTTI
ITALIA
VIA S. ANNA
CORSO VITTORIO VENETO
ROMA
P. ZA S. GIOVANNI
VIA GIUSEPPE GARIBALDI
VIA SALVATORE
VIALE DEL FANTE
P. ZA LIBERTA
VIALE TEN. LENA
P. ZA DEL POPOLO
VIALE SICILIA
VIA DANTE
VIA L. DA VINCI
VIA ARCHIMEDE
VIA BUONARROTI
CORSO
MARIANNINA SCHININA
VIA S. ANNA

the W, and the two became separate communities from 1865 to 1926 when they were reunited as a new provincial capital. The area is known for its asphalt mines. Oil was found here in 1953, and there used to be oil wells scattered about the upper town. Drilling now takes place offshore, and the oil is piped from Marina di Ragusa to Augusta. The Province has accused the oil companies of pollution and this remains one of the poorest areas on the island.

The centre of the well kept upper town of **RAGUSA** is Piazza San Giovanni around the monumental cathedral of **San Giovanni**, with its wide façade preceded by a scenographic terrace (with cafés beneath) and surround by a small garden. It was begun after 1694 by Mario Spada of Ragusa and Rosario Boscarino of Modica, and has a pretty campanile. It is closed for restoration. At its E end is the elegant 18C CASA CANONICA. Across Corso Italia is the COLLEGIO DI MARIA ADDOLORATA, with a handsome façade of 1801 next to its convent.

Corso Italia, the handsome long main street, lined with trees, descends very steeply to the edge of the hill above Ibla (see below). Uphill, above the Duomo, it crosses Via Roma (which to the right ends in a rotonda with a view of Ibla) which now leads left towards Ponte Nuovo (1937) which crosses the torrente Santa Domenica high above the public gardens of Villa Margherita with a good view (left) of Ponte dei Cappuccini (1835) and Ponte Papa Giovanni XXIII (1964) beyond. Across the bridge is Piazza Libertà, with buildings erected in the Fascist era.

Just before the bridge (right, below a 'Standa' department store) steps lead down to a building beneath the road viaduct which houses the **Museo Archeologico Ibleo** (open every day 9–14, 15–17.30; fest. 9–13, 15–17.30). The beautifully displayed collection has finds from the province, from prehistoric to Roman times. FIRST SECTION (Prehistory). The Bronze Age civilisation of 'Castelluccio' is particularly well documented. Here also is displayed material belonging to the Thapsos culture (1400–1270 BC).

SECOND SECTION (cases 5–14; finds from Camarina, from the Archaic to Classical period). Case 6. Two black-figured amphorae, one with a scene of wild boars and lions, and one showing Hercules and the lion; reconstructed necropolis of Passo Marinaro; finds from the necropolis (cases 9 and 10) include small red-figured vases of the 5C BC and a lekythos with a white ground. A statue of a kore was found in the Temple of Athena. Three levels of excavations have been reconstructed here. Case 13 contains terracotta statuettes of Demeter found in a deposit near a pottery oven (active from the end of the 5C to the beginning of the 3C BC).

THIRD SECTION, dedicated to indigenous centres inhabited by the Siculi (Archaic to Classical period). Cases 14–18 contain finds from Monte Casasia, and Licodia Eubea ware; in case 15 is a rare Ionic kylix with an inscription in the native language. Cases 17–18 display finds from the necropolis of Castiglione, N of Ragusa. Case 20 displays finds from the necropolis of Rito, including an Attic kylix with animals outside and a running warrior inside attributed to the circle of the 'Griffin bird painter' (c 550 BC).

FOURTH SECTION (Hellenistic centres). A potter's oven from Scornavacche has been reconstructed, and the terracotta figurines (cases 22–24) are particularly noteworthy. FIFTH SECTION (Roman and late Roman cities). Finds from Caucana, and mosaics from Santa Croce Camerina (with Christian motifs). Case 26 contains Roman glass. The SIXTH SECTION displays various material acquired from private collections.

From Piazza San Giovanni (see above) Corso Italia descends steeply past (right; No. 90) the fine 18C PALAZZO LUPIS to Piazza Matteotti. Here is the huge PALAZZO DEL COMUNE (1880; enlarged 1929) opposite the monumental Post Office (1930), with colossal statues on the top of the building. Corso Italia next crosses Via San Vito in which, on the right, is the fine Baroque PALAZZO ZACCO (in poor repair). Farther down Corso Italia is the late-18C PALAZZO BERTINI (No. 35) with three huge grotesque heads. The Corso ends at Via XXIV Maggio, with two palaces well sited at the corner, which narrows and becomes steeper as it begins the descent to Ragusa Ibla, now seen in its magnificent position on a separate spur. At the foot of an elegant little Baroque palace, a small tabernacle recalls a cholera epidemic here in 1838; in front wide steps descend to an interesting group of houses with courtyards, overlooking the valley. The road continues down past (left) the pretty Via Pezza, which runs along the hillside, and Via Ecce Homo which climbs uphill to the left, past a handsome little Baroque palace.

Via XXIV Maggio ends at the balcony beside the campanile of Santa Maria delle Scale with a superb bird's-eye view of Ragusa Ibla, with its beautifully coloured roof tiles which have been carefully preserved. Many fragments of the 15C structure of the church of SANTA MARIA DELLE SCALE survived the rebuilding of 1693. Outside, beneath the campanile is part of a Gothic doorway and the remains of an outside pulpit. Inside (usually closed) is an elaborate Gothic arch decorated with sculptures and (over a side altar) a relief (very ruined) of the Dormition of the Virgin in coloured terracotta, by the Gagini school (1538).

Ibla can be reached from here by the zigzag Corso Mazzini or on foot by various flights of steps, described below. The Discesa Santa Maria continues down straight ahead. On the road is a relief of the Flight into Egypt (15C–16C; restored in 1988), probably once part of a votive tabernacle. Across the road another flight of steps continues under the road, and then a walkway leads left in front of some houses. Just after rejoining the road, steps immediately to the left continue downhill and pass under the road twice before reaching the delightful *Palazzo Nicastro (or 'Vecchia Cancelleria'), erected in 1760 with tall pilasters, a decorative doorway, and windows with large balconies. To the left is the bell tower and little dome decorated with majolica tiles of the 18C church of SANTA MARIA DELL'IDRIA.

The Salita Commendatore continues down past (left) the 18C PALAZZO COSENTINI, with splendid Baroque pilasters, capitals, and more fantastic balconies. Its main façade is on Corso Mazzini which now continues right to PIAZZA DELLA REPUBBLICA at the foot of the hill of ***RAGUSA IBLA**, a beautifully preserved little town, with peaceful streets, which lends itself to exploration on foot. It is, however, suffering from depopulation, and many of the old houses have been abandoned.

To the left of the closed 17C church of the PURGATORIO Via del Mercato leads up round the left side of the hill with a view of Palazzo Sortino Trono above the road. Farther on it continues left past the old abandoned market building and has splendid views over the unspoilt valley, but this route instead follows the more peaceful (and nicely paved) Via XI Febbraio which diverges right for the centre of Ibla. On a bend there is a view left of the hillside covered with characteristic dry-stone walls. Via Sant'Agnese continues left, and then steps lead up to the wide Via Tenente Di Stefano near the church of Sant'Agnese beside a low 19C palace in a pretty group of houses. It continues uphill and soon narrows with a good view ahead of the 19C dome of the cathedral. On the left are the seven *balconies of PALAZZO

Ragusa Ibla from the upper town of Ragusa

LA ROCCA, beautifully restored as the seat of the 'APT' of Ragusa. It has an interesting double staircase in black 'pece' stone, and a little garden with citrus trees overlooking the unspoilt hillside.

The road continues round the the side of the Duomo into *PIAZZA DEL DUOMO, with a row of six palm trees. It slopes up to the magnificent three-tiered golden *façade of the cathedral of **San Giorgio** which rises above a flight of steps surrounded by a 19C balustrade. The church was built by Rosario Gagliardi in 1744. The neo-classical dome (hidden by the façade; it can be seen from the road behind or from the extreme left side of the piazza) dates from 1820.

The contemporary INTERIOR (entered by one of the side doors) is lit by the delightful dome which rises above its high drum with windows between the coupled columns. The stained glass dates from 1926. In the S aisle, above the side door (and behind glass), is an equestrian statue of St George; third altar, Vito d'Anna, Immacolata; fourth altar, Dario Guerci, Rest on the Flight into Egypt. In the N transept, St George and the dragon, also by Dario Guerci. In the sacristy is a lovely stone tarbernacle with the equestrian statue of St George between saints Ippolito and Mercurio, with ruined reliefs below. Above the side door in the N aisle is a silver reliquary urn. By the W door is a stone statue of St George by the school of Gagini. The organ in the nave is by the Serassi brothers.

PALAZZO AREZZI, in the piazza, has a delightful balcony over a side road. At the lower end of the piazza is a charming little fountain and the handsome Palazzo Veninata (early 20C). The fine neo-classical CIRCOLO DI CONVERSAZIONE (c 1850), which preserves an interesting interior, houses an exclusive club recently opened to women members. Next to it is PALAZZO DONNAFUGATA with its delightful little wooden balcony from which it was possible to watch the passers by in the road below without being seen. The palace contains a private art collection formed in the mid 19C by Corrado Arezzo de Spuches (admission only with special permission) and a little theatre built in the late 19C (150 seats; recently restored) where public performances are sometimes held.

The wide Corso XXV Aprile continues to Piazza Pola, with the splendid tall Baroque façade of the church of **San Giuseppe** (1590, probably by Gagliardi). In the oval domed interior there are pretty galleries once used by the nuns. The interesting pavement is made with black asphalt, mined locally. The altars are made of shiny painted glass. In the centre of the dome is a painting of the Glory of St Benedict by Sebastiano Lo Monaco (1793). Above the high altar, in an elaborate frame, Holy Family by Matteo Battaglia. The side altarpieces, including a Holy Trinity by Giuseppe Cristadoro, are in poor condition. Beside the church is the palace which served as town hall up to 1926 (now used as a post office).

Corso XXV Aprile continues to wind downhill past the closed church of the Maddalena and the high wall of SAN TOMMASO with a pretty bell tower. In the interior is an interesting font in black asphalt (1545). Just beyond, beside the church of St Vincent Ferrer (propped up with scaffolding) is the entrance to the **Giardino Ibleo** (open 8–20), delightful public gardens laid out in 1858, with a splendid palm avenue, and beds of lilies. It contains several small churches.

Beyond the colourful campanile of St Vincent Ferrer is the locked church of San Giacomo, founded in the 16C with a façade of 1902. At the end is the church of the CAPPUCCINI, now the seat of a restoration laboratory and of the Museo Diocesano (closed). It contains a very fine altarpiece with three paintings by Pietro Novelli. The beautifully kept gardens have fountains and views of the hills, and, beyond the War Memorial, can be seen the church of San Giorgio on the skyline with the large church of the Immacolata on the right. In an orchard below the balustrade ancient tombs can be seen excavated in the rock. Outside the entrance to the gardens, in Via Normanni, is the 15C Gothic side portal of the church of SAN GIORGIO VECCHIO (in very bad condition), with a relief of St George, behind a little garden. The church was destroyed in the earthquake of 1693.

From Piazza Pola (see above), with a view of the top of the façade of San Giorgio and its dome, Via Orfanotrofio leads past the church of SANT'ANTONIO (closed) with remains of a Gothic portal next to a little Baroque side doorway. Just beyond is the 18C PALAZZO DI QUATTRO with a balcony along the whole length of its façade. It has a pretty entrance and courtyard with a handsome double staircase (shown on request by the cabinet-maker who has his workshop here).

A road descends on the right past Santa Teresa to reach the Immacolata (closed), with a fine campanile. It contains interesting works in 'pece' stone. In Piazza Chiaramonte can be seen its Gothic portal in a little garden of orange trees. The narrow Via Chiaramonte leads up past the campanile to the back façade of PALAZZO BATTAGLIA (No. 40), a very original building. Beyond the arch on the left can be seen the main façade on Via Orfanotrofio, beside the church of the Annunziata. Just uphill from Largo Camerina, Via Conte Cabrera leads back past more interesting palaces, to Piazza del Duomo.

A road leads out of the other side of the piazza, under the arch of Palazzo Arezzi, to (left) the Salita Ventimiglia (steps) which lead down to the closed church of the GESÙ. The interior has stuccoes and frescoes by Matteo

Battaglia (1750). Behind the church is the PORTA WALTER, the only one of the five medieval gates of Ibla to have survived.

From Piazza Pola bus No. 3 (every half hour) runs (via Piazza della Repubblica) back up to the upper town of Ragusa (Corso Italia).

20

The province of Ragusa

The province of Ragusa, the smallest on the island, is one of the best preserved areas in Sicily. On an upland plain, with limestone outcrops, its distinctive landscape has numerous low dry-stone walls which divide the fields of pastureland and crops. These survive from the agricultural reforms introduced by the Spanish Henriquez-Caprera counts of Modica in the 18C, by which incentive was given to improve the productivity of each small holding. The fields are dotted with numerous lovely old grey-stone farm-houses and huge carob trees. Citrus fruits, olives, and almonds are cultivated here between hedges of prickly pear, and vineyards. The coast is crowded with market gardens, now disfigured by acres of plastic green-houses. Almost every town in the province was badly damaged, if not destroyed, by a terrible earthquake in 1693. They were all rebuilt in the following century, when the theatrical Baroque buildings were erected which characterise each of the towns (most of which also have one or two interesting 19C or early 20C buildings). There is a shortage of good hotels in the province, but all the places described below can be visited in a day from Ragusa.

Information Office. 'APT' Ragusa, 33 Via Capitano Bocchieri, Ragusa Ibla (Tel. 0932/621421).

A. Modica and environs

FROM RAGUSA TO MODICA, 15km, N115. There are two road approaches to Modica, one by the new fast road which leaves the modern town of Ragusa to the S and after 5km joins the bypass which crosses an extremely high viaduct on its way to Modica. The old road (N115), described below, is prettier. It runs along a ridge S of Ragusa, and there is a splendid view of the upper town, with its older houses below built into the rock face, and then of Ibla dominated by the conspicuous façade of San Giorgio. The road descends the steep Costa del Diavolo, a beautiful unspoilt wooded valley with characterisitic low dry-stone walls. Beyond the Irminio river are a few citrus fruit plantations and carob trees, and the black slag-heaps of asphalt mines. After crossing the railway, there is a view ahead of the Ragusa bypass carried over the valley on a huge viaduct built in 1984 and the highest in Europe (168 metres). From the upland plain a pretty minor read leads left through a remarkable landscape to Modica Alta, but it is simplest to continue straight on for Modica Bassa.

MODICA (50,000 inhab.) is an unusual town divided into two parts, Modica Bassa and Modica Alta, with decorative palm trees and elegant Baroque buildings many of them built when it was still a powerful county ruled by Spanish counts. Like many towns in this corner of Sicily it had to be rebuilt after the earthquake of 1693. The lower town occupies a valley at the confluence of two torrents, which were channelled and covered over in 1902 after a disastrous flood. On the steep spur between them the upper town rises in terraces above the huge church of San Giorgio.

Information Offices. 'APT' Ragusa, 33 Via Capitano Bocchieri, Ragusa Ibla (Tel. 0932/621421). 'Pro-Loco', Modica (Tel. 0932/762626; in summer: 0932/905803).

Railway Station, beyond Via Vittorio Veneto, 600m W of Corso Umberto I. On the line from Gela via Ragusa, Modica and Noto to Syracuse. Services to Syracuse in c 1hr 30mins.

Buses. Services run by 'AST' to Ragusa, Syracuse, Catania, etc.

Car Parking is very difficult in the upper town; in the lower town on Corso Umberto I or Viale Medaglie d'Oro.

Hotel. 3-star 'Motel di Modica', 1 Corso Umberto I.

Camping Site (open in summer) on the coast at Marina di Modica.

Restaurants. Modica is famous for its excellent cuisine. 1st-class restaurant 'Le Due Torri' in Modica Alta (near Santa Teresa); Trattoria 'La Rusticana' in Modica Bassa.

Cafés or bars ('pasticceria'). In Modica Alta: 'Colombo'; in Modica Bassa: 'Bonaiuto', 'Bonomo', and 'Iacono'. 'Di Lorenzo' (245 Corso Umberto I) sells delicious local sweets including 'mpanatigghi' (light pastry filled with minced meat, chocolate, and spices), 'cedrata' (honey and citron rind), and 'cobaita' (honey and sesame seeds), and chocolate.

Annual Festivals. Traditional processions during Easter week. The 'Festa di San Giorgio' in April, and the 'Festa di San Pietro' at the end of June, with a fair.

History. The site of Modica was occupied by the Siculi. The county of Modica, one of the most powerful fiefs of the Middle Ages, passed from the Chiaramonte in 1392 to the Spanish Cabrera family. In the 15C it ruled over Ragusa, Vittoria, Comiso, and the whole of the present-day province of Ragusa. After 1704 it came through Spanish connections to the seventh Duke of Berwick and Alba. At the end of the last century Modica was the fourth largest town in Sicily. It was the birthplace of the poet Salvatore Quasimodo (1901–68).

Modica Bassa, the lower town (300m), is traversed by **Corso Umberto I** which is unusually wide since it occupies the bed of a river torrent covered over in 1902. It is lined with handsome 18C and 19C palaces, and there is a splendid view of the monumental church of San Giorgio (described below) half-way up the hillside between the lower and upper town. On the extreme right, on top of a bare rock face, can be seen a round tower surmounted by a clock, all that remains of the castle of the Counts of Modica.

A monumental flight of steps, decorated with statues of the apostles, leads up to the church of SAN PIETRO (being restored), rebuilt after the earthquake of 1693. Nearby, off Via Clemente Grimaldi, is the inconspicuous entrance (usually kept locked) to a grotto used until recently as a storeroom. Here three layers of frescoes were discovered in 1989, the earliest of which may date from the 11C. They decorated an ancient church which has been given the name of SAN NICOLÒ INFERIORE.

At the centre of the town, where the two river torrents formerly united, the Corso forms a fork with Via Marchesa Tedeschi, which is also unusually wide since it is on the site of a river bed. Here is the Town Hall, next to the church of SAN DOMENICO which contains a 16C painting of the Madonna of the Rosary. On the other side of the Corso, in Via De Leva, is a fine Arab Norman doorway in a little garden, probably once part of a 13C palace. In Via Marchesa Tedeschi is the church of SANTA MARIA DI BETLEM (closed) which incorporates a beautiful chapel built in the 15C by the Cabrera. The elaborate crêche in the N aisle, with 60 terracotta statuettes, was made in Caltagirone in 1882.

On the other side of the Municipio (see above) Corso Umberto I continues past Piazza Matteotti with decorative palm trees. Here the 15C church of the CARMINE contains a marble group of the Annunciation by the Gagini school.

The Corso ends at Viale Medaglie d'oro above which in Via Mercè is the church of Santa Maria delle Grazie next to its huge ex-convent, the PALAZZO DEI MERCEDARI, restored as the seat of the Museo Civico and the Museo delle Arti e delle Tradizioni Popolari. On the ground floor is the **Museo Civico** (open daily 9–13 except fest.), with an archaeological collection formed at the end of the last century. It was catalogued and opened in 1960 by the local scholar Franco Libero Belgiorno (1906–71), after whom it has been named since it was rearranged here in 1990. The display is chronological, from the Neolithic era onwards, with finds from Cava d'Ispica and Modica. A bronze statuette of Hercules dating from the 4C BC has been removed for restoration.

On the top floor, in lovely vaulted rooms of the old convent, is the ***Museo Ibleo delle Arti e delle Tradizioni Popolari**, a private museum opened on request. This fascinating local ethnological collection of artisans' tools and utensils is displayed in reconstructed workshops (a smithy, shoemaker's shop, basket worker's store, a laboratory for making sweets, a cartwright's office, a saddlery, a carpenter's workshop, etc.). Local artisans will come to give demonstrations of their skills by appointment. A local farmhouse has also been faithfully reconstructed. There is a collection of Sicilian carts.

The huge church of ***San Giorgio** is reached from Corso Garibaldi which runs parallel to Corso Umberto I. Some 250 steps (completed in 1818) ascend to the church which was rebuilt in 1643 and again after 1693. The *FAÇADE (covered for restoration) is one of the most remarkable Baroque works in Italy. It has five original doorways and a very tall central bell tower. It is attributed by most scholars to Rosario Gagliardi (1702–38); the upper storey was added in the 19C.

In the INTERIOR, with double side aisles, the apse is filled with a huge polyptych attributed to the local painter Bernardino Niger (1573). The silver high altar was made in 1705. In the S aisle is a 16C painting of the Nativity and (on the second altar) an Assumption by Filippo Paladino (1610). At the end of the S side is a 14C silver reliquary urn. In the chapel to the right of the presbytery is a popular equestrian statue of St George. In the chapel to the left of the presbytery is a statue of the Madonna by Giuliano Mancino and Berrettaro. The fine Serassi organ dates from 1886–88.

On the left side of San Giorgio is the 18C PALAZZO POLARA from which there is a fine view of the lower town and the hillside beyond. Uphill behind San Giorgio, on Corso Francesco Crispi, is the Baroque PALAZZO TOMASI-ROSSI, with fine balconies.

Roads and lanes continue steeply uphill to **Modica Alta** which is well worth exploring. Its main street, the Corso Regina Margherita, has handsome 18C and 19C palaces. At the highest point of the hill stands its most important church, **San Giovanni**, preceded by another monumental flight

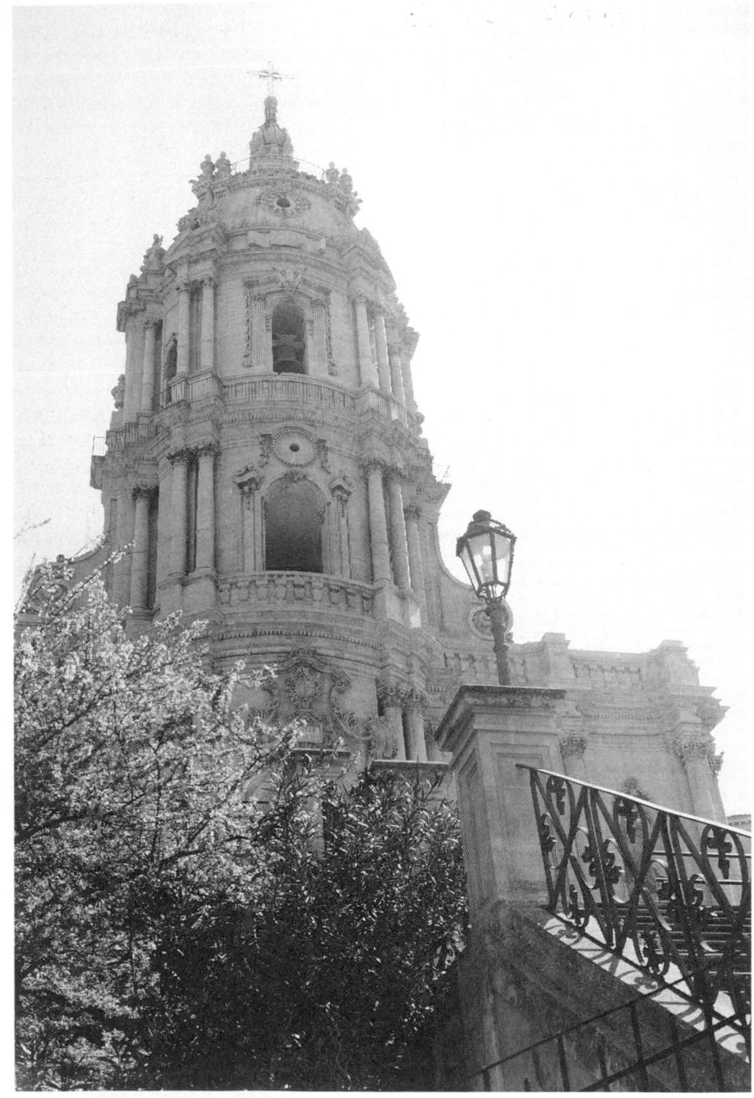

San Giorgio, Modica

of steps. Its façade was erected in the Baroque style in 1839. In another part of the upper town, within a prison enclosure (but visible from the outside), is the elaborate doorway of 1478 of the ruined church of SANTA MARIA DI GESÙ.

The **Cava d'Ispica** lies 11km E of Modica (signposted). It is a deep gorge 13km long which follows a river (now usually dry) with beautiful plants and trees. The sides of the canyon are honeycombed with prehistoric tombs and medieval cave-dwellings; here the presence of man can be traced from the earliest times to the most recent, although the valley was greatly damaged in the earthquake of 1693. Beside the entrance is a hut used as an office by the Soprintendenza alle Antichità of the region, and the site is being enclosed. It is usually open 8–14, but it is safer to telephone in advance to the Soprintendenza at Camarina (Tel. 0932/826004). Just below the entrance are extensive Christian catacombs known as 'LARDERIA' (4–5C AD). They extend for some 36m inside the rock.

Across the main road is the little church of SAN NICOLA (unlocked on request) with very damgaged traces of late-Byzantine frescoes. A path near here leads along the dry river bed to the prehistoric tomb of 'BARAVITALLA', dating from the Castelluccio period (1800 BC), and a Sicel tomb with a design of pilasters on its façade. Nearby traces of a hut village have been uncovered.

From the entrance (see above) a gravel road (c 400m) leads past numerous caves, including some on more than one storey, ruined by the earthquake. Outside the enclosure an overgrown path continues along the splendid valley, with luxuriant vegetation, for some 13km. It passes numerous rock tombs and dwellings, including the so-called 'Castello' on four floors. At the far end is the PARCO DELLA FORZA, best approached from Ispica, see below.

FROM MODICA TO ISPICA, 18km. The road leads SW from Modica across pretty countryside typical of this region of the island, with low dry-stone walls between fields of pastureland and crops, and small farmhouses built of the local grey stone.

Ispica (14,800 inhab.; 'Pro-Loco' information office, 21 Via Bellini) was rebuilt on its present site after the earthquake of 1693 destroyed the former town on the floor of the valley, and it has fine 18C and 19C buildings. It was known in the Middle Ages as *Spaccaforno*, but re-adopted its old name in 1935. The chalk eminence on which it stands is pierced with tombs and cliff dwellings. These can be seen in the PARCO DELLA FORZA (open 9–13, 15–17), which is at the S end of the Cava d'Ispica (see above). It has lovely vegetation and various cisterns, catacombs, etc., and a remarkable tunnel known as the 'Centoscale'.

In the little town, the church of SANTA MARIA MAGGIORE is a good building by Vincenzo Sinatra with 19C stuccoes and frescoes by Olivio Sozzi (1763–65), who is buried here. PALAZZO BRUNO DI BELMONTE, an Art Nouveau building by Ernesto Basile (1910) has been restored as the town hall. The church of the ANNUNZIATA is filled with stuccoes carried out in the mid 18C, attributed to Giuseppe Gianforma.

The main road continues from Ispica to Rosolini (5.5km) and Noto (17km), both in the province of Syracuse and described in Rte 22.

FROM MODICA TO SCICLI, 10km. The pretty byroad leads across an upland plain with low walls and carob trees. Before descending to Scicli, it passes the site of the old medieval town marked by the ruined church of SAN MATTEO, which was once its cathedral. Remains survive of its façade of 1762.

Scicli (25,000 inhab.; 'Pro-Loco' information office, 4 Via Castellana) has occupied the floor of the valley, surrounded by rocky cliffs, since the 14C. Prosperous under Saracen and Norman rule, it is another charming Baroque town rebuilt after the 1693 earthquake, with numerous churches. Here the annual festival of the 'Madonna delle Milizie' is celebrated in May, which commemorates the battle between the Normans and Saracens. In Piazza Italia, planted with trees and surrounded by some neo-classical buildings, is the 18C DUOMO. It contains a papier mâché 'Madonna dei Milici' which is carried in procession in May. Opposite is the Baroque PALAZZO FAVA with good balconies, on the corner of Via San Bartolomeo which opens out in front of the well sited church of SAN BARTOLOMEO, in front of a rock face. The pleasantly coloured façade, crowned with a cupola, was built at the beginning of the 19C by Salvatore d'Alì. It contains a crêche by Pietro Padula (1773–75).

Via Nazionale leads uphill and on the right, at the end of a short street, is the corner of PALAZZO BENEVENTANO, with remarkably eccentric Baroque details (in very poor repair). Off the other side of Via Nazionale is the prettily paved Via Mormino Penna with a few trees. Here is the Town Hall (1906) next to the elegant church of SAN GIOVANNI, with a fine façade. Via Penna winds on past SAN MICHELE with a well designed side door, past Palazzo Spadaro and the church of Santa Teresa.

Via Nazionale continues to Piazza Busacca, planted with palm trees, with a 19C statue by Benedetto Civiletti, of the philanthropist Pietro Di Lorenzo (died 1567). Here is the church of the CARMINE (1751–69), beside its convent with a decorative belcony. Beyond, to the right, is the church of SANTA MARIA DELLA CONSOLAZIONE, with another good façade. Beyond, surrounded by a rocky cliff, in an interesting old part of the town, is the church of SANTA MARIA LA NUOVA. The neo-classical façade (covered with scaffolding) dates from 1816. In the interior, decorated with stuccoes, is a high altarpiece of the Birth of the Virgin by Sebastiano Conca. The presbytery was designed by Venanzio Marvuglia. A silver statue of the Immacolata dates from 1844, and there is a Gaginesque statue of the Madonna. The coast to the S of Scicli is described in Rte 20C.

B. Comiso and Vittoria

A road leads W from Ragusa across a plateau (614m) from which there is a magnificent view of the coast extending as far as Licata. Beyond the junction with the Catania road (N514) it descends steeply in hairpin bends to the pretty Baroque town of **Comiso** (18km; 27,000 inhab.; 'Pro-Loco' information office, 26 Via Ferreri), dominated by the domes of the Chiesa Matrice and Santissima Annunziata. Some ugly new buildings have been built here in recent years, but the main streets preserve their handsome paving made out of the local stone which has the appearance of marble. The town became a centre of pacifist and disarmament demonstrations after 1983 when a NATO nuclear missile base was installed on the old airfield N of the town. This was dismantled in 1991 as a result of the treaty signed between the Soviet Union and America in 1987.

Three palm trees stand outside the church of the ANNUNZIATA, with a lovely blue dome, rebuilt in 1772–93. The light interior has stucco decoration in blue, grey, and white. It contains a wood 15C statue of St Nicholas on the first S altar, and a Crucifix attributed to Fra Umile da Petralia in the S transept. On the second N altar is a painting of the Transition of the Virgin by Narciso Cidonio (1605). The font is a fine work by Mario Rutelli (1913). The organ is by the Polizzi brothers of Modica.

Via Papa Giovanni XXIII leads downhill in front of the church, and Via degli Studi leads right to Piazza del Municipio with its amusing fountain (1937). The waters of the 'Fonte di Diana' were fabled to refuse to mix with wine when poured by unchaste hands; in Roman days they supplied a bath-house, with a mosaic of Neptune, the remains of which are visible beneath the Town Hall. Just out of the piazza rises the huge church of SANTA MARIA DELLE STELLE, the Chiesa Matrice, also with a dome. The fine façade (the top of which is covered for restoration) is attributed to Rosario Gagliardi. The interior, with a vault painted in the 17C attributed to Antonio Barbalunga, is closed for restoration. Below its terrace is Piazza delle Erbe, with a fountain, onto which faces the handsome MARKET, with a raised portico, built in 1867. It has been restored as the seat of the Biblioteca and Pinacoteca, entered from the delightful courtyard, with a fountain. The collection of paintings includes 19C portraits.

From Via Giovanni XXIII a road leads shortly (right) to the church of SAN FRANCESCO (if locked, ring at the convent), founded in the early 14C. The present church was built in 1478, and the *Cappella Naselli (1517–55) was added at the E end by Gaspare Poidomani, using a fascinating pastiche of architectural styles. Arab-Norman squinches support the dome, and classical details are incorporated in the decoration. It contains the funerary monument of Gaspare Naselli, attributed to Antonello Gagini. At the W end is a wood choir loft of the 15C. The 15C CASTELLO FEUDALE of the Naselli family, at the entrance to the town, was altered in 1575 (closed).

A straight road leads NE from Comiso past an old airfield, used from 1983 to 1991 as a NATO nulcear missile base, to **Chiaramonte Gulfi** (18km; 1st-class restaurant 'Maiore'), founded by Manfredi Chiaramonte for the inhabitants of Gulfi, a Saracenic town destroyed in 1299 by the Angevins. The town is famous for its salami, hams, etc. It has numerous churches and fine views. Remains of the castle survive. At the foot of the hill, at Scornavacche, remains have been found of a Greek colony, with numerous potteries. 17km E of Chiaramonte Gulfi is the little town of GIARRATANA, rebuilt on lower ground after the earthquake of 1693. Its three Baroque churches stand close together. MONTEROSSO ALMO (691m) lies 6km N of Giarratana. In the large central piazza are the church of San Giovanni Battista, attributed to Vincenzo Sinatra, and neo-classical palaces. Via Roma leads down to the Chiesa Madre, with a neo-Gothic façade. It contains a 12C stoup. Opposite is the church of Sant'Antonio Abate with 16C paintings.

Vittoria, 8km W of Comiso, a prosperous agricultural town (market garden produce and flowers), and centre of the wine trade (50,000 inhab.), was named after the daughter of the viceroy Marcantonio Colonna in 1607. It is situated on a plain overlooking the Ippari, a little river sung by Pindar, bordered by pine forests. Much illegal new building has taken place here in recent years.

In the main square the elegant neo-classical TEATRO COMUNALE (1869–77) stands next to the church of the MADONNA DELLE GRAZIE, with a good façade of 1754. The CHIESA MADRE, with an unusual façade (18C–19C), contains paintings by the school of Pietro Novelli. There are number of Art Nouveau palaces in the town, and Palazzo Traina is in the Venetian Gothic style.

A byroad leads NW from Vittoria to **Acate** (9km; 6700 inhab.), known as *Biscari* up until 1938, surrounded by olives and vineyards. In the central Piazza Libertà, surrounding a garden, is the huge 18C Castello dei Principi di Biscari, and the Chiesa Madre, rebuilt in 1859. The Palio di San Vincenzo is celebrated here after Easter.

C. The Castello di Donnafugata and the ruins of Camarina

A pretty byroad leads SW from Ragusa though lovely countryside with numerous farms to the **Castello di Donnafugata**, acquired by the Comune of Ragusa in 1982 and opened to the public in 1991 (9–12.30, except Mon). There is a trattoria in one of the outbuildings. It has its own railway station (one or two trains a day stop here, from Ragusa in 20 minutes); the Ragusa–Comiso line was diverted to the S in 1893 especially for the politician Baron Corrado Arezzo De Spuches (1824–95), owner of the estate.

On the site of a 17C building, the present 'castle' was constructed by Corrado Arezzo. It is a huge country villa, built in an eclectic style, with a Venetian Gothic loggia. Its delightful setting survives, with its farm surrounded by beautiful countryside. In the exotic *GARDEN, with splendid huge ficus trees, are a stone labyrinth entered over a miniature drawbridge guarded by a stone soldier, a coffeehouse, a little neo-classical temple above a grotto, and an amusing little chapel (no adm.). Nineteen of the 122 rooms of the castle are shown, most of them in poor repair, the most interesting of which is the Salone degli Specchi. The contents include some paintings of the Neapolitan school and a spinet. The 'Donnafugata' described in Lampedusa's book 'Il Gattopardo' was near Santa Margherita di Belice (see Rte 10).

A narrow road continues from the castle down towards the coast, past some fine old villas, including one in neo-Gothic style. Near the sea are market gardens (many covered with plastic greenhouses) and huge old carob trees.

The excavations of **Camarina** are signposted from the little town of SANTA CROCE CAMERINA, which has some Art Nouveau palaces. The road passes several enclosures with excavations (if closed, usually unlocked on request at the museum) before reaching the MUSEO REGIONALE (open 9–14, 15.30–17.30; fest. 9–13, 15–17.30).

Camarina was a Syracusan colony, founded c 598 BC, which suffered alternate sack and repopulation by Gela, Syracuse, and Carthage. It was finally destroyed by the Romans in 258 BC, but there are signs of occupation in the Republican and Imperial eras, and of a late Arab Norman settlement. The museum is housed in a restored 19C farmhouse built above the remains of a Temple of Athena. A room displays underwater finds made offshore where six ship-wrecks have so far been identified. These include a Greek bronze helmet (4C BC), and objects from Punic and medieval boats. In 1991 a hoard of some 1000 bronze coins was found from the treasure chest of a Roman cargo ship which sank offshore in 275 AD.

Outside in the courtyard, beneath a porch are sandstone sarcophaghi and a circular stone tomb. Beyond can be seen part of the cella wall of the temple. Another building contains a plan of the site and explanatory diagrams, and Bronze Age finds from the area. Material from the 6C BC includes a beautiful Corinthian black-figure vase with a hunting scene. In another building the foundations of the temple, dating from the early 5C BC, have been exposed. It was reused as a church in the Byzantine era. A room on two floors has a splendid display of amphorae, c 1000 of which were found in the oldest necropolis of Camarina known as Rifriscolaro (Corinthian, Carthaginian, etc.).

The various excavated areas, overlooking the sea, include fragments of the walls, part of the street lay-out and houses with three or four rooms opening onto a courtyard (built after 405 BC), and part of the agora. A necropolis has yielded a great number of tombs (mostly dating from the early 6C). Traces of the port have been found on the river Hipparis. There are plans to unite the entire area of excavations in one enclosure.

A road leads along the coast towards Gela (see Rte 13), following the Gulf of Gela, a long shallow bay whose beaches provided the chief landing place for the American assault forces on 10 July 1943. The land, watered by several rivers, is intensively cultivated with fields of cane, olives, oranges, market garden produce, and vineyards.

FROM CAMARINA TO PACHINO, 75km. A road follows the coast past a turning for the excavations of CAUCANA (signposted), a large harbour town mentioned by Procopius, where the fleet of Belisarius put in on the way to Africa. The road skirts the shore (there are a number of 3-star and 2-star camping sites here) through the simple little resort of (11km) PUNTA SECCA on Capo Scalambri, with its lighthouse, to (17km) **Marina di Ragusa** (two 3-star camping sites open in summer; luxury-class fish restaurants: 'Fumia', 'Alberto', and 'Da Carmelo'), a resort which grew up in the 1950s, with palm trees along the sea front. A fast 'superstrada' (24km) connects it to Ragusa (see Rte 19). Oil is drilled offshore and piped from here to Augusta (see Rte 23). There are good views ahead of the coastline. Beyond a stretch of reedy sand-dunes, the road passes Playa Grande and numerous plastic greenhouses.

25km **Donnalucata** is a pretty little resort (with an open fish market on the beach). Beyond Cava d'Aliga the road skirts an unspoilt sandy bay. Inland the landscape is dotted with huge carob trees, and hedges of prickly pear. Market garden produce is cultivated here together with olives and almonds. Among the characteristic low stone walls are some handsome country houses built of golden stone. Beyond Sampieri, there is a conspicuous ruined industrial building on the right of the road. 41km **Marina di Modica** (with a camping site open in summer). The little resort (signposted to the right) is known for its fish restaurants (Luxury-class: 'Le Alghe'. 1st-class: 'Serrauccelli', 3km outside the town).

A short stretch of double-lane highway continues into (49km) **Pozzallo**, a small port with a prominent square tower built in the 15C by the Cabrera (reconstructed after 1693), and a popular sandy beach. On the outskirts is an industrial plant. Ispica (described in Rte 20A) is 8km NE. The coast road continues past beaches hidden behind tree-covered dunes where cane fences control the sand. The road then deteriorates and becomes deserted as it turns inland and skirts some small lagoons. 75km **Pachino**, in the province of Syracuse, is described in Rte 22C.

21

Syracuse

SYRACUSE, in Italian SIRACUSA, is the successor (108,900 inhab.), of the once magnificent SYRACUSAE, which rivalled Athens as the largest and most beautiful city of the Greek world. It was one of the most delightful cities of Europe until the unattractive modern town expanded in a disorderly way on the mainland and the coastline was ruined by industrial plants and new buildings which have polluted the sea to the N and S. It has become more and more detached from the promontory of Ortygia, once the centre of the city, which is suffering from depopulation. The principal ruins of the Greek city, including the splendid theatre, survive in Neapolis, somewhat protected from the modern city by a park. The splendid archaeological collection was reopened in a fine new building in 1988. In the beautiful and peaceful town of Ortygia are many monuments of great interest. Cicero noted that Syracuse knew no day without sun, and it has a mild marine climate throughout the year. **Plan on pages 12–13 of atlas section**.

Information Offices. 'APT' Siracusa, 45 Via San Sebastiano (Tel. 0931/67710); the information office at San Niccolò at the entance to the archaeological zone of Neapolis has been temporarily closed. 'Azienda Autonoma', 33 Via Maestranza, Ortygia.

Railway Station (Pl.6). Services via Catania and Taormina to Messina (with some through trains to Rome); to Gela via Noto, Modica and Ragusa. The line from Noto to Pachino has been substituted by a bus service.

Buses. The city buses tend to be infrequent and only a few of them are useful to visitors. No. **1** from Riva della Posta (Ortygia) via Corso Umberto, Corso Gelone, and Viale Teracati for the main archaeological zone of Neapolis. No. **4** from Ortygia via Corso Umberto and Corso Gelone to Viale Teocrito (for San Giovanni and the new Museo Archeologico). No. **2** from Riva della Posta (Ortygia) via Corso Umberto and Via Agatocle to Via Montegrappa (for Santa Lucia). No. **11** every 40 minutes from Riva della Posta (Ortygia) via Corso Gelone to Castello Eurialo and Belvedere (and the Youth Hostel).

Country Buses run by 'AST' from Piazza Marconi (Pl. 7) daily to Catania, to Palermo (in 3hrs 15mins), and to Palazzolo Acreide. Services run by 'SAIS' from Piazza Marconi to Catania (in c 1hr) and Palermo; to Noto (in c 1hr) and Pachino. Daily express service run by 'SAIS' for Rome via Catania and Messina (in 12½hrs).

Car Parking is difficult. Best near the archaeologial zone, where a car-park is being constructed.

Maritime Services. Capitaneria di Porto, Piazzale 4 Novembre. The main quay is at Molo Zanagora (Pl. 11). 'Tirrenia Navigazione', 4 Via Mazzini. Services via Catania to Naples, and to Malta. BOAT TRIPS UP THE CIANE RIVER from Molo Zanagora (Signor Vella), or, if the water is too low, at the confluence of the Anapo and Ciane rivers (off N115).

Hotels are widely scattered about the modern town, many of them inconvenient for those without a car. 4-star: 'Jolly' (Pl. 7; a), 45 Corso Gelone. 3-star: 'Grand Hotel Villa Politi' (Pl. 4; b), 2 Via Politi. The 'Grand Hotel', 12 Viale Mazzini (Pl. 11; c) is closed for restoration. 2-star: 'Aretusa' (Pl. 6; e), 75 Via Crispi; 1-star: 'Milano' (Pl. 11; f), 10 Corso Umberto. YOUTH HOSTEL, 45 Viale Epipoli, at Belvedere, 7km NW of the town.

Camping Sites. The nearest site is the 1-star 'Agriturist Rinaura', 5km S of the town. In summer 2-star sites are open on the coast to the S: 'Fontane Bianche', and 'Sabbiadoro' (at Avola).

Restaurants. Luxury-class: 'Arlecchino', 5 Via dei Tolomei; 'Tavernetta del Papiro', 6 Via Tripoli. 1st-class: 'Don Camillo', 96 Via Maestranza; 'Il Nuovo Tevere', 8 Largo Empedocle. Trattorie: 'La Foglia' (vegetarian), 39 Via Capodieci; 'Il Teatro', 8 Via Agnello; 'Aretusa', 32 Via Santa Teresa.

Cafés or bars ('pasticceria'). 'Marciante', 39 Via Maestranze; 'Caffè del Duomo', Piazza del Duomo.

Picnic places at the Latomia del Paradiso, the Greek Theatre, and the Amphitheatre; in the gardens of Villa Landolina; and on the seafront near the Fonte Aretusa in Ortygia.

Public offices and learned Institutions. SOPRINTENDENZA AI BENI CULTURALI E AMBIENTALI, Piazza Duomo. ISPETTORATO DELLE FORESTE (for the nature reserves of Vendicari, and the Valle dell'Anapo), 7 Via San Giovanni alle Catacombe, Tel. 0931/462452. ISTITUTO NAZIONALE DEL DRAMMA ANTICO, Corso Matteotti. BIBLIOTECA COMUNALE, Via Santi Coronati. ASSOCIAZIONE CULTURALE ITALO-BRITANNICA, Via Maestranza.

Theatres. Biennial classical drama festival in the Greek Theatre (even years) in May and June. The Teatro Comunale has been closed for restoration for many years. Concerts in the auditorium of San Pietro al Carmine. Puppet Theatre, 14 Via Nizza (temporarily closed).

Annual Festivals. Santa Lucia, 13 December, procession from the cathedral to the church of Santa Lucia; also on the first and second Sundays in May. San Sebastiano, 20 January. Madonna delle Lacrime, 29 August–3 September. Procession on 8 December (Immacolata).

Topography (see the plan on p 220–1). Ancient Syracuse at the height of its power included five districts: ORTYGIA, the island now occupied by the older part of modern Syracuse, which lies between the Great Harbour, 640 hectares in area, extending S to the headland of Plemmyrium, and the Small Harbour on the N; ACHRADINA, occupying the area immediately adjoining on the mainland, TYCHE, called after a Temple of Fortune, to the NE of Achradina; NEAPOLIS (new town), to the NW of Achradina; and EPIPOLAE (upper district), stretching to the outer defences, inland on the N and W. Ortygia was a fortified citadel (linked to the mainland by a causeway c 550 BC); Achradina represented the commercial, maritime, and administrative centre, and Neapolis the social centre; Tyche was a residential area, while Epipolae was sparsely populated. The ancient buildings were built of an oolitic limestone quarried from the 'latomiae', now covered with luxuriant gardens.

History. This part of the coast of Sicily had a number of important Bronze Age sites. The Corinthian colony under Archias (734 BC) which drove out the Sicel (or perhaps Phoenician) inhabitants of Ortygia increased so rapidly in power and wealth that, within a century of its foundation, it was able to found three sub-colonies at Akrai, Kasmenai, and Camarina. Internal dissensions were put down by the firm government of Gelon, tyrant of Gela (c 485–478) who in 480 in alliance with Theron of Akragas, defeated the Carthaginians at Himera. Hieron I (478–c 467) helped the Cumaeans to overcome the Etruscan fleet (474) and welcomed to his court the poets Aeschylus, Pindar, Simonides, and Bacchylides; but Thrasybulus by misrule brought about his downfall and the establishment of a republic (466).

The increasing power of the republic provoked the jealousy of Athens, which despatched a hostile expedition (415) under Alcibiades and Nicias. Alcibiades was soon returned to Athens under political arrest, but escaped and deserted to Sparta. The Athenian operations were almost successful, as they tried to enclose the city within a double wall and blockade it by sea. But a reinforcement from Sparta under Gylippus (despatched by the rene-

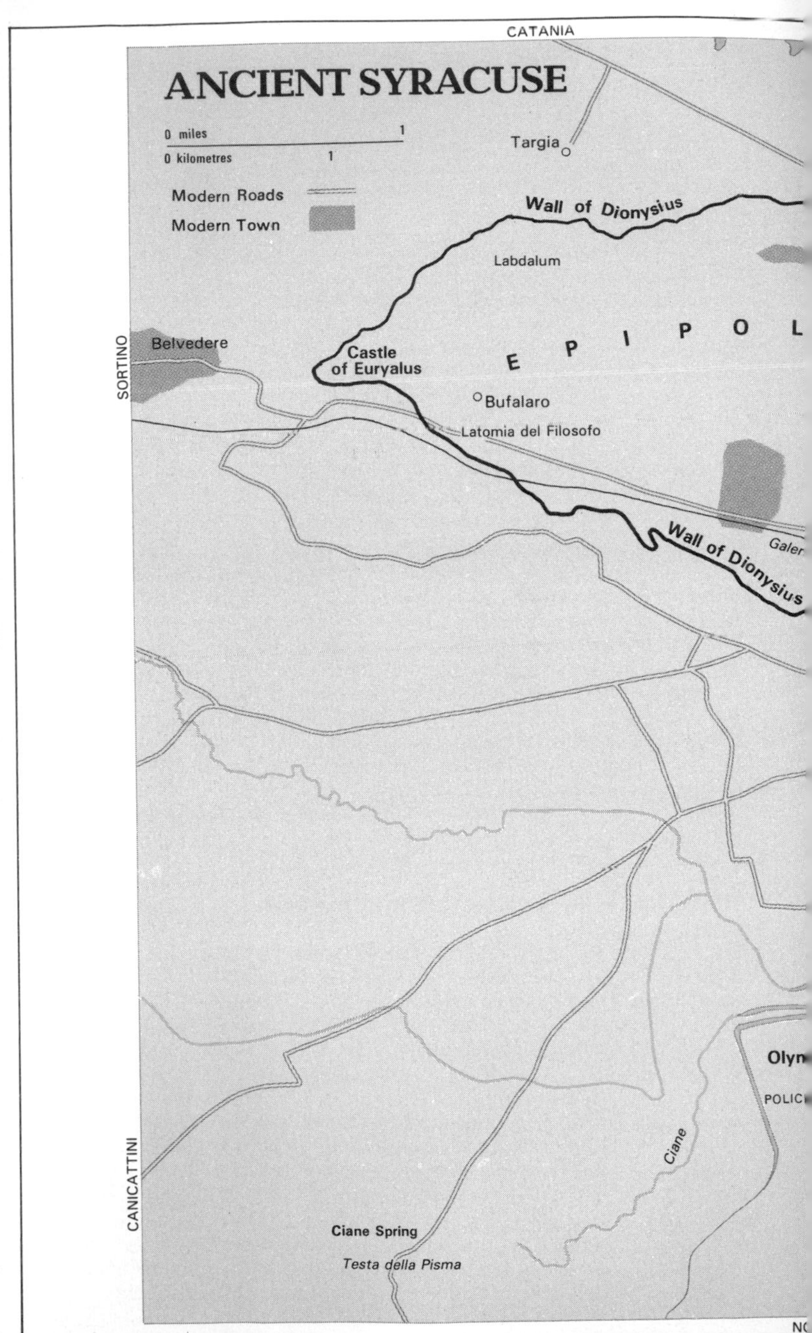

CATANIA
ANCIENT SYRACUSE
0 miles 1
0 kilometres 1
Modern Roads
Modern Town
Targia
Wall of Dionysius
Labdalum
SORTINO
Belvedere
Castle of Euryalus
E P I P O L
Bufalaro
Latomia del Filosofo
Wall of Dionysius
CANICATTINI
Ciane
Ciane Spring
Testa della Pisma

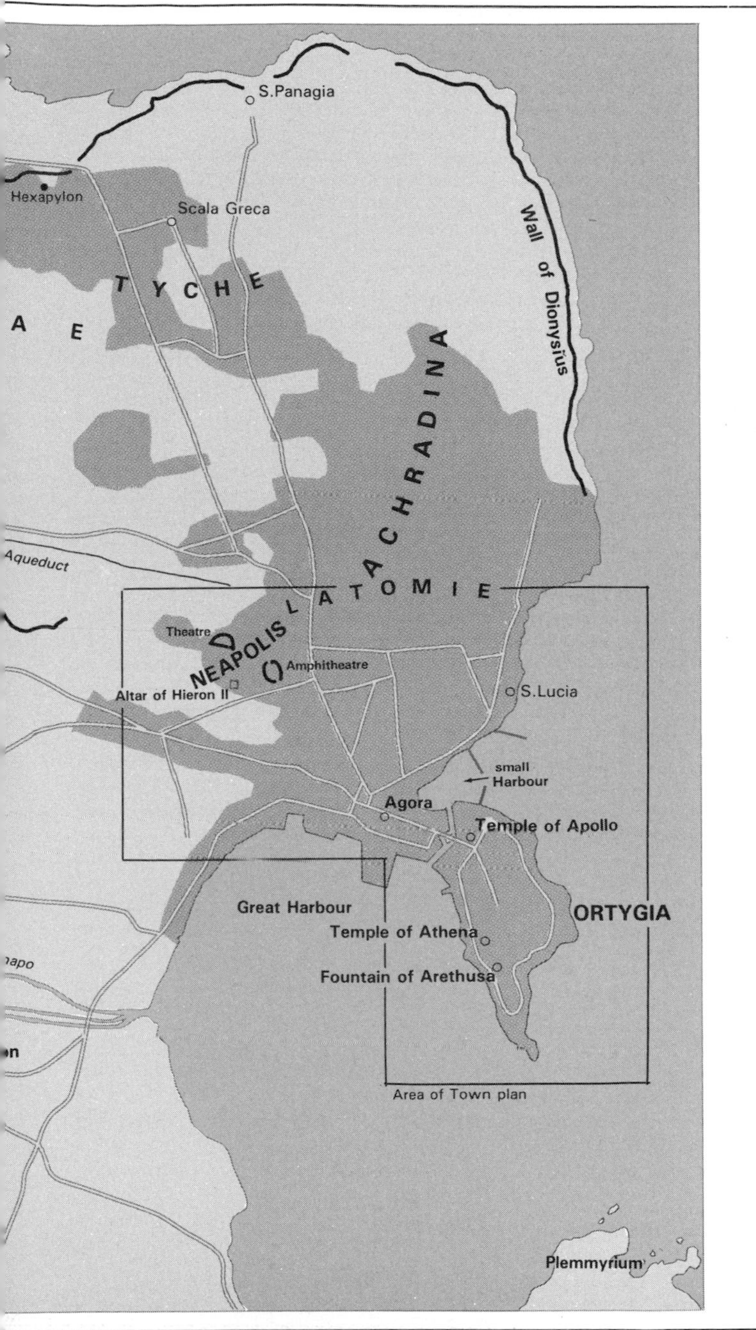

S.Panagia
Hexapylon
Scala Greca
TYCHE
A E
Wall of Dionysius
ACHRADINA
Aqueduct
LATOMIE
Theatre
NEAPOLIS
Amphitheatre
Altar of Hieron II
S.Lucia
small Harbour
Agora
Temple of Apollo
ORTYGIA
Great Harbour
Temple of Athena
Fountain of Arethusa
Area of Town plan
Plemmyrium

gade Alcibiades), together with the courage of the Syracusans under Hermocrates and Athenagoras, saved the city. Athenian reinforcements under Demosthenes were themselves blockaded and their fleet destroyed in the Porto Grande. A frantic attempt to escape led in 413 to the final defeat of the Athenian army on the Assinaros, and those who survived were put to death in the latomiae.

In 405, Syracuse, again threatened by Carthage, was led by Dionysius the Elder, who built the castle of Euryalus, defeated Himilco (397), and made Syracuse the most powerful city of Sicily and sovereign of the Western Mediterranean. Under his less successful son Dionysius II (367–343) the Carthaginians again threatened the city, but it was saved from both tyrants and its enemies by the successful hero Timoleon of Corinth, who briefly re-established a democracy and died an ordinary citizen (336). Agathocles, a man of humble birth but strong personality, took power in 317, carried the war against Carthage into Africa (310), and left Syracuse once more in a position of hegemony. Pyrrhus, king of Epirus, liberated the city from a Carthaginian siege and, on his departure from Sicily, left the whole island clear for Hieron II (276–215), who wisely allied himself with Rome. His successor, Hieronymus, reversed this policy, and the city fell to Marcellus after a two years' siege (c 214–212). The task of the besiegers was aggravated by the ingenious inventions of Archimedes, who was accidentally killed during the sack of the town while quietly pursuing his studies. The Roman booty included innumerable works of art, which gave the first impetus to the appreciation of classical art in Rome, and, according to Cato, were the earliest factors in the decline of the true Roman spirit. Under Roman occupation Syracuse was governed both by Verres, who further despoiled it, and Cicero, the accuser of Verres. St Paul stayed three days at Syracuse on his way from Malta to Rhegium in the Alexandrian ship 'Castor and Pollux' (Acts xxviii, 11–12).

After the Roman period, the power of Syracuse declined rapidly, though the Emperor Constans II resided here in 662–68. It was destroyed by the Saracens in 878, and freed for a time by George Maniakes (1038–40), the general of Basil II of Byzantium, who drove the Saracens off the island. The temporary importance Syracuse regained in 1361–1536 as the quasi-independent seat of the Camera Regionale was not maintained and in 1837, having rebelled unsuccessfully against the Bourbons, it even ceded for a time to Noto its rights as a provincial capital. After the conquest of Libya the port expanded again, and during World War II was a target first for the Allied air forces, and, after its capture on 10 July 1943, for German aircraft.

The most famous Syracusans of ancient times, besides Archimedes (287–212), are Theocritus (fl. 270 BC), the father of idyllic poetry, and Moschus (fl. 200 BC), another pastoral poet. Plato visited the city in c 397, and probably returned several years later on the invitation of Dionysius II to advise him on how to rule his kingdom. Corax of Syracuse and his pupil Tisias founded the Greek art of rhetoric in the 5C. The plot of Shakespeare's 'Comedy of Errors' hinges upon the supposed enmity of Syracuse and Ephesus. Elio Vittorini (1908–66), the writer, was born in Syracuse.

A. Ortygia

The promontory of ***Ortygia** is joined to the mainland by two bridges; in the channel are moored numerous small boats and part of the fishing fleet. This charming old town, best explored on foot, has delightful streets of Baroque houses with pretty balconies and numerous trees. Since the modern centre of Syracuse moved to the mainland, Ortygia has faced serious problems of depopulation, although there have been signs in the last few years of a return here, and numerous buildings are in the process of restoration.

Near Ponte Nuovo is the conspicuous Post Office (1934). Piazza Pancali with ficus trees leads to Largo XXV Luglio (Pl. 11), near the covered market place, a fine building of 1889–1900. Here, freed in 1938 from overlying structures, and surrounded with lawns, papyrus plants and palm trees, stand the remains of the **Temple of Apollo** (Pl. 12), peripteral and hexastyle, built of sandstone. It is the earliest peripteral Doric temple in Sicily, built c 575 and attributed to the architect Epicles. Some scholars identified it with the Artemision recorded by Cicero, but the inscription to Apollo cut in the steps of the stereobate seems conclusive. Two monolithic columns and part of the cella walls remain intact. Fragments of the polychrome terracotta cornice are preserved in the Museo Archeologico.

Via Savoia leads to the waterfront overlooking the Porto Grande, near the elaborate Camera di Commercio building. Here is the PORTA MARINA, a plain 15C gateway with a label in the Spanish Gothic style. The long promenade by the water's edge, planted with splendid ficus trees, is known as the FORO VITTORIO EMANUELE II. There is a lovely view across the harbour to the wooded shore. Within the gate to the left (in the street of the same name) is the attractive little church of SANTA MARIA DEI MIRACOLI (open 8–10, 17–19), with a fine doorway resting on little lions, with a sculptured lunette, and a worn tabernacle in the Gothic-Catalan style. The interior has a pretty 14C chancel, and a painting of St Corrado the Hermit attributed to Giovanni Maria Trevisano.

Ahead Via Ruggero Settimo emerges on a terrace above the trees of the Foro Italico, and Via del Collegio leads away from the sea skirting the tall flank, with its Corinthian pilasters and overhanging cornice, of the CHIESA DEL COLLEGIO (1635–87; closed), whose incomplete façade recalls that of the Gesù in Rome. The interior contains altars from the former Jesuit college in Palermo, moved here in 1927–31. The church faces Via Cavour, off which parallel streets run down towards the sea.

To the right opens **Piazza del Duomo**, with some fine Baroque buildings. To the left the MUNICIPIO occupies the former Seminario (begun in 1628 by Giovanni Vermexio). Here a small MUSEUM (admission 9–13 except Sun) in two rooms has an instructive display illustrating the building and history of Ionic temples, and fragments of unusual Ionic columns with a band at the base which was supposedly intended to bear sculpted reliefs. The custodian also shows excavations beneath the building where foundations of an Ionic temple, probably dedicated to Artemis, were found in 1963. Begun c 530 BC, it was probably never completed and some of the stones were used in the construction of the Doric temple of Athene nearby (see below). Here, too, may be seen various levels of occupation, from a dwelling of the 8C BC (the oldest Greek structure in Syracuse) to a 17C funerary crypt.

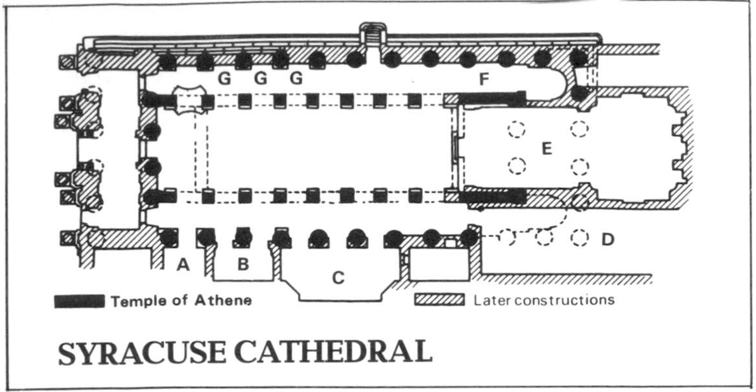

Across Via Minerva is the ***Duomo** (Pl. 12; Santa Maria del Piliero or delle Colonne; closed 12–16) reconstructed by Bishop Zosimus in the 7C from the ruins of the Doric **Temple of Athene**, erected in the 5C BC, probably to celebrate the victory of Himera. It became the cathedral of Syracuse later in the 7C, and was again rebuilt after the earthquake of 1693, when the Norman façade fell. In Via Minerva 12 columns of the splendid temple, with their architrave and triglyphs, punctuate the medieval N wall of the church, their cornice replaced by battlements. The FACADE of the cathedral, a graceful Baroque composition erected in 1728–54, was designed by Andrea Palma. The marble statues of Saints Peter and Paul flanking the steps are the earliest known works of Ignazio Marabitti; he also sculpted the statues (1754) on the façade. The entrance is through an elaborate vestibule.

The INTERIOR was stripped of its Baroque decoration in 1909–27, reducing the NAVE arcades to the plain massive piers formed by opening eight arches in the side walls of the cella. The inscription above, making an unwarrantable claim, dates from a bull of Leo X (1517), and the ceiling from the following year. The stained glass by Eugenio Cisterna (1862–1933) was restored in 1990. The stoups are by Gaetano Puglisi (1802). On the W wall are preserved two columns from the opisthodomos of the cella, and 19 columns of the peristyle are incorporated in the aisles, those on the N side being engaged.

SOUTH AISLE. First chapel (A). Font of antique marble with a Greek inscription (found in the Catacombs of San Giovanni), resting on seven miniature bronze lions (13C); on the wall are fragments of mosaics which survive from the earlier church. In the second chapel (B; 1711), closed by bronze gates, the work of Pietro Spagnuolo (1605), is a statue of St Lucy by Pietro Rizzo (1599; shown only on certain religious festivals and carried in procession on 13 December) backed by a carved altarpiece of Desio Furnò (1781) and supported on a coffer attributed to Nibilio and Giuseppe Gagini, all of silver. The two marble medallions are attributed to Ignazio Marabitti. The third chapel (C), closed by wrought-iron gates (1811), was designed in 1650–53, probably by Giovanni Vermexio. The altar frontal bears a beautiful relief of the Last Supper by Filippo della Valle (1762). Above is a ciborium by Luigi Vanvitelli (1752).

At the end of the aisle, in the CAPPELLA DEL CROCIFISSO (D), the painting of St Zosimus attributed to Antonello da Messina, after an attempted theft in 1973, was removed for restoration. The fine painting of St Marcian, by the school of Antonello, is also in restoration. From this chapel open the Treasury and the SACRISTY (both normally closed), which has stalls of 1489. Two paintings by Marco Costanzo (St Jerome and the Annunciation), and 13 panels of a polyptych of the school of Antonello have all been removed for restoration. There are long-term plans to exhibit them in a Diocesan Museum. The bronze candelabra in the CHANCEL (E) date from 1513. In the Byzantine apse (F) of the NORTH AISLE is a Madonna della Neve by Antonello Gagini. The end of the cella wall of the temple with its column can be seen here. The noticeable irregularity of the pillars is due to an earthquake of 1542. In the N aisle (G) are three statues with fine bases: St Lucy by Antonello Gagini; Madonna and Child by Domenico Gagini; and St Catherine of Alexandria by the school of the Gagini.

Excavations beneath the cathedral carried out by Paolo Orsi in 1912–17 revealed details of an archaic temple, demolished to make way for the later temple, and, at a lower level, pre-Greek huts of the 8C BC. Beside the steps of the Duomo more excavations are in progress. Beyond the PALAZZO ARCIVESCOVILE is the BIBLIOTECA ALAGONIANA (not open regularly to the public; 13C Greek, Latin, and Arabic MSS.), with a pretty hanging garden with palm trees behind a balustrade.

On the other side of the piazza, opposite the Municipio, is PALAZZO BENEVENTANO DEL BOSCO, a fine building by the local architect Luciano Alì (1778–88). Next to it is the curving pink façade of Palazzo Gaetani e Arezzo, and, beyond, the building of the 'Soprintendenza ai Beni Culturali e Ambientali' which used to house the Museo Archeologico (see Rte 21B), and still contains a superb *coin collection (not at present on view). At the end of the piazza, with a balcony on the corner, is Palazzo Impellizzeri and the church of SANTA LUCIA ALLA BADIA (closed), with a lovely façade begun c 1695, probably by Luciano Caracciolo (the upper storey was added in the mid 18C). Just out of the piazza is the church of MONTEVERGINE (also closed) with a façade by Andrea Vermexio.

From the piazza Via Picherale, passing the former Hotel des Etrangers (which may eventually be restored), which incorporates part of the medieval Casa Migliaccio, leads down to a charming terrace in a quiet spot on the waterfront surrounding the famous **Fonte Aretusa** (Pl. 15), the mythical spring of the nymph Arethusa celebrated by Pindar and Virgil. It now flows into a pond (built in 1843), planted with papyrus and abounding in fish and inhabited by ducks, beside a splendid old ficus tree. Arethusa is supposed to have reappeared here as a fountain after having plunged into the Ionian sea, pursued by the river-god Alpheus, in Elis in the Peloponnese. Alpheus, following her, sprang up as another fountain some 30m away. A fresh-water spring still wells up in the harbour, and is called the Occhio della Zillica. The spring of Arethusa diminished after the erection of the Spanish fortifications, and was mixed with salt water after an earthquake. Nelson claimed to have watered his fleet here before the battle of the Nile. There are walkways along the attractive sea front (closed to cars).

The end of the promontory, beyond Piazza Federico di Svevia with its barracks, has been closed to the public. The ***Castello Maniace** (Pl. 16), now belongs to the Comune and is in need of restoration. Visitors are only admitted with special permission. The castle was built c 1239 by Frederick II but named after George Maniakes, supposed in error to be its founder. The keep, c 52 sq m, with cylindrical corner-towers, has lost a third of its original height. On either side of the imposing Gothic doorway are two consoles, formerly bearing bronze rams, one of which is in the Museo Archeologico in Palermo. Overlooking the harbour are the remains of a large three-light window. Beneath the castle is the so-called Bagno della Regina (unlit staircase), an underground chamber of uncertain date, probably a reservoir.

Via Salomone and Via San Martino return past (right) the church of SAN MARTINO, founded in the 6C, with a doorway of 1338. The interior (being restored), dating from Byzantine times, contains a fine triptych by a local 15C master.

At the end of the street (left) stands the church of SAN BENEDETTO (usually locked), with a huge canvas by Mario Minniti, a local painter. Adjacent is **Palazzo Bellomo** (Pl. 16), where the **Galleria Regionale** is appropriately housed in a building combining elements of its Swabian construction (c 1234) with alterations of the 15C. The collection is well displayed and labelled; it was closed for restoration in 1993 and the arrangement may differ from the description given below when it reopens. It is normally open 9–14, fest. 9–13; closed Mon. The vestibule has a stellar vault with decoration recalling that of the Castello Maniace; the staircase in the courtyard is a good example of the Catalan style; a second court with two palm trees, to the N, containing the offices, formed part of the Benedictine monastery and dates from 1365. The walls are covered with 15–18C coats of arms.

The collection of SCULPTURE is displayed on the GROUND FLOOR. **Room I** (right). Sculptural fragments including 9C columns and capitals. **RII** (right). Fragment of a portal (11–12C); charming 14C altarpiece of the Annunciation, Adoration of the Magi, and the Crucifixion; and 11C stoup. **RIII** (off the left side of the courtyard). Tomb of Giovanni Cardinas, perhaps by Antonello Gagini; monument to Eleonora Branciforte (1525) by Giovanni Battista Mazzola; Madonna of the Bullfinch, attributed to Domenico Gagini; carved tomb-slab of Giovanni Cabastida (died 1472), and other interesting sculptures. In the loggia behind are two carriages (17C and 18C).

A pleasing outside staircase leads up to the FIRST FLOOR (PINACOTECA). **Room V** (right). 16–17C Graeco-Venetian icons; (in case) portable triptych (c 1590) by the school of 'Stroganow'. **RVI**. Madonnas by the local 15C school. **RVII** (left). Pere Serra (attributed; 14–15C), Madonna and Child enthroned with saints; 'Master of the Retable of St Lawrence' (early 15C), St Lawrence and stories of his life; Lorenzo Veneziano (attributed), St Leonard. While the *Annunciation (1474) by Antonello da Messina, brought from Palazzolo Acreide, and transferred to canvas, is being restored, the *Burial of St Lucy by Caravaggio (1608), from Santa Lucia (see Rte 21B) is exhibited here. **RVIII** incorporates a pretty window of the palace. Marco Costanzo (attributed; c 1496), Trinity and saints; tiny illuminated Book of Hours by the 16C Flemish school. **RR IX** and **X**. 16C works; an album of drawings by Filippo Paladino (c 1544–1614); Guglielmo Borremans, Immacolata.

The charming collection of SICILIAN DECORATIVE ARTS begins in **RXI**, which displays 18C statuettes, marble intarsia panels, and ecclesiastical objects. **RRXIII** and **XIV**. Sicilian presepio figures including a crib by Emanuele Moscuzza (1806–58); church vestments. **RXV**. 18C costumes and furniture. **RXVI**. Ceramics including Arab and Hispano-Moresque ware. **RXVIII**. Majolica from Caltagirone (16–17C), and 19C terracotta figurines by Bongiovanni Vaccaro. Old plans of Syracuse are displayed in **RXX**.

Via Roma, with delightful overhanging balconies, leads away from the sea front (pretty palace on the corner) N past the Teatro Comunale (being restored). On the corner of Via Crocifisso is the church of SANTA MARIA DELLA CONCEZIONE (1651) with a fine interior with a tiled floor. On the vault is a fresco by Sebastiano Lo Monaco, and the altarpieces on the N side and on the first S altar are by Onofrio Gabrielli. Its ex-monastery is being restored.

PIAZZA ARCHIMEDE (Pl. 12) was laid out in 1872–78 at the centre of Ortygia, with a fountain by Giulio Moschetti. Palazzo Lanza on the S side, and the courtyard of the Banca d'Italia on the W side preserve medieval elements. Off the square, reached by Via dei Montalto, is the complete façade of PALAZZO MONTALTO in the Gothic Chiaramonte style of 1397; it has been propped up with concrete bastions. From the car-park behind can be seen the shell of the building, with a fine loggia.

The interesting Via Maestranza leads E from the square towards the sea, past several good Baroque palaces and the church of the IMMACOLATA (or San Francesco) with an attractive little convex façade. It has a fine late 18C interior, with 12 small paintings of the apostles in the apse. On either side of the pretty Baroque E end two Gothic portals have been exposed. Beyond is the 18C Palazzo Rizza (No. 110). Via Vittorio Veneto, lined with smaller 17–18C Spanish palaces continues left. It emerges on the sea by the church of SAN FILIPPO (closed) next to the fine restored Gothic PALAZZO INTERLANDI. There is a view from here of the Bastion of San Giovanello.

Via Mirabella (with Palazzo Bongiovanni on the corner) leads away from the sea front past the CARMINE (closed) which preserves part of its 14C structure. Opposite the former church of the Ritiro, with a façade attributed to Pompeo Picherali (c 1720) is being restored. Nearby is the church of SAN PIETRO (open only for concerts), a small aisled basilica founded in the 4–5C, and altered in Byzantine times. It preserves a fine Gothic doorway. Via Vittorio Veneto ends near the Post Office and the bridges which lead back to the mainland.

B. The Mainland: Achradina and Tyche (and the Archaeological Museum)

The buildings of interest described below are widely scattered about the unattractive modern town; to cover the distances between them a bus is recommended where possible (listed above).

The part of the town on the mainland adjoining Ortygia corresponds to the ancient **Achradina**. From Piazza Pancali buses run across the bridge along Corso Umberto to the FORO SIRACUSANO (Pl. 7), a huge and busy square with a Pantheon war memorial (1936), and splendid trees. Here are some remains of the ancient AGORA; recent excavations have revealed other parts of the Agora near Corso Umberto and Corso Gelone (where dwellings of the late 8C BC have also come to light, the earliest so far found in Syracuse).

From Piazza Marconi, Via Crispi forks right to the Station, while Via Elorina (left) leads to the so-called **Ginnasio Romano** (Pl. 6; admission 9–18 except Sun), a complex ruin surrounded by lawns and palm trees. A portico surrounded on three sides an altar, a temple, and a small theatre. The portico on the N side, and part of the high temple podium remain. The orchestra of the theatre is now under water; a few of the lower steps of the cavea are visible. The buildings, all of Imperial date, probably formed part of a serapeum.

From the NE corner of the Foro, the ugly Viale Diaz leads towards Borgo Santa Lucia. On the left are two excavated sites, the first (straddled by a brown modern block of flats) includes a small bath-house of Byzantine date, possibly the BATHS OF DAPHNE in which the Emperor Constans II was assassinated in 668. The second, just beyond, behind railings marks the ARSENALE ANTICO, where the foundations can be seen of the mechanism used by the Greeks to drag their ships into dry dock. In a simple house at No. 11 in Via degli Orti di San Giorgio, a figure of the Virgin is supposed to have wept in 1953 (plaque in Piazza Euripide; the shrine of the 'Madonna delle Lacrime' is described below). The long narrow Riviera Dionisio il Grande continues N, seaward of the railway, through Santa Lucia.

A long way NE (bus No. 2) is the large piazza, surrounded by an avenue of ficus trees, in front of the church of **Santa Lucia** (Pl. 3). The façade, which recently collapsed without warning, has been faithfully reconstructed. It was begun in 1629 on a plan by Giovanni Vermexio, and completed in the 18C (perhaps by Rosario Gagliardi), on the spot where St Lucy (?281–304), patron saint of Syracuse, was martyred. The portal, the apses, and the base of the campanile are Norman work and the rose-window is of the 14C. Outside is the chapel of San Sepolcro (see below), with a pretty exterior. Inside the church, in a chapel off the left side, are two ancient crucifixes (one T-shaped). A painting of the *Burial of St Lucy by Caravaggio which belongs to the church is at present kept in the Museo Regionale (see Rte 21A).

A tunnel from the church leads past the entrance to the CATACOMBS (closed indefinitely). These are the oldest in Sicily, and the most extensive in existence, after those in Rome. Caverns in the limestone existed here before the Christian era; there are Christian remains of the 2C and fragmentary Byzantine paintings. The tunnel emerges in SAN SEPOLCRO (also closed for restoration), a domed octagonal chapel by Giovanni Vermexio, partly below ground. This was the burial place of St Lucy; and from here her body was taken to Constantinople in 1038 (the empty tomb remains behind the altar). The 17C statue of the saint is by Tedeschi; a 16C silver statue by Pietro Rizzo is kept locked in the Duomo (but exposed here for eight days in December).

The area of the city immediately to the N corresponds to the ancient **Tyche**. About 500m NW of Santa Lucia, on Viale Teocrito (bus No. 4 from Ortygia via Corso Gelone) are the gardens of the VILLA LANDOLINA, in a small latomia (stone quarry), which surround the new building, opened in 1988, of the ****Museo Archeologico Regionale Paolo Orsi** (Pl. 3), one of the most interesting archaeological collections in Italy, especially representative of the eastern half of Sicily, and one of the finest museums in Europe. The material from excavations made by Paolo Orsi, the director in 1895–1934, is outstanding. It is beautifully displayed in a handsome functional building by Franco Minissi. It was designed in 1967 and kept low in order to preserve the character of the gardens of the Villa Landolina, but since then it has been surrounded by ugly new buildings which tower above it. It is open 9–13, 15–18 except Mon; fest. 9–13.

The garden, with splendid palm trees, and some olives, pines, cypresses, and orange trees, and some antique remains, was used as a Protestant cemetery. Among the 19C British and American tombstones (reached by the upper path which encircles the garden) is that of August von Platen (1796–1835), the German poet.

Beyond the entrance hall the centre of the building has an introductory display illustrating the history of the museum. The Museo Civico of Syracuse which opened in 1811 under the supervision of Saverio Landolina, became a national museum in 1878. From 1895–1934 Paolo Orsi, the famous archaeologist, was director of the collection which was displayed in a building in Piazza Duomo in Ortygia until it was moved here.

The display is divided into three sections: Prehistory (A), Greek colonies in Eastern Sicily (B), and sub-colonies and Hellenized centres (C). On the upper floor the Hellenistic and Roman material is eventually to be displayed.

Section A: Prehistory. An introductory display illustrates the geology of Sicily, and in particular the Monti Iblei region. The fauna of the island is described including dwarf elephants (with their fossil bones and two models). The strictly chronological display in this section begins with the NEOLITHIC PERIOD, represented by the STENTINELLO culture, an Agrarian civilisation, characterised by fortified villages and the use of impressed pottery. It is particularly well represented on the E side of the island around Etna and Syracuse. Four moated villages have been identified at Stentinello, Matrensa, Megara Hbylaea, and Ognina. Plain unglazed pottery with impressed decoration, and tools made out of ossidian from Lipari are exhibited from Case 14 onwards. Cases 38–44 have Bronze Age finds from Sant'Ippolito (near Caltagirone), Valsavoia, Messina and Milazzo.

With Case 45 begins the display relating to the important Bronze Age site of CASTELLUCCIO (between Noto Antica and Palazzolo Acreide) including brown painted pottery, and interesting carved door slabs from rock-cut tombs. The pottery reveals trading links with Egypt and the Aegean, and shows Minoan-Mycenaen influences. Steps lead up to Cases 61–81 with Middle Bronze Age material from THAPSOS on the Magnisi peninsula. The necropolis was excavated by Paolo Orsi, but the inhabited area has only recently been excavated (1500 BC–900 BC). Finds include imported pottery (from Mycenae, Cyprus, and Malta) and a splendid display of large impasto storage *jars. Material from other coastal settlements of the Thapsos culture are also exhibited.

Cases 82–89. Material from PANTALICA, the most important Late Bronze Age site in Sicily, which was naturally defended. This seems to have been inhabited by the Sicels who are thought to have migrated here from the Italian peninsula c 1300 BC, and whose culture remained virtually unchanged until the arrival of the Greeks. There is a splendid display of the characteristic red impasto *vases, with shiny glaze, and numerous bronze artefacts. Other centres of this date are illustrated, including material from the necropolis of Madonna del Piano at Grammichele (the tombs have been reconstructed), and bronzes from Mendolito di Adrano. The finds from the Marcellino valley near Villasmundo include interesting pottery; the examples of imported Greek ware represent the earliest known examples (8C BC) so far found on the island. The last cases in this section contain finds from SANT'ANGELO MUXARO, with local and imported pottery, and Polizzello.

Section B: Greek colonization. This period begins in the mid 8C when colonists from Corinth, Rhodes, Crete, and the Chalcides arrive on the island. With the defeat of Carthage at Himera in 480 BC the Greek supremacy in the Mediterranean was established, and the great victory over Athens at Syracuse in 413 BC symbolised the importance Sicily attained in the Greek world. Finds are displayed from the earliest Greek colonies on the island: NAXOS, founded c 734 BC (cases 138–140), Mylai, Zancle, and Katane. The finds from LENTINI include a fine *kouros (late 6C BC). A large section is dedicated to MEGARA HYBLAEA. The pottery includes imported Greek ware and local products. The highly interesting archaic sculpture includes a Greek marble statue (c 560–550 BC), thought to be a funerary monument, with an inscription on the leg to the physician Sambrotidas, son of Mandrokles, and a *statue of a mother goddess suckling twins (mid 6C BC).

It is now necessary to go out into the central rotonda and re-enter the pavilion (still Section B) beside the splendid headless statue of ***Venus Anadyomene**, temporarily displayed here. This is an Imperial Roman adaption of a Hellenistic original of the 2C BC, remarkable for its anatomical perfection. It was found in Syracuse in 1804 by Saverio Landolina, and greatly admired by Guy de Maupassant when he visited Syracuse in 1885 (he left a vivid description of it). Here begins the section dedicated to SYRACUSE. Finds from Ortygia are arranged topographically, and include material from recent excavations in Piazza della Vittoria, where a sanctuary of Demeter and Kore of the late 5C and early 4C BC has been found. There are numerous votive statuettes and a polychrome bust in terracotta (case 185). Numerous pottery types are displayed. Finds from necropoli near Syracuse include those from Contrada Fusco, with proto-Corinthian ware (725–700 BC) and a fine bronze statuette of a horse, in the geometric style (Case 188; late-8C BC). The Temples of Apollo and Athena are reconstructed in models, and terracotta fragments from them exhibited. The frieze of seven lion-faced gargoyles comes from the Temple of Athena. The marble figure was part of its acroterion. The display of finds from sanctuaries outside the urban area, include an archaic limestone head from Laganello (near the Ciane spring).

It is now necessary to got out into the central rotonda and back towards the entrance to enter **Section C: sub-colonies and Hellenized centres**. The display begins with material from ELORO, including votive terracottas. Finds from AKRAI include statues, one of a female deity, and another of a male figure enthroned (7C–6C BC). KASMENAI is represented by a high-relief in limestone of Kore holding a dove (570–560 BC), and ex-votos. The finds from CAMARINA include a horse and rider (6C BC), used as part of the decoration of the roof of a temple. A marble torso by a Greek artist (c 500 BC) and a terracotta goddess enthroned (late 6C BC) come from GRAMMICHELE. There are numerous examples of local pottery and imported Greek ware. A votive desposit found recently at FRANCAVILLA DI SICILIA includes a remarkable series of *reliefs in terracotta (470–460 BC). A lovely little clay miniature altar bears a relief of the 6C BC showing a lion attacking a bull (case 280) from Centuripe. The bronze statuette known as the *'Ephebus of Mendolito' from Adrano dates from c 460 BC.

The last section is devoted to Gela and Agrigento. Finds from GELA include architectural terracottas, cinerary urns, and sarcophaghi. The *vases from Gela, include (case 297) an amphora with an onomachia, signed by Polygnotus (440 BC); part of a cup signed by Chachyrylion (520–510 BC); lekythoi depicting the struggle of Thetis and Peleus, and of Aeneas with Anchises (black-figured; 6C); lekythos with a Nike, signed by Duris (470–460 BC); bronze dish with relief of horses (from the Necropolis at Gela, 7C BC). Also, fragment by the 'Painter of Panaitos', and fine bronze kraters. The finds from AGRIGENTO (mostly made by Paolo Orsi) include votive terracottas, and busts of Demeter and Kore. Three rare wooden *statuettes of archaic type dating from the late 7C BC were found by a sacred spring at Palma di Montechiaro (Case 309).

The park to the S surrounds the vast circular sanctuary of the MADONNINA DELLE LACRIME, begun in 1970 to enshrine a miraculous sculpture of the Madonna. This mass-produced figure of the Virgin is supposed to have wept for five days in 1953 in a house in Achradina (see above). The church (by Michael Andrault and Pierre Parat), mostly below ground level has recently been completed with a huge conical spire (90m high), which towers above the high buildings of the city. It incorporates some remains of catacombs.

Adjoining it to the S, in PIAZZA DELLA VITTORIA, extensive excavations begun in 1973 during the construction of the church of the Madonna delle Lacrime, have revealed a group of Hellenistic and Roman houses, a Sanctuary of Demeter and Kore (late 5C BC or early 4C BC), and a monumental fountain of the 5C BC. These are visible from outside the fence. Several hundred terracotta votive statuettes found here are now exhibited in the Museo Archaeologico Regionale (see above).

Off Viale Teocrito, just to the W of Villa Landolina, Via San Giovanni leads right to **San Giovanni** (Pl. 3; open in summer at 10, 11, 12, 16, 17, and 18; in winter 10–12, 15–17; mid November–mid March, 10–12 only; closed Wed) a ruined church whose façade is preceded by three arches constructed of medieval fragments, now surrounded by modern buildings. It occupies the W portion of an old basilica, once the cathedral of Syracuse, which was reconstructed by the Normans in 1200, and reduced to ruins in 1673 by earthquake. A fine 14C rose-window survives; and the 7C apse may be seen from the garden.

The CRYPT (entered through the ruined church to the left), in the form of a Greek cross, with three apses, was the site of the martyrdom of St Marcian (c 254 AD): the sanctuary was transformed into a basilica at the end of the 6C or beginning of the 7C, and was probably destroyed by the Arabs in 878. The visible remains (which include faded frescoes) date from a Norman reconstruction. The fine Byzantine capitals with symbols of the Evangelists, are thought to have been reused from the earlier basilica. In one apse are traces of 4C and 5C frescoes from a hypogeum. The column against which the saint was martyred and his tomb surrounded by some of the earliest catacombs (cf. below) can be seen. An altar is said to mark the site of St Paul's preaching in Syracuse.

The extensive ***Catacombs of San Giovanni** (entered to the right of the entrance) were probably in use from the 3C to the end of the 6C. The galleries have been several times rifled and thousands of loculi have been despoiled of their treasures. From the 'decumanus maximus', or principal gallery, adapted from a disused Greek aqueduct, smaller passages lead to five circular chapels, known as the ROTONDE D'ADELFIA (from the sarcophagus now in the archaeological museum), DI EUSEBIO or DELLA SANTA AMPOLLA, DELLE SETTE VERGINI (with the rock-cut tombs of seven nuns, members of one of the first religious houses established after the persecutions in Syracuse), DI ANTIOCHIA (from the sarcophagus with a Greek inscription), and one without a name.

The LATOMIA CASALE (no admission), a few minutes N of San Giovanni, has luxuriant vegetation. To the E of Villa Landolina is the VIGNA CASSIA with 3C catacombs (also closed). To the NE, near the sea (bus No. 4 from Corso Umberto) are the **Latomia dei**

Cappuccini (Pl. 4), to the right of the former Capuchin convent. These have been closed indefinitely because of landslides, but can be seen in part from the road outside. One of the most extensive of the ancient quarries (cf. below), they are now overgrown by luxuriant vegetation. Adjacent is the Villa Politi hotel where Churchill stayed on his holidays in Syracuse. From Piazza dei Cappuccini, in front of the 17C church (recently restored), is a view of Ortygia.

Viale Teocrito leads W from Villa Landolina past a small private PAPYRUS MUSEUM (No. 66). This illustrates how papyrus was produced in ancient times and preserves a collection of ancient papyruses, and artefacts from Egypt made out of papyrus. There is also a section dedicated to the production of papyrus (which still grows at the Fonte Ciane, see Rte 22B) in Syracuse. Viale Teocrito leads into Neapolis. At the end of Viale Augusto (500m) is the entrance to the archaeological zone.

C. Neapolis: the archaeological zone

Bus No. 1 from the town centre. **Plan on p 12–13 of the atlas section**.

Off Viale Augusto a car-park and garden have been under construction on a piece of waste land for many years. Beside a splendid giant magnolia tree and a group of huge ficus trees is the little church of **San Nicolò** (see plan on p 12–13 of the atlas section). Here the funeral service of Jourdain, son of Count Roger, was held in 1093. It is closed for restoration (and normally houses an information office). Below it outside can be seen part of an aisled PISCINA, a reservoir used for flushing the amphitheatre (see below), to which it is connected by a channel.

A short road (closed to cars), overlooking the Latomia del Paradiso on the right and the Altar of Hieron on the left, continues to the ticket office and entrance to the ARCHAEOLOGICAL AREA (see plan inset, p 12–13 of atlas section), enclosed in a public park. The monuments were pillaged in 1526 to provide stone for the Spanish defence works. A single entrance gives access to the LATOMIA DEL PARADISO and the GREEK THEATRE (open daily 9–two hours before sunset).

A path leads through the beautiful garden with tropical fruit trees on the floor of the ***Latomia del Paradiso**, the largest and most famous of the huge deep quarries excavated in ancient times, and since then one of the great sites of the city. They are now all covered with luxuriant vegetation because of their sheltered positions. Their extent testifies to the colossal amount of building stone used for the Greek city; following the N limit of Achradina from here to the Cappuccini near the sea, they also served as a defensive barrier. They were used as prisons and according to Thucydides some 7000 Athenians were incarcerated here. Part of the rock face is now protected with scaffolding; this is the only latomia at present open to the public.

The path ends at the ***Orecchio di Dionisio** (ear of Dionysius), an S-shaped artificial cavern, 65m long, 5–11m wide, and 23m high, in section like a rough Gothic arch. Its name was given to it by Caravaggio in 1586, who referred only to the shape of the entrance; but, because of the amazing acoustic properties of the cavern, it has given rise to the legend that Dionysius used the place as a prison and from a small fissure in the roof at the upper end heard quite clearly the whispers of the captives at the lower end. The interior can be visited (torch useful). In the NW wall of the Latomia opens the GROTTA DEI CORDARI, named for the ropemakers who used to work here, a picturesque cavern supported by huge pillars and covered with maidenhair ferns and coloured lichens. Access has been prohibited since 1984 because of its perilous state (its partial disintegration has been caused by the infiltration of water, pollution from the air, and traffic vibrations).

Another path leads to the ***Greek Theatre**, the most celebrated of all the ruins of Syracuse, and one of the largest Greek theatres known (138m in diameter). Archaeological evidence confirms the existence on this spot of a wooden theatre as early as the 6C BC, and here it was that Epicharmus (c 540–450 BC) worked as a comic poet. About 475 BC Hieron I constructed a small stone theatre with a trapezoidal orchestra, in which shortly afterwards Aeschylus probably produced his 'Persae'. The semicircular form was adopted c 335 BC, when the theatre was enlarged under Timoleon by excavating deeper into the hillside; it was again enlarged under Hieron II (c 230 BC) by extending the cavea upward. Under the Romans the scena was altered and in the late Imperial period the orchestra was flooded for the production of naumachiae. A classical drama festival is held here every two years in May and June.

The existing cavea, with 42 rows of seats in nine wedges, is almost entirely hewn out of the rock. This is now believed to represent Hieron II's auditorium of 59 rows, less the upward extension which has been quarried. The extent of Timoleon's theatre before Hieron's excavations is marked by the drainage trench at the sixth row above the larger gangway. Around the gangway runs a frieze bearing, in large Greek characters, the names of Hieron (II), Philistis (his queen), Nereis (queen of Gelon II), and Zeus Olympius, which served to distinguish the blocks of seats. The foundations of the scena remain, successive alterations making it difficult to identify their function, except for the deep recess for the curtain. The trapezoidal shape of the earlier theatre can clearly be seen as a deep trough in the orchestra. The view from the upper seats was especially good in the early morning (the hour at which Greek drama was performed). Above the theatre were two porticoes (to provide shelter from the weather).

A path leads up behind the little two-storeyed house perched on a rock to the rock wall behind the theatre with recesses for votive tablets and a grotto (or nymphaeum) in which the abundant aqueduct which traverses Epipolae ends. There is a view of the port from here. At the left-hand end of the wall begins the STREET OF TOMBS (Via dei Sepolcri), rising in a curve 146m long. The wheel ruts in the limestone were made by carts in the 16C serving the mills which used to occupy the cavea of the theatre. The Byzantine tombs and Hellenistic niches in its rock walls have all been rifled. Its upper end (no admission) crosses the rock-hewn ACQUEDOTTO GALERMI, whose water comes from the Bottiglieria spring, 20km away. Immediately to the W of the theatre a SANCTUARY OF APOLLO TEMENITES has been discovered. A smaller, and probably older theatre lies to the SW.

Across the road from the ticket office (see above) is a good view of the foundations of the huge **Altar of Hieron II**, hewn out of the rock. The public have not been admitted since 1983 for preservation reasons. The altar, built between 241 and 215 BC, was used for public sacrifices. It was 198m long and 22.8m wide (the largest altar known), and was destroyed by the Spaniards. To the W is an Augustan portico.

Near San Nicolò (see above) is the entrance (somewhat hidden by souvenir stalls) to the ***Amphitheatre** (admission with the same ticket as for the Latomia del Paradiso and the Greek Theatre) approached past stone sarcophagi from cemeteries in Syracuse and Megara Hyblaea. An imposing Roman building probably of the 1C AD, partly hollowed out of the hillside, in external dimensions (140m by 119m) the amphitheatre is only a little inferior to that at Verona. The perfection of the masonry is probably attributable to a Syracusan architect. Beneath the high parapet encircling the arena runs a corridor with entrances for the gladiators and wild beasts; the marble blocks on the parapet have inscriptions recording the ownership of the seats. In the centre is a rectangular depression probably for the machinery used in the spectacles. The original entrance was at the S end, outside which a large area has been exposed, including an enclosure thought to have been for the animals, and a large fountain. Also here excavations have revealed an earlier roadway and the base of an Augustan arch.

There is a view of the archaeological park from VIALE RIZZO (Pl.2) above: in the foreground is the Theatre and the Latomia del Paradiso, beyond, the Altar of Hieron and the Amphitheatre, and in the distance the Porto Grande and Ortygia (obscured by modern tower blocks).

A short way to the N of the church of San Nicolò (see above) is the beautiful garden of the **Latomia di Santa Venera** (closed indefinitely after landslides), in whose walls are niches for votive tablets. Above it are the NECROPOLI DELLE GROTTICELLI, a group of Hellenistic and Byzantine tombs, one of which, with a Doric pediment, is arbitrarily known as the 'Tomb of Archimedes'. The new excavations here can be seen from the fence along the main road, Via Teracati.

22

Environs of Syracuse

Besides the places described below, the province of Syracuse includes the excavations of the ancient sites of **Megara Hyblaea**, c 20km N, and of **Lentini**, c 45km N, both described in Rte 23.

A. Castle of Euryalus

ROAD, 8km. Bus No. **11** (every 40mins) for Belvedere from Ortygia (Riva della Posta) via Corso Gelone.

North of the archaeological zone of Neapolis the Catania road leads through the ugly modern city. Soon the road for Belvedere (signposted) diverges left, and, after traversing more suburbs, emerges on the open barren plateau of Epipolae. It crosses the great ***Wall of Dionysius** (see the plan of ancient Syracuse) which defended the Epipolae ridge, the W limit of the ancient city. Begun by Dionysius the Elder in 401 BC after the Athenian siege, it was finished by 385; it stretches for 31km (the N line can be followed on foot from the Castle of Euryalus, see below). Just before the walls a path (50m) leads right (near a house and water deposit) to the LATOMIA DEL FILOSOFO (or Bufalaro), so-called from the legend that

Philoxenus of Cythera was confined here for expressing too candid an opinion of the verses of Dionysius. The quarry was probably used for the construction of the walls and the castle of Euryalus.

The main road winds up towards BELVEDERE; just after the signpost for the town, a road (signposted) leads right for the ***Castle of Euraylus** (more correctly 'Euryelos', i.e. broad-based; open every day 9am–one hour before sunset). The most complete and important Greek military work extant, it was begun under Dionysius the Elder in 402–397, and probably altered by Agathocles in 317. Archimedes is thought to have strengthened the defences in the late 3C, but his work was left unfinished because of the sack of the city in 212. Built on the highest point (172m) of the plateau of EPIPOLAE, it commands the W extremity of ancient Syracuse (as the view shows), at the most delicate point in the wall of Dionysius. A huge oil refinery now dominates the coast from Panagia to the Magnisi peninsula.

Three ditches precede the W front; the outermost (A) is near the custodian's house. Between the second (B) and the third (D) are the ruins of an outwork (C), whose walls have partly collapsed into the second ditch. A wooden staircase descends into the INNERMOST DITCH (D), the principal defence of the fortress which gave access to a labyrinth of casemates and passages to all parts of the fort. On the right the three piers of the drawbridge (E) are prominent. There are 11 entrances from this main ditch to the gallery parallel with it; from here three passages lead E; the longest, on the N (K; 174m long; closed since 1983) connects with the Epipolae Gateway (G; see below). The construction of the long gallery was accelerated by means of vertical shafts which were afterwards closed, but could be used as a means of escape in case the enemy occupied the castle. The gallery to the S (also partly blocked in 1993) leads to a ditch (J) outside the S wall of the castle and connects also with the advanced outwork.

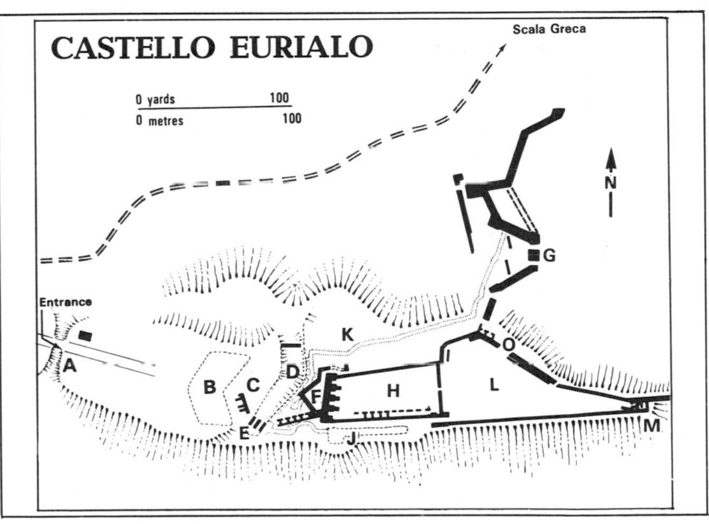

Castle of Euryalus, Syracuse

It is at present necessary to return up the wooden stairs and follow the path (right) round the S perimeter of the site to enter the CASTLE proper, which consisted of a keep (H) with an irregular outer ward (L) on the E. In these parts of the castle the barracks and cisterns were located. The KEEP (H), an irregular quadrilateral, has five prominent square towers on the W side and a pointed bastion in front. The towers were probably battlemented and decorated with lions' head gargoyles. On the NE side of the outer ward (L) was the main entrance (O) from the town; on the SE rose a tower (M) connected with the S Wall of Dionysius.

The N Wall of Dionysius is united to the keep by a complicated system of underground works, notable for their ingenious provisions for shelter and defence. The EPIPOLAE GATEWAY (G), is a 'pincer' type defence work on the spur of the N wall of Epipolae.

It is still possible to follow the line of the N Wall of Dionysius (5380m) on foot from the castle as far as Scala Greca, near the sea. Just below the entrance to the castle (reached from the main road for Belvedere; first turning on right), a track follows the line of walls (broken at intervals by towers and posterns) to the NE. At the water trough it is necessary to keep right. On the cliff above the Contrada Targia is the probable site of LABDALUM, the fort erected by the Athenians when they captured Epipolae. The city is re-entered at SCALA GRECA; in the white rock here can be seen many caves, in two of which a rock sanctuary of Demeter was found. To the W are the remains of what was perhaps the HEXAPYLON (gate of the six openings) of Dionysius, at the N extremity of Tyche. The main Catania road returns to the centre of town (Bus No. 33 to Corso Gelone and Corso Umberto).

B. The Olympieion and the river Ciane

BUS **24** in summer from Corso Gelone via Via Elorina for the Olympieion. There is no public transport to the source of the Ciane, although a BOAT can sometimes be hired (Sig. Vella) to go up the river from Molo Zanagora in Ortygia, or, if the water is too low, at the confluence of the Anapo and Ciane rivers (off N115).

The **Olympieion** or **Temple of Zeus**, on the right bank of the Ciane, is reached from the Noto road which crosses first the Anapo and then the Ciane (c 3km from Syracuse). After the Ciane the two columns of the temple can be seen among trees on the skyline of a low hill, the POLICHNE, a point of great strategic importance, invariably occupied by the besiegers of Syracuse. About 1km after the bridge, at the top of the rise, a road (right; signposted) leads in less than 1km (keep right) to the temple in a cypress grove. Built in the 6C, just after the Temple of Apollo (see Rte 21A), it is the second oldest Doric peripteral temple in Sicily. It was hexastyle and peripteral with 42 monolithic columns, two of which remain standing on part of the stylobate. There is a view of the promontory of Ortygia.

The source of the river **Ciane** (7km from the centre of Syracuse) is reached by car from the Canicattini Bagni road. After crossing the Anapo, a byroad (left; signposted) leads for 3km through a fertile valley with orange and lemon groves and magnificent old olive trees (and some 'pill-box' defences left over from the Second World War).

Beyond a tributary of the Ciane, a road (signposted) continues left to end in a grove of eucalyptus and cypress trees beside the romantic spring (the ancient 'Cyane'), overgrown with reeds and thick clumps of Egyptian papyrus. This plant grows in no other part of Europe, and is traditionally said to have found its way here as a gift from Ptolemy Philadelphus. In fact, it was probably introduced at the time of Hieron II, or later, by the Arabs. The name of the spring (in Greek, blue) describes the azure colour of its waters, but a myth relates how the nymph Cyane, who tried to prevent Pluto from carrying off Persephone, was changed into a spring and condemned to weep for ever. Beyond the bridge a path follows a fence along the reeds to the large pool, inhabited by numerous waterfowl. The spring called TESTA DELLA PISMA, and the smaller PISMOTTA spring, both also have pools planted with papyrus.

C. Noto

Noto can be reached from Syracuse by BUS ('AST' and 'SAIS'), c every hour in 45mins, or by TRAIN (on the Gela line) in c 35mins.

FROM SYRACUSE TO NOTO, N115, 32km. As far as Cassibile, a stretch of 7km of motorway is open, reached from the Canicattini 'superstrada'; instead the old road (N115) skirts the Porto Grande and crosses the Anapo. Just before it crosses the Ciane, two columns of the Temple of Zeus Olympieion (see Rte 22B) are conspicuous in the woods to the right. The road passes plantations of citrus fruits and crosses the base of the PENNISOLA DELLA MADDALENA, the ancient headland of 'Plemmyrium', which was the headquarters of Nicias after his defeat on Epipolae by Gylippus, in the famous battle between Athens and Syracuse in 415 BC. The bay to the S, the FONTANE BIANCHE, used to be one of the best bathing beaches on the island; it is now polluted by uncontrolled new buildings.

8km SANTA TERESA DI LONGARINI. Neolithic settlements have been found on the offshore islet of OGNINA (5km SE), where Neolithic and Early Bronze Age pottery finds suggest that it may have been a Maltese trading outpost. 14km CASSIBILE, where a huge Bronze Age necropolis and hut village yielded extremely interesting finds, now in the archaeological museum in Syracuse. In an olive grove near here on the afternoon of 3 September 1943, Generals Bedell Smith and Castellano signed the military terms of surrender to the Allies of the Italian army. Several 'pill-boxes' survive along the road and on the bed of the Anapo. The road touches the coast near the mouth of the Cassibile, the ancient 'Kakyparis', by whose banks the Athenian general DemosthenesDemosthenes, covering the rear of Nicias' forces during the retreat from Syracuse, was cut off and forced to surrender (see above). It now passes splendid old olive trees, carobs, almonds and citrus fruit plantations, with a range of low hills parallel to the road inland.

29km **Avola** (32,100 inhab.) is a prosperous agricultural town, and one of the most important centres of almond culture in Italy. It has expanded in a disorderly way around its interesting centre which retains the hexagonal plan on which it was built after 1693 by Fra Angelo Italia. In the centre is Piazza Umberto I with the Chiesa Madre (San Nicolò; being restored), which contains an 18C organ by Donato del Piano. Four smaller piazze open off the outer edge of the hexagon, one of which, Piazza Vittorio Veneto, has a fountain with three amusing 20C lions by Gaetano Vinci. The 18C churches include Sant'Antonio Abate and Santissima Annunziata (with a façade by Giuseppe Alessi) and there are a number of good Art Nouveau buildings. The church of the Cappuccini, outside the hexagonal centre, in Piazza Francesco Crispi, has a good 17C altarpiece. 32km Noto.

***NOTO** (23,300 inhab.) is the most charming and best preserved of the 18C Baroque cities of Sicily. It was built after the earthquake of 1693 when the former town of Noto (now Noto Antica, see below), 7km away, was abandoned. It is an excellent example of 18C town planning, and its architecture is exceptionally homogeneous. Many of the fine buildings, with theatrical exteriors, including numerous churches and convents, were built between 1715 and 1780 by Rosario Gagliardi, his pupil Vincenzo Sinatra, and Paolo Labisi. The fragile local white tufa has been burnt to a golden brown by the sun. After years of neglect by the local administration many of its major buildings threatened with collapse are now being slowly restored. Noto lends itself to exploration by foot.

Information Office of the 'APT' of Syracuse, Piazza XVI Maggio (Tel. 0931/836744).

Railway Station, 1.5km S of the public gardens, on the Syracuse–Gela line (trains from Syracuse in c 35mins). The branch line to Pachino has been substituted by a bus service.

Buses from Largo Pantheon ('AST' and 'SAIS') to Syracuse c every hour in 45mins. Services run by 'Caruso' to Noto Marina on the coast.

Car Parking outside Porta Reale.

Hotels. 1-star 'Stella', 44 Via Maiore (corner of Via Napoli). On the coast at Noto Marina, 3-star 'Helios' and two others.

Restaurants. Simple trattorie: 'Il Barocco', Via Cavour and 'Trattoria del Carmine', Via Ducezio.

Café or bar ('pasticceria'). 'Corrado Costanzo', 7/9 Via Silvio Spaventa.

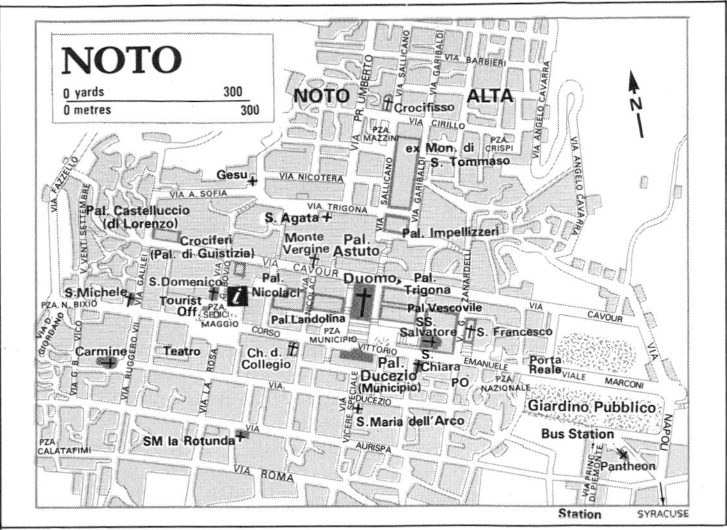

Picnic places in the public gardens outside Porta Reale.

Concerts are given in several churches in the town, including the convent of San Domenico and the church of Montevergine. International Classical Music Festival in July and August.

Annual Festivals. Festivities in honour of 'San Corrado' on 19 February, last Sunday in August, and the first Sunday in September. Procession of the 'Santa Spina' on Good Friday, and other religious ceremonies during Easter week. 'Infiorata' on the third Sunday in May, when Via Nicolaci is carpeted with fresh flowers.

History. After the earthquake of 1693 which severely damaged Noto Antica this new site was chosen in 1702 by a majority of the inhabitants. It is known that Giuseppe Lanza (Duke of Camastra), Giuseppe Asmundo, Giovanni Battista Landolina, and the Jesuit Angelo Italia, all played a part in planning the new city. In 1837–65 Noto displaced Syracuse as provincial capital. Since 1986 the Corso has been closed to traffic, and many buildings in the town have been propped up by scaffolding, and closed. The funds which have been allotted to the city by the government, Region, and UNESCO are at last being used to repair the easily eroded tufa and to carry out urgent restoration work.

At the E end of the town are the PUBLIC GARDENS where the thick evergreen ficus trees form an impenetrable roof over the road. PORTA REALE (being restored), erected by Orazio Angelini for the visit of Ferdinand II in 1838, leads into the **Corso** from which the town rises to the right and falls away to the left; by skilful use of open spaces and monumental flights of steps a straight and level street, 1km long, has been given a lively skyline and a succession of glimpses of the countryside. On the right opens a grandiose flight of steps which lead up to SAN FRANCESCO by Vincenzo Sinatra, with a good façade and a pretty white stucco interior. The huge convent of SAN SALVATORE (now a seminary) faces Via Zanardelli; the splendid long 18C façade and delightful tower (possibly designed by Rosario Gagliardi) have been covered for restoration for many years.

Opposite is the church of SANTA CHIARA (usually open on Sunday morning) with an oval interior by Gagliardi (1730–48), with a Madonna by

Antonello Gagini. In part of the convent there are plans to reopen the **Museo Civico**, which has been closed for many years. The contents include Bronze Age pottery from Canicattini, Castelluccio, and Licodia Eubea, and Bronze Age weapons (including volcanic glass, used as a fine cutting instrument) from Castelluccio and Noto. The finds from Eloro include the reconstruction of part of a Sanctuary of Demeter (in use from the 6C BC–3C BC), with votive statuettes attached to the outside wall by a coat of stucco. There is also a collection of Roman and Byzantine coins. Material from Noto Antica includes ceramics, sculptural fragments, and the damaged sarcophagus of Niccolò Speciale (died 1444) by the workshop of Andrea di Francesco Guardi (also attributed to Antonio Gagini). A bronze panther dates from the Norman period, and the head of a saint in hard wood from the 15C. There is a plan of the city made in 1783. Modern works include sculptures by Giuseppe Pirrone.

Beyond, in the centre of the city, the huge façade of the Cathedral above a splendid staircase looks down on PIAZZA MUNICIPIO with its symmetrical horseshoe hedges of ficus. The **Cathedral** (San Nicolò) was built in several stages throughout the 18C probably with the intervention of Gagliardi and Vincenzo Sinatra; the dome was rebuilt in the 19C. The interior has recently been reopened since its restoration. It is flanked by the Bishop's Palace and PALAZZO LANDOLINA (covered for restoration), once the residence of this important local family. Beyond the Bishop's Palace is the church of SAN SALVATORE (admission on request at the seminary next door). The façade was designed by Andrea Gigante of Trapani and probably built by Antonio Mazza (1791). The pretty polychrome interior, with a vault painting by Mazza, contains 18C paintings by Giuseppe Velasquez, and an organ of 1778 by Donato del Piano.

On the S side of the piazza, facing the Duomo, is ***Palazzo Ducezio** (the town hall), a splendid building begun as the Casa Senatorio in 1742 by Vincenzo Sinatra. The continuous raised classical portico is beautifully proportioned. The upper floor was added in 1951. Inside is a vault painting by Antonio Mazza. In the Corso is the *CHIESA DEL COLLEGIO (San Carlo), with a tower façade probably by Gagliardi (1730; restored by Vincenzo Sinatra in 1776). It has a pretty white stucco interior (being restored). Beyond, the long façade (propped up by scaffolding) of the EX-COLLEGIO DEI GESUITI (now a school) stretches as far as Piazza San Domenico (or Piazza XVI Maggio), with the TEATRO VITTORIO EMANUELE (1851; recently restored). Here in a delightful little garden with tall palms and monkey-puzzle trees, the fountain is surmounted with an 18C statue of Hercules. In the pavilion behind is the 'APT' information office. Above to the left is the charming convex *façade of **San Domenico** (1737–56) by Gagliardi, perhaps his most successful building in the town. Via Bovio mounts to the ex-convent of the CASA DEI CROCIFERI by Paolo Labisi (1750), finished by Vincenzo Sinatra. It has been restored as law courts.

From near Piazza Municipio (see above) Via Nicolaci is overlooked by the delightful Baroque balconies of the huge *PALAZZO NICOLACI (Villadorata; 1737–65), once the residence of Don Giacomo Nicolaci, a patron of the arts. He donated part of his huge library to the Biblioteca Comunale, which, since 1982, has been housed in a wing of the palace. The end of the street is closed by the façade of MONTEVERGINE, attributed to Vincenzo Sinatra, which contains paintings by Costantino Carasi. Via Cavour is another lovely 18C street, with the neo-classical PALAZZO CASTELLUCCIO (Di Lorenzo) at its W end. Next to the church is the beautiful PALAZZO ASTUTO

San Domenico, Noto

(late 18C; possibly the work of Vincenzo Sinatra or Paolo Labisi) which once housed the famous Museo Astuziano, a private museum dispersed in the mid 19C. Farther on, on the right, is the splendid PALAZZO TRIGONA (1781; restored by Bernardo Labisi), part of it renovated as a congress centre.

Beside Palazzo Astuto steps (Via Fratelli Bandiera) ascend to Via Sallicano and the upper part of the town known as **Noto Alta**. This simpler district was laid out on a different plan and orientation from the lower monumental district with its four long straight parallel streets running from east to west. Here is PALAZZO IMPELLIZZERI and the huge EX-MONASTERY OF SAN TOMMASO (now a prison; good façade in Via Trigona).

Beyond, on the summit of the hill in Piazza Mazzini, the centre of Noto Alta, is the church of the **Crocifisso**, by Gagliardi (1728) which contains a number of works of art from Noto Antica, including (in the right transept) a *Madonna della Neve signed by Francesco Laurana (1471), and two Romanesque lions. The Cappella Landolina (recently restored), with frescoes by Costantino Carasi, preserves a relic of the holy thorn (the 'Sacra Spina'). In Via Trigona (cf. the plan) is the church of SANT'AGATA attributed to Gagliardi and finished by Paolo Labisi. It contains stuccoes by Labisi and paintings by Costantino Carasi. Nearby is the GESÙ in a fine position. In front of Sant'Agata steps (Via Dante Alighieri) lead back down the hill to the lower town.

The pretty Via Ducezio runs parallel to the Corso to the south. It is closed at its W end by the delightful concave Baroque façade (with Rococo details) of SANTA MARIA DEL CARMINE (if closed ring at the door on the right), a late work by Gagliardi with a charming interior. At the other end of the street, on Via Vicerè Speciale, is the church of SANTA MARIA DELL'ARCO (1730), also by Gagliardi with an elegant portal, and a decorative stucco interior, with two stoups from Noto Antica. Nearby is an interesting Art Nouveau house. Via Vicerè Speciale, beautifully paved between two rows of steps mounts to the splendid rear façade of the Town Hall (see above). Via Aurispa, parallel to Via Ducezio on the S, is another pretty street with simpler buildings.

FROM NOTO TO NOTO ANTICA, 12km. The road (signposted for Palazzolo Acreide) leads uphill to the left from the public gardens. It traverses Noto Alta with pleasant streets of low Art Nouveau houses. Beyond the little town of SAN CORRADO DI FUORI, with more pretty early-20C houses, the road continues across a fine upland plain with old olive trees. It then descends to cross a bridge decorated with four obelisks.

9km, turning (left) for Noto Antica. The road is lined with early-20C Stations of the Cross on the approach to the large sanctuary of SANTA MARIA DELLA SCALA, next to a seminary, with a pleasant façade (1708) with three statues and a balcony. The road now descends to cross another bridge in a ravine. 12km **Noto Antica**, abandoned since the earthquake of 1693 and now utterly deserted. The scant ruins, mostly reduced to rubble, are almost totally overgrown and provide an eery romantic sight. This was a settlement that long antedates its legendary foundation by the Sicel chief Ducetius in 448 BC, and was the only Sicilian town that resisted the depredations of Verres. The last stronghold of Muslim Sicily, it gave its name to the Val di Noto, one of the three areas into which the Arabs divided up the island. It fell to the Normans in 1091. A flourishing medieval city, it was the birthplace of Matteo Carnelivari, the architect. After the terrible earthquake of 1693 the inhabitants decided to move their city to its present site (see above).

The entrance is through the monumental PORTA DELLA MONTAGNA (recently restored) with remains of the high walls on either side. A rough road continues through the site of the town for c 2km. It leads up past a round tower and along the ridge of the hill. The conspicuous wall on the left (the highest one to survive) belonged to the Chiesa Madre. After 1km, beside a little monument, the right fork continues (and the road deteriorates) to end beside the EREMO DELLA MADONNA, a little deserted chapel.

There is a good view of the surrounding countryside from here. There are plans to clear the site to some extent and put up signs on some of the ruins.

The main road (N287) continues, from the Noto Antica turning, through the pleasant little village of VILLA VELA, with some Art Nouveau villas. A byroad leads right for the CAVA GRANDE of the Cassibile river, where thousands of tombs (11C BC–9C BC) have been identified (finds in the Archaeological Museum in Syracuse). Huge plane trees grow on the banks of the river which was declared a nature reserve in 1984. Farther on the road reaches AVOLA ANTICA (10km), destroyed in 1693. The road traverses beautiful farming countryside with olives and carobs, and the view widens out as it joins the 'superstrada' from Syracuse to Palazzolo Acreide (see Rte 22D).

FROM NOTO TO PACHINO AND PORTOPALO, 29km. The road runs S through beautiful countryside past huge old olive trees, carobs, almonds, and citrus friut trees. Just outside Noto it crosses the Asinaro, the ancient Assinaros, where Nicias' retreating Greeks, trying to reach Heloros, were overtaken while drinking at the river and killed after the great battle between Syracuse and Athens in 415 BC. Byroads lead down to the little resorts of CALABERNARDO and LIDO DI NOTO (3-star hotel 'Elios') on the sea, with some of the best beaches on the E coast of the island. Beyond (3km) the Gioi, at the top of a rise, in lovely countryside, a road leads left for **Eloro** (*Helorus*; 3km), one of the first cities to be founded by Syracuse, probably at the beginning of the 7C BC.

After 2km, at a sharp bend in the road, an unsignposted rough track continues right under the railway bridge. The first road left continues to the top of a low hill, with the excavations in a lovely deserted position by the sea near the mouth of the Tellaro. There is a good view inland of the Pizzuta column (see below), with Noto beyond green rolling hills. The view along the unspoilt coastline extends to the S tip of the island. The road passes the basement of a temple perhaps dedicated to Asklepios. To the right of the road, in a large fenced enclosure sloping down to the canal, are a Sanctuary of Demeter with a larger temple and a monumental stoa. A theatre has been partially excavated nearby. To the left, beyond the custodian's house, is another enclosure of recent excavations. An ancient road continues to the walls and N gate. Outside the walls a Hellenic Sanctuary of Demeter was found; it has been reconstructed in the Noto Museum. The so-called PIZZUTA, a column over 10m high, can be reached by returning to the approach road beyond the railway bridge. From the road for the 'tourist village' of Eloro a rough road leads right through an almond and olive grove past the column. This was once thought to be a monument to the Syracusan victory (cf. above), but it is in fact a funerary memorial of the 3C BC.

From the main road, just after the bridge across the Tellaro, a road leads right for a farmhouse (conspicuous to the right of the road) in the locality of Caddeddi, less than 1km from the main road. Beneath the farmhouse a Roman villa of the second half of the 4C AD, known as the '**Villa del Tellaro**', was discovered in 1972. The farmer shows some of the splendid polychrome mosaics, reminiscent of those at Piazza Armerina, but the best ones have not been returned here since they were removed for restoration. Excavations continue. There is a distant view of Noto lying in the hills.

The main road continues S past almond trees to (8km) the turning (signposted) for the nature reserve of ***Vendicari**. Beyond the railway, a poorly surfaced road continues for c 1km past lemon groves to the entrance (open daily 9–dusk). This beautiful marshy area of the coast (1500 hectares; closed to cars), of the greatest interest for its wildlife (an oasis for migratory birds), has been protected since 1984 after local opposition succeeded in halting the construction of a vast 'tourist village' here. It was one of the first coastal areas on the island to become a reserve. Information is given at the entrance about the itineraries and regulations. It is a splendid place to picnic. At the S end is the 18C farmhouse of SAN LORENZO LO VECCHIO, with remains of a Hellenistic temple transformed into a Byzantine church. On the edge of the shore are ruins of a Norman tower, and a tuna fishery which closed down in 1943.

The road, now less pretty, continues past (20km) a byroad left for the fishing village of MARZAMEMI (2-star hotels). In the shallow bay here excavations, begun in 1959, have so far revealed 14 ancient shipwrecks (four Greek, five Roman, and five Byzantine ships).

22.5km **Pachino** (21,000 inhab.), a wine-producing centre. A road continues past almonds and olive trees skirting the sea and an inland lagoon, to the untidy fishing port of (29km) **Portopalo** (2-star and 1-star hotels and camping sites). There is a disused tuna fishery on the sea front next to an 18C palace. The landscape is ruined by numerous plastic greenhouses. The lighthouse stands on CAPO PASSERO, the ancient *Pachynus*, the SE horn of Sicily. A Roman necropolis has been excavated here, and the island of Capo Passero is of great interest for its vegetation. The southernmost point is the little ISOLOTTO DELLE CORRENTI, 6km SW of the cape. Sea turtles and pelicans used to be seen frequently on the shore here. For the coastal road between Pachino, Pozzallo and Camarina, see Rte 20.

At **Castelluccio**, c 25km W of Noto, is a prehistoric village (c 18–14C BC), that has given its name to the most important Early Bronze Age culture of SE Sicily. Nearby are a number of rock-tombs, which had carved portal slabs (now in the archaeological museum at Syracuse).

The main road (N115) for Ragusa descends S from Noto across the Asinaro and Tellaro via ROSOLINI, founded in 1713 (17,400 inhab.). A rock-hewn basilica of early Christian date lies beneath the Castello del Principe (1668) amid extensive catacombs (now used as a garage). Before reaching Ispica, the road enters the province of Ragusa, described in Rte 20.

D. Palazzolo Acreide

BUSES run by 'AST' from Syracuse to Palazzolo Acreide (Piazza del Popolo) c every hour in 40mins.

FROM SYRACUSE TO PALAZZOLO ACREIDE, 31km. A fast 'superstrada' known as the 'maremonti' begins on the outskirts of Syracuse and climbs past citrus fruit plantations and olives (with a retrospective view of the hill of Belvedere at the W limit of the ancient city and the huge conical spire of the new church of the Madonna delle Lacrime. 12.5km, turning for Floridia (right; see Rte 22E) and for Cassibile (left; see Rte 22C). Just beyond the crossroads, on the left of the road, is the GROTTA PERCIATA, the largest cave so far discovered in Sicily, where prehistoric artefacts have been found. The road continues to climb and bypasses (21km) CANICATTINI BAGNI, now surrounded by new buildings. Founded in 1678 it has interesting early-20C houses decorated in the local stone. 28km, junction with N287, which leads left for Noto (see Rte 22C), while this road continues into (31km) Palazzolo Acreide.

Palazzolo Acreide can also be reached from Syracuse by a prettier but slower road (N124) via Floridia, described in Rte 22E.

PALAZZOLO ACREIDE is the successor (9100 inhab.) to the Greek city of *Akrai*. It is a pleasant little town whose finest buildings were built after the earthquake in 1693. It also has some interesting 19C and early-20C palaces.

Information Office. 'APT' Syracuse, Tel. 0931/461477.

Buses ('AST') from Syracuse c every hour in 40mins.

Hotel. 3-star: 'Senatori' in contrada Pantana.

Restaurants. 1st class: 'Il Portico' and 'Valentino'. Simple trattorie: 'Zio 'Nzino' and 'La Casareccia'.

Annual Festival of San Paolo on 29 June.

History. Akrai was a sub-colony founded from Syracuse in 663 BC. In a treaty between Rome and Hieron II in 263 BC Akrai was assigned to Diodorus Siculus of Syracuse. There followed its period of greatest splendour, and its main monuments, including the theatre, were built at this time. It had a conspicuous Christian community, and was destroyed in the 9C by the Arabs. The name 'Palazzolo' was probably added some time in the 12C. It was governed from 1374 for two centuries by the Alagona family. It was damaged by earthquake in 1693 and bombed by the Allies in 1943 (with 700 casualties).

Just outside the town is the CIMITERO MONUMENTALE, an unexpected site, with elaborate funerary monuments erected in the mid 19C. In the lower town are the Duomo (recently restored but kept locked) next to SAN PAOLO, with a good *façade perhaps by Vincenzo Sinatra. In the interior are two late-19C carved thrones used for transporting a 16C statue of the saint and his relics in procession. The charming sacristy dates from 1778 with a pretty vault and its original furniture.

In Piazza Umberto I, nearby, is the red 18C Palazzo Zocco, with a decorative long balcony. A road leads downhill from the piazza towards the edge of the town and the church of the ANNUNZIATA, with a lovely 18C portal decorated with four twisted columns and vines and festoons of fruit. In the white interior, covered with stuccoes, is a fine high altar in pietre dure. The Annunciation by Antonello da Messina, now in Palazzo Bellomo in Syracuse, was commissioned for this church in 1474. From Piazza Umberto I Via Garibaldi leads uphill past Palazzo Caruso (No. 127), with monsters' heads beneath its balcony. Further uphill, after a flight of steps, is Palazzo Ferla with four good balconies. The Museo Archeologico in Via Gaetano Italia has been closed for many years.

The centre of the busier and more attractive upper part of the town is Piazza del Popolo. Here is the 18C church of SAN SEBASTIANO, with a scenographic façade and a portal by Paolo Labisi. In the interior is a painting of St Margaret of Cortona by Vito d'Anna (fourth N altar). The Town Hall dates from 1808. In Corso Vittorio Emanuele the 19C Palazzo Judica has an eccentric façade with vases on its roof.

Off the parallel Via Carlo Alberto, entered through a courtyard, is the CASA-MUSEO (being restored; but open daily 9–13; ring), a delightful local ethnographical museum created by the late Antonino Uccello and displayed in his 17C house. It was acquired by the Sicilian Region in 1983. The interesting material from the provinces of Syracuse and Ragusa includes farming utensils and implements, household objects, puppets, terracotta statuettes, etc., beautifully displayed. An oil press and a press used for making honey are also preserved here.

At the top of the road is San Michele, propped up with scaffolding. Via Acre continues uphill to the church of the IMMACOLATA with a convex façade, difficult to see, as the church is now entered through the courtyard at the E end (ring at the central door, at the house of the custodian of a school). It contains a *Madonna by Francesco Laurana.

Above the Immacolata a road continues up to the entrance to the Greek remains of **Akrai** (open daily 9–dusk), the first colony founded by Syracuse (663 BC). It is a beautifully kept site, although part of it is at present inaccessible. Excavations began here in 1824, and were continued in this century. The small *THEATRE, built in the late 3C BC, is well preserved. The scena was altered in Roman times, and in 600 AD a mill with round silos was built over the ruins. Nearby is an altar for sacrifices. Behind the theatre is the BOULEUTERION, a tiny council chamber (connected to the theatre by a passageway). From here (through a locked double gate) there is a good view of the recent excavations of the ancient city. There is a long stretch of the DECUMANUS constructed in lava (altered by the Romans), and parts of another road at right angles which passes close to a circular TEMPLE. Probably dedicated to Persephone, it is thought to date from the 3C BC. It was covered by a cupola with a circular opening in the centre, supported on girders of terracotta (no longer in situ, but preserved); the holes for them are visible in the circular walls, and the pavement survives. Excavations continue here in the area thought to have been the Agora.

The rest of the enclosure consists of a depression between two LATOMIE, or stone-quarries, showing traces of a Heroic cult and of later Christian occupation. On the face of the smaller latomia, nearest to the path, can be seen niches (formerly closed with commemorative plaques carved with reliefs and inscriptions) and an interesting funerary bas-relief of c 200 BC, showing two scenes, one Roman, with a warrior sacrificing, and one Greek, with a banquet scene. Farther on (at present kept locked) are extensive Byzantine CATACOMBS carved into the rock (some of them adapted by the Arabs as dwellings). The larger family chapels are decorated with unusual lattice-work transennae. From the other path can be seen the larger latomia, and near the theatre a monumental gateway. Beyond a locked gate is the basement of a TEMPLE OF APHRODITE. A 'strada panoramica' (above the entrance gate) circles the top of the Acropolis, with traces of its fortification walls. It gives a splendid idea of the site, and has wide *views.

On request, at the entrance gate, a custodian will accompany visitors (in their car) to visit the so-called ***Santoni**, interesting statues of Cybele, carved in a rock face. The road goes down the hill to the Ragusa road, off which a paved byroad (left) ends beside a gate (unlocked by the custodian). Steps continue down past 12 remarkable life-size statues dating from around the 3C BC representing the goddess Cybele, hewn out of the rock (protected by wooden huts). The goddess is shown between the two dioscuri on horseback; with Marsyas, Hermes, and other divinities; with her daughter Persephone; seated and flanked by two little lions; etc. They are extremely worn, and were wilfully disfigured in this century. There was a sanctuary here near a spring on the road to the necropolis across the valley from the city. It was reached via the TEMPLI FERALI, on the E side of the hill, in a vertical cliff. These temples of the dead, containing Greek inscriptions and votive niches survive, but it is not at present possible to visit them.

FROM PALAZZOLO ACREIDE TO GRAMMICHELE, 45km. A road corkscrews across the Anapo valley, with (8km) the hill town of BUSCEMI, rebuilt after 1693, on the right. 10km, junction with N124 (which leads right for Cassaro and Ferla, see Rte 22E). It continues across the barren PIANA DI BUCCHERI (820m), with Monte Lauro (986m), the highest point of the Monte Iblei, on the left, and a view of Etna to the N. Beyond (14km) BUCCHERI (820m), another little 18C town, it continues to (28km) Vizzini and (45km) Grammichele, both described in Rte 18.

E. Pantalica and the Valle dell'Anapo

The Valle dell'Anapo and Pantalica are reached from Syracuse by car via Floridia and Ferla; the road from Syracuse via Sortino has not been completed. The only public transport available from Syracuse is the bus to Sortino which is at least 5km from Pantalica.

FROM SYRACUSE TO THE VALLE DELL'ANAPO AND PANTALICA, N124, 56km. The road crosses the Anapo by Ponte Capocorso and leads straight to (12km) **Floridia** (19,400 inhab.), founded in 1628, with 18C churches. The Madonna delle Grazie was built by the Spaniards to celebrate the victory of 1720 over the Austrians. The road now climbs past huge carob trees to (16km) SOLARINO, founded in 1759 with a handsome neo-classical palace on the left of the road. A byroad (signposted) leads right for **Sortino** (20km), rebuilt after the earthquake of 1693, with interesting 18C churches. This byroad, 6km before reaching Sortino, passes an entrance to the Valle dell'Anapo (described below).

The main road now ascends steeply along a plateau to the S of the Anapo valley through pretty countryside with attractive farmhouses and low stone walls. Many of the fields are uncultivated and the barren landscape is dominated by huge carobs and olives. In the area are Byzantine tombs and caves showing evidence of Neolithic and Bronze Age occupation. 30km, turn for Cassaro and Ferla (N124 continues for another 12km into Palazzolo Acreide, described in Rte 22D). The Ferla road traverses uncultivated fields and passes numerous farm houses, all of identical design, built by the Fascist government of Mussolini. It then descends steeply into (36km) the Valle dell'Anapo. Beyond (44km) FERLA, a byroad ends at (56km) Pantalica.

The road from Syracuse to Ferla (described above) descends steeply into the Anapo valley and crosses a bridge. Beside the road (36km from Syracuse) is a car-park and a hut owned by the Forestry Commission, at the entrance (signposted) to the **Valle dell'Anapo** (open every day 9–16.30; summer 9–20). This beautiful deep limestone gorge, a protected area since 1988, is run by the Forestry Commission (information office in Buccheri, Tel. 0931/873093; or in Syracuse, Tel. 0931/462452). A map of the paths in the area is available at the hut. No cars are allowed but a van takes visitors for 8km along the rough road on the site of the old narrow-gauge railway track (and its tunnels) which used to run along the floor of the valley (on the Syracuse–Vizzini line).

The lovely vegetation includes ilexes, pines, figs, olives, citrus fruit trees, and poplars. The only buildings to be seen are those once used by the railway company. Horses are bred here, and may one day be used to transport visitors by carriage along the road. Careful replanting is taking place where fires have destroyed the plants. Picnic places, with tables, are provided. The van stops in the centre of the valley from where there is a good view of the tombs of the necropolis of Pantalica (see below) high up at the top of the rock face. There is another entrance to the valley from the

Sortino road (approached from Solarino), where another van accompanies visitors along the valley for some 4km before joining this road.

The road continues towards Ferla passing the site of the little town of Cassaro which moved after the earthquake of 1693 up to the top of the cliff face (seen above the road). On the approach to Ferla are terraces planted with orange trees, prickly pear, and pomegranate, some of which have been allowed to grow wild. FERLA, 44km from Syracuse, is a pretty little town traversed by one long main street which slopes steeply uphill past its four Baroque churches (three of them being restored) and interesting early-20C houses.

Half-way up the main street is the turning (right; signposted) for Pantalica. The lonely road leads for 12km along a ridge through beautiful remote farming country and pine woods to the remarkable prehistoric necropolis of ***Pantalica** (marked by a yellow sign), 56km from Syracuse, in totally deserted countryside. All around can be seen rock tombs carved in the cliffs. The huge unenclosed site is traversed by the road (which ends here) and footpaths (signposted from the road). The deep limestone gorges of the Anapo and Cava Grande almost encircle the plateau of Pantalica, occupied from the 13C to the 8C BC. In this naturally defended site Siculi from the Italian mainland settled c 1270 BC. Their way of life remained virtually unchanged up until the arrival of the Greeks in the second half of the 8C BC. The cliffs of the vast necropolis, the largest and most important in Sicily, are honeycombed with 5000 tombs of varying shape and size. Each cell was the tomb of a family, and there appears to have been an arrangement of the cells in groups. The objects discovered in them, including splendid pottery, are displayed in the Archaeological Museum in Syracuse. The city disappeared after the foundation of the Greek colony of Akrai (see

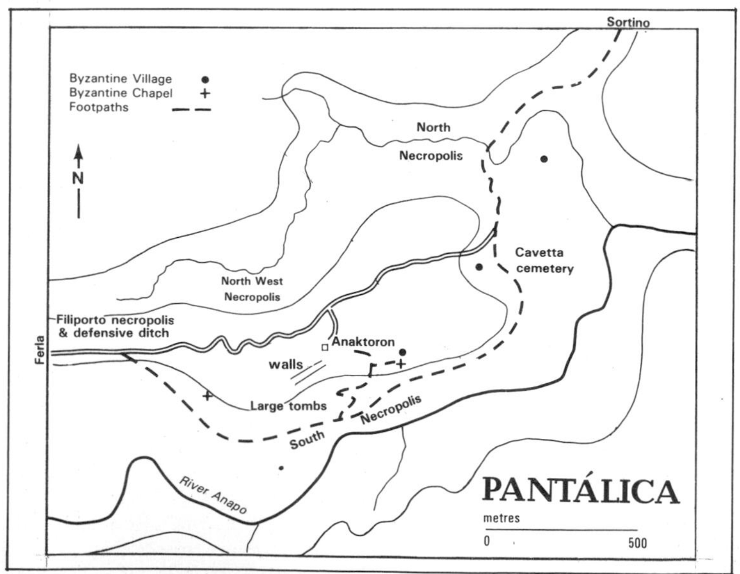

Rte 22D) in 663 BC, and some of the tombs were converted into cave-dwellings during the barbarian invasions, and were later inhabited by Christians.

An easy footpath (signposted 'Villaggio Bizantino') at the beginning of the road leads to a tiny Byzantine oratory carved in the rock (with traces of fresco) known as SAN MICIDIARIO, and the SOUTHERN NECROPOLIS. Off the road, farther on, a track leads up to the top of the hill and the so-called 'ANACTORON', a megalithic palace dating from the late Bronze Age, the foundations of which survive (35m by 11m). Nearby are short sections of wall and a defensive ditch, the only remains of the city, recently identified with the legendary *Hybla* whose king allowed the Megarian colonists to found Megara Hyblaea (see Rte 23). Far below can be seen the Anapo valley (described above), with a white track following the line of the old railway. Farther on, downhill, near the end of the road a signpost indicates the CAVETTA cemetery (9–7C BC), and another Byzantine village. A path leads towards the NORTHERN NECROPOLIS (beyond the stream in the valley). The road ends abruptly and the road from Sortino (see above), which has never been completed, can be seen across the valley. There is a view of Sortino in the distance.

23

Syracuse to Catania

Road, N114, 59.5km.—21km, turning for **Megara Hyblaea**—27km, crossroads for **Augusta** (right) and **Lentini** (left)—59.5km **Catania**. Parts of this road, which carries heavy traffic, are dual carriageway (near Augusta).

Bus ('SAIS'; see Rte 21) from Syracuse to Catania in c 1 hour.

Railway, via Lentini, 87km in c 1 hour.

Beyond the archaeological zone of Neapolis the road traverses the fast-expanding city of Syracuse and crosses the huge terrace once occupied by the ancient city. The road, now motorway, descends past Scala Greca (see Rte 22A) with a view left of the ridge of Epipolae with the Castle of Euryalus prominent, and the tall mast of Belvedere (Rte 22A). Capo San Panagia has been identified with ancient *Trogilus*. Fossils exist in the limestone caves and, in the over-lying clays, there are remains of Neolithic habitation. The shores of the GULF OF AUGUSTA, once lined by the ancient cities of Syracuse, Thapsos, and Megara Hyblaea are now a jungle of oil refineries, and oil tankers are anchored offshore. The industrial zone which grew up in the 1950s extends for 30km from here to Priolo and Augusta, and has the largest concentration of chemical plants in Europe. The 42 industries here (including Montedison, Esso, and Liquichimica) employ tens of thousands of workers. The pollution of the sea has caused the death of marine life, and because of the contaminated air the inhabitants (over 1000) of Marina de Melilli were evacuated in 1979 and the houses razed to the ground. Local protest has led to legal proceedings against those responsible for the pollution.

The road crosses the base of the low-lying peninsula of MAGNISI, the

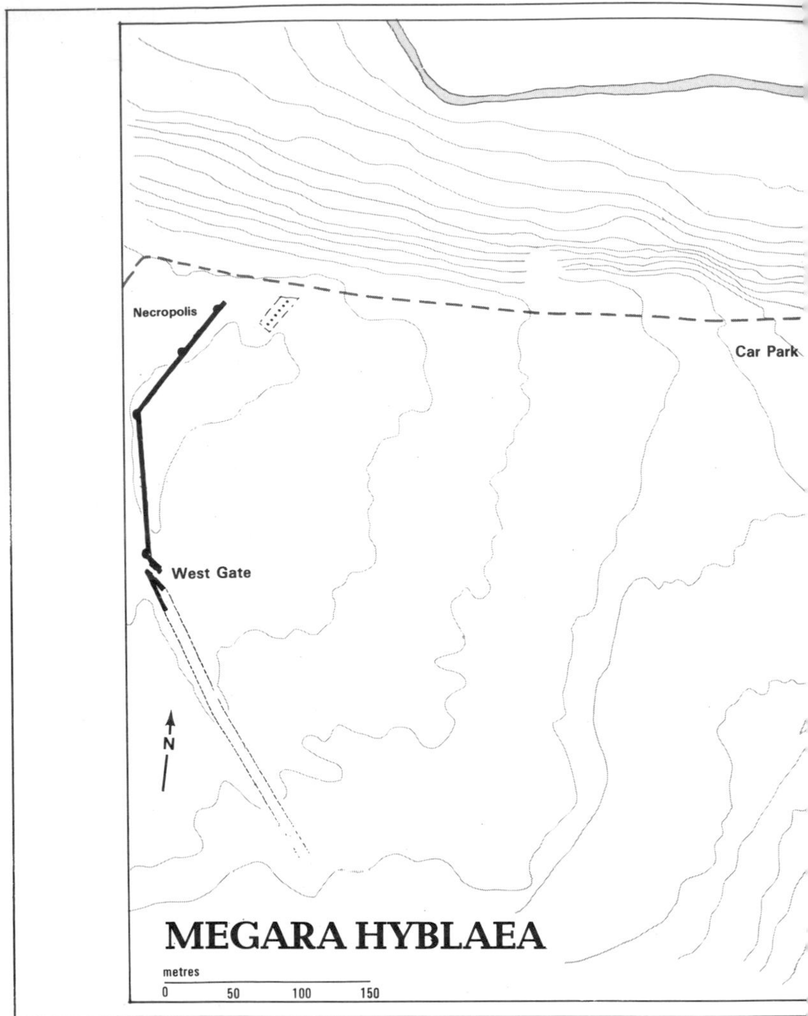

ancient **Thapsos**, under whose N shore the Athenian fleet anchored before the siege of Syracuse. It is almost an island (2km long and 700m wide), since its only connection with the mainland is a sandy isthmus 2.5km long and little more than 100m wide at one point. Near here also the fleet of Marcellus moored during the Roman siege of Syracuse. Finds from its vast necropolis have given name to a Bronze Age culture (cf. the Archaeological Museum in Syracuse) and interesting domed rock tombs line the shore W of the lighthouse. Two Mycenaean vases were found in here in 1974. The inhabited area, where the most recent excavations have taken place, shows three periods of occupation: c 1500–1400 BC, characterised by round huts; c 1300–1200 BC where the square houses are of the Mycenean type (a

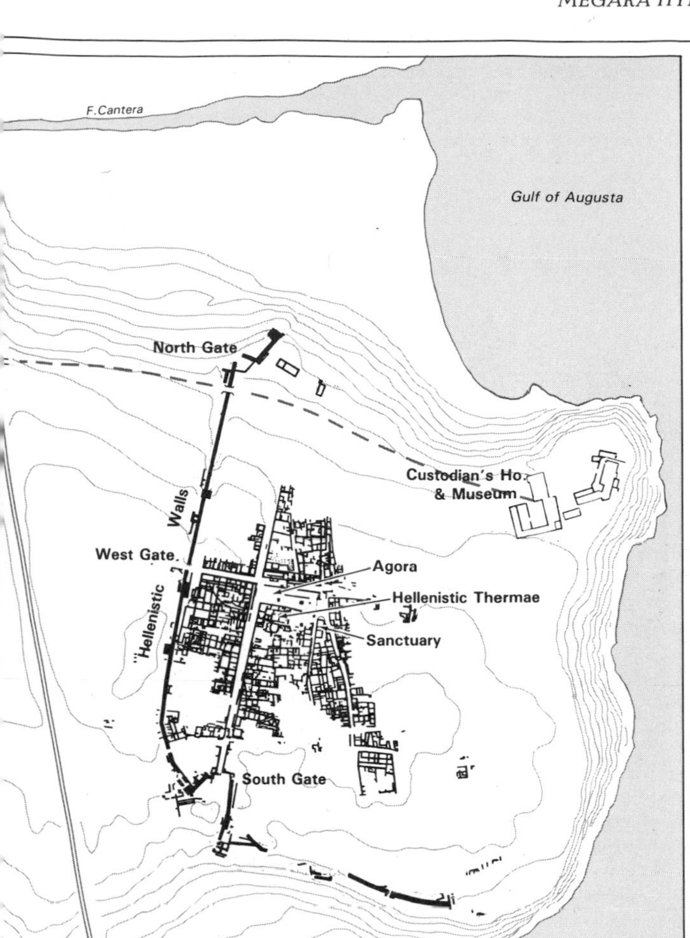

bronze bar with figures of a dog and fox, unique in prehistoric Sicily, and thought to be of Aegean origin, was found here); and a final period c 1100–900 BC, with finds of remarkable pottery (now in the Archaeological Museum in Syracuse).

Beyond the large port of (14km) PRIOLO, there is a view ahead of Etna. A fast motorway (signposted 'Zona industriale' and 'Catania via Litoreale') diverges right through a jungle of industrial plants. Yellow signposts indicate the way (2km) to the excavations of the ancient city of **Megara Hyblaea** (admission 9–14; fest. 9–13; or at any reasonable time on request at the custodian's house). Founded by the Megarians of Greece towards the end of the 8C BC, it was destroyed by Gelon in 483. A second city was founded by Timoleon in 340 BC, which in its turn was obliterated by the Romans in 214. In c 630 BC Pammilus was invited from Megara in Greece by the settlers to 'found' Selinunte. The site, still being excavated by the French School in Rome, is now surrounded by oil refineries which pollute the air.

The site is approached by a byroad which skirts a citrus fruit plantation behind a wall of cypresses. The road continues right (signposted 'scavi') and here in a group of pines is a stretch of ARCHAIC WALLS (6C BC) with four semicircular towers (a fifth has been destroyed). The walls can be followed on foot for some 250m as far as the ARCHAIC WEST GATE. A number of tombs have been placed near the walls, salvaged from excavations of the two necropoleis which are now covered by industrial plants. The third necropolis was located in the vicinity of these walls. Farther on, below ground level, is an oblong construction with seven bases for columns. Excavated in 1880, it is of uncertain significance. Just before the little bridge over the railway is a car-park; excavations were carried out near here in 1982 to prevent the laying of an oil pipe across the site. Cars can continue over the bridge along a rough road past some abandoned farmhouses.

The road passes over the second line of HELLENISTIC WALLS built around the Hellenistic town (they run along a line of cypresses, see below). To the left of the road here the HELLENISTIC NORTH GATE of the city has been identified near the remains of Archaic walls. The road ends at the custodian's house in a pretty little garden, with a small MUSEUM. Among the local finds here are a tomb with a decorative frieze; and there are excellent plans of the site. The important Archaic sculptures found here are now in the Syracuse Archaeological Museum.

The custodian indicates the path across a field to the main area of excavations: the complicated remains include buildings from both the Archaic and Hellenistic periods (the red iron posts indicate the Archaic areas, and the green posts the Hellenistic buildings). There are plans to restore and label the site. At the intersection of the two main roads is the AGORA, near which are a sanctuary, interesting HELLENISTIC THERMAE with good pavements, and a poorly preserved small DORIC TEMPLE of the 4C (protected by a roof). The main E–W road leads from the Agora to the narrow HELLENISTIC WEST GATE in the walls (with two square towers) along the line of cypresses. Near the gate, on a lower level to the S, are ovens and houses of the Archaic period. The main N–S road ends at the HELLENISTIC SOUTH GATE, a 'pincer' type defence work.

27km, crossroads for Augusta and Lentini. 10km E on the coast lies **Augusta** (2-star hotels), the most important oil port in Italy (cf. above), with 34,700 inhabitants. It stands on a rocky islet connected with the mainland by a long bridge. To the E and W are two capacious harbours, the Porto Xifonio and the Porto Megarese, the latter with two old forts (1595). Augusta was founded by Frederick II in 1232 as a refuge for the inhabitants of Centuripe and Montalbano. In 1269 it was sacked by Philip and Guy de Montfort. It was taken by the French in 1676 after the defeat in the bay of a Dutch fleet under De Ruyter by Admiral Duquesne. De Ruyter was mortally wounded in the action and died a few days later at Syracuse. Augusta was totally destroyed by the earthquake of 1693, and the modern town suffered severe damage from the air in the last war. Another earthquake hit the town and the provinces of Syracuse, Catania, and Ragusa in 1990, leaving 13,000 people homeless.

On the coast to the N (9km) is the ruined castle of BRUCOLI, erected by Giovanni Bastida in 1468. *Trotilon*, one of the oldest Greek settlements on the island, probably stood on the bay of Brucoli which has a vast holiday 'village'.

From the crossroads (cf. above) a road leads left for Carlentini and Lentini (18km). **Carlentini** (11,700 inhab.) was founded in 1551 by Charles V as a summer residence for the people of Lentini (cf. below). It is now an undistinguished town, surrounded by orange plantations, which was very badly damaged in an earthquake in 1990 (many of the inhabitants are still housed in containers, on the road to Agnone Bagni).

A poorly signposted road leads in 1km to the site of the Greek city of **Leontinoi** (open daily 9–14), founded by the Chalcidians of Naxos, in 730–728 BC, on the site of an earlier Sicel settlement. In the 6C BC Panaetius set himself up as tyrant of Leontinoi, the first such ruler in Sicily. In the early 5C it was taken by Hippocrates of Gela, and soon afterwards succumbed to the Syracusans. In 427 BC it despatched the orator Gorgias (480–c 380) to invoke the assistance of Athens against her tyrants. Hieronymus, the last native tyrant of Syracuse, was assassinated at Leontinoi in 215 BC. The excavations are in a nicely planted and well kept site. A path leads down from the entrance to the elaborate SOUTH GATE. Across the valley steps lead up to a path which skirts the walls to the top of the hill, from which there is a fine view of the site and the surrounding hills. The site of the prehistoric settlement, with a NECROPOLIS (6C–4C BC), and hut village, are not at present open to the public.

The road descends from the hills N to **Lentini**, an unattractive agricultural centre (31,700 inhab.). The medieval town was destroyed in the earthquake of 1693, and the modern town was again badly shaken in 1990. The CHIESA MADRE preserves an icon thought to date from the 9C. The churches of San Luca and Santissima Trinità have interesting 16C paintings. The MUSEO ARCHEOLOGICO (poorly signposted; open daily 9–14) has a well-arranged collection of local finds including three fine calyx-kraters, and a reconstruction of the South Gate of the ancient city.

N194 continues SW from Lentini towards Comiso. It bypasses **Francofonte** (14,200 inhab.), a hill town, damaged in 1990, where the Municipio occupies the 18C Palazzo Palagonia adjoining the medieval castle.

A road (16.5km) continues N from Lentini to rejoin this route at Ponte Primosole (cf. below).

35km AGNONE BAGNI. Near the railway station of Agnone di Siracusa, a little inland, are the remains of the Cistercian church of Roccadia, founded at Lentini in 1176, and moved here in 1224 by Frederick II. It was left unfinished, and the apse was fitted up as a church in 1707; since then it has been used mostly as a wine cellar. Just before (46.5km) Ponte Primosole the old road from Catania diverges left via Lentini (cf. above). Here begins the fertile PLAIN OF CATANIA, known to the Greeks as the 'Laestrygonian Fields', the home of the cannibal Laestrygones. Its vast citrus fruit plantations are watered by the Simeto and its tributaries, the Dittaino and the Gornalunga. The mouth of the Simeto, once an oasis for migratory birds, is now covered with new holiday villas. On its left bank stood the town of *Symaethus*, whose necropolis survives on the Turrazza estate. 59.5km **Catania**.

24

Catania

CATANIA, the most important town (376,000 inhab.) in Sicily after Palermo, stands at the S foot of Etna, by the eruptions of which it has been several times ruined. The spacious appearance of the centre, with long straight streets of imposing buildings, dates from the reconstruction that followed the earthquake of 1693. The black lava on which it stands has been used for the paving of the streets and as the material of almost all the buildings. The lava flows which reached the town in 1669 can still be seen from the ring-road ('Circonvallazione'). The most prosperous city on the island, it was known in the 1960s as the 'Milan of the South'. The life of the city has deteriorated drastically in the last two decades due to a chaotic local administration. Since 1980 it has become one of the strongholds of the Mafia on the island. Old Catania can be explored in a day, but the city is a good centre for visiting Etna and its foothills. It has a temperate winter climate. **Plan on p 7 of atlas section**.

Information Offices. 'APT' Catania (Pl. 6), Largo Paisiello (Via Pacini), Tel. 095/312124. Information offices at the Railway Station and the Airport.

Railway Stations. CENTRALE (Pl.8), for all services, on the line to Palermo via Enna (trains in 3½–4hrs) and on the coastal line between Syracuse and Messina (with some through trains to Rome). To Messina, in 1½hrs and to Syracuse in 1hr 20mins. CIRCUMETNEA STATION, Corso delle Provincie, off Corso Italia (Pl. 4), for the Circumetnea line.

Airport at Fontanarossa, 5km S (very poorly signposted). International and national services. AIR TERMINAL, 105 Corso Sicilia (Pl. 7). Bus (No. 24) from the railway station via the air terminal, every 10–15mins to the airport.

Buses. Nos **29** and **36** traverse the city from the station via Via Etnea; No. **24** from the railway station via the Air Terminal and Corso Sicilia to the airport; No. **22** for Ognina; No. **27** for La Plaia (and in summer 'D' from Piazza Verga and Via Etnea for the beaches).

Country Buses run by 'SAIS' from 181 Via d'Amico (Pl. 8) c every hour via the motorway for Palermo (in 2hrs 40mins) and Messina (in 1½hrs); less frequently via the motorway for Enna (in 1½ hours) and Caltanissetta (in 1½hrs); for Syracuse in c 1hr; Taormina (in 45mins–1hr); Agrigento (2½hrs); Noto (2½hrs). Services run by 'AST' from Piazza Giovanni XXIII outside the station (Pl. 8) to Gela, Vittoria, Ragusa, Modica, Noto, and Caltagirone. Buses run by 'Etnatrasporti' (185 Via D'Amico) to: Gela (in 1½hrs); Licata (2hrs 15mins); Piazza Armerina (2½hrs); Aidone (2hrs); Ragusa (2½hrs). For towns at the foot of Mount Etna, see Rte 25. Long-distance daily coach service to Rome (run by 'SAIS') in 11hrs.

Maritime Services. Ferries run by 'Tirrenia', 61 Via Androne. Once a week to Naples and Reggio Calabria, and three times a week to Malta (via Syracuse). HYDROFOILS in summer to Malta (in 3hrs).

Car Parking. Multi-storey car-park in Piazza Grenoble (Pl. 7). Garages in the centre charge reasonable tariffs.

Hotels. 4-star: 'Excelsior' (a; Pl.4), Piazza Giovanni Verga; 'Central Palace' (b; Pl.7), 218 Via Etnea; 'Jolly Trinacria' (c; Pl.3), Piazza Trento. 3-star: 'Moderno' (d; Pl. 10), 9 Via Alessi; 'Villa Dina' (e; Pl. 2), 129 Via Caronda. 2-star: 'Gresi', 28 Via Pacini; 'Centrale Europa', 167 Via Vittorio Emanuele; 'Savona', 210 Via Vittorio Emanuele. On the N outskirts of the city (for those with a car): 3-star 'Nettuno', 121 Viale Ruggero di Lauria (on the lungomare for Ognina). 4-star and 3-star hotels also at Aci-Castello and Acireale, see Rte 26.

Camping Sites. At OGNINA; 'Jonio', 38 Via Acque Casse (2-star); at LIDO DI PLAIA, on S outskirts of the city: 2-star: 'Villaggio Turistico Europeo', 91 Viale Kennedy; 1-star: 'Internazionale La Plaja', 47 Viale Kennedy and 'Villaggio Souvenir', 71 Viale Kennedy. Many other sites on the coast N of Catania.

Restaurants. 1st-class: 'La Cantinaccia', 245 Via Messina; 'Da Rinaldo', 59 Via Simili; 'Don Saro', 129 Viale Libertà, 'Enzo', 26 Via Malta. Simple trattorie: 'La Casalinga', 19 Via Biondi, 'Da Peppino', 43 Via Empedocle, 'Da Turi', 18 Piazza Bove. Outside the centre and at Ognina: Luxury-class: 'Costa Azzurra', 2 Via de Cristoforo; 'La Siciliana', 52 Viale Marco Polo, 'Pagano a Mare', 18 Via Acque Casse (Ognina), and 'Selene', 24 Via Mollica.

Cafés or Bars ('pasticceria'). 'Verona-Bonvegna', Via Asiago; 'Savia' and 'Spinella', Via Etnea (opposite Villa Bellini), 'Mantegna', Via Etnea, 'Ethel', Via Milano.

Picnic places in Villa Bellini.

Theatres. Massimo Bellini (Pl. 11), Piazza Bellini, for opera and concerts; Teatro Stabile Verga (prose performances), 35 Via dello Stadio, Musco, Metropolitan and Ambasciatori. Concerts are also held at the Metropolitan, where, from October–May the 'Associazione Musicale Etnea' give concerts, and there is a Jazz festival in November–April. In summer concerts are given in many of the Baroque churches of the city, and (open-air) in Villa Bellini. The 'APT' will supply information about these, and about PUPPET THEATRE performances.

Annual Festivals. The Festa di St Agatha is celebrated on 3–5 February with a traditional procession and dances.

History. Catania was perhaps a Sicel village when the first Greek colony (Chalcidians from Naxos) established itself here in 729 BC, and, as *Catana*, it soon rose to importance. Charondas (7C, or early 6C) here drew up a written code of laws which was eventually adopted by all the Ionian colonies of Sicily and Magna Graecia; the poet Tisias of Himera, called Stesichorus, died here (c 540); and Xenophanes, the pantheistic philosopher, adopted Catanian citizenship (c 530). Hieron of Syracuse took the city in 476 and exiled the inhabitants to Leontinoi, refounding the town with celebrations for which Aeschylus wrote his 'Women of Aetna'; the exiles returned and drove out his Doric colonists in 461. In 415 it was the base of the Athenian operations against Syracuse, but it fell to Dionysius in 403, when the citizens were sold as slaves. After the defeat of the Syracusan fleet at the Cyclopean Isles by Mago the Carthaginian it was occupied by Himilco. Catania opened its gates to Timoleon in 339 and to Pyrrhus in 278, and was one of the first Sicilian towns to fall to the Romans (263). Its greatest prosperity dated from the time of Augustus who rewarded it for taking his part against Pompey.

In early Christian days Catania was the scene of the martyrdom of St Agatha (238–253), the patroness of the city. In the Middle Ages it was wrecked by an earthquake (1169), sacked by Henry VI (1194), and again by Frederick II (1232), who built the castle to hold his rebellious subjects in check. Constance of Aragon, his empress, died here on 23 June 1222. The 17C saw the calamities of 1669 and 1693, the former the most terrible eruption of Etna in history, the latter a violent earthquake. In 1943 Catania was bombarded from the air and from the sea.

Natives of Catania include Vincenzo Bellini (1801–35), the composer; Giovanni Verga (1840–1922), the novelist; Mario Rapisardi (1844–1912), the poet; Giovanni Pacini (1796–1867), the composer; and Luigi Capuana (1839–1915), the writer. The writer Federico De Roberto (1866–1917) lived most of his life in Catania, and died here. Frederick III of Aragon died at Catania in 1377.

The old centre of the city is the well-proportioned PIAZZA DEL DUOMO (Pl.11). In the middle stands a fountain with an antique lava elephant (which has since become the symbol of Catania) and an Etyptian obelisk that was once perhaps a turning-post in the Roman circus, set up here in 1736 by Giovanni Battista Vaccarini, a native of Catania, who became the official municipal architect in 1730. It is modelled on the monument by Bernini in Piazza Minerva in Rome. The square is surrounded by 18C edifices, mostly by Vaccarini. The MUNICIPIO, begun in 1695 was finished by Vaccarini in 1741.

The **Duomo** (Pl. 11; closed 12.30–17), dedicated to St Agatha, was founded by Count Roger in 1094 and rebuilt after the earthquakes of 1169 and 1693. The granite columns on the lower story of its Baroque FACADE (by Vaccarini, 1736–58) come from the Roman theatre. The CUPOLA, by Battaglia, dates from 1804. The NORTH DOOR, with three statuettes, is attributed to Gian Domenico Mazzola (1577). The structure of the mighty black lava 11C APSES can be seen from No. 159 Via Vittorio Emanuele.

In the INTERIOR, during restoration work in the 1950s, the foundations of the 11–12C basilica were revealed beneath the nave. The fine antique columns (of late Imperial and Byzantine date) in the transepts and three apses have also been uncovered. SOUTH SIDE. Against the second pier is the tomb of Vincenzo Bellini (see below), by Giovanni Battista Tassara; its sole inscription is a well-known phrase from his opera 'La Sonnambula'. The second and third altarpieces are by Borremans. From the S transept a doorway by Giovanni Battista Mazzola (1545) admits to the Norman CAPPELLA DELLA MADONNA which preserves a huge Roman sarcophagus, with the figures (very worn) finely carved in the round, thought to come from Smyrna. It contains the ashes of Frederick II (died 1337), Louis (died 1355), Frederick III (died 1377), and other illustrious members of the House of Aragon. Opposite is the beautiful tomb of Queen Constance of Aragon (died 1363), wife of Frederick III, with contemporary scenes of Catania. The sculptured fragment above the door dates from the 15C.

The corresponding Norman CAPPELLA DEL CROCIFISSO is approached from the N transept through an arch designed by Gian Domenico Mazzola (1563). In the SACRISTY is a fresco painted in 1675 showing the destruction of Catania by the lava flow from Etna in 1669. On the right of the choir is the CAPPELLA DI SANT'AGATA (seen through a grille), containing a marble altarpiece (Coronation of the saint); the tomb (right) of the Viceroy Fernandez d'Acuña (died 1494), a kneeling figure attended by a page, by Antonello Freri of Messina; and (left) the treasury, with a rich collection of relics of St Agatha, including her reliquary bust by Giovanni di Bartolo (1376). These are exposed only on the saint's festival (12 February, 17 August, and, in procession, on 4 and 5 February). The stalls in the CHOIR, finely sculpted by Scipione di Guido of Naples (1588), represent the life of St Agatha and the adventures of her dead body. The excavations which exposed the earlier TERME ACHELLIANE, beneath the front of the cathedral, have been closed indefinitely.

Via Vittorio Emanuele II passes between the N side of the cathedral and the Baroque church of SANT'AGATA (open 8–11), another work by Vaccarini (1748–67; the Rococo interior was completed after his death). Beyond in a little piazza is the church of SAN PLACIDO (usually closed) with a façade of 1769 attributed to Stefano Ittar, and a pretty interior.

Via Museo Biscari leads out of the piazza past the huge PALAZZO BISCARI, the most impressive private palace in Catania. Here in the 18C the Prince of Biscari, Ignazio Paternò Castello, collected his famous museum, part of which is preserved in the Museo Civico (see below). The finest decoration of the exterior can be seen from Via Dusmet. In the lovely Rococo Salone della Musica concerts are occasionally held. Via Vittorio Emanuele II continues across Via Landolina (which leads left to the splendid TEATRO MASSIMO BELLINI, 1873–90) to the COLLEGIO CUTELLI (left), with a remarkable round courtyard designed by Vaccarini (1779). It ends in Piazza dei

Martiri, where a statue of St Agatha surmounts a column from the ancient theatre. Here a wide terrace overlooks the harbour.

From the N side of Piazza Duomo (see above) begins the handsome **Via Etnea**, nearly 3km long, the main street of the city (closed to private cars S of Villa Bellini), with numerous shops and some cafés, and always crowded. It rises to a splendid view of the peak of Mount Etna in the distance. Beyond the Municipio is the distinguished Piazza dell'Università, laid out by Vaccarini. The UNIVERSITY (Pl. 11) was founded in 1434 by Alfonso V of Aragon as the first university in Sicily, and rebuilt after the earthquake of 1693; the court was begun by Andrea Amato and finished in 1752 by Giovanni Battista Vaccarini. Just beyond is the COLLEGIATA, a royal chapel of c 1768 by Stefano Ittar. Via Etnea continues N to Piazza Stesicoro (see below).

The vista on the S side of Piazza Duomo is closed by the fine PORTA UZEDA (1696) which leads to a public garden and beyond to the harbour. Here a marble fountain (1867) closes the entrance to the characteristic meat market; the busy fish market is centred round a 16C archway farther S. Via Gemelli leads past a Baroque palace (right) to the simple little church of SANTA MARIA DELL'INDIRIZZO (Pl. 11). Behind it, in the courtyard of a school with a palm tree (seen from behind the railings) are the remains of Roman baths and a tiny domed Greek-cross building in black lava.

Via Auteri leads S to Piazza Federico di Svevia, where low houses surround the **Castello Ursino** (Pl. 14) built for Frederick II by Riccardo da Lentini. This was partly destroyed by the lava of 1669, which completely surrounded it, hardening into a natural esplanade. The castle was restored after 1837 and now houses the **Museo Civico** (closed since 1988), in which material taken from the monastery of San Nicolò was augmented by the archaeological treasure collected by the Prince of Biscari (cf. above) in the 18C. The arrangement will probably change and the description given below no longer be accurate when the museum reopens after much needed restoration.

From the fine HALL (see below) is the entrance (right) to **Room I** which contains architectural fragments from the Roman theatre. **RIII**, a fine vaulted hall, displays Roman and Hellenistic sculpture: (in the centre) sleeping nymph (2–3C AD); Eros riding a dolphin; torso of a Roman emperor; (at the end of the room) fragment of a commemorative column with reliefs of horsemen (1C AD); heads of Aphrodite and Roman portrait busts. **RIV**. Funerary reliefs; statuette of Dionysius (4C BC); two heads of Zeus (copies of 4C and 5C BC works); fine archaic head of 6–5C BC from Lentini (possibly belonging to the torso in the archaeological museum in Syracuse); mosaic pavement with the months of the year.

The ENTRANCE HALL exhibits arms and armour. **RXII**. 18C portrait busts, many copies of Roman works, and a series of dignitaries of Paternò. The octagon tower (**RXIII**), with a fine vault, contains more 18C sculpture, and a statuette of Aphrodite in basalt and onyx. **RXI**. Fine 14C tombstone of a woman, and of a young knight (16C); bust of an abbot, by Vitto Maria Amico (18C); 16C bust of a gentleman; statuette of St John Baptist by Domenico Gagini. Sculptural fragments from Catanian churches, including 14C and 15C funerary monuments, and a Romanesque font, are displayed in **RX**. **RIX**. Cinerary urns; Roman portrait heads (including women of the Trajan era). **RVII**. Inscriptions and Roman mosaics of 2C AD; head of a boy (3C). The second octagon tower (**RVIII**) displays Christian frescoes of Old and

New Testament subjects, and Byzantine candle-holders. A fine courtyard contains sculptural fragments and sarcophagi.

From the courtyard steps ascend to the FIRST FLOOR. **RXV** (Salone dei Paramenti) contains paintings: Gherardo delle Notti, Derision of Christ; Ribera (attributed), Deposition; Pietro Novelli, St Christopher; Domenico Feti, Melancholy; Van Dyck (attributed), St Sebastian; Simon de Worbrecht, Adoration of the Magi (signed and dated 1585). **RXVI** houses the interesting collection of Baron Zappalà Asmundo: Domenico Morelli, Death of Tasso (sketch); portraits by Mancini; Lorenzo di Credi, Madonna and Child; Giuseppe Sciuti, Visit of the Nurse; Spanish school, portrait of a lady; Sebastiano Guzzone, shepherd boy. In this room are exhibited two precious violins of Amati, and ceramics, including Sicilian and Capodimonte ware. **RXVIII**. Engravings, many of old Catania. The museum also contains a prehistoric collection, Greek ceramics, 17C bronzes, and 18C costumes.

Via Auteri, near the submerged railway line, leads out of the Piazza and crosses Via Gisira, scene of a daily street market, before reaching PIAZZA MAZZINI, charmingly arcaded with 32 columns from the Roman basilica (beneath Sant'Agostino; Pl. 10). The busy Via Garibaldi leads W in c 1km to the Baroque PORTA GARIBALDI (1768). To the N, across Via Vittorio Emanuele, is Piazza San Francesco (Pl. 10), where a large votive deposit of 6C BC pottery came to light in 1959. Facing the Baroque façade of San Francesco is the **Museo Belliniano** (open 9–13.30; fest. 9–12.30), Bellini's birthplace, with a charming small museum which contains mementoes of the composer. It preserves the original scores of 'Adelson e Salvini', 'I Capuleti ed i Montecchi' and 'I Puritani', besides fragments of all the remaining operas. The music library is open to students.

The handsome long, straight Via Vittorio Emanuele, with a number of Baroque church façades, continues W. On the left, in the short Via Sant'Anna (Pl.10), is VERGA'S HOUSE (No. 8; on the second floor approached by the stairs on the left). This charming little apartment (open weekdays 9–13), where Giovanni Verga lived and died in 1922, preserves many of its original furnishings including the writer's study, library and bedroom. It was bought and restored by the State and opened to the public in 1984. Autograph works preserved here include the manuscripts for 'I Malavoglia', 'Cavalleria Rusticana', and 'Mastro-don Gesualdo'.

On the other side of Via Vittorio Emanuele (No. 266) is the inconspicuous entrance to the **Teatro Romano** (Pl. 10; open daily 8–17; fest. 8–14), overlooked by houses. This is a Roman building on the site of the theatre where Alcibiades harangued the men of Catania to win them to the cause of Athens (415 BC). It has been restored and tidied up.The building is of lava, practically all of the marble facing having disappeared. The underground passageways which gave access to the cavea are well preserved. The cavea has nine wedges of seats in two main tiers; the diameter was 86m, the depth of the orchestra 29m. Adjoining was the small ODEION, a semicircular building used for the rehearsals of the chorus and for competitions. One colonnade of the FORO ROMANO (no admission) remains near Piazza San Pantaleone, to the SW. Via Sant'Agostino (with a view of the Odeion) leads up to Via Rotonda. Here (behind railings) can be seen remains of Roman baths and the primitive domed church of SANTA MARIA DELLA ROTONDA. Many of the adjacent houses have been converted from another bath-house.

From Piazza San Francesco (see above), beyond the arch of San Benedetto

(1702) begins ***Via Crociferi**, the prettiest 18C street in Catania, lined with Baroque churches, convents, and palaces, many of them approached by a short flight of steps. SAN BENEDETTO (left) has a good façade and vestibule of 1762. The pretty interior (entrance in Via San Benedetto; if closed ask at the convent opposite) has an elaborate nuns' choir, a frescoed barrel vault by Giovanni Tuccari (1726), and a good pavement. Opposite, SAN FRANCESCO BORGIA and the large Jesuit college (with four courtyards) are the work of Angelo Italia (1754). Farther on (right) SAN GIULIANO was begun in 1738 and continued by Vaccarini (who is responsible for the façade). In the fine elliptical interior is a 15C painted Crucifix. Next to it is a Baroque palace (No. 30) with a garden of banana trees.

Here Via Gesuiti, with herring-bone paving in large blocks of lava (typical of the side streets of the city), mounts past modest houses to the church of **San Nicolò** (Pl. 10), facing a simple little crescent of houses. This is the largest church in Sicily (105m long, transepts, 42m), rebuilt in 1735 by Francesco Battaglia, probably to the design of Antonino Amato; the striking façade with its gigantic columns was left uncompleted in 1798. The simplicity of the interior emphasises its good proportions; it has been restored, but was temporarily closed in 1993. The meridian line on the floor of the transept dates from 1841. The choir stalls are by Gaetano Francese and Nicolò Bagnasco. The huge organ (2916 pipes) has been partially dismantled for restoration. Its builder, Donato del Piano (died 1775), lies buried beneath. The dome, reached over the roof from the façade, has been closed indefinitely; it provides a good view of the city.

Part of the CONVENT, the largest in Europe after that of Mafra in Portugal, is sometimes shown by the custodian on Sundays. It was almost entirely rebuilt after 1693 to the design of Antonino Amato and his son Andrea; the rich detail of its Baroque ornamentation combines well with its simplicity of line. Of the two main courts, occupied by part of the University, the first is enhanced by a beautiful (enclosed) garden, the second, beyond a monumental neo-classical staircase (1794; by Antonino Battaglia), beautifully restored, has the more graceful arcade. Excavations here have been covered by a protective roof. The remainder of the conventual complex, beyond the apse, is occupied by the MUNICIPAL LIBRARY, one of the most valuable in Sicily, by the important ASTRO-PHYSICAL OBSERVATORY, and by part of the hospital. Outside the convent wall, to the left of the church façade, can be seen some remains of Roman buildings, recently excavated, below ground level (surrounded by railings).

Just out of the Piazza the long straight Via Antonio di Sangiuliano redescends to Via Crociferi which continues N towards the church of the SANTO CARCERE, flanked by a strong defence wall. Incorporated into the Baroque façade is a doorway, with grotesque animal heads, which dates from 1236; it was formerly in the façade of the cathedral. The prison of St Agatha, with a Roman barrel vault, is shown by the custodian. A road leads uphill to Via Maddalena with the entrance to SANT'AGATA LA VETERE which contains the eight 'ceri' of St Agatha carried in procession on her festival. A little to the N is the church of SAN DOMENICO (Pl. 6; open before 9.30 and 17–18.30; ring at the convent next door). It contains a beautiful Madonna by Antonello Gagini (1526), and a painting of St Vincent Ferrer by Olivio Sozzi (1757). Some way to the W, in Via Castromarina, in a poor district of the town, a tiny MOSQUE (Pl. 5; open 11–13; Fridays also 17–19) was built in 1980.

The 18C church of San Biagio faces the huge PIAZZA STESICORO (Pl. 6,7), the heart of modern Catania, with a monument to Bellini by Monteverde (1882). Here are the scant ruins of the **amphitheatre** in black lava, thought to date from the 2C AD. The external circumference was 389m, and the arena was one of the largest after the Colosseum in Rome. There were 56 entrance arches. The visible remains include a corridor, part of the exterior wall, and fragments of the cavea supported on vaults; the rest of the structure still exists in part beneath the surrounding edifices. Its destruction had already begun under Theodoric when it was used as a quarry; Totila made use of the stone in building the city walls in 530, and Count Roger stole its decorative elements to embellish his cathedral in 1091. In 1693 the municipality used the area as a dump for the ruins of the earthquake. Nearby, in Piazza della Borsa are remains of the 18C church of SANT'EUPLIO covering a 3C Roman hypogeum. It was partially restored in 1978 after its destruction in 1943 (for admission to the crypt apply at the Municipio).

Via Etnea (cf. above) runs through Piazza Stesicoro. To the N beyond the Post Office, steps lead up to the charming **Villa Bellini** (Pl. 2), a fine public garden laid out c 1870, crowded on sunny days. It contains a bust of Bellini and a monument to Giovanni Pacini (1796–1867), another Catanese musician. At the N end of the garden a gate leads out to Viale Regina Margherita, part of the modern E–W artery of the city, c 5km long.

To the N is a good BOTANICAL GARDEN (Pl. 2; open weekdays 9–13). The main entrance is on Via Etnea; but the usual entrance is on Via Longo. It is particularly famous for its cacti plants. About 500m W, surrounded by tall modern apartment blocks, is the church of SANTA MARIA DI GESÙ (Pl. 1), founded in 1442 and built in 1465. To the left is the pretty exterior of the Cappella Paternò which survived the earthquake of 1693. It is entered from the N aisle of the church through a doorway by Antonello Gagini (1519) with a Pietà in the lunette above. Inside is a fresco (transferred to wood) of the Madonna with St Agatha and St Catherine, by Angelo de Chirico (signed 1525). Above the main altar of the church is a Crucifix by Fra Umile di Petralia, and in the last N chapel, a Madonna with four angels in adoration by Antonello Gagini.

Viale Regina Margherita is continued E beyond Via Etnea by Viale Venti Settembre which runs into Piazza Giovanni Verga, a vast square dominated by PALAZZO DI GIUSTIZIA (Pl. 3; 1952) and the focus of a new and fashionable district. Farther E, in Corso Italia, PALAZZO DELLE SCIENZE (Pl. 4; 1942) houses the geological and volcanological collections (for admission apply at university) of the university. The Corso, passing close to the STAZIONE CIRCUMETNEA, terminates at the sea in Piazza Europa, with a shrine on top of a mound of lava. Via Lungomare leads from here through new housing to Ognina.

Via Etnea returns from Viale Regina Margherita towards the centre of the city. Beyond the Post Office Via Pacini leads left to Piazza Carlo Alberto (Pl. 7) filled with a daily market. The little church of SAN GAETANO ALLE GROTTE dates from 1700. The former church, built into a volcanic cavern beneath in 1262, has been made accessible (shown by custodian; offering). Photographs in the upper church of the contemporary frescoes help visitors identify them on the much ruined walls below, where the ancient altar survives. The Lucchesi-Palli barracks occupy a fine palazzo nearby; in the court an antique cella is pointed out as the tomb of Stesichorus.

25

Mount Etna and its foothills

A. Etna

****MOUNT ETNA**, to the NW of Catania, the highest volcano (c 3330m) in Europe and one of the largest in the world, forms a circular cone nearly 40km in diameter. From a distance it appears almost perfectly regular in shape (and the great width of its base detracts from its height); really the terminal cone with its crater rises from a truncated cone 2801m high on whose sides are c 200 groups of subsidiary craters. The latter are formed by lateral eruptions (one in 1971 opened three more craters) and are nearly always arranged along a regular line of fracture. On the SE side is a tremendous cleft, called the VALLE DEL BOVE, with precipitous sides 600–1200m high and strangely shaped volcanic dykes that look almost as though formed by artificial means. During the eruptions of 1978–79, 1986, and 1992 the lava flowed into this huge natural reservoir, thus avoiding the towns on the SE slopes. In 1981 Etna was designated a protected area in an attempt to preserve its unique vegetation and prohibit more new buildings; it S slopes have been covered in the last 20 years by holiday villas. In 1987 some 50,000 hectares of the mountainside were at last declared a National Park. **Plan on page 7 of the atlas section**.

History. Etna, called Aetna by the ancients and MONGIBELLO (from Monte and Jebel, the Arabic word for mountain) by the Sicilians (often simply 'La Montagna'), probably originated from a submarine eruption in the gulf that is now represented by the Piana di Catania. Some 130 eruptions have taken place in historical times. In ancient Greece it was held to be the forge of Vulcan or of the Cyclopes, or the mountain from beneath which the imprisoned Titan, Enceladus, for ever struggled to free himself. Empedocles was said to have thrown himself into the crater to create the belief that he was a god, but the mystery of his disappearance was revealed when the volcano cast up one of his bronze sandals.

Among early eruptions that of 475 BC has been described by Pindar and Aeschylus, while that of 396, whose lava reached the sea, is said to have prevented Himilco from marching on Syracuse. Hadrian climbed Etna to see the sunrise and the conical shape of the mountain reflected on the island. In 1169, 1329, and 1381 the lava again reached the sea, twice near Acireale, the third time (1381) at Catania.

The most famous of more recent eruptions took place in 1669 when an open cleft extended from the summit to Nicolosi and part of Catania was overwhelmed. The Monti Rossi were formed at this date. Since 1800 there have been some 30 eruptions, that of 1923 being the most destructive of the present century. Gladstone ascended the volcano in 1838 and has left a graphic account in his journal.

In 1847 Edward Lear wrote: 'From Catania we saw Etna and went up it; a task, but now it is done I am glad I did it; such extremes of heat and cold at once I never thought it possible to feel.'

In 1908 a huge pit opened in the Valle del Bove, from which lava streamed for 17 hours, reaching a distance of 5km; in 1910 a larger cleft appeared N of the Cantoniera at the foot of Monte Castellazzo. The six cones of the Monti Ricco (called after the then Director of the Observatory) were formed, and the lava descended to within 3km of Nicolosi. In 1911 there were two eruptions on the N side, creating a cleft 5km long and about 170 temporary craters; the double stream of lava interrupted the railway line near Castiglione. In May 1923 lava began to flow from the cleft of 1911, and in June a new cleft 9.5km long opened at the base of Monte Nero. A crater E of Monti Umberto e Margherita and others to the SE and S of Monte Nero poured out lava at a tremendous speed, which threatened to overwhelm Linguaglossa. It halted, however, at the Piano Miceli, having destroyed the railway stations of Castiglione and Cerro, the village of Cerro, and part of Catena. In 1928 a lava-stream destroyed a few hundred metres of the Ferrovia Circumetnea, overwhelmed the village of Mascali, and interrupted the railway from Catania to Messina. The eruption of 1947 threatened Passopisciaro, and that of 1950—51 menaced Rinazzo and Fornazzo before the lava halted.

The 1971 eruption destroyed the observatory and the second stage of the cableway on the summit, as well as vineyards and some houses near Fornazzo. The lava-stream cut several roads, and stopped just above Sant'Alfio. Eruptions on the Western slopes at a height of 1600m and 2850m took place in 1974–75. In 1978–79 four new cones erupted and the lava flowed into the Valle del Bove; the town of Fornazzo was again threatened. Nine people were killed by an explosion on the edge of the main crater itself in 1979. An eruption in 1981 caused considerable damage around Randazzo, crossing the main road for Linguaglossa. In the spring of 1983 activity started up on the opposite side of the mountain above Nicolosi and Belpasso (in the area of the 1910 lava flow). The main road up the S slopes from Nicolosi was damaged and the cableway above the Rifugio Sapienza. After several months dynamite was exploded in an attempt to divert the lava stream. In 1984 an earthquake damaged the little town of Zafferana Etnea, and in 1986 eruptions took place on the SE side near Milo; no damage was caused as the lava flowed into the Valle del Bove. In 1987 two people were killed by an explosion on the edge of the main crater. In 1991/2 eruptions took place for four months and threatened the town of Zafferana Etnea. Dynamite was exploded and huge blocks of reinforced concrete dropped from helicopters in an attempt to arrest the flow and divert it into the Valle del Bove. The lava halted within one kilometre of Zafferana Etnea.

Vegetation. Enormous quantities of lava having poured out of the craters at various dates (156,000 cubic metres in 1908; 28,317,000 cubic metres in 1669; 31,148,000 cubic metres in a prehistoric flow near Randazzo), the soil at the foot of Etna is extraordinarily fertile. In the cultivated zone (pedemontana) oranges and lemons are grown behind low, black, lava walls, on which poinsettias and bougainvillea grow wild. Higher up are groves of walnuts, cherries, apples, pistacchio, almonds and vineyards. At 1300m forest trees grow, especially oaks, chestnuts, pines and beeches. Above 2000m extends the 'desert zone', with a few junipers, and the spino santo (*Astragalus aetnensis*), which collects little heaps of earth round it, affording protection to a few violets in spring, and crocuses in autumn. An unusual lichen flourishes in the hot vapour of the large fumarole near where the observatory used to stand. Animal life is scarce. The heat of the rocks and the hot vapours of the terminal cone cause the snow to melt partly even in

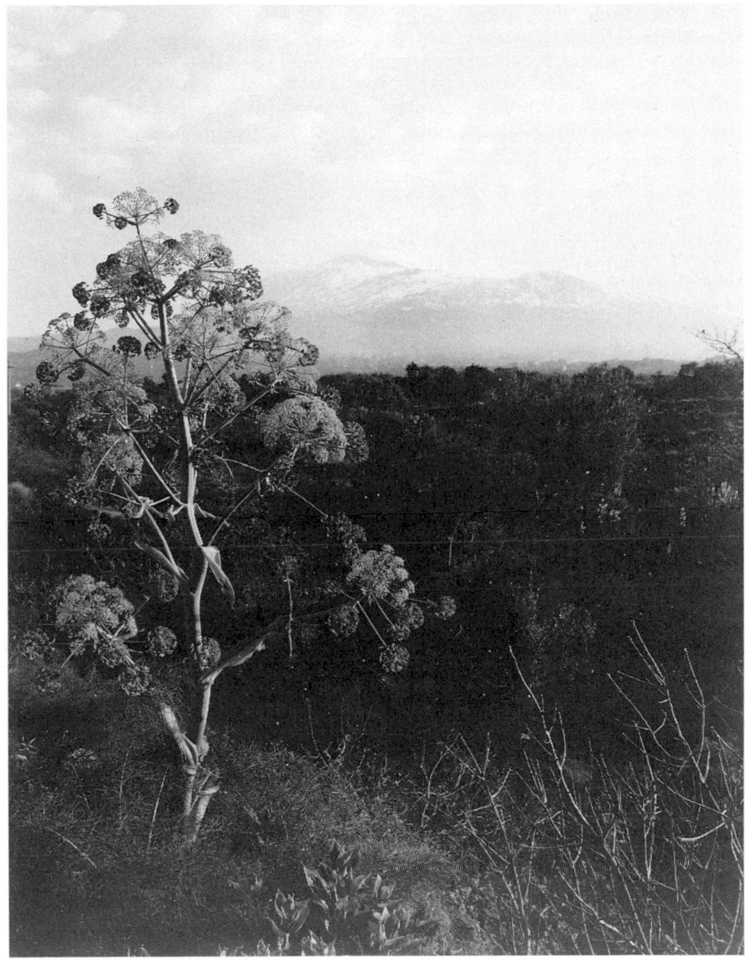

Mount Etna from the west

winter. In certain depressions with a N aspect the snow used to be preserved for refrigeration purposes throughout the summer by covering it with volcanic ash, and it was transported on mule-back in the eastern part of the island.

The ***Ascent of Etna**, although now easy and commonplace, is an experience which should not be missed, both because of the volcanic phenomena and the superb view. The extent of a visit is subject to the current volcanic activity, and the visibility determined by cloud conditions and the direction of the smoke from the main crater. Normally, however, it is possible to see smoking and gaseous craters and fissures, the main crater with its crumbling sulphurous edge and thick smoke, and sometimes even explosions. There is usually a strong smell of sulphur and much of the mountain-side is covered by yellow sulphur patches. The view, beyond the mountain's hundreds of subsidiary cones and craters, can extend across the whole of Sicily, the Aeolian Islands, and Calabria. The spectacle is unique owing to the enormous difference in height between Etna and the surrounding hills.

Information Offices. 'SITAS' at the Rifugio Sapienza (Tel. 095/914141) and at Nicolosi (45 Piazza Vittorio Emanuele, Tel. 095/911158).

Timetable. The journey by car (or bus; see below for times) from Catania to the Rifugio Sapienza (1910m) and back may be made easily in a day, and is strongly recommended. From the refuge a cableway climbs to a height of 2600m; the summit can be reached by jeep excursions in summer. The night can also be spent at the Rifugio Sapienza (114 beds), where night excursions can be arranged (by previous appointment; Tel. 095/914141), in order to see the red-hot lava glowing inside the crater, and the sunrise.

Ascent by foot. Before undertaking the climb advice must be obtained about weather conditions, etc. at the 'SITAS' offices at the Rifugio Sapienza, or at Catania (64 Via Vecchia Ognina), Nicolosi or Linguaglossa (where guides are available to accompany walkers). The temperature is always chilly, and warm clothing and strong shoes are essential. These can be hired at the Rifugio Sapienza. The easiest and most usual approach from Sapienza follows the jeep track. About 4 hours should be allowed for the return trip from the refuge. The most spectacular time for the ascent is before dawn (cf. above). Walkers are recommended to spend the night at Sapienza.

The Southern Slopes

The first stage of the ascent, from Catania to (34km) the Rifugio Sapienza, is made by car or bus. Every day a bus (run by 'AST') departs at 8am from Piazza Stazione in Catania and takes about 2 hours to reach the Rifugio Sapienza. In July and August a second service is run by 'AST', leaving Piazza Stazione at 11.15 for Nicolosi where a connecting bus continues to Rifugio Sapienza. A bus returns to Catania from the Rifugio Sapienza every day at 16.

The road leaves Catania by Via Etnea and Piazza Gioeni; the STRADA DELL'ETNA, opened in 1934 by Victor Emmanuel III bears left. 10km Gravina. On the right are the POMICIARI DI SANTA MARIA, craters formed in 1381, and above them the open cleft of that eruption. 11km MASCALUCIA (420m), centre of production of 'del Bosco' wine. At (13.5km) Massa Annunziata (539m), the road skirts the lava of 1669 planted with broom, oaks, and pistachio trees. On the left rises Mompilieri (765m), a prehistoric crater; behind it the Monti Rossi. 16km **Nicolosi** (990m; 3-star hotels 'Biancaneve' and 'Gemmellero', and 2-star camping site 'Etna'), a centre for excursions (5400 inhab.), with a 'SITAS' information office. To the W (reached from the road to Ragalna) are the craters of the MONTI ROSSI (949m). They represent one of the most important subsidiary groups of craters (over 3km round), formed in 1669.

Beyond Nicolosi the road (partly realigned since damage in 1983) climbs through lava-beds and woods, where many houses are being built. It crosses the lava flows of 1886 and 1910; the names of the craters on either side of the road are indicated. 31km, a loop road (left) diverges to the winter-sports fields of **Serra La Nave** (1750m), where much new building has taken place near the pine woods. Several ski-lifts were destroyed in the eruptions of 1983. From here there is one of the closest and best views of the summit, the line of the cableway, and some of the more recent lava-streams. The University OBSERVATORY here may be visited at certain times.

The main road continues to the CASA CONTONIERA (1882m), a small group of restaurants and cafés (and an information office). A little higher up (1910m) the road ends at a huge car-park (invaded with tourist booths) beside the **Rifugio Sapienza**, a refuge. Always open, it has sleeping accommodation, a restaurant, and guides. In the desert of clinker nearby several extinct volcanoes may be explored easily on foot.

At the Rifugio Sapienza tickets are purchased for the excursion to the summit (inclusive of the cableway, jeep ride, and guide). The cableway ascends to a height of c 2600m (in 15 minutes). A jeep continues from the cableway station (where four ski-lifts operate in winter and there is a restaurant) up the slopes of the MONTAGNOLA (2507m), a crater of 1763 through a desert of lapilli, to a height of 3000m (in 20 minutes). This is the site of the second cableway station and the old observatory, both destroyed in the eruption of 1971. The small Torre del Filosofo (2926m), a tower, said to have been the home of Empedocles, but more probably a Roman memorial commemorating Hadrian's climb to the summit, has also been destroyed in recent eruptions. Here guides are available to explore the summit. In good conditions (and in summer only), the jeep continues almost to the summit.

The last part of the climb is made on foot to the edge of the ***Crater** itself, a gulf whose reeking walls are coloured by sublimated chlorides and sulphates. A circuit of the edge is impracticable except for mountaineers. Its depth varies constantly (914m in 1874, 161m in 1897, 244m in 1916). From here Calabria, the Aeolian Isles, and the whole of Sicily may be seen spread out like a relief-map. The fan-like lava flows radiating from the centre are distinctly seen, and the hundreds of subsidiary cones with their great craters. To the SE, beyond the Torre del Filosofo is the CISTERNAZZA, an abyss formed in 1792, and the *VALLE DEL BOVE, an immense chasm, 19km in circumference, bounded on three sides by sheer walls of tufa and lava, in places 900m high.

An alternative descent may be made from the road which leaves the Strada dell'Etna, just S of Monte San Leo, 12.5km below Sapienza. This road continues down to Adrano (and another branch descends to Paternò), see Rte 25B.

The Eastern and Northern Slopes

FROM CATANIA TO LINGUAGLOSSA, 47km. The road runs parallel to the main Catania–Messina road but c 8km farther inland on the slopes of the mountain. Bus to Zafferana (frequent service in c 1 hour, run by 'AST'). Excursions run by 'Circumetnea' (from Piazza Teatro Massimo, Catania) by train and bus to Linguaglossa. Catania is left as for the ascent, but at the Barriera del Bosco the road diverges right, climbing through the villages and vineyards of the S slopes.

At (10.5km) SAN GIOVANNI LA PUNTA (3-star hotel 'Ares') this route crosses a road from Acicastello to Mascalucia. About 3km right is SAN GREGORIO DI CATANIA (2-star hotel 'Villa Fiorita'), which has interesting volcanic caves. The road divides. 16km **Trecastagni** on the upper branch (left), and VIAGRANDE, an equal distance on the lower branch (right), both lie on the Acireale–Nicolosi road. At Trecastagni the Chiesa Madre is perhaps the purest Renaissance building in Sicily, thought to be the work of Antonello Gagini. The Chiesa del Bianco has a good 15C campanile. The roads meet again shortly before (21km) Fleri.

25.5km **Zafferana Etnea** (600m; 3-star hotel 'Airone' and 2-star 'Del Bosco') was damaged by earthquake in 1986, and a lava flow in 1992 reached the outskirts of the town. It is the starting point for climbs towards the Valle del Bove (information office, 343 Via Roma). A road runs W to the Rifugio Sapienza (see above). On the approach to (30km) MILO (3-star camping site 'Mareneve') the huge chasm of the VALLE DEL BOVE may be seen (cf. above), into which the lava from several eruptions poured in 1978–9, in 1986, and again in 1992. A tongue of the lava stream of 1950 is crossed between Rinazzo and (32km) Fornazzo (840m). Near SANT'ALFIO (downhill to the right) is a famous giant *chestnut tree known as the 'Castagno dei Cento Cavalli', with a circumference of over 60m, hundreds of years old. The area was once a forest of chestnuts. A characteristic festival takes place here on 10 May.

At Fornazzo a road called the '**Mareneve**' (18km longer; and interrupted in 1986), diverges left to climb the eastern slopes of Etna before descending to Linguaglossa, reached more directly by the lower road. The mountain road passes beneath the Citelli refuge (12.5km; 1741m; closed after damage in 1983), and continues to PINETA DI LINGUAGLOSSA (18km), with ancient pine woods, of great interest to naturalists. PIANO PROVENZANA is the main ski resort on Etna, with a refuge, and five ski-lifts (1800m and 2300m). In January–April a ski-bus run by 'FCE' ('Ferrovia Circumetnea') leaves Catania on Sundays and fest. at 7am for Piano Provenzana (in 1½ hours), returning at 15.30. From May to October excursions are organised to the crater from the refuge by 'STAR' (233 Via Roma, Linguaglossa, Tel. 095/643180). Information from the 'Pro-Loco' at Linguaglossa, Piazza Annunziata, Tel. 095/643094. On the descent to Linguaglossa (see Rte 25B) the view widens to embrace Piedimonte Etneo and Taormina in the distance.

B. Round Etna

The road and railway round Etna traverse spectacular countryside, with rich vegetation.

Road. 134.5km, N121.—19km **Paternò**—34km **Adrano**. N284—48km Bronte—66km **Randazzo**. N120—85km Linguaglossa—96km Fiumefreddo di Sicilia. From there on N114 to Catania (134.5km), see Rte 26.

The **motorway** from Messina to Catania runs roughly parallel to the route described below from Fiumefreddo; it may be joined at Giarre, shortening the return journey to Catania by c 10km.

Railway. The 'Circumetnea', opened in 1898, provides a classic rail trip (although the line is being modernised). From Catania (Corso delle Provincie; Pl. 4) to Randazzo (74km) in c 2hrs, continuing less frequently to Giarre (114km) in c 1hr more; from there the direct return (30km; poor connections) may be made by the main Messina–Syracuse line (see Rte 26).

Frequent **bus** service from Catania to Paternò and Adrano.

Catania is left by Viale Mario Rapisardi (Pl. 1); the complicated one-way systems are eventually signposted to the Messina motorway. N121 (signposted for Misterbianco) diverges under the motorway ring-road and continues as a fast four-lane highway through the industrial suburbs of MISTERBIANCO. Its unusual name is derived from a Benedictine monastery, the 'monastero bianco', destroyed, together with the town, in 1669. A byroad diverges left for (5km) the village of MOTTA SANT'ANASTASIA perched on a rock, with a fine 11C Norman castle which preserves its crenellations.

The main road crosses the barren lava of 1669 and continues as a fast road to bypass (19km) **Paternò** (225m; 2-star hotel 'Sicilia'), with 46,100 inhabitants, where much new building sprawls at the base of a 14C castle. The austere tower built of volcanic rock commands the wide Simeto valley. Restored in 1900, with a fine hall and frescoed chapel (key at Municipio), the castle is used as a museum. From the terrace there is a fine view. Frederick II of Aragon died near Paternò while journeying to Enna. The churches of San Francesco and Santa Maria della Valle di Giosafat retain Gothic elements.

The bypass continues, now with good views of Etna, past (24km) Santa Maria di Licodia (with vestiges of a Roman aqueduct) and (29km) BIANCAVILLA. The best oranges in Sicily are produced here: beside the extensive orange plantations are fields of olive trees, and hedges of prickly pear.

34km **Adrano** (560m), with 35,000 inhabitants, represents the ancient *Adranon* founded by Dionysius the Elder. Overlooking the huge Giardino della Vittoria (with superb trees) is the ex-monastery of SANTA LUCIA, rebuilt in the 15–16C, and now a school, flanked by the towering façade of its church (1775), with a pretty oval interior.

The fine interior of the CASTLE, a foundation (1070) of Count Roger, is used as a delightful local MUSEUM (admission 8.30–13.30; fest. 9–12). The archaeological section includes prehistoric material from Stentinello and Castelluccio (ground and first floors). On the second floor the later finds from Mendolito (see below) include a hanging Ascos and bronze figurine, 'Il Banchettante' of the 6C BC. In a little Norman chapel, with an apse fresco, is a collection of coins from ancient Adrano. The third floor has paintings, most of them in very poor condition. The CHIESA MADRE has a skeleton campanile in reinforced concrete, left unfinished. The interior, of Norman origin, incorporates 16 basalt columns possibly from a Greek temple. In the N aisle is a painted crucifix of the 15C (much ruined) and a polyptych of the 16C Messina school hangs over the W door.

Remains of the Greek WALLS can be seen in fields outside the town to the E (in Contrada Cartalemi). About 4.5km NW, near the Simeto, are the remains of the walls and S gate of the ancient Sicel town of MENDOLITO. The road ends just before the PONTE DEI SARACENI, a 14C bridge with four unequal arches across the rocky bed of the Simeto. A huge experimental solar energy plant, financed by the European Economic Community, was opened 6km N of Adrano in 1981, in Contrada Contrasto (information office open 9–13, 14–18 except Mondays). CENTURIPE (described in Rte 16), visible across the Simeto valley, is 17km SW of Adrano.

The vegetation now includes pistachio trees as the road crosses several streams of lava short of (48km) **Bronte** (760m), a town of 19,800 inhabitants, where recent new building has obscured the battlemented steeples of its churches, once a characteristic aspect of the town. It gave its name to the dukedom bestowed on Nelson in 1799 by Ferdinand IV. The title and estates passed, by the marriage of Nelson's niece, to the family of Viscount Bridport; conspicuous signposts (for the 'Castello dei Nelson') indicate the way from Bronte to the former family seat which lies 12km to the N at

MANIACE, in a little wooded valley on the Saraceno, a tributary of the Simeto.

The **Castello Maniace** was bought from Viscount Bridport in 1981 by the Comune of Bronte, and it is now open to the public and shown by a custodian (10–13, 14.30–17.30; fest. 10–12.30, 14.30–17.30; closed Mondays). It was founded as a convent in 1173 by Margaret of Navarre, mother of William II, on the spot where George Maniakes defeated the Saracens in 1040, with the help of the Normans and perhaps of Harold Hardrada and the Varangian Guard. In the courtyard is a stone Cross memorial to Nelson. The 13C chapel (good portal) has a Byzantine Madonna and Child and two charming primitive reliefs of the Annunciation. The house, farm, and delightful gardens (with palm trees and cypresses) are shown. The vast estate with plantations of fruit trees was broken up and sold off in 1981. The Scottish writer William Sharp (who also published under the pseudonym Fiona Macleod) died here in 1905 and is buried beneath an Iona cross in the cemetery (shown on request).

B120 continues through a barren landscape, with numerous volcanic deposits, studded with little farm houses built of black lava; the countryside is used for grazing and the cultivation of vineyards. It rejoins the main road just outside (8km) **Randazzo** (see below).

Beyond Bronte the road becomes steeper and the railway tortuous as both surmount the large lava-stream of 1832, reaching summit levels above 945m near (54km) MALETTO, whose sandstone cliff (1140m) is the highest sedimentary rock on Etna (views). The low vineyards in this region produce an excellent red and white wine ('Etna rosso' and 'Etna bianco'). The road leaves the Simeto basin and enters that of the Alcantara near the little seasonal lake of Gurrida.

66km **Randazzo** (765m), above the Alcantara valley, is a lava-built town of great antiquity (11,700 inhab.), that has never in historic times suffered volcanic destruction. Its medieval history resolves itself into a rivalry between the three churches of Santa Maria, San Nicolò, and San Martino, each of which served as cathedral for alternate periods of three years. The parishioners (of Greek, Latin, and Lombard origin) of each church spoke different dialects until the 16C. It was damaged from allied bombs when, in August 1943, the Germans made it the strong-point of their last resistance in the island.

SANTA MARIA, the present cathedral, is a 13C church (attributed without foundation to Leone Cumier), with fine black lava apses and a three-storeyed S portal (approached by two flights of steps) in the Catalan-Gothic style of the 15C. The dome is attributed to Venanzio Marvuglia and the black-and-white tower was badly restored in 1863. The terrace, beyond the sacristy and canonica above a 16C portico, looks out over the Alcantara valley. The interior (1594) has fine black columns and capitals, one of which serves as an altar. Over the S door is a view of the town attributed to Girolamo Alibrandi (15C); over the N door is a fragment of a fresco of the Madonna and Child (13C). Five of the altar-paintings are by Giuseppe Velasquez. The treasury (usually closed) contains a chalice given to the church by Peter I of Aragon.

Via Umberto I leads past the S flank of Santa Maria to Piazza Municipio where the Palazzo Comunale (1610) is being restored. From here the narrow pretty Via degli Archi leads right to SAN NICOLÒ which dates mainly from the 16–17C (damaged in 1943). The apse, however, is original (13C). Inside is a statue of St Nicholas by Antonello Gagini signed and dated 1523.

Outside is an 18C copy of a curious antique figure, thought to symbolise the union of the three parishes (see above). Nearby is Palazzo Finocchiaro (1509). Via Umberto I continues to the district of San Martino, with evident signs of shell fire from the last war. The damaged church of SAN MARTINO preserves its fine 14C *campanile, and, inside, a marble font by Angelo Riccio da Messina (1447). In the road in front of the church the little CASTLE is being restored. Just beyond is Porta San Martino (1753) in the walls.

Via Duca degli Abruzzi leads NE from Santa Maria and leaves the old town by Porta Aragonese in the medieval walls. Beyond is the market place (market on Sundays). At the top of Via Santuario is the MUSEO VAGLIASINDI in an old people's home (officially open 8–14; fest. 9–12; closed Mondays). It contains some fine vases from a neighbouring Greek necropolis (5–2C BC), including a red-figure Oinochoe of the 5C; also coins, jewellery, etc. A festival is held in the town on 15 August. From Randazzo to Capo d'Orlando, see Rte 29.

The road continues across the railway and the huge lava flow of 1981 to (74km) PASSOPISCIARO where oaks and chestnuts begin to give place to vines and olives. On this last stretch of the road is some of the prettiest scenery, with numerous handsome old russet-coloured houses (many of them now abandoned) typical of the Etna foothills. The views of the volcano are magnificent; and to the left can be seen Moio Alcantara and Francavilla, with a background of wooded mountains.

From Passopisciaro a detour (17km farther) may be made to the N to MOIO ALCANTARA (5km), a little horticultural centre. Farther N, near Malvagna, is a tiny ruined Byzantine chapel in a field (not easy to find; footpath to 'La Cuba'), one of the few relics of the Eastern Empire in Sicily. Beyond Moio this route joins (11.5km) the road from Novara (Rte 29), but leaves it again at Francavilla (14.5km), turning S. Another Byzantine church in a ruined state (overshadowed by a factory) lies on this road near the S bank of the Alcantara, which is crossed by a medieval bridge. CASTIGLIONE DI SICILIA (20km), an ancient city of 4700 inhabitants, perched on a crag (621m), was once a stronghold of Roger of Lauria.

Just before ROVITTELLO there is another massive lava flow (1923) and, beyond the road from Castiglione (see above) another tongue of it is crossed. At (81.5km) CATENA oaks and chestnuts are prominent.

85km **Linguaglossa** (550m; 5500 inhab.; 2-star hotel 'Happy Day') is the best centre for excursions on the N slopes of Etna; the mountain road known as the 'Mareneve' begins here (see Rte 25A), and leads up through pine woods to the PINETA DI LINGUAGLOSSA and the ski-fields of PIANO PROVENZANA (1800m). Linguaglossa has some interesting churches.

The road crosses the Circumetnea railway several times before (90.5km) PIEDIMONTE ETNEO, another pleasant little town. From here the railway turns S to terminate at Giarre (see Rte 26), while the road descends steeply to the coast through splendid citrus fruit plantations, with views of Taormina and Castel Mola. It joins the Messina–Catania road at (101km) Fiumefreddo di Sicilia (Rte 26); from here to (134.5km) **Catania**, see below.

26

Catania to Messina

Road, N114, 99km.—16.5km **Acireale**—38.5km Fiumefreddo di Sicilia—50km Mazzarò (**Taormina**)—74.5km Ali Terme—99km **Messina**.

A **motorway** (90km; toll) runs parallel to N114; as a result, the road has been relieved of heavy traffic.

Bus (Rte 24) via the motorway direct from Catania to Messina in 1½hrs c every hour; by N114 via Taormina to Messina in 3hrs c every hour.

Railway, 95km in 1–1½hrs, on the main line with through trains from Syracuse to Villa San Giovanni, Naples, and Rome. To Taormina-Giardini, 48km in 45mins–1hr (the station is 5km from Taormina).

Information Offices. From Catania to Calatabiano, 'APT' Catania (Tel. 095/312124); from there to Messina 'APT' Messina (Tel. 090/674236).

The road, motorway, and railway run close together along the coast. Between Catania and Taormina there are spectacular views of Etna and its volcanic outcrops, and the fertile land is densely cultivated. Beyond Taormina the landscape changes and becomes more barren. Every drop of the scanty water-supply is utilised by means of aqueducts from springs, and subterranean channels in the broad 'fiumare' (cf. Rte 29), conspicuous features of the countryside.

Catania is left by Via Vecchia Ognina or Corso Italia (Pl.4). N114 continues through OGNINA, on a little bay, perhaps the Portus Ulixis of the 'Aeneid', half-filled with lava in the 15C. 9km **Aci Castello** (18,600 inhab.) has large 4-star and 3-star hotels. Its CASTLE on a splendid basalt rock of extremely interesting geological formation sticks sharply out of the sea. It was covered with lava in the eruption of 1169. It was rebuilt by Roger of Lauria, the rebel admiral of Frederick II (1297). Frederick succeeded in taking it by building a wooden tower of equal height alongside. It contains a MUSEO CIVICO, with interesting mineralogical, palaeontological, and archaeological material (well labelled).

In the sea between Aci Castello and ACI TREZZA (1st-class restaurant 'Da Federico') are the ISOLE DE' CICLOPI (or FARAGLIONI), the largest of which is the ISOLA LACHEA (or Isola di Aci), remarkable basalt rocks of volcanic origin. These were said to be the rocks which the blinded Polyphemus hurled at the ships of Ulysses. Aci Trezza was described by Giovanni Verga in 'I Malavoglia'.

16.5km **Acireale** (47,100 inhab.) a pleasant prosperous town in a good position above the sea (161m). It is in the midst of a fertile valley of Etna, intensely cultivated with citrus trees.

Information office. 'Azienda Autonoma', 177 Corso Umberto.

Buses to Catania, and via Viagrande (Rte 24A) to the foothills of Etna (in 40mins).

Hotels. In the centre: 4-star: 'Aloha d'Oro'; 3-star: 'Delle Terme' and 'Maugeri'. Large 3-star hotels on the outskirts on the sea, including 'Park Hotel Capo Mulini', and 'Santa Tecla'. 3-star and 2-star CAMPING SITES on the sea at Santa Maria La Scala and Pozzillo.

The **Puppet Theatre** in Via Alessi gives performances in summer. The town is famous for its **Carnival** (in February or March). Acireale and several neighbouring villages derive their name from the Aci, the mythical river which came into being on the death of Acis, the shepherd beloved by Galatea and killed by Polyphemus.

The town, which has long been visited as a spa, stands on seven streams of lava. It is interesting for its Baroque buildings, some of which date from the 17C; others were erected after the earthquake of 1693. At the S end of the town, near the railway station (opened in 1866) are the sulphur baths of SANTA VENERA in a park; the waters have been used since Roman times. The spa building of 1873 stands near the modern hotel Delle Terme.

The main Corso Vittorio Emanuele leads up to Piazza Vigo, where the church of SAN SEBASTIANO has a splendid 17C façade in the Spanish style with numerous statues and putti with garlands. The balustrade and statues are by Giovanni Battista Marino (1754). Opposite is the classical PALAZZO PENNISI DI FLORISTELLA, with a famous numismatic collection. Beyond, the main streets of the town meet at the long Piazza del Duomo. Here is the huge 17C PALAZZO COMUNALE and the church of SANTI PIETRO E PAOLO, with an early-18C façade. Beside it rises the 17C DUOMO; its neo-Gothic façade was added at the beginning of this century by Giovanni Battista Basile. Inside are 18C frescoes by Pietro Paolo Vasta.

Via Cavour leads to the church of San Domenico, near which at No. 17 Via Marchese di San Giuliano, is the BIBLIOTECA and PINACOTECA ZELANTEA. Founded in 1671, this is one of the most important libraries on the island. The small archaeological collection and art gallery are open on weekdays, 10–13. In this area are some good early-18C buildings. At the N end of the town is the BELVEDERE, a public garden laid out in 1848, with a good view. Nearby is the neo-classical church of SANTA MARIA DELL'INDIRIZZO, by Stefano Ittar.

A pleasant walk follows Via Romeo from the cathedral and the picturesque Strada delle Chiazzette to (2km) SANTA MARIA LA SCALA, a little fishing village with a port. From here there are boat trips to the basaltic GROTTA DELLE PALOMBE to the N, and (to the S) the FARAGLIONI or SCOGLI DEI CICLOPI (cf. above).

The main road turns inland while a secondary road follows close to the pretty shore known here as the 'Riviera dei Limoni'; citrus fruit plantations continue along the coast all the way to Taormina. Before (25.5km) Mangano the road crosses the fertile lava-stream of 1329. 30km **Giarre** (27,300 inhab.), where Sicilian folk art, ceramics, etc., are sold on the main road, forms one town with the little port of RIPOSTO (14,500 inhab.; 2-star camping site at Fondachello). Here the Circumetnea railway terminates. Etna towers above the road and the lava-stream of 1928 is crossed before (38.5km) FIUMEFREDDO DI SICILIA (9200 inhab.) amid plantations of oranges. Here is the junction with the road from Randazzo (Rte 24B).

The road passes below CALATABIANO dominated by a medieval castle high up on the right, which is not built on lava, despite the legend that Himilco was diverted here by a lava-stream from his direct march on Syracuse (396 BC). The road now enters the province of Messina, and just before Giardini-Naxos a road to Francavilla di Sicilia (Rte 24B) diverges up the valley of the Alcantara (Arab, El Kantara, bridge), with numerous orange groves.

Just before Motta Camastra (16km), the 'Gole Alcantara' are signposted (left; 50m). Beside the car-park is a lift (open daily) which descends into the **Alcantara Gorge**, an unexpectedly deep cleft of basalt prisms, now a protected area. Waders can be hired to explore the gorge, which can also be reached by a path, 150m farther on off the main road (signposted 'Strada Comunale').

The main road continues through **Giardini-Naxos** and then rounds the cape and traverses (50km) **Mazzaro** below **Taormina**, all described in Rte 27. 54km LETOJANNI has recently expanded as a resort (3-star hotels: 'Albatros', 'Antares', and 'San Pietro'; 2-star: 'Da Peppe'; and 1-star: 'Da Nino'. Camping sites: 'Marmaruca', 3-star, and 'Paradise', 2-star). A byroad runs up into the hills to MONGIUFFI and MELIA (9km), characteristic of the remote little upland villages reached by steep roads from the coast between here and Messina.

At (60km) Capo Sant'Alessio (with a last view back to Taormina) a road winds up to FORZA D'AGRO (4km; 420m), another little medieval village, from which the views extend along the straight coastline towards Messina, across the straights to Calabria, and south to Taormina. The coast road continues through SANT'ALESSIO SICULO (3-star hotel 'Kennedy' and 2-star camping site 'La Focetta') to (64.5km) SANTA TERESA RIVA, from where the church of Santi Pietro e Paolo d'Agro can be reached.

Just before the entrance to the town a byroad off the main road leads left below the railway bridge along the wide Fiumara d'Agro to SAN FRANCESCO DI PAOLA. From here the bed of the wide torrent can be followed (best on foot) inland to reach the church of Santi Pietro e Paolo (seen on a prominence above; c 45-minute walk from the end of the road). The church can also be approached by car by a less direct but prettier route (10.5km from Santa Teresa Riva) via SAVOCA (4km), a village in a saddle between two hills with spectacular views of the sea. 'Restorations' are in progress here and a local ethnographical museum has been arranged on the top floor of the town hall. Catacombs (signposted; ask locally for the key) preserve naturally mummified bodies.

The pretty road continues over cultivated hills and valleys up to CASALVECCHIO SICULO (7km) charmingly situated on the slopes of a hill. Less than 1km beyond the village a very narrow single-track road diverges left (signposted) to descend through lovely countryside to the old Basilian monastery of ***Santi Pietro e Paolo d'Agro** (10.5km). The imposing tall Norman edifice (custodian at neighbouring farm) was begun in 1116. An inscription over the door relates how Gerardo il Franco dedicated it to Saints Peter and Paul for the Basilian monks in 1172; it was probably also restored at this time. Built of brick and lava the exterior has notable polychrome decoration. The interior betrays Arab influence in the stalactite vaulting and the tiny domes in the apse and nave. The stucco has recently been removed from the walls to reveal the splendid brickwork.

The coast is now almost continually built up as far as Messina and the Calabrian coastline is in full view. At ROCCALUMERA is a 2-star hotel ('La Piramide'). Just before (74.5km) ALÌ TERME, with sulphur springs, a byroad leads inland to FIUMEDINISI (5.5km) where the Chiesa Madre has a wood statue of St Lucy by Rinaldo Bonanno (1589) and a painting of the Madonna of the Rosary by Agostino Ciampelli (both restored in 1985). Beyond Alì Terme is the last view back of Etna. At Marina d'Itala a road (signposted) leads up to ITALA (3km).

The road passes through delightful country with ancient olive trees and lemon groves up to the well preserved church of SAN PIETRO above the town. It was built in 1093 by Count Roger and has a handsome exterior with blind arcading and a dome. It is only open on Sundays.

The Messina road traverses the long narrow main street of the lower town of (83km) SCALETTA ZANCLEA; fishing boats are kept in the alleyways which lead down to the sea under the railway line. In the upper town the remains of a 13C castle lie beneath Monte Poverello (1279m), one of the highest of the Peloritani. 91km Mili Marina, on the outskirts of Messina.

A byroad (signposted left) leads up through a pretty wooded valley with terraced vineyards and orange groves to MILI SAN PIETRO (2.5km). On the outskirts of the village (by the school) the primitive little Norman church (1082), also founded by Count Roger, can be seen just below the road to the left. Steps descend to a farm, and under the arch to the left is the church (key at the parish church in the village).

The road continues close to the shore beneath the Monti Peloritani into the centre of (99km) **Messina**, see Rte 28.

27

Taormina and environs

TAORMINA is renowned for its magnificent position above the sea on a spur of Monte Tauro (206m) covered with luxuriant vegetation, commanding a celebrated view of Etna. With a delightful winter climate, it became a fashionable international resort at the end of the 19C. The small town (11,000 inhab.; with some 60 hotels), with one main street and many side lanes, is now virtually given over to tourism, and it is a more expensive place to visit than the rest of Sicily. Many of the villas and hotels, built in mock-Gothic or eclectic styles at the beginning of this century, are surrounded with beautiful subtropical gardens. The appearance of the medieval town has deteriorated in recent years and new houses have been allowed to cover the hillside above, and roads, on raised stilts, have spoilt some of the landscape below the town. It suffers from the proximity of the unattractive new holiday resort of Giardini-Naxos on the shore to the south.

Information Office. 'Azienda Autonoma', Palazzo Corvaja (Tel. 0942/23243).

Railway Station. 'Taormina-Giardini', a pretty building on the sea front and on the coast road (N114). With two battlemented towers, it is built in an eclectic Romanesque-Gothic style. It is on the busy line along the coast from Syracuse via Catania to Messina. Buses ('SAIS') and taxis up the hill to the town centre (via Via Pirandello; 5km).

Buses. From the Bus Terminal in Via Pirandello, services run by 'SAIS' to the railway station, Mazzarò, Giardini-Naxos, Castelmola, and Forza d'Agro. Long distance buses to Catania (and Catania airport) and Messina. Coach excursions in summer run by 'CIT', 'SAIS' and 'SAT' from the bus terminal to Etna, Syracuse, Piazza Armerina and Enna, Agrigento, Palermo and Monreale, and the gorge of Alcantara.

Approaches by Car. The most pleasant approach is by the old road, Via Pirandello (described below). Another approach road has been built to link up with the Catania–Messina motorway exit ('Taormina Nord'). This leaves the main coast road (N114) near Mazzarò and mounts on stilts past the huge car park of 'Lumbi' (closed while work is in progress on a tunnel beneath the town) to enter Taormina near the Stadium and join Via Pirandello. A third approach road (also on stilts), at the opposite end of the town, diverges from N114 in the locality of Villagonia between Giardini-Naxos and the railway station. It terminates at Porta Catania, beside the Excelsior hotel. It is not clear how the tunnel under construction beneath the town will resolve the traffic problems.

Car-parks. parking is usually difficult, especially in summer. The main street (Corso Umberto I) is totally closed to traffic at all times; motorists are strongly advised to park outside the gates. Most of the large hotels have car-parks (signposted). The car-park known as 'Lumbi', built in the late 1980s, on the N approach road from the motorway and connected by a staircase up to Via Fontana Vecchia (outside Porta Messina) has been closed during work on a tunnel. At the S end of the town there is very limited car parking in Piazza San Domenico.

To leave the town from Porta Catania (or the Circonvallazione) motorists take the pretty Via Roma (from Piazza San Domenico), one-way down, and rejoin Via Pirandello via Via Bagnoli Croce. The new road to Villagonia can also be used as an exit from the town.

Cableway (temporarily closed in 1993) from the foot of the hill at Mazzarò (car-park) to outside Porta Messina in 5mins.

Approaches on foot are described below.

Hotels. The principal hotels provide transport from the station; they also have car-parks. Many hotels are in quiet positions with fine gardens and views. Many of them are only open from April–October and from Christmas to the New Year. Among the 60 of so hotels are: 5-star: 'San Domenico Palace', an old monastery. 4-star: 'Timeo', 59 Via Teatro Greco (closed for restoration); 'Miramare', 40 Via Guardiola Vecchia; 'Excelsior Palace', 8 Via Toselli. 3-star: 'Isabella', 58 Corso Umberto; 'Villa Fiorita', 39 Via Luigi Pirandello; 'Villa San Giorgio', 46 Via San Pancrazio; 'Villa Sirina', Contrada Sirina; 'Andromaco Palace Hotel', Via Fontana Vecchia. 1-star; 'Soleado', 41 Via Dietro Cappuccini. **Rooms and apartments to let** all over the town (list from the 'Azienda Autonoma').

The bathing resort of **Taormina-Mazzarò** (described below) at the foot of the hill (cableway or road) also has numerous pleasant hotels including: 5-star: 'Mazzarò Sea Palace'; 4-star: 'Villa Sant'Andrea' and 'Ipanema'; 3-star: 'Park Hotel La Plage' and 'Villa Bianca'. Many large hotels in a much less attractive position at the new undistinguished resort of **Giardini-Naxos** (see below), 4km W of Capo Taormina. Among the smaller hotels here (all of them 2-star) are: 'Alexander', 'Sabbie d'Oro', 'Marika', and 'Villa Mora'.

Camping Site at San Leo (1-star).

Restaurants. Luxury-class: 'La Giara', 1 Via La Floresta, and 'Il Granduca', 170 Corso Umberto. Numerous 1st-class restaurants all over the town. **Picnic places** in the public gardens. In the environs, at the archaeological site of Naxos.

Anglo-American Church (St George's), Via Luigi Pirandello. A chaplain is shared with the Holy Cross in Palermo.

Annual Festivals. Classical dance and music festival in the Greek Theatre, July–15 September. International film festival in July.

History. *Tauromenium*, founded after the destruction of Naxos (see below) by Dionysius of Syracuse in 403 BC, was enlarged in 358 by a colony of Naxian exiles under Andromachus, father of the historian Timaeus. Its harbour was the landing place of Timoleon in 334 BC, and of Pyrrhus in 278. It was favoured by Rome during the early days of occupation, and suffered in the Servile War (134–132), but forfeited its rights as an allied city by taking the part of Pompey against Caesar. In AD 902 it was destroyed by the Saracens, though rebuilt shortly afterwards, and it was taken by Count Roger in 1078. Here the Sicilian parliament assembled in 1410 to choose a king on the extinction of the line of Peter of Aragon.

The town was visited and described by numerous travellers in the 18C and 19C. Goethe came here in 1787. John Henry Newman stayed in the town in 1833. In 1847 Edward Lear spent four or five days in 'Taormina the Magnificent'. In the latter part of the 19C it was already a famous resort: Augustus Hare complained that it had become a 'fashionable loafing place' and that the Hotel Timeo was 'usually besieged by its patrons before Christmas and held against all comers, except royalties, who have done so much to spoil Taormina'. Before World War I the town had a considerable Anglo-American, German, and Scandanavian colony, including the photographer Baron Wilhelm von Gloeden (1896–1931). The town attracted the attention of allied aircraft in July 1943 when it temporarily became Kesselring's headquarters.

The most pleasant approach is by the old road Via Pirandello which diverges from the main road (N114) at Capo Taormina and winds up the hill past lovely gardens (beware of coaches at the hair-pin bends). It passes the little 15C church of SANTI PIETRO E PAOLO (open only for services), the ruins of the huge 'Kursaal', and a series of Byzantine tomb-recesses in the wall below the ex-convent of Santa Caterina. Shortly after the junction with Via Bagnoli Croce (one-way down from the town) it passes the little BELVEDERE with a fine view. Beyond the Bus Terminal, on the right (No. 24), surrounded by a garden of date palms, is the Anglo-American church of ST GEORGE'S, built by the British community in 1922, with lava decoration on the exterior. It contains British and American funerary monuments, and memorials to the two World Wars. Beyond the cableway station (at present out of operation) Via Pirandello terminates outside Porta Messina, at the entrance to the town.

From Piazza Vittorio Emanuele on the site of the ancient Agora, Via Teatro Greco leads past a congress hall opened in 1990, to end at a group of cypresses covered with bougainvillea beside the Hotel Timeo, one of the oldest hotels in the town (closed indefinitely for restoration). Here is the entrance to the ***Theatre** (open every day, 9am–dusk), famous for its remarkable scenic position. First erected in the Hellenistic period, it was almost entirely rebuilt under the Romans when it was considerably altered. This is the largest antique theatre in Sicily after that of Syracuse (109m in diameter; orchestra 35m across). The cavea, as was usual, was excavated in the hillside; above the nine wedges of seats, a portico (partially restored in 1955) ran round the top, a few stumps of the 45 columns in front survive. The scena is in a remarkably fine state of preservation. The outer brick wall is pierced by three gates; the inner wall was once cased with marble. The foundations of the proscenium, or stage, remain, together with the parascenia, or wings, and traces of porticoes at the back (perhaps shelters from the weather). The theatre was famous for its acoustic properties, which can still be tested.

The celebrated *view from the top of the cavea (reached from the steps to the left), one of the most breathtaking in Sicily, has been described by countless writers: Goethe in 1787 exclaimed 'Never did any audience, in any theatre, have before it such a spectacle'. On a clear day Etna is seen at its most majestic. In the other direction the Calabrian mountains extend to the northern horizon, and inland the hills stretch behind Monte Mola. A small Archaeological MUSEUM (closed since 1988 for restoration), adjoining the custodian's house, contains the torso of a youth (Hellenistic); the financial tablets of Tauromenium (150 BC to the Empire); list of strategoi on white marble (2–1C BC); sculptural fragments including a leg, and foot with sandal, etc.; and a female head attributed to the school of Scopas.

In Piazza Vittorio Emanuele (see above) stands **Palazzo Corvaia** (late 14C), with good windows, a 14C side-portal, and a courtyard stair decorated with reliefs of Adam and Eve. The limestone ornamentation with black and white lava inlay is characteristic of Taormina. The building houses the tourist information office. The great hall, meeting place in 1410 of the Sicilian parliament and other rooms, are shown on request (9–13, 16–18). The church of SANTA CATERINA (usually closed) has three large white Baroque altars and a good painting of the Madonna and martyrs by the Messina school (very damaged). In the floor of the nave parts of the Odeon (cf. below) have been revealed. Stairs lead down to a macabre funerary chamber of 1662. Behind the church are the scant remains of the ODEON or TEATRINO ROMANO, incorporating part of an earlier Hellenistic temple.

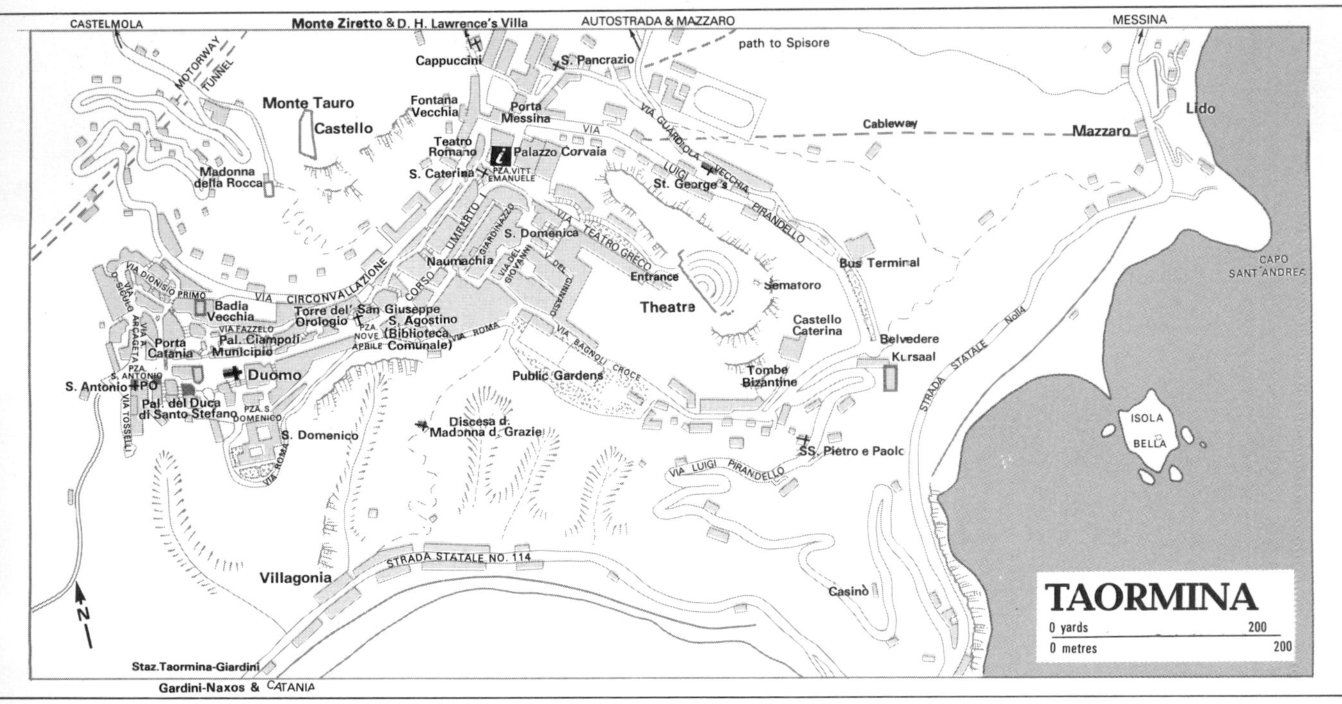

CASTELMOLA
Monte Ziretto & D. H. Lawrence's Villa
AUTOSTRADA & MAZZARO
MESSINA
path to Spisore
Cappuccini
S. Pancrazio
MOTORWAY
TUNNEL
Monte Tauro
Castello
Fontana Vecchia
Porta Messina
VIA LUIGI PIRANDELLO
VIA GUARDIOLA VECCHIA
Cableway
Mazzaro
Lido
Teatro Romano
Palazzo Corvaia
S. Caterina
PZA VITT. EMANUELE
St. George's
Madonna della Rocca
CORSO UMBERTO
GIARDINAZZO
S. Domenica
VIA TEATRO GRECO
Naumachia
VIA DEL GIOVANNI
V. DEL GINNASIO
Entrance
Bus Terminal
CAPO SANT ANDREA
VIA DIONISIO PRIMO
VIA D. SICULO
VIA CIRCONVALLAZIONE
Sematoro
Theatre
Badia Vecchia
Torre del' Orologio
San Giuseppe
S. Agostino (Biblioteca Comunale)
PZA. NOVE APRILE
VIA ROMA
Castello Caterina
VIA FAZZELO
VIA A. ARCAGETA
Porta Catania
Pal. Ciampoli
Municipio
VIA BAGNOLI CROCE
Belvedere
Kursaal
STRADA STATALE
Nolla
PZA. S. ANTONIO
Duomo
Public Gardens
Tombe Bizantine
S. Antonio
PO
VIA TOSSELLI
Pal. del Duca di Santo Stefano
PZA. S. DOMENICO
S. Domenico
Discesa d. Madonna d. Grazie
ISOLA BELLA
SS. Pietro e Paolo
VIA LUIGI PIRANDELLO
VIA ROMA
STRADA STATALE NO. 114
Villagonia
Casinò
N
TAORMINA
0 yards 200
0 metres 200
Staz. Taormina-Giardini
Gardini-Naxos & CATANIA

Recent excavations behind the barracks in the piazza have revealed public BATHS of the Imperial Roman period.

Outside Porta Messina, at the lower end of a large piazza, is SAN PANCRAZIO (open on Sunday morning), built on the ruins of a Greek temple to Isis, whose cella is still traceable. The pretty little arcaded forecourt has a palm tree, and there is a view up to the Castello (see below), towering above the town. Below the church is Villa San Giorgio, with its garden, built in 1908 by C.R. Ashbee, the founder of the Guild of Handicraft at Chipping Camden, many features of which are incorporated in its decoration, using local motifs and materials.

Via Costantino Patricio leads sharp left outside Porta Messina up to remains of a public fountain. On the right, beyond Porta Cappuccini, Via Fontana Vecchia continues past vestiges of an aqueduct and the Piscina Mirabile (left; under a school) to the church of the CAPPUCCINI, with a doorway similar to the N door of the cathedral. The road passes under the arch to the left of the campanile and Via Fontana Vecchia forks right, with (in front) a picturesque villa composed of ancient fragments. Just beyond the villa an unattractive staircase leads down to the huge 'Lumbi' car-park (closed). The hillside beyond has been ruined by new buildings in the last two decades: the red villa where D.H. and Frieda Lawrence lived from 1920–23 survives in an abandoned state as the only old house on the hillside. It can be seen from here clearly, to the right, in a clump of cypress trees on the ridge of a hill. It is now recorded only by the name of the street which approaches it.

Corso Umberto Primo (totally closed to traffic) runs the length of the town. To the right and left are glimpses of picturesque stepped alley-ways, with colourful plants. On the left, beyond a pretty doorway and tiny rose window (No. 42), steps (Via Naumachia) lead down to the so-called NAUMACHIA, a long brick wall (122m) with niches (formerly decorated with statues) of late Roman date, now supporting a row of houses. Behind it is a huge cistern (no adm.): it is thought to have been a monumental nymphaeum. The Corso opens into PIAZZA NOVE APRILE, with a superb S aspect open to the sea and Etna. Below can be seen the railway station and the unspoilt hillside. Several cafés here have tables outside.

On the left is the former church of SANT'AGOSTINO (1448), now the library, with a Gothic doorway, and to the right, approached by a pretty flight of steps, stands the 17C church of SAN GIUSEPPE, with a heavily decorated Rococo stucco interior. Beyond the TORRE DELL'OROLOGIO (?12C; restored 1679), is the so-called Borgo Medioevale; along the Corso are many little medieval palaces, with doors and windows where supposedly Saracenic influences linger among the 15C details of the Gothic-Catalan doorways and windows. The first house on the left (No. 154) has two columns from the Roman theatre. At No. 185 is the ex-church of San Giovanni (1533), which is now a club for war veterans and is full of trophies and photographs. A flight of steps leads up to PALAZZO CIAMPOLI built in 1412 and restored after war damage. In the garden the Hotel Palazzo Vecchio was built in 1926, modelled on Palazzo Vecchio in Florence (being restored).

Opposite the Municipio is the flank of the **Duomo** (San Nicolò), founded in the 13C, with battlements, and two lovely side portals (15C and 16C). The façade has a late rose-window and portal of 1636. In the interior with six monolithic antique pink marble columns are a painting of the Visitation by Antonino Giuffrè (1463), and a polyptych by Antonello De Saliba (1504; with a fine frame), from the former church of San Giovanni, both in the S aisle, and particularly fine works. In the chapel at the end of the S aisle, delicate tabernacle dated 1648, and an early 16C Madonna and Child in alabaster. In the N aisle, first altar, Madonna enthroned with saints (in very poor condition) by Alfonso Franco; on the second altar, 16C statue of

St Agatha; and on the third altar, Adoration of the Magi. In the piazza is a charming fountain of 1635, with the bizarre figure on the top of a female centaur with only two legs.

Steps on the right of the fountain ascend past a small black-and-white Roman mosaic (right; within an enclosure) and (left) the rebuilt church of the CARMINE with a pretty campanile. More steps lead up to the PORTA CUSENI (or Saraceni), the name given to the village outside the walls. Outside the gate steps continue up to Via Dionisio I which can be followed to the right to see the BADIA VECCHIA (restored) with its large crenellated tower. Beyond it is a neo-Gothic hotel, typical of the hotels built in the town at the beginning of this century. In the other direction Via Leonardo da Vinci leads past a wall in front of cypresses, bougainvillea and plumbago to CASA CUSENI (No. 5). It is preceded by terraced gardens and a fountain planted with papyrus. The villa was built by the painter Robert Kitson in 1907.

From Piazza del Duomo a street descends to the convent of SAN DOMENICO (now a hotel), with a late-16C cloister. Field-Marshal Kesselring set up his HQ here in July 1943, and many of his staff were killed by an allied air-raid, which destroyed the church (the exterior was reconstructed in 1973; the interior is used as a conference hall).

The Corso ends at PORTA CATANIA or Porta del Tocco (1440). Across the walls here the Normans built one of their last refuges in Sicily at the end of the 12C, the PALAZZO DEL DUCA DI SANTO STEFANO. It was restored in 1973 and is now used for exhibitions (8.30–13.30, 16–19). This area of the town suffered badly during the air-raids of July 1943 (see above), when the little church of SANT'ANTONIO (good Gothic portal) was damaged and the Barbican gate all but destroyed. The view from the terrace (Viale Toselli) in front of the neo-Saracenic Excelsior hotel, is spectacular, despite some ugly new buildings, and the new road, raised on stilts, which descends to the main coast road.

Walks in the vicinity of Taormina

There are a number of pretty walks (with signposted paths; cf. the plan) from the town down to the coast at Mazzarò, Spisone, and Villagonia. Above the town paths lead up to the Madonna della Rocca and the Castle. They all have good views and lead through luxuriant vegetation.

The beautifully kept PUBLIC GARDENS in Via Bagnoli Croce have exotic tropical plants, a pagoda, aviaries, and delightful 'follies'. They were created in 1899 as 'The Beehives' for Florence Trevelyan Cacciola (1852–1907), whose bust (a copy of her funerary monument) has been placed on the left of the main entrance on Via Bagnoli Croce. The gardens were given to the town in 1922. In 1992 a reproduction of a human torpedo used in 1941 to sink the British war ships 'Queen Elizabeth' and 'Valiant' in the port of Alexandria was installed here as a memorial to local sailors who lost their lives in service. From the terrace there is a view of Etna and the resort of Naxos.

Beyond the tennis courts is an exit from the garden, outside of which a narrow road with steps descends past a plaque (1908) which records the work of Mabel Hill (1866–1940), an Englishwoman who revived the traditional methods of making Taormina lace, and, with Robert Kitson, took an interest in local social conditions between the Wars. Beyond a modern hotel built on the steep hillside, a lane continues down to the coast at VILLAGONIA near the railway station.

Steps lead down from the other end of the Public Gardens (beside the Jolly Hotel) to Via Pirandello which can then be followed down hill by steps linking the loops in the road. VIA ROMA, which runs from the Public

Gardens to San Domenico, although open to cars, provides magnificent views over luxuriant vegetation and precipitous ravines to the sea.

A path descends from the BELVEDERE on Via Pirandello to MAZZARÒ opposite Capo Sant'Andrea. Another path, off the approach road from Mazzarò and the motorway, starts near the stadium and well-tended cemetery, part of which is reserved for non-Catholics and the town's foreign community (open 8–12, 14–16 except Friday; fest. 9–12). The path descends to LIDO SPISONE beyond Mazzarò.

Above the town, from the Circonvallazione, a path (signposted) leads up through plantations of sub-tropical trees to the MADONNA DELLA ROCCA and the CASTELLO (see below), from which there are wonderful views. The return can be made by the 738 steps that link the serpentine loops of the Castel Mola road (described below). MONTE ZIRETTO (579m) is also a fine view point.

Environs of Taormina

A. Castel Mola

From the Circonvallazione above Taormina the Castel Mola road (with many hairpin bends) climbs up past numerous new houses. A turning (right) leads to the MADONNA DELLA ROCCA and the CASTELLO (398m), with a ruined keep (view). 5km **Castel Mola** (550m), a small village with hotels (2-star 'Villa Sonia') and restaurants on top of a rock with a ruined castle, high above Taormina. In the little piazza, with a view from the terrace of Etna and the bay of Naxos, the café has an interesting collection of autographs. The village is famous for its almond wine. The façade of the parish church opens onto a balcony with another wonderful view. The view is still better from MONTE VENERE or VENERETTA (884m) reached by a long footpath from the cemetery of Castel Mola.

B. Giardini-Naxos

GIARDINI, 4km S of Capo Taormina, once a quiet fishing village, with a long main street parallel to the sea, has been developed in the last few decades into the large holiday resort of **Giardini-Naxos**. The wide bay is now lined with hotels, flats, and restaurants from Capo Schisò as far as the railway station of Taormina-Giardini, and tower blocks have been built wherever possible. The numerous large 3-star hotels cater mostly for package holiday tours. The smaller hotels are listed above.

From this bay Garibaldi, with two steamboats and 4200 men, set out on his victorious campaign against the 30,000 Bourbon troops in Calabria (19 August 1860). Signs to the museum lead to the point of the cape, CAPO SCHISÒ, formed by an ancient lava-flow which can still be clearly seen at the water's edge here, by the little harbour. This was a natural landing-place for the navigators rounding the 'toe' of Italy from the East, and it was the site of the Greek colony of **Naxos**. From the sea front there is a view of Taormina, with Castel Mola above to the left. Excavations of the Greek city (cf. below) continue here, and by the modern harbour wall an old Bourbon fort has been restored to house the **Museo Archeologico** of Naxos (open every day, 9–14; fest. 9–13).

The entrance is through a pretty little garden, through which runs the ancient lava-flow. The collection is beautifully displayed chronologically on two floors and is well labelled. GROUND FLOOR. Neolithic and Bronze Age finds from the Cape (Stentinello ware, etc.); Iron Age finds from the necropolis of Mola including geometric style pottery. FIRST FLOOR. Terracottas and architectural fragments from a sanctuary at Santa Venera (6C BC); material found in the area of the ancient city including a fine antefix with polychrome decoration, and Attic pottery; votive object of uncertain purpose decorated with sphinxes in relief (late 6C BC?); statuette of a goddess (end of 5C BC); rare marble lamp from the Cyclades found in the sea (end of 7C BC); finds from a tomb near Santa Venera of the 3C BC, including four pretty vases; bronze objects (helmet of 4C BC, etc.). In the garden there is a stretch of Greek walls, and a little museum of underwater finds has been arranged in a small fort. It contains anchors (7C BC–4C BC), amphorae, etc.

There are long-term plans to connect the museum with the excavations of Naxos across the fields to the S. At present it is necessary to return inland and follow the signs for the excavations around a complicated one-way system through the new resort. The ***excavations of Naxos** (open daily 9am–dusk) are situated in a beautiful orchard with lemon trees, palms, olives, orange trees, eucalyptus, and medlar trees; between which flower bougainvillea, hibiscus, and jasmine.

The foundation date of the Greek settlement (Chalcidians from Euboea and Ionians from Naxos) is thought to be 734–733 BC. It was the first Greek colony on the island, closely followed by Syracuse and Megara Hyblaea. The town surrendered to Hippocrates of Gela (495) and to Hieron of Syracuse in 476. It was finally destroyed by Dionysius I in 405–4. Excavations were first carried out here in 1953. From the entrance a path follows the line of the CITY WALLS in black lava (c 500m) past an area of recent excavations, to the WEST GATE, where a plan of the well-labelled site is displayed. The city area, not yet fully excavated, lies to the left (N).

A path leads through the W gate to the original entrance to the AREA SACRA, and remains of the 7C and 6C, including part of the walls, an altar, and a TEMENOS OF APHRODITE. A 'sacello' or simple temple, constructed towards the end of the 7C was built over by a larger temple at the end of the 6C. Under cover are preserved two KILNS, a circular one for pithoi, and a rectangular one for tiles; both were in use during the late 6C and 5C BC. Beyond is the SEA GATE with a fine polygonal lava wall. The pretty high wall, which blocks the view of the sea, was built during excavation work. Exceptionally fine Greek coins, dating from 410–360 BC were found here, many of them bearing the head of Dionysius.

C. Mazzarò

Mazzarò is a pretty bathing resort on CAPO SANT'ANDREA beneath the hill of Taormina, well supplied with hotels (see above). Three beaches of fine shale and pebbles are separated by rocky spurs. Offshore is the ISOLA BELLA, of great natural beauty, finally acquired as a protected area by the Sicilian Regional government in 1987. Off CAPO TAORMINA 35 Roman columns lie submerged: they are unworked quarried stone, probably destined for a temple or the portico of a villa, which must have been lost in in a shipwreck. Footpaths (signposted) and a cableway (not in operation in 1993) mount from Mazzarò to Taormina.

28

Messina

MESSINA, on the western shore of the Strait bearing its name, extends along the lowest slopes of the Monti Peloritani above the splendid harbour, one of the deepest and safest in the Mediterranean. The port, at the entrance to the island, is always busy with the movement of the ferries from the mainland. The city (270,000 inhab.) remains the third largest town in Sicily despite the terrible earthquake that completely wrecked it in 1908, when 84,000 people died out of a population of 120,000. Rebuilt with exceptionally broad streets planted with trees and low buildings to minimise the danger of future earthquakes, the centre of Messina combines sea, sky, and hills in a pleasant open townscape. Unattractive higher buildings have been constructed on the outskirts in recent years.

Information Offices. 'APT' Messina, Via Calabria, (corner of Via Capra), Tel. 090/675356. 'Azienda Autonoma', 45 Piazza Cairoli.

Train-ferries, car-ferries, and hydrofoils from the Italian mainland. CAR FERRIES from Villa San Giovanni run by the State railways in connection with trains in 40mins; other car ferries ('Caronte', 'Tourist Ferry Boat') c every 20mins in 20 mins. From Reggio Calabria car ferries run by the State railways in connection with trains in 50mins; other car ferries approximately every hour. Frequent HYDROFOIL services in 15mins from Reggio Calabria run by 'SNAV'. The ferries run by the State railways from Villa San Giovanni and Reggio Calabria arrive at the STAZIONE MARITTIMA, going on to the STAZIONE CENTRALE, the station for Catania and Palermo. Other car ferries and hydrofoils moor at the various jetties on the water-front parallel to Via Vittorio Emanuele II and Via della Libertà. There is a hydrofoil service once a day (in c 90mins) to the Aeolian Islands (see Rte 30).

Buses from the station via Corso Cavour to Museo Nazionale and Punta del Faro (**8**); via Corso Garibaldi to Museo Nazionale (**7** black); from Piazza Cairoli to the Cemetery (**2** and **7**). COUNTRY BUS services run by 'SAIS' (terminal in Piazza della Repubblica) to Catania (direct via the motorway) in 90mins (going on to Catania airport); to Taormina (via N114) in 90mins; and to other towns in the province; to Rome in 9½hrs. Coach service run by 'Cavalieri' (from Piazza Duomo) in connection with internal flights from Reggio Calabria Airport (via Piazza Duomo and Piazza Stazione). From April–September services by 'Giuntabus' from 8 Via Terranova to Milazzo (for the Aeolian islands; see Rte 30).

Car Parking is difficult in the centre of Messina: space sometimes available in Via La Farina and near the Fiera di Messina. A new car-park is under construction in Piazza Cavallotti.

Hotels. 4-star: 'Jolly dello Stretto', 126 Via Garibaldi. 3-star: 'Excelsior', 32 Via Maddalena, and, N of the town at Ganzirri: 'Villa Morgana' and 'Giardino delle Palme'. 2-star: 'Milano' 65 Via dei Verdi'. 1-star: 'Roma', 3 Piazza Duomo.

Restaurants. Luxury-class: 'Alberto', 95 Via Ghibellina; 'Fico d'India', Via Placida; 'Piero' 121 Via Ghibellina; 'La Trappola', 39 Via dei Verdi. 1st-class: 'Briganndì', Via La Farina; 'Donna Giovanna', 16 Via Risorgimento; 'Siglari', Via Lascaris (corner of Viale Boccetta). There are numerous restaurants and trattorie at Lago Ganzirri, N of the town.

Cafés or bars ('pasticceria'). 'Irrera', Piazza Cairoli; 'Billé', Piazza Cairoli; 'Casaramola', 242 Viale San Martino.

Theatres. 'Vittorio Emanuele', Corso Garibaldi (for music and prose). 'Teatro San Carlino', Via Calapso, for prose.

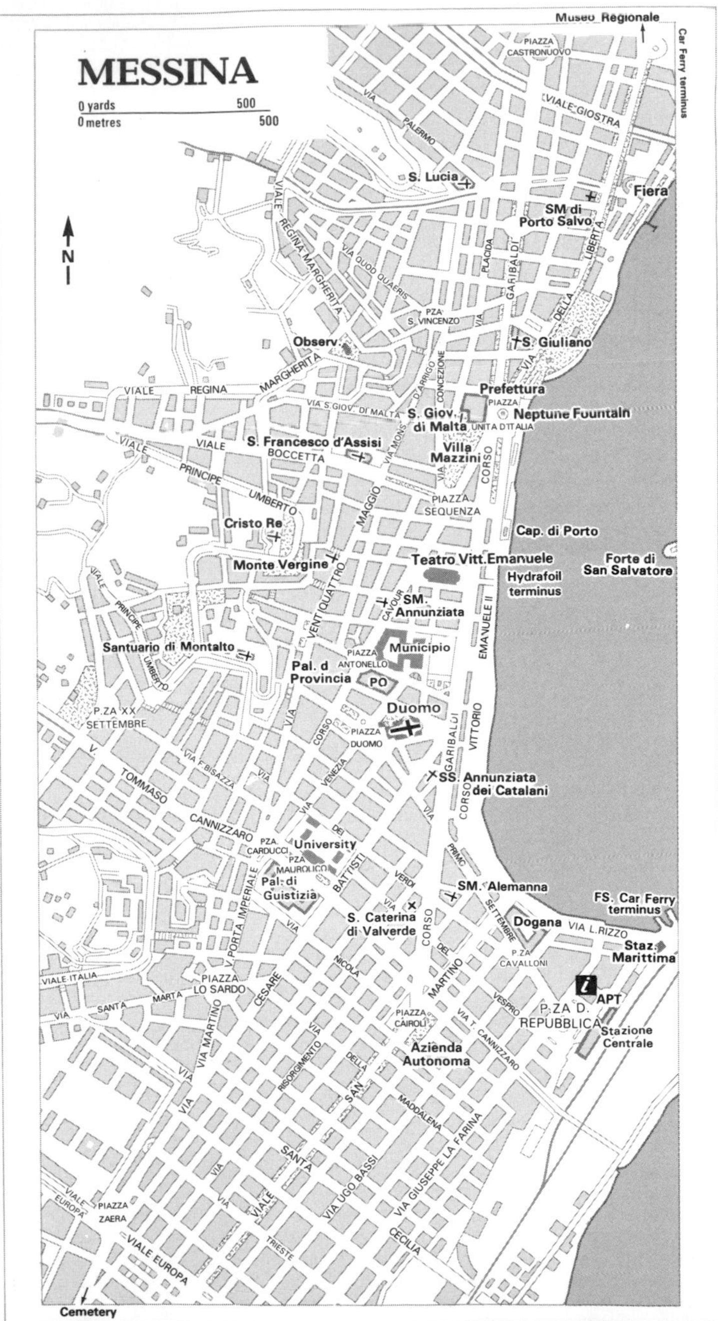
MESSINA
0 yards 500
0 metres 500
N
Museo Regionale
Car Ferry terminus
PIAZZA CASTRONUOVO
VIA PALERMO
VIALE GIOSTRA
S. Lucia
Fiera
SM di Porto Salvo
VIALE REGINA MARGHERITA
VIA QUOD QUAERIS
PLACIDA
GARIBALDI
DELLA LIBERTÀ
PZA S. VINCENZO
S. Giuliano
Observ.
MARGHERITA
VIALE REGINA
CONCEZIONE
D'ARRIGO
Prefettura
PIAZZA
VIA S. GIOV. DI MALTA
S. Giov. di Malta
Neptune Fountain
UNITA D'ITALIA
VIALE BOCCETTA
S. Francesco d'Assisi
VIALE PRINCIPE UMBERTO
VIA MONS.
Villa Mazzini
CORSO
MAGGIO
PIAZZA SEQUENZA
Cristo Re
Cap. di Porto
Monte Vergine
Teatro Vitt. Emanuele
Forte di San Salvatore
Hydrafoil terminus
VENTIQUATTRO
SM. Annunziata
CAVOUR
VIALE PRINCIPE UMBERTO
EMANUELE II
Santuario di Montalto
Municipio
PIAZZA ANTONELLO
Pal. d Provincia
PO
Duomo
P.ZA XX SETTEMBRE
VIA
VITTORIO
PIAZZA DUOMO
GARIBALDI
V. TOMMASO CANNIZZARO
VIA F. BISAZZA
VIA VENEZIA
CORSO
SS. Annunziata dei Catalani
CORSO
VIA DEI
PZA CARDUCCI
University
PZA MAUROLICO
PRIMO
BATTISTI
VERDI
Pal. di Guistizia
VIA PORTA IMPERIALE
SM. Alemanna
SETTEMBRE
FS. Car Ferry terminus
VIA
S. Caterina di Valverde
CORSO DEL
Dogana
VIA L. RIZZO
Staz. Marittima
VIA NICOLA
MARTINO
P.ZA CAVALLONI
VIALE ITALIA
PIAZZA LO SARDO
VIA SANTA MARTA
CESARE
V. MARTINO
VIA
APT
VESPRO
PIAZZA CAIROLI
VIA T. CANNIZZARO
P.ZA D. REPUBBLICA
Stazione Centrale
VIA RISORGIMENTO
DELLA
Azienda Autonoma
SAN
MADDALENA
VIA
VIA SANTA
VIA UGO BASSI
VIA GIUSEPPE LA FARINA
VIALE EUROPA
PIAZZA ZAERA
VIALE
TRIESTE
CECILIA
VIALE EUROPA
Cemetery

Annual Festivals. The 'Fiera di Messina', a trade fair during the first 15 days of August coincides with the traditional processions of the 'Giganti' on 13 and 14 August and the 'Vara' (cart with tableau) on the Assumption (15 August). Other processions on 3 June (Madonna della Lettera, protectress of the city), on Good Friday ('Varette') and on Corpus Domini ('Vascelluzzo'). Exhibitions are held (especially in winter) in various galleries.

History. *Zancle*, as Messina was called by the Greeks in allusion to the sickle-shaped peninsula enclosing its harbour, was probably a settlement of the Siculi before its occupation by the Cumaeans and later by a colony from Chalcis. In 493 BC it was captured by Anaxilas, tyrant of Rhegium, and renamed *Messana*, in honour of his native country of Messenia in the Peloponnese. It took part in local wars against Syracuse and then against Athens, and was destroyed by the Punic general Himilco. Rebuilt by the Syracusans, it was occupied by the Campanian mercenaries of Agathocles, who called themselves Mamertini. These obtained the alliance of Rome against the Carthaginians and Messina prospered with the fortunes of Rome. Under the Normans it was renowned for monastic learning and important as a Crusader port. Richard Palmer, an Englishman, who had arranged the marriage of William the Good to Joan Plantagenet in 1177, was Archbishop of Messina from c 1183 to his death in 1195. In 1190–91 Richard Coeur de Lion built the Castle of Mategriffon (in 1282 the stronghold of Herbert of Orleans, governor of Sicily) and wintered in the town, which he sacked as a warning to Tancred to surrender Joan and the Plantagenet share of William's inheritance. The Emperor Henry VI died of dysentery at Messina in 1197. After a heroic and successful resistance to Charles of Anjou in 1282, the city flourished until it lost its privileges by rebelling against Spanish misrule in 1674.

From then on its story is one disaster after another: plague in 1743, earthquake in 1783, naval bombardment in 1848, cholera in 1854, another earthquake in 1894, culminating in the catastrophe of 1908. The earthquake, which took place early on the morning of 28 December, not only ruined almost the entire city, but caused the shore to sink over half a metre. The subsidence caused a violent tidal wave which swept the coast of Calabria, rising to a height of 6m; its effects were felt at Malta 24 hours later. A series of lesser shocks continued almost daily for two months. Of the 100,000 victims, 84,000 lost their lives in Messina and its environs. Reconstruction, though assisted by liberal contributions from all over the world, was by no means complete when the city was again devastated in 1943 by aerial bombardment (when 5000 people lost their lives). In 1955 a preliminary agreement was signed by the 'six' in Messina to found the European Economic Community.

Antonello da Messina (c 1430–79), who perfected the art of painting in oil by the Flemish method and added his own delicate sense of light, was one of the masters of the Italian Renaissance, and perhaps the greatest southern Italian painter. In 1492 Pietro Bembo came to Messina at the age of 22 in order to study Greek under Constantine Lascaris, and stayed two years. From Messina Cervantes sailed in the 'Marquesa' to Lepanto (1571) and in Messina hospital recovered from the wound received in the battle. The action of Shakespeare's 'Much Ado' is set in Messina. The French geologist Dolomieu (1750–1801), returning from Napoleon's Egyptian expedition, was captured and imprisoned for two years (1799–1801) in Messina.

Piazza del Duomo was spaciously laid out in the 18C. Beside the cathedral the elaborate modern campanile overshadows the delicate *ORION FOUNTAIN, a masterpiece by Montorsoli (1547; covered for restoration). The **Duomo** (closed 12–16), despite successive reconstructions, retains much of the appearance of the original medieval structure.

Originally built by Roger II, and consecrated in 1197 in the presence of Henry VI, the cathedral was shattered in 1908, when the roof collapsed and the 26 monolithic granite columns, brought, it is believed, from the Temple of Neptune at the Punta del Faro, were smashed to pieces. The N corner of the façade and some of the mosaics and monuments survived, with the contents of the treasury, and the building was carefully restored following the Norman lines, only to be even more thoroughly devastated by a fire, which, started on 13 June 1943, by incendiary bombs, raged for three days.

Many of the treasures were completely destroyed including the mosaics and frescoes, the royal tombs, and the stalls. But everything that could be salvaged was replaced in position in the rebuilt church; damaged works were painstakingly restored; and, where possible, lost works accurately reconstructed.

The lower part of the FACADE (covered for restoration) preserves much of the original sculptured decoration including panels in relief with delightful farming scenes, and three fine doorways, by 15C and 16C artists. The central *doorway has a tympanum by Pietro da Bonitate (1468). The S doorway is by Polidoro da Caravaggio; beyond a pretty wall with fine Gothic Catalan windows is the entrance to the TREASURY, particularly rich in 17C and 18C objects (which has been closed indefinitely for many years).

The majestic basilican INTERIOR, in pink and grey tones, was remarkably well reconstructed after the fire. The side altars (copies of originals by Montorsoli), the columns, the marble pavement, and the painted wood roof were all restored. In the S AISLE is a statue of St John the Baptist by Antonello Gagini (1525; being restored). At the end of the aisle is the 14C Gothic arcaded tomb of five archbishops, and (on the nave pillar in the transept) the fragmented tomb slab of Archbishop Palmer (died 1195; cf. above). Outside the right apse chapel, elaborately decorated in marble, is the tomb of Archbishop De Tabiatis by Goro di Gregorio (1333). The sumptuous high altar bears a copy of the venerated Byzantine Madonna della Lettera (destroyed in 1943). The baldacchino, the stalls (designed by Giorgio Veneziano in 1540), and the bishop's throne have all been reconstructed. The mosaic in the apse has been recomposed. The monument to Bishop Angelo Paino (1870–1967), to the left of the apse, was sculpted by M. Lucerna. In the left apse chapel is the only original mosaic to have survived in the church from the 14C.

In the N transept the tomb effigy of Bishop Antonio La Lignamine is surrounded by 12 fine small panels of the Passion sculpted by the Gagini school. Nearby is a 17C bust of Archbishop Proto, and part of the tomb of Archbishop Bellorado by Giovanni Battista Mazzola (1513). In the N AISLE, beside the doorway, is a 16C relief of St Jerome (the exterior of the 15C N doorway can be seen here). At the end of the aisle, the baptistery, with a reconstructed font, contains a striking wood Crucifix.

The CAMPANILE was designed by Francesco Valenti to house an astronomical *clock, the largest of its kind in the world, built by a Strasbourg firm in 1933. At noon a cannon-shot heralds an elaborate movement of mechanical figures.

A short way N of the Duomo is the circular Piazza Antonello, laid out in 1914–29 with a group of monumental buildings: the Post Office, the Palazzo della Provincia, the Municipio (its façade faces Corso Garibaldi), and an arcade with cafés and shops. In Via Cavour is the circular domed church of SANTA MARIA ANNUNZIATA DEI TEATINI (1930). To the S, reached by Via Venezia, the UNIVERSITY (1927), with a fine library dating from the foundation in 1548, faces PALAZZO DI GIUSTIZIA, a monumental neo-classical building in ochre stone by Marco Piacentini (1928).

From Piazza Duomo, Via I Settembre (stone on the corner recording the outbreak of the Sicilian revolution in 1847) leads towards the Station. It passes two Baroque corner fountains which survived the earthquake near (left) the church of ***Santissima Annunziata dei Catalani** (now the University chapel; open for services only), a 12C Norman church, shortened under the Swabians. It has been carefully restored. The exterior is remarkably fine. The apse, transepts, and cupola, with beautiful arcading, date from the 12C, while the three doors at the W end were added in the 13C. The interior has a pretty brick apse and dome in yellow and white stone, and tall dark grey columns with Corinthian capitals. The windows and nave arches are decorated with red and white stone. The large stoup is made up from two capitals. In the piazza is a statue of Don John of Austria, by Andrea Calamech (1572).

Via I Settembre crosses Corso Garibaldi, a long broad thoroughfare, which continues S. Just off it, to the left, is SANTA MARIA ALEMANNA (c 1220), interesting as one of the few Gothic churches in Sicily. It is in a state of neglect. On the opposite side of the Corso, the church of the SANTA CATERINA DI VALVERDE contains a painting of the Madonna dell' Itria between Saints Peter and Paul by the local artist Antonello Riccio (restored in 1985). Corso Garibaldi ends in the huge PIAZZA CAIROLI, the centre of the town, where one or two famous cafés survive. The splendid evergreen ficus trees have remarkably thick foliage.

Farther S, Viale San Martino, one of the main shopping streets, traverses an area of well laid out streets, with homogeneous low buildings. It ends at the public gardens beside the monumental CEMETERY, designed in 1872 by Leone Savoia. The luxuriant garden built in terraces on the slopes of the hill, has a lovely view of Calabria. The 'Famedio', or Pantheon, was damaged by the earthquake, but almost all the smaller family tombs were left intact; 80,000 victims of the disaster are buried here among the flowers. In 1940 the British cemetery, founded during the Napoleonic wars, was transferred here (reached by a path on the extreme left side of the cemetery) by the Italian authorities when its original site near the harbour was needed for defence works. It was the subject of a scandal in 1992 when legal proceedings were begun against those responsible for 're-ordering' the site in an attempt to reduce it in size and use part of it for other purposes.

From Piazza Cairoli (see above), Corso Garibaldi runs N, parallel to Corso Vittorio Emanuele and the water front, with a good view of the busy harbour, and the 'sickle', with the FORTE DI SAN SALVATORE, erected by the Spaniards in 1546. On its ancient wall rises a column (60m) surmounted by a Madonna. The E side of the harbour is a naval base. The TEATRO VITTORIO EMANUELE (1852; by Pietro Valente), on Corso Garibaldi, was reopened in 1985 after its reconstruction. The two parallel streets end in PIAZZA UNITÀ D'ITALIA, with the NEPTUNE FOUNTAIN by Montorsoli (1557; the figures of Neptune and Scylla are 19C copies; the originals are kept in the Museo Regionale, see below). Behind it is the huge PALAZZO DEL GOVERNO (Prefettura), designed by Cesare Bazzani in 1920 (being restored). Nearby the little church of SAN GIOVANNI DI MALTA (c 1590; by Camillo Camilliani and Giacomo del Duca) has also been reconstructed. Also facing the piazza is Palazzo Carrozza built in the 1930s in an eclectic style. There is a garden with pines and ficus trees facing the water front, and, behind, the public gardens of VILLA MAZZINI, with an aquarium.

Viale Boccetta leads inland to the church of SAN FRANCESCO D'ASSISI (restored). The exterior has an interesting apse; the deeply recessed arches retain some of the original masonry.

Viale della Libertà (bus, see above), which follows the shore in full view of the Calabrian coastline, passes the site of the Messina Fair, opposite which is the church of Santa Maria di Porto Salvo with red domes in the Norman style, near the pretty Villino Tricomi-Sergio, built in the 1920s.

The road skirts the beach to reach (c 3km from the Duomo) the ***Museo Regionale** (daily 9–13.30; fest. 9–12.30; Tues, Thurs and Sat also 15–17.30) founded to house works of art saved from the earthquake. This remarkable collection of local art is particularly interesting for its fine examples of 15C and early 16C paintings (many of them recently restored). It was beautifully re-arranged in 1980–83. A new building under construction beside the present museum is to be used to expand the exhibition space.

The OUTER COURT contains architectural fragments from the old city; the INNER COURT has statues of Ferdinand II and Charles III of Bourbon. **Room 1** contains works of the Byzantine and Norman periods. 12C sculptural fragments; two fonts; the sarcophagus of the archimandrite Luke; a mosaic niche of the *Madonna and Child, called 'La Ciambretta' (13C); Madonna and Child of the Byzantine type; fragments salvaged from the Duomo of the medieval painted wood ceiling; mosaic head of an apostle; marble bas-relief of the Virgin orante (13C, Byzantine); a fine capital from the Duomo; painting of San Placido; damaged mosaic of the Madonna and Child. **Room 2**. Gothic period. fragment of a 14C painting of the Madonna and Child; 'Master of the Sterbini Diptych' (attributed), triptych of the Madonna and Child between Saints Agatha and Bartholomew (very damaged); Goro di Gregorio, *Madonna 'degli Storpi' (1333; a seated statue from the Duomo); 14–15C Veneto-Marchigiana school, polyptych of the Madonna and Child with four saints (damaged).

Room 3. Early 15C. Wood *Crucifix; architectural fragments from the Duomo; Della Robbian tondo of the Madonna and Child; bas-reliefs including St George and the dragon (attributed to Domenico Gagini) and the Madonna and Child (attributed to Desiderio da Settignano). **Room 4**. **Antonello da Messina**, his school, and Flemish and Spanish works. Displayed on its own is the *polyptych of the Madonna with Saints Gregory and Benedict and the Annunciation, by Antonello da Messina (1473). It was much damaged in the earthquake but has been restored since. Also here: 15C Flemish school, Madonna and Child; Francesco Laurana, (attributed), *statue of the Madonna and Child (restored in 1983); school of Antonello, Madonna of the Rosary (1489); Salvo d'Antonio (attributed), Madonna and Child between Saints John the Evangelist and Peter; Flemish 'Master of the St Lucy Legend' (attributed), Pietà and symbols of the Passion; Giovannello da Itala, St Clare and stories from her life, St Thomas of Canterbury; Antonello de Saliba, Madonna and Child; 16C Spanish school, fragment of a triptych; school of Antonello, Madonna and Child; Antonello Freri, funerary monument of admiral Angelo Balsamo (restored in 1983–4); Jacob Cornelisz van Costzanen, triptych; Colijn de Coter, Deposition.

Room 5. Girolamo Alibrandi and the early 16C. 16C statue of St Catherine of Alexandria (restored in 1983); Vincenzo Catena, *Holy Family and St George; Girolamo Alibrandi, Last Judgement, *St Catherine of Alexandria, St Peter, St Paul; statue of St Anthony of Padua (1534; restored in 1983); Girolamo Alibrandi, *Circumcision, *Presentation in the Temple (1519; restored in 1983–4); Giovanni Battista Mazzolo, head of archbishop Pietro Bellorado (from his funerary monument, 1513); Antonello Gagini, ciborium, Madonna and Child. Rooms 6–9 contain works of the 16–17C. **Room 6**. Stefano Giordano, St Benedict between Saints Mauro and Placido (1541); Polidoro da Caravaggio, Adoration of the Shepherds (1533); Montorsoli, Scylla (the original from the Neptune fountain; restored in 1983–84); Deodato Guinaccia, Resurrection, and works by Mariano Riccio and Stefano Giordano. **Room 7**. Deodato Guinaccia, Adoration of the Shepherds; and a case of majolica (from the Casteldurante and Venetian workshops). **Room 8**. Funerary monument of Francesca Lanza Cibo (1618); Alessandro Allori, Madonna of Istria (1590); Antonio Biondo, Marriage of St Catherine.

Room 9. Antonio Catalano il Vecchio, Madonna appearing to saints Francis and Clare (1604); Giovan Simone Comandè, miraculous draught of fish; Filippo Paladini, St Francis receiving the stigmata; Antonio Catalano il Giovane, Madonna 'della Lettera' (1629).

Room 10 contains two masterpieces by **Caravaggio**, both late works painted during his stay in Messina in 1608–09: *Nativity (commissioned by the Senate of Messina) and *Raising of Lazarus. Works by Sicilian artists of his school displayed here include: Alonzo Rodriquez (meeting between Saints Peter and Paul, restored in 1984); Mario Minniti, miracle performed by Christ for the widow of Nain; and works by Matteo Stomer. **Room 11**. The 17C works here include marble intarsia panels, and paintings by Domenico Marolì, Giovanni Battista Quagliata, Mattia Preti (tondo of the Dead Christ), Giovanni Fulco, and Agostino Scilla. **Room 12**. 18C works including Giovanni Tuccari (Marriage at Cana, restored in 1985); Filippo Tancredi; Sebastiano Conca; and a state coach by Domenico Biondo.

From R 12 stairs lead up to a mezzanine floor where the **Treasury** has recently been arranged. It includes vestments, altar frontals, church silver (16–18C), a 17C ivory and ebany cabinet; an 18C silver altar frontal; and ceramics.

The rest of the collection is to be displayed in a newly-built pavilion in the garden. This will contain the archaeological material and sculpture including: Greek, Roman, and Byzantine coins; marble head of strategos (1C AD, copy of a 5C original); fragment of an Egyptian statue (c 1413 BC); Bronze Age pithos; statue of Igea (3–2C BC) found in Piazza Duomo; a Roman sarcophagus showing Leda and the swan; Roman portrait busts; a sarcophagus with Icarus (mid 3C AD); Bronze Age pithos from the Aeolian Islands; and a bronze mirror showing Eros in repose. Also to be displayed here is Montorsoli's statue of Neptune (from his fountain; cf. above).

On the slopes of the hillside above the town is CRISTO RE (1939), a centrally planned church with a cupola standing on a prominence, and the conspicuous SANTUARIO DI MONTALTO (1930); nearby is the BOTANIC GARDEN. The long winding avenue here (Viale Italia, Principe Umberto, and Regina Margherita), marked by an almost continuous line of pine trees, used to provide a fine view of the Straits before new high building took place.

PUNTA DEL FARO (14km N; bus No. 8), at the extreme NE tip of the island, can be reached by the old road lined with a modest row of houses facing the sea front, which, however, traverses the ambitiously named suburbs of Paradiso, Contemplazione, and Pace, where more high building has taken place. The new fast road ('Panoramica dello Stretto') which starts from Viale Regina Elena and runs along the hillside above has a better view of the Calabrian coast; it is to be extended as far as Mortelle. Just short of the cape is the fishing village of **Ganzirri** (many restaurants and some hotels) on two little lagoons (the 'Pantano Grande' and the 'Pantano Piccolo') once famous for mussels, but now polluted. There are still mussel beds on the smaller lagoon, but no fishing takes place now in the prettier Pantano Grande, one side of which is lined with palm trees.

At PUNTA DEL FARO is a lighthouse and a tower bearing the Sicilian end of the cable that brings electricity from Calabrian power stations, over 229m high. Sword-fishing has taken place off the coast here since ancient times; it was for long considered one of the 'sights' of Messina. The traditional method of harpooning the fish from characteristic small boats with tall look-out masts, has been carried out since the 1960s with modern equipment and motor boats. The catch usually takes place here in June and July.

FROM MESSINA TO THE BADIAZZA AND THE MONTI PELORITANI, N113. The road is well signposted from the centre of Messina ('Colle San Rizzo', 'Portella Castaneo', 'Santa Maria Dinnamare' and 'Badiazza'). Off N113 a very poor road (almost impassable in places) leads right (signposted) past Sant'Andrea, a little church built in 1929 and slums to the head of the valley. Here, in a group of pine trees, is LA BADIAZZA (also called 'Santa Maria della Scala' or 'Santa Maria della Valle'). This fine 13C church (abandoned) belonged to a ruined Cistercian convent and has an interesting exterior with lava decoration.

The main road continues uphill to enter all that remains of the forest which once covered the slopes of the **Monti Peloritani**. Thick pine woods survive here. The road sign indicating Palermo (250km) is a reminder that this was the main road to Palermo before the motorway was built. At COLLE SAN RIZZO (460m) is a crossroads. From here a spectacular road (signposted 'Santuario di Maria Santissima di Dinnamare) leads for 9km along the crest of the Peloritani range to a height of 1130m. The first stretch is extremely narrow and dangerous but further on the road improves. The *views on either side are splendid: on the right Milazzo can be seen and on the left the toe of Italy. There are delightful picnic places and beautiful vegetation. Beyond a television mast is a car-park (signposted). The church of MARIA SANTISSIMA DI DINNAMARE, built in the 18C and restored in 1886, was rebuilt in 1899. The aerial *view, one of the most remarkable in Sicily, takes in the whole of Calabria, the port of Messina, and the tip of Punta del Faro. On the other side can be seen the Aeolian islands including Stromboli (beyond Milazzo), and Mount Etna.

From the Colle San Rizzo crossroads (see above) the road signposted to Castanea leads through fine pine woods (with views down of the port of Messina, and left of the Aeolian islands, and the motorway in hills). In May MONTE CICCIA is on the migratory route from Africa to central Europe for hundreds of birds, especially falcons. On the approach to the village of CASTANEA DELLE FURIE is a castellated villa. Castanea has two churches, one with a primitive dome. The road continues down to SPARTÀ past olives and pines. As the road nears the sea there is a wonderful view of Stromboli.

The coast road can be followed from here back to Messina past some pleasant houses and a few orange plantations, with clear views of Calabria, via Punta del Faro and Ganzirri (described above).

29

Messina to Cefalù (and the Nebrodi mountains)

Road, 184km N113, SETTENTRIONALE SICULA, the line of which follows almost exactly that of the Roman Via Valeria joining Messina to Lilybaeum. Beyond Barcellona the road becomes prettier, running close to the sea, through rich vegetation. The heavy traffic near Messina has been alleviated by the construction of a MOTORWAY (A20; toll) which runs parallel to this route, and continues to Palermo. However a gap in the middle of 72km has been awaiting completion for years (although work has recently been resumed on it). The motorway is at present open from Messina as far as (90km) Rocca Capri Leone.

N113.—40km, byroad for **Milazzo**—67.5km **Tindari**—104km Capo d'Orlando—152km Santo Stefano di Camastra (for the **Nebrodi mountains**)—184km **Cefalù**.

Railway, to Cefalù, 164km in 2½hrs; to Tindari, 61km in 1–1½hrs (the stations of 'Oliveri-Tindari' and 'Patti-San Piero Patti' are both c 12km from the site). Almost all services on this line are through trains from Milan, Turin, Rome or Naples and are therefore subject to delay, although the line is being modernised. After the first 12km and except for a few kilometres at Milazzo the road and railway run together.

Information Office. 'APT' Messina, Tel. 090/675356.

From Messina the road and motorway climb NW amid the slopes of the Monti Peloritani, once covered with thick forests. The steep and winding mountain road (described at the end of Rte 28) climbs to Colle San Rizzo on the main ridge (465m) from which there is a splendid view of both coasts, while the spectacular motorway traverses deserted country (where some pine groves survive), negotiating the mountains by a series of tunnels. On the descent to the N coast, the peninsula of Milazzo and the islands of Vulcano and Lipari come into view, with the distant cone of Stromboli. N113 continues along the coast through a series of unattractive small towns.

At VILLAFRANCA TIRRENA is a 1-star hotel ('Al mio albergo'). At sea off (30km) VENETICO, Agrippa defeated the fleet of Pompeius at the battle of Naulochos (36 BC). At 33km a byroad leads inland for ROCCAVALDINA, where a remarkably well preserved 16C pharmacy, complete with its jars, survives in Piazza Umberto I (admission by appointment at the Comune, Tel. 090/9977086).

40km **MILAZZO** is a port (32,100 inhab.) with pretty buildings and an attractive sea front, standing on the isthmus of a narrow peninsula, 7km NW of the main road. It is the port for the Aeolian islands. On the outskirts is a huge oil refinery and much new building.

Information Office. 'Azienda Autonoma', Piazza Duilio (Tel. 090/9222865).

Railway Station, Piazza Marconi, near the port. Services on the Messina–Palermo line.

Maritime Services to the Aeolian Islands, see Rte 30.

Hotels. 3-star: 'Silvanetta Palace', 1 Via Mangiavacca; 'Riviera Lido', Strada Panoramica (località Corrie).

Camping Site (2-star) 'Sayonara', at Gronda.

Restaurants. Luxury-class: 'Villa Marchese', Strada Panoramica; 1st class: 'Covo del Pirato', Lungomare Garibaldi; 'Al Pescatore', 119 Via Marina Garibaldi.

History. Milazzo was the ancient *Mylai*, founded by Greeks from Zancle in 716 BC. Here Duilius defeated the Carthaginians in a sea-fight (260 BC), and here in 1860 Garibaldi successfully assaulted the castle, garrisoned by Bourbon troops, promoting J.W. Peard, a Cornish volunteer, to the rank of colonel on the field.

The road for the centre passes the station and the port, where the boats and hydrofoils for the Aeolian islands dock. In Via Crispi is the MUNICIPIO built at the end of the last century by Salvatore Richichi. On the other side of the building (reached through the courtyard) is Piazza Duilio, with a copy made in 1990 of the 'Fontana della Mela' (the original made in 1762 by Giuseppe Buceti was destroyed in the Second World War). Here is the pleasant red façade of the former convent of the CARMELITANI (16C; recently restored), with the 'Azienda Autonoma' information office. Next to it is the Baroque façade of the CARMINE (1574; rebuilt in 1726–52), and, on the other side, a handsome neo-classical palace. Opposite is Palazzo Proto which was Garibaldi's headquarters for a time in 1860 (cf. above).

The Lungomare, planted with trees, continues Via Crispi along the sea front. The 18C church of San Giacomo is well sited at a fork in the road which leads inland to the DUOMO NUOVO (1937–52) which contains paintings by Antonello de Saliba and Antonio Giuffrè. Farther on, Via Colombo leads away from the sea past two little Art Nouveau villas, now surrounded by unattractive buildings.

From Piazza Roma Via Impallomeni leads up towards the castle past the pretty 18C church of SAN FRANCESCO DI PAOLA, which contains six paintings of miracles of the saint by Letterio Paladino (restored). The 17C church of the Immacolata can be seen above on the left, and on the right is the closed church of San Salvatore. Pretty low houses surround the double walls of the ***Castle**, built by Frederick II in 1239, enlarged by Charles V and restored in the 17C. The walls date from the 16C and enclose a large area including an imposing keep with a Gothic doorway and great hall. The castle has been 'in restoration' for many years but when the custodian is available it is open daily except Monday, on the hour, from 9–12, and from 14.30–15.30 (17–19 in summer). The DUOMO VECCHIO, within the castle enclosure, is an interesting building of the early 17C, attributed to Camillo Camilliani or possibly Natale Masuccio. It was abandoned when the new Cathedral was begun in 1937 (see above). The 16C walls survive here.

A pretty road (c 12km) runs round the unspoilt peninsula of Capo Milazzo, known as BARONIA. It passes 19C and early 20C villas and ends by a group of olive trees. There is a light house, and paths descend to the rocky shore. The vegetation includes prickly pear, palms and olive trees. From the Cape the view (on a clear day) encompasses the two active volcanoes of Etna and Stromboli.

Santa Lucia del Mela (1st-class restaurant 'Dal Pellegrino') lies 5.5km inland off N113, in an open position, but now surrounded by new buildings beneath its prominent castle.

A narrow road leads up to the fine DUOMO (if closed ring at No. 3 Via Cappuccini), with a lovely 15C portal and an interesting interior. In the S aisle, the first altarpiece of the martyrdom of St Sebastian (in poor condition) is attributed to Zoppo di Ganci; on the second altar is a painting of St Mark the Evangelist by Deodato Guinaccia (1581) and a statuette of the Ecce Homo attributed to Ignazio Marabitti. In the S transept, St Blaise by Pietro Novelli. In the chapel to the right of the sanctuary, marble statue of St Lucy (1512). The high altarpiece of the Assumption is by Fra' Felice da Palermo (1771). In the chapel to the left of the sanctuary is an unusual little sculpted Last Supper in the front of the altar attributed to Valerio Villareale. The altarpiece in the left transept is by Filippo Iannelli (1676), and on the third N altar is an 18C Crucifix. The font dates from 1485.

Also in the piazza is PALAZZO VESCOVILE, with a little collection of works of art (closed after thefts in 1992). Other churches of interest (open only for services) include: SANTISSIMA ANNUNZIATA with a campanile of 1461 and a painting of the Madonna and Child of c 1400; SANTA MARIA DI GESÙ (or Santa Cuore) with a Crucifix by Fra Umile da Petralia; and the sanctuary of the MADONNA DELLA NEVE (1673) with a Madonna and Child by Antonello Gagini. The CASTLE of 1322, now a seminary, has a round tower.

A mountain road (surfaced as far as Calderado) leads into the Peloritani mountains as far as Pizzo Croce (1214m).

At frequent intervals the coast road crosses 'fiumare' (not unlike the 'wadis' of the Syrian deserts), wide flat-bottomed torrent-beds filled with gravel, usually waterless and standing out conspicuously in the surrounding landscape. In flood time the water descends these channels in spate, carrying a considerable quantity of alluvial matter. 45.5km BARCELLONA (3-star and 2-star hotels; and 2-star camping site 'Centro Vacanze Cantoni'), with a lot of unattractive new buildings (34,400 inhab.).

A byroad mounts to **Castroreale** (9km; 313m), an upland town (3560 inhab.; Youth Hostel 'Delle Aquile'), the favourite residence of Frederick II of Aragon from whose castle (1324; now in ruins) it gets its name. Despite damage in the earthquake of 1978 the little town is unusually well preserved thanks to the efforts of its inhabitants. The numerous churches contain 16–17C works of art: notable are the CHIESA MATRICE, with a St Catherine by Antonello Gagini (1534); the CANDELORA, with a 17C carved wood altarpiece; SANTA MARIA DEGLI ANGELI with interesting paintings and two sculptures (St John the Baptist by Andrea Calamech, 1568; and a Madonna by Antonello Freri, 1510); SANTA MARINA; SANT'AGATA, with an Annunciation by Antonello Gagini, dated 1519; and the 15C church of SANTA MARIA DI GESÙ. A charming MUSEO CIVICO is in the course of arrangement in the restored ex-Oratorio dei Filippini. The collection of sculpture and paintings from local churches includes the sarcophagus of Geronimo Rosso by Antonello Gagini (1507), a wood 15C Crucifix (restored in 1981), and a Madonna enthroned with angels by Antonello de Saliba. A Crucifix on a 'vara' as high as the Chiesa Matrice is carried in procession through the little town on Good Friday.

The main road continues through (51km) CASTROREALE TERME, now part of the new commune of TERME VIGLIATORE (3-star 'Grand Hotel Terme' and 2-star hotels; 4-star camping site 'Bazia' at Furnari), a thermal resort, with a tourist port. The main road passes under a railway bridge at San Biagio, W of the town, and, just beyond on the left (well signposted), protected by a plastic roof, are the remains of a large ROMAN VILLA of the 1C AD (admission daily 9–dusk). The rooms have black-and-white mosaics, mostly geometric, but one floor has a lively fishing scene, with dolphins, sword fish, and other fish still found off the coast here. The main hall has a fine opus sectile pavement.

A byroad leads S to Rodi (3.5km), just beyond which, near MILICI, is the site of ancient LONGANE. A Sicel town of some importance, it was no longer inhabited in the 5C BC. Traces of the walls survive and the foundations of a sacred building.

FROM CASTROREALE TERME TO FRANCAVILLA DI SICILIA, N185, 50km. This road, which connects the Tyhrrenian coast with the Ionian sea at Naxos, is fairly well engineered, and carries very little traffic. Rising to a height of 1100m, it has some of the best scenery on the island.

Just beyond Terme Vigliatore N185 diverges left and follows the wide Mazzarrà and Novara valleys on the beds of which are extensive citrus fruit plantations and some 'pill-box' defences from the last war. The road passes (5.5km) MAZZARRÀ SANT' ANDREA surrounded with nurseries. Gravel is extracted from the grey waterless river bed here, beside which oranges are grown. A few lovely old abandoned farmhouses survive. Farther on there is a good view back of Tindari with its sanctuary on a promontory on the coast.

19.5km NOVARA DI SICILIA (675m), the ancient *Noae*, is now a quiet little town below the main road. From Largo Bertolami, with a bronze statue of David by Giuseppe Buemi (1882), Via Duomo leads up to the 16C Duomo. In the right aisle is a wood statue of the Assumption by Filippo Colicci. Across the valley much new building has taken place at San Basilio. The road passes beneath the fantastic bare horn-shaped ROCCA NOVARA (1340m), at the end of the Peloritani range. The road now enters thick woods of pine and fir as it climbs up to the pass at (30km) SELLA MANDRAZZI (1125m). The view back takes in the coastline and the sanctuary of Tindari on its promontory, beyond the conspicuous Rocca Novara.

The scenery is particuarly fine here, and picnic places are provided. The fine mountain road now descends through deserted country which provides pasture for sheep and goats. Almost all the farmhouses here are abandoned. On a clear day there is a spectacular *view of Etna, and of the river torrents on the hillsides. The road continues to descend and there are now some vineyards, persimmon trees, and prickly pears. It crosses a bridge before reaching (47km) the junction with the road from Moio Alcantara (described in Rte 26), near an abandoned villa. The Francavilla road continues left along the side of the valley and then descends through orange groves.

50km **Francavilla di Sicilia**. Above the cemetery on the outskirts is the well-signposted Convento dei Cappuccini (admission only for services), where the church has 17C and 18C works. A pretty road continues past numerous orange groves and the Gola dell'Alcantara (described in Rte 25) to Giardini Naxos on the coast (see Rte 27).

Another very winding minor road leads SW from Terme Vigliatore to MONTALBANO ELICONA (27km), a little hill town (900m), in a fine position surrounded by woods, with a castle (1302–11) open for exhibitions and concerts.

The coast road climbs across (67.5km) CAPO TINDARI (278m), a headland (2km right) crowned by a conspicuous sanctuary. A huge new church was built onto the old in 1957–79 to house a seated statue of a black Virgin of Byzantine origin which has been greatly venerated since the 16C (pilgrimage on 8 September). The old sanctuary, with a portal of 1598, on the seaward side, is no longer visible.

The road continues from the sanctuary to the ruins of ***Tyndaris** (open daily 9–dusk), just beyond. Excavations were begun in the 19C and resumed from 1949–64. A path leads down through a little garden to the site in a grove of olives and pines planted with bougainvillea and prickly pear, with delightful views of the sea and the Aeolian Islands. Unusual currents in the shallows at the foot of the cliffs produce pretty formations of sand and gravel and areas of temporary marshland of great interest to naturalists. On the left is a small MUSEUM (open 9–dusk; fest. 9–14) with a plan of the excavations and finds from the site including two fragments of Hellenistic statues of winged victories, 4–1C BC statuettes, a colossal head of the emperor Augustus (1C), two female draped statues, vases, reliefs, a capital of 1C BC, and a theatrical tragic mask.

The paved DECUMANUS MAXIMUS is flanked by remains of houses (some with mosaics). To the right is a conspicuous building, once called the 'GINNASIO', but now thought to have been a monumental entrance to the public buildings. Its façade, which fell in Byzantine times, was excellently restored in 1956. It is an unusual building with barrel vaulting across the main road of the city: formerly dated in the 1C BC it is now thought to have been built in the 4C AD. The agora lies beneath the modern village. To the left of the entrance is the THEATRE, a Greek building adapted by the Romans to gladiatorial uses. The Greek WALLS (3C BC), obscured by vegetation on the seaward side, survive in a good state of preservation to the S (beside the approach road below the sanctuary), extending, with interval towers, for several hundred metres on either side of the MAIN GATE, a dipylon with a barbican.

76.5km **Patti** (11,500 inhab.; 3-star hotels: 'La Playa' and 'Park Philip', 2-star hotel: 'Villa Romana'; and two 2-star camping sites; 'APT' information office, 17 Via Agrigento), on a hill, damaged by earthquake in 1978. In the Cathedral (damaged) is the Renaissance tomb of Adelaide (died 1118), queen of Roger I. During the construction of the motorway from Messina part of a large ROMAN VILLA (4C AD) was uncovered here in 1973;

excavations are still in progress (follow the signs for Marina di Patti and the motorway: the entrance to the site is beneath the motorway viaduct; open daily 9am–dusk). The beautiful polychrome mosaic floors (protected by a roof, and seen from walkways), similar to those at Piazza Armerina, have geometric designs and hunting scenes. A small museum (not yet open) has been built to house finds from the site. The road tunnels through the steep Capo Calavà.

89km GIOIOSA MAREA, now a seaside resort (2-star hotels: 'Baia Calavà', 'Cani Cani', 'Villa Giulia', 'Maddalena', 'Villa Smeralda', and 'Capo Calavà', and 2-star camping sites. 1st-class restaurant 'Cani-Cani). The island of Vulcano is only 19km offshore. The town was built in the 18C after an earthquake destroyed the medieval town of GIOIOSA GUARDIA, the ruins of which survive high up (828m) on a hill beyond the motorway. A winding road leads up to the old town from which there are wonderful views. At PIRAINO-GLIACA is a 3-star hotel ('Calanovellamare' and a 3-star camping site).

104.5km **Capo d'Orlando** (3-star hotels 'Il Mulino' and 'La Meridiana' and 2-star hotels; 'Azienda Autonoma' information office, 71 Via Piave), another little seaside resort (9300 inhab.), lies below its cape, off which Frederick II of Aragon was defeated in 1299 by Roger of Lauria, commanding the allied fleets of Catalonia and Anjou. The promontory, already occupied in the Greek era, is noted for its sudden storms. It is crowned by a 14C castle and a sanctuary. The town became famous in Italy in 1991 for the courageous stand its shopkeepers took against the Mafia racket.

The Nebrodi Mountains

FROM CAPO D'ORLANDO TO RANDAZZO, 65.5km, N116. 11.5km **Naso**, a small town of 5300 inhab., has 15–17C tombs in the church of the MINORI OSSERVANTI, including a monument to Artale Cardona (died 1477). The road continues to climb through the **Nebrodi Mountains**, a protected area of great natural beauty which may become the PARCO DEI NEBRODI. The mountain range, which stretches from the Peloritani on the E to the Madonie on the W, has an average height of 1200–1500m and is interesting as the largest forested area to survive on the island. The trees include oak, elm, ash, beech, holm oak, and yew, and are especially fine in the Caronia forest. The area has numerous mountain torrents, small lakes and springs. The upland plains provide pasturelands, and horses of the 'San Fratello' breed run wild here. The road from Naso continues to climb to (45km) FLORESTA (1275m), the highest village in Sicily, with winter sports facilities. It reaches a summit level of 1280m before descending in full view of Etna to (65.5km) RANDAZZO (described in Rte 25B).

The main road continues, and at 116.5km a byroad leads up to SAN MARCO D'ALUNZIO, where Robert Guiscard built the first Norman castle in Sicily in 1061 (it survives in ruins at the top of the hill). At the entrance to the town is the Temple of Hercules, dating from the Hellenistic era, transformed into a church in the Middle Ages.

121km SANT'AGATA DI MILITELLO (hotels) is a seaside resort (12,600 inhab.), from which climbing expeditions may be made in the Monti Nebrodi (see above). A museum relating to the Nebrodi is open here on weekdays (9–13.30).

FROM SANT'AGATA DI MILITELLO TO CESARÒ, N289, 51km. The lovely road leads S through the Nebrodi mountains past (14km) SAN FRATELLO, a Lombard colony founded by Adelaide, queen of Roger I, with a 12C Norman church. The ancient 'Festa dei Giudei' is celebrated here on Maundy Thursday and Good Friday in traditional costume. The road continues to climb, reaching (33.5km) a summit level of 1524m below MONTE SORO (1847m), the highest peak of the Nebrodi. The road now begins to descend, and at (36km) the PORTELLA DI MIRAGLIA is a 2-star hotel ('Villa Miraglia'). 51km **Cesarò**, see Rte 16C.

142km, byroad for CARONIA (4km) which preserves a privately owned Norman castle. On the outskirts the site of the Greek and Roman colony of KALACTE has been identified. The byroad continues up into the Nebrodi through the splendid forest of Caronia to Capizzi, 33km S, described in Rte 16. 152km SANTO STEFANO DI CAMASTRA, noted for its ceramics, which are sold on the streets. Here begins N117, another fine road through the Nebrodi which passes MISTRETTA (950m), 17km S, a pretty old town (6600 inhab.) the ancient *Amestratus*. The carved S portal of the church has been ascribed to Giorgio da Milano (1493). A small museum is usually open here in the mornings. This magnificent mountain road continues S to Nicosia (46km), described in Rte 16.

160km CASTEL DI TUSA (3-star hotel 'L'Atelier sul Mare'). On the byroad to Tusa just E of the town is the site of HALAESA on a hill (signposted 'Scavi' and approached beyond a gate by a paved road which ends at a chapel and the custodian's farmhouse). The site (open 9–14) commands a fine view of the Tusa valley. Remains of the Greek city founded in the 5C BC by Archonides, tyrant of Herbita, include part of the W side of the agora, as well as a bath, two temples, and stretches of the walls. Excavations begun in 1952–56 were interrupted in 1972.

Vast incongruous modern sculptures set up in the wide 'fiumare' of the

Tusa river in 1989 were ordered to be demolished by a court ruling in 1991. The hills rise steeply from the rocky and deserted shore, and the villages, some kilometres inland, can be approached only by their individual tortuous roads; TUSA, and SAN MAURO CASTELVERDE have churches with good sculptures by Domenico and Antonello Gagini.

176km Castelbuono Station and turning (see Rte 3). The limestone crag concealing Cefalù becomes more and more prominent. 184km **Cefalù**, described, together with the road from here to Palermo in Rte 3.

30

The Aeolian Islands

Information Office. 'Azienda Autonoma del Turismo delle Eolie', 202 Corso Vittorio Emanuele, Lipari (Tel. 090/9880095).

Approaches. The most convenient starting point in Sicily for the islands is Milazzo (cf. Rte 29). Throughout the year FERRIES (run by 'Siremar' and 'Navigazione Generale Italiana' leave twice a day from Milazzo for the Islands (to Lipari in c 2hrs). A HYDROFOIL service operates at least three times a day (more frequently in summer) from Milazzo (run by 'SNAV', 'COVEMAR, and 'Siremar') in 45mins. An overnight ferry from Naples (with sleeping accommodation and restaurant) operates two or three times a week; it calls at Stromboli, Panarea, Salina, Lipari, and terminates at Messina. In summer hydrofoil service from Messina and Reggio Calabria to Lipari. Although the timetables are subject to change, there is also usually a hydrofoil service in summer from Palermo to Vulcano and Lipari, and from Naples to Stromboli and Lipari (also, sometimes, from Cefalù).

Sailing Times. Timetables vary annually and according to season, and ferry and hydrofoil sailings are subject to sea conditions; the time of departure should always be checked locally. Some ticket offices on the islands open 30mins before sailing. Information from the 'Azienda Autonoma', 202 Corso Vittorio Emanuele, Lipari. Sleeping accommodation on the ferry from Naples to Messina can be booked at the Agenzia Carlo Genovese, 78 Via de Pretis, Naples.

Inter-island Communications. All the islands are connected by ferry and hydrofoil services most days of the week; the services to Alicudi and Filicudi are less frequent. It is advisable to purchase return tickets for day excursions between the islands as space is limited on hydrofoils. Extra hydrofoil services operate from Lipari to Vulcano (several times daily) and Salina, both of which can also be reached by local boat excursions. The ferries are slower and often less direct than the hydrofoil service, but are comfortable and provide an opportunity of seeing the coastal regions of the islands. The hydrofoils are relatively more expensive, and less reliable as they cannot sail in rough weather. It should not be overlooked that on some islands the ferries call at several ports: Lipari, Canneto, and Acquacalda (on Lipari); Santa Marina, Lingua, Rinella, and Malfa (on Salina); Stromboli and Ginostra (on Stromboli); and Filicudi Porto and Filicudi Pecorini (on Filicudi). Fishing boats may be hired on all the islands, and the trip around the coast of most of the islands is strongly recommended.

Cars are allowed on Lipari, Vulcano, Filicudi and Salina; a car ferry runs from Milazzo. However, visitors are not advised to take a car as distances are short, and local transport good. A car hire service operates on Lipari. On the other islands small motor vehicles are used to transport luggage.

The ***AEOLIAN ISLANDS** or Lipari Isles form an archipelago of seven islands (Lipari, Salina, Stromboli, Panarea, Vulcano, Alicudi, and Filicudi) and numerous rocks. The alternative titles are derived from the name of the main island of the group, and from Aeolus, the Greek god of the winds, who was fabled to keep the winds imprisoned in his cave here. The islands are remarkable for their spectacular scenery and geological and archaeological interest. Several prehistoric sites have been excavated, and the fine archaeological museum in Lipari is one of the most important collections of its kind in Europe. No visitor can fail to be struck by the variety and beauty of the rock formations, and the volcanic phenomena of Stromboli (still active) and Vulcano. The islands are increasingly visited in the summer months for sea bathing. A lively fishing industry supplies the archipelago with a variety of fish. The local style of architecture adds charm to the picturesque villages on the smaller islands.

History. The islands were important in ancient times because of the existence of obsidian, a hard volcanic glass used as a tool and exported in the Mediterranean. The earliest traces of settlement found belong to the Stentinello culture of the Neolithic age. In the Middle Bronze Age the islands were on the main trade routes between the Aegean islands and the Western Mediterranean. The Greeks colonised Lipari in c 600 BC, and in the following centuries the islands were attacked by the Athenians and the Carthaginians. They fell to Rome in 252 BC. From then on their history has been closely related to that of Sicily.

Vegetation. The tropical plants which thrive on the rocky soil include prickly pear, carob trees, and palms. Huge old olive trees survive on some of the islands. In spring, broom flourishes, and the wild flowers, particularly on Panarea, are particularly beautiful. Capers and excellent wine are exported from the islands.

Accommodation. Good hotels are now to be found on most of the islands; the standard of accommodation is often higher than the official categories would suggest (especially in Panarea and Lipari). It is essential to book in advance in the summer months, and advisable to do so at all times of the year. All the islands have numerous flats and rooms to let. **Camping sites** are open in summer on Lipari, Filicudi, Salina and Vulcano.

LIPARI (37 sq km), the chief island of the group and about 40km from Milazzo on the Sicilian mainland, has become a popular summer resort. About half its 8580 inhabitants are concentrated in the lively little town of **Lipari**.

Information Offices. 'Azienda Autonoma del Turismo delle Isole Eolie', 202 Corso Vittorio Emanuele, with a subsidiary office at the Marina Corta.

Boats from Naples, Messina, and Milazzo, and the inter-island ferries (cf. above) dock at the MARINA LUNGA. The **Hydrofoil** services operate from the MARINA CORTA, 10mins S of the main harbour.

Buses. Services from the Corso Vittorio Emanuele to Canneto (every 2hrs) and to the pumice quarries and Acquacalda (every 3hrs); to Quattrocchi, Pianoconte, and Quattropani (every 3hrs).

Hotels. 4-star: 'Meligunis'; 3-star: 'Gattopardo', 'Carasco', and 'Giardino sul Mare'; 2-star: 'Filadelfia'. Apartments to rent at 'Residence La Giara'. YOUTH HOSTEL on the Acropolis. 2-star CAMPING SITE 'Baia Unci' at Canneto.

Restaurant. 'Filippino', Piazza Municipio; and numerous trattorie.

Sailing regattas and underwater fishing contests are held in summer.

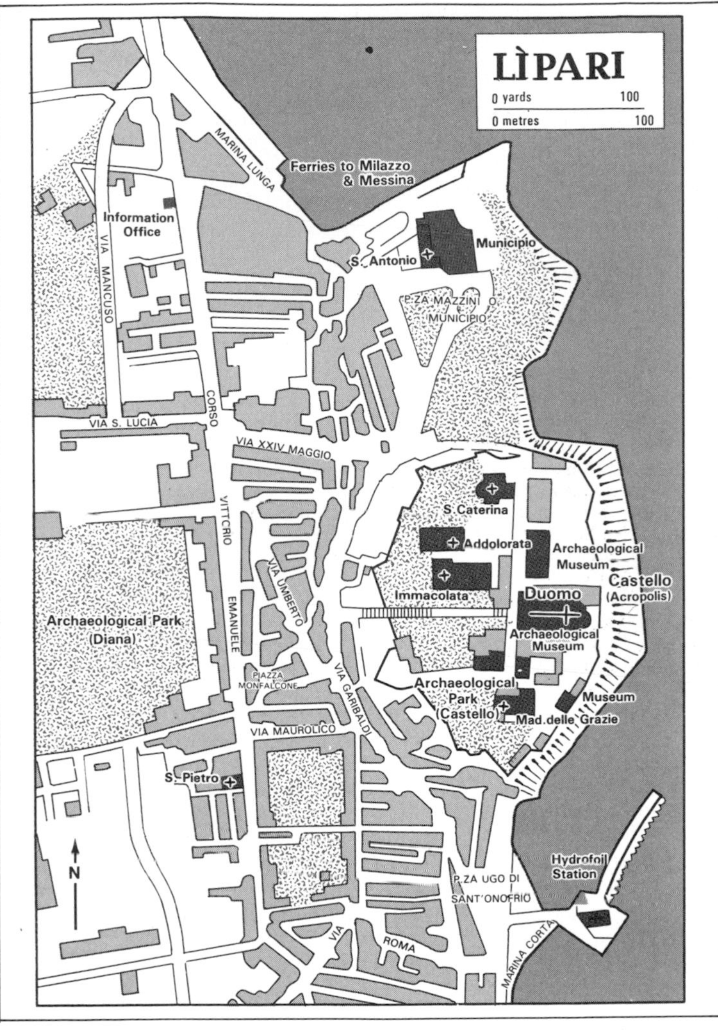

The **Acropolis** (or **Castello**) commands the shore above the town, and separates the two harbours. The impressive entrance through its 16C Spanish fortifications incorporates Classical fragments. On the summit excavations have revealed a remarkable sequence of levels of occupation uninterrupted from the Neolithic Age when the islands were first inhabited. The unique pottery strata (reaching a depth of 9m) make the acropolis the key dating site of the central Mediterranean. The different levels are well labelled and explained by diagrams; the finds are displayed in the museum.

The ***Museo Archeologico** (open daily 9–14; fest. 9–13; if closed, ring for the custodian in one of the three buildings) is housed in the former episcopal palace (17C) on the acropolis, and in two buildings nearby. The superb collection, beautifully displayed in chronological sequence, contains finds from Lipari and other islands in the Aeolian group (as well as from Milazzo and Southern Italy).

FIRST BUILDING. **Rooms I–III** contain Neolithic finds from Lipari, including painted vases, 'Serra d'Alto' style pottery (resembling Southern Italian forms), and red pottery of the 'Diana' style. **RVI** displays objects belonging to the Capo Graziano (1800–1400 BC) and Milazzese (c 1400–1250 BC) cultures, showing Greek influences. Notable are the vessels on tall pedestals, thought to have been used from a sitting position on the floor. The Ausonian culture is represented in **RRVII–IX**; the finds show the influence of the Italian mainland, and the vessels have a great variety of strangely shaped handles. Here also are the remains of a small cooking device, and a large impasto pot, the repository of over two-hundredweight of bronze objects of the 9C BC. **RX**. Greek and Roman period. Couchant lion (c 575 BC) carved from volcanic rock, which probably guarded a votive deposit; Roman *statue of a girl of the 2C AD, found in the bishop's palace; statuette of Asklepios (4C BC). A case displays Hellenistic and Medieval ceramics. A door leads out to the garden where the EPIGRAPHIC PAVILION contains funerary inscriptions of 5–1C BC.

SECOND BUILDING (MUSEO DELLE ISOLE MINORI) contains finds from Panarea (from the Calcara and Milazzese sites), Stromboli, Filicudi, and Salina. In a group of old houses nearby the GEOLOGICAL SECTION has recently been arranged.

THIRD BUILDING. **Room XVII** contains finds from Milazzo displayed in chronological sequence from the Middle Bronze Age to the 3C BC; reconstruction of a burial site, with the pithoi in situ. The Piazza Monfalcone necropolis (1125–1050 BC) in Lipari is reconstructed in **RXVIII**. A superb collection of sarcophagi from Lipari fills **RXIX**. Among the Greek and Roman tombs is a sarcophagus found in the Contrada Diana (2–1C BC); perfectly preserved, it is thought to have been made by the sculptor as his own tomb.

Upstairs, beyond several more rooms is R XX which contains a fascinating *collection of tragic masks and theatrical terracottas (early 4C–mid 3C BC) found on Lipari. Note especially the statuettes of dancers, and Andromica with her child. **RXXI** has finds from a sanctuary of Demeter and Kore, including statuettes and bas-reliefs, and funerary pottery on a black ground (end of 4C BC). Here, and in **RXXII** are displayed the brightly-coloured *vases by the 'Lipari Painter', a master who excelled in the representation of the female figure. The southern Italian vases include a krater with Dionysius watching a nude acrobat and two actors, and a bronze hydra with a female bust (early 5C BC). **RXXIII** has theatrical masks (some of them painted), and Hellenistic gold jewellery (note the ring of the 4C BC with a female nude). The Roman glass includes elaborate funerary vases. **RXXV** consists of a reconstruction of part of the necropolis of Lipari, with pithoi and situlae. The underwater finds, fished up off Capistello (Lipari), and near Filicudi and Panarea, are displayed in **RXXVI**. They include a fine series of amphorae.

Outside, the extensive excavations are surrounded by a number of churches; opposite the Baroque façades of the ADDOLORATA and the IMMACOLATA stands the **Cathedral**, first built on this site by King Roger (c 1084). Inside, the vault has 18C frescoes and in the N transept is a Madonna of the Rosary, attributed to Girolamo Alibrandi. The statue in silver of San Bartolomeo dates from 1725 (carried in procession through the streets on 24 August).

SW of the museum a small ARCHAEOLOGICAL PARK (with fine views) incorporates a large number of Greek and Roman sarcophagi. These were found in the necropolis of Contrada Diana (late 5C and 4C BC), at the foot of the acropolis (now covered by the modern town). There is a second ARCHAEOLOGICAL PARK in the town W of the Corso in CONTRADA DIANA where two Roman hypogeum were found, and where recent excavations have revealed part of the Greek walls (5–4C BC) of the ancient city, and Roman houses.

A road (26.5km) encircles the island. It leads N from Lipari via (5.5km) CANNETO to traverse huge white *cliffs of pumice, with deep gallery quarries. The loading jetties protrude into the sea, here washed clean by the pumice stone. Beyond (8.5km) PORTICELLO the road crosses red and black *veins of obsidian, some of which reach the sea. The beaches are covered with pumice and obsidian, and some of the paths in the villages are cut out of obsidian. A road connects (12km) Acquacalda with (17km) Quattropani. 21.5km PIANO CONTE, where lava battle axes and Bronze Age weapons have been found. Near the coast (reached by a byroad, 3km) are the ancient hot springs of SAN CALOGERO with remains of Roman baths and a thermal spa (open July–September). An ancient tholos has come to light here. The road returns to (26.5km) Lipari past the view-point of Quattrocchi. MONTE SANT'ANGELO (594m; view), in the centre of the island, is an extinct stratified volcano of unusual form.

VULCANO (21 sq km; 717 inhab.) is the most southerly of the isles (separated from the S tip of Lipari by a channel less than 1km wide) and easily reached from the Sicilian mainland (cf. above) or by frequent hydrofoil services from Lipari (and by local boat excursions). A spectacular volcanic landscape of rugged peaks rises above the beaches where the boats anchor; the small plain has been marred in recent years by indiscriminate new building.

An INFORMATION OFFICE is open in summer at Porto Levante. HOTELS: 4-star: 'Les Sables Noirs'; 3-star: 'Eolian'; 2-star: 'Conti'. Rooms to let at 'Residence al Porto' and 'Sea Houses Residence'. The N part of the island is much visited by holiday-makers. Hot springs in the sea provide good bathing, and there are facilities for under-water swimming. A solar energy plant was opened here in 1984.

Vulcano is of outstanding interest because of its geological structure. The last volcanic eruption occurred in 1890. A steep path leads up from the untidy plain to (c 1 hour) the *GRAN CRATERE (375m), whose rim steams with sulphur vapours. The cone may be descended. On a clear day the ***view** embraces most of the Aeolian islands. The N tip of the island consists of VULCANELLO, an excellent example of a volcanic cone which rose out of the sea in 183 BC. Near the FARAGLIONE DELLA FABBRICA, a lofty rock with alum quarries, are the hot springs of Acqua Bollente and Acqua del Bagno. A road ascends to MONTE ARIA (499m). Between Vulcano and Lipari are some striking basalt stacks, including the *PIETRALUNGA, an obelisk of rock, 72m high.

SALINA, 4km NW of Lipari, is the highest of the islands (962m), and is formed by two volcanic cones and the saddle between them (27 sq km). It has been identified with Homer's 'Siren Island', and was anciently called

'Didyme'. Its population (2300 inhab.) is divided into several picturesque villages; SANTA MARINA (1-star hotels), MALFA (3-star hotels and rooms to let), and LENI (2-star hotel). The island is famous for malvasia wine. On the E coast, near the Santa Marina lighthouse, a Middle Bronze Age village has been excavated, and traces of Roman houses were found nearby.

***PANAREA** lies to the NE (15km from Lipari), towards Stromboli. It is perhaps the most charming of all the islands, and its natural beauty and the style of the local architecture has been carefully preserved by its 317 inhabitants. It is 3.5 sq km in area. 3-star hotels: 'Cincotta' and 'La Piazza'; 2-star hotels: 'Lisca Bianca', 'Raya', 'Residence', 'Tesoriero' and 'Cincotta'; 1-star: 'Bottari'. Electricity was brought to the island in 1982. Near the fishing harbour hot spring water mixes with the sea.

An easy walk (c 30 minutes) leads to a naturally defended promontory on the S tip of the island. On this superb site the Bronze Age village of MILAZZESE (probably inhabited in the 14C BC), with 23 huts, was excavated in 1948. Mycenaean ceramics and native vases showing Minoan influences were brought to light (now in Lipari Museum, cf. above).

At the opposite end of the island, near the last houses on the coast, a path descends to the shore at CALCARA where the fumarole emit sulphureous gases. Nearby are traces of Neolithic pits made from boulders and volcanic clay, probably used for offerings. A Greek wreck was found offshore here in 1980, and from then until 1987 some 600 pieces of ceramics were recovered from its cargo of precious terracotta vases (5C–4C BC), some of which are now exhibited in the Lipari museum.

In the sea near the island the beautifully coloured rocks of LISCA BIANCA and BASILUZZO (with many traces of Roman occupation) provide a foreground to the ever-changing view of Stromboli. In hot weather, when the sea is very calm, the volcano takes on the appearance of a 'floating isle' (cf. 'Odyssey', x, 3).

STROMBOLI (12.5 sq km; c 28km from Lipari) is the most famous island of the archipelago on account of its continual volcanic activity. It consists of a single cone (926m); the present active crater is 200m below the summit. It has been several times abandoned after severe eruptions, but is now again increasing in population (407 inhab.). It is visited by many tourists, especially from Germany.

The main village of STROMBOLI is on the NE coast (3-star hotel 'La Sirenetta'; 2-star: 'Zurro'; and 1-star: 'Villa Petrusa'; and rooms to let. Information office, open in summer, at Ficogrande). The boats also call at GINOSTRA, an attractive small group of houses (including several simple 'locande') on a rocky headland on the SW tip of the island. The construction of a port here in 1991 was blocked in an attempt to preserve the beauty of the coast. Eruptions occur on the NW side of the volcano and are not visible from either of the villages. The cone may be ascended with a guide (c 3 hours); but an easy footpath from Stromboli (San Vincenzo) ascends as far as the 'Semaforo' (c 1½ hours), from which point the explosions can usually be seen. Normally a small eruption occurs at frequent intervals; on days of unusual violence the spectacle (best seen at night from the sea) of the volcanic matter rushing down the SCIARA DEL FUOCO into the sea is unforgettable.

Off the NE coast is the striking rock of STROMBOLICCHIO, a steep block of basalt (43m) ascended by a rock-hewn stair and commanding an unparalleled *view of the islands and of Calabria. Around Strombolicchio are certain mysterious currents, sometimes violent enough to incline the vertically anchored fishing nets to an angle of 45 degrees. Shoals of flying fish can occasionally be seen offshore.

The remote and picturesque island of **Filicudi** (9.5 sq km) lies 19km W of Salina. Anciently called *Phoenicoessa*, it has 301 inhabitants (3-star hotel). Two prehistoric villages have been excavated on Capo Graziano; on the point (Montagnola) 12 huts were uncovered showing evidence of rebuilding before their destruction in the Milazzese period, while just inland, three oval huts yielded Bronze Age vases. Off the Cape in 1975 a hoard of Bronze Age ceramics was found on the site of a shipwreck.

The most westerly isle is **Alicudi** (1-star hotel). Its 5 sq km support a dwindling population of 102 inhabitants. Electrictiy was bought to the island in 1990.

View of Stromboli from Mark Twain's 'The Innocents Abroad' (1895)

INDEX TO ARTISTS

INDEX

Topographical names are printed in CAPITALS (modern, ancient, and medieval names), names of people, sub-indexes and other entries in roman type.

ATLAS AND TOWN PLANS

2

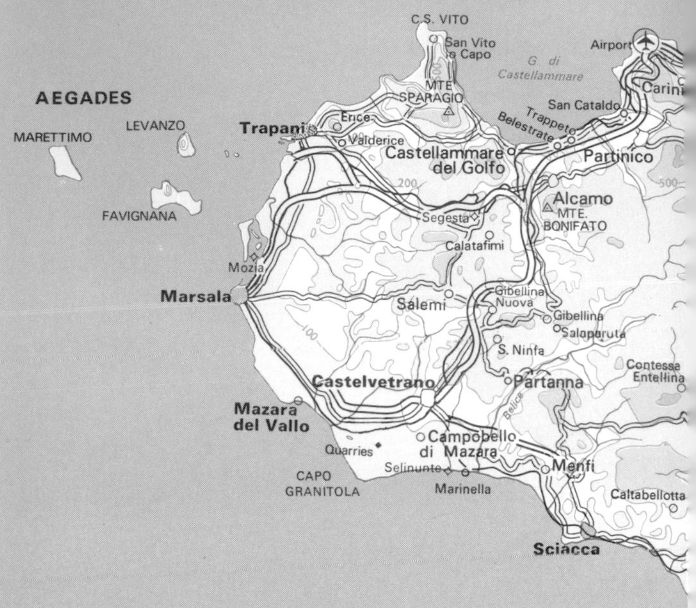
USTICA
C.S. VITO
San Vito lo Capo
Airport
G. di Castellammare
AEGADES
MTE SPARAGIO
Carini
San Cataldo
LEVANZO
Trapani
Erice
Trappeto
Belestrate
MARETTIMO
Valderice
Castellammare del Golfo
Partinico
200
500
Alcamo
MTE. BONIFATO
FAVIGNANA
Segesta
Calatafimi
Mozia
Marsala
Salemi
Gibellina Nuova
Gibellina
Salaparuta
100
S. Ninfa
Contessa Entellina
Castelvetrano
Partanna
Mazara del Vallo
Belice
Campobello di Mazara
Quarries
Selinunte
Menfi
CAPO GRANITOLA
Marinella
Caltabellotta
Sciacca

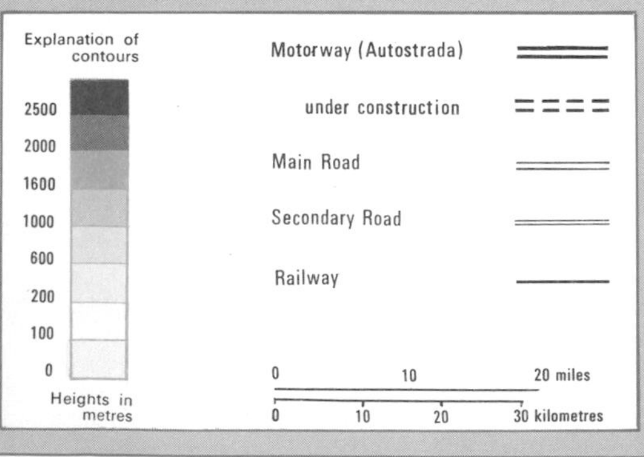
Explanation of contours
2500
2000
1600
1000
600
200
100
0
Heights in metres
Motorway (Autostrada)
under construction
Main Road
Secondary Road
Railway
0
10
20 miles
0
10
20
30 kilometres

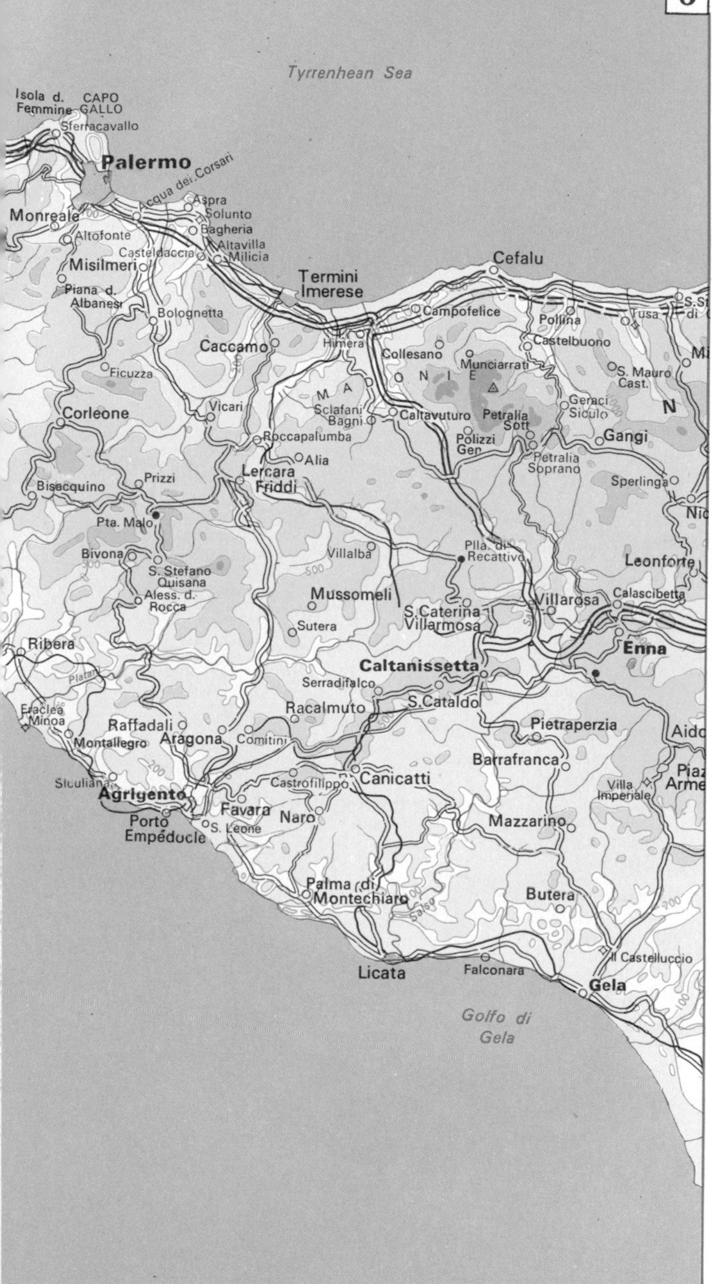
3
Tyrrenhean Sea
Isola d. Femmine
CAPO GALLO
Sferracavallo
Palermo
Acqua dei Corsari
Monreale
Aspra
Solunto
Bagheria
Altofonte
Casteldaccia
Altavilla Milicia
Misilmeri
Piana d. Albanesi
Termini Imerese
Cefalu
Bolognetta
Campofelice
Pollina
Tusa
Caccamo
Himera
Castelbuono
Collesano
Munciarrati
S. Mauro Cast.
Ficuzza
M A D O N I E
Sclafani Bagni
Caltavuturo
Petralia Sott
Geraci Siculo
Corleone
Vicari
Polizzi Gen
Gangi
Roccapalumba
Petralia Soprano
Alia
Lercara Friddi
Sperlinga
Prizzi
Bisacquino
Pta. Malo
Villalba
Plla. di Recattivo
Leonforte
Bivona
S. Stefano Quisana
Aless. d. Rocca
Mussomeli
Villarosa
Calascibetta
S. Caterina Villarmosa
Sutera
Ribera
Enna
Caltanissetta
Serradifalco
Eraclea Minoa
Racalmuto
S. Cataldo
Raffadali
Pietraperzia
Montallegro
Aragona
Comitini
Barrafranca
Siculiana
Castrofilippo
Canicatti
Villa Imperiale
Agrigento
Favara
Naro
Mazzarino
Porto Empedocle
S. Leone
Palma di Montechiaro
Butera
Licata
Falconara
Il Castelluccio
Gela
Golfo di Gela

4

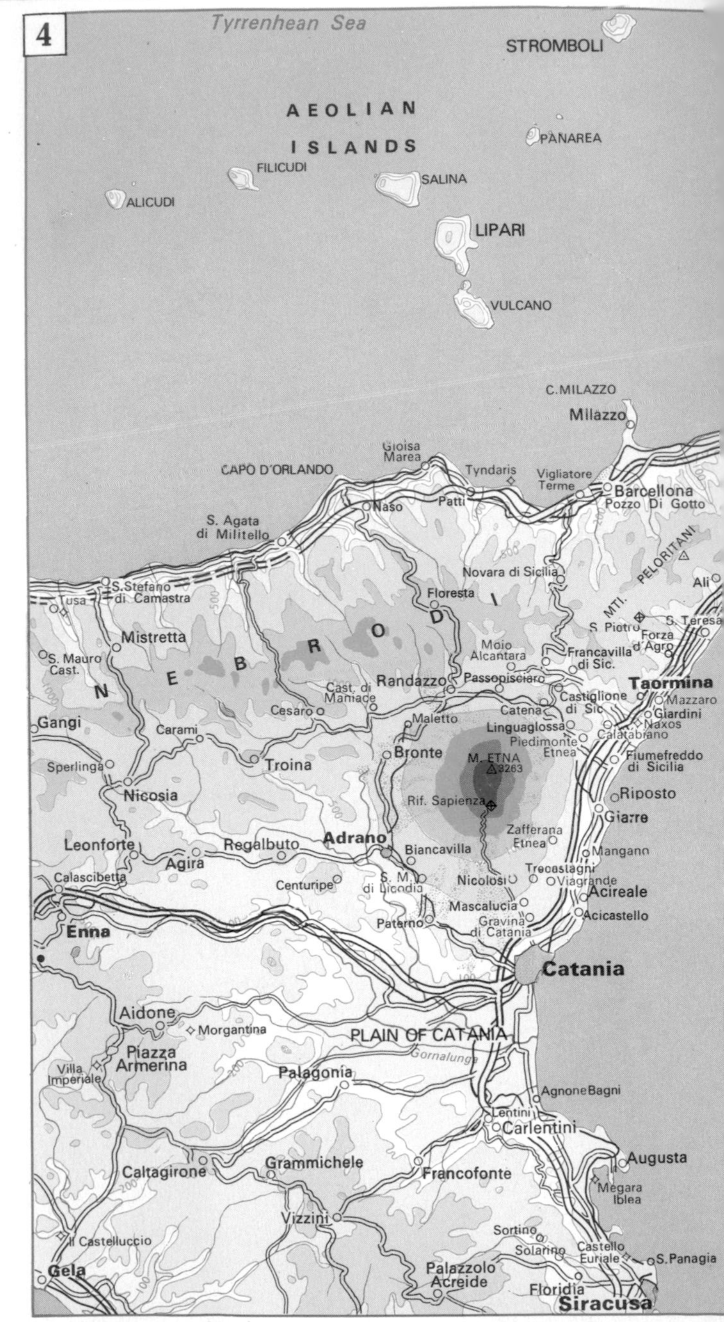
Tyrrenhean Sea
STROMBOLI
AEOLIAN
ISLANDS
PANAREA
FILICUDI
SALINA
ALICUDI
LIPARI
VULCANO
C.MILAZZO
Milazzo
Gioisa Marea
CAPO D'ORLANDO
Tyndaris
Vigliatore Terme
Barcellona Pozzo Di Gotto
Naso
Patti
S. Agata di Militello
MTI. PELORITANI
Novara di Sicilia
S.Stefano di Camastra
Tusa
Floresta
Alì
NEBRODI
S. Pietro
S. Teresa
Forza d'Agro
Mistretta
Moio Alcantara
Francavilla di Sic.
S. Mauro Cast.
Randazzo
Passopisciaro
Taormina
Cast. di Maniace
Castiglione di Sic.
Mazzaro
Catena
Giardini
Cesaro
Maletto
Naxos
Gangi
Carami
Linguaglossa
Calatabiano
Piedimonte Etnea
Bronte
M. ETNA
3263
Fiumefreddo di Sicilia
Sperlinga
Troina
Nicosia
Riposto
Rif. Sapienza
Giarre
Zafferana Etnea
Leonforte
Regalbuto
Adrano
Biancavilla
Mangano
Agira
Trecastagni
Calascibetta
S. M. di Licodia
Nicolosi
Viagrande
Centuripe
Acireale
Mascalucia
Acicastello
Paterno
Gravina di Catania
Enna
Catania
Aidone
Morgantina
PLAIN OF CATANIA
Piazza Armerina
Gornalunga
Villa Imperiale
Palagonia
Agnone Bagni
Lentini
Carlentini
Augusta
Caltagirone
Grammichele
Francofonte
Megara Iblea
Vizzini
Sortino
Il Castelluccio
Solarino
Castello Euriale
S.Panagia
Gela
Palazzolo Acreide
Floridia
Siracusa

Pizzo
Vibo Valentia
CAPO VATICANO
Mileto
Soriano
Nicotera
Serra S. Bruno
Golfo di Gioia
Rosarno
Gioia Tauro
Polistena
Cinquefrondi
Taurianova
Cittanova
Gioiosa Ionica
Palmi
Seminara
Bagnara Calabra
Sparta
Punta Faro
Sinopoli
Gerace
Villafranca
Ganziri
Locri
Villa S. Giovanni
Messina
ASPROMONTE
Reggio di Calabria
Scaletta Zanclea
Melito di P. Salvo
Ionian Sea

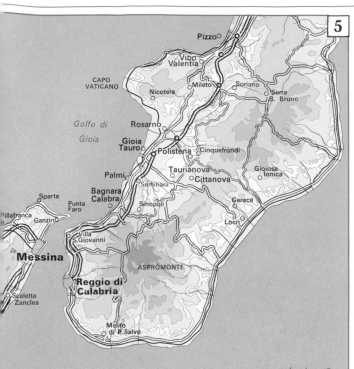

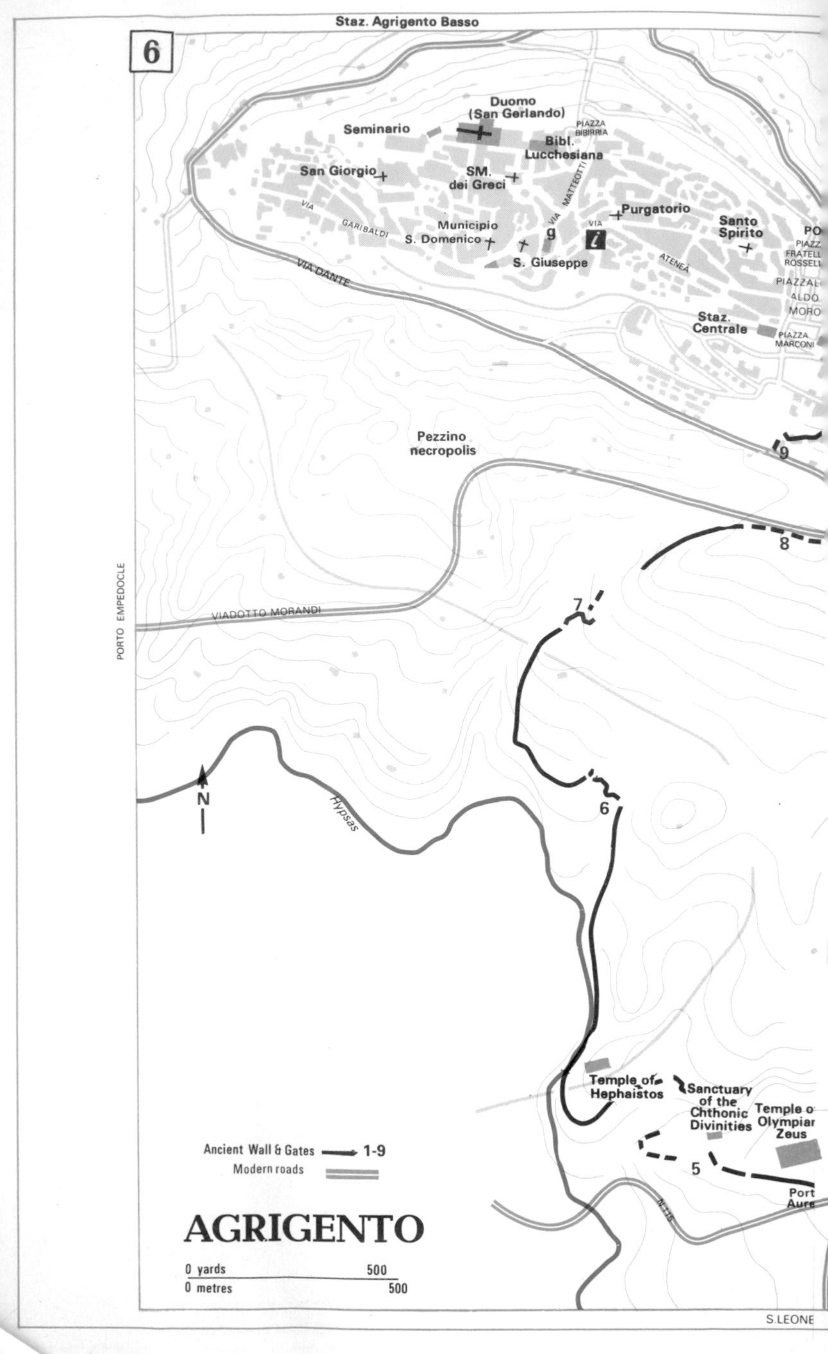

Staz. Agrigento Basso
6
Duomo
(San Gerlando)
Seminario
PIAZZA
BIBIRRIA
Bibl.
Lucchesiana
San Giorgio
SM.
dei Greci
VIA MATTEOTTI
VIA
GARIBALDI
Purgatorio
Santo
Spirito
Municipio
S. Domenico
g
VIA
ATENEA
S. Giuseppe
VIA DANTE
PIAZZA
FRATELLI
ROSSELLI
PIAZZALE
ALDO
MORO
Staz.
Centrale
PIAZZA
MARCONI
Pezzino
necropolis
9
8
7
VIADOTTO MORANDI
PORTO EMPEDOCLE
N
Hypsas
6
Temple of
Hephaistos
Sanctuary
of the
Chthonic
Divinities
Zeus
5
Ancient Wall & Gates 1-9
Modern roads
N 115
AGRIGENTO
0 yards 500
0 metres 500
S.LEONE

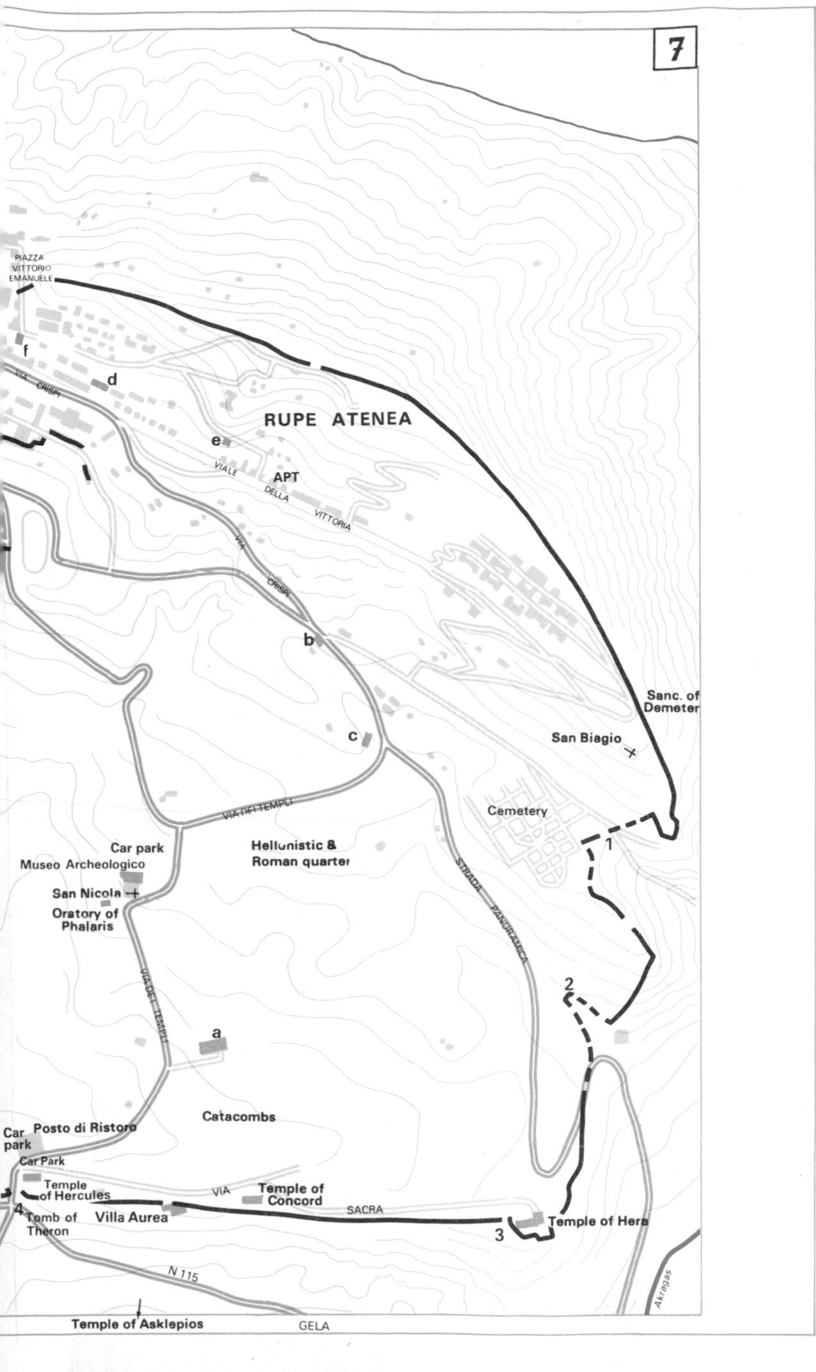

7
PIAZZA VITTORIO EMANUELE
f
d
VIA CRISPI
RUPE ATENEA
e
APT
VIALE DELLA VITTORIA
VIA CRISPI
b
Sanc. of Demeter
San Biagio
c
Cemetery
VIA DEI TEMPLI
Car park
Museo Archeologico
Hellenistic & Roman quarter
1
STRADA PANORAMICA
San Nicola
Oratory of Phalaris
VIA DEI TEMPLI
2
a
Catacombs
Car park
Posto di Ristoro
Car Park
Temple of Hercules
VIA
Temple of Concord
4
Tomb of Theron
Villa Aurea
SACRA
Temple of Hera
3
N 115
Akragas
Temple of Asklepios
GELA

8
CATANIA
0 yards 400
0 metres 400
N
ETNA
Orto Botanico
S. Maria di Gesu
Villa Bellini
APT
S. Domenico
Mosque
Anfiteatro
S. Biagio
S. Agata La Vetere
S. Carcere
Biblioteca
Osservatorio Astrofisico
S. Nicolo
SM. d. Gesuiti
Rotunda
S. Benedetto
Odeon
Bellini s Ho
Teatro Romano
SS.Trinita
Verga's House
Porta Garibaldi
Castello Ursino (Museo Civico)
San Giuliano
VIA BECCARIA
VIA RASPAGLIESI
VIA R. FRANCHETTI
VIA MARIO RAPISARDI
PIAZZA S. MARIA DI GESU
PIAZZA V. LANZA
VIA MUSCATELLO
VIA A. LONGO
PIAZZA ROMA
VIALE REGINA
VIA CARONDA
VIA MOROSOLI
VIA SALVATORE TOMASELLI
VIA ETNEA
VIA G PAOLA
VIA BASILE
VIA MOGADISCIO
VIA F. FILZI
VIA LAGO DI NICITO
VIA DOTTOR CONSOLI
VIA ANDRONE
VIA UGHETTI
VIA ROCCA ROMANA
VIA N. MARTOGLIO
VIA ORTO S. CLEMENTE
VIA CASTROMARINA
VIA CARLO FORLANINI
VIA CAPPUCCINI
PZA. D. BORSA
VIA EUPLIO
VIA PLEBISCITO
VIA ANTICO CORSO
VIA S. MADDALENA
VIA PENNINELLO
VIA M. VERGINE
VIA S. ELENA
VIA BAMBINO
VIA A.DI SAN GIULIANO
VIA CROCIFERI
PZA. VACCARINI
PZA DANTE
VIA GESUITI
VIA ROTONDA
VIA S.M CATENA
VIA GRASSI
VIA TEATRO GRECO
VIA S. AGOSTINO
PIAZZA SAN FRANCESCO
VIA S. ANNA
PIAZZA MAZZINI
VIA FASSARI
VIA VITT EMANUELE II
PZA. MACHIAVELLI
VIA POZZO MOLINO
VIA GARIBALDI
VIA S. DAMIANO
VIA GISIRA
VIA AUTERI
VIA CAST. URSINO
VIA TRANSITO
VIA CONS. D. SETA
VIA S.S. TRINITA
VIA ITTAR
VIA NAUMACHIA
PIAZZA FEDERICO DI SVEVIA
PATERNO
PZA. PALESTRO
VIA SACCHERO
VIA PORTINO VECCHIO
PZA. S. CRISTOFORO
VIA REITANO
VIA GISMONDO
VIA CONSTANTINO
VIA ZUCCARELLI
VIA D. CALCARE
VIA TESTULLA
VIA BELFIORE
VIA S.M. DELLE SALETTE
VIA MOLINO A VENTO
VIA GRAMIGNANI
1
2
5
6
9
10
13
14

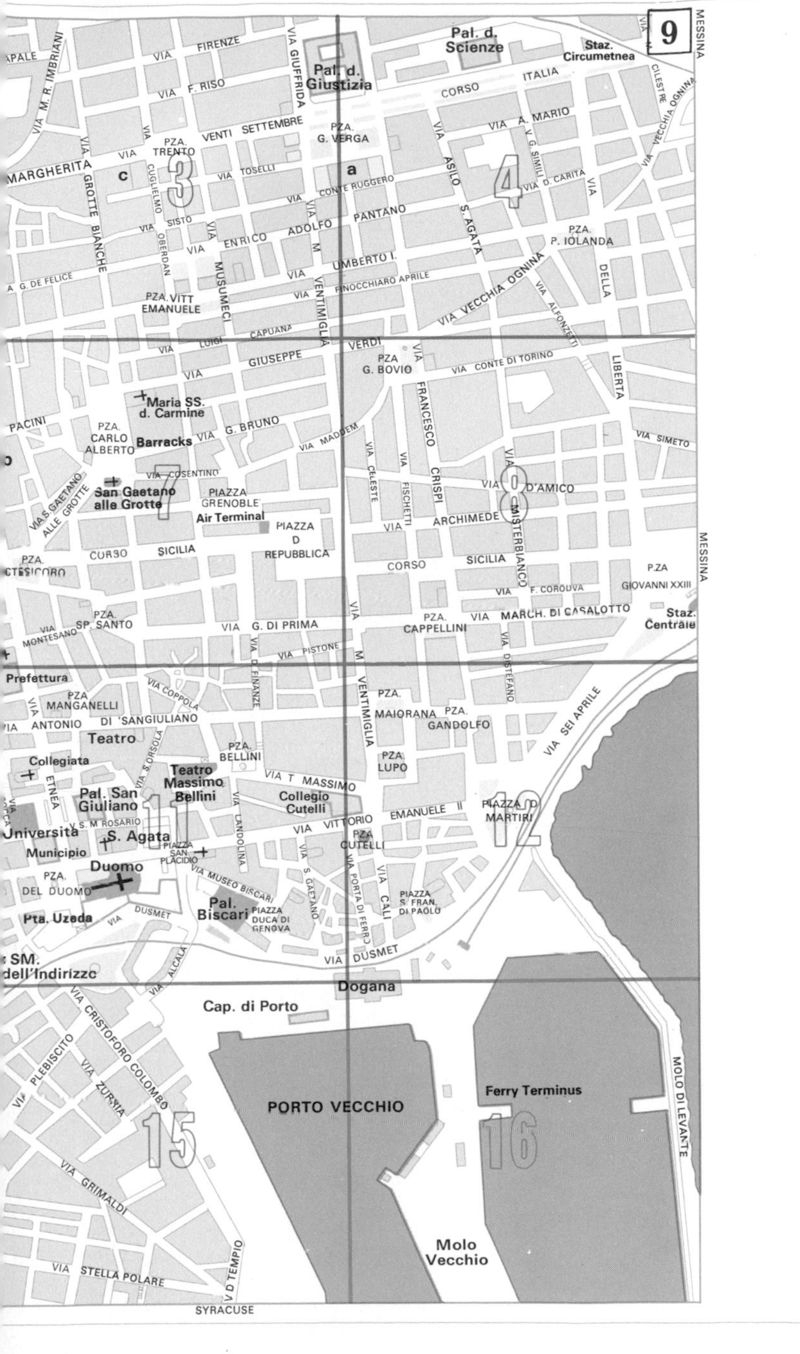
9
Pal. d. Scienze
Staz. Circumetnea
Pal. d. Giustizia
MESSINA
VIA FIRENZE
VIA F. RISO
VIA GIUFFRIDA
CORSO ITALIA
VIA M. R. IMBRIANI
PZA. TRENTO
VENTI SETTEMBRE
PZA. G. VERGA
VIA A. MARIO
MARGHERITA
VIA GROTTE BIANCHE
VIA TOSELLI
CONTE RUGGERO
ASILO
S. AGATA
V. G. SIMILI
VIA D. CARITA
VIA VECCHIA OGNINA
SISTO
OBERDAN
CUGLIELMO
VIA ENRICO
ADOLFO
PANTANO
PZA. P. IOLANDA
DELLA
UMBERTO I.
G. DE FELICE
MUSUMECI
VENTIMIGLIA
FINOCCHIARO APRILE
VIA VECCHIA OGNINA
VIA ALFONZETTI
PZA. VITT EMANUELE
CAPUANA
LUIGI
VERDI
PZA. G. BOVIO
VIA CONTE DI TORINO
LIBERTA
VIA GIUSEPPE
Maria SS. d. Carmine
FRANCESCO
PACINI
PZA. CARLO ALBERTO
Barracks
VIA G. BRUNO
VIA MADDEM
VIA CELESTE
VIA FISCHETTI
CRISPI
VIA SIMETO
VIA COSENTINO
San Gaetano alle Grotte
VIA S. GAETANO ALLE GROTTE
PIAZZA GRENOBLE
Air Terminal
PIAZZA D REPUBBLICA
VIA ARCHIMEDE
VIA D'AMICO
MISTERBIANCO
PZA. CTESICORO
CORSO SICILIA
CORSO SICILIA
P.ZA GIOVANNI XXIII
VIA F. CORODVA
PZA. SP. SANTO
VIA MONTESANO
VIA G. DI PRIMA
PZA. CAPPELLINI
VIA MARCH. DI CASALOTTO
Staz. Centrale
VIA PISTONE
VIA DI FINANZE
VIA DISTEFANO
Prefettura
VIA COPPOLA
PZA MANGANELLI
VIA ANTONIO DI SANGIULIANO
PZA. MAIORANA
PZA. GANDOLFO
VIA SEI APRILE
Teatro
VIA S. ORSOLA
PZA. BELLINI
Collegiata
Teatro Massimo Bellini
PZA. LUPO
VIA T MASSIMO
ETNEA
Pal. San Giuliano
VIA LANDOLINA
Collegio Cutelli
PIAZZA D MARTIRI
V. S. M ROSARIO
Universita
S. Agata
VIA VITTORIO EMANUELE II
PZA CUTELLI
Municipio
PIAZZA SAN PLACIDO
PZA. DEL DUOMO
Duomo
VIA MUSEO BISCARI
VIA S. GAETANO
VIA PORTA DI FERRO
VIA CALI
PIAZZA S. FRAN. DI PAOLO
Pta. Uzeda
VIA DUSMET
Pal. Biscari
PIAZZA DUCA DI GENOVA
VIA DUSMET
SM. dell'Indirizzo
VIA ALCALA
Dogana
Cap. di Porto
VIA CRISTOFORO COLOMBO
VIA PLEBISCITO
VIA ZURRIA
PORTO VECCHIO
Ferry Terminus
MOLO DI LEVANTE
VIA GRIMALDI
Molo Vecchio
VIA STELLA POLARE
V D TEMPIO
SYRACUSE
3
4
7
8
11
12
15
16
a
c

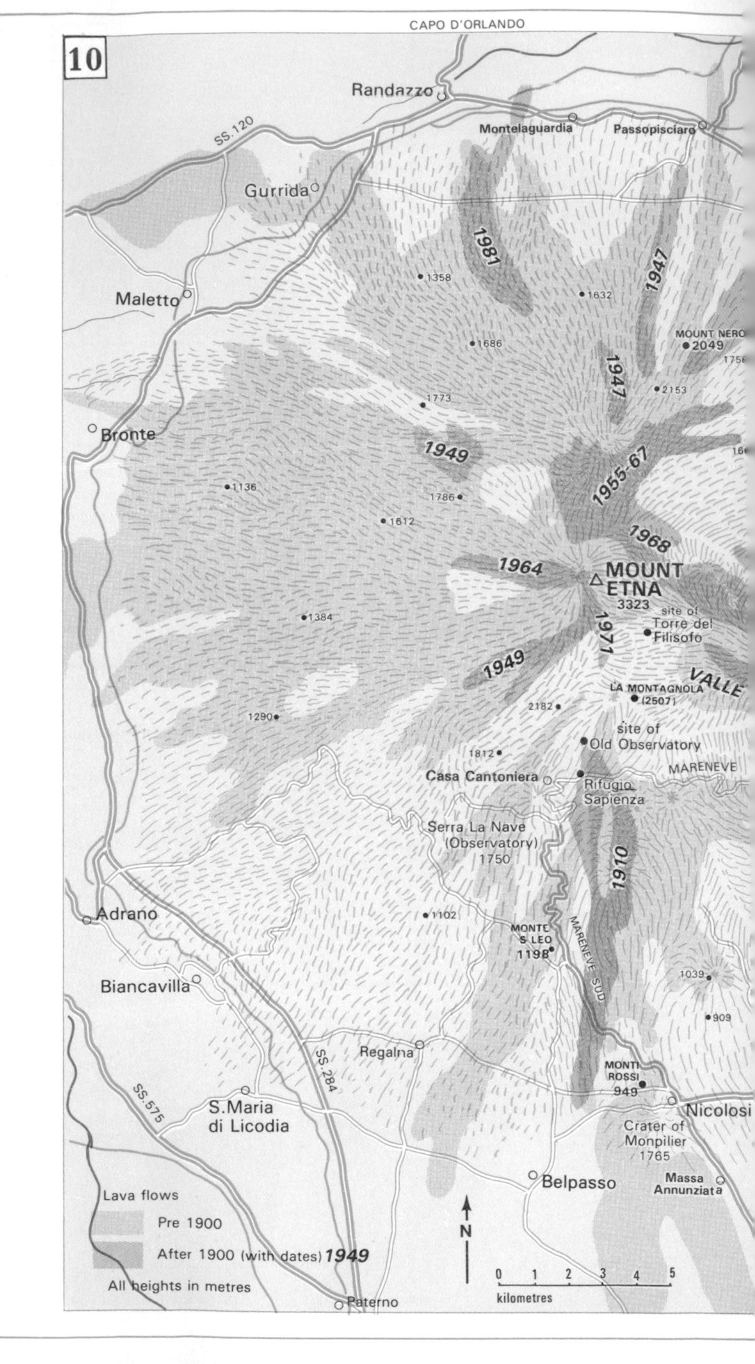

CAPO D'ORLANDO
10
Randazzo
Montelaguardia
Passopisciaro
SS.120
Gurrida
Maletto
Bronte
1981
1947
1358
1632
MOUNT NERO
2049
1686
1947
2153
1773
1949
1955-67
1136
1786
1612
1968
1964
MOUNT
ETNA
3323
site of
Torre del
Filisofo
1971
1384
1949
VALLE
LA MONTAGNOLA
(2507)
2182
1290
site of
Old Observatory
1812
Casa Cantoniera
MARENEVE
Rifugio
Sapienza
Serra La Nave
(Observatory)
1750
1910
Adrano
1102
MONTE
S LEO
1198
MARENEVE SUD
Biancavilla
1039
909
SS.284
Regalna
MONTI
ROSSI
949
SS.575
S.Maria
di Licodia
Nicolosi
Crater of
Monpilier
1765
Belpasso
Massa
Annunziata
Lava flows
Pre 1900
After 1900 (with dates) 1949
All heights in metres
N
0 1 2 3 4 5
kilometres
Paterno

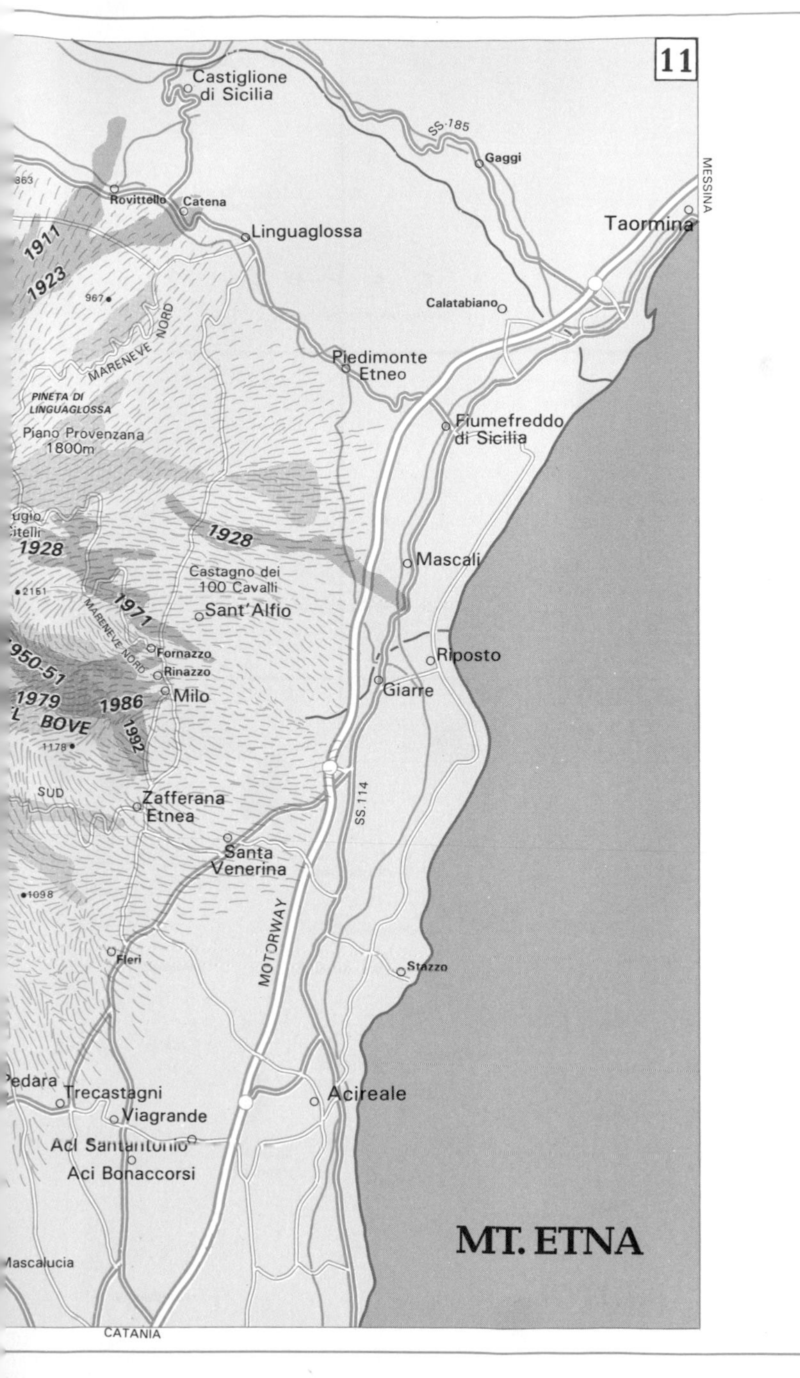
11
Castiglione di Sicilia
SS.185
Gaggi
MESSINA
Rovittello
Catena
Linguaglossa
Taormina
1911
1923
967
Calatabiano
MARENEVE NORD
Piedimonte Etneo
PINETA DI LINGUAGLOSSA
Fiumefreddo di Sicilia
Piano Provenzana 1800m
1928
1928
Mascali
Castagno dei 100 Cavalli
2151
1971
Sant'Alfio
MARENEVE NORD
Fornazzo
Riposto
Rinazzo
Giarre
1979
1986
Milo
BOVE
1992
1178
SUD
Zafferana Etnea
SS.114
Santa Venerina
1098
MOTORWAY
Fleri
Stazzo
Pedara
Trecastagni
Acireale
Viagrande
Aci Santantonio
Aci Bonaccorsi
MT. ETNA
Mascalucia
CATANIA

12

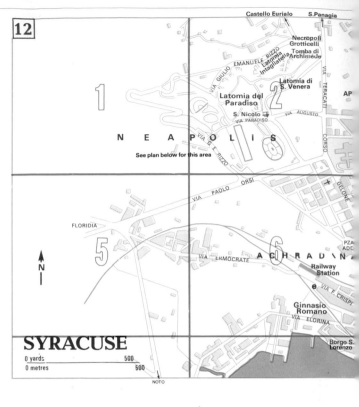

Castello Eurialo
S.Panagia
Necropoli Grotticelli
Tomba di Archimede
VIA GIULIO EMANUELE RIZZO
Latomia Intagliatella
Latomia di S. Venera
VIA TERACATI
1
2
Latomia del Paradiso
S. Nicolo
VIA PARADISO
VIA AUGUSTO
N E A P O L I S
VIA G. E. RIZZO
See plan below for this area
CORSO
VIA PAOLO ORSI
GELONE
FLORIDIA
5
6
N
VIA ERMOCRATE
A C H R A D I N
Railway Station
VIA F. CRISPI
Ginnasio Romano
VIA ELORINA
Borgo S. Lorenzo

SYRACUSE

0 yards 500
0 metres 500
NOTO

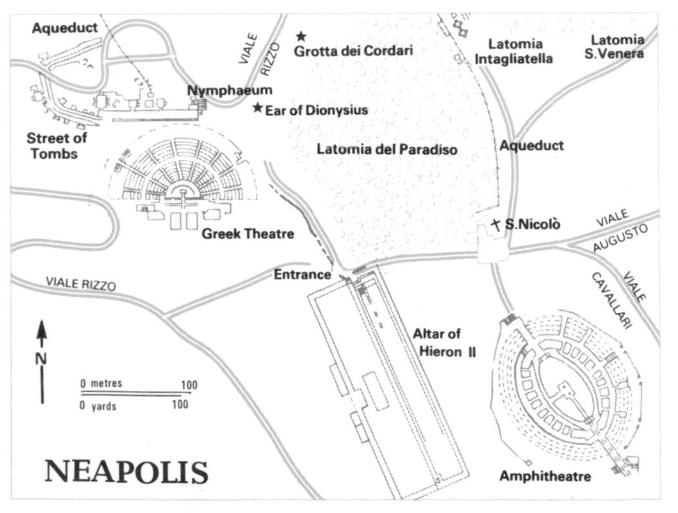

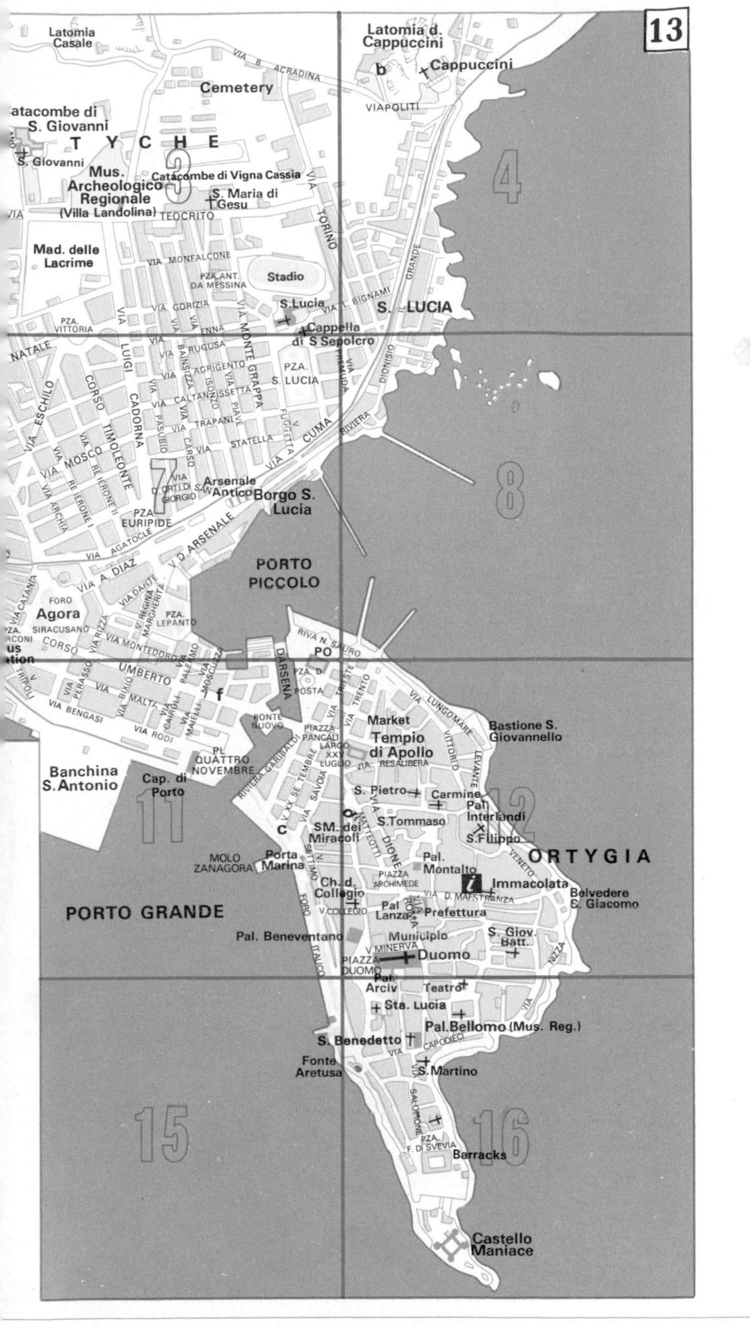
13
Latomia Casale
Latomia d. Cappuccini
Cappuccini
Cemetery
Catacombe di S. Giovanni
S. Giovanni
T Y C H E
Mus. Archeologico Regionale (Villa Landolina)
Catacombe di Vigna Cassia
S. Maria di Gesu
VIAPOLITI
Mad. delle Lacrime
Stadio
S.Lucia
S. LUCIA
Cappella di S Sepolcro
PZA. S. LUCIA
Arsenale Antico
Borgo S. Lucia
PZA. EURIPIDE
PORTO PICCOLO
Agora
FORO SIRACUSANO
PZA. LEPANTO
DARSENA
PO
Market
Tempio di Apollo
Bastione S. Giovannello
PL QUATTRO NOVEMBRE
Banchina S.Antonio
Cap. di Porto
S. Pietro
Carmine
Pal. Interlandi
S.Tommaso
SM. dei Miracoli
S.Filippo
ORTYGIA
MOLO ZANAGORA
Porta Marina
Pal. Montalto
Immacolata
Belvedere S. Giacomo
Ch. d. Collegio
PORTO GRANDE
Pal Lanza
Prefettura
Pal. Beneventano
Municipio
S. Giov. Batt.
Duomo
Pal. Arciv
Teatro
Sta. Lucia
Pal.Bellomo (Mus. Reg.)
S. Benedetto
Fonte Aretusa
S.Martino
Barracks
Castello Maniace
VIA ACRADINA
VIA TEOCRITO
VIA TORINO
VIA MONTE GRAPPA
CORSO GELONE
CORSO TIMOLEONTE
VIA CUMA
RIVIERA DIONISIO
VIA CATANIA
CORSO UMBERTO
VIA ROMA
VIA MAESTRANZA
VIA NIZZA
VIA SALOMONE
FORO ITALICO
RIVIERA GARIBALDI
VIA LUNGOMARE
3
4
7
8
11
12
15
16

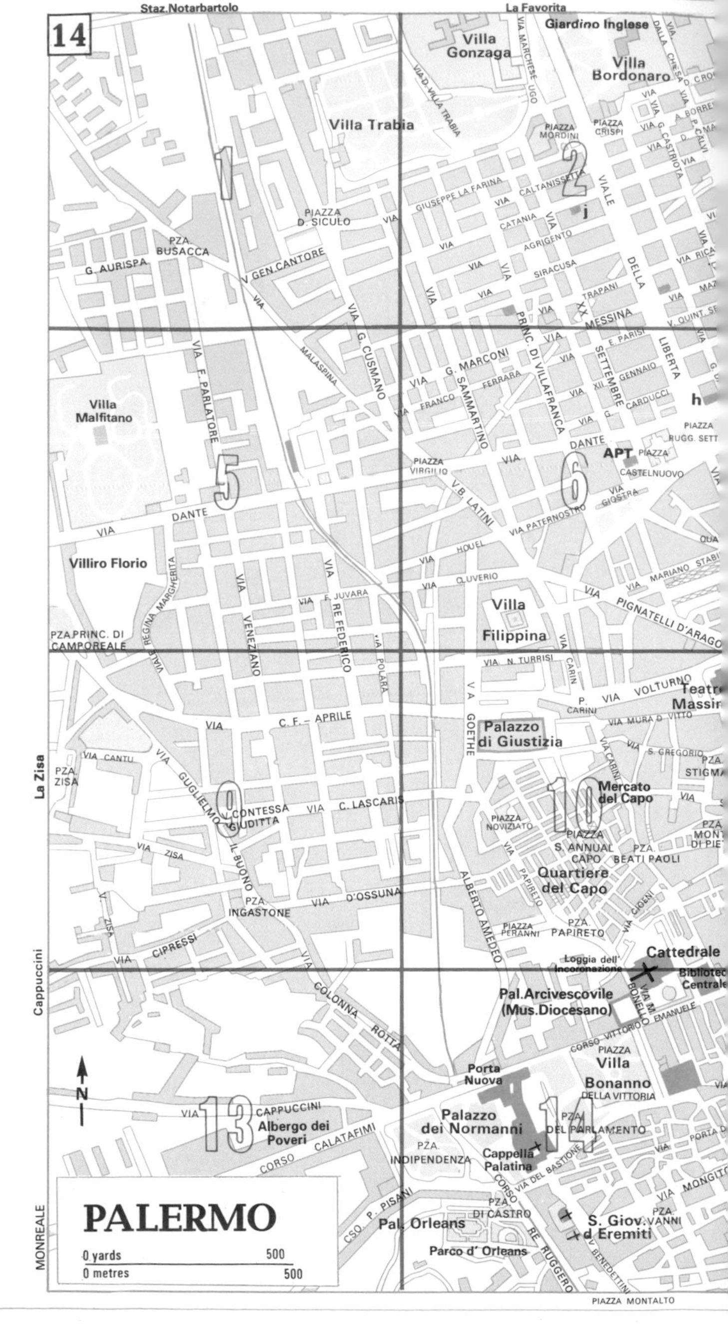
14
PALERMO
0 yards 500
0 metres 500
Staz.Notarbartolo
La Favorita
Giardino Inglese
Villa Gonzaga
Villa Bordonaro
Villa Trabia
Villa Malfitano
Villiro Florio
Villa Filippina
Palazzo di Giustizia
Mercato del Capo
Quartiere del Capo
Cattedrale
Loggia dell' Incoronazione
Pal.Arcivescovile (Mus.Diocesano)
Porta Nuova
Palazzo dei Normanni
Cappella Palatina
Villa Bonanno
Albergo dei Poveri
Pal. Orleans
Parco d' Orleans
S. Giov. d Eremiti
APT
Teatro Massimo
La Zisa
Cappuccini
MONREALE
PIAZZA MONTALTO

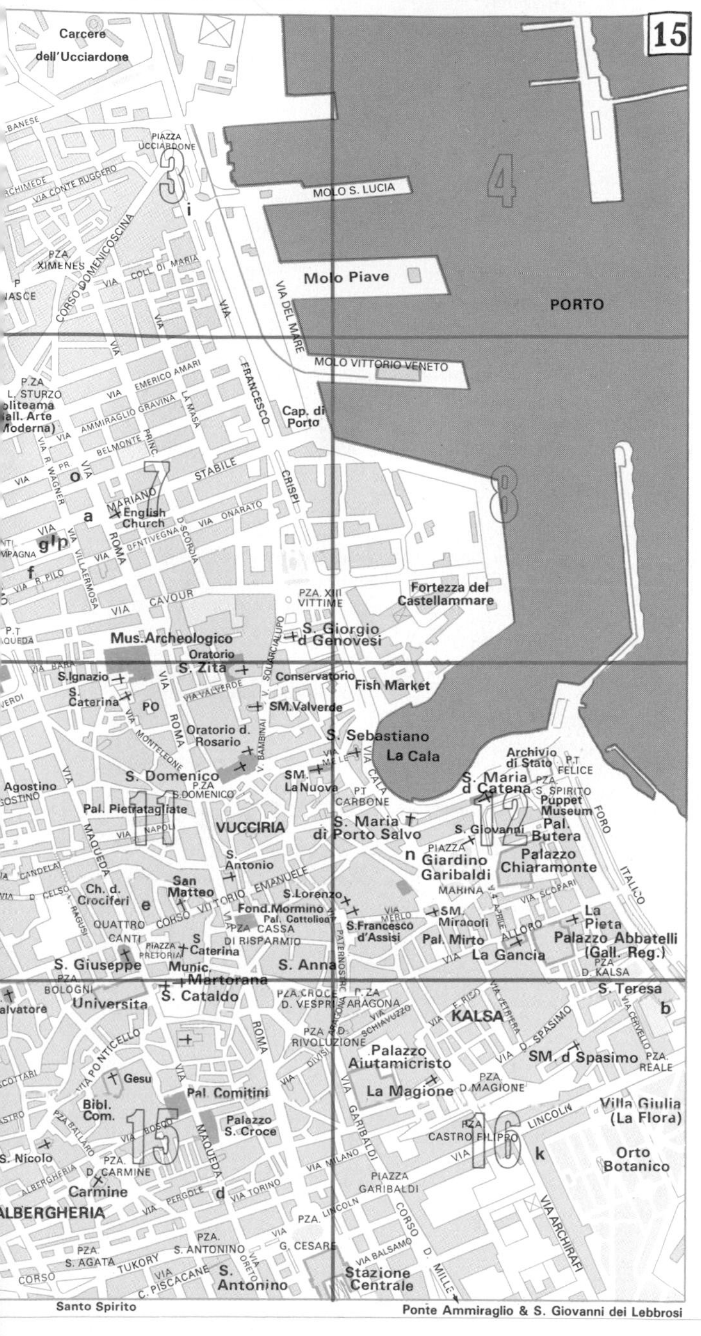
15
Carcere dell'Ucciardone
PIAZZA UCCIARDONE
MOLO S. LUCIA
Molo Piave
PORTO
VIA DEL MARE
MOLO VITTORIO VENETO
Cap. di Porto
VIA FRANCESCO CRISPI
PZA. XIII VITTIME
Fortezza del Castellammare
S. Giorgio d Genovesi
Conservatorio
Fish Market
S. Sebastiano
La Cala
Archivio di Stato
P.T FELICE
S. Maria d Catena
PZA. S. SPIRITO
Puppet Museum
FORO ITALICO
Pal. Butera
Palazzo Chiaramonte
S. Giovanni
PIAZZA Giardino Garibaldi
MARINA
VIA SCOPARI
La Pieta
Palazzo Abbatelli (Gall. Reg.)
PZA. D. KALSA
S. Teresa
b
KALSA
SM. d Spasimo
PZA. REALE
Villa Giulia (La Flora)
Orto Botanico
k
VIA ARCHIRAFI
VIA LINCOLN
PZA. CASTRO FILIPPO
PZA. D. MAGIONE
La Magione
Palazzo Aiutamicristo
PZA. D. RIVOLUZIONE
P.ZA ARAGONA
PZA. CROCE D. VESPRI
VIA GARIBALDI
PIAZZA GARIBALDI
CORSO D. MILLE
Stazione Centrale
PZA. G. CESARE
VIA BALSAMO
VIA MILANO
VIA TORINO
S. Antonino
PZA. S. ANTONINO
VIA C. PISCACANE
TUKORY
CORSO
PZA. S. AGATA
ALBERGHERIA
Carmine
PZA. D. CARMINE
S. Nicolo
PZA. BALLARO
Bibl. Com.
Gesu
Pal. Comitini
Palazzo S. Croce
MAQUEDA
d
VIA PONTICELLO
Universita
PZA. BOLOGNI
S. Cataldo
Martorana
Munic.
S. Giuseppe
PIAZZA PRETORIA
S Caterina
QUATTRO CANTI
S. Anna
DI RISPARMIO
PZA CASSA
Fond. Mormino
Pal. Cattolica
S. Lorenzo
S. Francesco d'Assisi
SM. Miracoli
Pal. Mirto
La Gancia
VIA PATERNOSTRO
CORSO VITTORIO EMANUELE
San Matteo
S. Antonio
Ch. d. Crociferi
e
VUCCIRIA
S. Maria di Porto Salvo
n
P.T CARBONE
SM. La Nuova
S. Domenico
PZA S. DOMENICO
Pal. Pietratagliate
VIA NAPOLI
Agostino
Oratorio d. Rosario
SM. Valverde
VIA VALVERDE
PO
S. Caterina
S. Ignazio
S. Zita
Oratorio
Mus. Archeologico
VIA CAVOUR
VIA ROMA
VIA MONTELEONE
VIA BAMBINAI
VIA SQUARCIALUPO
English Church
a
g/p
f
o
VIA MARIANO STABILE
VIA ONARATO
VIA BENTIVEGNA
D. SCORDIA
VIA R. PILO
VIA VILLAERMOSA
VIA R. WAGNER
VIA BELMONTE
PRINC.
VIA AMMIRAGLIO GRAVINA
LA MASA
VIA EMERICO AMARI
P.ZA L. STURZO
Politeama (Gall. Arte Moderna)
VIA COLL. DI MARIA
CORSO DOMENICO SCINA
PZA. XIMENES
VIA CONTE RUGGERO
i
Santo Spirito
Ponte Ammiraglio & S. Giovanni dei Lebbrosi

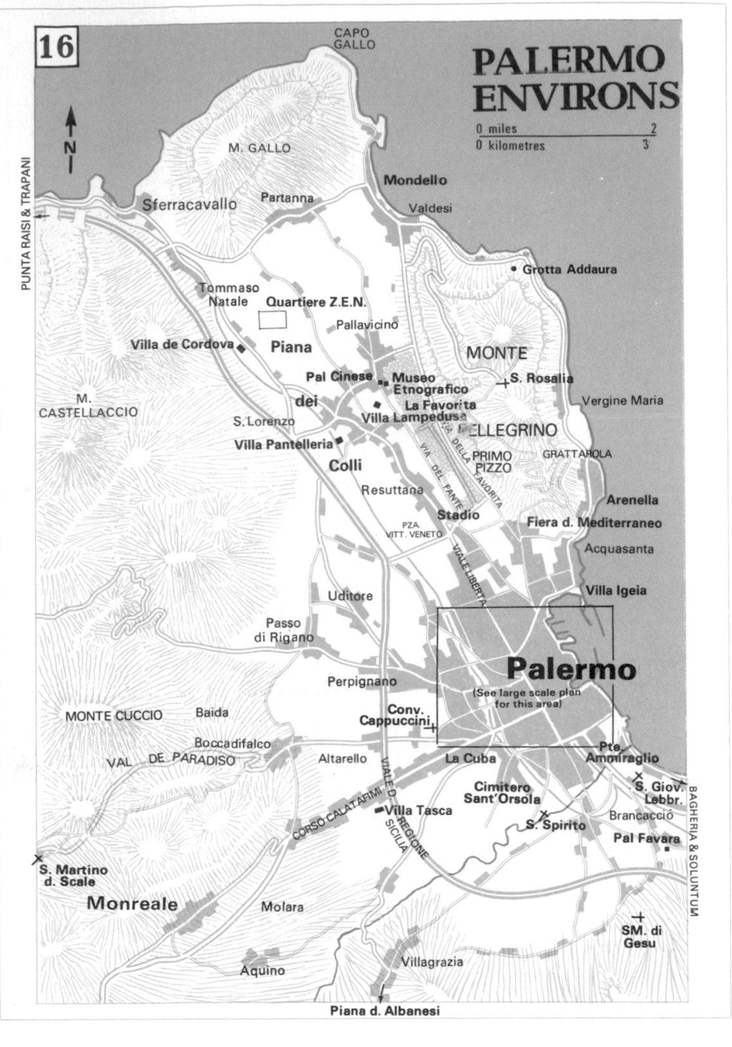
16
PALERMO
ENVIRONS
0 miles 2
0 kilometres 3
N
CAPO
GALLO
M. GALLO
Mondello
Valdesi
Sferracavallo
Partanna
PUNTA RAISI & TRAPANI
Grotta Addaura
Tommaso
Natale
Quartiere Z.E.N.
Pallavicino
Villa de Cordova
Piana
dei
Colli
MONTE
PELLEGRINO
Pal Cinese
Museo
Etnografico
S. Rosalia
La Favorita
Villa Lampedusa
Vergine Maria
M.
CASTELLACCIO
S. Lorenzo
Villa Pantelleria
PRIMO
PIZZO
GRATTAROLA
VIA DEL FANTE
VIA DELLA FAVORITA
Resuttana
Arenella
Stadio
PZA.
VITT. VENETO
Fiera d. Mediterraneo
Acquasanta
VIALE LIBERTA
Villa Igeia
Uditore
Passo
di Rigano
Palermo
(See large scale plan
for this area)
Perpignano
MONTE CUCCIO
Baida
Conv.
Cappuccini
Boccadifalco
VAL DE PARADISO
Altarello
La Cuba
Pte.
Ammiraglio
Cimitero
Sant'Orsola
S. Giov.
Lebbr.
BAGHERIA & SOLUNTUM
CORSO CALATAFIMI
VIALE D. REGIONE SICILIA
Villa Tasca
S. Spirito
Brancaccio
Pal Favara
S. Martino
d. Scale
Monreale
Molara
SM. di
Gesu
Villagrazia
Aquino
Piana d. Albanesi